Shells and Shores of Texas

The Elma Dill Russell Spencer Foundation Series/Number 5

Shells and Shores of Texas

by Jean Andrews

Foreword by William J. Clench

University of Texas Press/Austin and London

Publication of this book was assisted in part
by a grant from the Caesar Kleberg Foundation
for Wildlife Conservation

Library of Congress Cataloging in Publication Data

Andrews, Jean.
Shells and shores of Texas.

(The Elma Dill Russell Spencer Foundation series; no. 5)
First published in 1971 under title: Sea shells of the Texas coast.
Bibliography: p.
Includes index.
1. Shells—Texas—Gulf region—Identification.
2. Shells—Mexico, Gulf of—Identification.
I. Title. II. Series.
QL415.T4A64 1977   594'.04'7   76-41321
ISBN 0-292-77519-9

Design/Eje Wray & Jean LeGwin
Typeset/G&S Typesetters
Print & Bind/Kingsport Press
Color printing/University of Texas Printing Division

To Robin, my seafaring son, who soars with his own wings far above the crowd

Contents

Illustrations

Foreword

In our world of systematic zoology, there are two distinctive types of research, monographic and geographic. The monographic procedure is to study animals by groups; these groups can be the species of a single genus, a family, or even under higher categories. Here the various species are described in detail—in the Mollusca, not only the shells but also their soft anatomy, their relationship to one another, ranges of distribution, and a series of localities where they have been found. In studies of this sort their distribution can be local or limited, as the Atlantic coast of North America, or even world-wide. References to a multitude of other subject matter pertaining to the group are usually mentioned and these references are added to the bibliography.

The geographic type of research is that of locality, be it a state, a zoographic province, a mountain range, a river system, an island, or a given body of water. This geographic approach in our field of Mollusca has a very important impact on students as it covers a multitude of species within any given area. It has a direct interest to teachers of biology as it covers in detail a group of animals in which they are concerned. The identification of a species gives a name to it and this in turn leads to far more information if needed.

Monographic and geographic studies are of great value to museum curators as they give immediate aid to the various sections of their collections which may need this new knowledge.

Dr. Jean Andrews has added much to our knowledge of the marine Mollusca of the northern Gulf of Mexico. She has drawn freely on the data brought together by a host of scientists and trained amateurs in the Texas region.

William J. Clench

Preface

Most people in this twentieth century are keenly aware that we exist in a world of constant change—a world of process, where everything is relative. Gone is the Newtonian scheme of things based on the idea of simple location—matter in a definite region of space, throughout a definite duration of time, apart from any reference to the relations of that piece of matter to other regions of space or to other durations of time. The doctrines of evolution and relativity have wiped out those long-held "truths."

Today scientific theory is outrunning common sense. Who knows when more of yesterday's nonsense, such as Buck Rogers and his spaceship, will become tomorrow's demonstrated truth? The world is operating on a higher imaginative level, not because we have keener imaginations but because we have better instruments. In biology, one such instrument, the scanning electron microscope (SEM), has opened new frontiers of study. So much information is being accumulated at such a rapid rate that often it is not assimilated before it is outdated.

This rate of change became strongly apparent to me when I was asked to revise *Sea Shells of the Texas Coast*. The first edition, which went to the editor in February of 1970, is now virtually obsolete. Biologists are no longer satisfied to simply classify organisms; they are using their new instruments to study the structure of the organism, the environment in which the organism

lives, the effect of that environment on the organism, and the effect of the organism on its environment. *Ecology*, a word almost unheard of fifteen years ago, is now on the tip of every tongue. One does not have to be an Einstein to understand relativity; it has become evident to thinking people that nothing exists in "simple location." A "thing" is part of its space and its space is part of it as it moves through time.

And so it is with the mollusks, these creatures that were known to earliest man, that had existed in the eons before, at the time when most life on earth was little more than distant pulsations of emerging being. Their fossilized shells tell the story of this earth from the time they appeared as highly evolved organisms when the first fossils were formed at the opening of the Cambrian period 600 million years ago. Yet, little is known of the animals that created these shells and that have fascinated and helped to feed humans since they crawled from the primordial ooze.

Though Aristotle made accurate studies of the reproduction of the molluscan octopus, those who followed him were more interested in his science of classification than in anatomical studies. They have been satisfied to group and regroup the mollusks on the basis of their shell characters alone. Today that approach is changing. Improved methods of collection, preservation, examination, comparison, and so on have brought the soft body of the

mollusk under the hard scrutiny of the biologist, and long-unanswered questions are beginning to find answers. The conchologist, one who studies the shell, now prefers to be called a malacologist, one who studies the organism. This change is coming slowly—but it is coming.

While the scientific investigation has been changing, others have become absorbed with the beauty of the shell. Where once a colorful, spiral gem or a fragment of a cockle only gathered dust as a reminder of a summer at the beach, now, it would seem, almost any coffee table in America displays a prized specimen—a stunningly coiled nautilus, a porcelainlike cowrie, or a radiating flame-colored scallop. Every decorator's shop, gift shop, jewelry store, discount mart, and import house is burgeoning with these gifts from the sea. So great is the demand for their beauty that we are no longer satisfied to wait for them to wash up on the shore. Now, we go out and tear them from their natural habitat, while the animal is still living, in order to meet the demand. The question is, Will this creature, which predates most forms of known life on our planet, survive the onslaught long enough for others to learn of the animal who made the shell?

Some states have laws to protect their marine mollusks, but freshwater species are rapidly becoming extinct. Each new dam and inland waterway seals their fate. Texas does not have protective laws except for the oyster. Even so, it is diminishing rapidly as pollutants make bays uninhabitable. Texas coastal waters provide such an inhospitable environment for the mollusks that they do not occur in quantities sufficient to elicit such protective measures. Many collectors can recall the days before the early sixties, when they could walk along a line of drift on a winter's beach and gather numbers of shells of many varieties (it is not an ecological crime to pick up a shell that has been stranded on a beach, for it can never reenter its world). However, that was before Hurricanes Carla (1961), Beulah and her floods (1967), Celia (1970), and Fern (1971) joined forces with a killing freeze (1962) to virtually eliminate the molluscan populations from the shallow coastal waters of central and south Texas. They are slowly and modestly returning. Leave them to reproduce! Perhaps, then, Texas coastal waters will once again offer the variety they did in the recent past.

However, the elimination of molluscan populations is not a new phenomenon. Myriads of dead snail shells—*Tegula, Vermicularia,* and *Modulus*—line the bays, even though they have not been seen living there during recorded history, to perplex scientists and to attest the effect that severe climatic conditions have had on the Texas shores throughout history.

At a reception held when *Sea Shells of the Texas Coast* first appeared six years ago, my friend Aalbert Heine, director of the Corpus Christi Museum, said with his kindly Dutch humor, "We shall be looking forward to 'Son of Sea Shells.'" This, then, is the new offspring, which has, it is to be hoped, taken the best from his parent, gathered to him new perceptions

from the world he lives in, and moved on through time. It is the nature of this changing world that a "Grandson of Sea Shells" will one day supercede the son. May the lovely, lowly mollusks live to tell their story to those who will pick up where our duration ends.

There are many to whom I am greatly indebted. Jean Bowers Gates of Austin, Texas, is responsible for most of the black-and-white shell photographs. After their appearance in the first edition, *American Scientist* called them "the finest available in a popular book on American molluscs." Few can imagine the degree of skill and patience required for the tedious task.

In addition to those who helped me with *Sea Shells*—identifying material, correcting names, suggesting references, supplying other information, giving financial assistance, proofreading—there are those who have sent me suggestions for improvement, reprints of papers, answers to my inquiries, letters of encouragement, and much, much more. There are too many to acknowledge individually without the risk of omitting someone. However, there is one to whom I am especially obliged, Dr. Dwight W. Taylor, for generosity with his time and library, for encouragement, for admonishment, but most of all for his scholastic example.

To Sam and Leonarda Cowan, whose hospitality made a period of research possible for me, goes a special thanks. Ed Harte made it financially possible for me to do the color photography, and Don Raymond Schol, photography teacher at North Texas State University, provided the facilities and technical advice for my work. The retracing of my route along the *long* Texas coast was made a happy time

by my young friend and able driver, Martha "Missy" Camp. Again, my erudite, long-time friend Carol Issensee Kilgore read reams of edited manuscript with me. Librarian Ellie N. Whitmore and the interlibrary loan of North Texas State University searched for and supplied me with a vast array of literature from over the entire country. The Bureau of Economic Geology of the University of Texas, under the direction of Dr. L. F. Brown, Jr., generously provided the base maps of their *Environmental Geologic Atlas of the Texas Coastal Zone* for my use, as well as recommendations concerning the terminology used in the geologic ranges.

Those who have freely furnished shells from their collections for photographs in this book are Manette Wilson, Carl Young, Adelaide Johnstone, Yvonne Canine, and Theresa Stelsig of Corpus Christi, Texas; Dr. Henry Hildebrand and Dr. John Wesley Tunnell of Texas A&I University; Dr. Harold W. Harry and Clyde A. Henry of Texas A&M University; Dr. Paul Boyer of Fairleigh Dickinson University; Dr. D. W. Taylor of the University of the Pacific; and the late Dan Steger of Tampa, Florida.

The patience of my editor, Barbara Spielman, who skillfully and uncomplainingly pieced together a manuscript that was written and illustrated concurrently with my classwork, teaching activities, and the preparation of a Ph.D. dissertation on a totally different subject, should not go unrecognized. These were trying times which may have led to some errors and omissions, but I hope that those who so unstintingly gave their help will not be let down. To all of these go my heartfelt thanks.

Introduction

Before civilization dawned, early man used sea shells for implements, food, adornment, and fetishes, and as a medium of exchange. Kitchen middens and grave sites throughout the world bear witness to the dependency of man on mollusk.

Much has been written about the way man has employed the shell. Peter Dance, in his book *Shell Collecting*, R. Tucker Abbott, in *Kingdom of the Seashell*, and Roderick Cameron, in *Shells*, devote much space to this interesting relationship. They cite the use of mollusks by primitive man as axes, spears, utensils, ornaments, knives, and trumpets as well as a staple of diet. The ancient Phoenician empire was dependent for its existence as a world power on a dye, Tyrian purple, produced by a mollusk of the Murex family.

Although the use of shells as ornaments and tools was most important, their employment as a medium of exchange cannot be overlooked. This practice has not become completely obsolete, for even in recent times England imported tons of cowries for export to West Africa, there to be exchanged for native products.

In North America, Indians manufactured shell money, or wampum, by a laborious process. Wampum consisted of strings of cylindrical shell beads, each about a quarter of an inch in length and half that in breadth. The beads were of two colors, white and purple, the latter being more valuable. *Mercenaria mercenaria*, a common clam, furnished the largest part of the material for wampum. The trade routes of North America can be traced by marine shells transported by trade into areas far from their native habitats.

Museums, as well as curio shops, are replete with items decorated with shell. In the priceless pre-Columbian trumpet displayed in a Mexico City museum, one is thrilled to recognize the large spired horse conch from the Gulf. Beads, bracelets, rattles, drums, and trumpets from carved shells all found popularity with early man. However, primitive man is not alone, for what woman can resist a beautiful cameo carved from the colorful shell of the cassis snail. Cameo carving is still an important industry in Italy. Mounted shells and shells transformed into silver-rimmed boxes, or worked into precious jewelry as they were in the sixteenth and seventeenth centuries, are staging a resurgence in popularity and today are to be found in expensive specialty shops throughout America.

Perhaps the veneration of the chank shell, *Turbinella pyrum* (Linné), by the Hindus of India is one of the strangest uses of a shell. These shells are considered sacred, being symbolic of the many-armed Hindu god, Vishnu, and all images of Vishnu bear a chank shell in one hand.

Not only did the Renaissance artist depict shells in his paintings but he also found a practical use for them as containers for his paint after he had mixed his pigments. Georges Cuvier used sepia from cephalopods he had dissected to make the drawings used to illustrate his anatomy of the Mollusca in 1817. While sepia ink from the Mediterranean cuttlefish is the most highly prized cephalopod ink, artists and writers have used ink from various cephalopods for at least two thousand years to record their work. It is not permanent, however, and modern substitutes have largely replaced true sepia ink.

The mollusk appears frequently in art and literature, as throughout history shells were often used as symbols. The crusaders adapted the Jacob's scallop from Europe as their emblem when they invaded the Middle East. Afterward they made pilgrimages to the tomb of the Apostle James, supposedly at Santiago de Compostela in Spain, where they found scallop shells on the nearby beaches. They carried them home as a sign that they had reached their goal. Soon people began selling scallop shells at other places, and finally, in order to stop the racket in shells, the Pope decreed that anyone who sold scallop shells at any place but Santiago de Compostela would be excommunicated.

This same scallop shell, *Pecten jacobeus*, has become the familiar trade mark of a Dutch petroleum company that began long ago importing shells to sell to collectors and to be traded to natives in outly-

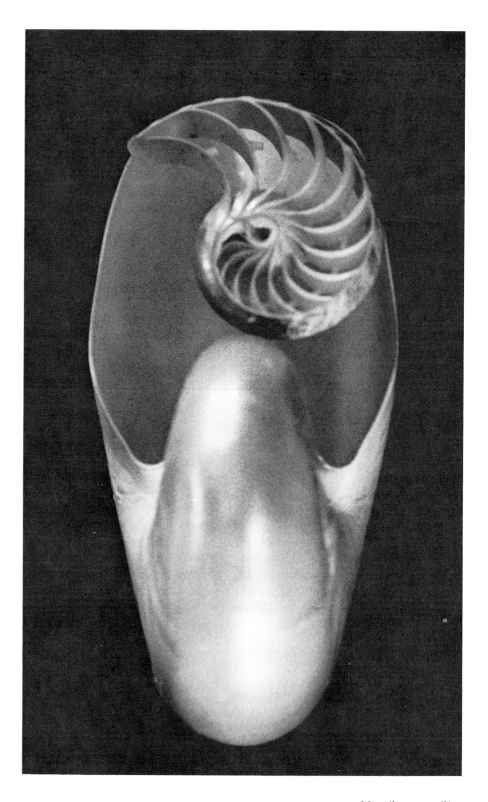

Nautilus pompilius

ing colonies for use as money. As a sideline, the company began selling petroleum products. The origin of the company is but a memory, even though today the tankers owned by the company are each named for and decorated with a sea shell. The southwest Pacific is the home of the pearly chambered nautilus, whose faultless symmetry has inspired design the world over.

Pearls produced by the family Pteriidae, the pearl oyster, have been prized by man since time began. Except for use as food, perhaps the most important industry employing shell is the pearl industry. The iridescent, nacreous layer, or "mother-of-pearl," from certain mollusks is used in the manufacture of buttons, knife handles, inlays, studs, and brooches. Natural pearls result from a foreign body entering the shell and causing an irritation to the animal. In its attempt to protect itself by coating the irritant with a smooth covering of nacre, the mollusk produces a pearl. Perfect pearls formed this way are highly treasured. The production of cultivated pearls is a large industry in Japan, where foreign particles are inserted into the living mollusk, forcing it to produce a pearl. Other shells produce pearls and "mother-of-pearl" but those of the Pteriidae are of the greatest commercial value.

In Texas it is possible to trace similar uses of shell by man. Around Copano Bay, to name but one coastal site, numerous mounds of oystershell abound, affirming the importance of this delicacy in the diet of the Karankawas who lived there. Around these kitchen middens and mounds may be found awls and drills made from the columella of the *Busycon*, beads from *Oliva sayana*, and scrapers from the *Busycon* and the *Callista nimbosa*. Due to the lack of rock, arrowheads in this region were occasionally made of shell. Cabeza de Vaca, acting as a trader for the coastal tribes, found shells a valuable item of exchange.

In the smoothly scraped older cemeteries in areas of rural Texas that were colonized by Anglo-Americans from the southern part of the United States, one will find primitive grave mounds that have been ornamented with shells. The German and Mexican settlers have used this symbol of a mother-goddess cult also, but it was adopted from the Anglos and is not typical of their culture except in Texas. Unless there is proximity to the Gulf of Mexico, the shells used are from streams and rivers in the vicinity.

In modern Texas, as in early times, the most important use of the mollusk is as food. The commercial oyster in Texas is *Crassostrea virginica* (Gmelin). Much research has been done on this oyster, and a bulletin on the subject by the Texas Game and Fish Commission, now the Parks and Wildlife Service, is worthy of study (Hofstetter 1959). Several important game fishes depend on oyster beds for their subsistence, and whatever endangers the oysters endangers their dependents, including sportsmen and sporting goods dealers.

Not only is the oyster important as food, but also its discarded shell is of great value as building material. Shell, primarily oyster, is used in an unaltered state in the building of railway and highway roadbeds, although controversies have arisen in recent years over dredging for this purpose. The high calcium content of oystershell (98–99% as compared to 96% in limestone) made it a good source of lime in the manufacture of Portland cement. Chemical companies along the coast use it in the production of caustic soda and other chemicals. In the Rockport area many roofs are covered with shell, as are driveways and sidewalks. Veritable mountains of oystershell can be seen being transported by barges on the Intracoastal Canal.

Before the Civil War, a material called "shellcrete" was used in building many of the early homes in Corpus Christi. The Centennial House, 411 North Broadway, built in 1848–49, is the oldest building standing and the first two-story home erected in Corpus Christi. Its foundation walls are made of this material. To produce shellcrete, oystershell was gathered along the bay front and then burned in shallow pits to be converted into lime, which, while still in a solid form, was placed in barrels to be air-slaked. This lime was used with an aggregate of crushed shell, sand, and water and was formed in wooden molds to make building blocks. Old buildings of this construction have walls twelve to eighteen inches thick that can be demolished only with dynamite.

Mollusks have always been considered a delicacy, and their cultivation for food dates back to Roman times, when runners sped fresh oysters from the Mediterranean to the Caesars and from the Pacific to the Moctezumas. In America, however, the mollusk is used less as a form of food than in other countries of the world with the exception of England. Many mollusks found in the Gulf waters are edible, but none except the oyster is found in commercial quantities. The *Donax*, or coquina shell, of the island surf can become a delicate chowder, while the adductor muscle of the *Atrina*, or pen shell, rivals the Eastern scallop. The *Mercenaria* of wampum fame also produces a succulent chowder when enough can be gathered. Clam digging is not a productive pastime on the Texas coast, because of the limited supply in waters within easy access.

Shells are sometimes harmful to man. Some, like the *Teredo*, or shipworm, destroy wooden structures in the sea by burrowing into the center of exposed wood. The shipworms were so devastating in 1917 in San Francisco that ferry slips collapsed and warehouses and freight cars crashed into the bay, with destruction reaching catastrophic proportions. Losses in this one disaster were estimated at $25 million. Damage by this family of mollusks probably exceeds the total income from the sale of mollusks for food and all other purposes. The onslaught of boring mollusks can be retarded by the application of creosote and other chemicals, but there is no sure defense against the attack. As yet, the *Teredo* is not a major problem on the Texas coast, but its control is a continuous struggle.

In some areas of the world, diseases carried by shells are a serious menace. The carrier is usually a fresh-water mollusk. Several species that carry schistosomiasis are under study at the Southwest Foundation for Research and Education in San Antonio, Texas. Contamination is another danger, but state health regulations regarding the handling and packaging of seafoods make poisoning by contaminated mollusks a negligible problem.

A minor industry on the Texas coast is the manufacture of curios incorporating shells, most of which are shipped in from the Pacific and Florida. Many lovely natural forms are converted into grotesque animals, lamps, or ashtrays to remind a tourist of his visit to the shores of Texas. Often a shell that never saw the waters of Texas when living tenders "Greetings from Padre Island."

The severe extremes of the physical factors found in Texas tend to make it an inhospitable environment for the shell makers. Still a profusion of molluscan life can be found. Admittedly, the Texas coast does not rival the western coast of Florida, but it has enough specimens to keep the enthusiast busy for many a day. More than 50,000 molluscan species are known in the world, of which 6,000 are found in North American waters. Known to be living in the bays of Texas and within a mile or two offshore are approximately 400 to 600 species. An exciting aspect of shell collecting in Texas is the possibility of having a complete collection of all known local shells or even of being the proud discoverer of a species not previously known to be an inhabitant of these shores.

Shells and Shores of Texas

1. The Texas Coast

Texas, the home of great ranches with their cowboys and oil wells, is seldom thought of as a land of windswept beaches and soaring sea gulls. The second state of the United States in land area, Texas ranks third in length of coastline, containing one-twelfth of the total in the country. The land along this coastline—extending between the Sabine River, at latitude 30° N and longitude 93° 31' W, and the Rio Grande, at latitude 25° 50' N and longitude 97° W—is a vast coastal plain only slightly above sea level. The principal ports on the coast—Corpus Christi, Galveston, and Brownsville—are respectively 35, 20, and 57 feet above sea level. (Houston is an inland port.) The Gulf of Mexico, which forms this coastline, deepens gradually, and along most of the coast lie long barrier islands of sand, enclosing lagoons and bays. Between these islands and the mainland runs the Gulf Intracoastal Waterway. Four hundred and twenty-three miles of the total eleven hundred of this waterway lie in Texas waters, bringing an inexpensive form of transportation to the booming industries of Texas.

Historical Background

Fossil remains of man on the Texas coast date back eight thousand years. However, the first European known to view the Texas shore was probably Alonso Alvarez de Pineda while on a mapping expedition for Francisco de Garay, the governor of Jamaica. In 1519 Pineda sailed along the coast of the Gulf of Mexico from Florida to Veracruz searching for the Strait of Anian, which would lead the treasure-hungry Spaniards to the riches of Cathay and India. While on this journey he careened his four vessels for a needed overhaul at what is now the Rio Grande, the southern boundary of Texas. There, in the fall of 1519, he spent forty days and noted numerous Indian villages along the lower Rio Grande. These same Indians drove Diego de Camargo away in 1520 when he attempted to found a colony near Pineda's landing site.

Pánfilo de Narváez was commissioned to sail from the Río de las Palmas to the Cape of Florida and to establish two colonies along his route. On his staff, as treasurer, was Alvar Núñez Cabeza de Vaca, whose chronicle of the events following the shipwreck of the expedition in 1528 gives us our earliest account of life in the area now known as Texas. It is thought the survivors landed somewhere on Galveston Island. Starvation soon reduced the Spaniards to cannibalism. De Vaca survived the hardships and passed eight years as captive, trader, and medicine man among the Indians, leaving to us an exciting record of his experiences.

The Karankawa Indians of the Texas coast were a primitive tribe, without clothing, arts, or houses, and practicing ritualistic cannibalism. Having come to this region in about A.D. 1400, they were well established and had lived primarily on fish and oysters for many generations when the first white man sighted these shores. Eventually driven out by the gun and sword, they left the European colonist an untouched source of wealth. These Indians were reported by early settlers to be as treacherous and inhospitable as the islands they inhabited. Their primary locale between 1536 and 1821 was from Galveston Island to the northern tip of Padre Island. Shell mounds, shell implements, and primitive arrowheads are still found to attest their former presence (fig. 1).

The Karankawas, "water walkers," were a vile-smelling group as a result of their practice of smearing their bodies with alligator fat or any other odorous material they could find to ward off the tormenting mosquitoes. Although usually hungry, they did not resort to cannibalism when threatened with starvation. Contrary to popular opinion resulting from early Spanish reports, these coastal Indians were not cannibals in the true sense of the word but practiced the custom of eating human flesh for reasons of revenge or for magical purposes. They were lazy and pre-

3

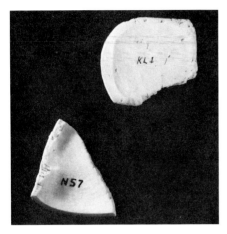

A

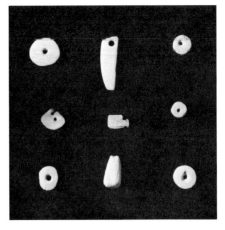

B

C

ferred to suffer hunger and naked-ness in order to be at liberty in the inland woods or on the beach.

Even though the Karankawas were said to be the largest American Indians, they were no match for their invaders. They were extermi-nated by the usurpers of their terri-tory. The remnants eventually drifted into Mexico, where they were absorbed by local tribes. Kuykendall reports (1903, p. 253): "In the year 1855 the once formida-ble tribe of Karankawas had dwin-dled to six or eight individuals who were residing near San Fernando, State of Tamaulipas, Mexico."

Their neighbors to the east and into Louisiana across the Sabine River were the Atakapans. The French officer Simars de Bellisle left us a reliable account of this people after he was captured in 1719 and lived among them for three years. Closely related to the Karankawas, they were, as the translation of their name indicates, "maneaters." Their territory was more hospitable than that of the larger Karankawas, but they, too, moved in seasonal rhythms, gathering roots and nuts, hunting and fishing. Both tribes led a beachcombing, scavenger type of existence, and neither survived modern civilization.

The coast south of the last Karan-kawa camp was largely uninhabited because of its inaccessibility. Occa-

sional bands of Coahuiltecans would prowl its southern limits from their territory to the west. In-habiting the country inland from Galveston Bay to the Rio Grande and west to San Antonio, they had few usable natural resources in their southern zone and were constantly on the move looking for food. It was this never-ending search that brought them to the coast at times in attempts to supplement their usual diet of cacti, mesquite beans, nuts, sotol, and agave. Ritualistic cannibals, they probably did not re-sort to cannibalism for food but ate only captives and their own people who died of natural causes.

The Spaniards, prospering from their conquest of the fabled Aztecs in Mexico, were sending vast treas-ure fleets back home with their loot. In 1553 vessels laden with such a cargo, as well as a thousand proud conquistadors and their families, sailed from Veracruz for Spain via Havana. Before reaching the Bahama passage they were hit by a tropical hurricane that sank four ships on the spot and drove thirteen across the Gulf to crash in the pounding surf off Padre Island. Only three finally straggled to safety.

At Devil's Elbow, about forty miles from the southern tip of Texas, three hundred men, women, and children staggered ashore.

They saved much of the food sup-ply from the wrecked vessels and had been on the beach for six days when a hundred Karankawa In-dians arrived bearing fresh fish and making signs of peace. While the survivors were eating the meal pre-pared for them, the Indians at-tacked. Crossbows salvaged from the wreckage drove them away but not until many of the Spaniards were dead.

The next day the survivors headed south down the island, abandoning most of their supplies because they thought they were near the Pánuco River and a Span-ish outpost. Five days later when they arrived at Brazos Santiago Pass, they built rafts and crossed but in doing so lost the weapons overboard. The Indians attacked again at the pass and only two hun-dred disaster victims managed to reach the Rio Grande, half of them wounded. Thinking they could ap-pease the Indians so that they would go away, the foolhardy Spaniards gave them all their cloth-ing, leaving themselves exposed to the vicious sun and wind.

In desperation they stumbled on, dogged at every step by the Indians, who killed all stragglers. Only two survived to tell the tale. One of these men reached the Pánuco in spite of festering wounds from ar-rows that were to remain in his

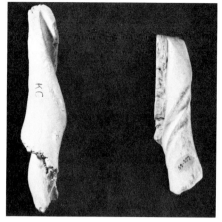

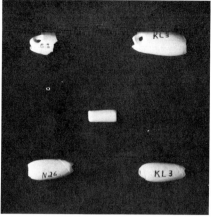

D

E

Fig. 1. Indian shell artifacts collected along the coastal bend by Sam Fitzpatrick, a Corpus Christi geologist and archeologist:
A. two scrapers made from *Busycon*
B. beads and pendants made from various shells
C. shell arrowheads dating from A.D. 11 to A.D. 1500
D. archaic *Busycon* columella gouges
E. beads of olive shells (the fish type is very rare)

body until he was carried to Mexico City. The other was found a year later at the site of the catastrophe when Spanish ships returned to salvage the wrecks. Twelve of the ships were located and most of the treasure recovered, but the precious cargo of the thirteenth has defied man's search until this day. ¿Quien sabe?

Only hapless victims of the sea came to the Texas coast to fall prey to the merciless Karankawas until René Robert Cavelier, Sieur de la Salle, discoverer of the Mississippi and a hero of France, arrived in 1685. He claimed that the purpose of his journey was the establishment of a colony near the mouth of the Mississippi, but it is believed by some research students that he was on a mission to conquer New Spain and that the stated plan was only a cover. In order to facilitate a French invasion, he needed to be based nearer Spanish territory. He sailed on until he reached Matagorda Bay. One of his four vessels went aground there and the others sailed back to France after bitter arguments between La Salle and one of his captains.

Between 180 and 220 unskilled artisans and soldiers were in the remaining group. They built a fort on a high bluff on the west bank of Garcitas Creek about five or six miles upstream. La Salle named the fort St. Louis and the nearby bay La Vaca. He made two long overland expeditions from the fort in search of rumored Spanish settlements. His people were dying and hopeless by the time he attempted a third march, and he was murdered near the Brazos River by one of his men.

In the meantime the Spanish had heard of the French colony in Texas and had begun to send expeditions by land and sea attempting to locate it. When Alonso de León, coming north from Mexico, arrived at the ill-fated French fort in 1689, he found only the bodies of the few who had remained to fall victims of the Karankawas.

De León's penetration of the country as far as the Guadalupe River marked the beginning of the European settlement of Texas. The Spaniards realized they must establish colonies to hold the land and so began their period of mission building.

As years went by, the French, Spanish, and Americans sailed up and down the Gulf coast, landing or being shipwrecked. To the southern end of what is now called Padre Island, in the year 1804 came a Spanish seafaring priest named Nicolás Balli (pronounced Baayee). He and his alleged nephew, Juan José Balli, lived there until the padre went to Matamoros, Mexico, to establish a church. The two men es-

tablished the Santa Cruz ranch about twenty-six miles north of Point Isabel and in 1829 received a grant to the land. In 1852 a special act of the Texas legislature made the grant permanent. It is for this adventurous priest, Padre Nicolás Balli, that the longest of the Texas islands is named.

The offshore islands, worlds of incessant change, linked with piracy and tales of sunken and buried treasure and lost Spanish galleons, have inspired reams of romantic lore. Some fact, some fiction. It is a fact that Louis Aury, a famous pirate, called Galveston his base until 1816. He was succeeded by Jean Lafitte, who raided Spanish shipping and sold slaves from Galveston until 1821.

Colonists from the United States began to come to Texas early in the nineteenth century, and by 1836 they were strong enough to fight a bloody war and win their independence from Mexico, which had only a dozen years earlier overthrown the Spanish yoke. The Treaty of Velasco, ending this conflict, was signed May 14, 1836, at the temporary capital located on the beach at the mouth of the Brazos River, now Surfside.

For ten years following the Texas Revolution both the new Republic of Texas and Mexico claimed the territory between the Nueces River and the Rio Grande. Into this void sailed the army of the United States in the form of several thousand troops led by General Zachary Taylor. On July 26, 1845, the first U.S. flag in Texas was flown on San José Island, where the troops had landed. In his journal (1847, p. 14), Captain W. S. Henry recorded the event with these words: ". . . on top of the loftiest sand hill was erected a pole, from the top of which was unfurled the star spangled banner. It floats over a rich acquisition, the most precious Uncle Sam has yet added to his crown."

The stars and stripes were waving over the Karankawa's old hunting grounds, and hunting grounds they were. The men marveled at the fish and game so easily taken and at how rapidly melons and potatoes would grow. Deer and wild mustangs, ducks and geese, oysters and fish of every description abounded. Foul-tasting but potable water could be had by digging a few feet into the sand and shoring the hole with a barrel. These young soldiers and their camp women frolicked in the surf before moving across the bay and settling down to the business of training for a war.

The camp was set up in what is now the northern part of downtown Corpus Christi. From this base the soldiers fought the mosquitoes and the elements for seven months and eleven days. During this period Texas statehood was made official, and in December 1845 the republic became the twenty-eighth state, the Lone Star State.

After sending a reconnoitering party down Padre Island, Taylor decided it would be better to march his men inland to a site opposite Matamoros. In their trek across the "Wild Horse Desert" on the trail used by the Mexicans as they retreated from San Jacinto, the men suffered from heat, dust, and lack of water. Soon after their arrival at Fort Brown, they engaged and overwhelmingly defeated the larger

Mexican army on the flats nearby in two battles—the first, Palo Alto, on May 8, 1846, and the second on the following day at the Resaca de la Palma. From there Taylor and his young West Point lieutenants, among them Ulysses S. Grant, went on to win the territory for the United States.

With the Mexicans whipped and Texas in the Union, ranchers and planters from the States began to move in. Gone were the treasure fleets and pirates, but perhaps the real treasures of these coastal islands are the grass and abundant fresh water that have made ranching profitable since the days of Balli.

This grass and water made life possible for the family of John V. Singer, which was shipwrecked on the southern tip of Padre in 1847 (Writer's Round Table 1950, p. 158). They landed near the padre's old ranch headquarters, now covered by the shifting sand hills. The family built a home from their wrecked schooner and soon prospered by ranching and salvaging until they were ordered from the island by the Confederate army in 1861.

The Civil War brought considerable activity to the coast of Texas. The Union navy attempted to blockade the almost limitless coast in order to cut off Confederate shipments of cotton and hides. Numerous skirmishes took place between the two forces, but lack of communications and remoteness made achieving this blockade an almost impossible task. The shanty town of Bagdad sprang up on the south side of the mouth of the Rio Grande, and the beach was covered with bales of cotton awaiting shipment to Europe.

Attesting the isolation of this area at that dramatic time in history is the fact that the last battle of the Civil War was fought at Palmito Hill near the southern tip of the coast, on May 12–13, 1865, thirty-four days after Lee had surrendered at

Appomattox. Ironically, the Confederates were the victors. We wonder if, when word of the battle reached the federal commander in chief, Ulysses S. Grant, he remembered the place where he had fought as a young lieutenant, only a stone's throw from Palmito Hill. Twenty years later it was still in isolation.

Reports made soon after the war by the hardy engineer R. E. Halter brought about the establishment of a series of lighthouses along the coast and make interesting reading for those who marvel at the fiber of the men who defied the elements on these islands long ago.

It was cheaper and easier to have shallow-draft lighters built in the East and shipped by schooner to Texas than to attempt to have them made in Corpus Christi or Galveston in the mid–nineteenth century. Traffic behind the islands went by flat-bottomed scows through the bays to Indianola or through Aransas Pass into Corpus Christi along a channel that had been dredged to a depth of six feet.

Between 1840 and 1880 an active business sprang up in the coastal area in slaughtering the wild mustangs and cattle for their hides, tallow, and bones. Packing houses dotted the coast from Galveston to Flour Bluff, and salt was in demand to pack the hides in. The trade boomed, then died. Also, during this period the area supported a large green-turtle fishery; in 1890 more than 83,000 pounds were produced. This creature no longer inhabits the Texas bays.

Near where La Salle had landed, on Lavaca Bay, the prime entry point for colonists coming to Texas from over the world developed. It was called Indianola. In 1875 Indianola, grown to six thousand population, was heavily damaged by a severe tropical storm; finally, in 1886, the town was wiped from the map by a hurricane. Here, from this flat, featureless shore, countless numbers of pioneering souls streamed to the frontiers of Texas. There were the Germans who followed the rivers, establishing along the banks settlements that bear their imprint to this day. Here, too, came much of the building material for early Texas homes, along with the camels for the ill-fated dream of using these beasts as transportation for the army in the "deserts" of west Texas.

Gone, too, are many other settlements. Throughout history northers and hurricanes, like those at Indianola, have made the barrier islands of Texas inhospitable for permanent settlements, although several have survived. The city of Galveston has clung to the sands of Galveston Island since the early nineteenth century in spite of having been the victim of the worst natural disaster ever to strike the continental United States. The hurricane of 1900 left about six thousand dead in the havoc that visited the island.

Port Aransas and South Padre Island are the other incorporated towns on the islands. A colony is growing near the northern end of Padre, private ranches thrive on mid–San José and southern Matagorda islands, and the air force, until recently, practiced bombing at a range on northern Matagorda. All these establishments receive repeated attacks from Mother Nature, but a better understanding of the environment, more efficient hurricane warning systems, and increased knowledge of construction principles are easing the blows.

After the building of the lighthouses was completed, between 1852 and 1856, and the activity of the Civil War had subsided, the beaches of Texas lapsed into their early ways, unmolested except for a few cattlemen who came after the Ballis and the Singers, fattening their cattle on the lush grasses of their unfenced domains.

The Singers were followed by the Kings, Kenedys, and Dunns on Padre. Each island along the coast was a series of large privately owned ranches—kingdoms populated by cattle, deer, coyotes, turkeys, cranes, herons, and the skittish ghost crab. The barbed-wire en-tanglements that covered the beaches in World War II only made these kingdoms more secure for a while.

Each of the barrier islands has been privately owned at least once. Today, however, 69.5 miles of Padre have become a national seashore. The plan to conserve the region, begun in 1954 by the National Park Service, is now a reality. Development is progressing slowly, but it is reassuring to know that a part of this coastline will be kept as it was when the Karankawas, the Spaniards, the French, the pirates, Taylor's troops, the Confederates, and the cattle barons roamed its shores. It is hoped that this seashore, along with the large national wildlife refuge on Aransas Bay near Matagorda Island, will be a haven for the abundant wildlife of the area. Where the shore birds soared over the heads of the tall Karankawas, the giant turtles, and the wild mustangs, modern man is striving to reestablish the almost extinct whooping crane before he too is driven from his native shores.

Physical Description

The 370 miles of coastline plus the bays and tidewater flats make an impressive 624 miles of beach for the shell collector in Texas to investigate. The barrier-island chain has been described as the longest in the world. Geologically, it is of the Holocene period. Located in a semitropical climate, these islands have a minimum width of a few hundred feet to a maximum of nearly four and one-half miles. The southern ends of the islands are usually narrower than the northern ends. The white sand beach slopes gently beneath the Gulf surf. The slope of the continental shelf is only about six feet per mile. Beyond the beach is a ridge of sand dunes that reaches a height of fifty feet in some places. Behind the dunes the terrain breaks into a scattering of lower dunes and finally into a tidal flat that eventually disappears beneath the waters of the bays and lagoons. (See figs. 2 & 3; table 1.)

Naturally, there are variations. Let us begin at the Sabine River and make our way southwestward to the Rio Grande. (Reference to the maps in chapter 4 will aid in following this description of the coast.) We are concerned here only with the shallow waters and not the offshore shelves and their fauna. However, those extremely broad, muddy shelves extending out into the Gulf have caused the beach collecting to be less productive than in some other localities of the United States. This fact, coupled with the lack of natural rock formations and coral reefs close to shore, contributes to the brevity of our species list. Nevertheless, the list is rapidly being added to due to the growing interest in the Texas coast for serious students of marine biology. Actually, the greatest part of the coast is relatively inaccessible to all except the well-equipped and endowed researcher.

Perhaps of less interest to the collector is that part of the coast between the jetties at Sabine Pass and Galveston. Because longshore currents here carry large amounts of silt from the Mississippi, the water is seldom the clear blue that it is off the Florida and southern Texas coasts. Salt marsh extends from the Sabine to MacFadden Beach near Galveston, and oyster grass (*Spar-*

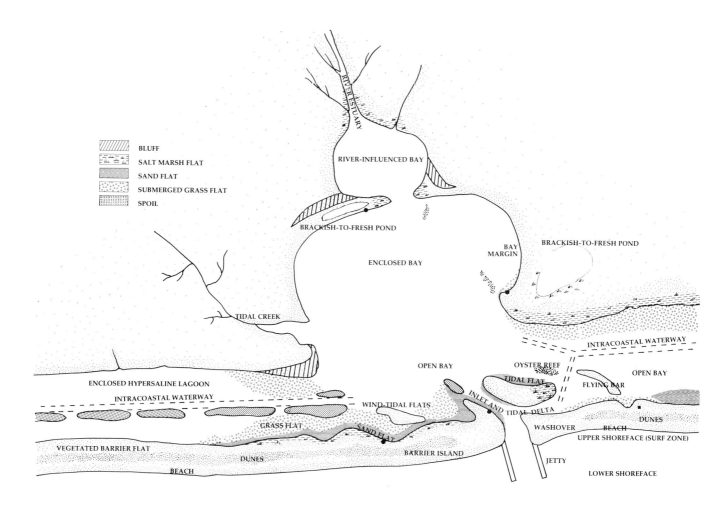

BLUFF
SALT MARSH FLAT
SAND FLAT
SUBMERGED GRASS FLAT
SPOIL

RIVER ESTUARY

RIVER-INFLUENCED BAY

BRACKISH-TO-FRESH POND

ENCLOSED BAY

BAY MARGIN

BRACKISH-TO-FRESH POND

TIDAL CREEK

INTRACOASTAL WATERWAY

OPEN BAY

OYSTER REEF

OPEN BAY

TIDAL FLAT

FLYING BAR

ENCLOSED HYPERSALINE LAGOON

INTRACOASTAL WATERWAY

WIND-TIDAL FLATS

INLET AND TIDAL DELTA

DUNES

GRASS FLAT

SAND FLAT

WASHOVER

BEACH

UPPER SHOREFACE (SURF ZONE)

VEGETATED BARRIER FLAT

DUNES

BARRIER ISLAND

JETTY

BEACH

LOWER SHOREFACE

Fig. 2. Generalized Texas coastal area

tina alterniflora) grows in the intertidal zone, which is chiefly marsh clay.

State Highway 87, from Sabine Pass to Bolivar Pass, closely follows the beach ridge, which has been stabilized by grasses, and the beach slope is almost imperceptible. The near-shore Gulf bottom is largely clay covered with a few inches of sand. Toward Bolivar Pass the beach on this narrow peninsula separating East Bay from the Gulf of Mexico begins to slope gently, and a wide sand flat occurs at the pass. This flat is a favorite spot for collectors in this area.

At Bolivar Pass we find the second jettied inlet. The area adjacent to the pass encompasses the city of Galveston, which is protected by a ten-mile-long sea wall. Continuing westward, this offshore island is

separated from a barrier spit by San Luis Pass, which was long an obstacle to driving along the beach from Galveston to Freeport. A new toll bridge now spans the gap. Along this route the beach slopes very gently and the foreshore area (the area between the tide lines) is wide. Low dunes, seldom more than six feet in height, have formed along the beach ridge on the backshore. San Luis Pass is the only channel opening from West Bay to the Gulf. There is a wide sand flat here that becomes a special haunt of the shell collector at low tides.

In the vicinity of Freeport the coast again becomes a part of the mainland and the Velasco jetties act to divert the Brazos River so that its channel can be utilized by the many industrial plants located here. In good weather the beach is crowded

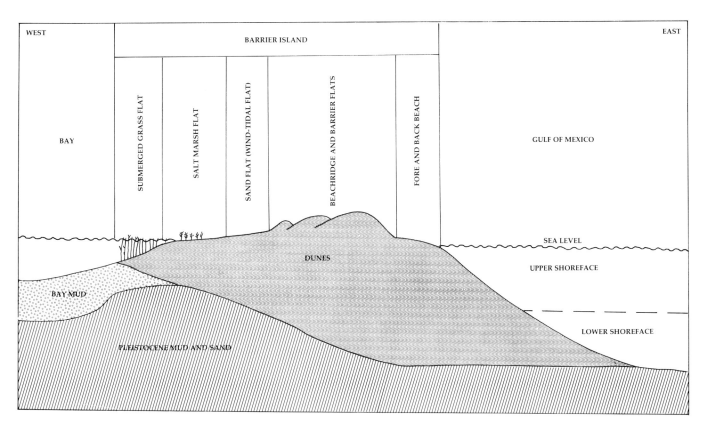

WEST   EAST

BARRIER ISLAND

SUBMERGED GRASS FLAT · SALT MARSH FLAT · SAND FLAT (WIND-TIDAL FLAT) · BEACHRIDGE AND BARRIER FLATS · FORE AND BACK BEACH

BAY · GULF OF MEXICO

SEA LEVEL

DUNES

UPPER SHOREFACE

BAY MUD

LOWER SHOREFACE

PLEISTOCENE MUD AND SAND

in spite of the fact that the Gulf is generally muddy from waters entering it from the Brazos and San Bernard rivers. From here to Sargent Beach, the next point readily accessible to the collector, the beach is eroding badly. A road has been completed to the mouth of the San Bernard and a proposed bridge may soon add another access to the Gulf shore. Between the San Bernard and Sargent Beach are several places where fossil marsh clay is exposed in the intertidal zone. At Sargent Beach, sandstone and beach rock almost completely replace the sand. Instead of a beach ridge, there is a cut bank two to three feet in height. The beach slopes gently away from the bank. Some cottages on stilts line the beach and are separated from the Intracoastal Waterway by a marshy area.

From Sargent Beach, near Brown Cedar Cut, south to the Colorado River, the surrounding land is low and is cut by bayous on its bay

shores. The beach nearest Brown Cedar Cut is covered with heavy shell, and the beach ridge has a greater variety of plants than is found to the south. Brown Cedar Cut prevents a four-wheel-drive vehicle from traveling the beach between the Colorado and Farm Road 457 at Sargent Beach. Those who drive northeast on the beach from the Colorado River along Matagorda peninsula will find a wide, flat beach and low dunes.

The bayside is cut by numerous bayous. An amazing amount of driftwood litters the beach ridge; most of this wood floats down the Colorado River. A log jam that accumulated over a period of at least fifty years once choked the river for a distance of forty-six miles upstream. This jam was dynamited and cleared between 1926 and 1930. In 1936 a man-made channel was dredged across the barrier peninsula to the Gulf. This diversion of the major source of fresh water into Matagorda Bay changed the bay

Fig. 3. Modern barrier-bar environments and facies (cross section after Bernard and LeBlanc 1970)

Table 1. Coastal Environmental Units

Inner continental shelf

Coastal barriers

Beach and shoreface
Fore-island dunes and vegetated
barrier flats
Active dunes
Washover areas
Swales
Tidal flats

Bays, lagoons, and estuaries

Tidal inlet and tidal delta
Tidally influenced open bay
Enclosed bay
Mobile bay-margin sands
Reef and reef-related areas—living
Reef and reef-related areas—dead
Grass flats
River estuary, river-influenced bay
Spoil areas
Wind-tidal flats

Coastal wetlands

Salt marsh
Fresh-water marsh
Brackish marsh
Brackish marsh (closed)
Swamp

Made land and spoil

Biotopes

Coastal Gulf
Gulf beach and shoreface
Dune and barrier flat
Spoil bank
Jetty and bulkhead
Oyster reef
Thalassia (grass flat)
Spartina (salt-water marsh)
Juncus (fresh-water marsh)
Mud flat
Sand flat
Blue-green algal
Hypersaline
River mouth
Bay plantonic
Channel

Source: Based on Texas Governor's Office 1973.

from an estuarine environment to one with a salinity more typical of the Gulf of Mexico.

Matagorda Peninsula is isolated and difficult to reach except at the point near the Colorado River where State Highway 60 follows the east bank of the river. Fishing craft are unable to use the river as an exit to the Gulf except on very calm days, due to the shallow water over the longshore sand bars; otherwise the area would be more extensively developed. The new Matagorda ship channel, maintained by the Corps of Engineers, cuts the peninsula about three miles north of Pass Cavallo. From this pass to the Rio Grande, the Gulf coast is a chain of barrier islands that front a series of shallow coastal bays.

In general the islands' outer shorelines are almost straight. The beach is corrugated with temporary serrations, or cusps, sometimes several hundred feet apart, which are caused by storm action but may be smoothed out by later storms. According to Hedgpeth (1953), the inner shoreline is irregular, scalloped by washover fans or prolonged into spits, which, on the Texas coast, usually point to the southwest. Some of the spits may persist as "flying bars" of small chain islands, for example, the Bird Islands of the Lagunda Madre and Mud Island in Aransas Bay. In less humid regions to the south, there is a development of clay dunes fifteen to twenty feet high.

The northernmost two islands in the main barrier chain are privately owned and can be reached only by boat or light plane. Matagorda Island is approximately thirty-four miles long and is bounded on the north by Pass Cavallo and on the south by Cedar Bayou. Matagorda Island receives more rain than the islands to the south and, except at the southern end, dunes are not a conspicuous part of the landscape. The sea oats (*Uniola paniculata*) so familiar to the visitor on Padre Island are replaced here by wiregrass (*Spartina patens*) as the dominant plant on the beach ridge. The beach is fine sand and slopes very gently. Fences cut the beach at frequent intervals on the southern two-thirds, and small bomb craters left from the days of the air force pock the wide, flat beach on the northern portion. The rusting hulk of a large ship rests in the surf about mid-island. The absence of beachcombers on this island has permitted driftwood, bottles, and other wreck to accumulate in quantities on the beach. The area behind the dunes on this most isolated of the barrier beaches is a wonderland. Here man has developed the natural resources without despoiling nature. The acres of lush grasslands are crossed by shell-paved roads from which can be seen incredible quantities of wildlife mingling with the vast herds of cattle. Small, fenced-in wooden tepees, serving as quail covers, dot the flat terrain, which is devoid of the brush these birds naturally choose for protection and nesting.

San José Island is bounded on the north by Cedar Bayou and on the south by Aransas Pass, an inlet jettied in 1887, through which the ocean-going freighters bound for the port of Corpus Christi must pass. The island is approximately twenty miles long and inhabited only by a few ranch employees. Previously, in winter and early spring, commercial beach seiners from Port Aransas, using nets over twenty feet in length, worked the outer beach. This practice is against the law in or on any of the waters of the Gulf of Mexico within one mile of the Horace Caldwell Pier located on Mustang Island and the Bob Hall Pier on Padre Island and within one thousand feet of the shoreline of Padre Island in Nueces County. The owners of San José could and often did bar this practice because there is no public access to the island. Early in 1969 they chose to put a stop to

the commercial seining.

The southernmost five miles of San José Island comprise an open flat where the dunes have not developed. The natural shifting of Aransas Pass during the ages before it was stabilized by the jetties occurred over this stretch of beach. The lighthouse that stands on Harbor Island was built in 1852 to guard the pass. During the Civil War a village of two thousand people flourished on San José opposite the lighthouse. Through the years following the destruction of the village during that war, the pass gradually shifted to the south, creating a vast flat and leaving the lighthouse nothing to guard. It was deactivated in 1952 and the old pass site is called North Pass. This island was named San José by the Spaniards but has long been known as St. Joseph Island. In January 1973 the Texas legislature restored the original title.

In Lydia Ann Channel, the western boundary of San José, the wreckage of a World War II Victory ship, *The Worthington*, lies next to the island's bay shore opposite the old light. This ship, torpedoed by German submarines in the Gulf, was being towed to Corpus Christi for salvage. Considered a hazard to navigation by port authorities, it was denied entry, and the owners anchored it across from the lighthouse, where it was sunk to protect navigation. It is now a favored spot for anglers. On the shore nearby, fragments of the shellcrete foundations of the former village can be found.

The northern end of the island is covered with sand dunes in the foreshore area. It differs from Mustang Island in that the small active drifts common at the base of the dunes on Mustang are rare or absent on most of San José. Vegetation is similar to that on Padre Island, but the backshore growth is denser with large clumps of mesquite trees.

Mustang Island is separated from

the southern tip of San José by the Aransas Pass jetties. The fishing-resort town of Port Aransas is located on the northern end and is connected with the town of Aransas Pass by a ferry and a causeway and with Corpus Christi by a road (completed in 1954) down the center of the island to the John F. Kennedy Causeway. The University of Texas maintains its Marine Science Institute at Port Aransas.

The foreshore of Mustang Island is a gently sloping beach of fine sand and is passable to passenger cars at times during low tides. This fine sand is one of the first things a visitor notices, for it is more highly sorted than most beach sand in this country. The backshore, that area between high tide and the base of the dunes, is approximately 150 feet wide. The fore dunes are nearly all stabilized by sea oats. However, the small dunes at their seaward base are in their first stages of development and are more or less active. Prior to the opening of the Mustang Island Water Exchange Pass, Mustang and Padre islands had been joined ever since the dredging of the ship channel at Port Aransas except when storm tides opened Corpus Christi Pass. This new jetty, dedicated February 6, 1971, and opened August 3, 1972, has permanently separated the two islands.

Padre Island, a low, barren, stormswept strip of sand for 113 miles, is the longest barrier island in the world. It separates the Laguna Madre from the Gulf of Mexico. There are few landmarks for the beach traveler. Causeways built at the northern end in 1950 and the southern end in 1974 link it to the mainland. Nueces County in the north and Cameron County to the south have developed parks at either extremity. Twelve miles south of Nueces County Park, the Padre Island National Seashore Area has been established and is being developed with federal funds. A causeway is proposed in Willacy

County to link the island to Port Mansfield, 78 miles south of Bob Hall Pier. We shall designate this pier in Nueces County Park "mile zero" when indicating the location of the prominent features south of it on Padre Island.

The topography of Padre Island, like that of the other barrier islands, is shaped by the wind and the sea. The most conspicuous features are the sand dunes and the washovers. Washovers are open, flat areas or shallow channels formed by the spilling of water across the barrier island during the times of storm tides. Sand soon closes the seaward opening and the remaining areas appear to be dry washes. There are no washovers on the northern end of Padre Island, but beginning about 50 miles from the pier and extending to the southern end they become numerous. Vegetation invades the washovers only very slowly and, since there is little or no vegetation, dunes do not form.

The first plant to invade the shore is sea purslane. Hildebrand and Gunter (1955) have described a dune's development as being based on this plant. As the purslane grows, sand collects around its base and builds a mammilliform mound, or coppice dune. After this mound reaches a certain height, and if it is not dissolved by a storm tide, it is invaded by other plants, usually sea oats. However, in very wide washovers, such as the old North Pass on San José Island, where there are no other plants adjacent, coppice dunes up to six feet in height are built solely on sea purslane. Normally other plants would crowd out the purslane before the coppice dune was three feet high. The dunes on Padre do not reach a great height, probably no more than thirty to forty feet. Behind the beach dunes are grass flats and smaller dunes. The shore along the Laguna Madre is a poorly defined area of mud flats that merge with the waters of the lagoon.

About 8 miles south of the pier the Chevron offshore oil field can be seen. The entrance to the seashore area is at the 12-mile point. A paved road has been constructed down the center of the island to these facilities at Malaquite Beach and is projected for the entire island. In the meantime the beach traveler in a passenger car can safely go only about 20 miles, or to the beginning of Little Shell, a section that is difficult to delimit but has been so called by fishermen because of the large deposit of small clam shells on the foreshore. At the long-closed Yarborough Pass (28.3 miles), the beach becomes streaked with blackish lines caused by magnetite, or iron oxide, in the sands. About three miles south of this pass, Big Shell commences and extends 10 to 12 miles farther south. In Big and Little Shell the steep, high-tide crest and the soft shell on the backshore make passage difficult. Big Shell differs from Little Shell in being composed only of large, heavy shell. Mostly, however, the shells are fragmented and the fragments form ridges and cusps on an otherwise steep beach. Old, badly worn, heavy clam shells almost form a pavement as one nears the Mansfield jetties, where an outcropping of clay is encountered in the foreshore.

The barrier islands are paralleled by two or three rows of sand bars with troughs between them that are called longshore bars and longshore troughs. One difference in the foreshore of mid–Padre Island is that the longshore bars do not parallel the shore but form what the fishermen call "blind guts" along the shore. The absence of the bars also accounts for the area called Big Shell. Without the bars the full force of the waves strikes the beach, fragmenting all but the large, heavy shell so characteristic of this stretch of shore (fig. 4). The probable reason for the absence of sand bars is the abrupt curve that the coastline makes in this mid-region. It not

only changes direction in relation to the prevailing winds but also becomes the meeting place of the longshore currents.

The same approximate area is referred to by Leipper (1954) as a "graveyard of ships" (fig. 5). This 100-square-mile area of current convergence is 20 miles east and 40 miles south of Aransas Pass. If one examines the wrecked boats along the shore, he is impressed by the fact that they are most numerous in the vicinity of Yarborough Pass, which lies in the convergence region. A beached shrimp boat being pounded by the waves is a familiar sight in this area. At times it is possible to see an abrupt change in the color of the Gulf, as if there were a line of demarcation in the sea with cloudy, blue water to the north of it and clear, aqua water to the south.

Three and two-tenths miles below Yarborough Pass, which is recognized by the radio tower at an oil company camp near the bay side, one can find a ranch road behind the dunes. This simple trail extends 13 miles down the center of the island and reenters the beach at the 44.4-mile point. This road is inundated following rains and storms.

The only other significant landmark seen before arriving at the Mansfield jetties is the boiler of the *Nicaragua*, a six-hundred-ton Mexican coastal steamer that ran aground during a storm on October 18, 1918. The crew of this hapless vessel was rescued five days later. According to local tradition, the ship was running guns to be used in the Mexican revolution, but it was probably a banana boat on its regular run. Her remains protrude from the surf 65.5 miles south of the pier, and a small park ranger station can be seen here back in the dunes.

A point on the beach about 2.8 miles north of the Mansfield jetties is a haunt of the metal-detector-equipped treasure hunter because Spanish galleons lie offshore. An

A

B

C

Fig. 4. Big Shell:
A. beach ridges only occurring here
B. broken heavy shell covering
C. detail of shell

Fig. 5. Big Shell, the "graveyard of ships": a wrecked shrimp boat in the pounding surf at the point on Padre Island where a convergence has produced a historic hazard to navigation

out-of-state company began salvage operations in 1969 on one of the 415-year-old treasure ships, an action that may put an end to the thrill of catching the gleam of an ancient doubloon in the sand. Laws were promptly passed in the state legislature to protect such treasures, and the Texas Antiquities Committee is making plans for the preservation and display of the artifacts (Antiquity Code, Article 6145-9; passed September 10, 1969).

The jetties, 77.6 miles south of the pier and 36 miles north of Brazos Santiago Pass, were completed in May 1962. Prior to that it was possible to drive the entire length of the island. There is talk of a causeway to connect this section of the island to the mainland, but at present these jetties are accessible only by boat or four-wheel-drive vehicle. Here the water is generally clear because no rivers empty into the Laguna Madre, which is opened by this cut.

South of the Mansfield jetties the driving is difficult until one reaches the pavement about five miles north of Isla Blanca Park; then it is an easy drive to the Port Isabel jetties and the well-developed resort facilities at this end of Padre. Fine hotels and cottages as well as more modest

motels and trailer parks dot the sands of this almost tropical part of the island.

Brazos Island, the last and smallest in the chain, can be reached by going inland and taking State Highway 4, which goes directly to Boca Chica Beach. As one goes through the town of Port Isabel, the old Point Isabel lighthouse (1852–1905) can be seen. The pass this historic light guarded is said to have been named El Paso de los Brazos de Santiago (the Pass of the Arms of St. James) by Pineda in 1519.

The road passes near the site of the last battle of the Civil War fought on the barren flats of Palmito Hill. At present there is no development at the beach although hundreds of people visit it every summer to fish and swim. The Boca Chica inlet, which is often closed, forms the southern boundary of Brazos Island. From this inlet to the mouth of the fabled Rio Grande (10 miles from the jetty) the beach becomes progressively more silty and muddy. In the immediate vicinity of the river, which empties directly into the Gulf, marsh grasses grow into the edge of the water. The flow of the Rio Grande has been greatly reduced by dams along its course; therefore, the supply of fresh water

entering the Gulf has a negligible effect on the ecology of the region.

The most conspicuous and biologically significant feature of the shoreline is the chain of passes we have described as we proceeded down the coast: Sabine, Bolivar, San Luis, Matagorda, Cavallo, Cedar Bayou, Aransas, Corpus Christi, Port Mansfield, and Brazos Santiago. These passes become stabilized at the extreme southern ends of the bays into which they open. Related to these inlets are the tidal deltas built up by deposition of sediment carried from the direction of the barrier island northeast of the inlet. Thus the delta is built up at the northern end of the island, that is, south of the inlet.

Harbor Island at Port Aransas and the islands at Pass Cavallo are examples of the tidal delta. Pass Cavallo is probably the most stable natural pass on the Texas coast. We will recall that La Salle entered Matagorda Bay through Pass Cavallo, which has been shown on charts since 1690, and that the German pioneers of Texas braved its treacherous shoals to reach Indianola.

The barrier islands, formed between two and five thousand years ago, earn their name because they

1

2

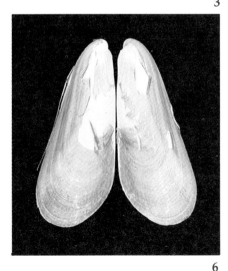

5

3

4

6

7

1. The lion's paw, *Lyropecten nodosus*, a glowing inhabitant of the 7½ Fathom Reef and similar offshore habitats, runs the gamut of warm hues from deep red to orange.

2. This minute jewel, *Mitrella lunata*, hides its neatly patterned shell under old shell in the bays.

3. The gregarious *Ischadium recurvum* nestles in crannies between clumps of *Crassostrea virginica*, which form the "reefs" in shallow bays.

4. The sturdy, large *Cymatium parthenopeum* occurs along the southern reaches of the Texas coast.

5. The racy design on the shell of the tiny *Tricolia affinis cruenta* is a match for many larger, more familiar beauties.

6. An iridescence gleams through the green periostracum of the delicate bay-dwelling *Amygdalum papyria*.

7. The color of this tiny shell, *Simnialena marferula*, is determined by its diet of red or yellow coral.

8

9

8. A beach still life on Padre Island sand brings together (clockwise) *Janthina janthina, Trachycardium isocardia, Murex fulvescens,* and a golden *Strombus alatus.*

9. The black-bodied *Murex fulvescens* stretches from its shell in search of a clam.

10. The large valves of the giant Atlantic cockle *(Laevicardium robustum)* are in sharp contrast in both size and color to the other bivalves stranded on the beach.

11. The predatory Florida rock shell, *Thais haemastoma floridana,* is actively attacking a juvenile *Laevicardium robustum.*

12. The grinning tun dominates a group that includes tiny coquinas, a *Strombus alatus, Oliva sayana, Janthina janthina, Dosinia discus, Tonna galea,* and *Anadara brasiliana.*

13. Only a real emerald can compare with the colorful beauty of its namesake, the emerald nerite *(Smaragdia viridis viridemaris),* when it is spotted amid the dingy rubble of beach drift.

14. This beautifully fringed, unidentified, little nudibranch lives among floating *Sargassum.* (Photo by Carl Young)

15. The little ark shell, *Anadara brasiliana,* is so ordinary that its true sculptural qualities are usually overlooked.

16. Emerald nerites glow amid the colorful valves of *Donax variabilis roemeri,* purple sea snails *Janthina janthina* and *J. globosa,* the white *Epitonium angulatum,* and the striped *Neritina virginea.*

17. As if covered with a veil of chiffon, a *Polinices duplicatus* glides into view.

18. The winds of March catch the floats of the pelagic purple sea snail, *Janthina globosa,* and blow it ashore. Finding one is a matter of being in the right place at the right time.

12

15

10

11

13

14

16

17

18

19

20

21

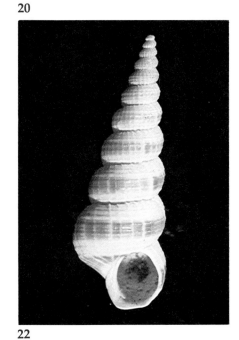

22

19. Nature was fraught with indecision when she created the multipatterned *Neritina virginea*.

20. Some of the most colorful shells are minute, like the beautifully patterned *Anachis semiplicata*.

21. An uprooted colony of coquinas, *Donax variabilis roemeri*, busily burrows in the surf zone.

22. *Amaea mitchelli* is the most sought-after shell in Texas. Until recently it was thought to be endemic to our shores, but it is now known from as far away as Panama.

23. Late-afternoon sunlight glows on the golden apertures of a trio of *Busycon perversum pulleyi*.

24. One of the largest shells found on Padre Island beaches is that of *Cypraea cervus*. The polished surface of this beauty is hidden from view by an enveloping mantle when the animal is not disturbed.

23

24

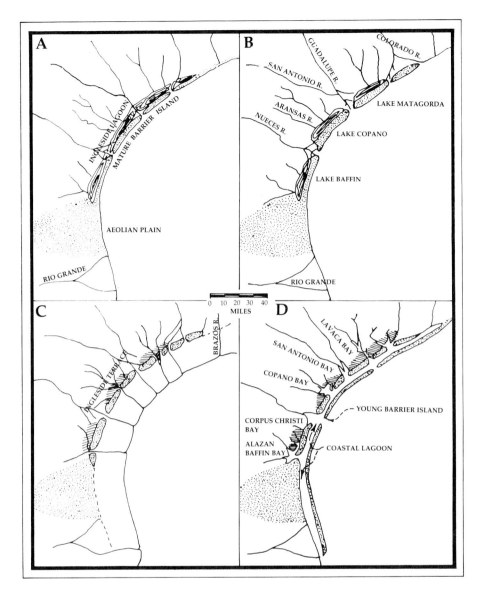

Fig. 6. Theoretical stages in the development of the barrier islands of Texas (after Price 1933):
A. master streams flow directly into Gulf
B. period of delta building
C. fall in sea level entrenches streams
D. rise in sea level widens the estuaries of master streams into bays

make a barrier between the Gulf of Mexico and a series of shallow coastal bays and lagoons (fig. 6). The bottoms of these bays are for the most part mud; the Laguna Madre, however, has a predominately sandy bottom. Behind the coastal bays is a system of inner bays, of lower salinity than the coastal or outer bays, which are in turn lower in salinity than the Gulf. These coastal bays are connected to the Gulf of Mexico by the series of passes previously listed. Seven of these passes—Sabine, Bolivar, Matagorda, Aransas, Mustang, Port Mansfield, and Brazos Santiago—have been stabilized as navigable

channels with jetties maintained by the United States Army Corps of Engineers.

Across the bays from the islands the shores are wind-tidal flats and the surface is only a few feet above sea level. The greatest fluctuation of water level in the bays is caused by the wind, and these changes in water level are called "wind tides." The wind tide, especially after the passage of a cold front, leaves large areas of shoreline exposed, and these exposed flats are referred to as "wind-tidal flats."

Indications are that this area, now a part of the mainland, was once a chain of barrier islands. The bays

that separate the ancient from the new barrier islands vary from five to six miles in width. These lagoons and large embayed (indented) river mouths are dotted with small islands and spoil banks, thrown up from the dredging of the Intracoastal Waterway, and have become nesting grounds for countless thousands of birds.

The seasonal temperature of the area rivals that of Florida, and the sea breezes make even the hot Texas summers pleasant. The average reading in the spring is 73.2 degrees, while the summer average is 81.8, fall 77.4, and winter 65.5. According to the *Texas Almanac*, temperatures of 32 degrees or lower occur only four years out of ten in Brownsville, the southernmost tip of the coastal range. Killing freezes, those of long duration, occur about once every ten years. August is the hottest month, and late spring and early fall are the wettest times.

Perhaps the fear of hurricanes with their great property damage has been the largest single factor in retarding the development of this beautiful, semitropical coastal area. Tropical cyclones, the largest and most destructive storms that affect the Texas coast, have been occurring in the Gulf of Mexico since long before the time of man. Ancient languages spoken in the area had a word for them: Mayan, *hunrakin*; Guatemalan, *hurakan*; Carib Indian, *aracan*, *urican*, and *huiranvucan*.

Of the approximately ninety-nine tropical cyclones affecting Texas during the period 1766–1961, only sixteen have been designated "major," that is, with maximum winds of 101 to 135 miles per hour; however, two-thirds of them have had winds over 74 miles per hour. Mass mortality of near-shore marine fauna due to hurricanes is significant on the Texas coast.*

Flora and Fauna

Vegetation on the coast of Texas is sparse because of the wind and the high salinity of both air and soil. On the barrier islands, the plant growth is confined to the dune area and the sand barrens behind bare beaches. On and near the dunes you will see the silvery beach croton, *Croton punctatus* Jacq.; waving sea oats, *Uniola paniculata* Linné; the large, purple flowers of the trailing goat-foot morning-glory, or railroad vine, *Ipomoea pes-caprae* Linné; the smaller white-flowered *Ipomoea stolonifera* Gmelin; the spreading fleshy sea purslane, *Sesuvium portulacastrum* Linné; the yellow beach evening primrose, *Oenothera drummondii* Hook, which opens in late after-

noon; the dune sunflower, *Helianthus argophyllus* Torr. & Gray, with silky, silver leaves; wiry dune sedge, *Fimbristylis spadicea* Vahl; a common but unspecifiable mushroom, and several other varieties of sand-strand vegetation.

In late August and early September when the sea oats are at their prime, they wave their heavy heads from atop the dunes, casting long shadows across the rippled, white sands to make an unforgettable sight. They do not extend through the eastern half of the Texas coast.

On the barrens of the islands and across the bays on the shores of the mainland the saltwort, *Salicornia bigelovii* Torr., whose succulent stems take on a reddish tinge in the fall; the round-leaved pennywort, *Hydrocotyle bonariensis* Lamarck; and the fleshy, green *Batis maritima* Linné sparsely cover the salt-glinting ground. In more marshy areas the flora is dominated by clumps of a grass the Mexicans call *sacahuiste*, *Spartina spartinae* Merr., which forms a dull green background for the bright wild flowers that dot the area seasonally. Indian blanket, *Gallardia pulchella* Foug, the yellow aster, *Machaeranthera phyllocephala* Shinners, and a daisy, *Borrichia frutescens* Linné, are but a few of the latter. Cat tails, *Typha domingensis* Pers., stand guard in ditches and low spots.

Isolated motts (a term introduced by Irish colonists, according to Jordan 1972) of live oak, *Quercus virginiana* Mill, offer a rare patch of shade, and their wind-sculptured forms add variety to an otherwise flat terrain. The sweet bay, *Persea borbonia* Speng., whose leaves add zest to a good seafood gumbo, the false willow, *Baccharis angustifolia* Michx., and the groundsel, *Baccharis halimifolia*, to the east, are some of the first woody invaders of a salt marsh. Scattered about with the usual chaparral-type (thorny brush) vegetation of the shell ridges

one sees the stately Spanish dagger, *Yucca treculeana* Carr., whose massive shafts of white flowers begin to bloom in February; the prickly pear, or nopal, *Opuntia lindheimeri* Engelm., the fruit of which formed an important staple in the diet of the Karankawas during summer and fall; and the Turk's-cap, *Malvaviscus drummondii* T. & G., which adds a dash of red to the fall landscape.

There are other plants that are submerged in the shallow waters of the bays and marshes but whose importance to the ecology of the area cannot be underestimated. Not only do they provide cover and protection in the nursery grounds of game fish and mollusks, but they also are responsible for the development of the coastal prairie. As the plants die and decay, the substratum is built up, the water becomes shallower, and reed-swamp plants take over. These are succeeded by marsh grasses, which in turn are followed by the prairie grasses. Here the most prominent submerged grasses are widgeon grass, *Ruppia maritima* Linné; a type of eelgrass, *Halodule beaudettei* (den Hartog) [*Diplanthera wrightii* of authors]; turtle grass, *Thalassia testudinum* Koenig & Sims; manatee grass, *Syringodium filiforme* Kutzing; and clover grass, *Halophila engelmannii* Aschers.

The grass prairies and salt marshes that once extended to the water's edge are being invaded by thorny brush. This brush may be deplored by stockmen of the region, but this extension of subtropical jungle plants has saved thousands of acres from erosion and complete denudation. These vast coastal prairies and salt marshes are not as extensive as they once were due to overgrazing by early pioneers, drainage, and cultivation (fig. 7). It is an ecological tragedy because a salt marsh has a higher rate of primary production, that is, the manufacture of plant material by photosynthesis, than any other crop in

A

B

Fig. 7. Salt marsh flats:
A. marsh grass at low tide near Pass Cavallo
B. close-up of marsh with *Littorina* snails, *Abra* clams, and pelican feather
C. close-up of marsh grass with *Littorina* on leaf and *Mercenaria* in sand

C

the world except sugar cane. *Spartina*, without cultivation by man, yields three times as much as the best wheat lands. The shoreline marshes, wastelands to many, actually produce much of the nourishment for many forms of life in the coastal seas. Destroying the marshes by draining or filling to provide industrial sites can bring disaster to the fauna of shore and ocean.

The coast of Texas is a birdlover's paradise. It would be foolish in a book of this nature to try to elaborate on a subject that has been so well covered by Harry C. Oberholser in *The Bird Life of Texas*

and Roger Tory Peterson in his *Field Guide to the Birds of Texas*. It is common knowledge that the area falls in one of the major flyways of this hemisphere, and the late Connie Hagar in Rockport did more than any other one person to record the birds' activities.

While shelling on our coasts one can see avian hordes that include the great blue heron, roseate spoonbills, snowy egrets, reddish egrets, cattle egrets, wood ibis, white pelicans, laughing gulls, herring gulls, curlews, avocets, terns, skimmers, and cormorants. Racing at the water's edge are the smaller species, such as sanderlings,

sandpipers, willets, turnstones, and dowitchers. Behind the dunes one might find a huge flock of the giant sandhill cranes or, on a coastal roadside in the spring, watch a pair of prairie chickens perform their ritual mating dance.

A still greater thrill can be had between October and March when your boat glides near the almost legendary whooping cranes as they feed along the edge of the Intracoastal Waterway behind Matagorda Island. The quail and turkeys are almost unbelievably abundant. The turkeys on San José were introduced by the late owner of the ranch, who built weird roosts with metal flanges to protect them from preying coyotes, since no natural roosts exist on the island barrens.

On rare occasions a giant frigate bird strays our way from faraway Yucatán to soar effortlessly over the Texas shore. It is not an uncommon sight while searching for a shell to come upon a speckled egg in an indentation in the sand. If it is that of a black skimmer, the mother bird will make shrieking divebomb attacks on the unwary beachcomber. At times the small spoil islands in the bays appear to be paved with eggs, some of which are laid so carelessly that they roll off the low banks and break.

Such landbirds as the mockingbird, falcon, cardinal, barn swallow, hummingbird, meadow lark, horned lark, and warblers, to name but a few, inhabit the land. Ducks raft on the bays by the thousands and geese fly in honking formations overhead. It is a birdwatcher's paradise.

The mammals and reptiles are not so numerous. The wily coyote comes to the water's edge in the evening to scavenge for food. Spotted ground squirrels, kangaroo rats, grasshopper mice, jack rabbits, pocket gophers, badgers, and deer hide in burrows or under clumps of grass during the day. Cattle stand amid the sea oats on top of the dunes or bunch together in the breeze at the water's edge through the night to avoid the mosquitoes behind the dunes. Lizards, turtles, and rattlesnakes sun themselves on a winter's day on the lee side of a dune. The tracks of these animals tell tales of hunting and being hunted on the smooth, white sand.

In 1860 W. S. Gilbert, who made a coastal survey for the United States government, wrote in his description of the San Antonio Bay area, "The scattered 'motts' within the same limits afford a refuge for the wild animals that infest the

country. Panthers, tiger cats and mustangs abound" (p. 355). Perhaps panthers and mustangs no longer roam the region, but nature, unspoiled, is still visible at every turn on the barrier islands of Texas.

The Coastal Waters

The previous sections describe the shores one walks in search of a sea shell; in this section the many factors influencing the variety and number of marine animals will be examined. The tides, waves, and currents, the salinity, temperature, and turbidity, and the substratum all have an influence on the marine fauna. The combined effects of variations in these factors make the long Texas coast a relatively inhospitable environment for marine mollusks.

Temperature

Perhaps the greatest controlling factor in the distribution of marine animals is temperature. The temperature of the ocean has a very limited range; consequently, comparatively small changes in temperature have a very decided effect on marine organisms. In the ocean, temperature creates as much of a barrier to the dispersal of animals as a mountain range does to land animals. The maximum and minimum temperatures each animal can tolerate limit marine animals to certain regions of the seas.

Texas is renowned for its "blue northers." In reality these are rapidly moving cold fronts that sweep across the land, dropping temperatures as much as thirty to forty degrees in a few hours. An officer in Taylor's army described a typical norther (Henry 1847, p. 45)—"Hast thou, dear reader, ever felt a norther? Heard tell of one? No. Well, your northern cold is nothing to it. It comes 'Like a thief in the night,' and all but steals your life. I'll venture to say there is no part of the U.S. cursed with such a variable one in the winter. Oh

Texas, if we have not 'fought, bled and died for you,' we have done as Dick Riker (peace to his ashes) did, 'suffered some.'" In the century and a quarter since that was written the northers have not changed and the beach is a miserable place to be during one.

The extremely rapid onset of the northers, accompanied by sharp drops in water temperature, occasionally causes massive mortality of marine life. Texas bays are invaded by such subtropical animals as the commercial shrimp, *Penaeus setiferus* and *P. aztecus*, in the spring and summer; in the fall and winter they return to the Gulf. The lingering strays seldom survive a Texas winter.

Biologists have determined that if the damaging cold waves are preceded by other, lesser freezes their destructive effects are lessened. Some animals escape to deeper water if the onset of the cold wave is slow. However, the slow-moving or attached mollusk has little opportunity to escape. The marine life in the shallow bays must be able to withstand temperature changes far greater than animals in corresponding positions in deeper water on the outer coast.

According to Pulley (1952b) and Moore (1961) the coast from South Texas to Cape Hatteras, North Carolina (excepting southern Florida), is considered a single biogeographic area, the Carolinian Province (fig. 8). The climate in this zone is warm temperate; the tropical element is scanty. Hedgpeth (1953) has suggested that the boundary between the Carolinian and the Caribbean provinces is at a point near latitude 27°N, but this line of demarcation probably cannot be established that precisely, due to the movement of tropical and temperate water masses north and south during particular seasons of the year. The organisms associated with these water masses move also,

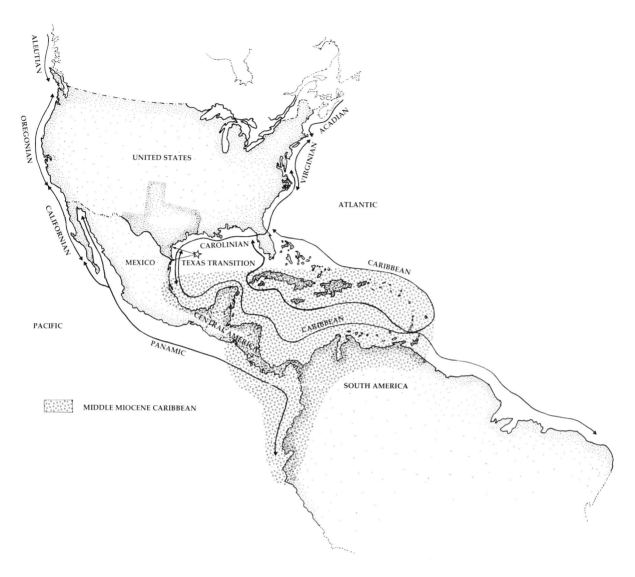

MIDDLE MIOCENE CARIBBEAN

Fig. 8. Faunal provinces

but generally we may expect the benthic (bottom-dwelling) forms south of this point to be more Caribbean in nature and seldom found alongshore north of it. Tunnell's studies (1974) indicate that the Carolinian elements might extend farther south into Mexico to a point near Cabo Rojo, Veracruz, which is about sixty miles south of Tampico (see fig. 10).

Only those forms able to withstand wide extremes of temperature during the year can survive along the Texas coast. Cold winter winds greatly lower the temperature of inshore and bay waters, but the waters of the continental shelf may never get below 65° or 70°F. This

stable offshore temperature results in a shelf fauna almost entirely West Indian in character (Pulley 1952b), while the shoreline fauna in the northern Gulf is similar to that of the Carolinas. The broad range of environmental factors that characterize the estuarine, bay, and coastal waters of Texas produces a mixed invertebrate fauna containing both temperate Atlantic and tropical Caribbean species, with a very low endemic component (Hedgpeth 1953).

The Caribbean faunal province contains many species that can be found in the Pacific, either as identical or strikingly similar (vicariant) remnants of Miocene populations

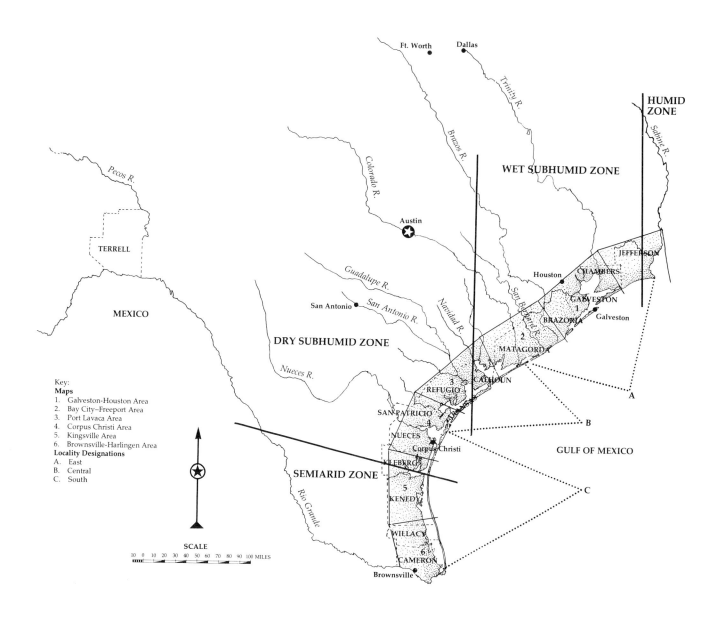

Fig. 9. Climate and geographic divisions

that existed when the Atlantic and Pacific were connected prior to the ascent of the Panama land bridge during the Pleistocene time. Each of these modern twins was probably the same species in the Miocene, having moved from the Caribbean to the Pacific through an opening between Central and South America. When the Panama land bridge arose in the Miocene the passage of larvae was halted and slight differences developed over the ages. Increasing attention is being given to the significance of those species, which have been called "twins," "analogs," "cognates,"

"allopatric," or "vicariant" (Croizat et al. 1974).

Climate and Salinity

The surface climate of the Texas coast has a direct effect on the water temperature and the salinity of the bays and lagoons. From Sabine to Galveston we find a humid climate with a slight surplus of moisture (fig. 9). The next climatic zone is the wet subhumid, extending from Galveston to Port Lavaca. Here moisture supply and loss are in balance. This condition is not always true in the case of the next zone, from Port Lavaca to Corpus Christi, a dry subhumid belt. The transition

Table 2. Salinity Designations

Classification of approximate geographic divisions, salinity ranges, types, and distribution of organisms in estuaries

Divisions of estuary	Salinity ranges ($^o/oo$)	Zones	Types of organisms and approximate range of distribution in estuary, relative to divisions and salinities
		Venice system	**Ecological classification**
River	0.5	limnetic	limnetic
Head	0.5–5	oligohaline	oligohaline
Upper reaches	5–18	mesohaline	mixohaline · true
Middle reaches	18–25	polyhaline	estuarine
Low reaches	25–30	polyhaline	stenohaline marine · euryhaline marine · migrants
Mouth	30–40	euhaline	

Source: Adapted from Day 1951, 1964; and Venice System, Symposium on the Classification of Brackish Waters, 1959.

between the dry subhumid region and that of the semiarid portion is very gradual. The remainder of the coast is characterized by a permanent moisture-deficient climate, almost desert (Hedgpeth 1953).

Along the Texas coast these climatic zones are roughly correlated with rainfall, but in the bays this correlation breaks down due to the drainage of rivers into the bay systems. If there has been extensive rain and flooding along the watersheds of the rivers that drain into a bay system, the salinity will be lowered in spite of the fact that there has been little or no rain in the bay area itself. At present the annual rainfall on this coastline ranges between 15 and 40 inches per year, with, of course, a trend toward a drier, more arid climate in south Texas.

Normal Gulf salinity is usually 36 parts per thousand (36 $^o/oo$). (See table 2 for terms used to describe the degree of salinity of a body of water.) Salinity conditions are nearly stable at Port Isabel, where the monthly averages range from 30.4 to 37.5 $^o/oo$. This fact permits mollusks that are only found offshore in other, less stable areas of the coast to move in closer to shore here. Variation is the rule, however, in most of the other tidal waters of the Texas coast. Salinities can rapidly decrease after heavy rains and flooding along the rivers. Hurricane Beulah, in 1967, is an extreme example of the devastation to sessile (sedentary or attached) marine life produced by sustained flooding and reduced salinities over a long period. The animals that inhabit estuarian waters are more adaptable than those of other, more stable regions but they, too, will succumb if the water stays "fresh" for too long a period. It is usually about eighteen months after the water returns to its normal salinity before the bottom fauna becomes reestablished.

A rapid change in the proportions of salt in the water will interfere with the mollusk's process of osmosis, during which water with a lower concentration of dissolved salts moves through a membrane into a region of greater concentration and in doing so sets up a considerable pressure known as osmotic pressure. When a marine mollusk is placed in fresh water, the fresh water rushes into its cells, which have a higher concentration, causing expansion and rupture of the cell tissues. If the change is gradual the mollusk might be able to adjust its enzyme output and thus prevent immediate death due to breakdown of its membranes. Such bivalves as *Pholadidae* (angel wings), which are unable to completely close their shells, are particularly susceptible.

If certain marine invertebrates are not forced into a sudden salinity change they are able to make considerable adjustment. For example, the dilution of sea water by fresh water from rains or from a limited amount of flooding of the rivers may have little effect on marine animals. A reverse process of gradually raised salinities due to evaporation and drought may also have little effect. But, if great amounts of fresh water are introduced into a bay or if portions of it

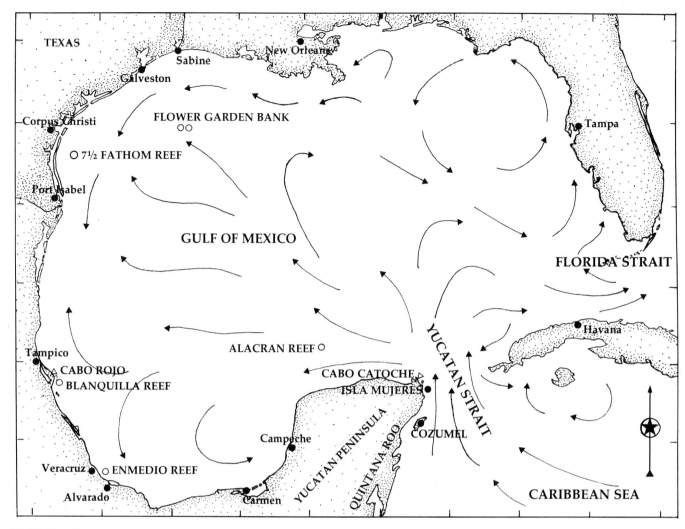

TEXAS
Sabine
Galveston
Corpus Christi
FLOWER GARDEN BANK
○○
○ 7½ FATHOM REEF
Port Isabel
New Orleans
Tampa

GULF OF MEXICO

FLORIDA STRAIT

ALACRAN REEF ○
Havana

Tampico
△ CABO ROJO
○ BLANQUILLA REEF
CABO CATOCHE
ISLA MUJERES
YUCATAN STRAIT

Campeche
YUCATAN PENINSULA
COZUMEL
QUINTANA ROO

Veracruz ○ ENMEDIO REEF
Alvarado
Carmen
CARIBBEAN SEA

FEBRUARY

Fig. 10. Surface currents in the Gulf of Mexico from U.S. Naval Oceanographic Office pilot charts (after Nowlin 1971):
February: a loop current and a northwestward flow over the central and eastern Gulf
August: less well defined flow in the eastern Gulf and a more pronounced convergence of flow into the northwestern Gulf

become cut off and evaporation goes on until the salinity becomes exceedingly high, all the strictly marine animals will die.

A look at the map of Texas shows at least nine rivers emptying into the waters of this area. Extended droughts, alteration of the drainage pattern by reclamation projects, or agricultural diversions along these rivers cause low river runoff with accompanying increases of the salinity in landlocked bays. Normally, these bays are less saline than the open Gulf; consequently, when the salinity increases they are invaded by many marine or open-Gulf species of invertebrates, and the low-salinity or brackish-water mollusks disappear. As the salinity of the bay water approaches Gulf sa-

linity, from either a fresh or a hypersaline condition, the number of species present increases and the number of individuals of each species decreases (Keith & Hulings 1965).

Flooding by the rivers emptying into the bays, bringing an influx of fresh water, on the one hand, and summer evaporation, on the other, causes variable and often extremely low and high salinities. Normal salinity for Aransas Bay is about 19 to 30 ⁰/₀₀ as compared with 31 to 36 ⁰/₀₀ for the open Gulf. It consistently rises during the summer months and was recorded as high as 42 ⁰/₀₀ in August 1951. Port Isabel, a more stable area, has no river drainage into its lagoons, and the flow of the Rio Grande (10 miles south) has

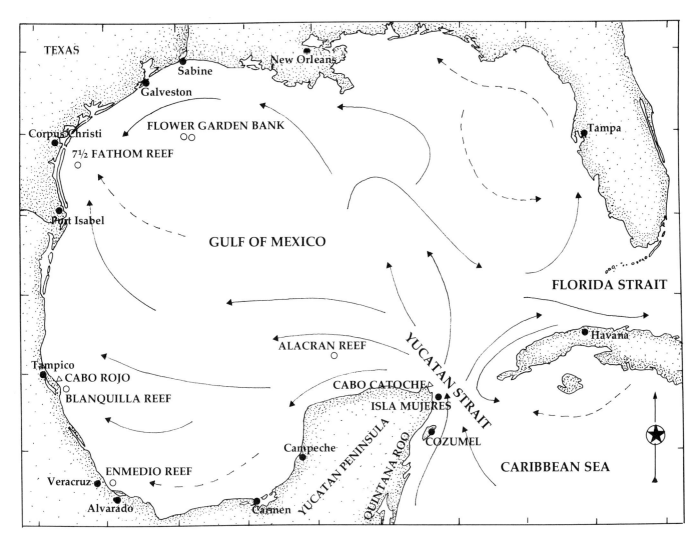

AUGUST

been reduced to but a trickle due to up-stream damming. The Baffin Bay of the Laguna Madre is one of the saltiest bodies of water on earth. During the late thirties it was rivaled only by the Dead Sea and the Great Salt Lake.

Mass mortality due to killing cold spells in the winters, high salinity in the summer droughts, and flooding of the bays or estuaries have been characteristic features of this area since Pleistocene times (about 1 million years ago); yet man and animal on the Texas coast still find the adjustment difficult.

Currents

Currents, or movements of water, are related to the productivity of the sea. Currents help to distribute not only nutrients for both plants and animals, but also the animals themselves. Of primary concern to the area under consideration are the inshore currents. As yet they have not been studied in sufficient detail, but it would seem that the Mississippi Current follows the coast southwestward, getting narrower toward Tamaulipas, Mexico, and is the principal force in governing the productivity of the region. With respect to the current system of the Caribbean and western Atlantic as a whole, the currents of the Gulf of Mexico, exclusive of the main system of the Florida Current, comprise an eddy (fig. 10).

It would be well to consider briefly the general nature of the currents that may be expected in the Gulf. Sverdrup (1942) lists three different groups of currents, each of which is represented in the Gulf of Mexico. These are as follows:
1. Currents that are related to the distribution of density in the sea
2. Currents that are caused directly by the stress that the wind exerts on the sea surface
3. Tidal currents and currents associated with internal waves
No body of water of comparable size has generated as much difference of opinion regarding its current patterns as has the Gulf of Mexico. It is a field under study, and only a few general remarks can be made about the Gulf currents.

In the northern hemisphere the Coriolis force (force due to the rotation of the earth) acts toward the right of the flow of water which results from the movement of water of higher density into water of lower density. Temperature, salinity, and atmospheric pressure determine the relative density of water. Hence, in this hemisphere the more dense water is on the left of a person standing with his back to the current.

Surface or wind currents involving frictional and Coriolis force will become better understood when studies being made from data gathered on the oil-drilling platforms off the Gulf coast are analyzed.

Tidal currents are horizontal movements of water that have the effect of raising the sea level at a given location. On the Gulf the bays and lagoons have restricted outlets, or passes, to the sea. All the water necessary to bring about a change in level of the bays must flow through these passes. At certain stages of the tide these tidal currents become quite strong through the passes.

The sands that pile up on the south side of the jetties are part of the evidence that the prevailing set of inner coastal currents is westward and southward, or counterclockwise, in the northwestern part of the Gulf, at least to Big Shell on Padre Island, where there seems to be a convergence with a northward current along the shore. Mounds of driftwood and storm debris at Big Shell attest this convergence.

One does not think of the currents of the Gulf of Mexico without a reference to the Gulf Stream. On either side of the equator is a zone where the wind blows constantly in one direction. These winds, trade winds, drive surface waters before them. South of the equator these wind-blown waters form the South Equatorial Current, and north of the equator, the North Equatorial Current. The latter is driven across the Atlantic by northeast trade winds to be divided into two currents. Half of the North Equatorial Current joins the South Equatorial waters near the Windward Islands and continues northwestward across the Caribbean through the Yucatán Strait into the Gulf of Mexico. Here a pressure wall turns the current to the northeast out through the Florida Strait. This current becomes the Gulf Stream. As the warm and salty waters of this stream flow along the southern Atlantic coast of North America, they are reinforced by the remainder of the North Equatorial Current. Opposite Cape Hatteras the Gulf Stream begins its long journey eastward across the Atlantic.

The action of the Gulf Stream on the waters of the Gulf of Mexico, combined with other factors, sets up a whirlpoollike current, or drift, in a clockwise direction. This eddy tends to carry some of the sediments from the rivers northward and eastward toward the Florida coast. A brief study of these currents will aid the beachcomber in following the travels of his "treasure" from its far-away source. According to Sweet (1971) the Gulf of Mexico may be divided into two major circulatory provinces east and west, each distinguished by different flow regimes. As stated previously, water enters the Gulf via the Yucatán Strait and leaves via the Florida Strait. Nowlin's studies (1971) show

a general circulation pattern consisting of a clockwise Loop Current flowing from the Yucatan to the Florida Strait in the eastern Gulf, but no strong, semi-permanent currents in the western Gulf. Finally, indications of the degree of variability of these circulation patterns come from recent cruises. Large current rings, or eddies, form from the Loop Current. And a well-defined pattern of winter flow contrasts with a highly variable summer pattern for the western Gulf. . . . In contrast to the eastern Gulf, which is dominated by one major current system and occasional rings, the western Gulf seems characterized by generally minor currents. (See fig. 10)

In other words, there is much to be learned about the currents off the shores of Texas. However, it is known that there is only a slight and slow exchange of water between the Gulf and its neighboring bodies of water (Atlantic and Caribbean). This rate of exchange is a contributing factor to the higher overall salinity of the Gulf of Mexico compared to that of the Atlantic and Caribbean.

Tides

Tides are one of the factors that keep the ocean in motion. They may be simply explained as twice-daily waves that move like the hour hand of a clock about a central point mid-ocean. These waves run twelve hours and twenty-five minutes apart; their crests are high tides and the troughs are low tides. They are the response of the waters of the ocean to the gravitational pull of the moon and the more distant sun. These heavenly bodies set the seas in motion, but the local nature of tides is determined by the underwater topography of the area—the width of an inlet's entrance, the depth of the channel, or the slope of the bottom. In the open ocean underwater structures are hardly significant, but closer to the shore the continental shelf acts as a wedge against the wave to produce the kind of tide that man notices.

The moon, closer to the earth, has a stronger pull than the sun. When sun and moon are in line with the earth and pull together, the high tide is highest and the low tide is lowest. The extreme tides that accompany a full moon are known as *spring tides*, and the moderate tides on the quarters of the moon are called the *neap tides*. The Gulf of Mexico has only one- or two-foot tides; elsewhere they may be four to eight feet or more. Compare this with Juneau, Alaska, where the tide is more than twenty-three feet. What the Gulf of Mexico tides lack in impressiveness, they make up for in complexity.

There are three types of tides to be found in the world, and the Gulf of Mexico has all three. They are daily, semidaily, and mixed. Marmer (1954, p. 110) describes them by saying:

The semidaily type of tide includes all those in which the tidal cycle is completed in half a day; that is, there are two high and two low waters a day with only little difference between corresponding morning and afternoon tides.

The daily type of tide includes tides in which only one high and one low water occur in a day. The mixed type of tide includes those tides which feature two high and two low waters a day but with considerable difference between the two high waters and/or between the two low waters.

Due to the revolution of the moon about the earth in twenty-eight days, the times of either high or low tides are about fifty minutes later each day. Several factors affect the clocklike regularity of the tides, but the declination of the moon is the most important factor affecting the Texas tides. As the moon revolves around the earth from east to west, it also has a north-south movement. The declination is the measurement in degrees of latitude that the moon is north or south of the equator. The plane of the moon's orbit is not in the same plane as the equator; therefore, the declination of the moon is constantly changing. Another factor that affects tides is the shape of the basin. In the Gulf of Mexico this shape is such that it, combined with the moon's declination, responds better to daily forces than to semidaily forces. Meteorological conditions, such as winds and pressure, as well as the shape

of the coastline, affect this regularity. On open coasts like those of Texas, the tide is usually less than eight feet, but in funnel-shaped bays, like the Bay of Fundy in Nova Scotia, the tides may rise thirty to forty feet.

It has been pointed out that there are two kinds of daily tides and that they are affected by the declination of the moon. In the moon's fortnightly change from maximum northerly to maximum southerly declination, the differences between morning and afternoon tides are greatest near the times the moon is over the equator. Those at maximum declination are known as *tropical tides* and those at minimum declination as *equatorial tides*. The water-level variation coincident with the cycle of tropical and equatorial tides is probably the most important as far as the lagoons and bays of Texas are concerned. It is this variation that is responsible for the largest regular exchange of water between bay and Gulf. This exchange causes the tidal currents in the narrow inlets that affect the migrations of organisms through the passes. Molluscan larvae are transported primarily by these tidal currents.

Sessile mollusks, such as mussels, oysters, and pen shells, owe their existence to the flow of the tides, which brings them the food they are unable to go in search of. The breeding rhythms of certain mollusks coincide in some unknown way with the phases of the moon and the stages of the tide.

In the bays the periodic tide is negligible and follows the Gulf tide about an hour later. The water level of these landlocked bodies is dependent principally on the wind. The north winds that push the water out through the passes often cause extremely low tides in the winter months. There are five natural passes along this coast that are kept open by this scouring action of wind and water. Annual

migration of marine life in this area between the bays and the Gulf is dependent on the tidal current in these passes.

If a norther occurs at the time of very low, or minus, tide, the collector has a field day in the bays. To determine when a minus tide is due check the annual book of tide tables published by the United States Coast and Geodetic Survey. The daily paper in the area where you wish to collect also will give the hour of each high and low tide.

Waves and surf

When one thinks of the ocean he thinks of waves. They may appear low and regular or high and frightening. Waves are not actually regular but differ in size and form. The inconsistency of the wind has much to do with the irregularity of the waves. Wave motion is largely a surface phenomenon, the wave motion decreasing rapidly with increasing depth. As the wave nears the shore, the friction of the bottom causes it to rise higher until it dips forward and breaks. The breaker rushes to the beach until its energy is exhausted. Wave action can also set up currents and undertows along the beaches.

The size of the unbroken water area plus the velocity and direction of the wind determine the size of waves. Obviously, waves in the Gulf of Mexico could not compare in size to those of the Pacific coast. In closed bays and lagoons, there is almost no surf. A gently sloping beach and broad continental shelf such as ours do not produce crashing surf. They deprive the wave of a considerable amount of its energy because bottom friction is increased so slowly that the wave remains stable most of its way to the shore. By then its force is largely spent. This is the type of wave that surfers love to ride. Ours is a wide surf zone with a series of sand bars and troughs that have big breakers on the outer bar and smaller ones on each succeeding bar toward shore.

A

The action of the waves on a sandy beach tends to move the sand, making it a more inhospitable habitat than a rock shore. Only those animals which can burrow rapidly in the sand and can remain buried for some time are to be found on a sandy beach. Where the surf is an important factor, only those animals which have developed structures that will minimize the impact of the breakers against their bodies, or the means of holding securely to rocks and seaweed, have been able to live.

The shell collector may wonder why on some days he finds greater numbers of the right valves of clams and on other days left valves. This variation is a result of wave action; the shape of the shell is the determining factor. Waves approaching from the right as you face the sea tend to deposit right valves.

Turbidity
As a factor governing marine life, turbidity has had little study on the Texas coast. Turbidity is expressed by the percentage of light transmission through a sample of water. Dirty or disturbed water affects the amount of light transmitted. The shallowness of the Texas bays permits turbulence to the bottoms by a minimum amount of wave action. Particles suspended in the water cut out light as well as put a strain on animals that must filter water for their food. Insufficient light discourages plant and algal growth, and animals dependent on these sun-loving forms will disappear when the plants die. Silting of the rivers from erosion in the watersheds, industrial wastes, and drilling in the bays contributes to the turbidity of Texas bay waters, but the most important factor is the minute size of the particles that make up the bottom sediments.

Substratum
Two major faunal divisions exist in Texas waters, one in open-shelf, unprotected waters and the other in the protected waters of the bays and lagoons (fig. 11). Within these two divisions the substratum becomes one of the important factors in limiting the distribution of mollusks. The inshore area has a sandy bottom, the water is usually turbulent, and the temperature reflects that of the air. An unprotected sandy beach is sparsely populated by a few forms of burrowing animals and is not the place where one can expect to find more than a few species of live mollusks, except after a storm or a hard freeze, when inhabitants of the open shelf are stranded on the beach.

On the outer shores it is not always easy to group marine animals into communities, but in the bays and estuaries with their mud or sand bottoms the animals are characteristically grouped. Many areas have rocky shores, but on the Texas coast the man-made jetties at the major inlets furnish the only rocky habitat (fig. 12). On the jetties the universal problems of rocky shores exist—wave shock and the development of powerful attach-

B

C

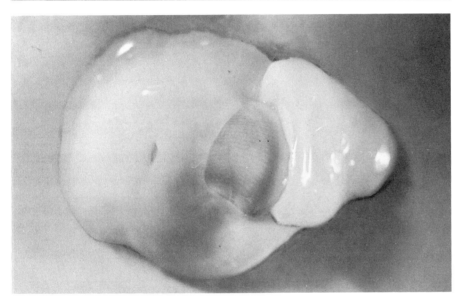

D

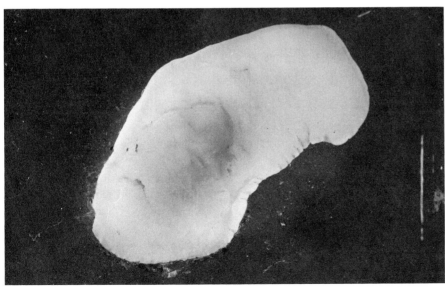

Fig. 11. Offshore and inlet-influenced areas:
A. Cypraea cervus, an inhabitant of 7½ Fathom Reef
B. the large Atlantic cockle, *Laevicardium robustum*, invades the bays during periods of increased salinity.
Two views of *Sinum perspectivum*, which envelops its small shell:
C. contracted, and
D. extended while moving on a mucus trail

A

B

C

D

E

Fig. 12. Rocky shores:
A. a typical Texas jetty, south jetty
at Port Aransas
B. close-up of jetty rock with *Lit-
torina lineolata* and *Siphonaria pec-
tinata*, dwellers of the splash zone
C. rock fill at Cline's Point, Port
Aransas, uncovered by low tide
D. close-up of fill rock with *Thais*
snails and false limpets
E. another inhabitant of the jetty
area, *Cantharus cancellarius*

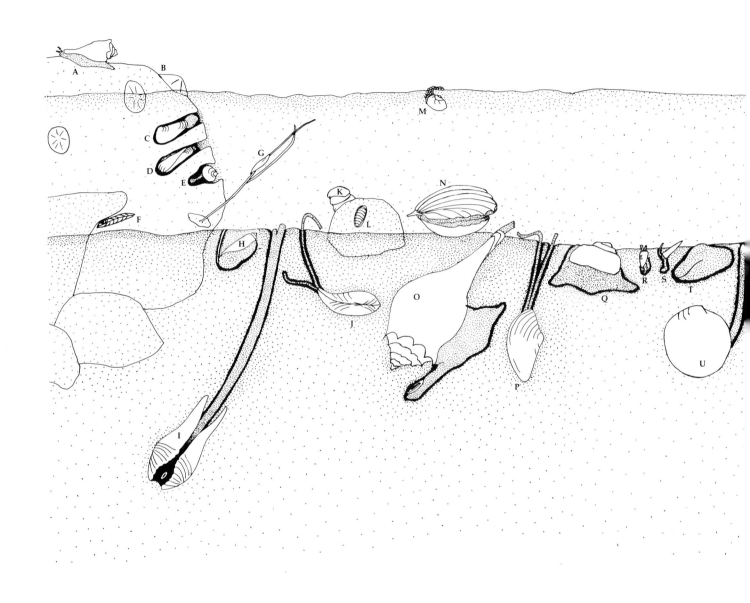

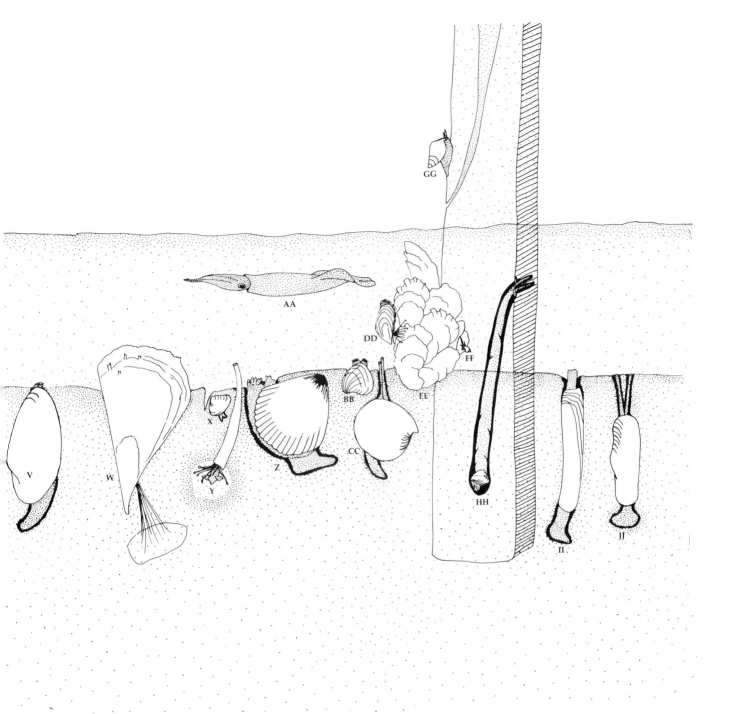

Fig. 13. Various mollusks are depicted in this highly generalized diagram showing relative habitats:

A. *Thais*
B. *Siphonaria*
C. *Hiatella*
D. *Lithophaga*
E. *Diplodonta*
F. *Isognomon*
G. *Simnialena*
H. *Oliva*
I. *Cyrtopleura*
J. *Macoma*

K. *Crepidula*
L. *Ischnochiton*
M. *Janthina*
N. *Pecten*
O. *Busycon*
P. *Tellina*
Q. *Polinices*
R. *Donax*
S. *Terebra*
T. *Sinum*
U. *Codakia*
V. *Callista*
W. *Atrina*

X. *Nucula*
Y. *Dentalium*
Z. *Laevicardium*
AA. squid
BB. *Chione*
CC. *Dosinia*
DD. *Ischadium*
EE. *Crassostrea*
FF. *Odostomia*
GG. *Littorina*
HH. *Teredo*
II. *Ensis*
JJ. *Tagelus*

31

A

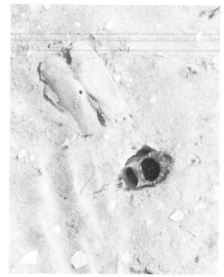

B

Fig. 14. Tidal flats:
A. collectors digging in the muck for the beautiful angel wing clam
B. next to the open valves of *Tagelus plebeius* can be seen the exhalant and inhalant siphons of *Cyrtopleura costata*, the angel wing, which resides about eighteen inches below the surface in the black mud
C. an angel wing with the siphon contracted—in feeding position the siphon is extended as much as three times the length of the shell
D. the siphon holes of an angel wing are in the lower left, and a *Polinices duplicatus* leaves a trail in the sand as it glides past its fluted collar of eggs and sand
E. following severe northers, *Atrina serrata*, the large pen shell, is frequently stranded by the hundreds in long windrows along the outer beaches
F. P. duplicatus with mantle fully extended

C

D

E

F

ment devices. The jetties have been constructed by covering a fill of rubble and small stones with large quarry blocks, forming a long wall that is triangular in cross section. These structures are about three to five feet above mean low water, and the slopes are covered with green algae. During storms and in the spring, when waves break over them, the jetties become slick and dangerous to walk on. Because they project hundreds of yards into the open Gulf, they are favorite spots for anglers. Life on the jetties is sparse, since they have been available for colonization less than one hundred years. The shifting sand base, wave shock, sudden variations in salinity, and low winter temperatures of the region limit the colonization to very hardy forms from various sources. The jettied passes are highways by which fish, crabs, and shrimp migrate from the bays to the Gulf to spawn.

The type of substratum has a great deal of influence on the mol-luscan populations (fig. 13). Most of these animals are incapable of rapid movement and might be kept from an area by the size of the grains of sand on the bottom. Many mollusks that can live in sand cannot exist in mud. Much of the area near the mouths of rivers is mud with a surface layer of fine unconsolidated material that is easily stirred by waves. Most mollusks are unable to keep silt from clogging their gills and as a consequence are unable to maintain life in these regions; however, certain clams like the delicate angel wing and some snails have adapted to the mud flat (fig. 14). The lack of attachment sites in mud flats also makes for a rather specialized fauna. Some snails crawl around on top of the mud at low tide, but most of the mollusks burrow to rather unusual depths. Food-getting becomes a problem and the lack of oxygen is another hazard to which the animal must adapt.

Sand flats in quiet waters with no shoal grass are ideal locations for many marine animals (fig. 14). Here the substratum is soft enough so that feeble burrowing powers will suffice and yet not so soft as to require special adaptations to avoid suffocation. There is no attachment problem, for a small amount of burrowing is sufficient to assure that the animal will not be washed out, and a little more burrowing protects it from the drying winds and bright sunlight. Overpopulation is the main problem that develops in this area.

Submerged grass flats can be on either sand or muck in warm, clear, shallow water (fig. 15). Eastern Texas coastal waters have sparse marine plant growth, but the lower coastal lagoons are rich with many algae and grasses. The establishment of a bed of marine grass is an important step in the conversion of an ocean region into wet meadow and then into dry land. Turtle grass (*Thalassia testudinum* Koenig & Sims) and eelgrass (*Halodule beau-*

A

B

C

Fig. 15. Submerged grass flats:
A. a bed of *Ruppia maritima* Linné at low tide with empty *Busycon* shell
B. to the left are small snail trails in the sand, while a gelatinous mass of mollusk eggs can be seen on the grass just above and to the right of the shell
C. Argopecten irradians amplicostatus in feeding posture (photo by Carl Young)
D. Willcox's sea hare, *Aplysia willcoxi,* swimming quietly in the shallows
E. Busycon perversum pulleyi in active pursuit of a meal
F. Bulla striata gliding along on a trail of mucus

D

E

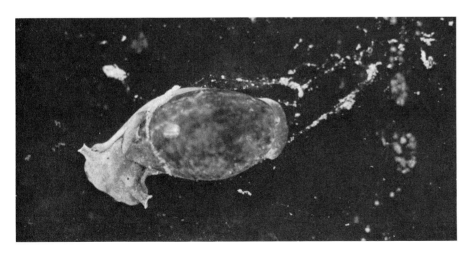

F

A

Fig. 16. Pilings and wood:
A. a protected, barnacle-covered piling with stranded *Mercenaria* clam and cabbagehead jellyfish
B. wood after being tunneled by *Teredo*, the destructive bivalve known as the shipworm
C. wood that has been broken apart to expose its inhabitants, the *Martesia*

B

C

dettei [den Hartog]) support a group of mollusks that live on the blades, about the bases, and among the roots. Summer sunlight or extremes in temperature cause the animals that live among grasses to move downward for protection against exposure; as a result the flats seem quite barren at certain times.

These tidal flats are a meeting ground between the sea and the land, a tension zone where the reaction of animals and their environment can be observed as nowhere else. The communities, or groupings, found in the flats are the result of the complicated interplay of the physical factors of environment— influx of fresh water, tidal action and currents, salinity and temperature—and the biological factors imposed by the animals on their environment. A change in any one of these factors will affect the various communities. Consequently, in an area like Redfish Bay, the communities will change from year to year.

Here on the tidal flats, a change in the factors could wipe out the species as it did following the influx of fresh water from Hurricane Beulah in 1967, but the territory is rapidly restored when the balance is reestablished.

Man-made wharf pilings may be considered a distinct type of substratum and are generally considered under two headings: (a) exposed and (b) protected (fig. 16). All wharves and pilings are built in relatively protected positions, but the

A

B

Fig. 17. Oyster reefs:
A. an extreme low tide exposes the commercial oyster *Crassostrea virginica* in Aransas Bay
B. the oyster reef provides a home for many plants and animals, such as the mussel *Ischadium recurvum*, which can be seen in the left center of the large clump of oysters
C. close view of *I. recurvum* nestling between the shells

C

outer pilings experience more pounding during storms. On the outer pilings marine growth will be rather sparse and almost flush with the wood. The animal most associated with wooden pilings is the wood-boring *Teredo*, or shipworm. As mentioned earlier, this small clam is the bane of shipping throughout the world. It is completely helpless outside the protected life in timber, but it can reduce an untreated pile to the collapsing point in six months. The life of a pile may be prolonged to three or four years by chemical treatment; however, nothing permanently protects pilings from the shipworm, which, unseen, works on the inside of a piece of wood.

Oyster reefs occur in shallow water, many of them aligned perpendicular to the prevailing currents (fig. 17). The conditions that promote the formation of an oyster reef are salinities ranging from about 12 to 25 $^o/_{oo}$, a firm bottom, and temperature cool enough in winter to permit a resting period in their reproductive activities. The living as well as the dead oyster reefs provide shelter and food for many kinds of organisms.

---

*During the ten-year period in which I worked on the material for the first edition of this book, three major hurricanes struck the Texas coast: Carla on September 11, 1961, Beulah on September 20, 1967, and Celia on August 3, 1970. The first two had a marked effect on the marine life of the coast, but the last primarily affected man and his structures. Finding myself alone in my home on that afternoon in August with the edited copy of the manuscript and the only carbon copy, I became frantic looking for a way to protect them. As my windows broke and water poured through the ceiling, the light fixtures, and each slight orifice, I tried to recall scenes of other natural disasters. The vision I conjured up as my home shook and leaked was of fallen walls with a lone refrigerator standing in their midst. In haste and desperation I pulled the contents from my refrigerator and replaced them with the manuscript and its copy—there they remained until I remembered them several days later. When the door was opened the light did not come on as usual, but the papers were dry and safe; that is quite a bit more than I could say about the rest of my home. Celia will be long remembered by those caught in its unpredictable, devastating path.

CLASS: APLACOPHORA · POLYPLACOPHORA · CEPHALOPODA · BIVALVIA · SCAPHOPODA · GASTROPODA · MONOPLACOPHORA

ERA	PERIOD	EPOCH	MILLIONS OF YEARS BEFORE THE PRESENT	SUCCESSION OF LIFE
CENOZOIC	QUATERNARY (BEFORE THE)	HOLOCENE / PLEISTOCENE	0–1	Man. Mammals spread with development of grasses
CENOZOIC	TERTIARY	PLIOCENE / MIOCENE / OLIGOCENE / EOCENE / PALEOCENE	1–63	Mollusks much the same as today, important on land and sea
MESOZOIC	CRETACEOUS		63–135	Decline of dinosaurs and ammonites. Development of modern invertebrates
MESOZOIC	JURASSIC		135–181	Earliest birds. Reptiles abundant. Cephalopods
MESOZOIC	TRIASSIC		181–230	Comeback of ammonites
PALEOZOIC	PERMIAN		230–280	Decline of ammonites. Extinction of trilobites. Plants, insects, and marine invertebrates
PALEOZOIC	CARBONIFEROUS — PENNSYLVANIAN		280–345	Crinoids, blastoids, and brachiopods important. Trilobites waning
PALEOZOIC	CARBONIFEROUS — MISSISSIPPIAN			Brachiopods, corals, first land plants, fishes
PALEOZOIC	DEVONIAN		345–405	Brachiopods, corals, crinoids, trilobites
PALEOZOIC	SILURIAN		405–425	Trilobites, corals, graptolites, crinoids, and nautiloids important
PALEOZOIC	ORDOVICIAN		425–500	
PALEOZOIC	CAMBRIAN		500–600	Trilobites, inarticulate brachiopods, and gastropods important. Mollusks already evolved. Widespread fossils occur
PRE-CAMBRIAN			600–4,500	
PRE-CAMBRIAN	PROTEROZOIC ERA		3,900–4,300	Origin of life
PRE-CAMBRIAN	ARCHEOZOIC ERA		4,300–4,500	Origin of earth

Tree (phylogeny) labels: ACULIFERA · PLACOPHORA · CONCHIFERA · MOLLUSKS · ANNELIDS · FLATWORMS · PROTO-PROTOSTOME

2. General Features of the Mollusk

The mollusk was one of the earliest forms of life on this planet. Six hundred million years ago in the Cambrian period, when the earliest fossils were laid down, all classes of mollusk were already evolved. Today, the fossil remains of their shells are important to the study of the earth's geologic past.

The phylum Mollusca contains about fifty thousand living species and is out-numbered only by the Arthropoda and Nematoda (Boss 1971, p. 97). Many theories concerning the origin of the mollusks have been advanced in the past. Some have referred to them as descendants of the Platyhelminthes (flatworms), while others have felt their ancestor to be the annelids (segmented worms). Some malacologists constructed a hypothetical ancestral mollusk (Morton 1967), but more recent research supports the abandonment of these theories and a movement toward the concept of a very distant but common ancestor for the mollusks, flatworms, annelids, and arthropods—the "protoprotostome." This common antecedent resembled none of them but was probably a tiny vermiform

organism somewhat like an expanded version of the tubellarian Platyhelminthes. As yet there is no single answer to the question of molluscan origin (phylogeny); the solutions offered are hypothetical because the initial evolutionary stages of the Mollusca took place more than 600 million years ago in the Precambrian and were unrecorded by fossil evidence (fig. 18).

A theory of mollusk evolution has been advanced by Stasek (1972) in which he suggests that most of the broad features that distinguish the Mollusca as a phylum have come about in direct relation to a single evolutionary accomplishment—"the secretion of a cuticle over the dorsal body surface, together with trends toward increase in size." This "cuticle" evolved into the calcified shell (fig. 19).

A dramatic discovery was made in 1957 off the northwest coast of Central America by the Danish *Galathea* expedition, which stimulated interest in the phylogeny of the Mollusca. From a depth of 3,590 meters (2.01 miles) several specimens of a limpetlike shell, *Neopilina*, were recovered and described by Dr. Henning Lemche. Previously, the members of the class Monoplacophora were known only as fossils from the Cambrian to the Devonian periods (600 million to 345 million years ago) and they had been absent from the fossil record for approximately 370 million years. More recent findings of six or seven

other species of *Neopilina* have shed more light on the class, but further investigation is needed: as yet a living specimen has not been studied. With the discovery of *Neopilina* all but three of the approximately ten classes of mollusks have living representatives (see Stasek 1972; Stasek & McWilliams 1973; Harry 1968*a* & *b*; Solem 1974).

It is virtually impossible to generalize the characteristics of the recent mollusks due to the enormous diversity of the members of the phylum. The usual concept of a mollusk is that of an animal with a soft, slippery body and a hard shell, but there are many exceptions, for some, such as the octopus and the sea slug, have no adult shell. However, they all have a soft, fleshy body that is referred to in the name Mollusca, "soft bodied."

The various classes of molluscan animals include chitons that cling to rock; clams that burrow, anchor, or skip; snails that float, dig, or climb; the tooth shell that burrows its wide end into the sand; the jet-propelled octopus that zips through the water leaving a smoke screen of ink in its wake; the primitive, wormlike Aplacophora; and the abyssal-dwelling *Neopilina*. They may be found in any habitat—deserts, trees, rivers, lakes, mud, gardens, coral reefs, the depths of the sea, inside or attached to other animals, and buried in the ground. In all of the animal kingdom their variety is rivaled only by the chordates.

Fig. 18. Phylogeny of the molluscan classes (based on Stasek 1972) correlated with the divisions of geologic time and compared with the major events in the evolution of life on earth

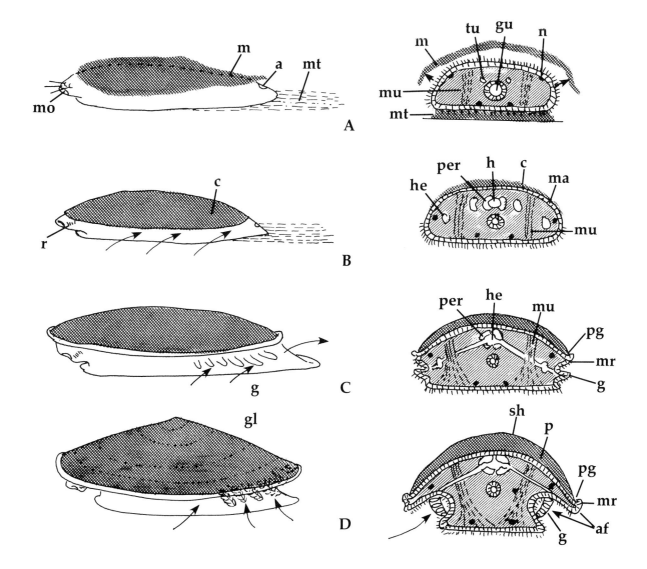

Fig. 19. Four stages in the evolution of the molluscan framework from flatwormlike stock, all shown in lateral and cross-sectional aspects:

A. Proposed ancestral form with complete gut and ability to secrete mucus as a protective measure and as a locomotory track.

B. Transitional stage with radula and cuticle. The cuticle is thin at the periphery where marginal growth takes place, but, because the cuticle is retained throughout life, it becomes thicker in the older portions.

C. Transitional molluscan stage with an incipient mantle cavity. The cuticle arises from a shallow per-iostracal groove beyond which the mantle rim extends.

D. Advanced molluscan stage with calcified layers laid down under the uncalcified periostracum. The mantle rim is still simple.

a - anus
af - accessory fold of mantle associated with production of mucus
c - cuticle
g - ciliated gill
gl - growth lines
h - heart
he - unlined blood spaces
m - protective mucus coat
ma - mantle
mo - mouth
mr - mantle rim
mt - mucus track
mu - dorso-ventral muscles from which pedal muscles were derived
n - longitudinal nerve cords
p - thin periostracum derived from the original cuticular layer
per - pericardium
pg - periostracal groove
r - radula
sh - shelly layers of calcified cuticle
tu - gonoducal tubules form the heart and pericardium in later stages
arrows in B–D indicate respiratory flow of water.
(From Stasek 1972. © Academic Press)

Table 3. Major Differences between Major Classes of Mollusks

Activity	Polyplacophora (chitons)	Bivalvia (clams)	Cephalopoda (squids, octopuses)	Scaphopoda (tusk shells)	Gastropoda (snails)
Sensing the outer world	Through their shell	Mantle edge and siphons	Eyes and tentacles	Tentacles	Head and siphon
Food gathering	Browsing on rocks	Filtering	Grab and bite	Grab and scrape	Mostly scrape, some grab, suck, or spear
Food source	Life on rocks	Microscopic life	Larger animals	Microscopic burrowers	Almost everything
Movement	Crawl	Burrow or attached, rarely swimming	Swim by jet or scramble	Burrow	Crawl or swim, some burrowers

Source: Solem 1974, p. 27. (Reprinted by permission)

Basic Molluscan Pattern

The enormous diversity of the Mollusca makes it difficult to formulate a basic pattern that will apply to all members of the group and still be confined to a brief description. They do have certain biological characters that distinguish them from other phyla, but to include all their known characters is beyond the scope of this book. A basic pattern can only be suggested with the help of a stock of qualifying words like *probably*, *often*, and *certain*. A chart by Solem (1974) is helpful in comparing how each class performs the basic activities (table 3).

The unsegmented molluscan body generally contains a variation of three regions: (1) the *head*—sensory-feeding area, (2) the *foot*—locomotor area, and (3) the *visceral hump*—body mass. The tripartite division of the molluscan body is the rule in nearly all mollusks and is not recognizable in any other group of animals (Harry 1968a, p. 176). The shell may take many forms or it may be enclosed by the mantle, which is a flap extending from the visceral hump; it may be reduced in

size; or it may be completely absent. Among the higher groups of mollusks there is a trend toward the loss of the shell.

Most mollusks have a well-developed head with eyes and tentacles; however, it is not present in bivalves. The head contains the mouth, which leads into a *buccal cavity* usually containing the characteristic molluscan *radula*, a horny ribbon with teeth used to rasp food. Most of the special sense organs are found in the head region.

The foot is common to practically all mollusks in one form or another. This organ of locomotion is located on the ventral side of the animal and is typically a tough, broad, muscular structure. It may contain special glands for secreting the gastropod operculum and, in certain bivalves, the byssus threads for attachment. In burrowing forms, the foot is highly developed. Snails creep by a succession of muscular waves or by cilia on the sole of the flattened foot. The expanded parts of the foot stay fixed to the surface with mucus while the contracted

area is in forward motion. Many bivalves move over the bottom of the sea by extending the foot and then contracting the muscles violently, producing a jumping motion. Other clams dig or creep by extending the foot forward, then drawing the body after it. In certain pelagic forms, such as the pteropods, the foot is much modified into fan-shaped, finlike structures, which aid in swimming; the octopus foot is modified into tapering arms, and the scaphopods use it as an aid in feeding.

All mollusks have a dorsal visceral mass (coiled in Gastropoda), in which the internal organs are concentrated and which remains permanently within the shell and enveloped by the mantle. The *mantle* (or *pallium*) is an overgrowing sheet of tissue extending out and downward from the visceral hump. The mantle secretes the calcareous shell, and its edges may be modified by prolonging into *siphons*. The siphon is, on the whole, best developed in carnivorous gastropods and infaunal bivalves. It has been

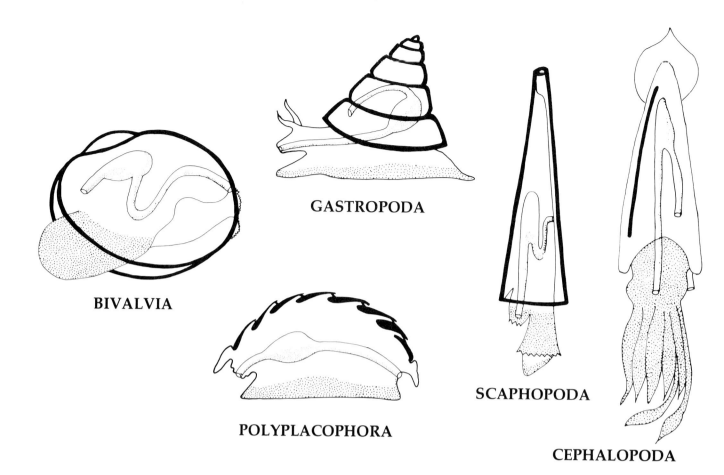

GASTROPODA

BIVALVIA

POLYPLACOPHORA

SCAPHOPODA

CEPHALOPODA

Fig. 20. The molluscan body plan in various classes. The shell is indicated by a heavy line, the digestive tract by small stipples, and the foot by heavier stippling (after Buchsbaum 1967).

shown that in the primitive mollusk the mantle's mechanism for shell growth was a prime factor in severing the ties with the original vermiform ancestor and in establishing the Mollusca as a definite phylum (Stasek & McWilliams 1973; see also fig. 19).

The *mantle cavity*, a distinctly molluscan feature, characteristically developed as a pocket or groove enclosed by the mantle skirt. This space constitutes the respiratory chamber and usually contains the *gills* (*ctenidia*) when present. The anus and the reproductive and excretory systems often open into the mantle cavity. It has been referred to as the main "vestibule and center of commerce" of the molluscan body (Fretter & Graham 1962). The mantle cavity also provides space so that the head and foot may be withdrawn to safety.

The exterior of some smooth and

glossy shells, such as the cowry and olive, is completely enveloped by the mantle. In clams the mantle lines each of the two valves it has secreted. The mantle edges are joined where the valves of the shell are joined and are generally free along the other edges; however, some are fused together along all or most of the lower margins, with openings for the foot and siphon.

The calcareous *exoskeleton*, or *shell*, when present, is secreted by the mantle, that is, by the epithelial covering of the visceral hump and mantle skirt, and it has, therefore, the same shape as that part of the animal's body. The shell may be external, partly external and partly internal, or completely absent. Its shape is a poor guide to natural relationships. The shell is made in three or more highly variable layers: the outer, periostracum, is unpregnated conchiolin (flexible protein);

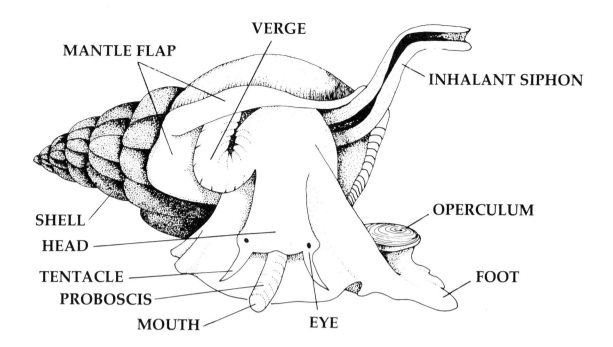

MANTLE FLAP

VERGE

INHALANT SIPHON

OPERCULUM

SHELL

HEAD

TENTACLE

PROBOSCIS

MOUTH

EYE

FOOT

the middle, prismatic, is conchiolin impregnated with crystals of argonite; and the inner, nacreous, is impregnated with the crystalline form of prisms of calcite. Sculpturing or ornamentation of the shell, such as spines and flutings, is only produced at the edge of the mantle.

At the time of its formation, all shell ornamentation followed the edge of the outer lip. Successive stages of growth (additions to the shell at the ventral or apertural edge) remain marked on the surface by distinct growth lines. From a study of the growth lines it is possible to reconstruct the shape of the outer lip of the shell even when the lip has been damaged. When the shell is not protected by the mantle, the outer layer, or periostracum, is a horny, rough, sometimes hairy coating that prohibits marine growths and acids from damaging the shell. The periostracum is a remnant of the primitive cuticle and soon disappears after the animal dies.

In shelled snails, the animal is held in its shell by a columellar muscle that originates on the axial columella, follows the right side of the body into the foot, and attaches

to the under side of the operculum. This muscle retracts the animal into the shell. The head precedes the foot, and if there is an operculum on the rear of the foot it partially or completely closes the aperture. Bivalves are held in their shells by strong adductor muscles that act to close the valves. In scallops and oysters there is only one adductor muscle. In mussels there is one large muscle near the posterior end and a small one near the anterior. In clams there are two adductor muscles, one near the anterior end and one near the posterior.

The shell's color, which is only on the surface of most shells, is influenced by light and temperature. The secretion of color pigment is actually a part of the disposal of the waste products of metabolism. Thus, many gastropods harmonize with the seaweeds or corals on which they live and feed (e.g., *Simnialena marferula* and *Gorgonia*). Color patterns are not necessarily protective, because many of the most elaborately colored shells are obscured with a coating of periostracum or by the mantle in actual life. Species from clear tropical waters are more highly col-

Fig. 21. A coiled gastropod shell with head-foot mass protruded, anterior view (after Cox 1960; courtesy of the Geological Society of America and the University of Kansas).

45

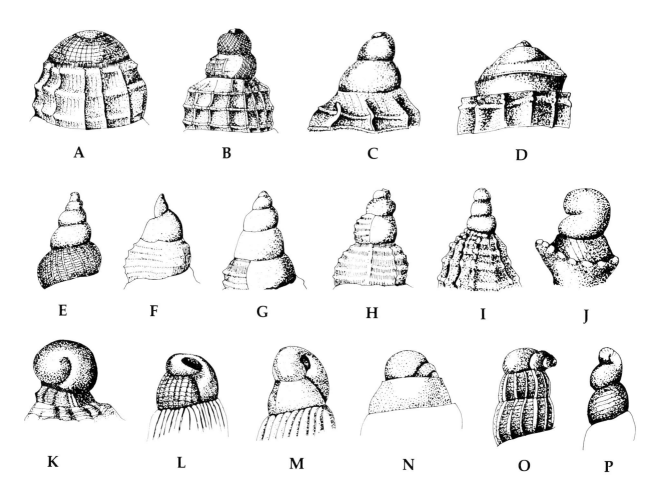

Fig. 22. Various gastropod protoconchs:

A. domelike, paucispiral, with reticulate ornament, *Melatoma*
B. with decussate ornament, *Daphnella*
C. with papillose ornament, *Murex*
D. obtusely conical, *Nassarius*
E. conical, *Scala*
F. disjunct with erect tip, *Charonia*
G. conical, multispiral, *Cymatium*
H. mammillated, *Clavilithes*
I. mammillated, *Cerithiopsis*
J. deviated, paucispiral, *Columbarium*
K. deviated, paucispiral, *Pterospira*
L. heteroscopic and submerged, *Partulida*
M. heteroscopic, *Turbonilla*
N. heteroscopic, *Odostomia*
O. heteroscopic, *Odostomia*
P. heteroscopic, *Eulimella* (after Cox 1960; courtesy of the Geological Society of America and the University of Kansas)

ored than those from colder climates.

The shell grows rapidly at first if the food supply is abundant. In most cases it continues to grow during the lifetime of the animal. The largest gastropod, the horse conch of the Gulf of Mexico, attains a length of two feet; the giant squid, a cephalopod, reaches fifty-five feet; and the *Tridacna* clam may grow to four or five feet and weigh several hundred pounds. The lifetime of a mollusk may range from less than one to twenty-five years depending on the species; however, the *Tridacna* clam is thought to live one hundred years. The majority of the mollusks die at an early age, one year or less, due to changes in salinity or temperature, exhaustion from egg laying, or falling prey to another organism. Many snails form a thickened lip when adulthood is reached; others form a varix or

transverse axial ridge along the edges of the shell between periods of growth and rest. In the latter most of life is spent in the varix stage because additional growth takes place relatively quickly.

A rudimentary shell is present in the larval stage or within the egg. The protoconch of marine snail shells usually consists of two to three smooth whorls that remain clearly delimited in the adult shell (fig. 22). In some families, such as the Pyramidellidae, the protoconch is coiled in a direction different from the remainder of the shell and is described as *heterostrophic*. The immature, or juvenile, shells are usually thin, with thin lips, and are often so different from the adult that they are mistaken for different species.

The shell acts as support or protection for some, but when the shell is nonexistent the animal may have such adaptations as protective coloration or ink sacs that expel a "smoke screen" when danger approaches. Some species develop long, sharp spines on the shell to keep other animals from swallowing them or to help them anchor in the substratum, and others have chemical exudates as defense.

The *digestive system* consists basically of a tube leading from the mouth to the anus. In carnivorous forms the mouth is in a snout, or proboscis, on the head and leads into the enlarged buccal cavity, which contains the mandibles, or jaws, and the openings of the salivary glands. From the buccal cavity the esophagus leads to the stomach, located near the base of the visceral mass. Also in the buccal cavity is the radula, a ribbonlike organ with rows of rasplike teeth that tear food and draw it into the mouth. In some species it contains a device to poison the victim, thus quieting it to make feeding easier. In other species the teeth and rasping motion of the radula are used to drill holes in bivalves through which the soft parts of the victim are eaten. The type of hole can be used to determine the kind of gastropod that drilled it. The arrangement of the minute teeth on this organ is often so distinctive that it may be used as a reliable means of identification of a species, and the present arrangement of the prosobranch gastropod families is based largely upon the radula.

The pulleylike motion of the radula aids the mandibles in scraping and biting the food. The food then passes through the esophagus by means of muscular contractions into the stomach and then into the intestine. In the more complex mollusks, the intestine forms loops and folds. The intestine ends in the anus through which wastes are expelled.

Many snails are carnivorous, feeding on mollusks or other animals; others are vegetarians (herbivores); some are not selective as to plant or animal matter (omnivores); and others are parasites. Clams have only a simple mouth and use their gills as the main organ of feeding. The majority take minute particles of food from the water in one of two ways: suspension, or filter, feeding (pumping water through the mantle cavity); or by deposit, or detritus, feeding (sucking up food from the muddy bottom with the siphon). Detritus is comprised of minute particles of decaying plant and animal material and bacteria commonly found on the surface of mud flats, estuaries, and ocean bottoms (see Appendix E for feeding forms).

The *circulatory system* usually contains a heart that receives aerated blood from the respiratory organs and propels it to every part of the body. When arteries are present they carry the blood from the heart to the other parts, and the veins return the blood to the respiratory organs after it passes through the kidneys, where waste materials are extracted. The blood is usually colorless or faintly blue, but a few species have red blood.

The *respiratory apparatus* consists of branchiae, or ctenidia (gills), which aerate the blood on its way to the heart. In clams water is pumped in through the incurrent siphon, carried over the gills by cilia, and then forced out the excurrent siphon. In some clams these two siphons are joined, while in others they may be long and separate. Epifaunal bivalves do not have siphons. Many snails have a tubelike projection of the shell (siphonal canal) to protect the siphon. The gills are so distinctive in position and character that many divisions of the mollusks are named for these characteristics.

The *nervous system*, which is less complicated in bivalves, consists of a nerve ring with three pairs of swellings, or concentrations, of ganglia: (1) the cerebral ganglia controlling mouth, mantle, and eyes; (2) the visceral ganglia controlling the adductor muscles and visceral mass; and (3) the pedal ganglia controlling the foot.

The sense of touch is well developed in only a few species. The foot is the most sensitive area, then the edges of the mantle, the tentacles, and the skin surface. Taste is present to some extent in all head-bearing mollusks.

Sight is a curious sense in many mollusks. The range in development is great—from the highly developed eye of the octopus down to the simple light-sensitive spots in some clams. It is believed that only a few snails and the cephalopods use their eyes to observe. In head-bearing marine mollusks the "eyes" are generally in the region of the tentacles but not on the tips. Usually pelagic, burrowing, and deep-sea mollusks have no eyes. The intertidal species are the most light sensitive, a sense they use for protection against man and diving birds. Bivalves may have light-sensitive spots scattered over the surface of the mantle, concentrated around the siphon, or, as in the scallop, highly developed ocelli on the edge of the mantle.

Perhaps one of the most important senses to the mollusk is that of smell. The osphradium, or smell organ, is situated next to the gills. The carnivorous gastropods have the most highly developed sense of smell, while the bivalves apparently do not have this sense. Very little is known about the hearing sense of the mollusk.

In Mollusca, *reproduction* is invariably from an egg, which is developed in the ovary of the female and usually fertilized by the spermatozoa of the male. The sperm may be implanted directly into the female by the verge, a copulatory organ, or they may be discharged freely into the sea. Ejecting eggs and sperm into the water promiscuously is a risky business. To counteract some of that risk the mollusks produce and dispense huge numbers of sperm and eggs. The number of eggs is highest among the bivalves and in the case of *Ostrea edulis* can be as many as 60 million. The sea hare, a naked gastropod, deposits 41,000 eggs per minute, or half a million in one seventeen-week laying period; on the other hand, the abalone lays only one egg at a time. The breeding period is determined by such factors as water temperature, lunar phases, proximity of the opposite sex, winds, and tides.

A great number of male gastropods have external copulatory organs, but none of the bivalves are so equipped. Some univalves and most bivalves are of separate sexes, but certain groups of mollusks have dual sexuality (hermaphroditism). Sex change in an individual is not uncommon. In these hermaphroditic forms mutual impregnation between two individuals may take place; that is, each of the two may function as both male and female at the same time and thus fertilize the other. However, in most such cases one individual assumes the role of male and the other that of female during mating. Some hermaphrodites have a special sac for storing live sperm to be used later when the eggs mature.

In order to protect their eggs, the mollusks have developed a variety of protective coverings. The female snail may deposit eggs inside strings of leathery cases, enclosed in bladdery capsules, glued with grains of sand into sand collars, in jellylike masses or ribbons on seaweed, attached to the underside of floats, or attached to the outside of their own shell (figs. 23 & 24). The foot is often used to shape complicated, horny strings of egg cases like those of the whelk. Some bivalves hatch their eggs within the mantle cavity and allow the veliger to grow within the protection of the gills. Many snails give birth to live young.

The fertilized egg develops in four ways: *indirectly* into (1) planktotrophic larvae with a long larval life of up to three months, (2) planktotrophic larvae with a short swimming life of never more than a week, or (3) lecithotrophic larvae that take no food in the plankton but hatch from yolky eggs and swim little, or (4) *directly*, as in many gastropods that develop completely in the egg capsule and are nonpelagic. The functions of the larvae are to disperse the species and to locate a settling spot before metamorphosis takes place. The characteristic larval shell, the veliger, may differ completely from the adult shell. The size and number of embryonic whorls differ according to the length of time the larvae passed in the plankton. The more whorls, the longer the life in the planktonic stage.

Only a small number of the eggs develop into adult mollusks; some serve as nurse eggs for the few cannibalistic survivors that hatch at the crawling stage and others fall prey to plankton feeders. The adult also has many enemies. Birds, including crows, gulls, and other aquatic birds, are the main enemies. Gulls have been seen flying into the air with a clam and letting it drop to the ground, repeating the process until the shell has broken so that the bird can have its meal. A crow holds a snail on a limb with its foot and expertly crushes the shell with its strong beak. Fish, such as the bottom-feeding catfish, drum, and flounder, find mollusks a staple of diet. Parasitic worms cause great havoc in some mollusks, principally the fresh-water varieties. Snails are one of the greatest enemies of the bivalves. Carnivorous species, such as *Polinices* and *Thais*, drill holes in other mollusks and eat the flesh. The *Thais*, or oyster drill, is one of the plagues of the oyster reef. Man as an enemy also must not be forgotten.

To overcome these enemies, the mollusk has developed many passive modes of resistance. When danger approaches, the clams "clam-up" by snapping their valves shut and the snail draws into its shell, sealing the opening with the operculum. Some hide in a nest they have constructed of marine refuse held together with byssus threads. The *Xenophora*, or carrier shell, glues bits of shell and rocks to the top of its shell and is thus difficult to locate. To keep fish from swallowing them, many mollusks have developed a variety of spines. The vulnerable sea slug, or nudibranch, produces an exudate that makes it distasteful to its predators. The cones are able to inject poison into their prey or their enemies, while other mollusks can only rely on blending into the surroundings. Some become active and leap about with their strong foot, while the shell-less sea hares and octopuses resort to a cloudy screen of ink to avoid predators.

The phylum Mollusca is, indeed, quite distinct from other modern groups. For further reading on their biology, see Morton 1960, R. C. Moore 1960–, Fretter & Graham 1962, Wilbur & Yonge 1964, Hyman 1967, and Purchon 1968.

Identifying the Shell

One of the most rewarding features of an interest in the field of natural history, whether it be insects, wildflowers, or sea shells, is the pleasure to be had from identifying one's collection. Once the collector is able to name his shell he can compare his observations of the habits of the animal with studies by others. Simply, he can communicate.

Identification of a shell is not al-

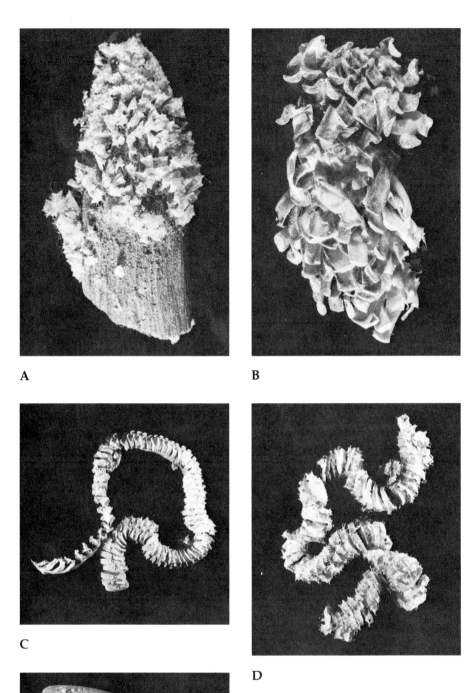

A

B

C

D

E

F

Fig. 23. Gastropod egg cases:
A. *Cantharus* egg capsules attached to wood
B. the purplish egg cases of a *Thais*
C. a rope of horny egg capsules constructed by the female *Busycon perversum pulleyi*
D. *B. spiratum plagosum* constructs capsules with serrated edges
E. the tulip shell, *Fasciolaria*, has attached vase-shaped egg capsules to a pen shell
F. a spongelike mass of egg capsules produced by *Murex pomum*

Fig. 24. Gastropod egg cases:
A. *Littorina irrorata*
B. *L. lineolata*
C. *L. meleagris*
D. *L. angulifera*
E. *L. nebulosa*
F. *Nerita*
G. *Phalium*

H. *Trivia*
I. *Cantharus*
J. *Epitonium*
K. *Aplysia*
L. *Fasciolaria*
M. *F. tulipa*
N. *F. lilium*
O. *Pleuroploca*

P. *Nassarius*
Q. *Diastoma*
R. *Busycon*
S. *B. perversum pulleyi*
T. *B. spiratum plagosum*
U. *Cancellaria*
V. *Polinices*

ways a simple task. A look at illustrations may spot the shell or a near relative so that a reference to the text will point out the real identity. Although the shell of the mollusk may be unsatisfactory as a basis of classification, it is convenient for identification because one seldom has the live animal.

Within a species there might be great variation in color or shape because marine mollusks are extremely responsive to varying environmental conditions. Conversely, some species may be so similar to others that only an anatomical study of the animal will prevent misnomer. Quite often the differences caused by environment are difficult to distinguish from the inherent characteristics of a species.

For the ability to find their way around at all, within the multiplicity of forms, collectors are indebted to the great Swedish naturalist Carolus Linnaeus, or Karl von Linné (1707–1778). It was he who established the first useful system of classification for the whole of the plant and animal kingdoms. His introduction of the two-word symbol for designating species gave descriptive natural science a new tool.

Taxonomy (systematics) is composed of two distinct parts: *nomenclature*, which deals with the assigning of name, and *classification*, which deals with relationships and the various categories (species, genus, family, etc.) to which organisms are assigned. Classification is grouping, whereas identification is the recognition of an organism as being similar to other organisms that have already been named (Schenk & McMasters 1958).

Standardized names, which can be recognized by students throughout the world, are used to discuss the many kinds of mollusks. Because these names are in international use, Latin or Latinized forms are employed for nomenclature. No one, not even professional malacologists, can remember all of them, but it adds to the pleasure of collecting to be able to recall a few of the more common species.

Like people, a mollusk is given a name of two parts—a binomial. The generic name, always capitalized, is used like the surname, such as Jones or Smith—for example, *Tellina*; the trivial, or specific, name, which is not capitalized and which follows the generic name, corresponds to the first name, such as Jane or George—for example, *texana*. Both of these names are italicized. The name of a person, printed in Roman type, and a date follow the scientific name—for example, *Tellina texana* Dall, 1900—indicating the person who first described the species (the author) and the year in which it was described. This information is helpful in tracing the original description. If the author's name is in parentheses, it indicates that someone has since studied that particular species and placed it in a different genus from that assigned by the original author. Thus, the common rangia, first described as *Gnathodon cuneatus* Gray, 1831, is now written as *Rangia cuneata* (Gray, 1831). Once an animal has been named, the specific name becomes unchangeable unless it has already been used within that genus. The species may be transferred to another genus but the specific name remains the same.

If there is a subgeneric name it is capitalized and placed in parentheses following the generic name. If there is a subspecific name it follows the specific name without separation by sign or symbol. Thus, *"Genus (Subgenus) species subspecies* Author, date."

The generic name is one word written in the form of a singular noun. It is preferable that the specific name be in the form of an adjective which agrees grammatically with the generic name, but it may be patronymic (given in dedication) or another noun which further explains the generic noun.

The name may describe some characteristic of the mollusk, may indicate geographic localities in which it is found, or may be either the name of a person who has made an important contribution to this field of science or a mythological name. Some names are without definite meaning, but usually the name selected is a store of information about the organism and not nonsense.

The names of classes, orders, and families (collective classification) always end in plurals of Latinized nouns. Families have the suffix *-idae* and subfamilies have *-inae* added to the stem of their type genus. These names originate in three ways:
1. Adoption directly with appropriate modifications in spelling from Greek, Latin, and other languages
2. Composition by compounding and affixation
3. Outright or arbitrary creation without use of evident antecedent root or stem material

The International Commission for Zoological Nomenclature devised the rules by which animals are named. The starting point of zoological nomenclature and the Law of Priority is accepted as the date of January 1, 1758, when Linné's *Systema Naturae* was published. According to Article 25 of the Rules of Zoological Nomenclature, the valid name of a genus or species may be only the name by which it was first designated. As our knowledge of mollusks increases and old papers are reinvestigated, it often becomes necessary to change a name to an older, little used name which has priority. When these names are based on identical material they become *synonyms*. In some instances, when the junior synonym has been in long usage the commission may rule to preserve it as a *nomen conservandum* even if it does not have priority.

In spite of the care taken by this august body, the seemingly constant switching of scientific names is a perplexing problem for the amateur. In 1905 David Starr Jordan said in his *Guide to the Study of Fishes*: "In taxonomy it is not nearly so important that a name be pertinent or even well chosen as that it be stable. In changing his own established names, the father of classification, Linnaeus, set a bad example to his successors, one which they did not fail to follow."

When it has been determined that a new genus or species has been found, a specimen of the shell is placed under lock and key in a type collection, such as those located at the United States National Museum and other major study centers. The various type categories are shown in Appendix B.

Pronunciation of the genus and species names is a personal matter, but it is generally based on Latin and Greek pronunciations. Words of two syllables are accented on the first; those of more than two syllables are accented on the penult (next to last). The purpose of pronunciation is to be understood. If the name is a patronymic (formed from a proper name), the pronunciation of the area or the person's name is retained regardless of how it is syllabicated.

Many mollusks have common, or popular, names. These names may vary for the same shell according to region, but in most cases they are names in use by local collectors and fishermen. Abbott (1974) has listed more than eleven hundred popular names of American sea shells and in so doing has gone a long way toward their standardization. However, many small shells are too little known to have been given a common name. Actually, the common names are superfluous and only add to the confusion.

The development of a species is a gradual and continuous process. Ernst Mayr in his *Systematics and the Origin of Species* (1942) defines species as groups of actually or potentially interbreeding natural populations, which are reproductively isolated from other such groups by geographical, physiological, or ecological barriers.

A genus is merely an arbitrary and convenient grouping of related species. This is also true of the higher categories, subfamily and family, which are groupings of related genera. Whatever the faults of the system, it is extremely useful. With the generic system we may arrange the species in our collections in a biological and evolutionary sequence (classification). The usual order is kingdom, phylum, class, order, family, genus, species, and subspecies. The chart in figure 25 illustrates the classification of mollusks.

Until recently much molluscan classification was done on the basis of shell characteristics, but contemporary scientific work emphasizes the study of the organism. The result has been reclassification of many species and the end is not near. Biologists are becoming aware of unique research potentials and amateurs have an increasing interest in studying the mollusk as a living animal.

The differences in characteristics of a mollusk may be morphological (form and structure), physiological (pertaining to function), or genetic (hereditary). The morphological features of a mollusk include many besides the characters most commonly used to identify the shell. Such characteristics as spines, color, and number of whorls are used to distinguish species; therefore, it will be necessary to become acquainted with the names of these features in order to identify one's shells. The use of technical words is unavoidable because many of these terms have no counterpart in our daily language. Familiarization with such terms as operculum, periostracum, umbones, and beaks is gained easily with a few trial identifications using the illustrations and glossary provided in this book.

The amateur should understand taxonomy/systematics (the art or science of classification) and should try to identify his collection because it adds to its value, but taxonomy should not be his primary interest. Today we are bogged down in a tangle of names—one shell may have many synonyms; even the experts are often stumped. Without an extensive library or a large collection from many locations the amateur is greatly handicapped.

This does not mean that he cannot make a significant contribution to the science of *malacology* (anatomical), or *conchology* (shell). (Dance 1966, p. 270, discusses the problem of usage of conchology vs. malacology.) The amateur probably has more opportunity to observe the living mollusks than does the busy professional malacologist who often teaches or directs a museum. Much information is needed as to the type of bottom that the animal is associated with, its spawning habits, how it feeds, and so on. Consider the mollusk as a living animal in a particular environment, record your observations—they could be important contributions to science. The science of ecology is less than one hundred years old and growing in importance; your perceptions could advance it. But, without data the most prolonged study of an animal's habits is worthless. Record and date your observations, but do not stop there. Make certain your locality data are accurate by including enough information for a complete stranger to locate the spot on a standard map.

Fig. 25. Classification chart for mollusks

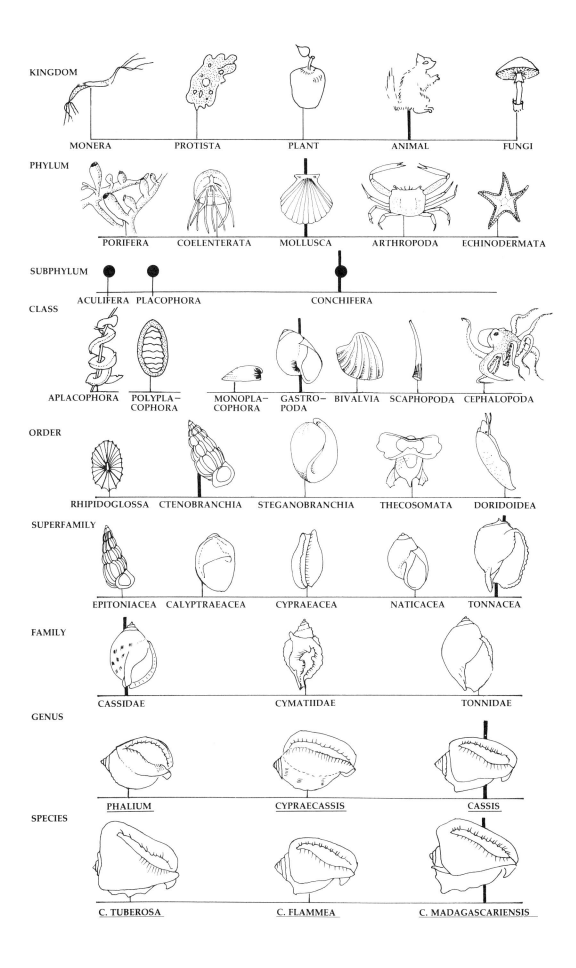

KINGDOM   MONERA   PROTISTA   PLANT   ANIMAL   FUNGI

PHYLUM   PORIFERA   COELENTERATA   MOLLUSCA   ARTHROPODA   ECHINODERMATA

SUBPHYLUM   ACULIFERA   PLACOPHORA   CONCHIFERA

CLASS   APLACOPHORA   POLYPLA-COPHORA   MONOPLA-COPHORA   GASTRO-PODA   BIVALVIA   SCAPHOPODA   CEPHALOPODA

ORDER   RHIPIDOGLOSSA   CTENOBRANCHIA   STEGANOBRANCHIA   THECOSOMATA   DORIDOIDEA

SUPERFAMILY   EPITONIACEA   CALYPTRAEACEA   CYPRAEACEA   NATICACEA   TONNACEA

FAMILY   CASSIDAE   CYMATIIDAE   TONNIDAE

GENUS   PHALIUM   CYPRAECASSIS   CASSIS

SPECIES   C. TUBEROSA   C. FLAMMEA   C. MADAGASCARIENSIS

53

The Conchifera

Recent evaluation of the interrelationships of the molluscan classes has caused the introduction of three new subphyla—Aculifera, Placophora, and Conchifera—based on the thesis that all living Mollusca are the offspring of three separate lineages stemming from unrecorded pre-Mollusca (Stasek 1972, p. 40). The first subphylum has one known member in Texas, the second but two known members; however, the third is represented by five classes encompassing the Texas fauna. Stasek suggests that the subphylum Conchifera is composed of the Monoplacophora (none in Texas) and its four descendant classes—Gastropoda, Bivalvia, Scaphopoda, and Cephalopoda (table 4).

Class Gastropoda: Snails

The name Gastropoda means "stomach-footed ones" (L. *gaster* stomach; Gk. *pod* foot). The gastropod shell, which consists of one unit, is called a univalve. The gastropod is distinct from the other classes of the phylum because of its asymmetrical, spirally coiled, visceral mass and shell. Gastropods are the most diverse group of mollusks. They have adapted for life in both marine and fresh water as well as on land. The primitive forms may browse on algae or minute animals, but others have become scavengers, parasites, and grazers, as well as active carnivorous predators. Adaptations in form probably were based on the requirements of the feeding pattern.

When moving, the gastropod carries its shell with the opening (*aperture*) forward; hence, the aperture is considered *anterior/abapical* and the pointed end (*apex*) is considered *posterior/adapical*. When you examine the shell, it is conventional to hold it in a position with the aperture toward you and the apex uppermost, with the axis vertical. Look at the outline of the shell in this position to determine the shape. Some of the most typical of the varied shapes of snail shells and the terms applied to them are illustrated in figure 26.

The external parts of the gastropod shell have been given names that are useful in describing your shell. In the following discussion, some of the terms more frequently used are given in italics and are illustrated in figure 27. The *apex* at the *adapical* (*posterior*) end of the shell is where the *nucleus* (*proto-conch*) is located. The *protoconch* is the larval shell; growth proceeds from it to accommodate the increasing size of the visceral hump of the growing animal; on adult shells it is often eroded.

The protoconch, secreted during embryonic life, is the only part of the shell formed by the simultaneous deposition of calcium carbonate and conchiolin; it may be without ornament or have ornament quite different from the later additions. The additions, as the shell grows, are added spirally around the protoconch, which acts as a point of origin, forming *whorls*. The diameter of each new whorl becomes larger, and the youngest and largest is the *body whorl*, which contains the head and foot. The remainder of the whorls make up the spire where the visceral mass is located. The spire and body whorls exclusive of the protoconch comprise the *teleoconch*. The entire conical tube is the *helicocone*. It is not always easy to count the whorls. The diagrams in figure 27 may help more than words.

Each successive whorl is separated by an indentation, or *suture* (fig. 28). The sutures may be shallow or deeply cut, wavy or regular,

Table 4. Summary of Molluscan Relationships

Phylum MOLLUSCA Cuvier, 1797
   Subphylum ACULIFERA Hatscheck, 1891
      Class APLACOPHORA von Ihering, 1876*
   Subphylum PLACOPHORA von Ihering, 1876
      Class POLYPLACOPHORA Blainville, 1816*
   Subphylum CONCHIFERA Gegenbaur, 1878
      Class MONOPLACOPHORA Wenz, 1940
      Class GASTROPODA Cuvier, 1797*
      Class BIVALVIA Linné, 1758*
      Class SCAPHOPODA Bronn, 1862*
      Class CEPHALOPODA Cuvier, 1797*

* Relevant to the Texas fauna.

Fig. 26. Diagrammatic illustrations of typical gastropod shell shapes

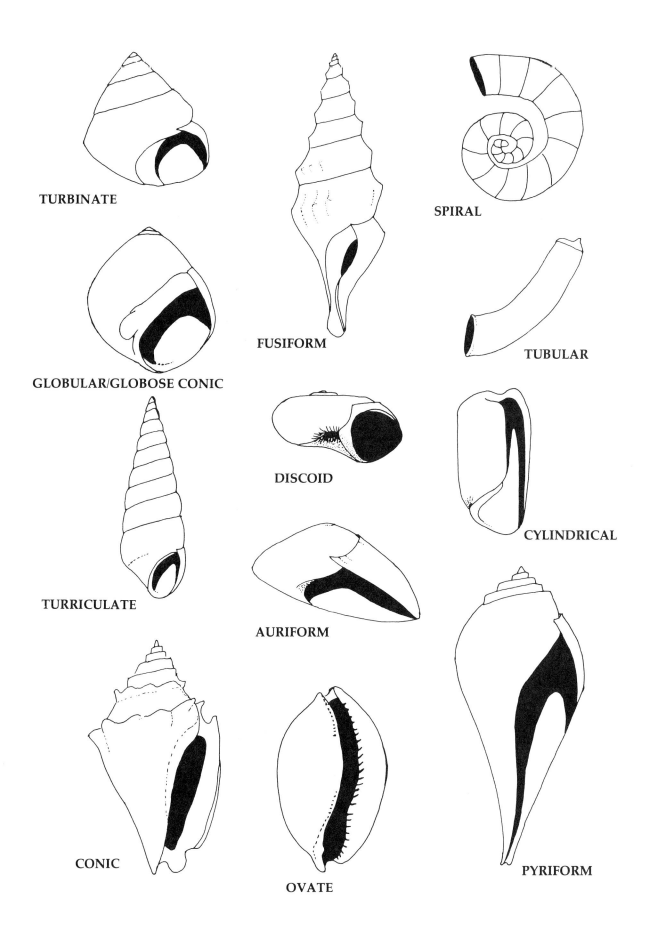

TURBINATE

FUSIFORM

SPIRAL

GLOBULAR/GLOBOSE CONIC

TUBULAR

TURRICULATE

DISCOID

CYLINDRICAL

AURIFORM

CONIC

OVATE

PYRIFORM

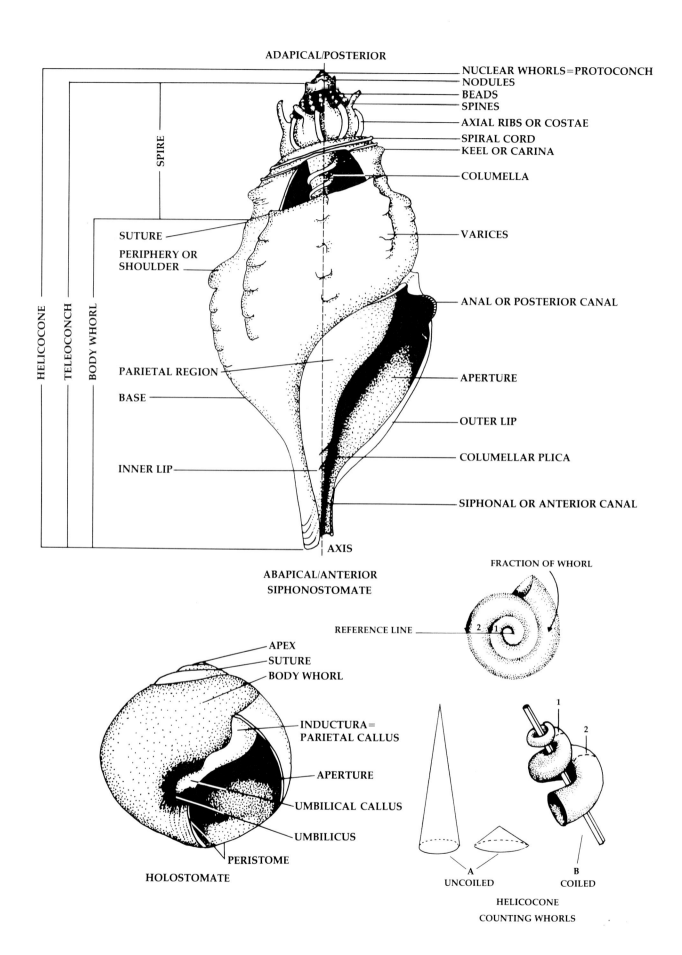

ADAPICAL/POSTERIOR

NUCLEAR WHORLS=PROTOCONCH
NODULES
BEADS
SPINES
AXIAL RIBS OR COSTAE
SPIRAL CORD
KEEL OR CARINA

COLUMELLA

SPIRE

HELICOCONE
TELEOCONCH
BODY WHORL

SUTURE
PERIPHERY OR
SHOULDER

VARICES

ANAL OR POSTERIOR CANAL

PARIETAL REGION

BASE

APERTURE

OUTER LIP

COLUMELLAR PLICA

INNER LIP

SIPHONAL OR ANTERIOR CANAL

AXIS

ABAPICAL/ANTERIOR
SIPHONOSTOMATE

FRACTION OF WHORL

REFERENCE LINE

2 1

APEX
SUTURE
BODY WHORL

INDUCTURA=
PARIETAL CALLUS

APERTURE

UMBILICAL CALLUS

UMBILICUS

PERISTOME

HOLOSTOMATE

1

2

A
UNCOILED

B
COILED

HELICOCONE
COUNTING WHORLS

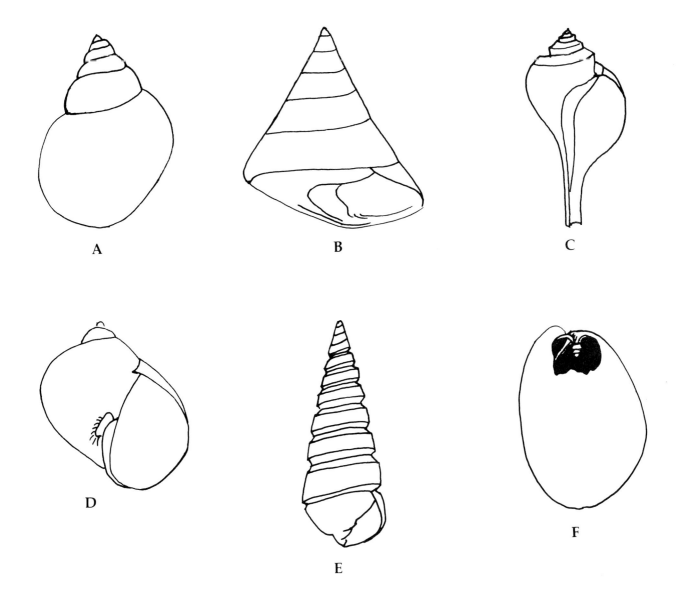

A

B

C

D

E

F

Fig. 27. Parts of the gastropod shell. In this composite shell the columella is seen through a cutaway section. *Counting whorls*: The apical end of the whorl in the diagram is semicircular with the reference line forming approximate right angles at the sutures. The suture is the line of contact of successive whorls and is perpendicular to the reference line. If there is no coil, there is no whorl, e.g., the limpet. The completion of the first turn is the completion of the first whorl; it does not coincide with the termination of the protoconch.

Fig. 28. Types of gastropod sutures:
A. impressed
B. flush
C. tabulate and canaliculate
D. adpressed
E. grooved
F. involute, not visible

marking the juncture of each whorl. The whorls may be ornamented with pointed spines, ridges, flutings, or color patterns. At the abapical end of the shell is the *aperture*, an opening through which the body of the gastropod extends. The edges, or lips, of the aperture are the growing zone of the shell. The margin of the aperture is the *peristome*. The peristome is said to be *entire* (*holostomate*) if it is not interrupted by a siphonal canal or by the parietal area of the body whorl and *siphonostomate* if it is.

The aperture varies greatly in shape, being round, oval, or a long narrow slit, as in the olive shell. The edge of the body whorl adjoining the aperture is the *outer lip*. At the end of each growth period the outer lip may become thickened to form a *varix*, and at adulthood it might become extremely flared or ornate. The mantle can remove these varices or other portions of the shell when no longer needed, as well as adding to the interior of the shell to thicken the walls or to repair damages to the shell.

The side of the aperture opposite the outer lip is known as the *inner lip* and consists of two parts, the *columellar lip* and the *parietal lip*. The *columella* is a central pillar formed by the rotations of the growing shell. To it is attached the columellar muscle, which draws the head and foot into the shell. The columella may be smooth or marked with folds, which are referred to as *teeth*, *folds*, or *plicae* that may provide attachment for the muscle fibers. The parietal lip may be coated with a smooth shelly layer known as the *inductura* (*callus*).

In siphonostomate shells there is an outlet for the siphon, the *siphonal canal*, which is a prolongation of the aperture.

The *sculpture* (*ornament*) found on the exterior of the shell—spines, costae, indentations, nodules, cords, threads, and colored bands—may be put into two basic groups: (1) the *spiral sculpture*, which is spirally arranged in the direction of the suture between the whorls; and (2) the *transverse* (*axial*) sculpture, which is ribs, lines, or nodules that run across the whorl from suture to suture parallel with the axis. Growth lines, varices, and the outer lip are transverse features. *Growth lines* refer to lines in the shell that mark temporary cessations of growth. Each growth line was once the outer lip of the shell.

When whorls are not wound closely at their abapical side, an opening is left in the shell, the *umbilicus*. Such shells are *umbilicate*, or *phaneromphalous*. Only about a fourth of the gastropods have this feature, but it can be quite distinctive in those that are umbilicated. Shells without an umbilicus are *anomphalous*.

The *operculum* is a solid accessory to the gastropod shell constructed by the foot. There are about twenty forms within three main types of opercula, but they are not present in all adult gastropods (fig. 29). In many of the more advanced families there has been a reduction or complete disappearance of the operculum; however, it is present in the larval stage of all gastropods. This horny or calcareous plate is carried on the rear dorsal surface of the foot. It closes the aperture when the head and foot are withdrawn into the shell and may even aid in locomotion, as in *Strombus*.

Often the outer layer of the shell is a horny coating known as the *periostracum*. In some cases this layer, composed of protein, may be thin and almost transparent like a coating of varnish; in others it might be thick and hairy; and in some groups, such as the olives, it is entirely absent. It serves to protect the shell from chemical action, boring animals, and erosion.

Class Bivalvia: Clams

The Bivalvia (Pelecypoda), or "two-valved ones" (L. *bi* two, *valvae* folding doors), contain fewer genera and species than the Gastropoda, but in number of individuals may outweigh all other classes of Mollusca and are the most important economically. All bivalves are aquatic filter feeders on detritus and plankton (for more on feeding, see Appendix E). Their mode of feeding has limited them to strictly aqueous environments. On the Texas coast in the areas known as Big Shell and Little Shell on Padre Island, the wind and waves have banked the shore with incredible numbers of the shells of the coquina, the arks, and others of this class.

The environments of the bivalves have been classified by Kauffman (1969, n.141) into three habitat categories:
1. *Epifaunal* bivalves, normally living exposed above the surface of the substratum (sea floor); they may be:
   a. Byssate free-swinging forms (*Pteria*)
   b. Byssate, closely attached, exposed forms; solitary (*Modiolus*) and gregarious (*Mytilus*)
   c. Byssate nestlers (*Arca*, *Barbatia*)
   d. Byssate fissure dwellers (some *Chlamys*, *Lima*)
   e. Cemented form (*Ostrea*, *Chama*)
   f. Free-living epifaunal; swimmers (*Pecten*) and nonswimmers (*Glycymeris*, in part)
2. *Semi-infaunal* bivalves
   a. Sessile (*Pinna*)
3. *Infaunal* bivalves, normally concealed in the substratum
   a. Mobile detritus feeders (*Tagelus*)
   b. Sessile detritus feeders (*Tellina*)
   c. Filter feeders (*Chione*)
   d. Borers (*Lithophaga*)

The bivalves invariably have two shells usually external on either side of the body. Typically, the two valves are of equal convexity (*equivalve*), but in some forms this symmetry has been lost and the valves will differ in size to a varying degree (*inequivalve*). These valves are held together dorsally by a

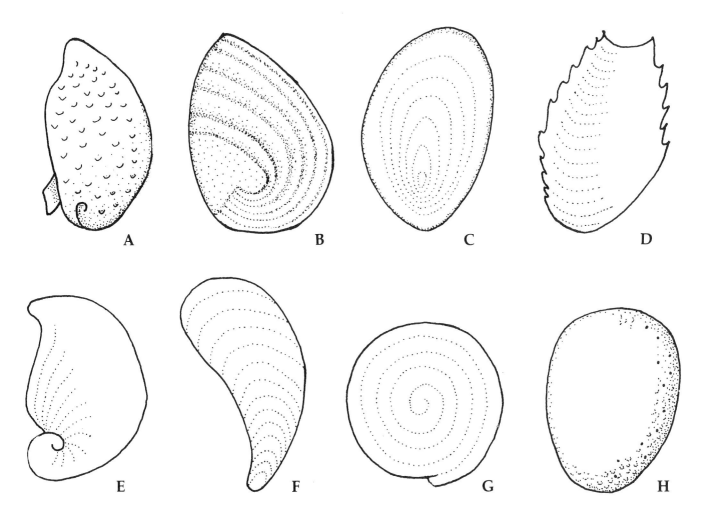

leathery, brown, elastic *ligament*. Some of the characteristics of the bivalve shell are illustrated in figure 30 and are described in the following text.

The two valves are joined at their *dorsal margin* but are open along their *anterior*, *posterior*, and *ventral margins*. The ventral margin is opposite the dorsal margin. The valves are closed by action of the *adductor muscles* attached to the inner face of each. When the two valves do not meet at the ventral margin when closed, they are said to *gape*.

Along the dorsal margin will be found the *beak*, or *umbo* (plural, *umbones*), which is the point where growth of the shell began. If the adult shell has a beak that occupies a position close to the middle of the length of the shell, the shell is said

to be *equilateral*, but if the beak lies closer to one end or the other it is said to be *inequilateral*. The *umbonal cavity* is that part of the interior of the valve which lies within the umbones.

Along the dorsal margin are also found the *hinge teeth*. These teeth function to prevent any rocking or shearing movements of the valves. Infaunal bivalves, with their more sheltered lives, do not require the stronger, interlocking teeth of epifaunal genera, such as *Spondylus*. *Cardinal teeth* are those immediately below the umbones; the *anterior* and *posterior laterals* are those on the respective sides of the cardinals. Often in the case of inequilateral bivalves the teeth have become so distorted that they are difficult to distinguish. The dentition is a prin-

Fig. 29. Gastropod opercula:
A. calcareous, paucispiral with apophysis
B. calcareous, paucispiral
C. horny, concentric
D. horny, lamellar with serrated edge
E. horny, paucispiral
F. horny, unguiculate
G. horny, multispiral
H. calcareous

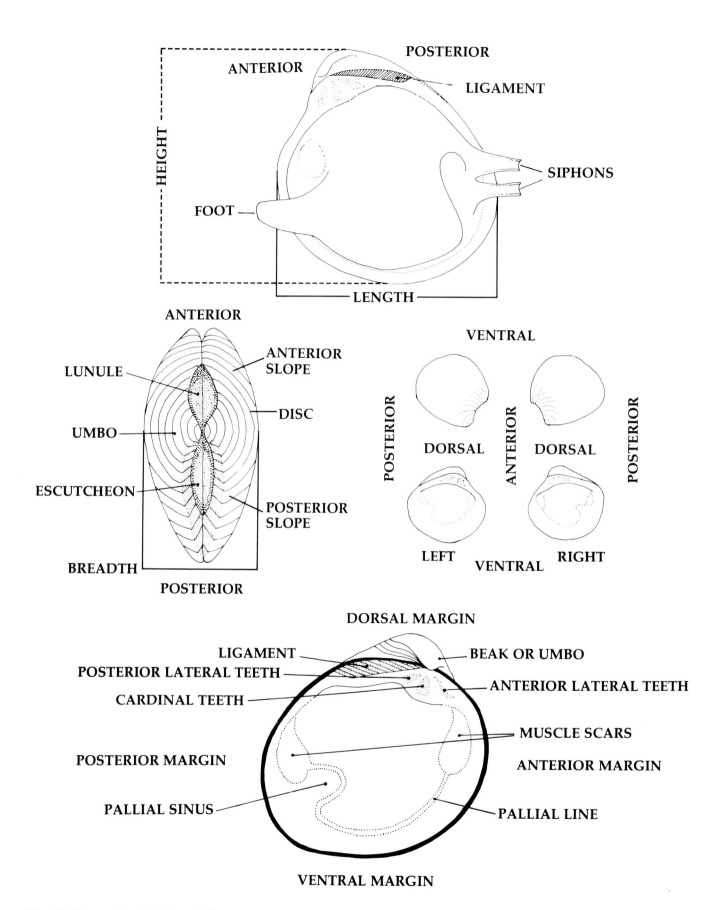

Fig. 30. Parts of the bivalve shell

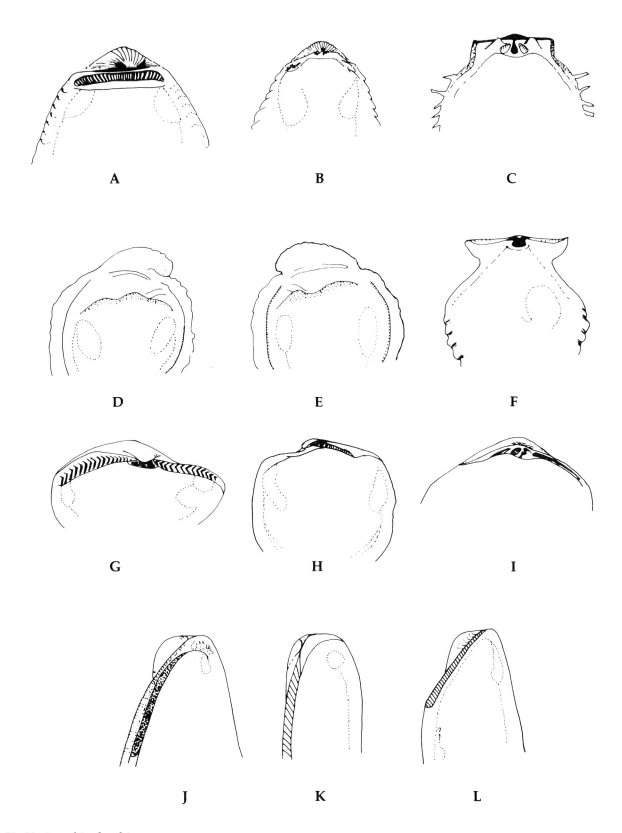

Fig. 31. Various bivalve hinges:
A. *Anadara*, taxodont
B. *Cardium*, heterodont
C. *Spondylus*, isodont
D. *Chama*, pachyodont
E. *Pseudochama*, pachyodont
F. *Pecten*, isodont
G. *Nuculana*, taxodont
H. *Anodontia*, edentulous
I. *Mactra*, heterodont
J. *Brachidontes*, dysodont
K. *Lithophaga*, edentulous
L. *Modiolus*, edentulous

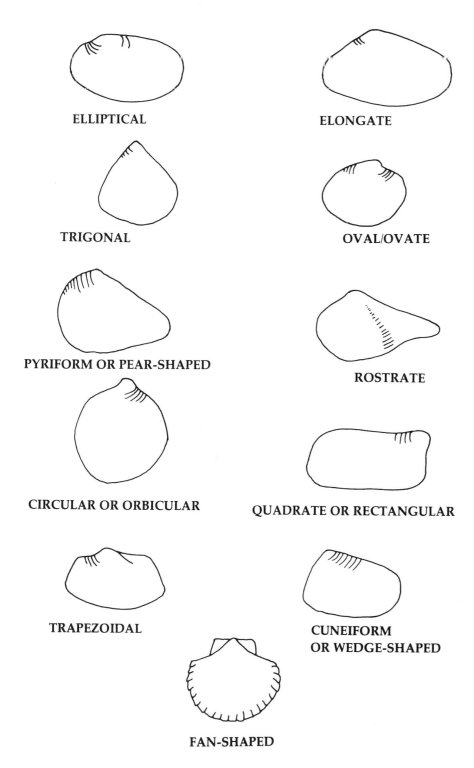

ELLIPTICAL

ELONGATE

TRIGONAL

OVAL/OVATE

PYRIFORM OR PEAR-SHAPED

ROSTRATE

CIRCULAR OR ORBICULAR

QUADRATE OR RECTANGULAR

TRAPEZOIDAL

CUNEIFORM
OR WEDGE-SHAPED

FAN-SHAPED

Fig. 32. Diagrammatic illustrations
of typical bivalve shell shapes

cipal basis of classification within the class Bivalvia.

Two characteristic features of the umbonal area to be found in infaunal bivalves are the *lunule* and the *escutcheon*. The lunule is a heart-shaped impression anterior to the beaks, while the escutcheon is a similar depression posterior to the beaks. The significance of these two features has not yet been adequately interpreted.

The interior of the shell bears an impression, or *pallial line*. This line running parallel and close to the shell margin is a band, or series, of pits made by the insertion of muscles attaching the mantle to its shell. This line may be *continuous* or *discontinuous* and farther within the shell, as in many epifaunal bivalves. The deeper location is correlated with longer muscle fibers, used to withdraw the mantle far into the shell of the more vulnerable epifaunal species.

An obvious feature of the pallial line is a U-shaped embayment, or indentation, the *pallial sinus*, always located posteriorly close to the siphons. The sinus will only be found in infaunal bivalves, but the very short siphons of some infaunal clams do not produce a sinus. If the pallial line is without a pallial sinus it is described as a *simple* pallial line.

The primary adaptive function of the bivalve shell is supportive, secondarily protective, but an accessory structure of the valves may share either function. The forms in which the shell does not completely enclose the soft parts often show such adaptations as deep burial, secretion of tubes, building of nests, or other structural and ecologic modifications of the usual bivalve pattern.

The shape and convexity of infaunal bivalves are closely correlated with the depth to which they burrow in the substratum. In general the more obese bivalves will be found nearer the surface of the substratum than those of more stream-

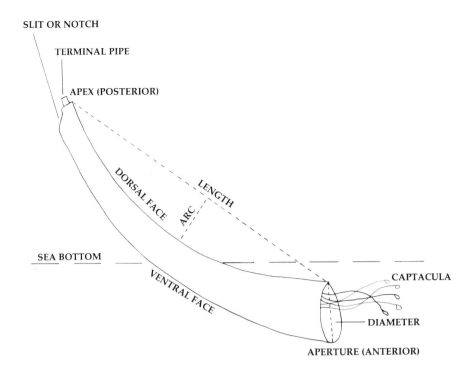

SLIT OR NOTCH

TERMINAL PIPE

APEX (POSTERIOR)

DORSAL FACE

LENGTH

ARC

SEA BOTTOM

VENTRAL FACE

CAPTACULA

DIAMETER

APERTURE (ANTERIOR)

Fig. 33. General features of the Scaphopoda

lined shell shapes.

The exterior sculpture of the shell reflects environmental demands and is strikingly similar in even distantly related genera that occupy the same type of environment. Epifaunal groups are more variable than those of the infauna, showing greater variety in their modes of life and habitats. Ornamentation, such as spines, costae, lamellae, and flutes, function to strengthen the shell, to provide support and anchorage in the substratum, to keep the feeding margin elevated above the bottom, to support sensory extensions of the mantle margin, and to discourage predators. The exterior sculpture may be classified as (1) the *concentric* sculpture, arranged parallel to the margins of the valves, generally indicating former growth and resting stages; and (2) *radial* sculpture, running fanlike across the shell from the umbones to the ventral margins of the valves. When both concentric and radial sculpture occur a *cancellate* sculpture is formed. Most bivalves have an external layer of *periostracum*.

To identify the bivalve shell, it is often necessary to determine which valve is the right valve and which is the left (see fig. 30). This identification is more difficult in the siphonless epifaunal forms than in the infaunal. Hold the paired shells of a bivalve with the ventral margins down, the dorsal region (*beaks*) up, and the anterior end (usually the flatter end) away from you; the beaks will usually be pointed toward the anterior end, and the ligament will be found posterior to the beaks in most cases. Holding the shell in this manner, you will find the right valve on your right and left valve on your left. A method for distinguishing the right valve from the left of infaunal bivalves (*Tellina*, *Mactra*) is to lay the open shell on the table with the beaks uppermost, or away from you, and the interior of the shell up. In this position it is possible to locate the U-shaped pallial sinus. If the sinus is indented or open toward the right, it is a right valve, and if to the left, a left valve. The indentation is always nearest the posterior end where the siphons are located. The posterior margin is nearest the surface when the siphons are extended for feeding.

To determine the length of a bivalve shell, a straight line from the extreme anterior margin to the extreme posterior margin is measured; the height is measured on a line from the umbones to a point directly opposite on the ventral margin. The greatest distance between the sides of the closed valves determines the thickness.

Class Scaphopoda

Tusk shells, forming the small class Scaphopoda (Gk. *scapha* boat, *pod* foot), burrow with a foot shaped like the prow of a boat. These semi-infaunal marine mollusks feed on detritus and microorganisms with the help of *captacula* and the foot. The captacula are long, ciliated filaments which originate near the mouth. This class was long thought to be marine worms with calcareous tubes. The shells are tubular, open at both ends, slightly curved but in one plane, and tapered toward the posterior end (tusk-shaped). Growth takes place at the wider anterior end. The foot extends through the anterior end of the shell; the posterior end of the shell protrudes just above the surface of the substratum. They have no operculum or periostracum.

Class Cephalopoda

The Cephalopoda (Gk. *cephalos* head, *pod* foot), or "head-footed ones," are the most highly developed of the phylum Mollusca. These strictly marine animals are found in all the oceans of the world. Today there are about 150 known species, but fossil evidence shows that the class abounded in prehistoric seas. These primeval cephalopods bore coiled and many-chambered shells, but only the nautilus of the southwestern Pacific produces this kind of shell today. The "shell" of the argonaut is an egg case, not an exoskeleton.

Members of the subclass Nautiloidea deviate from the usual pattern of the class in characteristics other than the shell; they have up to ninety arms and four gills. The other subclass, Coleoidea, contains the orders Vampyromorpha, Octopoda, Teuthoidea, and Sepioidea—all with two gills, two kidneys, and three hearts with blue blood.

The Vampyromorpha are strange creatures long thought extinct but now known by several surviving members. One species, a jet-black animal with ten arms, *Vampyroteuthis infernalis* Chun, 1903, was recovered from the Gulf of Mexico by the *Atlantis* expedition. These deep-water inhabitants have been monographed by G. E. Pickford (1949).

The Octopoda, "eight footed," range in size from two inches to thirty-two feet. However, the body of the "giant" octopus is only eighteen inches long. They are inhabitants of rocky shores or reefs and occupy a permanent lair. The crab is the favorite food of this eight-armed carnivore, which is capable of changing color to match its background. Octopuses have a globular body that narrows slightly into a "neck." Eight arms arise from the head and are united at their base by a membranous web. These arms are often incorrectly referred to as tentacles (Lane 1960). The octopus is the best known of all cephalopods, and the most studied species of octopus are inhabitants of shallow water, where they live in natural holes or lairs of their own construction. The octopus captures its prey by snaring the victim with its sucker-clad arms and enveloping it in the membranous web while holding on securely with the other arms. It actively stalks prey at night and uses its beak to open clams, another principal item of its diet. By some unknown method, the octopus quiets its victim with a nerve poison, or venom, secreted from the salivary glands; then it breaks it apart and picks the shell clean.

Recently the order Decapoda, "ten footed," has been separated into two groups, the Teuthoidea and the Sepioidea (in litt. G. L. Voss). The first includes squid and cuttlefish. At present there are no living cuttlefish known from American waters (Harry & Snider 1969; Voss 1974), but the squid is familiar to all fishermen, who find it a choice bait. This mollusk has a cigar-shaped, or fusiform, body with one end or two side fins at the posterior end. The head bears eight arms and two tentacles used to seize prey. The mantle covers a chitinous shell called a pen. Most squid live in deep water by day and rise to the surface to feed at night.

The squid feed on plankton, crustaceans, and fish. They reach out and catch their prey with their two long tentacles, hold it with the suckers on their arms, and then bite it with their sharp beaks.

The Sepioidea is represented by the deep-water dweller *Spirula spirula*, which has a spirally coiled internal shell. This shell, freed from the body of the animal, is often found by the thousands on the beaches. The animal that formed this beautiful, white coil was long a mystery. Prior to 1920 only 13 live animals had ever been recovered. A Danish expedition in search of the breeding place of the American and European river eel in the Sargasso Sea netted 188 *Spirula* about a quarter of a mile below the surface of the sea. The shell is constructed to resist great pressure, enabling it to rise from the depths and float unbroken to distant shores.

Although Aristotle described the reproduction of the cephalopods, it was not studied again until the middle of the nineteenth century and it is still imperfectly known except in a few species. In most members of the class the male, which is smaller, has one or more of the arms modified into a sex organ, the hectocotylus, which he uses to transfer the sperm to the female. The female usually lays her eggs inshore in clusters attached to rocks or debris and guards them until they hatch. Squid lay their eggs in gelatinous strings, which they often attach to other squid egg masses or seaweed. The female does not brood her eggs but awaits death in a very weakened state after she has performed her biological function.

Cephalopods display luminescence by a variety of means. This ability is more developed in deep-sea squid, such as the *Spirula*, than in shallow-water species. This bioluminescence, light without heat, may be produced by any one of the following means:
1. Intracellular: intrinsic, depending on the animal's own biochemical processes and taking place within luminescent cells or photocytes
2. Extracellular: intrinsic, from the discharge of luminous secretions
3. Bacterial: from symbiotic luminous bacteria
Bioluminescence is one of the most striking characteristics of these strange creatures.

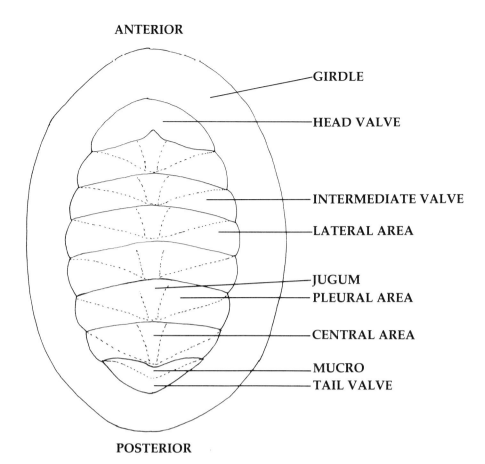

ANTERIOR

GIRDLE

HEAD VALVE

INTERMEDIATE VALVE

LATERAL AREA

JUGUM

PLEURAL AREA

CENTRAL AREA

MUCRO

TAIL VALVE

POSTERIOR

Fig. 34. General features of the Polyplacophora

Class Monoplacophora

The Monoplacophora are limpet-shaped mollusks long considered extinct but found living in 1957. They all occur in very deep marine water and none have yet been found in the Gulf of Mexico. The other four conchiferan classes have their origin in the Precambrian Monoplacophora (Stasek 1972, p. 19).

Other Mollusks

The other two subphyla, Aculifera and Placophora, which include vermiform, marine-dwelling Aplacophora and the chitons of the Polyplacophora, were formerly grouped with the Monoplacophora in the class Amphineura. Study has proved them to be so distinct that they rate classification as subphyla. The very deep water dwelling Aplacophoras have only recently been discovered in the Gulf of Mexico. Dr. John S. Holland of the University of Texas Marine Science Institute at Port Aransas, Texas, has reported (in litt.) that a yet unidentified, minute species of *Chaetoderma* has been found during collections for the Bureau of Land Management Project (L. P. Parker 1976). In 1975 the shell-less, wormlike mollusk was first recovered from the Gulf of Mexico off the south Texas coast in benthic samples collected by a research team from the University of Texas under the direction of Dr. Holland and has been partially identified by Granvil D. Treece.

Two small chitons have been found living along the Texas coast. The Polyplacophora, or chitons, have a many-plated shell similar in appearance to that of the garden pill bug. The chiton lives on solid substrata where it feeds on algae and minute animals, while moving about by slow muscular waves of the broad foot. It prefers relatively shallow water. Each of the eight plates of its shell is greatly arched and overlaps the valve next behind it. These valves are held together by a leathery tissue, or girdle, that surrounds the entire periphery of the lapped valves. This flexible girdle permits the chiton to roll up into a ball as the armadillo does and to hold itself closely to the rocks for protection. Often the interior of the valves is beautifully colored pink, blue, or green, while the exterior is camouflaged so that detection is difficult.

3. Systematic Descriptions

History of Malacology in Texas

Nineteenth Century

There is no record of shell collecting in Texas during the earliest period of European colonization; perhaps those hardy first settlers were too busy gaining a foothold in a new and hostile environment to be concerned with a systematic study of nature. However, as nature and the Indians began to be tamed, thought turned to inventorying the flora and fauna of this wild, new territory. It was during the period of the Republic of Texas (1836–1845) that the German paleontologist Dr. Ferdinand Roemer (1818–1891) came to study this frontier land that was attracting so many settlers from his native country. For one and a half years he conducted an expedition in that new republic and recorded his findings in his book *Texas*. Most of his collection of marine mollusks was obtained in the Galveston area and the material was identified by the German conchologist Rudolf Amandus Philippi (1808–1904).

The next list was made by Joseph Daniel Mitchell (1848–1922), a state representative and amateur naturalist from Victoria, Texas. Mitchell's list was based on specimens he collected from Matagorda Island to Padre Island. This most able collector had his material identified by William Healey Dall and privately published one list of his findings in about 1894. Another list was published in the *Natural Science News* in 1895.

William Healey Dall (1845–1927), honorary curator of the United States National Collection of Mollusks, Smithsonian Institution, listed the shells from Texas in the Blake report of 1889.

The historically elusive John Allen Singley (dates unknown) spent sixteen years in Texas during which he collected for the 1892 *Geological Survey of Texas*, which was published in 1893. His material came from the entire coast and was included in the Dall report.

Twentieth Century

During this century the most important lists have been those of C. J. Maury (1920–1922) when she relisted and updated the previous lists. In 1935, J. K. Strecker's personal collection plus those of Singley and Mitchell were published together. C. W. Johnson brought Dall's catalogue up to date in 1934. H. B. Stenzel (1940) listed the mollusks from Point Isabel, and J. W. Hedgpeth (1950) surveyed those from the waters of the Aransas Wildlife Refuge. The jetty molluscan fauna was listed by H. L. Whitten et al. in 1950; the shallow waters of the bays from Baffin through Matagorda were covered by H. S. Ladd (1951); then T. E. Pulley (1952) published his illustrated list of mollusks from the entire coast. Those that occur in the grounds of the brown shrimp were listed by H. H. Hildebrand (1954); Abbott's *American Seashells* (1954, revised 1974) included Texas. In 1955 and 1959, R. L. Parker covered the central Texas coastal bays and in 1960 the northwest Gulf of Mexico. In 1962 and 1965, W. H. Rice and L. S. Kornicker catalogued those found on the Campeche Bank in the southern Gulf of Mexico. Most recently, J. W. Tunnell (1972) added the mollusks of the 7½ Fathom Reef; those found in the Corpus Christi, Copano, and Aransas bays system were reported by Holland et al. (1974); D. A. Lipka (1974) compiled those found on Flower Garden Bank; and A. A. Ekdale (1974) listed those from Yucatán. H. Odé has begun to list the Mollusca in the northwest Gulf of Mexico (1974–).

Data Used in the Descriptions

The basis for the present book is knowledge of Texas molluscan life derived from a long period of field work and continued study of the accumulated information available. Collecting over a period of ten years (1960–1970) was confined to the shallow-water, or littoral, fauna and included beach specimens and drift material. Smaller species were obtained by picking through algae and sorting drift material with the aid of a stereomicroscope. No dredging was undertaken. A number of small species and euthyneuras have been omitted from the list due to lack of data, identification, or a suitable specimen to photograph—their omission will not keep the casual collector from being able to identify the shells one is most likely to gather on a Texas beach. Although nearly 350 species were determined, this in no way implies a complete survey. If the species was collected living, the habitat, together with additional remarks of interest, is given. Many species were not found alive and are indicated as "in beach drift" or "beach shell."

The classification of mollusks is still a matter of debate and several systems are currently in use. The order used here is basically that of J. Thiele (1929–1935), a standard in the field. The classification of the gastropods is based on a revision in progress by Taylor of D. W. Taylor and N. F. Sohl (1962–1964) and the Siphostomatan [Neogastropod] families of W. F. Ponder (1973). The outline of classification of the bivalves is that of L. McCormick and R. C. Moore in *Treatise on Invertebrate Paleontology* (ed. Moore, 1969 *a* & *b*; 1971). The cephalopods are arranged according to a revision by G. L. Voss (in press).

Some of the abbreviations used in the text are cf. (*confer*), compare; s.l. (*sensu lato*), in the broad sense; ex gr. (*ex grupo*), of the group of; s.s. (*sensu stricto*), in the strict sense; ibid. (*ibidem*), the same reference; sp., species; syn. (synonym), other scientific names that have been applied or may apply; in litt. (*in litteris*), personal communication; and coll., collection. A single capital letter in the generic position of a name represents the genus under discussion.

Listing of synonyms has been avoided unless it was felt there was a need for a reference in order to prevent confusion when making comparisons with other popular

Table 5. Metric System Conversion

		Metric		U.S.	
Millimeter	(mm)	0.001	m	0.03937	in.
Centimeter	(cm)	0.01	m	0.3937	in.
Decimeter	(dm)	0.1	m	3.937	in.
Meter	(m)	1.0	m	39.37	in.
Kilometer	(km)	1,000.0	m	0.6213	mi.
Fathom	(fm)	1.829	m	6.0	ft.

shell books or recent changes in taxonomy. If a species was first described in a different generic combination, the author's name and date of publication appear in parentheses, for example (Say, 1922). In some cases, for the sake of clarity, some former combinations are given in brackets, for example [*Cyphoma intermedium*]. The principal source of the original citation of a species described before 1850 is Sherborn (1902–1933) and the abbreviations used are his.

The size given is the length of an average specimen. Dimensions are given in the metric scale (1 inch = 25.4 mm; 1 foot = 304.8 mm; see also table 5). The general geographic ranges outside Texas are a compilation from published literature; García-Cubas 1963, Rios 1970, Waller 1973, Abbott 1974, and Ekdale 1974 have been the primary range references. The range in Texas is from both published and unpublished records of collectors known to me, the northernmost listed first, the southernmost last.

Relative abundance, or occurrence, is given according to the occurrence on the beach and does not reflect the quantity to be found where the mollusks live. *Rare, uncommon, fairly common*, and *common* are the categories used. These are subjective estimates, for there are wide variations, and the use of these categories will serve only as a general guide.

Locality is usually designated as east, central, south, or entire. *East* refers to that section of the coast

from the Sabine to the Colorado River, where humid and subhumid climates prevail. *Central* is from the Colorado to Padre Island and represents the subhumid river-bay complexes. Padre Island and the Laguna Madre comprise the semiarid *south* region (fig. 9). Some localities overlap more than one region and are therefore described more explicitly; for example, *southern half of coast* indicates from Port O'Connor south. After noting the habitat of the species and studying the various maps in this book, the collector will learn that estuarine, or river-influenced, fauna does not occur in the southern range, because no rivers empty into this area; that shelf marine species will not occur naturally in the enclosed bays; and so on. Continued study of the coast is broadening these ranges. The maps in chapter 4 show the collecting sites mentioned in the text for Texas, and the current map (fig. 10) indicates those mentioned in Mexico. With few exceptions, the mollusks described inhabit depths of less than thirty meters. Further information, synonymies, biology, and so on may be found for many of the species in the monographs or other studies listed in "Remarks." It has been impossible to review the hundreds of papers on mollusks that have been published annually since 1968, and oversights have not been deliberate.

The sources of the shells used in the photographs are noted in "Remarks," with the full names given in the Preface. A shell from a location other than Texas was photographed only as a last resort when a good specimen collected in Texas was not available, even though it is well represented in the local fauna. There are less than two dozen examples of this and those were included with regret but with the idea that such a photograph was better than no illustration. Except as just noted, all photographed specimens were collected in Texas by me and are at the Corpus Christi Museum.

The identification of several families of minute mollusks was checked by authorities: Vitrinellas, D. R. Moore; Odostomias, J. X. Corgan; Ovulidids, C. N. Cate; and small brackish species, D. W. Taylor.

When information has been available, the geologic range of a species is presented. That information has been hard to come by, and I invite material that would help to fill the voids.

Of interest to collectors of modern mollusks as well as to paleontologists and geologists is the addition of four new fossil and one previously known species. These have been included because these late Pleistocene mollusks are the only recorded inland occurrence of Vitrinillidae and of *Rangia cuneata* in the world. The recent discovery of these marine fossils in the Pecos River valley of Texas should prompt collectors to be on the lookout for others or their close relatives living in the northwestern Gulf, perhaps on the less studied northern Mexican coast, since one of them (*Rangia*) is represented in the modern fauna.

In 1899 Charles Hedley remarked that "by some strange unwritten law these conchologists have invariably maintained a proportion between the size of a shell and its illustration. Thus, a large shell, however simple in structure, demanded a large figure; and a small shell, however complex its details, a small drawing. Had this school encountered *Pachyderms* or *Foraminif-*

era one or both would surely have fallen beyond the focus of their vision." Heeding Hedley, no attempt has been made to maintain a proportion between the size of the shell and its illustration; as a result, a specimen only 7 mm in length may be shown the same size as one whose length is 7 inches. The actual size is the first category in the accompanying descriptions.

This book describes more than 325 mollusks. You might wonder, as I did, who first described each species. It is interesting to note that only about a dozen people were responsible for naming more than half of these mollusks, yet about 130 authors' names appear in the descriptions. Listed in order of frequency, those who first described five or more Texas shallow-water marine mollusks are:

Thomas Say
(1787–1834)
American malacologist, Philadelphia Academy of Natural Sciences: 31 species

Carolus Linnaeus
(Karl von Linné)
(1707–1778)
Swedish naturalist and botanist; originated biological systematics: 25 species

William Healey Dall
(1845–1927)
American naturalist, United States National Museum and United States Geological Survey; prolific writer in many fields: 22 species

Timothy Abbott Conrad
(1803–1877)
American paleontologist, Philadelphia Academy of Natural Sciences: 22 species

Jean Baptiste Pierre Antoine de Monet de Lamarck
(1744–1829)
French naturalist; revised the Linnean system, proposing many new genera: 15 species

Alcide Charles Victor Dessalines d'Orbigny
(1802–1857)
French biologist and geologist; conducted expedition to South America: 15 species

Charles Baker Adams
(1814–1853)
American naturalist, Amherst College: 14 species

Johann Friedrich Gmelin
(1748–1804)
German naturalist, student of Linné; published thirteenth edition of Linné's *Systema Naturae*: 13 species

Paul Bartsch
(1871–1960)
American malacologist, United States National Museum: 9 species

Paul P. McGinty
(1877–1957)
American collector and writer: 7 species

Rudolf Amandus Philippi
(1808–1904)
German conchologist and writer: 7 species

Henry Augustus Pilsbry
(1862–1957)
American, Philadelphia Academy of Natural Sciences; prolific writer, supplied 5,600 new names: 7 species

Sowerby family
British writers, illustrators, and publishers who published books in parts and sold them separately over a period of years. Thus, it is difficult to determine dates for an article's composition or to say which Sowerby wrote the article, and it is equally hard to find the true date of publication. The Sowerbys were:
James
(1757–1822), father
James de Carle
(1787–1871), son
George Brettingham I
(1788–1854), son
George Brettingham II
(1812–1884), son of G. B. I
George Brettingham III
(1843–1921), son of G. B. II
Altogether, they described 7 species

P. C. Sander A. L. Rang
(1784–1859)
French; wrote *Histoire naturelle . . . des mollusques-pteropodes*: 6 species

Lovell Augustus Reeve
(1814–1865)
British; wrote *Conchologia iconica*, a large set of illustrated volumes on world-wide sea shells: 6 species

Peter Friedrich Röding
(1767–1836)
German; catalogued the Bolten collection: 5 species

John Edward Gray
(1800–1875)
English zoologist, British Museum: 5 species

Harald Alfred Rehder
(b. 1907)
American curator of mollusks, United States National Museum: 5 species

Phylum MOLLUSCA Cuvier, 1797

Subphylum ACULIFERA Hatscheck, 1891

Class APLACOPHORA Von Ihering, 1876

Order CHAETODERMATIDA Simroth, 1893
Family CHAETODERMATIDAE Von Ihering, 1876

A minute, yet unidentified specimen of the family Chaetodermatidae was found in deep water off Padre Island in 1975 by Dr. J. S. Holland of the University of Texas Marine Science Institute at Port Aransas.

Subphylum PLACOPHORA Von Ihering, 1876

Class POLYPLACOPHORA Blainville, 1816 = [AMPHINEURA Von Ihering, 1876, in part]

Ischnochiton papillosus

Chaetopleura apiculata

Order NEOLORICATA Bergenhayn, 1955
Suborder ISCHNOCHITONINA Bergenhayn, 1930
Family ISCHNOCHITONIDAE Dall, 1889

Genus *Ischnochiton* Gray, 1847

Mesh-Pitted Chiton

Ischnochiton papillosus (C. B. Adams, 1845), *Proc. Boston Soc. Natur. Hist.* 2:9.
Gk. *ischnos* slender, *chiton* girdle; L. *papilla* nipple.
SIZE: 8–12 mm.
COLOR: Whitish, mottled with olive green.
SHAPE: Oval.
ORNAMENT OR SCULPTURE: Girdle narrow, alternately white and olive. Upper surfaces of valves sculptured with microscopic pittings. End valves with concentric rows of fine, low beads. Lateral areas with fine, sinuous, longitudinal lines. Posterior valve is concave with 9 slits.
HABITAT: High-salinity lagoons on shell and reefs.
LOCALITIES: Entire.
OCCURRENCE: Fairly common.
RANGE: Tampa to lower Keys; Texas; West Indies.
GEOLOGIC RANGE: ? to Holocene.
REMARKS: Look under old shell in the bays.

Subfamily CHAETOPLEURINAE Plate, 1899

Genus *Chaetopleura* Shuttleworth, 1853

Chaetopleura apiculata (Say, 1839), *Amer. Conch.* 7:appendix.
Gk. *chaete* long, flowing hair, *pleura* sides; L. *apicula* small bee.
SIZE: 7–20 mm.
COLOR: Variable from ashy gray or brown to buff; interior white or grayish.
SHAPE: Oval.
ORNAMENT OR SCULPTURE: Dorsum is carinate. Intermediate valves have well-marked oblique lines separating the central area from the lateral area which bear numerous rounded beads. The girdle is narrow, mottled, with scattered transparent hairs.
HABITAT: High-salinity lagoons on jetty and reef.
LOCALITIES: Entire.
OCCURRENCE: Uncommon.
RANGE: Cape Cod; both sides of Florida; Texas.
GEOLOGIC RANGE: Pleistocene to Holocene.
REMARKS: More common offshore. Figured specimen collected in Florida by Steger; unfortunately, the fifth valve is broken.

Subphylum CONCHIFERA Gegenbaur, 1878

Class MONOPLACOPHORA Wenz, 1940

To date no member of this class has been found living in the Gulf of Mexico.

Class GASTROPODA Cuvier, 1797

Subclass PROSOBRANCHIA Milne Edwards, 1848 = [STREP-TONEURA Spengel, 1881]
Infraclass DIOTOCARDIA Mörch, 1865 = [ARCHAEOGAS-TROPODA Thiele, 1925]
Order RHIPIDOGLOSSA Mörch, 1865
Suborder ZEUGOBRANCHIA Von Ihering, 1876
Superfamily FISSURELLACEA Fleming, 1822
Family FISSURELLIDAE Fleming, 1822
Subfamily DIODORINAE Odhner, 1932

Genus *Diodora* Gray, 1821

Keyhole Limpet

Diodora cayenensis (Lamarck, 1822), *Hist. Natur. Anim. sans Vert.* 6:12. Gk. *dia* through, *dora* hide, covering; Cayenne, the capital of French Guiana.
SIZE: 25–51 mm.
COLOR: Varies from pinkish, whitish, to dark gray. Interior white or blue gray, polished.
SHAPE: Conic, oblong oval; rather thick shell; like a coolie hat.
ORNAMENT OR SCULPTURE: Orifice keyhole-shaped, just in front of and slightly lower than apex. Every fourth rib noticeably larger. Ribs crossed by concentric, lamellar ridges.
APERTURE: Oval with heavy callus. Margins irregularly and finely crenulated. Interior smooth.
OPERCULUM: None.
PERIOSTRACUM: Not preserved.
HABITAT: Intertidal to moderately deep water. Mainly on underside of rocks, jetties. Attached epifaunal.
LOCALITIES: Entire.
OCCURRENCE: Uncommon in east, becoming common south to Mexico.
RANGE: Bermuda; Maryland to southern half of Florida; Texas; Gulf of Mexico to Quintana Roo; Surinam; Brazil.
GEOLOGIC RANGE: Holocene with related species to Miocene.
REMARKS: Exterior usually covered with algae, making live specimens difficult to see. *See* Farfante 1943*b*, p. 5.

Diodora cayenensis

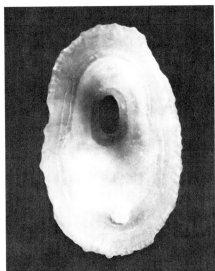

Lucapinella limatula

Calliostoma (Kombologion) euglyptum

Genus *Lucapinella* Pilsbry, 1890

File Fleshy Limpet
Lucapinella limatula (Reeve, 1850), *Conch. Icon.* 6:15.
Dim. of related genus *Lucapina* beetle; dim. of *lima* file.
SIZE: 15 mm.
COLOR: Dull white with brownish mottlings.
SHAPE: Oblong conic with almost central apical hole.
ORNAMENT OR SCULPTURE: Radial ribs alternately large and small. Growth lines form concentric lamellations, or scales, as they cross ribs.
APERTURE: Large. Interior smooth, white, porcelaneous. Callus rounded, smooth, with crenulate margins.
OPERCULUM: None.
PERIOSTRACUM: Not preserved.
HABITAT: On rocks, jetties, oyster reefs. Attached epifaunal.
LOCALITIES: Port Aransas, south.
OCCURRENCE: Uncommon.
RANGE: North Carolina to southern half of Florida; Texas; Yucatán; West Indies; Brazil.
GEOLOGIC RANGE: Pliocene to Holocene.
REMARKS: This tiny snail lives entirely underwater. Coll., Young. *See* Farfante 1943*a*, p. 19.

Suborder AZYGOBRANCHIA Spengel, 1881
Superfamily TROCHACEA Rafinesque, 1815
Family TROCHIDAE Rafinesque, 1815
Subfamily CALLIOSTOMATINAE Thiele, 1921

Genus *Calliostoma* Swainson, 1840
Subgenus *Kombologion* Clench & Turner, 1960

Sculptured Top-Shell
Calliostoma (Kombologion) euglyptum (A. Adams, 1854), *Proc. Zool. Soc. London* 22:38.
Gk. *kalos* beauty, *stoma* mouth; L. *eu* well, *glyphein* to carve.
SIZE: Height 25 mm.
COLOR: Pinkish brown, often mottled with white.
SHAPE: Turbinate.
ORNAMENT OR SCULPTURE: Seven and one-half whorls, with rounded keel. Periphery of whorls rounded. Spire extended. Anomphalous. Six large, beaded, spiral cords with smaller, intermediate, weakly beaded cords on each whorl.
APERTURE: Subquadrate; outer lip simple and produced at angle from base. Interior nacreous. Columella white, arched near base.
OPERCULUM: Thin, corneous, circular, golden brown, multispiral.
PERIOSTRACUM: Not preserved.
HABITAT: Low water to 57.6 meters (32 fathoms). Epifaunal.
LOCALITIES: On offshore oil-rig platforms and 7½ Fathom Reef off Padre Island.
OCCURRENCE: Rare beach shell.
RANGE: North Carolina to Florida; Texas; Mexico.
GEOLOGIC RANGE: Cretaceous to Holocene.
REMARKS: Though this species is very common on the offshore rigs, it is found only rarely on Padre Island. Coll., Hildebrand. *See* Clench & Turner 1960, p. 48.

Tegula fasciata

Tricolia affinis cruenta

Subfamily MONODONTINAE
Cossmann, 1916

Genus *Tegula* Lesson, 1835

Smooth Atlantic Tegula
Tegula fasciata (Born, 1778), *Index Mus. Caes. Vind.*, p. 337.
L. *tegula* tile, *fasciata* banded.
SIZE: Width 12–18 mm.
COLOR: Background light or reddish brown; mottled with reds, browns, blacks, white. Callus and umbilicus white.
SHAPE: Turbinate.
ORNAMENT OR SCULPTURE: Twelve postnuclear whorls sculptured with 3 or more fine spiral threads. Umbilicus deep, round, smooth.
APERTURE: Rounded with 2 teeth at base of columella.
OPERCULUM: Corneous, multispiral.
PERIOSTRACUM: Not preserved.
HABITAT: On *Thalassia* grass and algae in shallow water. Epifaunal.
LOCALITIES: Entire, more to south.
OCCURRENCE: Common in beach drift.
RANGE: Southeastern Florida; Texas; Gulf of Mexico to Quintana Roo; Costa Rica; West Indies to Brazil.
GEOLOGIC RANGE: Pliocene to Holocene.
REMARKS: To date, this species has not been reported alive on the Texas coast, although old shells are abundant in bay drift around Port Isabel and Port Aransas. Figured specimen is typically worn. Panamic vicariant is *T. cooksoni*.

Family PHASIANELLIDAE Swainson, 1840

Genus *Tricolia* Risso, 1826

Checkered Pheasant
Tricolia affinis cruenta Robertson, 1958, *Johnsonia* 3(37):267.
L. *tri* three, *colis* stalk, *affinis* adjacent, *cruenta* stain with blood.
SIZE: 6.2 mm.
COLOR: Background white or pale orange patterned with spiral rows of squarish, dark red spots.
SHAPE: Inflated, conic.
ORNAMENT OR SCULPTURE: Four and one-half smooth, rounded whorls. Apex rounded. Suture impressed. Umbilicus only a chink.
APERTURE: Elongate ovate. Columella with thick, white callus. Outer lip smooth.
OPERCULUM: Calcareous, white with dark olive green at margin.
PERIOSTRACUM: Not preserved.
HABITAT: Shallow bays on algae. Epifaunal.
LOCALITIES: San José Island, south.
OCCURRENCE: Fairly common.
RANGE: Texas; Yucatán; Quintana Roo; Caribbean coast of Central America; northern South America; Brazil. Sporadic along western Gulf of Mexico.
GEOLOGIC RANGE: Lower Miocene to Holocene.
REMARKS: This tiny, herbivorous mollusk may be dependent on specific plants. *See* Robertson 1958, p. 267; Marcus & Marcus 1960.

Nerita fulgurans

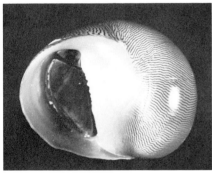

Neritina (Vitta) reclivata

Suborder PLANILABIATA
Stoliczka, 1868
Superfamily NERITACEA Rafinesque, 1815
Family NERITIDAE Rafinesque, 1815

Genus *Nerita* Linné, 1758

Antillean Nerite
Nerita fulgurans Gmelin, 1791, *Syst. Natur.*, 13th ed., p. 3685.
Gk. *nerites* pertaining to a coastline; L. *fulgar* lightning.
SIZE: 18–25 mm.
COLOR: Dark gray to black with occasional blurred markings.
SHAPE: Globose conic; body whorl expanded, spire low.
ORNAMENT OR SCULPTURE: Strong spiral cords. Heavy shell.
APERTURE: Large, rounded with 2 prominent teeth on inside of outer lip. Inner lip yellowish white, toothed, with decklike, porcelaneous callus.
OPERCULUM: Calcareous, light gray to yellowish gray. Has clawlike projection, or apophysis, that fits under edge of columella, permitting tight fit when shell is exposed.
PERIOSTRACUM: None visible.
HABITAT: Marine. Jetties and pilings near high-tide mark. Epifaunal.
LOCALITIES: Port Aransas, south.
OCCURRENCE: Uncommon.
RANGE: Southeastern Florida; Texas; Yucatán; Costa Rica; West Indies; northeastern Brazil.
GEOLOGIC RANGE: ? to Holocene.
REMARKS: A newcomer to Texas with the jetties. Can live around 75 days out of water. Places its eggs on its own shell or those of other mollusks (fig. 24).

Genus *Neritina* Lamarck, 1816
Subgenus *Vitta* Mörch, 1852

Olive Nerite
Neritina (Vitta) reclivata (Say, 1822), *J. Acad. Natur. Sci. Philadelphia* 2(1):244.
Dim. of *nerita*, L. *reclinis* leaning back, sloping.
SIZE: 12 mm.
COLOR: Brownish green or brownish yellow background with numerous transverse lines of brown, purple, or black.
SHAPE: Globular with expanded body whorl.
ORNAMENT OR SCULPTURE: Smooth, polished. Spire usually eroded away.
APERTURE: Semilunar. Parietal area smooth, white to yellowish with variable number of small, irregular teeth on columellar edge.
OPERCULUM: Calcareous, black, with apophysis that fits into corresponding indentation on inner lip.
PERIOSTRACUM: None visible.
HABITAT: Brackish to fresh water. Epifaunal.
LOCALITIES: Entire.
OCCURRENCE: Rare.
RANGE: Florida to Texas; West Indies.
GEOLOGIC RANGE: Pleistocene to Holocene.
REMARKS: Look for it near river mouths.

Neritina (Vitta) virginea

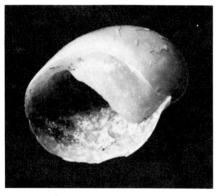

Smaragdia viridis viridemaris

Virgin Nerite
Neritina (Vitta) virginea (Linné, 1758), *Syst. Natur.*, 10th ed., p. 778. Dim. of *nerita*, L. *virgineus* maidenly.
SIZE: 4–12 mm.
COLOR: Color and pattern variable: background may be olive, white, gray, red, yellow, purple, or black with black and/or white waves, stripes, dots, lines, or mottlings.
SHAPE: Globular with expanded body whorl.
ORNAMENT OR SCULPTURE: Smooth, polished.
APERTURE: Semilunar. Parietal area smooth, convex, white to yellow, with variable number of small, irregular teeth.
OPERCULUM: Calcareous, usually black, smooth.
PERIOSTRACUM: Thin, greenish.
HABITAT: Bay margins and grass flats. Epifaunal.
LOCALITIES: Entire.
OCCURRENCE: Common, more to south.
RANGE: Bermuda; Florida to Texas; Gulf of Mexico to Quintana Roo; Costa Rica; West Indies; Surinam; almost all of Brazilian coast.
GEOLOGIC RANGE: Pleistocene to Holocene.
REMARKS: Lays its eggs in winter on its own shell or that of other mollusks. The eggs are in clustered, yellowish, gelatinous capsules. More easily found at night or on cloudy days. Patterns so varied one might think that each is a different species. More colorful in brackish water than in more saline water.

Genus *Smaragdia* (Maury, 1917)

Emerald Nerite
Smaragdia viridis viridemaris (Maury, 1917), *Bull. Amer. Paleontol.* 5:316. Gk. *smaragdos* emerald, *maris* of the sea; L. *viridis* green.
SIZE: 6–16 mm.
COLOR: Bright pea green with few fine, broken white lines near apex; these outlined in maroon color in some specimens.
SHAPE: Obliquely oval, subglobular, low spire.
ORNAMENT OR SCULPTURE: Glossy, smooth.
APERTURE: Simple, semilunar; outer lip thin, sharp. Parietal area green with 7 to 9 minute teeth.
OPERCULUM: Calcareous, green, smooth except for microscopic lines. Apophysis on columellar edge.
PERIOSTRACUM: None visible.
HABITAT: Grass flats in shallow bays. Epifaunal.
LOCALITIES: Port Aransas, south.
OCCURRENCE: Uncommon.
RANGE: Bermuda; southeastern Florida; Texas; Gulf of Mexico to Quintana Roo; Costa Rica; West Indies.
GEOLOGIC RANGE: Miocene to Holocene.
REMARKS: Animal is green. More abundant in late afternoon or when cloudy. First reported living in Texas by me (Wasson 1963).

Pomacea flagellata

Littorina (Littorinopsis) angulifera

Infraclass MONOTOCARDIA
Mörch, 1865 = [CAENOGAS-
TROPODA Cox, 1959]
Order CTENOBRANCHIA
Schweigger, 1820 = [PECTINI-
BRANCHIA Blainville, 1814]
Suborder HOLOSTOMATA Flem-
ing, 1828
Superfamily VIVIPARACEA Gray,
1847
Family PILIDAE Conolly, 1927 =
[AMPULLARIIDAE Gray, 1824]

Genus *Pomacea* Perry, 1811

Apple Snail
Pomacea flagellata (Say, 1829).
L. *pomum* apple, *flagellum* a whip.
SIZE: Up to 50 mm.
GEOLOGIC RANGE: ? to Holocene.
REMARKS: This species does not belong on a Texas list, but because this
conspicuous fresh-water snail is
often washed up on south Texas
beaches from its tropical home it is
shown here. Due to its comparatively large size it is mistaken for a
marine gastropod; for this reason it
is figured so that the lucky finder of
this beautiful snail can investigate it
further if so desired. Shrimp
fishermen off Puerto Alvaro Obregón, Tabasco, Mexico, have
dredged dead specimens from 36
meters (20 fathoms) after they had
been carried down inland streams.
Gases from the rotting animal are
sealed in, keeping it afloat until
waves loosen the operculum. It is a
common shell in Mayan middens in
Yucatán, Mexico. *See* Rehder & Abbott 1951, p. 66; E. W. Andrews
1969.

Superfamily LITTORINACEA
Gray, 1840
Family LITTORINIDAE Gray, 1840
Subfamily LITTORININAE Gray,
1840

Genus *Littorina* Férussac, 1821
Subgenus *Littorinopsis* Mörch, 1876

Angulate Periwinkle
Littorina (Littorinopsis) angulifera
(Lamarck, 1822), *Hist. Natur. Anim.
sans Vert.* 7:54.
L. *littus* seashore, *angulifera* bearing
an angle.
SIZE: 25–30 mm.
COLOR: Background varies: bluish
white, orange yellow, dull yellow,
reddish brown, or grayish brown.
SHAPE: Conic with elongate spire;
higher than wide.
ORNAMENT OR SCULPTURE: Darker
elongated spots on ribs, often fused
to form oblique stripes on body
whorl. Early whorls have regularly
spaced, vertical white spots below
suture. About 6 convex whorls;
body whorl about one-half of
height; slightly channeled sutures.
Spiral sculpture of irregular, in-
equidistant incised lines. Anomphalous.
APERTURE: Rounded oval; outer lip
smooth, does not flare, sharp and
nearly horizontal at body whorl.
Inner lip with thin deposit over
body whorl. Columellar area
smooth, moderately wide, with central groove in lower portion.
OPERCULUM: Corneous, light brown,
thin, flexible.
PERIOSTRACUM: None visible.
HABITAT: Brackish water. Mangrove
thickets. Epifaunal. On the black
mangrove. Climbs high into the tree
and can spend much time out of
water. At times on pilings and
rocks. *Avicennia nitida*, the black
mangrove, is subject to freeze in
this area.

Littorina (Littorinopsis) irrorata

LOCALITIES: On rocks at Corpus Christi Naval Air Station and Port Isabel area.
OCCURRENCE: Uncommon.
RANGE: Bermuda; southern half of Florida; Texas; West Indies; Brazil; Pacific Panama; central west Africa.
GEOLOGIC RANGE: ? to Holocene.
REMARKS: After hard freezes this species disappears. Coll., Young. *See* Bequaert 1943, p. 23; Bandel 1974.

Marsh Periwinkle
Littorina (Littorinopsis) irrorata (Say, 1822), *J. Acad. Natur. Sci. Philadelphia* 2(1):239.
L. *littus* seashore, *irror* bedewed, dotted.
SIZE: 25 mm.
COLOR: Grayish white with tiny, short streaks of reddish brown on spiral ridges. Opaque, dull.
SHAPE: Elongate conic; longer than wide.
ORNAMENT OR SCULPTURE: Eight to 10 gradually increasing, flat whorls. Suture weak. Body whorl about one-half of total height. Numerous, regularly shaped spiral grooves. Shell thick.
APERTURE: Oval. Columella and callus usually pale reddish brown. Outer lip stout, sharp, with tiny, regular grooves on inside edge.
OPERCULUM: Corneous, dark brown.
PERIOSTRACUM: None visible.
HABITAT: On marsh grass in low-salinity bays. Epifaunal.
LOCALITIES: East, central.
OCCURRENCE: Common.
RANGE: New Jersey to central Florida to Texas.
GEOLOGIC RANGE: Upper Miocene to Holocene.
REMARKS: Herbivorous on algae. When tide is out, animal withdraws into shell, which may remain dry and exposed to sun for many hours. Often seen completely out of water on stems of marsh grass where it leaves a trail of mucus. *See* Bequaert 1943, p. 6; Bingham 1972; J. R. Hall 1974; Bandel 1974.

Littorina (Austrolittorina) lineolata

Littorina (Littoraria) nebulosa

Subgenus *Austrolittorina* Rosewater, 1970

Zebra Periwinkle
Littorina (Austrolittorina) lineolata
Orbigny, 1840, *Voy. dans l'Amér.
Mérid.* 5(3):392.
L. *littus* seashore, *linea* lined.
SIZE: 12–25 mm.
COLOR: Background gray with ob-
lique zigzag lines of dark brown.
Apex reddish brown.
SHAPE: Elongate conic.
ORNAMENT OR SCULPTURE: Six to 8
gradually increasing convex whorls.
Body whorl more than one-half of
total height, more convex than
other whorls. Suture well marked.
Male smaller and more strongly
sculptured with spiral grooves than
female.
APERTURE: Pear-shaped. Outer lip
not flaring, edge sharp and thin.
Meets body whorl at sharp angle.
Columellar area long, wide, slant-
ing inward, smooth. Anomphalous.
Purple to mahogany brown.
OPERCULUM: Corneous, dark brown.
PERIOSTRACUM: None visible.
HABITAT: Intertidal on rocks, jetties,
pilings (fig. 12). Often in large col-
onies in crevices. Epifaunal.
LOCALITIES: Entire.
OCCURRENCE: Common.
RANGE: Bermuda; southern half of
Florida to Texas; Costa Rica; Brazil.
GEOLOGIC RANGE: Upper Miocene to
Holocene.
REMARKS: This species has been mis-
identified as *L. ziczac* (Gmelin, 1790)
in Texas. *L. lineolata* is darker in
color, is smaller, and has a wider
apical angle. *See* Abbott 1964, p. 65;
Borkowski & Borkowski 1969; Ban-
del 1974.

Subgenus *Littoraria* Gray, 1834

Cloudy Periwinkle
Littorina (Littoraria) nebulosa
(Lamarck, 1822), *Hist. Natur. Anim.
sans Vert.* 7:54.
L. *littus* seashore, *nebulosus* misty,
cloudy.
SIZE: 15 mm.
COLOR: Background bone yellow or
white with bluish tinge; early
whorls have spotting of white and
reddish brown, which stops abruptly on sixth or seventh whorl.
Variable in juveniles.
SHAPE: Elongate conic.
ORNAMENT OR SCULPTURE: Seven to
9 gradually increasing convex
whorls. Body whorl about two-
thirds of total height. Nuclear
whorls usually eroded in adults. Suture well marked, smooth or
slightly crenulate behind outer lip.
Spiral engraved lines become evident on fourth whorl, becoming
numerous and more regularly
spaced on body whorl. Strong
transverse striations cross spiral
lines at angles.
APERTURE: Subcircular; outer lip not
flaring; edge thin, sharp, smooth,
meeting body whorl at sharp angle.
Slight callus over body whorl. Columella long, wide, smooth. Anomphalous. Mouth yellowish brown to
pale purplish within; outer lip
whitish. Columella white.
OPERCULUM: Corneous, pale
mahogany brown.
PERIOSTRACUM: None visible.
HABITAT: Pilings and jetties in more
saline waters. Epifaunal.
LOCALITIES: Entire.
OCCURRENCE: Fairly common.
RANGE: Bermuda; Texas; Caribbean
coast of Central America; West Indies; northern South America;
Pacific Panama.
GEOLOGIC RANGE: ? to Holocene.
REMARKS: Prefers wooden jetties,
wreckage, and logs. Avoids rocks
exposed to heavy surf. Seldom survives Texas winters. Greatly reduced
since killing freeze of 1962. *See*
Bequaert 1943, p. 11; Bandel 1974.

Littorina (Melarhaphe) meleagris

Rissoina (Schwartziella) catesbyana

Subgenus *Melarhaphe* Menke, 1828

Spotted Periwinkle
Littorina (Melarhaphe) meleagris
(Potiez & Michaud, 1838), *Gal. Moll.
Dovai* 1:311.
L. *littus* seashore; Gk. *meleager*
guinea fowl.
SIZE: Height 7.5 mm, width 4.8 mm.
COLOR: Light to dark brown with
more-or-less spiral rows of white
spots giving checkered appearance.
Spots may be faded on body whorl.
SHAPE: Elongate conic.
ORNAMENT OR SCULPTURE: Five to 6
rapidly increasing convex whorls;
nuclear whorls not eroded; suture
well marked, smooth. Body whorl
about two-thirds of total height and
more convex than other whorls.
Surface smooth or with faint spiral
striations; transverse striations very
weak. Crescent-shaped umbilical
slit.
APERTURE: Pear-shaped. Outer lip
not flaring; edge smooth, sharp,
thin but slightly thickened within;
meets body whorl at sharp angle.
Inner lip has slight callus over body
whorl. Reddish brown within. Columellar area long, moderately wide,
smooth, usually flat; inner edge
long, nearly straight but not ending
abruptly below; very sharp outer
ridge, less sharp where it merges
evenly with bowlike basal lip. Inner
lip whitish.
OPERCULUM: Corneous, dark
mahogany brown.
PERIOSTRACUM: Thin and often
worn.
HABITAT: Intertidal zone on rocks
and pilings in quiet water. Epifaunal.
LOCALITIES: Port Aransas, south.
OCCURRENCE: Uncommon to rare.
RANGE: Southern Florida; Texas;
West Indies; central west Africa.
GEOLOGIC RANGE: ? to Holocene.
REMARKS: Look in algae on the jetties. Coll., U.T. Marine Science Institute. *See* Bequaert 1943, p. 19;
Rosewater & Vermeij 1972; Bandel
1974.

Superfamily RISSOACEA Gray,
1847
Family RISSOIDAE Gray, 1847
Subfamily RISSOINAE Gray, 1847

Genus *Rissoina* Orbigny, 1840
Subgenus *Schwartziella* Nevil, 1884

Catesby's Risso
Rissoina (Schwartziella) catesbyana
Orbigny, 1842, *Hist. d'Ile de Cuba*
2:24.
Dim. of *Rissoa*, a genus dedicated to
the French collector A. Risso
(1777–1845); dedicated to Catesby, a
pre-Linnean malacologist.
SIZE: 3–5 mm.
COLOR: Shiny white.
SHAPE: Elongate conic.
ORNAMENT OR SCULPTURE: Eight
whorls, slightly rounded; suture
fairly deep. About 14 strong ribs to
each whorl.
APERTURE: Oval, slightly oblique.
Strong tooth on inner side of outer
lip.
OPERCULUM: Corneous, light brown.
PERIOSTRACUM: Thin.
HABITAT: *Thalassia* grass beds in
brackish, shallow, inshore waters.
Epifaunal.
LOCALITIES: Entire.
OCCURRENCE: Fairly common in
beach drift.
RANGE: Bermuda; North Carolina;
Florida; Texas; Gulf of Campeche;
Campeche Bank; Quintana Roo;
Costa Rica; West Indies; Brazil.
GEOLOGIC RANGE: Pliocene to
Holocene.
REMARKS: Pronounced "riss-o-ee-
na." *R. chesneli* Michaud, 1830, of
authors. *See* D. R. Moore 1969.

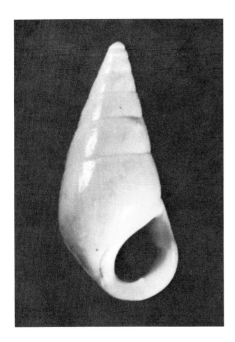

Zebina browniana

Assiminea cf. *A. succinea*

Genus *Zebina* H. & A. Adams, 1854

Smooth Risso
Zebina browniana (Orbigny, 1842),
Hist. d'Ile de Cuba 2:28.
Dedicated to Captain Thomas
Brown (1785–1862), conchologist.
SIZE: 4 mm.
COLOR: Shiny white or pale amber.
SHAPE: Elongate conic.
ORNAMENT OR SCULPTURE: Nine to
10 slightly convex whorls, smooth.
Suture shallow. Apex small, promi-
nent.
APERTURE: Oval, entire. Outer lip
thickened.
OPERCULUM: Corneous, light amber
color.
PERIOSTRACUM: Thin, transparent.
HABITAT: Under shell and debris in
grassy bottom beyond littoral zone.
Epifaunal.
LOCALITIES: Entire.
OCCURRENCE: Common in beach
drift.
RANGE: Bermuda; North Carolina to
Gulf of Mexico; Texas to Quintana
Roo; Costa Rica; West Indies.
GEOLOGIC RANGE: Lower Miocene to
Holocene.
REMARKS: Syn. *Rissoina laevigata* (C.
B. Adams, 1850). [*Rissoina brown-
iana*]. *See* D. R. Moore 1969.

Family ASSIMINEIDAE H. & A.
Adams, 1856

Genus *Assiminea* Fleming, 1828

Assiminea cf. *A. succinea* Pfeiffer,
1840, *Zeitschr. für Malakozool.*, p. 76.
Named for Oriental scholar Joseph
Simon Assemani (1687–1768); L.
succinea like amber.
SIZE: 5 mm.
COLOR: Pale brown, translucent.
SHAPE: Conic.
ORNAMENT OR SCULPTURE: No or-
nament other than microscopic
striae. Five to 5¾ whorls. Regularly
rounded, sutures shallow.
APERTURE: Pyriform, simple. Induc-
tura overlaps preceding whorl.
Anomphalous.
OPERCULUM: Thin, corneous, trans-
lucent, paucispiral, pale brown.
PERIOSTRACUM: Thin, shiny,
chestnut brown.
HABITAT: Salt marshes where there
is moisture and protection from
sun. Lives just out of water. Epi-
faunal.
LOCALITIES: Entire.
OCCURRENCE: Common.
RANGE: Boston to Texas; Quintana
Roo; Brazil.
GEOLOGIC RANGE: ? to Holocene.
REMARKS: D. W. Taylor found quan-
tities of these living on the flats just
north of the high bridge at Corpus
Christi, Texas, in 1973.

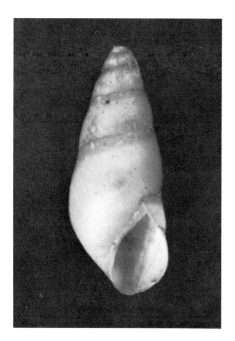

Texadina barretti

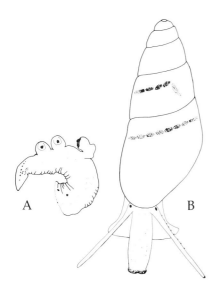

A, verge, 125×
B, dorsal view, 65× (after Taylor 1973)

Family LITTORIDINIDAE Thiele, 1929

Genus *Texadina* Abbott & Ladd, 1951

The genus is classified by Thompson (1968) in the Heleobia tribe, which is mainly South American. The only other North American genus of the tribe, *Heleobops* Thompson, 1968, found on the peninsula of Florida, Antros (Bahamas), and Haiti, has a bifurcate verge and apocrine glands depressed flush with the surface along the right ventral side. *Texadina* has no bifurcation of the verge, and the glands are borne on short, broad stalks. A further possible distinction is clusters of strong cilia on the left side of the left tentacle. Both species of *Texadina* are found in brackish coastal waters of Texas, one ranging eastward to Mississippi, the other southward along the coast of Mexico.

Texadina barretti (Morrison, 1965), *Proc. Biol. Soc. Washington* 78:220. From Texas and reference to the related genus *Littoridina*; dedicated to Ronny Barrett, assistant to Viosca.
SIZE: 2.1 mm.
COLOR: Vitreous.
SHAPE: Ovate conic.
ORNAMENT OR SCULPTURE: About 5½ whorls. Flat-sided whorls separated by linear almost unimpressed suture. Apex subtruncate; nuclear whorl rounded, with dividing suture moderately incised. After first 2 whorls, suture impression disappears with extreme flattening of whorls. Sculpture smooth, glossy, with minute growth striae only which slant forward at suture.
APERTURE: Generally oval; columellar and parietal walls at slight angle to each other, posterior angle distinctly narrowed. Lip very slightly thickened within but in no way reflected.
OPERCULUM: Corneous, paucispiral.
PERIOSTRACUM: Not preserved.

HABITAT: Soft mud in river-influenced areas.
LOCALITIES: Probably entire, known living only in east and central.
OCCURRENCE: Common.
RANGE: Mississippi to Texas.
GEOLOGIC RANGE: ? to Holocene.
REMARKS: This is the same as [*Odostomia barretti* Morrison, 1965] and [*Hydrobia booneae* Morrison, 1973].
ADDITIONAL REMARKS: Observations and drawings of living specimens are based on a series from Galveston Bay, Harris County, Texas, collected about 100 meters north of the Houston Yacht Club, Shore Acres, by H. W. Harry and D. W. Taylor, 15-VII-1973.

The most conspicuous external differentia is the pink color of the body. The pink buccal mass is vivid, as the snout lacks other coloration, and, further, the columellar area, base of tentacles, and head have a pink flush. When the snail is withdrawn into its shell, the pink columellar area is readily visible through the translucent operculum.

On the left side of the left tentacle, along the proximal two-thirds, is visible a series of low, uniform, and equidistant swellings that bear clusters of cilia. At the tip of each tentacle is a similar cluster of short bristles, or setae.

The verge was examined after excision from 4 live specimens. It is a flattened blade bearing 3–5 broadly stalked apocrine glands along the right venter. In general the verge is like that of *T. sphinctostoma* but differs by having (1) fewer glands, (2) broader openings to the glands so they appear cup-shaped, and (3) the pink flush of the head-foot tissue also present in the blade of the verge.—D.W.T.

Texadina sphinctostoma

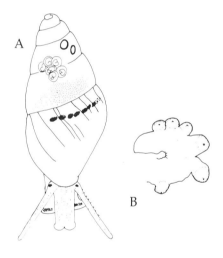

A, dorsal view with eggs, 65×
B, verge, 65×

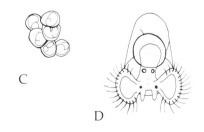

C, eggs, 65×
D, veliger (after Taylor 1973)

Texadina sphinctostoma (Abbott & Ladd, 1951), *J. Washington Acad. Sci.* 41(10):335.

From Texas and reference to the related genus *Littoridina*; Gk. *sphinkter* binder, *stoma* mouth.

SIZE: 2–3 mm.

COLOR: Translucent gray alive; opaque white dead.

SHAPE: Ovate conic.

ORNAMENT OR SCULPTURE: About 5 convex whorls, thin but strong. Whorls increase regularly in size until last third of body whorl, which becomes constricted and in some specimens detached. Surface smooth except for minute growth lines. Suture fine, moderately impressed. Omphalous. Juvenile specimens may be keeled at base of body whorl.

APERTURE: Oval to round. May be free from parietal wall.

OPERCULUM: Thin, smooth, transparent yellowish, paucispiral. Size and shape of aperture.

PERIOSTRACUM: Thin, smooth, translucent, grayish to yellowish.

HABITAT: Soft mud in river-influenced areas.

LOCALITIES: Entire.

OCCURRENCE: Common.

RANGE: Mississippi; Louisiana; Texas; Gulf of Campeche; Yucatán.

GEOLOGIC RANGE: Pleistocene to Holocene.

REMARKS: Lives associated with *Rangia cuneata* (Gray, 1831). Holotype collected by H. S. Ladd at San Antonio Bay on July 15, 1940.

ADDITIONAL REMARKS: Observations and drawings are from specimens collected in Hynes Bay at Austwell, Calhoun County, Texas, by D. W. Taylor, 29-VI-1973.

The animal is pale, and through the thick translucent shell little can be seen except the darkly pigmented stomach and fecal pellets in the intestine. The rostrum is unpigmented; within it the buccal mass is readily visible. In contrast to *T. barretti*, the buccal mass is generally unpigmented but sometimes suffused with pale pink. The tentacles are not quite so slender as in *T. barretti*, bear cilia as in that species, but lack terminal bristles.

The verge is a flattened blade with 5–6 apocrine glands along the right venter.

Numbers of the snail shells had egg capsules on them. These are simple, nearly hemispherical, and laid singly or in clusters. During the period of observation several veligers emerged; these had shells of about ¾ to 1 whorl.—D.W.T.

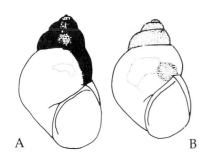

Littoridinops sp. A & B
L. sp. A: *A*, female; brown ovarian follicles in spire; lack of pigmentation in digestive gland
B, male; dark melanin pigmentation over digestive gland

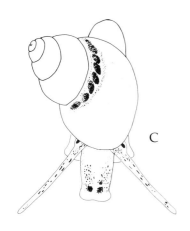

C, dorsal view; fecal pellets in intestine, granules, and ctenidum (50×)

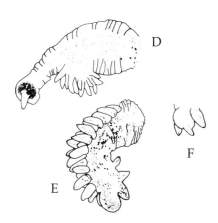

D, verge

L. sp. B: *E*, verge
F, head of verge (after Taylor 1973)

Genus *Littoridinops* Pilsbry, 1952
This genus falls into what Thompson (1968) called the Hydrobia tribe, although that group is here redefined slightly and does not include Hydrobia. The group is characterized by a verge with (1) a terminal papilla through which the vas deferens opens, the papilla being seated in (2) a distal bulbous, melanin-pigmented enlargement thought to be an ejaculatory structure, and (3) glandular papillae, broadly conical to narrowly elongate in form, each with an external opening from its lumen, situated on one or both sides of the verge and varying from few to numerous.

Two species as yet undescribed have been found recently in brackish waters of the Texas coast, and others may be expected in the area. Thompson (1968) recognized *Littoridinops* from central Georgia to the panhandle of Florida and the Bahamas but anticipated that the range would prove much more extensive.

Littoridinops sp. A.
Related to the genus *Littorina*.
SIZE: 3.5 mm.
COLOR: Translucent white.
SHAPE: Conic.
ORNAMENT OR SCULPTURE: Four to 5 rounded whorls. Smooth with microscopic spiral striations, otherwise featureless. Sutures shallow.
APERTURE: Oval, simple, entire. Thin inner lip leaving small umbilical opening.
OPERCULUM: Thin, corneous, brownish, paucispiral.
PERIOSTRACUM: Thin, pale brown.
HABITAT: Brackish water associated with *Cerithidea* and *Mytilopsis*.
LOCALITIES: Sunset Lake, Corpus Christi, Texas.
OCCURRENCE: Not determined.
RANGE: Unknown.
GEOLOGIC RANGE: ? to Holocene.
REMARKS: The upper part of the body as seen through the shell is a different color in the two sexes. The spire appears black in the male and pale in the female. There is a gray

band near the tip of each long, slender tentacle. Two conspicuous patches of yellow granules in the snout. D. W. Taylor located a colony of these in the summer of 1973.
ADDITIONAL REMARKS: Collected from Sunset Lake, San Patricio County, Texas, 1½ miles southwest of Portland along U.S. highway 181 by D. W. Taylor, 16-VI-1973.

This species was found commonly at first in the then-brackish water. Only a few weeks later the water level had subsided, salinity had increased, and no *Littoridinops* could be found. This species is probably found in brackish water around the mouths of streams tributary to Corpus Christi Bay, at least, but will not be described until a suitable type locality where a more stable population occurs can be found.

The verge is a bulky, blade-shaped organ that fills much of the mantle cavity. On its left side is a fan-shaped group of apocrine glands that share a common base and are directed laterally. In 21 specimens examined, the number of glands ranged from 8 to 27.

Pigmentation in the spire showed sexual dimorphism. The spire in males is black, in females pale brown.—D.W.T.

Littoridinops sp. B
The conical shell is identical to that of *Littoridinops* sp. A.
ADDITIONAL REMARKS: Found in a roadside pond 0.7 mile northeast of Aransas National Wildlife Refuge headquarters, Aransas County, Texas, by D. W. Taylor, 29-VI-1973. One specimen only.

The verge has 39 glands on the right (convex) margin, 3 on the left side toward the tip. Further differences from the verge of *L.* sp. A are that the terminal papilla is relatively immobile and is not seated in a depression in the terminal bulb.

The shell could not be distinguished from that of the common, associated *Pyrgophorus* nor from that of *L.* sp. A.—D.W.T.

Vioscalba louisianae

Truncatella caribaeensis

Family STENOTHYRIDAE Fischer, 1885

Genus *Vioscalba* Morrison, 1965

Vioscalba louisianae Morrison, 1965, *Proc. Biol. Soc. Washington* 78:217. Dedicated to Percy A. Viosca; from Louisiana.
SIZE: 3.3 mm.
COLOR: Polished, translucent.
SHAPE: Elongate ovate.
ORNAMENT OR SCULPTURE: Four and one-half slightly convex whorls, separated by distinct but very shallow suture, microscopically spirally striate, and with minute growth lines. Spire narrowly obtuse, first 3 whorls rapidly increasing; last whorl deflected, increasing rapidly only in height, almost three-fourths of shell height, and abruptly constricted at aperture. Entire shell appears subcylindrical, or pupiform. Abrupt (downward) constriction of last whorl at aperture causes heavy variciform thickening of lip to appear to fill upper angle of whorl, producing an almost evenly elliptic peritreme in adults.
APERTURE: Entire, slightly oblique; umbilicus narrow, distinct slit.
OPERCULUM: Thin, corneous, paucispiral, of about 2½ turns.
PERIOSTRACUM: Not preserved.
HABITAT: Brackish water. Epifaunal.
LOCALITIES: Entire.
OCCURRENCE: Common.
RANGE: Louisiana; Texas.
GEOLOGIC RANGE: Pliocene? to Holocene.
REMARKS: Named for Percy Viosca, Jr. (1892–1961), of the Louisiana Wildlife and Fisheries Commission. This species may be the same as *V. protera* Pilsbry, 1953 = [*Probythinella protera* Pilsbry, 1953].

Family TRUNCATELLIDAE Gray, 1840
Subfamily TRUNCATELLINAE Gray, 1840

Genus *Truncatella* Risso, 1826

Truncatella caribaeensis Reeve, 1842, *Conch. Syst.* 2:94, pl. 182, fig. 2.
L. *truncatus* cut off; from the Caribbean.
SIZE: 5.5–7.5 mm.
COLOR: White to pale amber, shiny.
SHAPE: Elongate conic.
ORNAMENT OR SCULPTURE: Four to 4½ convex whorls. Deeply impressed suture. Seventeen or more poorly developed transverse costae; some specimens may be nearly smooth. Costae appear only on upper part of whorl. Mature specimens appear very different from young due to loss of early whorls.
APERTURE: Ovate, somewhat flaring, entire. Angled above and rounded below. Outer lip simple, thin, thickened at union with body whorl. Columella not apparent. Anomphalous.
OPERCULUM: Corneous, paucispiral with thin calcareous plate on outer surface.
PERIOSTRACUM: Thin, brownish.
HABITAT: In bays above high-tide and inlet areas. Epifaunal but under wet debris.
LOCALITIES: Entire.
OCCURRENCE: Fairly common.
RANGE: Bermuda; southeastern United States; Texas; Carmen, Campeche, Mexico; Gulf of Campeche; Quintana Roo; West Indies; northeastern Brazil.
GEOLOGIC RANGE: ? to Holocene.
REMARKS: According to A. de la Torre (1960), formerly misidentified in Texas as *T. pulchella* Pfeiffer, 1839. Look for it out of the water in damp spots under driftwood along bay margins. *See* A. de la Torre 1960, p. 79.

Vitrinella floridana

Vitrinella helicoidea

Family VITRINELLIDAE Bush, 1897

Genus *Vitrinella* C. B. Adams, 1850

Vitrinella floridana Pilsbry & McGinty, 1946, *Nautilus* 60(1):16. Dim. of genus *Vitrina*; from Florida.
SIZE: 1.8 mm.
COLOR: White.
SHAPE: Slightly turbinate.
ORNAMENT OR SCULPTURE: Umbilicus broadly open. Protoconch slightly elevated. Two postnuclear whorls. Prior whorls can be seen; walls convex.
APERTURE: Circular, oblique. Columella slightly thickened.
OPERCULUM: Circular, thin, flexible.
PERIOSTRACUM: Not preserved.
HABITAT: Inlet-influenced areas and near shore. Epifaunal.
LOCALITIES: Entire.
OCCURRENCE: Fairly common in beach drift.
RANGE: Southern Florida and Texas to Campeche Bank; Quintana Roo.
GEOLOGIC RANGE: ? to Holocene.
REMARKS: The uncarinated umbilicus differentiates this from *V. helicoidea*. Figured specimen collected in Florida by Steger. *See* D. R. Moore 1964, p. 59.

Helix Vitrinella
Vitrinella helicoidea C. B. Adams, 1850, *Monogr. Vitrinella*, p. 9.
Dim. of genus *Vitrina*; Gk. *helico* spiral, coil.
SIZE: 2.7 mm.
COLOR: White.
SHAPE: Thin, turbinate.
ORNAMENT OR SCULPTURE: Two and one-half whorls. A spiral cord next to suture of first whorl. May be low spiral sculpture on periphery to first 1½ whorls. Umbilicus narrow, deep, flat-sided, angled where it meets base.
APERTURE: Round, slightly oblique. Columella curved inward.
OPERCULUM: Circular, multispiral.
PERIOSTRACUM: Not preserved.
HABITAT: Under rocks and near shore. Epifaunal.
LOCALITIES: Entire.
OCCURRENCE: Fairly common in beach drift.
RANGE: Bermuda; southeastern United States to West Indies; Texas; Quintana Roo; Costa Rica; Panama.
GEOLOGIC RANGE: ? to Holocene.
REMARKS: *See* D. R. Moore 1964, p. 56.

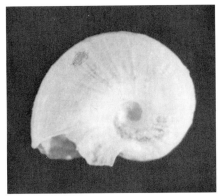

Vitrinella texana

Cyclostremiscus (Ponocyclus) jeaneae

Vitrinella texana D. R. Moore, 1965, *Nautilus* 78(3):76.

Dim. of genus *Vitrina*; from Texas.

SIZE: 1.72 mm.

COLOR: White.

SHAPE: Turbinate.

ORNAMENT OR SCULPTURE: One and one-fourth postnuclear whorls. Nuclear whorls glassy, with a narrow but distinct varix at their termination. Spire flat. Sculpture consists of many revolving dorsal grooves and low radiating ribs on base. Base flattened. Several grooves in umbilicus. Umbilicus narrow, deep.

APERTURE: Oblique. Parietal callus heavy with groove at upper inner angle.

OPERCULUM: Circular, multispiral.

PERIOSTRACUM: Not preserved.

HABITAT: Inlet areas. Epifaunal.

LOCALITIES: Port Aransas, south.

OCCURRENCE: Uncommon in beach drift.

RANGE: Florida; southern Texas.

GEOLOGIC RANGE: ? to Holocene.

REMARKS: To date, this species has only been found near the inlet area to Aransas Bay. Holotype collected by Winnie Rice at Port Aransas, Texas, in 1959. *See* D. R. Moore 1964, p. 66.

Genus *Cyclostremiscus* Pilsbry & Olsson, 1945

Subgenus *Ponocyclus* Pilsbry, 1953.

Jeanne's Vitrinella

Cyclostremiscus (Ponocyclus) jeaneae Pilsbry & McGinty, 1946, *Nautilus* 59(3):82.

Gk. *kyklos* circle, *trema* hole or aperture; dedicated to Dr. Jeanne S. Schwengel, contemporary Florida malacologist.

SIZE: 1.8 mm.

COLOR: Translucent white.

SHAPE: Discoid.

ORNAMENT OR SCULPTURE: Three and one-half whorls. Penultimate whorl has medial keel extending on to first part of last whorl. Last whorl has strong upper and lower carina with submedian keels or 4 keels. Umbilical region funnel-shaped with strongly keeled base.

APERTURE: Rounded pentagonal, slightly oblique.

OPERCULUM: Not preserved, probably circular.

PERIOSTRACUM: Not preserved.

HABITAT: Offshore. Epifaunal.

LOCALITIES: South.

OCCURRENCE: Not reported.

RANGE: Both sides of Florida to Texas; Costa Rica; Panama.

GEOLOGIC RANGE: ? to Holocene.

REMARKS: Living on 7½ Fathom Reef off Port Mansfield. Coll., Tunnell. *See* Pilsbry & McGinty 1946; D. R. Moore 1964.

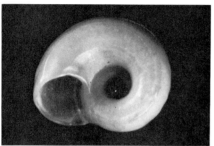

Cyclostremiscus (Ponocyclus)
pentagonus

Cyclostremiscus (Ponocyclus)
suppressus

Trilix Vitrinella

Cyclostremiscus (Ponocyclus) pentagonus (Gabb, 1873), *Proc. Acad. Natur. Sci. Philadelphia* 24:243.

Gk. *kyklos* circle, *trema* hole or aperture, *penta* five, *gonia* angle.

SIZE: 2.1 mm.

COLOR: White, glassy.

SHAPE: Discoid; nuclear whorls projecting.

ORNAMENT OR SCULPTURE: Postnuclear whorls almost flat on top and sculptured with 3 keellike ridges (tricarinate). Base flattened. Umbilicus open, deep, bordered with spiral ridge. Faint spiral lines within umbilicus.

APERTURE: Oblique. Lip incomplete.

OPERCULUM: Circular, multispiral.

PERIOSTRACUM: Not preserved.

HABITAT: Along shore in surf zone on sandy mud. Epifaunal.

LOCALITIES: Entire.

OCCURRENCE: Common in beach drift.

RANGE: Southeastern United States to West Indies and Texas.

GEOLOGIC RANGE: ? to Holocene.

REMARKS: Syn. *C. trilix* (Bush, 1885). *See* D. R. Moore 1964, p. 138.

Cyclostremiscus (Ponocyclus) suppressus (Dall, 1889), *Mus. Comp. Zool. Bull.* 18(1):361–362.

Gk. *kyklos* circle, *trema* hole or aperture; L. *suppressus* low or sunken.

SIZE: 1.7 mm.

COLOR: White.

SHAPE: Discoid.

ORNAMENT OR SCULPTURE: One and three-fourths postnuclear whorls sculptured with 3 narrow, sharp keels on periphery. Central keel higher than other 2. Less conspicuous keel near suture. At suture, which is covered by a thin callus of shell, is another ridge, which is peripheral keel of prior whorl. Base flat with raised ridge around umbilicus. Umbilicus narrow with flat wall. Last half of body whorl twisted so that umbilical ridge joins aperture in middle of base.

APERTURE: Oblique. Parietal callus heavy with groove at upper inner angle.

OPERCULUM: Thin, multispiral.

PERIOSTRACUM: Not preserved.

HABITAT: With grass in bays and inlets. Epifaunal.

LOCALITIES: Entire.

OCCURRENCE: Fairly common in beach drift.

RANGE: Lower eastern coast and entire western coast of Florida; Texas.

GEOLOGIC RANGE: ? to Holocene.

REMARKS: *Circulus suppressus* of some authors. *See* D. R. Moore 1964, p. 144.

Anticlimax (Subclimax) pilsbryi

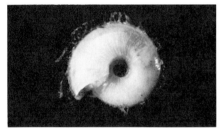

Episcynia inornata

Genus *Anticlimax* Pilsbry &
  McGinty, 1946
Subgenus *Subclimax* Pilsbry &
  Olsson, 1950

Anticlimax (Subclimax) pilsbryi
(McGinty, 1945), *Nautilus* 54(4):142.
Anti = not the genus *Climax*; dedicated to Henry A. Pilsbry (1862–
1959), American malacologist.
SIZE: 3.4 mm.
COLOR: White.
SHAPE: Discoid, spire slightly
dome-shaped.
ORNAMENT OR SCULPTURE: Two and
one-half postnuclear whorls
sculptured with numerous, fine
zigzag spiral grooves. More grooves
on dorsal side than on base. Pe-
riphery just above base marked
with strong keel. Umbilicus partly
filled with heavy callus; may be entirely filled.
APERTURE: Oblique. Lip slightly
thickened in adults. Parietal callus
thick, on preceding whorl.
OPERCULUM: Not preserved.
PERIOSTRACUM: Not preserved.
HABITAT: On muddy bottom in shallow water; shore. Epifaunal.
LOCALITIES: Entire.
OCCURRENCE: Fairly common in
beach drift.
RANGE: Southern Florida; Texas;
Quintana Roo.
GEOLOGIC RANGE: ? to Holocene.
REMARKS: The callus-filled umbilicus often causes confusion with
the *Teinostoma*. Look for the zigzag
grooving. *See* D. R. Moore 1964, p.
165.

Genus *Episcynia* Mörch, 1875

Hairy Vitrinella
Episcynia inornata (Orbigny, 1842),
Hist. d'Ile de Cuba 2:67.
Gk. *epi* upon; L. *scynium* skin above
the eyes, *in* without, *orno* decora-
tion.
SIZE: 3.4 mm.
COLOR: White, glassy.
SHAPE: Trochiform.
ORNAMENT OR SCULPTURE: Four and
one-half postnuclear whorls
sculptured with narrow peripheral
keel fringed with minute projecting
teeth. Umbilicus narrow, flat-sided,
deep with stepped appearance.
APERTURE: Flattened oval. Lip in-
complete.
OPERCULUM: Not known.
PERIOSTRACUM: Distinctive, thin,
yellowish brown, fringed at the pe-
riphery.
HABITAT: Offshore and along shore.
Epifaunal.
LOCALITIES: Port Aransas, south.
OCCURRENCE: Uncommon in beach
drift.
RANGE: Texas; Campeche Bank;
Greater Antilles.
GEOLOGIC RANGE: ? to Holocene.
REMARKS: Peripheral sculpture is
jewellike. *See* D. R. Moore 1964, p.
105.

?*Parviturboides interruptus*

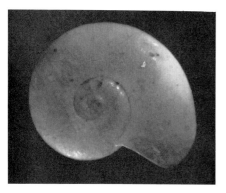

Solariorbis (Solariorbis) blakei

Genus *Parviturboides* Pilsbry &
McGinty, 1950

?*Parviturboides interruptus* (C. B.
Adams, 1850), *Monogr. Vitrinella*,
p. 6.
L. *parvus* small, *turbo* a top, *interruptus* broken apart.
SIZE: 1.43 mm.
COLOR: White.
SHAPE: Trochiform.
ORNAMENT OR SCULPTURE: One and
three-fourths postnuclear whorls
sculptured with 8 or 9 distinct spiral
ridges and several indistinct ones.
Low threadlike transverse sculpture
between ridges. Suture not impressed. Nuclear whorls large and
prominent. Base rounded. Umbilicus a narrow chink bordered by
ridge joining base of columella.
APERTURE: Circular, oblique, slightly
angled. Lip incomplete.
OPERCULUM: Thin, multispiral, circular.
PERIOSTRACUM: Not preserved.
HABITAT: Shallow water in rocks
and crevices. Epifaunal.
LOCALITIES: Port Aransas, south.
OCCURRENCE: Fairly common in
beach drift.
RANGE: South Carolina; Florida;
Texas; Mexico; Panama; Puerto
Rico; Haiti; Jamaica.
GEOLOGIC RANGE: ? to Holocene.
REMARKS: Provisionally listed in this
family; awaiting further study. *See*
D. R. Moore 1964, p. 156.

Genus *Solariorbis* Conrad, 1865
Subgenus *Solariorbis* s.s.

Solariorbis (Solariorbis) blakei Rehder,
1944, *Nautilus* 57(3):97.
L. *solarium* sundial, *orbis* circle;
Blake, a ship used for the United
States coast survey 1877–1878.
SIZE: 1.45 mm.
COLOR: White.
SHAPE: Discoid.
ORNAMENT OR SCULPTURE: One and
one-half postnuclear whorls
sculptured with microscopic spiral
grooves and brief transverse wrinkles fanning from suture. Suture
only slightly impressed. Nuclear
whorls project slightly. Base broad,
smooth, evenly rounded. Umbilicus
may be nearly or entirely closed;
however, there is always a narrow
chink and it never looks like *Teinostoma*.
APERTURE: Oblique, rounded.
Parietal callus extends beyond aperture.
OPERCULUM: Multispiral, round.
PERIOSTRACUM: Not preserved.
HABITAT: Inlets and bays. Epifaunal.
LOCALITIES: Entire.
OCCURRENCE: Fairly common in
beach drift.
RANGE: Eastern coast of United
States; Florida; Gulf states; Mexico.
GEOLOGIC RANGE: ? to Holocene.
REMARKS: The thickening around
the umbilicus is the most distinctive
characteristic of this genus. Figured
specimen collected in Florida by
Steger. *See* D. R. Moore 1964,
p. 122.

Solariorbis (Solariorbis) infracarinata

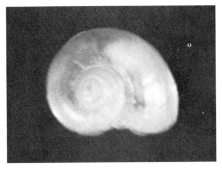

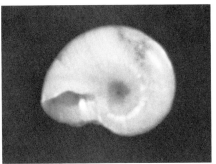

Solariorbis (Solariorbis) mooreana

Solariorbis (Solariorbis) infracarinata Gabb, 1881, *J. Acad. Natur. Sci. Philadelphia* 8(2):365.
L. *solarium* sundial, *orbis* circle, *infra* below, *carina* keel.
SIZE: 2.0 mm.
COLOR: White.
SHAPE: Discoid.
ORNAMENT OR SCULPTURE: One and two-thirds postnuclear whorls, which are carinate on periphery and sculptured with low radial waves on first whorl. Nuclear whorls project slightly. Below peripheral keel are three spiral ridges. Largest next to periphery and smallest nearest umbilicus. Largest usually beaded on inner surface, with beads disappearing on last half whorl. Umbilicus constricted, with strong ridge occupying lower part of umbilical wall.
APERTURE: Oblique. Parietal callus fairly heavy.
OPERCULUM: Multispiral, circular.
PERIOSTRACUM: Not preserved.
HABITAT: Bays and inlets. Epifaunal.
LOCALITIES: Entire.
OCCURRENCE: Fairly common in beach drift.
RANGE: Both sides of Florida; Texas to Campeche Bank; Central America.
GEOLOGIC RANGE: ? to Holocene.
REMARKS: Spiral sculpture of this shell is not visible from above. Syn. *S. euzonus* Pilsbry & McGinty, 1950. *See* D. R. Moore 1964, p. 113.

Solariorbis (Solariorbis) mooreana Vanatta, 1903, *Proc. Acad. Natur. Sci. Philadelphia* 55:758.
L. *solarium* sundial, *orbis* circle; dedicated to Clarence B. Moore, Florida archaeologist.
SIZE: 2.75 mm.
COLOR: White.
SHAPE: Discoid.
ORNAMENT OR SCULPTURE: Two and one-half postnuclear whorls, which are sculptured with about 8 spiral ridges on upper half of shell crossed with fine axial threads strongest near suture. Base smooth, rounded. Umbilicus narrow, deep.
APERTURE: Oblique. Parietal callus heavy. Columella thick.
OPERCULUM: Multispiral, circular, thin, light tan in color.
PERIOSTRACUM: Not preserved.
HABITAT: Near shore on sandy bottom. Epifaunal.
LOCALITIES: Entire.
OCCURRENCE: Uncommon to rare in beach drift.
RANGE: Cape San Blas, Florida, to Aransas Bay, Texas.
GEOLOGIC RANGE: ? to Holocene.
REMARKS: To date, the animal is unknown. *See* D. R. Moore 1964, p. 119.

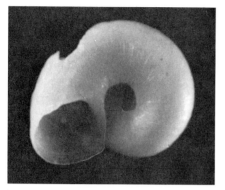

Solariorbis sp. A

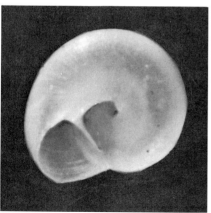

Solariorbis sp. B

Solariorbis sp. A
SIZE: Diameter 1.2 mm, height 0.7 mm.
COLOR: White.
SHAPE: Discoid with low spire.
ORNAMENT OR SCULPTURE: Two whorls, evenly rounded, sculptured with fine, oblique growth lines and inconspicuous spiral striae. Base slightly flattened. Umbilicus narrow, flat-sided, constricted by narrow ridge that joins inner edge of inner lip at base.
APERTURE: Oblique. Inner lip straight, outline evenly rounded elsewhere. Parietal callus thin, continuing into expanded inner lip at inner base of aperture.
OPERCULUM: Not preserved.
PERIOSTRACUM: Not preserved.
HABITAT: Might have been fresh water but perhaps saline from effect of underground salt deposits.
LOCALITIES: Terrell County, Texas.
OCCURRENCE: Not determined.
RANGE: Known from single locality in Terrell County, Texas.
GEOLOGIC RANGE: Late Pleistocene only.
REMARKS: Fossil found along the Pecos River in Terrell County by D. W. Taylor.

Solariorbis sp. B
SIZE: Diameter 1.1 mm, height 0.6 mm.
COLOR: White, translucent.
SHAPE: Low conic.
ORNAMENT OR SCULPTURE: Two postnuclear whorls, broadly rounded toward periphery, slightly flattened on base and toward suture, and sculptured with fine, irregular growth lines. Numerous fine, spiral raised threads about as strong as weaker growth lines override growth lines. Umbilicus narrow with concave walls, overhung by narrow ridge that widens to join inner edge of inner lip at base.
APERTURE: Body whorl descends in last one-tenth whorl to oblique aperture. Inner lip slightly curved, meeting outer lip with angles above and below, of uniform width from upper end to abrupt junction with callus ledge at base.
OPERCULUM: Not preserved.
PERIOSTRACUM: Not preserved.
HABITAT: Not known.
LOCALITIES: Terrell County, Texas.
OCCURRENCE: Not determined.
RANGE: Known from single locality in Terrell County, Texas.
GEOLOGIC RANGE: Late Pleistocene only.
REMARKS: Fossil found along the Pecos River in Terrell County by D. W. Taylor.

Pleuromalaxis balesi

Teinostoma biscaynense

Genus *Pleuromalaxis* Pilsbry &
McGinty, 1945

Bales' False Dial
Pleuromalaxis balesi Pilsbry &
McGinty, 1945, *Nautilus* 59(1):10.
Gk. *pleure* side, *homalos* even,
smooth; dedicated to Dr. Blenn R.
Bales (1876–1946).
SIZE: 1.6 mm.
COLOR: White.
SHAPE: Turbinate, depressed.
ORNAMENT OR SCULPTURE: One and
three-fourths postnuclear whorls.
Suture slightly impressed. Base flat-
tened. Two spiral keels on pe-
riphery with concave space be-
tween. Transverse riblets on both
top and bottom of whorls terminate
at peripheral keels, giving keels a
nodulose appearance. Umbilicus
shallow, widely open.
APERTURE: Circular, oblique.
OPERCULUM: Circular.
PERIOSTRACUM: Not preserved.
HABITAT: Inlet areas, under rocks,
offshore. Epifaunal.
LOCALITIES: Port Aransas, south.
OCCURRENCE: Uncommon in beach
drift.
RANGE: Florida; Texas; Cuba; Puerto
Rico.
GEOLOGIC RANGE: ? to Holocene.
REMARKS: Figured specimen col-
lected in Florida by Steger. *See* D. R.
Moore 1964, p. 77.

Subfamily TEINOSTOMATINAE
Cossmann, 1917

Genus *Teinostoma* H. & A. Adams,
1854

Teinostoma biscaynense Pilsbry &
McGinty, 1945, *Nautilus* 59(1):5.
Gk. *teine* to stretch, *stoma* mouth;
from Biscayne Bay south of Miami,
Florida.
SIZE: 1.9 mm.
COLOR: White.
SHAPE: Discoid.
ORNAMENT OR SCULPTURE: Three
and one-half whorls in adult shell
very smooth. Both spire and um-
bilicus covered with shelly callus.
Umbilical callus convex, fills entire
cavity.
APERTURE: Oblique. Parietal callus
thickened. Upper inner angle of lip
has a small groove.
OPERCULUM: Circular, multispiral.
PERIOSTRACUM: Not preserved.
HABITAT: Inlet areas and surf zone.
Epifaunal.
LOCALITIES: Entire.
OCCURRENCE: Fairly common in
beach drift.
RANGE: Southern and western
Florida; Texas.
GEOLOGIC RANGE: ? to Holocene.
REMARKS: Occasional specimens are
minutely striate. Coll., Wilson. *See*
D. R. Moore 1964, p. 95.

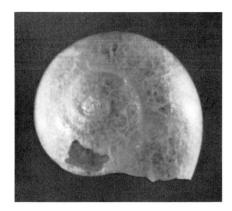

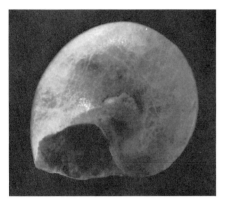

Teinostoma leremum

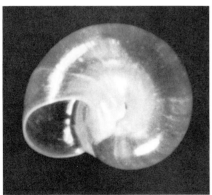

Teinostoma parvicallum

Teinostoma leremum Pilsbry & McGinty, 1945, *Nautilus* 59(1):6. Gk. *teine* to stretch, *stoma* mouth, *lerema* a trifle.
SIZE: 1.12 mm.
COLOR: White.
SHAPE: Discoid.
ORNAMENT OR SCULPTURE: Two nuclear whorls and but little more than 1 postnuclear whorl, which are smooth and glassy except for axial wrinkles adjoining suture. Umbilicus completely covered by shelly callus.
APERTURE: Oblique, round. No groove at upper inner angle.
OPERCULUM: Multispiral, circular.
PERIOSTRACUM: Not preserved.
HABITAT: Bays and inlets. Epifaunal.
LOCALITIES: Entire, more to south.
OCCURRENCE: Fairly common in beach drift.
RANGE: Florida Keys; northwestern Florida; Texas; Mexico; Virgin Islands.
GEOLOGIC RANGE: ? to Holocene.
REMARKS: Very similar to *T. biscaynense* but smaller, and the spire is not covered by a thin shelly callus. Figured specimen collected in Florida by Steger. *See* D. R. Moore 1964, p. 83.

Tiny-Calloused Teinostoma
Teinostoma parvicallum Pilsbry & McGinty, 1945, *Nautilus* 59(1):4. Gk. *teine* to stretch, *stoma* mouth, *parvus* small; L. *callum* hard skin.
SIZE: 1.7 mm.
COLOR: White.
SHAPE: Slightly turbinate.
ORNAMENT OR SCULPTURE: Two and one-half rounded postnuclear whorls, which are smooth and glassy. Nuclear whorls slightly elevated. Periphery and base both rounded. Chinklike umbilicus may not be covered with shelly callus until maturity.
APERTURE: Oblique, rounded with a small groove at upper inner angle. Heavy parietal callus.
OPERCULUM: Multispiral, circular.
PERIOSTRACUM: Not preserved.
HABITAT: Along shore. Epifaunal.
LOCALITIES: Entire.
OCCURRENCE: Rare in beach drift.
RANGE: Florida; Texas; Puerto Rico.
GEOLOGIC RANGE: ? to Holocene.
REMARKS: This minute shell is more rounded than *T. leremum* and *T. biscaynense*. *See* D. R. Moore 1964, p. 85.

Caecum (Micranellum) pulchellum

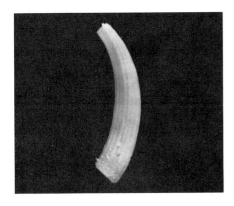

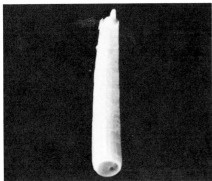

Caecum (Elephantulum) imbricatum

Family CAECIDAE Gray, 1850

Genus *Caecum* Fleming, 1813
Subgenus *Micranellum* Bartsch, 1920

Beautiful Little Caecum
Caecum (Micranellum) pulchellum
(Stimpson, 1851), *Proc. Boston Soc.
Natur. Hist.* 4:112.
L. *caecus* blind gut, *pulcher* fair,
beautiful.
SIZE: 2 mm.
COLOR: Translucent tan and shiny
when living; mat white when dead.
SHAPE: Tubular, cucumberlike.
ORNAMENT OR SCULPTURE: Twenty-
five to 30 fine, closely arranged axial
ribs; plug rounded.
APERTURE: Round, thin lipped.
OPERCULUM: Corneous, concave
with 8 whorls.
PERIOSTRACUM: Not preserved.
HABITAT: In crevices and under
stones; intertidal and offshore. Epi-
faunal.
LOCALITIES: Entire.
OCCURRENCE: Common in beach
drift.
RANGE: Cape Cod to North Carolina;
Texas; Carmen, Campeche, Mexico;
Gulf of Campeche; Yucatán; Quintana Roo; Costa Rica; West Indies;
eastern and southern Brazil.
GEOLOGIC RANGE: Pleistocene to
Holocene.
REMARKS: Develops in 3 stages. In
the first the shell is spiral; this part
is discarded after formation of second tubular stage. The adolescent
tube is discarded after the formation
of a similar curved tube closed by a
septum. *See* D. R. Moore 1962.

Subgenus *Elephantulum* Carpenter,
1857

Cooper's Caecum
Caecum (Elephantulum) imbricatum
Carpenter, 1858, *Proc. Zool. Soc.
London* 26:422.
L. *caecus* blind gut, *imbricatus* over-
lapping.
SIZE: 4–5 mm.
COLOR: Glossy, opaque, white.
SHAPE: Curved, tubular.
ORNAMENT OR SCULPTURE: Longitu-
dinal sculpture consists of about 24
rounded ribs crossed by numerous
rings. More prominent near aper-
ture, giving a cancellate appear-
ance. Apical plug has prong to one
side. Fairly heavy shell.
APERTURE: Round.
OPERCULUM: Corneous, concave,
round, spiral.
PERIOSTRACUM: Not preserved.
HABITAT: Offshore on sand and shell
banks.
LOCALITIES: Port Aransas, south.
OCCURRENCE: Uncommon in beach
drift.
RANGE: South of Cape Cod to north-
ern Florida and Texas; Campeche
Bank; Quintana Roo; Bahamas;
West Indies.
GEOLOGIC RANGE: Pliocene to
Holocene.
REMARKS: Syn. *C. cooperi* (S. Smith,
1870). *See* D. R. Moore 1972*b*, p. 891.

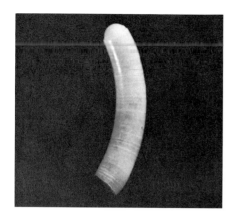

Caecum (Brochina) johnsoni

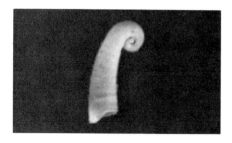

Caecum (Meioceras) nitidum
first stage after it has dropped off

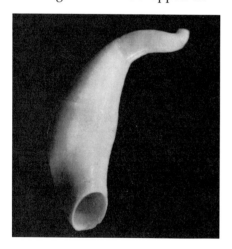

second and third stages

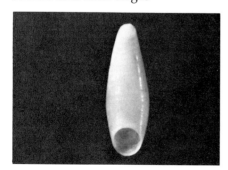

third stage

Subgenus *Brochina* Gray, 1857

Johnson's Caecum

Caecum (Brochina) johnsoni Winkley, 1908, *Nautilus* 22(6):54.
L. *caecus* blind gut; dedicated to Charles William Johnson (1863–1932), American malacologist.
SIZE: 4.5 mm.
COLOR: White.
SHAPE: Curved, tubular.
ORNAMENT OR SCULPTURE: Shell narrow, thin, smooth, subdiaphanous; aperture not contracted or tumid, white; septum without appendage (Tryon 1885).
APERTURE: Circular, not constricted.
OPERCULUM: Externally convex, corneous.
PERIOSTRACUM: Not preserved.
HABITAT: Bays and oyster reefs. Epifaunal.
LOCALITIES: Entire.
OCCURRENCE: Common in beach drift.
RANGE: Europe; North Carolina to Florida; Texas.
GEOLOGIC RANGE: Miocene to Holocene.
REMARKS: First reported for Texas by Hulings (1955). Lays eggs in capsules attached to bottom. *C. glabrum* Montagu, 1803, a European species, is often confused with this species. *See* Abbott 1974, p. 93.

Subgenus *Meioceras* Carpenter, 1858

Little Horn Caecum

Caecum (Meioceras) nitidum Stimpson, 1851, *Proc. Boston Soc. Natur. Hist.* 4:112.
L. *caecus* blind gut, *nitidus* glossy, sleek.
SIZE: 2.5 mm.
COLOR: Shiny white or brownish with irregular mottlings of opaque white.
SHAPE: Tubular with swollen center.
ORNAMENT OR SCULPTURE: Smooth, polished. Apical plug convexly rounded with tiny projection to one side.
APERTURE: Round, oblique, sharp edged. Larger than apical end.
OPERCULUM: Corneous.
PERIOSTRACUM: Not preserved.
HABITAT: Intertidal. Epifaunal.
LOCALITIES: South.
OCCURRENCE: Fairly common in beach drift.
RANGE: Southern half of Florida; Texas; Quintana Roo; West Indies; northeastern Brazil.
GEOLOGIC RANGE: Upper Miocene to Holocene.
REMARKS: According to D. R. Moore (in litt.), the center figure shows the second and third stages of growth after the protoconch drops off: "The second stage usually drops off when the third stage is about half grown. However, in some areas, especially Aransas Bay, the second stage is retained with all three stages. The septum that seals the posterior end of the shell forms before drop off. After the septum is formed, the poorly calcified line that marks the separation point is no longer in contact with living tissue. This area then begins to deteriorate and allows separation of the two stages." *See* D. R. Moore 1962; 1972b, p. 892.

Macromphalina palmalitoris

Cochliolepis parasitica

Superfamily TORNACEA Kuroda, Habe, & Oyama, 1971
Family TORNIDAE Sacco, 1896

Genus *Macromphalina* Cossmann, 1888

Macromphalina palmalitoris Pilsbry & McGinty, 1950, *Nautilus* 63(3):86. Gk. *macro* long, *omphalos* umbilicus; L. *palma* palm, *littus* seashore (palm-lined shore).
SIZE: 1.7 mm.
COLOR: White.
SHAPE: Auriform; nuclear whorls projecting.
ORNAMENT OR SCULPTURE: One and three-fourths postnuclear whorls, which are sculptured with recurved radial riblets that continue over periphery into base. Numerous fine, spiral grooves on entire shell. Base rounded. Umbilicus shallow, wide.
APERTURE: Oblique oval.
OPERCULUM: Not preserved.
PERIOSTRACUM: Not preserved.
HABITAT: On algae, in deeper water offshore. Epifaunal.
LOCALITIES: Port Aransas, south.
OCCURRENCE: Rare in beach drift.
RANGE: Southeastern and northwestern Florida; Texas.
GEOLOGIC RANGE: ? to Holocene.
REMARKS: Figured specimen has sand grains in umbilicus. Coll., Tunnell. *See* D. R. Moore 1964, p. 179.

Genus *Cochliolepis* Stimpson, 1858

Cochliolepis parasitica Stimpson, 1858, *Proc. Boston Soc. Natur. Hist.* 6:308.
L. *cochlea* snail shell, spiral; Gk. *lepis* scale; L. *parasitus* parasite.
SIZE: 3.55 mm.
COLOR: White, glassy.
SHAPE: Discoid.
ORNAMENT OR SCULPTURE: Two postnuclear whorls smooth except for occasional growth line. Spire flat and partially covered with thin callus of shell from each successive whorl. Umbilicus shallow, broadly open.
APERTURE: Oblique. Lip incomplete. Parietal callus thin.
OPERCULUM: Thin, flexible.
PERIOSTRACUM: Not preserved.
HABITAT: Shallow coastal bay. Commensal with a worm. Epifaunal.
LOCALITIES: Entire, more to south.
OCCURRENCE: Uncommon in beach drift.
RANGE: Beaufort, North Carolina; Charleston, South Carolina; western coast of Florida; Texas.
GEOLOGIC RANGE: Pliocene to Holocene.
REMARKS: Smaller than *C. striata*. Heavy growth lines give nautiloid appearance to shell. Animal is red. Syn. *C. nautiliformis* (Holmes, 1860). This shell is not the parasite that the name would indicate but a herbivore, or detritus feeder, which lives commensally with the tube worm *Polydontes lupina*. *See* D. R. Moore 1964, p. 171; 1972a, p. 100.

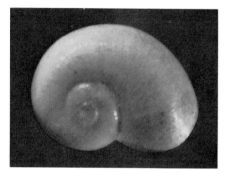

Cochliolepis striata

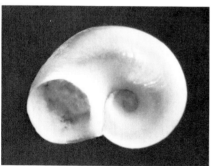

?Cochliolepis sp.

Cochliolepis striata Dall, 1889, *Mus. Comp. Zool. Bull.* 18(1):360.
L. *cochlea* snail shell, spiral; Gk. *lepis* scale; L. *striae* lines.
SIZE: 6.5 mm.
COLOR: White.
SHAPE: Discoid.
ORNAMENT OR SCULPTURE: Thin shell has 4 whorls sculptured with numerous spiral striations. Base smooth, but umbilicus striated. First nuclear whorl slightly projecting, while remainder covered by thin callus from succeeding whorls. Umbilicus slightly constricted.
APERTURE: Oblique. Lip thin, incomplete. No parietal callus.
OPERCULUM: Thin, flexible.
PERIOSTRACUM: Not preserved.
HABITAT: Shallow coastal bays; probably commensal with a worm. Epifaunal.
LOCALITIES: Entire.
OCCURRENCE: Uncommon in beach drift.
RANGE: North Carolina to Caribbean; western coast of Florida; Texas.
GEOLOGIC RANGE: Pliocene to Holocene.
REMARKS: This species will probably be reclassified into another family and genus. *See* D. R. Moore 1964, p. 173.

? Cochliolepis sp.
SIZE: Diameter 1.2 mm, height 0.6 mm.
COLOR: Translucent.
SHAPE: Discoid; spire flat to slightly projecting, base concave.
ORNAMENT OR SCULPTURE: Nuclear whorl with spiral sculpture of inconspicuous fine raised lines. One and one-fourth postnuclear whorls polished, shiny, with sculpture of fine, irregular growth lines. Broadly open umbilicus nearly flat-sided, bordered by narrowly rounded base of whorl. Irregular, discontinuous spiral striae on sides of umbilicus more conspicuous in shallow concavity just inside narrow base of whorl.
APERTURE: Body whorl descends in last one-tenth whorl to oblique aperture. Outer lip broadly curved, meeting inner lip at base and above with narrowly rounded angle. Inner lip gently curved, nearly straight below, scarcely touching previous whorl.
OPERCULUM: Not preserved.
PERIOSTRACUM: Not preserved.
HABITAT: Lower Pecos River valley in late Pleistocene, perhaps in saline water.
LOCALITIES: Terrell County, Texas.
OCCURRENCE: Not determined.
RANGE: Known from single locality in Terrell County, Texas.
GEOLOGIC RANGE: Late Pleistocene only.
REMARKS: May represent a new genus. Fossil found along the Pecos River in Terrell County by D. W. Taylor.

Heliacus bisulcata

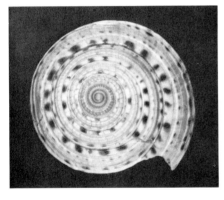

Architectonica nobilis

Superfamily ARCHITEC-
TONICACEA Gray, 1850
Family ARCHITECTONICIDAE
Gray, 1850

Genus *Heliacus* Orbigny, 1842

Orbigny's Sundial
Heliacus bisulcata (Orbigny, 1842),
Hist. d'Ile de Cuba 2:66.
Gk. *helico* spiral, coil; L. *bis* twice,
sulcare to furrow.
SIZE: 6–12 mm.
COLOR: Tan to dull gray.
SHAPE: Broadly conic; spire only
slightly elevated.
ORNAMENT OR SCULPTURE: Whorls
flat, more strongly sculptured than
Architectonica. Spiral sculpture of
revolving beaded cords; on pe-
riphery are 2 rows of stronger
beads. Base sculptured in similar
fashion. Umbilicus deep, wide,
with crenulated edge.
APERTURE: Round. Lip thin, irregu-
larly crenulated.
OPERCULUM: Corneous, spiral with
several turns and fringed edge.
PERIOSTRACUM: Not preserved.
HABITAT: Intertidal on rocks, jetties,
probably on tunicates and soft cor-
als. Epifaunal.
LOCALITIES: Port Aransas, south.
OCCURRENCE: Rare beach shell.
RANGE: Bermuda; southeastern
United States; Texas; Yucatán;
Costa Rica; West Indies; Surinam;
Brazil.
GEOLOGIC RANGE: ? to Holocene.
REMARKS: This species has been
found alive on the Port Aransas jet-
ties on the base of sea whip coral.
Coll., Young.

Genus *Architectonica* Röding, 1798

Common Sundial
Architectonica nobilis (Röding, 1798),
Mus. Boltenianum, p. 78.
L. *architecton* master builder, *nobilis*
famous or noted.
SIZE: 25–51 mm.
COLOR: Background cream with
orange brown spots spirally arranged, more prominent next to suture. Porcelaneous.
SHAPE: Broadly conic; spire low.
ORNAMENT OR SCULPTURE: Early
whorls marked with spiral cords
that appear beaded due to growth
lines of spire. Four or 5 prominent
sulcations and traces of others on
remaining whorls. Base flat, more
strongly sculptured than topside.
Umbilicus deep, wide, surrounded
with strongly crenulated spiral
cord.
APERTURE: Subquadrate. Lip thin,
irregularly crenulated. Interior
white.
OPERCULUM: Brown, paucispiral,
corneous.
PERIOSTRACUM: None visible.
HABITAT: Along shore with sea pan-
sies. Epifaunal.
LOCALITIES: Entire.
OCCURRENCE: Common.
RANGE: Southeastern United States
to West Indies; Texas; Campeche
Bank; Surinam; all of Brazilian
coast; western Mexico to Peru; eastern Pacific.
GEOLOGIC RANGE: Miocene to
Holocene.
REMARKS: This is a Miocene species
that survives on both sides of the
Panama land bridge. Syn. *A.
granulata* (Lamarck, 1816). *See* Ban-
del 1976, p. 256.

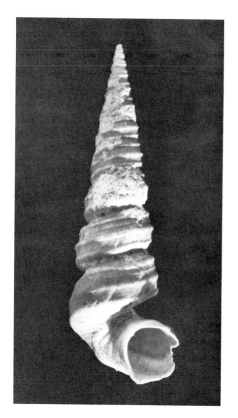

Vermicularia cf. *V. spirata*

Modulus modulus

Superfamily TURRITELLACEA
  Woodward, 1851
Family VERMETIDAE Rafinesque,
  1815
Subfamily VERMICULARIINAE
  Kimoshita, 1932

Genus *Vermicularia* Lamarck, 1799

West Indian Worm Shell
Vermicularia cf. *V. spirata* Philippi,
1836, *Arch. für Natur.* 2(1):224.
L. *vermis* worm, *spiralis* coil.
SIZE: 18–25 mm.
COLOR: Light brown, paler toward
aperture.
SHAPE: Very elongate conic or turriculate.
ORNAMENT OR SCULPTURE: About 6
regular whorls closely coiled; later
whorls detached, giving a wormlike
appearance. About 3 spiral cords
form keels at sutures of later
whorls. Weak, irregular transverse
growth lines. Fine spiral threads between major cords.
APERTURE: Round, thin lipped.
OPERCULUM: Corneous, circular;
closes aperture completely.
PERIOSTRACUM: Not preserved.
HABITAT: Intertidal, attached to
rocks, in mud, in bays. Attached
epifaunal.
LOCALITIES: Entire, more to south.
OCCURRENCE: Common in beach
drift.
RANGE: Southeastern Florida; Texas;
Carmen, Campeche, Mexico; Yucatán; Quintana Roo; Caribbean.
GEOLOGIC RANGE: Pleistocene to
Holocene.
REMARKS: This species has not been
found living on the Texas coast recently, but vast quantities of shells
occur along the bay shores of the
southern half. Panamic vicariant is
V. frisbeyae McLean, 1970. Syn. *V.
fargoi* Olsson, 1951. *See* Gould 1968;
1969.

Superfamily CERITHIACEA Fleming, 1822
Family MODULIDAE Fischer, 1884

Genus *Modulus* Gray, 1842

Atlantic Modulus
Modulus modulus (Linné, 1758), *Syst.
Natur.*, 10th ed., p. 757.
L. *modulus* a measure.
SIZE: Height 12 mm.
COLOR: Grayish white spotted with
brown.
SHAPE: Turbinate.
ORNAMENT OR SCULPTURE: About 3
small whorls in spire; body whorl
large with sloping shoulders and
keeled base. Upper portion of shell
marked with low spiral ridges and
oblique, transverse growth lines.
Five strong cords on base. Um-
bilicus deep, small.
APERTURE: Round with thin, slightly
crenulated outer lip that is thick-
ened and marked with low ridges
within; white, porcelaneous. Columella short with distinctive single
tooth near base.
OPERCULUM: Corneous, circular,
reddish brown, multispiral, thin.
PERIOSTRACUM: Not preserved.
HABITAT: On *Thalassia* grass; intertidal. Epifaunal.
LOCALITIES: Entire, more to south.
OCCURRENCE: Common in beach
drift.
RANGE: Bermuda; Florida Keys to
West Indies; Texas; Gulf of Mexico
to Quintana Roo; Costa Rica; almost
all of Brazilian coast.
GEOLOGIC RANGE: Pliocene to
Holocene.
REMARKS: No live specimens have
been reported in recent years. The
abundant shells along the Aransas
ship channel are all badly worn as is
the figured specimen. Panamic vicariant is *M. disculus* (Philippi,
1846). *See* Abbott 1944, pp. 1–6.
Bandel 1976, p. 258.

Cerithidea (Cerithideopsis) pliculosa

Family POTAMIDIDAE H. & A. Adams, 1854
Subfamily POTAMIDINAE H. & A. Adams, 1854

Genus *Cerithidea* Swainson, 1840
Subgenus *Cerithideopsis* Thiele, 1929

Plicate Horn Shell

Cerithidea (Cerithideopsis) pliculosa (Menke, 1829), *Conch. Samml. Malsburg*, p. 27.
Gk. *keration* little horn; L. *plicare* to fold.
SIZE: 25.6 mm.
COLOR: Dark brown or brownish black with bone yellow varices; sometimes grayish yellow spiral band through middle of whorls.
SHAPE: High conic or turriculate with siphonal notch.
ORNAMENT OR SCULPTURE: Eleven to 13 slightly convex whorls. Unevenly spaced transverse ribs, 18 to 25 per whorl. Many fine, uneven spiral striations. On body whorl ribs stop below periphery at strong cord; 6 to 9 spiral cords continue over base. Five to 8 prominent varices are characteristic feature of adult, usually beginning with sixth whorl.
APERTURE: Subcircular; outer margin convex, columellar margin concave. Shallow indentation at base near columella for siphon. Outer lip greatly thickened, forming raised, rounded varix.
OPERCULUM: Corneous, subcircular, spiral, closely coiled about central nucleus.
PERIOSTRACUM: None visible.
HABITAT: Mud flats in bays. Semi-epifaunal.
LOCALITIES: Entire.
OCCURRENCE: Common.
RANGE: Louisiana; Texas; Yucatán; West Indies.
GEOLOGIC RANGE: Pliocene to Holocene.

REMARKS: Juvenile specimens without strongly developed varices are easily confused with other Ceriths. Before Hurricane Beulah in 1967, they could be seen crawling on the mud flats of Aransas Bay at low tide, but the huge influx of fresh water resulting from the storm decimated the population; it is returning in the Portland area. A favorite food of water birds. Panamic vicariant is *C. albonodosa* Gould & Carpenter, 1857. *See* Bequaert 1972, p. 4.

Cerithium (Thericium) atratum

Cerithium (Thericium) lutosum

Family CERITHIIDAE Fleming, 1822
Subfamily CERITHIINAE Fleming, 1822

Genus *Cerithium* Bruguière, 1789
Subgenus *Thericium* ('Rochebrune') Monterosato, 1890

Florida Cerith
Cerithium (Thericium) atratum (Born, 1778), *Index Mus. Caes. Vind.*, p. 329.
Gk. *keration* little horn; L. *atratus* in mourning, in black.
SIZE: 37 mm.
COLOR: White with narrow, spiral brown bands.
SHAPE: Elongate conic or turriculate with siphonal canal.
ORNAMENT OR SCULPTURE: Eleven to 13 slightly convex whorls. Two to 3 white former varices on each whorl. Several rows of beaded spiral cords on each whorl with finer granulated cords separating them. Beads fairly regular, giving neat appearance.
APERTURE: Oval, oblique. Outer lip thickened into crenulated varix. Parietal area glossy white. Anterior siphonal canal short and upturned. Posterior canal simple fold where lip joins body whorl.
OPERCULUM: Corneous, brown, thin, paucispiral.
PERIOSTRACUM: Not preserved.
HABITAT: Littoral, on sea grasses. Epifaunal.
LOCALITIES: Entire.
OCCURRENCE: Uncommon beach shell.
RANGE: North Carolina to southern half of Florida; Texas; Yucatán; northeastern and eastern Brazil.
GEOLOGIC RANGE: Pliocene to Holocene.
REMARKS: To date, none have been reported living in Texas; probably fossil. Syn. *C. floridanum* Mörch, 1876. *See* Houbrick 1974*a*, p. 22, and *b*, p. 54; Bandel 1976, p. 161.

Muddy Cerith
Cerithium (Thericium) lutosum (Menke, 1828), *Syn. Meth. Moll.*, p. 86.
Gk. *keration* little horn, *lutosum* one fond of bathing.
SIZE: 6–12 mm.
COLOR: Brown black or grayish white with mottlings of reddish brown. Nuclear whorls whitish.
SHAPE: Elongate conic, turriculate.
ORNAMENT OR SCULPTURE: Eight slightly convex whorls; sutures distinct; 7 to 8 beaded, spiral cords on body whorl interspaced with fine striations. Repeated but fewer in number on remaining whorls. One to 2 former varices on each whorl.
APERTURE: Oval; outer lip thin on edge with thickened varix behind edge. Parietal area white and glossy but thin. Columella short, edged in white with brief upturned siphonal canal. Only slight posterior canal.
OPERCULUM: Corneous, light brown.
PERIOSTRACUM: None visible.
HABITAT: Littoral, on algae and marine grass; in shallow bays. Semi-epifaunal.
LOCALITIES: Central, south.
OCCURRENCE: Common.
RANGE: Bermuda; southern Florida; Texas; Gulf of Mexico to Quintana Roo; Costa Rica; West Indies.
GEOLOGIC RANGE: ? to Holocene.
REMARKS: Syn. *C. variabile* (C. B. Adams, 1845). Prior to Hurricane Beulah in 1967, this was the most common cerith on the Texas coast and could be found on the submerged grasses and crawling along the mud flats of the Aransas Pass area in great numbers. More abundant in summer. Animal black with white mottlings; eyes behind base of tentacles. Sexes separate. Secretes mucus thread to suspend itself. Lays eggs in gelatinous strings. *See* Houbrick 1970, p. 74, 1974*a*, p. 17, and *b*, p. 74; Bandel 1976, p. 260.

Diastoma varium

Alabina cerithidioides

Subfamily DIASTOMATINAE
Cossmann, 1895

Genus *Diastoma* DeShayes, 1850

Variable Bittium
Diastoma varium (Pfeiffer, 1840),
Arch. für Natur. 6:256.
Gk. *dia* through, *stoma* mouth; L.
varius diverse.
SIZE: 5–6 mm.
COLOR: Grayish brown.
SHAPE: Elongate conic, turriculate.
ORNAMENT OR SCULPTURE: Seven to
8 slightly convex whorls, sutures
definite. Numerous rounded,
curved transverse ribs crossed by
spiral grooves that give nodulose
appearance to sculpture. Base has
spiral grooves but no ribs.
APERTURE: Oval, thin with varix ad-
jacent. Anterior siphonal canal
poorly developed.
OPERCULUM: Corneous, light brown.
PERIOSTRACUM: None visible.
HABITAT: On marine grass; in bays.
Epifaunal.
LOCALITIES: Entire.
OCCURRENCE: Common.
RANGE: Maryland to Florida; Texas
to Gulf of Campeche; Yucatán;
Quintana Roo; Costa Rica; West Indies; Brazil.
GEOLOGIC RANGE: Pliocene to
Holocene.
REMARKS: During the warm months
before Hurricane Beulah in 1967,
this snail could be collected in vast
numbers from blades of marine
grass in Aransas Bay. The plethora
of this shell in the drift samples
confuses the novice micromollusk
fan. Food for drum. [*Bittium varium*
Pfeiffer, 1840].

Genus *Alabina* Dall, 1902

Miniature Horn Shell
Alabina cerithidioides (Dall, 1889),
Mus. Comp. Zool. Bull. 18(1):22, 258.
Dim. of genus *Alaba*, in the form of a
cerith.
SIZE: 2–4 mm.
COLOR: Cream to light brown.
SHAPE: Elongate conic.
ORNAMENT OR SCULPTURE: Eight to
10 whorls, first 3 smooth. Remain-
ing whorls with narrow, curved
axial ribs and faint revolving
threads.
APERTURE: Somewhat rounded,
outer lip thin. Columella weakly
curved and ending in slight lip be-
low, behind which is small narrow
umbilicus.
OPERCULUM: Corneous.
PERIOSTRACUM: None visible.
HABITAT: Inlet areas. Epifaunal.
LOCALITIES: Entire, more to south.
OCCURRENCE: Common in beach
drift.
RANGE: Florida; Texas; Campeche
Bank; Quintana Roo; West Indies.
GEOLOGIC RANGE: Pliocene to
Holocene.
REMARKS: This snail is most difficult
to separate from *Diastoma varium*
and juvenile *Cerithium lutosum*.
[*Finella cerithidioides*] *Finella dubia*
(Orbigny, 1842) may be syn.

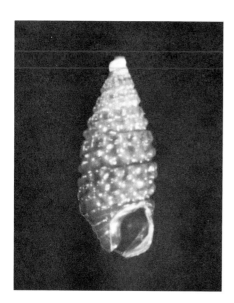

Cerithiopsis greeni

Cerithiopsis (Laskeya) emersoni

Subfamily CERITHIOPSINAE H. &
A. Adams, 1854

Genus *Cerithiopsis* Forbes & Hanley,
1849

Green's Miniature Cerith
Cerithiopsis greeni (C. B. Adams,
1839), *Boston J. Natur. Hist.* 2(2):287.
Gk. *keration* little horn, *opsis* appearance; dedicated to Jacob Green
(1790–1841), American naturalist.
SIZE: 3 mm.
COLOR: Glossy brown.
SHAPE: Elongate conic, turriculate.
ORNAMENT OR SCULPTURE: Nine to
12 convex whorls; nuclear whorls
smooth; remaining whorls with 3
rows of glassy beads joined by spiral and transverse threads.
APERTURE: Oval, lip thin. Columella
arched in juveniles but straight with
slight, flaring anterior notch in
adults.
OPERCULUM: Corneous, brown.
PERIOSTRACUM: Not preserved.
HABITAT: Bays, inlets, shelly sand.
Epifaunal.
LOCALITIES: Entire.
OCCURRENCE: Fairly common in
beach drift.
RANGE: Bermuda; Cape Cod to both
sides of Florida and Texas; Gulf of
Mexico to Quintana Roo; Costa
Rica.
GEOLOGIC RANGE: Pliocene to
Holocene.
REMARKS: Sexes separate. Lives on
marine plants. Can be confused
with *Diastoma*, but whorls are more
convex and siphonal canal better
developed.

Subgenus *Laskeya* Iredale, 1918

Awl Miniature Cerith
Cerithiopsis (Laskeya) emersoni (C. B.
Adams, 1839), *Boston J. Natur. Hist.*
2(2):284.
Gk. *keration* little horn, *opsis* aspect,
appearance; dedicated to George B.
Emerson of Boston.
SIZE: 12–18 mm.
COLOR: Light brown with suture
sometimes darker.
SHAPE: Slender, elongate conic,
awl-shaped.
ORNAMENT OR SCULPTURE: Ten to 14
flat-sided whorls, sutures distinct.
Three strong spiral rows of raised,
roundish beads, revolving thread
between beaded rows. Faint axial
ribs may connect the beads. Middle
row of beads is less prominent than
others. Base is concave with
cordlike spiral ridges and fine
transverse growth lines.
APERTURE: Oval. Lip thin. Short,
slightly flared anterior siphonal canal.
OPERCULUM: Corneous, brown.
PERIOSTRACUM: Not preserved.
HABITAT: Inlet, shelly sand along
shore. Epifaunal.
LOCALITIES: Central, south.
OCCURRENCE: Uncommon in beach
drift.
RANGE: Massachusetts to West Indies; Texas; Costa Rica.
GEOLOGIC RANGE: Upper Miocene to
Holocene.
REMARKS: Syn. *C. subulata* (Montagu, 1808). Looks like an elongated
C. greeni at first glance. *See* Clench &
Turner 1950*a*, p. 278.

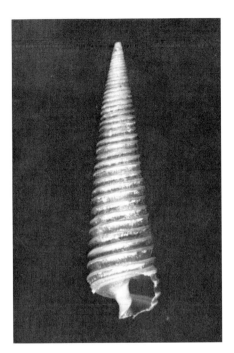

Seila adamsi

Alaba incerta

Genus *Seila* A. Adams, 1861

Adams' Miniature Cerith
Seila adamsi (H. C. Lea, 1845), *Trans. Amer. Philos. Soc.* 2(9):42.
Gk. *seira*? cord, string; dedicated to A. Adams.
SIZE: 10 mm.
COLOR: Brown.
SHAPE: Elongate conic, nearly cylindrical.
ORNAMENT OR SCULPTURE: About 12 flat-sided whorls, regularly increasing in size. Three strong, flattened spiral ridges on each whorl. Concave spaces between them marked with fine spiral striations and delicate transverse lines that do not cross ridges. Base of shell concave. Sutures only wider spaces giving initial impression of continuous ridges.
APERTURE: Oval. Outer lip crenulated to correspond with external sculpture. Columella short, ending in centrally located siphonal canal, slightly recurved.
OPERCULUM: Corneous, oval, brown, paucispiral.
PERIOSTRACUM: None visible.
HABITAT: Under shell in hypersaline bays and inlets. Epifaunal.
LOCALITIES: Entire.
OCCURRENCE: Fairly common.
RANGE: Bermuda; Massachusetts to Florida; Texas; Carmen, Campeche, Mexico; Gulf of Campeche; Campeche Bank; Yucatán; Costa Rica; West Indies; Brazil.
GEOLOGIC RANGE: Lower Miocene to Holocene.
REMARKS: Can be found in Aransas Bay by turning broken shell and examining attached algae. Sexes separate. Chalky and bleached when dead.

Genus *Alaba* H. & A. Adams, 1853

Uncertain Miniature Cerith
Alaba incerta (Orbigny, 1842), *Hist. d'Ile de Cuba* 1:218.
Gk. *alaba* coal dust or soot; L. *incertus* uncertain.
SIZE: 6 mm.
COLOR: Nucleus glossy brown; remainder whitish with light brown spots. Translucent.
SHAPE: Elongate conic, slender.
ORNAMENT OR SCULPTURE: About 13 rounded whorls, gradually increasing in size. Shell thin and smooth except for numerous very fine spiral striations. Raised former varices characteristic on whorls.
APERTURE: Oval. Lip barely thickened, smooth inside. Siphonal canal not well developed.
OPERCULUM: Corneous.
PERIOSTRACUM: None visible.
HABITAT: Among rocks in inlets and offshore. Epifaunal.
LOCALITIES: Central, south.
OCCURRENCE: Fairly common in beach drift.
RANGE: Bermuda; southeastern Florida to Lesser Antilles and Central America; Texas; Yucatán; Quintana Roo; Bahamas; Brazil.
GEOLOGIC RANGE: ? to Holocene.
REMARKS: Only reported recently, but at times can be found readily in beach drift near the jetties at Port Aransas. *See* Bandel 1976, p. 261.

Litiopa melanostoma

Triphora perversa nigrocinta

Subfamily LITIOPINAE H. & A. Adams, 1854

Genus *Litiopa* Rang, 1829

Brown Sargassum Snail
Litiopa melanostoma Rang, 1829, *Annu. Sci. Natur.* 16(63):307.
Gk. *litos* simple, *melanos* black, *stoma* mouth.
SIZE: 12–18 mm.
COLOR: Dark brown, translucent.
SHAPE: Moderately elongate conic.
ORNAMENT OR SCULPTURE: Seven whorls; body whorl expanded and about half length of shell. Appears smooth but covered with numerous microscopic spiral lines more strongly incised on base. Nuclear whorls have regularly spaced, vertical striations.
APERTURE: Semilunar with slightly convex columella. Strong ridge on inside edge of columella is characteristic.
OPERCULUM: Corneous, round, paucispiral.
PERIOSTRACUM: Thin, brown.
HABITAT: Pelagic with *Sargassum natans* Orbigny. Epifaunal.
LOCALITIES: Entire.
OCCURRENCE: Common in beach drift.
RANGE: Same as *Sargassum*, including Yucatán and Quintana Roo; both sides of Panama land bridge.
GEOLOGIC RANGE: ? to Holocene.
REMARKS: Looks very much like the berry on the *Sargassum*. Can be found by shaking *Sargassum* or by sifting beach drift. Dead, faded specimens are cream colored with small brown spots on shoulder of whorl and a brown band bordering the exterior of the aperture.

Family TRIPHORIDAE Gray, 1847

Genus *Triphora* Blainville, 1828

Black-Lined Triphora
Triphora perversa nigrocinta (C. B. Adams, 1839), *Boston J. Natur. Hist.* 2(2):286.
Gk. *tri* thrice, *phoren* to bear, bearing 3 rows; L. *perversum* turn wrong way, *niger* black, *cincta* encircled.
SIZE: 5–10 mm.
COLOR: Dark brown.
SHAPE: Elongate conic, somewhat cylindrical.
ORNAMENT OR SCULPTURE: Ten to 12 slightly convex whorls tapering to acute apex. Sutures slightly excavated. Three spiral rows of rather evenly spaced, glossy beads that appear lighter under lens. Keeled base has strong revolving cords.
APERTURE: Oval, oblique, brown with thin, crenulated outer lip. Well-developed posterior notch and short recurved anterior canal; in adults both of these become tubular. Sinistral.
OPERCULUM: Corneous, brown.
PERIOSTRACUM: Not preserved.
HABITAT: High-salinity reefs on algae. Epifaunal.
LOCALITIES: Entire.
OCCURRENCE: Fairly common in beach drift.
RANGE: Massachusetts to Florida; Texas; Carmen, Campeche, Mexico; Gulf of Campeche; Yucatán; West Indies; Brazil.
GEOLOGIC RANGE: ? to Holocene.
REMARKS: At a glance this shell is easily confused with *C. greeni*, but the "left-handed" aperture always sets it apart.

Amaea (Amaea) mitchelli

Superfamily EPITONIACEA S. S. Berry, 1910

Family EPITONIIDAE S. S. Berry, 1910

The members of this beautiful family, known as wentletraps or spiral-staircase shells, are a confusing lot. (*Wentletrap* is the Dutch equivalent of spiral staircase.) The Texas coast can boast a large number of these elegant little shells, but most collectors will find them difficult to separate. Juveniles are virtually impossible to group.

The tendency of the characteristics of one species to merge with those of another compounds the problem. Any two species have extremes that are readily recognized with a hand lens, but in between the differences are not clear-cut, especially if the distinguishing pattern is based on sculpture.

The wentletraps may be found by screening beach drift, or the lucky collector may happen on an occasional population washing in on the outer beaches. These populations have been of mixed species, thought to be onshore migrations for spawning purposes (Fretter & Graham 1962, p. 574).

Most of these shells secrete a purple dye, an indication that they are carnivorous, in spite of the fact that they do not sport the siphonal canal that usually characterizes the carnivore. It is thought by some that they feed on sea anemones, worms, and foraminifera because they are frequently associated with them.

The Epitoniidae is one of the few prosobranch families that are hermaphroditic. Eggs are produced in beadlike strings consisting of chitinous capsules made of agglutinized sand grains. Generally, the nuclear whorls are smooth and amber colored.

Clench and Turner have grouped the genera as to those that have spiral sculpture and those that exhibit only the typical axial costae. On taxonomic grounds, that is an artificial but very convenient distinction—and a great starting point for the beginner.

Genus *Amaea* H. & A. Adams, 1854
Subgenus *Amaea* s.s.

Mitchell's Wentletrap

Amaea (Amaea) mitchelli (Dall, 1896), *Nautilus* 9(10):112.

An invented word, may be Gk. *a* without; L. *maea* a crab; dedicated to J. D. Mitchell (1848–1922), early Texas naturalist.

SIZE: 25.6–51 mm.

COLOR: Pale ivory with dark brownish band at periphery and solid brownish area below basal ridge.

SHAPE: Elongate conic, turriculate.

ORNAMENT OR SCULPTURE: Fifteen strongly convex whorls gradually increasing in size from apex to base. Twenty-two irregular, low costae per whorl; spiral sculpture of fine threads produces definite reticulated pattern. Thickened ridge and brownish color define basal area.

APERTURE: Subcircular. Thickened but nonreflected lip. Columella short, arched.

OPERCULUM: Corneous, thin, dark brown.

PERIOSTRACUM: Not preserved.

HABITAT: Offshore. Epifaunal.

LOCALITIES: Entire.

OCCURRENCE: Broken pieces not uncommon but good specimens rare.

RANGE: Texas to Yucatán; Caribbean coast of Panama; Surinam.

GEOLOGIC RANGE: ? to Holocene.

REMARKS: One of the largest of the wentletraps and, until the R/V *Pillsbury* expedition to the Gulf of Panama in 1967 under the direction of Dr. Gilbert Voss, thought to be indigenous to this area (Bayer & Voss 1971, p. 132). Collectors vie with each other for this one and even prize broken pieces. After a severe cold snap in early 1966, it was found in unusual numbers in the Port Aransas area. It is used as the symbol of the Coastal Bend Shell Club. Holotype collected ca. 1894 on Matagorda Island, Texas, by J. D. Mitchell. *See* Dall 1896; Clench & Turner 1950*b*, p. 243.

Epitonium (Epitonium) albidum

Epitonium (Epitonium) angulatum

Genus *Epitonium* Röding, 1798
Subgenus *Epitonium* s.s.

White Wentletrap
Epitonium (Epitonium) albidum (Orbigny, 1842), *Hist. d'Ile de Cuba* 2:17.
Gk. *epitonion* peg, turncock; L. *albidus* white.
SIZE: 20 mm.
COLOR: Shiny white.
SHAPE: Elongate conic, turriculate.
ORNAMENT OR SCULPTURE: Nine to 11 gradually increasing, moderately convex whorls, attached by costae only. Bladelike transverse costae rather low and generally fused with costae on previous whorl. Body whorl contains 12 to 14 unangled costae. May be microscopic spiral threads but not strong enough to be grouped with those considered to have spiral striations. Anomphalous.
APERTURE: Subcircular. Outer lip expanded, reflected; parietal area narrow, slightly thickened, held away from body whorl by costae. Nearly holostomatous.
OPERCULUM: Corneous, subcircular, thin, paucispiral.
PERIOSTRACUM: Not preserved.
HABITAT: Intertidal to 360 meters (200 fathoms). Epifaunal.
LOCALITIES: Entire.
OCCURRENCE: Fairly common in beach drift.
RANGE: Bermuda; southern Florida; Texas; Costa Rica; West Indies; Surinam; south to northern Argentina; west Africa.
GEOLOGIC RANGE: ? to Holocene.
REMARKS: The low ribs of this rather "fat" little *Epitonium* appear to form continuous oblique lines from bottom to top. *See* Clench & Turner 1952, p. 260.

Angulate Wentletrap
Epitonium (Epitonium) angulatum (Say, 1831), *Amer. Conch.* 3.pl. 27.
Gk. *epitonion* peg, turncock; L. *angulatus* angled.
SIZE: 19–25 mm.
COLOR: Glossy white.
SHAPE: Elongate conic, turriculate.
ORNAMENT OR SCULPTURE: Eight moderately convex whorls gradually increasing in size from apex. Sculpture on whorls consists of numerous reflected, bladelike costae. Costae form angles on shoulder of each whorl that are stronger on early whorls, a little less to almost absent on later whorls. Costae in line with those on whorl above and fused where they meet. Anomphalous.
APERTURE: Subcircular. Outer lip thickened, held away from body whorls by costae. Columella not defined.
OPERCULUM: Corneous, brown, paucispiral.
PERIOSTRACUM: None visible.
HABITAT: Intertidal to moderate depths with sea anemones. Epifaunal.
LOCALITIES: Entire.
OCCURRENCE: Common in beach drift.
RANGE: Bermuda; eastern end of Long Island to Florida (excluding lower Keys); Texas; Brazil.
GEOLOGIC RANGE: Pleistocene to Holocene.
REMARKS: This shell can fool you because some specimens are more slender than the typical form and can be confused with *E. humphreysi* (Kiener). The juvenile shells are more strongly angulated than the adult; as the shells reach maturity the costae become more thickened and rounded. Late one afternoon in the spring of 1961, I happened on a mixed assemblage of *Epitoniums* washing in the surf near Horace Caldwell Pier at Port Aransas. In a few minutes I picked up over 300 living wentletraps of five species. I

Epitonium (Epitonium) cf. E.
humphreysi

had to leave for an hour, and when I returned, there was not a trace of the large colony. *E. angulatum* was the most abundant species. *See* Clench & Turner 1952, p. 271.

Humphrey's Wentletrap
Epitonium (Epitonium) cf. *E. hum-*
phreysi (Kiener, 1838), *Iconogr. Coq.*
Viv. 10:15.
Gk. *epitonion* peg, turncock; dedicated to G. Humphrey, eighteenth-century London shell dealer.
SIZE: 12–20 mm.
COLOR: Flat white.
SHAPE: Elongate conic, turriculate.
ORNAMENT OR SCULPTURE: Nine to 10 strongly convex whorls. Numerous bladelike to rounded costae on whorls, also serve to connect whorls. Suture deep. Costae more bladelike on early whorls, becoming thickened and rounded with maturity. They may be reflected and some are angled at whorl shoulder, especially on early whorls. Body whorl has 8 to 9 costae. Anomphalous.
APERTURE: Subcircular. Outer lip expanded; usually thickened. Parietal lip thin, tightly pressed to body whorl. Columella short, arched.
OPERCULUM: Corneous, thin, dark brown, paucispiral.
PERIOSTRACUM: None visible.
HABITAT: Inlet areas and along shore on sandy bottoms. Epifaunal.
LOCALITIES: Entire.
OCCURRENCE: Fairly common in beach drift.
RANGE: Cape Cod south to Florida (not lower Keys) and west to Texas; Carmen, Campeche, Mexico.
GEOLOGIC RANGE: Miocene to Holocene.
REMARKS: This shell is hard to distinguish from *E. angulatum* (Say). If typical, it is more narrow, costae more rounded, with less developed shoulder angle but very variable. *See* Clench & Turner 1952, p. 268.

Epitonium (Epitonium) cf. E. tollini

Epitonium (Gyroscala) rupicola

Tollin's Wentletrap

Epitonium (Epitonium) cf. E. tollini
Bartsch, 1938, *Nautilus* 52(1):34.
Gk. *epitonion* peg, turncock; dedicated to Oscar Tollin, who sent the specimen to Bartsch.
SIZE: 14 mm.
COLOR: White.
SHAPE: Elongate conic, turriculate.
ORNAMENT OR SCULPTURE: Nine to 10 convex whorls that can be adpressed or separated and attached by costae only. Numerous bladelike costae, 11 to 16 on body whorl. Spacing of costae irregular and they do not always line up with those on whorl above. They are even in height throughout with an occasional thick one, especially on body whorl. They are not angled at shoulder and there is no spiral sculpture. Suture deep. Anomphalous.
APERTURE: Subcircular. Outer lip thickened, reflected. Parietal area thin, pressed closely to body wall. Columella short, arched.
OPERCULUM: Corneous, yellowish brown, paucispiral.
PERIOSTRACUM: Not preserved.
HABITAT: Probably intertidal. Epifaunal.
LOCALITIES: Entire.
OCCURRENCE: Common in beach drift.
RANGE: Western Florida from Marco Island north to Gasparilla Island; Texas.
GEOLOGIC RANGE: ? to Holocene.
REMARKS: Look for the mismatched costae and the occasional large one. This shell is the most common *Epitonium* in the northern part of the range, less so to the south. *See* Clench & Turner 1952, p. 266.

Subgenus *Gyroscala* Boury, 1887

Brown-Banded Wentletrap

Epitonium (Gyroscala) rupicola (Kurtz, 1860), *Cat. Rec. Marine Shells*, p. 7.
Gk. *epitonion* peg, turncock; L. *rupes* rock, *incola* to inhabit.
SIZE: 12–20 mm.
COLOR: White to cream with 2 brownish, spiral bands at suture. Costae white.
SHAPE: Elongate conic, turriculate.
ORNAMENT OR SCULPTURE: Eleven globose whorls attached at sutures. Suture deep. Transverse sculpture consists of numerous low, bladelike costae, interspersed with rounded varices. Height and number of costae variable and they do not line up with costae on adjoining whorl. Basal ridge well defined with thin, threadlike line.
APERTURE: Subcircular. Lip slightly thickened, reflected. Nearly entire.
OPERCULUM: Corneous, thin, yellowish, paucispiral.
PERIOSTRACUM: Not preserved.
HABITAT: Below low water to 36 meters (20 fathoms). Epifaunal.
LOCALITIES: Entire.
OCCURRENCE: Fairly common in beach drift.
RANGE: Massachusetts south to Florida and west to Texas; Surinam.
GEOLOGIC RANGE: Pliocene to Holocene.
REMARKS: Look for the brown bands of color. Olsson, Harbison, et al. (1953) have placed *E. rupicola* under the genus *Clathrus* and subgenus *Pitoscala. See* Clench & Turner 1952, p. 284.

Epitonium (Asperiscala) cf. E. apiculatum

Epitonium (Asperiscala) multistriatum

Subgenus *Asperiscala* Boury, 1909

Dall's Wentletrap

Epitonium (Asperiscala) cf. E. apiculatum (Dall, 1889), *Mus. Comp. Zool. Bull.* 18(1):310.
Gk. *epitonion* peg, turncock; L. *apicula* small bee.
SIZE: 4.5 mm.
COLOR: White.
SHAPE: Elongate conic, turriculate.
ORNAMENT OR SCULPTURE: Nine convex whorls attached by costae only. Axial sculpture consists of numerous bladelike costae. Eleven costae on body whorl; nuclear whorls smooth; first 3 postnuclear whorls possess costae which are low, cordlike, and far more numerous than those on remaining whorls. Spiral, threadlike cord only on first 3 postnuclear whorls. Later whorls have strong bladelike costae.
APERTURE: Circular with thickened, expanded lip. Umbilical area partially closed by parietal thickening. Columella short, arched.
OPERCULUM: Unknown.
PERIOSTRACUM: Not preserved.
HABITAT: Probably along shore. Epifaunal.
LOCALITIES: Entire.
OCCURRENCE: Uncommon in beach drift.
RANGE: South Carolina; Texas; Puerto Rico.
GEOLOGIC RANGE: Pleistocene to Holocene.
REMARKS: This could be an aberrant form of some other species, which may explain the limited distribution. *See* Clench & Turner 1952, p. 290.

Multiribbed Wentletrap

Epitonium (Asperiscala) multistriatum (Say, 1826), *J. Acad. Natur. Sci. Philadelphia* 5(1):208.
Gk. *epitonion* peg, turncock; L. *multi* many, *striatus* lined.
SIZE: 15 mm.
COLOR: White.
SHAPE: Elongate conic, turriculate.
ORNAMENT OR SCULPTURE: Eight to 10 strongly convex whorls, later ones unattached. Suture deep. Transverse sculpture consists of very numerous cordlike to low bladelike costae not angled at shoulder. Between these are many finely incised lines that do not cross ribs. Apical whorls much smaller in proportion to later ones and have more ribs. Anomphalous.
APERTURE: More oval than round with very narrowly expanded lip. Columella not defined; parietal lip tightly pressed to parietal area.
OPERCULUM: Corneous.
PERIOSTRACUM: Not preserved.
HABITAT: Offshore. Epifaunal.
LOCALITIES: Entire.
OCCURRENCE: Common in beach drift.
RANGE: Bermuda; Massachusetts south to Cape Canaveral and west to Texas; Brazil.
GEOLOGIC RANGE: Pleistocene to Holocene.
REMARKS: This shell is more delicate in appearance than the other *Epitoniums* and the many ribs make it easy to recognize. *See* Clench & Turner 1952, p. 292.

Epitonium (Asperiscala) novangliae

Epitonium (Asperiscala) sericifilum

New England Wentletrap
Epitonium (Aperiscala) novangliae
(Couthouy, 1838), *Boston J. Natur. Hist.* 2:96.
Gk. *epitonion* peg, turncock; L. *novus* new, Anglia=England.
SIZE: 14 mm.
COLOR: White, banded with light brown above and below periphery of whorl. Often light brown throughout.
SHAPE: Elongate conic, turriculate.
ORNAMENT OR SCULPTURE: Eight to 10 strongly convex whorls gradually increasing in size from apex, later whorls attached by costae only. Numerous bladelike to cordlike costae, latter as a result of costae being reflected back and down. Body whorl has 9 to 16 costae that are angled or hooked at shoulder. Spiral sculpture has reticulated pattern formed by numerous spiral threads crossed by finer transverse lines. Magnification may be needed to detect latter. No basal ridge.
APERTURE: Subcircular with narrow expanded lip. Parietal lip only moderately thickened, pressed to body whorl above umbilicus.
OPERCULUM: Corneous, dark brown, paucispiral.
PERIOSTRACUM: Not preserved.
HABITAT: Offshore. Epifaunal.
LOCALITIES: Entire.
OCCURRENCE: Common in beach drift.
RANGE: Bermuda; Massachusetts; Virginia south to Campeche Bank; Brazil.
GEOLOGIC RANGE: Pliocene to Holocene.
REMARKS: This is the most common *Epitonium* on southern Padre Island. Look for the spiral striations between costae. *See* Clench & Turner 1952, p. 306.

Epitonium (Aperiscala) sericifilum
(Dall, 1889), *Mus. Comp. Zool. Bull.* 18(1):313.
Gk. *epitonion* peg, turncock; L. *sericum* silk, *filum* thread.
SIZE: 5.1–10 mm.
COLOR: Mat white.
SHAPE: Slender, elongate conic, turriculate.
ORNAMENT OR SCULPTURE: Ten convex whorls, gradually increasing from apex. Suture moderately defined. Transverse costae numerous, oblique, low. Spiral threads numerous but do not cross costae. No basal ridge. Anomphalous.
APERTURE: Subcircular. Outer lip slightly thickened. No parietal shield.
OPERCULUM: Corneous.
PERIOSTRACUM: Not preserved.
HABITAT: Inlet areas. Epifaunal.
LOCALITIES: Entire.
OCCURRENCE: Uncommon in beach drift.
RANGE: Texas; Honduras.
GEOLOGIC RANGE: ? to Holocene.
REMARKS: Little is known of this species; lip of figured specimen is broken. It is easily recognized by the close, oblique ribs and angled periphery of whorls. *See* Clench & Turner 1952, p. 217.

Depressiscala nautlae

Janthina (Jodina) globosa

Genus *Depressiscala* Boury, 1909

Depressiscala nautlae (Mörch, 1874),
Forening i Kjöbenhavn 17:265.
L. *depressus* press down, *scala* stair-case, *nauta* sailor.
SIZE: 15 mm.
COLOR: Reddish brown, darker at early whorls with whitish ribs.
SHAPE: Slender, elongate conic, tur-riculate.
ORNAMENT OR SCULPTURE: Ten to 21 convex, attached whorls. Trans-verse costae numerous, low, irregu-lar width with slight angles on shoulder of whorls. No spiral sculpture; no basal ridge. Anom-phalous.
APERTURE: Oval with slightly thick-ened lip. Parietal area smooth, tightly pressed to body whorl. Col-umella short, arched.
OPERCULUM: Corneous, thin, yellow brown, paucispiral.
PERIOSTRACUM: Not preserved.
HABITAT: Offshore. Epifaunal.
LOCALITIES: Extreme south.
OCCURRENCE: Rare in beach drift.
RANGE: North Carolina; Florida; Texas; southern Mexico; Bahamas; Cuba (discontinuous).
GEOLOGIC RANGE: ? to Holocene.
REMARKS: The all-over brown color and white ribs make this shell easily recognizable. *See* Clench & Turner 1952, p. 329.

Family JANTHINIDAE Leach, 1823

Genus *Janthina* Röding, 1798
Subgenus *Jodina* Mörch, 1860

Dwarf Purple Sea Snail
Janthina (Jodina) globosa Blainville, 1822, *Dict. Sci. Natur.* 24:155.
Gk. *janthinos* violet colored; L. *globus* ball.
SIZE: 6–19 mm.
COLOR: Deep violet.
SHAPE: Globose ovate.
ORNAMENT OR SCULPTURE: Thin shell faintly striated, with striae follow-ing edge of aperture. At indentation of latter they curve, forming distinct keel on last whorl.
APERTURE: Outer lip deeply indent-ed at mid-whorl point.
OPERCULUM: None.
PERIOSTRACUM: None visible.
HABITAT: Pelagic.
LOCALITIES: Entire.
OCCURRENCE: Uncommon.
RANGE: Worldwide.
GEOLOGIC RANGE: ? to Holocene.
REMARKS: The float is comparatively small. Egg cases of this hermaphro-dite are pear-shaped and contain about 75 eggs. Abbott (1974) refers to this species as *J. exigua* Lamarck, 1816, while Keen (1971) calls it *J. globosa*. Syn. *J. umblicata* Orbigny, 1940; "*J. exigua* Lamarck" of authors, not Lamarck, 1816. *See* Laursen 1953; Bayer 1963; Bingham & Al-bertson 1974.

Janthina (Janthina) janthina

Janthina (Janthina) pallida

Subgenus *Janthina* s.s.

Common Purple Sea Snail

Janthina (Janthina) janthina (Linné, 1758), *Syst. Natur.*, 10th ed., p. 772.
Gk. *janthinos* violet colored.
SIZE: 32 mm.
COLOR: Purple on basal part of shell, lavender or white above. (Floats with purple side up.)
SHAPE: Low conic; body whorl very large and gently angular.
ORNAMENT OR SCULPTURE: Smooth, very fragile.
APERTURE: More or less subquadrate with columellar edge almost vertical. Outer lip very delicate, lower edge horizontal.
OPERCULUM: None.
PERIOSTRACUM: None visible.
HABITAT: Pelagic in warm seas.
LOCALITIES: Entire.
OCCURRENCE: Seasonally common.
RANGE: Pelagic in most warm seas.
GEOLOGIC RANGE: ? to Holocene.
REMARKS: The foot builds a float by trapping air bubbles in mucus. The animal exudes a purple stain when disturbed. Hermaphrodite. Viviparous. Carnivorous, feeding on Portuguese men-of-war, *Velella*, and other violet-colored coelenterates. It is "feast or famine" for the collector: a strong southeast wind in the spring will literally cover the beach with them; the next year they might not appear at all. Beware of the Portuguese men-of-war that wash in with them (see chapter 5). *See* Laursen 1953; Bayer 1963; Bingham & Albertson 1974.

Pale Purple Sea Snail

Janthina (Janthina) pallida (Thompson, 1841), *Annu. Natur. Hist.* 5:96.
Gk. *janthinos* violet colored; L. *pallidus* pale.
SIZE: 12–18 mm.
COLOR: Purplish white with pale lavender on early whorls and along margin of outer lip.
SHAPE: Globose conic.
ORNAMENT OR SCULPTURE: Appears smooth but has fine, irregular axial growth lines. Body whorl large, rounded, swollen.
APERTURE: Subquadrate, somewhat flaring at base. Thin outer margin of lip slightly sinuate near center where float is attached. Interior violet along columella and base, fainter over remainder.
OPERCULUM: None.
PERIOSTRACUM: None visible.
HABITAT: Pelagic in warm seas.
LOCALITIES: Entire.
OCCURRENCE: Uncommon, seasonal.
RANGE: Pelagic in most warm seas.
GEOLOGIC RANGE: ? to Holocene.
REMARKS: Very easily confused with *J. prolongata*. Only recently recognized as occurring in this area. Attaches eggs to bottom of float. Hermaphrodite. Coll., Wilson. *See* Laursen 1953; Bayer 1963.

Janthina (Violetta) prolongata

Recluzia rollaniana

Subgenus *Violetta* Iredale, 1929

Globe Purple Sea Snail
Janthina (Violetta) prolongata Blainville, 1822, *Dict. Sci. Natur.* 24:155.
Gk. *janthinos* violet colored; L. *prolongare* long.
SIZE: 12–18 mm.
COLOR: Deep violet throughout.
SHAPE: Globose with low spire; body whorl very large.
ORNAMENT OR SCULPTURE: Smooth, very fragile. Very fine growth lines.
APERTURE: Subquadrate, very large. Columella vertical. Outer lip has sinuous margin; indentation marks point of attachment of float.
OPERCULUM: None.
PERIOSTRACUM: None visible.
HABITAT: Pelagic in warm seas.
LOCALITIES: Entire.
OCCURRENCE: Fairly common.
RANGE: Pelagic in warm waters; both coasts of United States.
GEOLOGIC RANGE: ? to Holocene.
REMARKS: Syn. *J. globosa* (Swainson, 1823) [not Blainville, 1822]. Attaches eggs to float. This shell does not occur in the numbers that *J. janthina* does after a windy spring day and is even more delicate than the others. Live specimens are best cleaned by "watering out" (see chapter 4, section on cleaning). Left in the sun they will fade and get dull. Coll., Wilson. *See* Laursen 1953; Bayer 1963; Bingham & Albertson 1974.

Genus *Recluzia* Petit de la Saussaye, 1853

Brown Sea Snail
Recluzia rollaniana Petit, 1853, *J. Conch.* [Paris] 5(4).
Dedicated to C. A. Récluz (d. 1873); dedicated to Rolland du Roguan (1812–1863).
SIZE: Diameter 13 mm, height 22 mm.
COLOR: White, but periostracum makes it appear brown.
SHAPE: Moderately elongate conic.
ORNAMENT OR SCULPTURE: Body whorl large, globose. Spire somewhat extended. Appears smooth but has fine, oblique growth lines. Fragile.
APERTURE: Oval, large. Lip very thin.
OPERCULUM: None.
PERIOSTRACUM: Thin, brown, completely coating shell, lacquerlike.
HABITAT: Pelagic in warm seas.
LOCALITIES: Port Aransas, south.
OCCURRENCE: Rare.
RANGE: Pelagic in most warm seas.
GEOLOGIC RANGE: ? to Holocene.
REMARKS: Looks like a large sargassum snail and more like a land snail than a marine snail. Uses its brown float as do *Janthina*. Feeds on *Minyas* sea anemones. Animal is yellow. Coll., Wilson. *See* Abbott 1963, p. 151.

Niso aegless

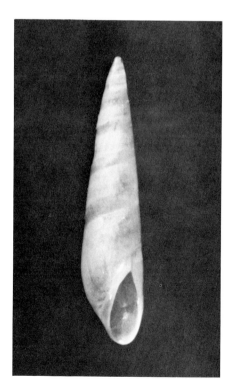

Eulima cf. *E. bilineatus*

Superfamily EULIMACEA Risso, 1826
Family EULIMIDAE Risso, 1826

Genus *Niso* Risso, 1826

Niso aegless Bush, 1885, *Annu. Rep. U.S. Comm. Fish.*, p. 155.
Gk. Nissus, king of Megara, *aegless* bright.
SIZE: 18 mm.
COLOR: Pale brown background with occasional mottlings of darker brown. Reddish brown line near base of suture on each whorl. Highly polished.
SHAPE: Elongate conic; apex acute.
ORNAMENT OR SCULPTURE: Ten to 11 flat-sided whorls. Angled at base. Base slightly convex. Transversely marked with fine reddish brown growth lines.
APERTURE: Pyriform. Sharp outer lip. Outlined with fine reddish brown line. Deeply omphalous with conical depression.
OPERCULUM: Corneous, pale yellowish brown; closes aperture.
PERIOSTRACUM: None visible.
HABITAT: Parasitic. Shallow bay areas, inlet influence. Epifaunal.
LOCALITIES: Aransas Bay.
OCCURRENCE: Rare.
RANGE: Cape Hatteras to Gulf of Mexico; Texas; Campeche Bank; Surinam; West Indies to Brazil.
GEOLOGIC RANGE: Pleistocene to Holocene.
REMARKS: Active white animal readily moves forward and backward. Formerly called *N. interrupta* (Sowerby, 1834). Coll., Young.

Genus *Eulima* Risso, 1826 = [*Strombiformis* of authors, not Da Costa, 1778]

Two-Lined Melanella
Eulima cf. *E. bilineatus* (Alder, 1848), *Moll. Northumberland & Durham*, p. 47.
Gk. *eu* good, original; L. *lima* file, *bis* twice, *lineatus* lined.
SIZE: 8 mm.
COLOR: Whitish with two brownish lines on each whorl. Polished.
SHAPE: Elongate conic, very slender.
ORNAMENT OR SCULPTURE: Ten flattened whorls, sutures fairly distinct. Gradually tapers to sharp apex that may be deflected.
APERTURE: Elongated pyriform. Entire. Outer lip sharp. Columella concave.
OPERCULUM: Corneous.
PERIOSTRACUM: Thin, black.
HABITAT: Thought to be ectoparasitic on holothurians in shallow waters. Epifaunal.
LOCALITIES: Entire.
OCCURRENCE: Uncommon in beach drift.
RANGE: Europe; North Carolina to West Indies; Texas; Brazil.
GEOLOGIC RANGE: ? to Holocene.
REMARKS: Animal has a long proboscis used to suck the juices of its prey. There is no gill or radula. [*Strombiformis bilineata*].

Balcis cf. *B. arcuata*

Balcis cf. *B. jamaicensis*

Genus *Balcis* 'Gray,' Leach 1847 =
[*Melanella* of authors]

Curved Melanella
Balcis cf. *B. arcuata*, C. B. Adams,
1850, *Contr. Conch.* 7:110. Balkis, the
Arabic name for the Queen of
Sheba; L. *arcus* curved.
SIZE: 4 mm.
COLOR: Glossy white.
SHAPE: Ovate conic.
ORNAMENT OR SCULPTURE: Ten con-
vex whorls with lightly impressed
suture. Fine impressed spiral line
above suture marks smooth shell.
Spire with axis curved to extraordi-
nary degree in upper whorls.
APERTURE: Rather long ovate.
OPERCULUM: Not preserved.
PERIOSTRACUM: Not preserved.
HABITAT: Ectoparasitic on sea
cucumbers. Epifaunal.
LOCALITIES: Central and south.
OCCURRENCE: Uncommon in beach
drift.
RANGE: North Carolina; Texas; West
Indies.
GEOLOGIC RANGE: Pliocene to
Holocene.
REMARKS: The type specimen has
been lost. [*Melanella arcuata*].

Jamaica Melanella
Balcis cf. *B. jamaicensis* (C. B.
Adams, 1845), *Proc. Boston Soc.
Natur. Hist.* 2:6. Balkis, the Arabic
name for the Queen of Sheba; from
Jamaica.
SIZE: 6–12 mm.
COLOR: Glossy white.
SHAPE: Elongate conic.
ORNAMENT OR SCULPTURE: Twelve to
14 flat-sided whorls. Polished
whorls taper to sharp apex that is
slightly bent. Sutures not well de-
fined. Anomphalous.
APERTURE: Pyriform, slender. Outer
lip thin but slightly thickened at
base. Columella concave.
OPERCULUM: Corneous.
PERIOSTRACUM: Thin, black.
HABITAT: Ectoparasitic. Bays. Epifaunal.
LOCALITIES: Entire.
OCCURRENCE: Fairly common in
beach drift.
RANGE: Florida; Texas; Carmen,
Campeche, Mexico; Gulf of Campeche; Costa Rica?; West Indies.
GEOLOGIC RANGE: Pliocene to
Holocene.
REMARKS: This may be *Melanella in-
termedia* Cantraine, 1835, but according to Abbott (1958*b*, p. 106) it is
not. It has been referred to as *B.
conoidea* Kurtz & Stimpson, 1851,
but it lacks the distinct basal ridge
and rhomboidal aperture of that
species. *See* Clench & Turner 1950*a*,
p. 296; Perry & Schwengel 1955, p.
116; Abbott 1958*b*, p. 106.

Graphis underwoodae (Bartsch 1947, pl. 1)

Henrya goldmani (Bartsch 1947, pl. 3)

Family ACLIDIDAE G. O. Sars, 1878

Genus *Graphis* Jeffreys, 1867

Graphis underwoodae Bartsch, 1947, *Smithsonian Misc. Coll.* 106(20):6. Gk. *graphis* writing; dedicated to Mrs. A. V. Underwood, Florida collector.
SIZE: 2.9 mm.
COLOR: Yellowish white.
SHAPE: Elongate turriculate.
ORNAMENT OR SCULPTURE: Nucleus single, well-rounded, smooth turn forming blunt apex. Postnuclear whorls rather high between summit and suture, strongly rounded. Sculpture consists of strong, sinuous, almost vertical axial ribs with 30 on body whorl. Spiral sculpture consists of 9 threads about half the thickness of axial ribs, producing a reticulated pattern. Suture strongly constricted. Base inflated, strongly rounded, marked with weak continuations of ribs and threads. Anomphalous.
APERTURE: Oval. Outer lip thin; inner lip concave, slightly reflected.
OPERCULUM: Light yellow, suboval.
PERIOSTRACUM: Not reported.
HABITAT: Shallow water, in littoral-level debris. Epifaunal.
LOCALITIES: Entire.
OCCURRENCE: Rare.
RANGE: West coast of Florida; Texas.
GEOLOGIC RANGE: ? to Holocene.
REMARKS: On casual examination this species appears to be a *Turbonilla*, but examine the protoconch carefully—it is normal and not heterostrophic. Reported in *Texas Conchologist* 7(5):53. I have not collected this one yet.

Genus *Henrya* Bartsch, 1947

Henrya goldmani Bartsch, 1947, *Smithsonian Misc. Coll.* 106(20):14. Dedicated to Henry G. Bartsch, author's son; dedicated to E. A. and L. G. Goldman, collectors.
SIZE: 2 mm.
COLOR: Translucent.
SHAPE: Elongate conic.
ORNAMENT OR SCULPTURE: Nucleus consists of single, strongly rounded, glassy turn which forms very blunt apex. Postnuclear whorls very strongly rounded and marked by incremental lines which on early turns form faint, hairlike, slanting riblets. Suture strongly constricted. Base well rounded, narrowly phaneromphalous, marked with incremental lines only.
APERTURE: Oval. Outer lip thin; inner lip reflected over the base. Parietal wall covered by thick inductura.
OPERCULUM: Not reported.
PERIOSTRACUM: Not reported.
HABITAT: Hypersaline lagoons.
LOCALITIES: Entire.
OCCURRENCE: Fairly common in beach drift.
RANGE: Texas; Yucatán.
GEOLOGIC RANGE: ? to Holocene.
REMARKS: This species has been found alive on mud flats near Port Aransas. Reported in *Texas Conchologist* 1971, 7(8):90. I have not yet collected this one.

Strombus alatus

Superfamily STROMBACEA
Rafinesque, 1815
Family STROMBIDAE Rafinesque,
1815

Genus *Strombus* Linné, 1758

Fighting Conch
Strombus alatus Gmelin, 1791, *Syst.
Natur.*, 13th ed., p. 3513.
Gk. *strombos* a spiral shell named by
Aristotle; L. *alatus* winged.
SIZE: 75–100 mm.
COLOR: Dark reddish brown to
lighter brown; some mottled or with
zigzag markings.
SHAPE: Conic.
ORNAMENT OR SCULPTURE: Spire has
8 whorls; body whorl is four-fifths
of total length of heavy, solid shell.
Wide shoulders with or without
short spines. Spiral striations near
base. Sutures distinct. Anompha-
lous.
APERTURE: Long, narrow. Lip has
broad outward flare. Interior
polished. Somewhat flared siphonal
notch at base and rounded notch in
lip just above it.
OPERCULUM: Corneous, clawlike;
does not close aperture.
PERIOSTRACUM: Thin, velvetlike
coating.
HABITAT: Intertidal to about 18 meters (10 fathoms). Epifaunal.
LOCALITIES: Entire.
OCCURRENCE: Uncommon beach
shell.
RANGE: South Carolina; both sides
of Florida; Texas.
GEOLOGIC RANGE: Miocene to
Holocene.
REMARKS: This grazing scavenger
has well-developed eyes on long
eye stalks on the head. The long,
narrow foot tipped with its clawlike
operculum moves the animal about
in awkward leaps. With this hop-
ping motion it can right itself and
return to the water if stranded by a
wave. Hurricane Carla (1961)
stranded thousands on the southern half of Padre Island. Sexes are
separate; the male brings his heavy
shell up alongside the female until
the shells touch, then fertilizes the
female with a long verge that is
thrust under her shell. Eggs are laid
in gelatinous ribbons. *See* Clench &
Abbott 1941, pp. 1–16.

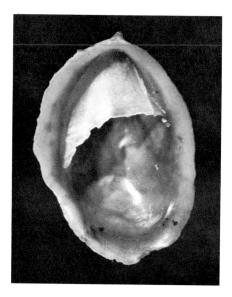

Crepidula (Crepidula) convexa

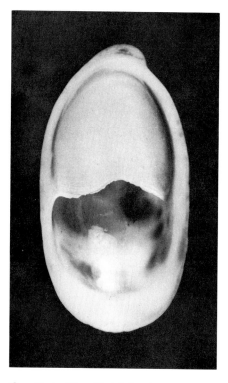

Crepidula (Crepidula) fornicata

Superfamily CALYPTRAEACEA Blainville, 1824
Family CALYPTRAEIDAE Blainville, 1824
Subfamily CREPIDULINAE Fleming, 1799

Genus *Crepidula* Lamarck, 1799
Subgenus *Crepidula* s.s.

Faded Slipper Shell
Crepidula (Crepidula) convexa Say, 1822, *J. Acad. Natur. Sci. Philadelphia* 2(1):226.
L. *crepidula* a small sandal, *convexus* vaulted.
SIZE: Length 12 mm, width 8 mm.
COLOR: Translucent tan or mottled with reddish brown. Internal septum white.
SHAPE: Limpetlike, low, oval with the apex near the margin. Varies corresponding to the shape of attachment site.
ORNAMENT OR SCULPTURE: Smooth with centrally located apex.
APERTURE: Very large oval with thin margin. Internal deck, or septum, deep-seated, convex; supports soft parts.
OPERCULUM: None.
PERIOSTRACUM: None visible.
HABITAT: Intertidal to moderate depths on shell, rocks, grass. Epifaunal.
LOCALITIES: Entire.
OCCURRENCE: Common.
RANGE: Bermuda; Massachusetts to Florida; Texas; Yucatán; Quintana Roo; West Indies; California.
GEOLOGIC RANGE: Upper Miocene to Holocene.
REMARKS: Many are found on *Argopecten amplicostatus* in the bays. *See* Franz 1970; Bandel 1976, p. 264.

Common Atlantic Slipper Shell
Crepidula (Crepidula) fornicata (Linné, 1758), *Syst. Natur.*, 10th ed., p. 1257.
L. *crepidula* a small sandal, *fornicata* vaulted.
SIZE: 51 mm.
COLOR: Dirty white to tan with mottlings of brown shades.
SHAPE: Limpetlike, oval oblique; curved to fit place of attachment.
ORNAMENT OR SCULPTURE: Smooth except for fine growth lines. Body whorl major part of shell. Apex turned to one side.
APERTURE: Oval, oblique, with thin margin. Polished interior. Deck occupies about half of aperture; white margin sinuous.
OPERCULUM: None.
PERIOSTRACUM: None visible.
HABITAT: One to 8 meters (6 fathoms). Epifaunal on exoskeleton.
LOCALITIES: Entire.
OCCURRENCE: Common.
RANGE: Canada to Florida and Texas; Yucatán; introduced to California and England.
GEOLOGIC RANGE: Lower Miocene to Holocene.
REMARKS: Mucociliary feeding. The adult shell is sedentary and tends to pile up in stacks of up to 19 individuals that gradually diminish in size. Frequently, on dead olive shells. The stack of protandric mollusks will have the right margin of each member in contact with the right margin of the one it is on. The bottom and larger animals are female, the top are males, and those in between are in transitional stages. The eggs are brooded in the female mantle cavity. *See* J. K. Johnson 1972; Bandel 1976, p. 264.

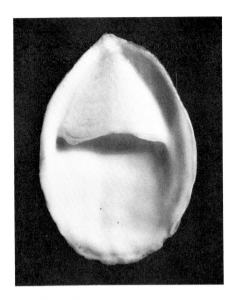

Crepidula (Ianacus) plana

Lamellaria cf. *L. leucosphaera*

Subgenus *Ianacus* Mörch, 1852

Eastern White Slipper Shell
Crepidula (Ianacus) plana Say, 1822, *J. Acad. Natur. Sci. Philadelphia* 2(1):226.
L. *crepidula* a small sandal, *planus* level, flat.
SIZE: Length up to 30 mm.
COLOR: White.
SHAPE: Elongate oval, flat; conforms to attachment site.
ORNAMENT OR SCULPTURE: Smooth except for fine growth lines. Apex depressed.
APERTURE: Large, oval with thin margin. Deck about half length of shell, notched to one side. Polished.
OPERCULUM: None.
PERIOSTRACUM: Thin, yellowish.
HABITAT: Intertidal to moderate depths. Epifaunal.
LOCALITIES: Entire.
OCCURRENCE: Common.
RANGE: Bermuda; Canada to Florida; Gulf states; Texas; Gulf of Mexico to Quintana Roo; rare in West Indies; Surinam; Brazil.
GEOLOGIC RANGE: Lower Miocene to Holocene.
REMARKS: Not as particular as to attachment site as are *C. fornicata* and *C. convexa*—dead shell, old bottles, piers, oysters, tires, all will do. As a result the shape of this flat shell can be quite varied. Eggs are brooded under the shell. *See* Bandel 1976, p. 265.

Superfamily LAMELLARIACEA Orbigny, 1841
Family LAMELLARIIDAE Orbigny 1841 = [VELUTINIDAE Gray, 1840]
Subfamily LAMELLARIINAE Orbigny, 1841

Genus *Lamellaria* Montagu, 1815

Rang's Lamellaria
Lamellaria cf. *L. leucosphaera* Schwengel, 1942, *Nautilus* 56(1).
L. dim. of *lamina* plate, leaf; Gk. *leukos* white, *sphaera* globe.
SIZE: 6 mm.
COLOR: Translucent, glassy, white. Nearly invisible.
SHAPE: Auriform, like *Sinum* but more globose.
ORNAMENT OR SCULPTURE: Very fragile, thin. Two and one-half to 3 whorls; body whorl very large. Surface has fine, irregular growth lines.
APERTURE: Very large, slightly oblique oval. Columella very thin.
OPERCULUM: None.
PERIOSTRACUM: None.
HABITAT: On living whip coral, other ascidians, *Hydrozoa* and *Alcyonaria*. Epifaunal.
LOCALITIES: Port Aransas to Port Isabel.
OCCURRENCE: Rare.
RANGE: Gulf of Mexico; Puerto Rico.
GEOLOGIC RANGE: Holocene.
REMARKS: Animal envelops the shell. Looks like a small bit of milky jelly when found alive. Difficult to detect. Carnivorous on ascidians; deposits eggs in crevices of these colonial animals. Coll., Young. *See* Schwengel 1942.

Trivia (Pusula) suffusa

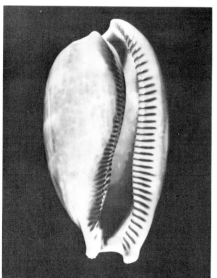

Cypraea (Macrocypraea) cervus

Superfamily TRIVIACEA Gray,
1852
Family TRIVIIDAE Gray, 1852
Subfamily TRIVIINAE Troschel,
1863

Genus *Trivia* Gray, 1852
Subgenus *Pusula* Jousseaume, 1884

Suffuse Trivia

Trivia (Pusula) suffusa (Gray, 1832),
Conch. Illus. no. 7, fig. 41.
Trivia, a surname of Diana, goddess
of the hunt; L. *suffusus* suffused.
SIZE: 12 mm.
COLOR: Pinkish with suffused
brownish mottlings and specks.
Underside white.
SHAPE: Ovate.
ORNAMENT OR SCULPTURE: Dorsal
groove well defined. Ribs beaded.
APERTURE: Long, narrow, polished.
Canals at both ends, touched with
pink. Lip rolled inward, sculptured
with 18 to 23 fine ribs.
OPERCULUM: None.
PERIOSTRACUM: None.
HABITAT: Offshore on tunicates and
rock. Epifaunal.
LOCALITIES: Entire.
OCCURRENCE: Rare beach shell.
RANGE: Southeastern Florida; Texas;
Campeche Bank; West Indies;
Brazil.
GEOLOGIC RANGE: Miocene to
Holocene.
REMARKS: Carnivorous on tunicates.
Lays eggs in walls of tunicates (fig.
24). Coll., Young.

Superfamily CYPRAEACEA
Rafinesque, 1815
Family CYPRAEIDAE Rafinesque,
1815
Subfamily CYPRAEINAE Rafin-
esque, 1815

Genus *Cypraea* Linné, 1758
Subgenus *Macrocypraea* Schilder,
1930

Atlantic Deer Cowrie

Cypraea (Macrocypraea) cervus Linné,
1771, *Mant. Plant.* 2:548.
L. Cypris, Venus, *cervus* deer.
SIZE: 75–125 mm.
COLOR: Polished light brown, with
large, round, white spots on dorsal
side. Whitish dorsal line.
SHAPE: Elongate oval; spire con-
cealed.
ORNAMENT OR SCULPTURE: Smooth,
polished.
APERTURE: Long, narrow. Outer lip
rolled inward, brownish without
spots. Edge outlined with regular,
small, alternating brown and white
riblets. Similar but less distinct riblets on inner lip. Purplish on interior.
OPERCULUM: None.
PERIOSTRACUM: None.
HABITAT: Offshore reefs. Epifaunal.
LOCALITIES: Port Aransas, south.
OCCURRENCE: Uncommon beach
shell.
RANGE: Southeastern Florida to
Yucatán; Brazil.
GEOLOGIC RANGE: ? to Holocene.
REMARKS: The mantle which envelops the shell is mottled, pinkish
brown and mauve white, entirely
covered with short papillae (fig. 11).
At rest, the shell is covered, but
when touched the animal draws
into the shell. The female lays eggs
in a gelatinous mass of 500 to 1,500
capsules, which she broods. This
carnivore grazes on algae and colonial invertebrates. Tunnell (1974)
reports nocturnal habits. The occasional shell found on the beach will
usually have a smooth worn place
on the underside parallel to the
aperture. Panamic vicariant is *C.
cervinetta* Kiener, 1843. *See* Crovo
1971, p. 292.

Simnialena marferula

Simnialena uniplicata

Family OVULIDAE Gray, 1853

Genus *Simnialena* Cate, 1973

Sea Whip Simnia
Simnialena marferula Cate, 1973, *Veliger* 15:suppl., 75.
Simnia, according to Risso, one of the Nereids; Gk. *leno* anything with a troughlike cavity; L. *mar* sea, *ferula* whip.
SIZE: 8.4 mm.
COLOR: Orange yellow to medium rose, glossy.
SHAPE: Elongate, tapering at both ends.
ORNAMENT OR SCULPTURE: Smooth, with numerous irregularly incised, transverse lines covering entire dorsal area. Base finely transversely striate throughout.
APERTURE: Broad, widening even more to front. Outer lip fairly heavily, roundly calloused. Outer surface uneven, subcrenulate.
OPERCULUM: None.
PERIOSTRACUM: None.
HABITAT: On sea whip coral *Leptogorgia setacea*. Epifaunal.
LOCALITIES: Entire.
OCCURRENCE: Common in beach drift.
RANGE: Texas coast.
GEOLOGIC RANGE: ? to Holocene.
REMARKS: Cate (in litt.) says that this has been called *Neosimnia uniplicata* (Sowerby II, 1848). The latter is a long slender form which does not have any dorsal striation but is striated at each end of the shell. *See* Cate 1973, p. 75.

Simnialena uniplicata (G. B. Sowerby II, 1848), *Thes. Conch.*, p. 478.
Simnia, according to Risso, one of the Nereids; Gk. *leno* anything with a troughlike cavity; L. *uni* one, *plicatus* folded.
SIZE: 20.2 mm.
COLOR: Deep rose brown overall, except that outer lip, front base, adaxial carina, and portions of rear terminal beak white.
SHAPE: Long, narrow, subcylindrical; ends tapering.
ORNAMENT OR SCULPTURE: Smooth, glossy except for incised striae restricted to either end.
APERTURE: Broad, flaring toward front. Outer lip thinly, roundly thickened, with weak callus shouldering above.
OPERCULUM: None.
PERIOSTRACUM: None.
HABITAT: On soft coral *Eugorgia virgulata*. Epifaunal.
LOCALITIES: Port Aransas, south.
OCCURRENCE: Uncommon in beach drift.
RANGE: Virginia to both coasts of Florida; possibly Honduras and east coast of Central America.
GEOLOGIC RANGE: ? to Holocene.
REMARKS: Previously misidentified (J. Andrews 1971, p. 98) as *Neosimnia acicularis* (Lamarck, 1810), which is *Cymbula acicularis*. Coll., Young. *See* Patton 1972; Cate 1973, p. 77.

Pseudocyphoma intermedium

Polinices (Neverita) duplicatus

Genus *Pseudocyphoma* Cate, 1973

Single-Toothed Simnia
Pseudocyphoma intermedium (G. B. Sowerby I, 1828), *Zool. J. London* 4:158.
Gk. *pseudo* false *Cyphoma*; L. *inter* between, *medius* middle.
SIZE: 30 mm.
COLOR: White, glossy.
SHAPE: Shell ovate oblong (diamond-shaped), somewhat acuminated at both ends, rather more so at the upper than at the lower.
ORNAMENT OR SCULPTURE: Back with transverse, raised rounded angle rather above middle; smooth, semi-glossy, except for fine transverse striae above either end.
APERTURE: Narrow at upper end, broader at lower. Columellar lip with single oblique plait. Outer lip thickened; inner edge smooth, without teeth.
OPERCULUM: None.
PERIOSTRACUM: None.
HABITAT: On soft corals. Epifaunal.
LOCALITIES: Port Aransas.
OCCURRENCE: Rare.
RANGE: Texas; Dominican Republic; West Indies; Surinam.
GEOLOGIC RANGE: ? to Holocene.
REMARKS: Figured twice and identified as *Cyphoma intermedium* and misidentified as *C. mcgintyi* (Pilsbry, 1939) in J. Andrews (1971, pp. 98–99). Washed in alive on the beach with the colorful, maculated animal enveloping the shell following a severe freeze in January, 1962. It lived in an aquarium for several months until consumed by an anemone. Less humped specimens are found in spoil banks along the ship channel. *See* Cate 1973, p. 69.

Superfamily NATICACEA (Swainson), Gray, 1840
Family NATICIDAE (Swainson), Gray, 1840
Subfamily POLINICINAE Gray, 1847

Genus *Polinices* Montfort, 1810
Subgenus *Neverita* Risso, 1826

Shark's Eye
Polinices (Neverita) duplicatus (Say, 1822), *J. Acad. Natur. Sci. Philadelphia* 2(1):247.
Gk. Polinices, son of Oedipus; L. *duplicatus* doubled.
SIZE: Diameter 26–37 mm.
COLOR: Porcelaneous, glossy, gray to tan, often strikingly marked with orange brown. Underside whitish. Callus in bay specimens often rich purple.
SHAPE: Globose, low spire, expanded body whorl; bay specimens have higher spires than Gulf ones.
ORNAMENT OR SCULPTURE: Smooth with fine growth lines.
APERTURE: Large, subcircular. Outer lip thin. Columella oblique; umbilicus deep, partly closed by heavy callus. No siphonal canal.
OPERCULUM: Corneous, thin, dark amber color, with shiny silver margin when fresh.
PERIOSTRACUM: Thin, glossy.
HABITAT: Shallow waters of both bay and Gulf. Infaunal.
LOCALITIES: Entire.
OCCURRENCE: Common.
RANGE: Cape Cod to Florida and Gulf states.
GEOLOGIC RANGE: Miocene to Holocene.
REMARKS: This predator has a propodium that is thrown over the head as it plows through the sand in search of bivalves and snails. It wraps its foot about the prey and begins the slow process of drilling a neat, round hole in the shell, inserting the proboscis, and rasping out

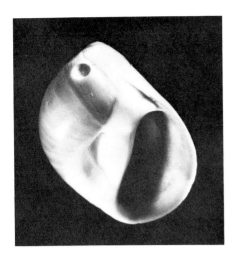

Polinices (Polinices) hepaticus

the soft parts with its radula. It often tires before completing a hole and will not feed unless buried. The female builds a collar of mucus and sand over the margin of her aperture when she spawns (fig. 14). *See* Hanks 1953; H. J. Turner 1958, p. 1; Huebner 1972.

Subgenus *Polinices* s.s.

Brown Moon Shell
Polinices (Polinices) hepaticus (Röding, 1798), *Mus. Boltenianum*, p. 21. Gk. Polinices, son of Oedipus; L. *hepaticus* the liver, liver brown.
SIZE: 25–51 mm.
COLOR: Exterior purplish brown and orange brown.
SHAPE: Globose, elongate oval.
ORNAMENT OR SCULPTURE: Polished, heavy. About 3 whorls. Body whorl dominates shell. Fine, irregular growth lines.
APERTURE: Semilunar. Columella and interior of shell white. Umbilicus white, large, deep.
OPERCULUM: Corneous, light brown, thin, paucispiral.
PERIOSTRACUM: Thin and glossy.
HABITAT: Shallow, sandy bottoms offshore. Infaunal.
LOCALITIES: Port Aransas, south.
OCCURRENCE: Rare beach shell.
RANGE: Southeastern Florida; Texas; West Indies; Surinam; Brazil.
GEOLOGIC RANGE: ? to Holocene.
REMARKS: Predatory carnivore. Bores holes in bivalves with radula. Deposits eggs in sand collars (fig. 24). Figured specimen has a hole begun by another predatory snail. Coll., Corpus Christi Museum.

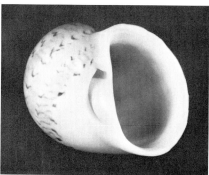

Natica (Naticarius) canrena

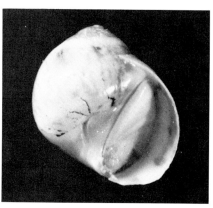

Natica (Tectonatica) pusilla

Subfamily NATICINAE Swainson, 1840

Genus *Natica* Scopoli, 1777
Subgenus *Naticarius* Dumeril, 1806

Colorful Atlantic Natica
Natica (Naticarius) canrena (Linné, 1758), *Syst. Natur.*, 10th ed., p. 776.
L. *natica* buttock; *canrena* from natives of Malay Archipelago, meaning unknown.
SIZE: 25–51 mm.
COLOR: White or cream with variable brown markings that may be axial zigzag marks superimposed over spiral bands alternating tan and white.
SHAPE: Subglobular.
ORNAMENT OR SCULPTURE: Smooth; spire depressed; body whorl expanded. Faint waves near sutures.
APERTURE: Large, semilunar. Thin outer lip. Callus large, white, entering deep umbilicus. Brownish on interior.
OPERCULUM: Calcareous, 10 spiral grooves on exterior. White outside, brownish inside. Columellar margin finely serrate.
PERIOSTRACUM: Glossy, thin.
HABITAT: Sandy bottoms beyond low tide. Infaunal.
LOCALITIES: Entire.
OCCURRENCE: Rare beach shell.
RANGE: Bermuda; southeastern United States to West Indies; Texas; Campeche Bank; Yucatán; Surinam; Brazil.
GEOLOGIC RANGE: Miocene to Holocene.
REMARKS: Lives offshore, seldom reaches the beaches. Is a predator on bivalves. Coll., Corpus Christi Museum.

Subgenus *Tectonatica* Sacco, 1890

Miniature Natica
Natica (Tectonatica) pusilla Say, 1822, *J. Acad. Natur. Sci. Philadelphia* 2(1):257.
L. *natica* buttock, *pusilla* very small.
SIZE: Diameter 6–8 mm.
COLOR: White to fawn brown, faint reddish brown markings.
SHAPE: Subglobular; spire depressed, body whorl expanded.
ORNAMENT OR SCULPTURE: Smooth with fine growth lines, porcelaneous.
APERTURE: Large, semilunar. Outer lip thin. Columella oblique. Callus strong, practically covering umbilicus, but often has small opening next to umbilical callus.
OPERCULUM: Calcareous, smooth.
PERIOSTRACUM: Thin, glossy.
HABITAT: Shallow inlet areas. Infaunal.
LOCALITIES: Entire.
OCCURRENCE: Fairly common.
RANGE: Eastern United States; Gulf states; Carmen, Campeche, Mexico; Gulf of Campeche; West Indies; Surinam; northeastern Brazil.
GEOLOGIC RANGE: Pliocene to Holocene.
REMARKS: This tiny *Natica* can be confused with juvenile *Polinices duplicatus*, but the operculum of *Polinices* is corneous.

Sinum maculatum

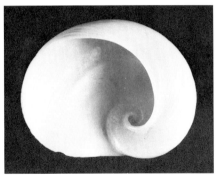

Sinum perspectivum

Subfamily SININAE Woodring, 1928

Genus *Sinum* Röding, 1798

Maculated Baby's Ear
Sinum maculatum (Say, 1831), *Amer. Conch.*, p. 176.
L. *sinus* a bend or curve, *macula* spotted.
SIZE: Diameter 25–51 mm.
COLOR: All brown or blotched with brown.
SHAPE: Auriform, slightly elevated.
ORNAMENT OR SCULPTURE: About 3 whorls. Sutures only slightly impressed. Very weak spiral growth lines on top of whorls.
APERTURE: Large, rounded. Outer lip sharp. Columella curved.
OPERCULUM: Corneous.
PERIOSTRACUM: Thin, yellowish brown.
HABITAT: Offshore. Infaunal.
LOCALITIES: Extreme south.
OCCURRENCE: Rare beach shell.
RANGE: Southeastern United States to West Indies; Texas; Brazil.
GEOLOGIC RANGE: ? to Holocene.
REMARKS: Shell heavier and more elevated than *S. perspectivum*.

Common Baby's Ear
Sinum perspectivum (Say, 1831), *Amer. Conch.*, p. 175.
L. *sinus* a curve or fold, *perspectivus* to look through with perspective.
SIZE: Diameter 25–51 mm.
COLOR: White.
SHAPE: Auriform, greatly flattened; apex on same plane as body whorl.
ORNAMENT OR SCULPTURE: About 3 whorls. Sutures slightly impressed. Many fine spiral growth lines on top of whorls.
APERTURE: Large, rounded. Outer lip sharp. Columella curved.
OPERCULUM: Corneous, minute.
PERIOSTRACUM: Thin, yellowish brown.
HABITAT: Along outer beaches and inlet areas in sand. Infaunal.
LOCALITIES: Entire.
OCCURRENCE: Common.
RANGE: Bermuda; southeastern United States; Gulf states; Campeche Bank; West Indies; Surinam; Brazil.
GEOLOGIC RANGE: Miocene to Holocene.
REMARKS: Lives on sandy bottom in shallow water. Animal almost completely envelops the shell (fig. 11). Exudes a surprising quantity of clear mucus when touched. At low tides raccoon tracks have been found leading to and from freshly cleaned shells.

Phalium (Tylocassis) granulatum granulatum

Superfamily TONNACEA Suter, 1913
Family CASSIDAE Latreille, 1825

Genus *Phalium* Link, 1807
Subgenus *Tylocassis* Woodring, 1928

Scotch Bonnet
Phalium (Tylocassis) granulatum granulatum (Born, 1780), *Test. Mus. Caes. Vind.*, p. 248.
Gk. *phalias* with white patches; L. *granulatum* granulated.
SIZE: Length 25–100 mm.
COLOR: Background white or cream with spiral bands of regularly spaced yellowish brown squares.
SHAPE: Oval with slightly extended spire.
ORNAMENT OR SCULPTURE: Body whorl about three-fourths of shell length. Some specimens have small nodules on shoulder edge. Deeply grooved spirally, raised spiral cords are slightly convex and wider than spaces between them. Transverse sculpture of fine lines gives overall reticulated pattern. Occasionally a specimen will have varices on early whorls.
APERTURE: Semilunar, length of body whorl. Outer lip thickened, reflexed with regular, small teeth on both edges. Interior fawn colored. Parietal wall glazed, smooth with lower area pustulose. Short siphonal canal upturned to left.
OPERCULUM: Corneous, small, thin, semilunar, light brown.
PERIOSTRACUM: Thin, pale amber.
HABITAT: Just offshore in warm seas. Epifaunal.
LOCALITIES: Entire, more to south.
OCCURRENCE: Fairly common.
RANGE: Bermuda; North Carolina to Gulf states; West Indies; Surinam; Brazil.
GEOLOGIC RANGE: Pleistocene to Holocene.

REMARKS: Will live in the passes after a storm has reopened them. The predatory animal is cream colored with close dark spots of color and feeds on sand dollars and sea urchins. Eggs are laid in a tower of horny capsules (fig. 24). Panamic vicariant is *Cassis centiguadrata* (Valenciennes, 1832). *See* Clench 1944, p. 6; Abbott 1968*a*, pp. 157–159.

Cypraecassis testiculus

Tonna galea

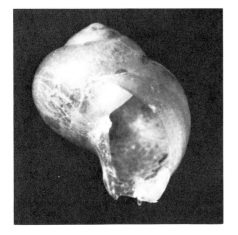

juvenile

Genus *Cypraecassis* Stutchbury, 1837

Reticulated Cowrie Helmet
Cypraecassis testiculus (Linné, 1758),
Syst. Natur., 10th ed., p. 736.
L. Cypris, Venus, *cassis* helmet, *testiculus* testicle, obovate shape.
SIZE: 25–75 mm.
COLOR: Pale orangish brown with white and purplish brown blotches.
SHAPE: Narrow oval with low spire.
ORNAMENT OR SCULPTURE: Seven to 8 rather solid whorls. Body whorl almost entire length. Early whorls spirally grooved; body whorl reticulated. Suture slightly indented.
APERTURE: Long, narrow. Outer lip thickened, reflexed, with teeth on inner margin. Parietal area heavily glazed, irregularly plicate. Parietal wall and outer lip creamy with 2 or 3 bright orange streaks.
OPERCULUM: None in adults.
PERIOSTRACUM: Not preserved.
HABITAT: Offshore reefs. Epifaunal.
LOCALITIES: Extreme south.
OCCURRENCE: Rare.
RANGE: North Carolina to Texas; Costa Rica; West Indies; Brazil.
GEOLOGIC RANGE: ? to Holocene.
REMARKS: Feeds on echinoderms. Female lays eggs under rocks or broken shell in greenish brown clusters of 100 or so capsules. Never found in large colonies. Animal is light brownish orange. Usually only fragments found on beach. *See* Clench & Abbott 1943, p. 1; Abbott 1968*a*, p. 71.

Family TONNIDAE Suter, 1913

Genus *Tonna* Brunnich, 1772

Giant Tun Shell
Tonna galea (Linné, 1758), *Syst. Natur.*, 10th ed., p. 734.
L. *tonna* a cask, *galea* helmet.
SIZE: Up to 160 mm.
COLOR: Creamy white to light coffee brown, generally uniform.
SHAPE: Globose; spire slightly extended, thin.
ORNAMENT OR SCULPTURE: Seven to 7½ very convex whorls. Body whorl dominates shell. Suture deep, channeled. Spiral sculpture consists of 19 to 21 rather broad, flattened ridges. Usually a finer ridge between 2 of larger ones on upper half of whorl. Fine axial growth lines. Umbilicate.
APERTURE: Subovate, large. Outer lip thin, crenulate until maturity. At maturity becomes reflexed and develops thickened ridge well below lip margin. Parietal area glazed. Columella short, twisted with ridge along outer edge that ends at siphonal canal.
OPERCULUM: None in adults.
PERIOSTRACUM: Thin, golden brown, somewhat deciduous.
HABITAT: Near-shore sandy bottoms and inlet areas. Epifaunal.
LOCALITIES: Entire.
OCCURRENCE: Uncommon to rare. Rarely taken alive in vicinity of Aransas ship channel.
RANGE: North Carolina to Florida; Gulf states; Campeche Bank; West Indies; Surinam; Brazil; Indo-Pacific; Mediterranean.
GEOLOGIC RANGE: ? to Holocene.
REMARKS: The free-swimming, pelagic young may be found in the spring in beach drift. These embryonic shells are smooth, golden brown in color, and somewhat flexible. They have 3 to 4 whorls and the aperture is closed with a tightly fitting operculum. In winter months on the upper Mexican Gulf

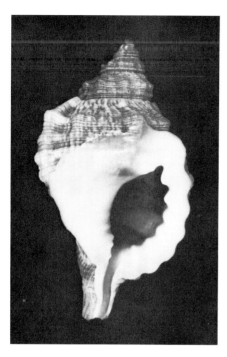

Cymatium (Gutturnium) muricinum

beaches, the drift will be lined with young tuns about the size of an egg. The animal has a large foot and long proboscis, is yellowish in color, and is heavily mottled with black. *See* R. D. Turner 1948, p. 178.

Superfamily CYMATIACEA
?Iredale, 1913
Family CYMATIIDAE Iredale, 1913

Genus *Cymatium* Röding, 1798
Subgenus *Gutturnium* Mörch, 1852

Knobbed Triton
Cymatium (Gutturnium) muricinum (Röding, 1798), *Mus. Boltenianum*, p. 133.
Gk. *kymation* dim. of *kyma* wave; L. *muricatus* pointed, murex shape.
SIZE: 25–75 mm.
COLOR: Gray to brown with reddish-brown colored spiral bands on last whorl. White underside.
SHAPE: Conic with extended siphonal canal.
ORNAMENT OR SCULPTURE: Five to 7 postembryonic convex whorls. Sutures irregular, slightly indented. Spiral sculpture consists of numerous nodulose cords of unequal strength with finer threadlike striations. Transverse sculpture of 7 to 8 knobbed varices with 2 to 3 nodulose ridges in between giving shell rough appearance.
APERTURE: Oval with greatly thickened outer lip. Parietal area forms large shield. Both areas glazed white. Outer lip has 7 strong teeth. Convex columella has 4 to 5 plicae near base. Siphonal canal variable in length, upturned at angle. Interior of aperture deep reddish brown.
OPERCULUM: Corneous, unguiculate; nucleus apical; numerous concentric growth rings.
PERIOSTRACUM: Light brown, deciduous, produced in rows of thin, low blades.
HABITAT: Intertidal reefs in warm seas. Epifaunal.
LOCALITIES: Extreme south.
OCCURRENCE: Rare beach shell.
RANGE: Bermuda; southeastern Florida; Texas; Mexico; West Indies; Brazil; Indo-Pacific.
GEOLOGIC RANGE: ? to Holocene.
REMARKS: Predatory on other mol-

Cymatium (Cymatriton) nicobaricum

lusks and starfish. Occurs in both Indo-Pacific and western Atlantic. Coll., Young. *See* Clench & Turner 1957, p. 225.

Subgenus *Cymatriton* Clench & Turner, 1957

Gold-Mouthed Triton
Cymatium (Cymatriton) nicobaricum (Röding, 1798), *Mus. Boltenianum*, p. 126.
Gk. *kymation* dim. of *kyma* wave; from Nicobar Islands in Bay of Bengal.
SIZE: 31– 51 mm.
COLOR: White or gray, mottled with reddish brown. Reddish brown on spiral threads.
SHAPE: Conic ovate with siphonal canal; spire extended at 45-degree angle.
ORNAMENT OR SCULPTURE: About 7 whorls, strongly convex. Six strong spiral cords. Noduled cords interspaced with fine threadlike cords. Five to 8 transverse varices with 3 to 5 knobs between each pair of varices. Anomphalous.
APERTURE: Obliquely oval. Bright orange with 7 single, large white teeth on inside of outer lip. Outer lip thickened, crenulated. Teeth extend into aperture, may be single or divided. Parietal lip narrow with numerous low lamellae. Columella curved convexly. Siphonal canal not long, usually upturned.
OPERCULUM: Broadly oval; subcentral nucleus with concentric growth lines.
PERIOSTRACUM: Thin, reddish brown, deciduous.
HABITAT: Offshore. Epifaunal.
LOCALITIES: Port Aransas, south.
OCCURRENCE: Rare beach shell.
RANGE: Bermuda; southeastern Florida; Texas; Campeche Bank; Yucatán; West Indies; northeastern Brazil; Indo-Pacific.
GEOLOGIC RANGE: ? to Holocene.
REMARKS: Predatory on other mollusks and starfish. Occurs in both Indo-Pacific and western Atlantic regions. Formerly known as *C. chlorostomum* (Lamarck, 1822). Coll., Young. *See* Clench & Turner 1957, p. 210.

Cymatium (Septa) pileare

Cymatium (Linatella) cingulatum

Subgenus *Septa* Perry, 1810

Atlantic Hairy Triton
Cymatium (Septa) pileare (Linné, 1758), *Syst. Natur.*, 10th ed., p. 749.
Gk. *kymation* dim. of *kyma* wave; L. *pilus* hair.
SIZE: Up to 131 mm.
COLOR: Grayish brown to golden brown, banded with alternating light and dark bands.
SHAPE: Elongate conic with extended siphonal canal.
ORNAMENT OR SCULPTURE: Seven to 8 whorls, shoulder of body whorl about midway. Suture slightly indented. Spiral sculpture consists of numerous, unequal, nodulose cords. Transverse sculpture of fine lines and 3 to 5 strongly knobbed varices.
APERTURE: Elliptical. Outer lip thickened into varix. Outer lip reddish brown with 12 to 14 whitish plicae, generally paired. Parietal area dark chocolate brown, with numerous fine, irregular, white lamellae. Columella convex. Siphonal canal short, upturned.
OPERCULUM: Corneous, unguiculate, numerous concentric growth ridges. Nucleus marginal and brown in color.
PERIOSTRACUM: Golden brown, rough, hairy.
HABITAT: Deep-water offshore reefs. Epifaunal.
LOCALITIES: Port Aransas, south.
OCCURRENCE: Rare beach shell.
RANGE: Bermuda; Florida to Tortugas; Texas; Veracruz, Mexico; Campeche Bank; Costa Rica; West Indies; Surinam; Brazil; both sides of Panama land bridge; Indo-Pacific.
GEOLOGIC RANGE: ? to Holocene.
REMARKS: A long veliger stage permits wide distribution. The embryonic shell is very different from the adult. Predatory and bisexual. Coll., Young. Syn. *C. martinianum* Orbigny, 1845. *See* Clench & Turner 1957, p. 216.

Subgenus *Linatella* Gray, 1857

Poulsen's Triton
Cymatium (Linatella) cingulatum (Lamarck, 1822), *Hist. Natur. Anim. sans Vert.* 7:216.
Gk. *kymation* dim. of *kyma* wave; L. *cingulum* girdle.
SIZE: 31–62 mm.
COLOR: Light brown to straw yellow, occasionally banded with brown.
SHAPE: Globose conic with extended siphonal canal.
ORNAMENT OR SCULPTURE: Four postembryonic whorls; convex; body whorl slightly shouldered. Suture slightly indented. Spiral sculpture consists of 18 to 20 flattened cords with fine threads in between. Shoulder cord might be slightly beaded. Transverse sculpture of fine growth lines; some have thin, bladelike varix. Anomphalous.
APERTURE: Subelliptical. Outer lip crenulated, slightly expanded. Parietal area glazed. Columella arched inward, continuing as margin of siphonal canal. Canal variable, moderately long, upturned.
OPERCULUM: Corneous, thin, subcircular, with concentric growth lines around eccentric nucleus.
PERIOSTRACUM: Thin; consists of numerous axial blades from which extend hairlike processes; deciduous.
HABITAT: Offshore to 411 meters (209 fathoms). Epifaunal.
LOCALITIES: Central, south.
OCCURRENCE: Rare beach shell.
RANGE: Bermuda; North Carolina; Florida south to West Indies to Venezuela; Texas; Mexico; Surinam; southern Brazil.
GEOLOGIC RANGE: ? to Holocene.
REMARKS: This shell is said to be rare, but at times it can be picked up by bushelfuls along the Mexican coast just south of the Rio Grande. The specimens there have thinner shells than those occasionally found on the Texas coast. Syn. *C. poulsenii* Mörch, 1877. Coll., Young. *See* Clench & Turner 1957, p. 198.

Cymatium (Monoplex) parthenopeum

Subgenus *Monoplex* Perry, 1811

Von Salis's Triton
Cymatium (Monoplex) parthenopeum
(Von Salis, 1793), *Reisen in Versch.
Prov.* 1:370.
Gk. *kymation* dim. of *kyma* wave; L.
Parthenop, old name of Naples.
SIZE: Up to 90 mm.
COLOR: Usually light brownish yellow; may have spiral bands of slightly darker brown becoming darker on varices.
SHAPE: Conic with extended siphonal canal.
ORNAMENT OR SCULPTURE: Seven to 8 postembryonic whorls, convex, shouldered. Spire moderately extended. Suture slightly indented. Spiral sculpture consists of 5 or 6 broad, low, often nodulose cords, with many finer threads in interspaces and on cords. Transverse sculpture of fine growth lines with 2 low varices in adults.
APERTURE: Subelliptical. Outer lip bordered with paired teeth opposite grooves between external spiral cords. Parietal wall dark reddish brown with numerous, irregular, white plications. Anal canal bordered with ridge on parietal wall. Short siphon, upturned, with columella extending into it at parietal margin.
OPERCULUM: Corneous, unguiculate; nucleus terminal, sculptured with concentric growth lines.
PERIOSTRACUM: Thin, brown, and produced in numerous fringed axial blades; deciduous.
HABITAT: Below low water to 63 meters (35 fathoms). Epifaunal.
LOCALITIES: Extreme south.
OCCURRENCE: Rare.
RANGE: Bermuda; North Carolina; Florida; Texas; Mexico; West Indies; Surinam south to Brazil; Uruguay; Indo-Pacific; Japan.
GEOLOGIC RANGE: Pleistocene to Holocene.

REMARKS: Syn. *C. costatum* Born, 1778. This is more often found on the beach south of the Rio Grande. Found on both sides of the Panama land bridge. *See* Clench & Turner 1957, p. 228.

Distorsio (Rhysema) clathrata

Genus *Distorsio* Röding, 1798
Subgenus *Rhysema* Clench &
   Turner, 1957

Atlantic Distorsio
Distorsio (Rhysema) clathrata
(Lamarck, 1816), Bruguière, *Encycl.
Méth.* 1:pl. 413, p. 4.
L. *distortus* deformed, *clathratus*
barred, latticed.
SIZE: 25–75 mm.
COLOR: Grayish white.
SHAPE: Conic with siphonal canal.
ORNAMENT OR SCULPTURE: Ten irregular, convex whorls. Spire extended. Suture slightly impressed,
irregular. Spiral sculpture consists
of numerous low cords interspaced
with fine spiral threads. Transverse
sculpture of numerous cords that
cross spiral cords, producing reticulated pattern with small knobs at
point of crossing. Seven to 9 varices.
APERTURE: Auriculate with thickened outer lip. Outer lip has 10
denticles; third below anal canal
largest and opposite deep parietal
embayment. Inner lip has numerous plicae. Two large parietal plicae
border posterior canal. Spiral cords
thickened in parietal embayment,
continuing as plicae on columella,
which is nearly straight and upturned. Wide, thinly glazed parietal
shield bordered by thin varix ridge.
OPERCULUM: Small, corneous, unguiculate; submarginal nucleus with
numerous concentric growth lines.
PERIOSTRACUM: Thin, yellowish
brown, reticulate, with numerous
fine hairlike processes over the surface and coarse hairlike processes
on the knobs.
HABITAT: Just below low water to 54
meters (30 fathoms) in warm seas.
Epifaunal.
LOCALITIES: Entire.
OCCURRENCE: Uncommon beach
shell.
RANGE: Southeastern United States;
Gulf states; Campeche Bank; Caribbean; Surinam; Brazil.
GEOLOGIC RANGE: Pleistocene to
Holocene.

REMARKS: The very distorted aper-
ture is the basis for its name. Frag-
ments are not too uncommon on
Mustang and Padre islands.
Panamic vicariant is *D. constricta*
(Broderip, 1833). *See* Clench &
Turner 1957, p. 236; Lewis 1972.

Cancellaria reticulata

Crassispira (Crassispirella) tampaensis

Suborder SIPHONOSTOMATA Blainville, 1824 = [STENO-GLOSSA Troschel, 1848, and NEOGASTROPODA Thiele, 1925]
Superfamily CANCELLARIACEA Gray, 1853
Family CANCELLARIIDAE Forbes & Hanley, 1853

Genus *Cancellaria* Lamarck, 1799

Common Nutmeg
Cancellaria reticulata (Linné, 1767), *Syst. Natur.*, 12th ed., p. 1190.
L. *cancellare* a lattice, *reticulatus* reticulate.
SIZE: 25–41 mm.
COLOR: Cream background with mottlings and irregular bands of reddish brown.
SHAPE: Conic with globose body whorl.
ORNAMENT OR SCULPTURE: About 6 very convex whorls. Sutures distinct. Body whorl large; whorls of spire gradually decreasing in size toward acute apex. Strong, regular spiral cords and similar, oblique riblets give very reticulate pattern.
APERTURE: Elongate, suboval, glazed white inside. Outer lip thin with crenulations on inner surface. Columella somewhat twisted with 2 strong folds. Top fold marked with several smaller ridges. Siphonal canal short, upturned.
OPERCULUM: None; uses mucus and sand to close aperture.
PERIOSTRACUM: Not preserved.
HABITAT: Offshore, shallow water to several fathoms. Epifaunal.
LOCALITIES: Central, south.
OCCURRENCE: Rare beach shell.
RANGE: North Carolina to both sides of Florida; Texas; West Indies; northern and eastern Brazil.
GEOLOGIC RANGE: Pleistocene to Holocene.
REMARKS: Found only after severe weather on outer beaches and in spoil deposits.

Superfamily CONACEA Rafinesque, 1815
Family TURRIDAE H. & A. Adams, 1853
A family of small gastropods that have generally been grouped into one single family but now appear to be many unrelated genera. Information which has accumulated describing the radula offers means by which the genera may be more accurately classified. Two major groups have been suggested: (1) the true turrids with a radular ribbon used for rasping; (2) the toxoglossate turrids whose radular teeth are designed to deliver toxin to their prey. Sorting and identification of these little shells on the basis of shell characteristics is difficult. The notch in the abaxial margin of the outer lip and the short siphonal canal aid in separating turrids from similar-appearing small gastropods. *See* McLean 1972.

Subfamily CRASSISPIRINAE

Genus *Crassispira* Swainson, 1840
Subgenus *Crassispirella* Bartsch & Rehder, 1939

Oyster Turret
Crassispira (Crassispirella) tampaensis Bartsch & Rehder, 1939, *Proc. U.S. Nat. Mus.* 87(3070):136.
L. *crassus* thick, fat, *spira* coil, twist; from Tampa, Florida.
SIZE: 8–22 mm.
COLOR: Pale yellow brown to chestnut.
SHAPE: Turriculate.
ORNAMENT OR SCULPTURE: About 10 to 12 convex, slightly shouldered whorls. Sutures distinct. Apex acute. Single strong spiral cord just below suture; about 20 beaded axial ribs begin at base of cord. Numerous regular spiral threads give beaded effect to convex ribs.
APERTURE: Narrow, oval. Outer lip thin, crenulate with posterior anal notch and short siphonal canal at base. Narrow callus on parietal wall. Phaneromphalous.

Kurtziella (Kurtziella) cf. *K. atrostyla*

OPERCULUM: Corneous, apical nucleus, dark.

PERIOSTRACUM. Not preserved.

HABITAT: Inlet influence to 162 meters (90 fathoms).

LOCALITIES: Port Aransas.

OCCURRENCE: Rare, probably fossil in beach drift.

RANGE: North Carolina to southern half of Florida; Texas; Cuba.

GEOLOGIC RANGE: ? to Holocene.

REMARKS: This species may be syn. with *Clathodrillia ostrearum* (Stearns, 1918). Olsson, Harbison, et al. (1953) present evidence to support the claim that this genus is *Clathrodrillia* Dall, 1918. Coll., U.T. Marine Science Institute.

Subfamily MANGELIINAE Fischer, 1883

Genus *Kurtziella* Dall, 1918
Subgenus *Kurtziella* s.s.

Brown-Tipped Mangelia
Kurtziella (Kurtziella) cf. *K. atrostyla* (Tryon, 1884), *Manu. Conch.* 6(3):310.

Dedicated to Lt. J. D. Kurtz, American conchoiogist; Gk. *atro* black; L. *stilus* slender, pointed writing instrument.

SIZE: 7–8 mm.

COLOR: Varies from yellowish white to dark brown, wholly or in stripes and bands.

SHAPE: Turriculate.

ORNAMENT OR SCULPTURE: Six postnuclear whorls with strong shoulders. Suture deeper than *K. limonitella*. Only 8 axial ribs; last forms strong varix.

APERTURE: Long; notch shallow; canal short.

OPERCULUM: None known.

PERIOSTRACUM: Not preserved.

HABITAT: Offshore. Epifaunal?

LOCALITIES: Port Aransas, south.

OCCURRENCE: Rare.

RANGE: Cape Hatteras to Antilles; Texas.

GEOLOGIC RANGE: Pliocene to Holocene.

REMARKS: Dead in beach drift. [*Mangelia atrostyla* Dall, 1889].

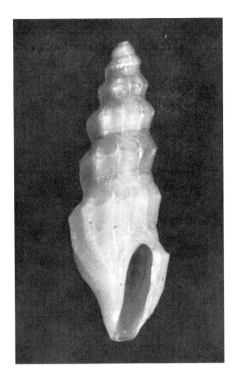

Kurtziella (Kurtziella) cf. *K. cerina*

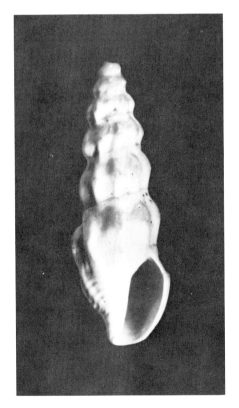

Kurtziella (Kurtziella) cf. *K. limonitella*

Kurtziella (Kurtziella) cf. *K. cerina*
(Kurtz & Stimpson, 1851), *Proc. Boston Soc. Natur. Hist.* 4:115.
Dedicated to Lt. J. D. Kurtz, American conchologist; L. *cerinus* wax colored.
SIZE: 9 mm.
COLOR: Waxen white to ash color on upper whorls. No lines of color.
SHAPE: Turriculate.
ORNAMENT OR SCULPTURE: Spire equal to last whorl. Five postnuclear whorls, flattish, angulated on shoulder. Small larval whorls, smooth except for last, which has 4 nodulous spiral lines. Granulous spiral sculpture. Nine swollen transverse riblets. No varix. Suture adpressed, undulated.
APERTURE: Narrow, oblique, about one-half length of body whorl. Notch well marked, away from suture. Canal very short.
OPERCULUM: None.
PERIOSTRACUM: Not preserved.
HABITAT: Mud flats between tides; hypersaline lagoons and inlet areas. Epifaunal?
LOCALITIES: Entire.
OCCURRENCE: Fairly common in beach drift.
RANGE: Massachusetts; North Carolina; both sides of Florida; Texas.
GEOLOGIC RANGE: Miocene to Holocene.
REMARKS: Specimens are usually worn and difficult to identify. [*Mangelia cerina*].

Punctate Mangelia
Kurtziella (Kurtziella) cf. *K. limonitella*
(Dall, 1884), *Proc. U.S. Nat. Mus.* 6(384):113.
Dedicated to Lt. J. D. Kurtz, American conchologist; L. *limon* lemon colored.
SIZE: 9 mm.
COLOR: Whitish, lineated spirally with yellow brown. Some brown on outside of canal.
SHAPE: Turriculate.
ORNAMENT OR SCULPTURE: Spire trifle shorter than last whorl. Five postnuclear whorls, rounded angulated behind periphery. Spiral sculpture granulose. Twelve narrow, transverse riblets. No varix. Ribs obsolete on fasciole. Suture hardly adpressed or undulated.
APERTURE: Narrow, oblique. Notch shallow, deepest at angulation. Canal not distinct from aperture.
OPERCULUM: None.
PERIOSTRACUM: Not preserved.
HABITAT: Offshore banks and mud flats between tides; hypersaline lagoons and inlets. Epifaunal?
LOCALITIES: Entire.
OCCURRENCE: Fairly common.
RANGE: North Carolina to both sides of Florida; Texas.
GEOLOGIC RANGE: Miocene to Holocene.
REMARKS: This species does not have the little beads on the last nuclear whorl that *K. cerina* has. [*Drillia limonitella*], [*Mangelia limonitella*].

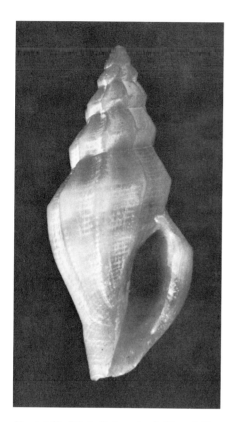

Kurtziella (Rubellatoma) cf. K. rubella

Cryoturris cf. C. cerinella

Subgenus *Rubellatoma* Bartsch & Rehder, 1939

Reddish Mangelia
Kurtziella (Rubellatoma) cf. *K. rubella* (Kurtz & Stimpson, 1851), *Proc. Boston Soc. Natur. Hist.* 4:115.
Dedicated to Lt. J. D. Kurtz, American conchologist; L. *rubellus* reddish.
SIZE: 6–8 mm.
COLOR: Cream with chestnut brown bands.
SHAPE: Turriculate.
ORNAMENT OR SCULPTURE: Narrow band below suture and broad band covering anterior half of body whorl. About 7 whorls with angled shoulders. Fairly heavy, sutures distinct. Spiral sculpture consists of fine lines. Transverse sculpture, about 9 rounded ribs that are highest at periphery of whorl shoulder. Spaces between ribs wider than ribs.
APERTURE: Elongate oval. Outer lip slightly thickened but edge thin, with weak posterior notch near summit. Parietal lip narrow, polished. Siphonal canal moderately extended.
OPERCULUM: None.
PERIOSTRACUM: Not preserved.
HABITAT: Inlet areas to moderate depths in warm seas. Epifaunal?
LOCALITIES: East, central.
OCCURRENCE: Rare in beach drift.
RANGE: North Carolina to southeastern Florida; Texas.
GEOLOGIC RANGE: Pliocene to Holocene.
REMARKS: This little carnivore is rather rare in its entire range. *See* Bartsch & Rehder, 1939*b*.

Genus *Cryoturris* Woodring, 1828

Wax-Colored Mangelia
Cryoturris cf. *C. cerinella* (Dall, 1889), *Mus. Comp. Zool. Bull.* 18(1):112.
L. *turris* tower, *cerinus* wax colored.
SIZE: 10.5 mm.
COLOR: Whitish toward apex, ashy on intermediate, orangish on body whorl. Never striped or spotted.
SHAPE: Turriculate, drawn out and slender.
ORNAMENT OR SCULPTURE: Seven postnuclear whorls, angulate at periphery and sloping either way from it. Granulose spiral sculpture. Six or 7 transverse ribs. Suture less adpressed and undulated than *Kurtziella cerina*.
APERTURE: Long, narrow, oblique. Hardly any indentation for notch. No canal to speak of.
OPERCULUM: None.
PERIOSTRACUM: Not preserved.
HABITAT: Mud flats between tides; hypersaline lagoons and inlets. Epifaunal?
LOCALITIES: Entire.
OCCURRENCE: Fairly common in beach drift.
RANGE: North Carolina to both sides of Florida; Texas.
GEOLOGIC RANGE: Pleistocene to Holocene.
REMARKS: Beach specimens are very worn. [*Kurtziella cerinella*].

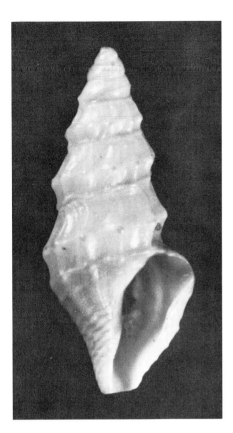

Nannodiella cf. *N. vespuciana*

Pyrgocythara plicosa

Genus *Nannodiella* Dall, 1919

Nannodiella cf. *N. vespuciana* (Orbigny, 1842), *Hist. d'Ile de Cuba* 2:175.
Nannodiella, a dwarflike creature; from Americus Vespucius.
SIZE: 5 mm.
COLOR: Yellowish white, tinged with brown just below suture and on anterior part of body whorl.
SHAPE: Fusiform.
ORNAMENT OR SCULPTURE: Eight postnuclear whorls strongly angulated just below middle, ornamented with about 9 rather prominent, straight transverse ribs, commencing at periphery and extending to suture; these, with their wide, concave interspaces, are crossed by 3 strong, rounded, equally distant threads, the third defining suture. Where these cross ribs, nodules are formed. Nucleus smooth, glassy. Surface granulose.
APERTURE: Narrow ovate, pinched up anteriorly into short, rather narrow, straight canal. Outer lip thickened, with conspicuous varix and thick, smooth, rounded, irregularly curved, light brown edge. Deep, narrow sinus considerably below suture, at angle of shoulder. Columella slightly curved.
OPERCULUM: None.
PERIOSTRACUM: Not preserved.
HABITAT: Probably offshore. Epifaunal?
LOCALITIES: East, central.
OCCURRENCE: Uncommon in beach drift.
RANGE: North Carolina; Gulf states.
GEOLOGIC RANGE: ? to Holocene.
REMARKS: This species was reported by Hulings (1955) as being in the Sabine area and has recently been identified from Port Aranas. Syn. *Mangelia oxytata* Bush, 1885.

Genus *Pyrgocythara* Woodring, 1928

Plicate Mangelia
Pyrgocythara plicosa (C. B. Adams, 1850), *Contr. Conch.* 4:54.
L. *pyrgo* tower, *cythra* Venus, *plicare* to fold.
SIZE: 6–8 mm.
COLOR: Reddish brown. Dead shells wax colored.
SHAPE: Turriculate; spire about one-half of length.
ORNAMENT OR SCULPTURE: Six to 7 whorls. Sutures distinct. Only slightly shouldered. Spiral sculpture consists of strong, regularly spaced cords. Eleven to 12 transverse ribs made nodulose by spiral cords.
APERTURE: Semilunar. Outer lip thickened with very pronounced posterior notch below suture. Interior dark. Parietal lip narrow. Siphonal canal short.
OPERCULUM: None.
PERIOSTRACUM: Thin, grayish.
HABITAT: Shallow, hypersaline lagoon on grass or mud bottom. Epifaunal?
LOCALITIES: Entire.
OCCURRENCE: Common.
RANGE: Cape Cod to western Florida; Texas.
GEOLOGIC RANGE: Pliocene to Holocene.
REMARKS: Female of this little carnivore produces smooth, transparent, lens-shaped egg capsules about 0.16 mm in diameter. The posterior notch makes this easy to identify. [*Mangelia plicosa*].

139

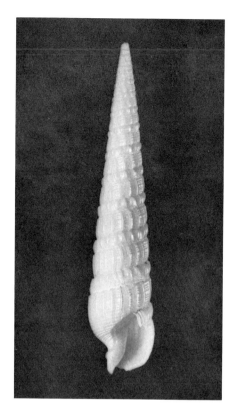

Terebra dislocata

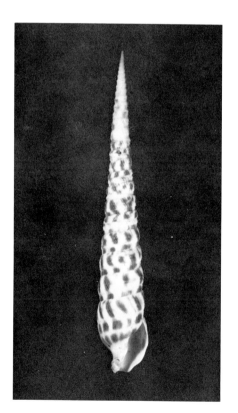

Terebra taurina

Family TEREBRIDAE Mörch, 1852

Genus *Terebra* Bruguière, 1792

Common Atlantic Auger
Terebra dislocata (Say, 1822), *J. Acad. Natur. Sci. Philadelphia* 2(1):235.
L. *terebra* a boring tool, auger, *dislocatus* dislocated.
SIZE: 37–51 mm.
COLOR: Grayish white to orangish white.
SHAPE: Turriculate.
ORNAMENT OR SCULPTURE: Numerous slightly convex whorls with about 15 axial ribs per whorl. Sutures distinct with beaded spiral band just below and fine spiral striae between ribs.
APERTURE: Small, subovate. Outer lip thin with recurved siphonal notch at base. Columella short. Narrow parietal area polished.
OPERCULUM: Corneous, thin, yellow brown.
PERIOSTRACUM: Thin, brownish.
HABITAT: Inlet areas. Infaunal.
LOCALITIES: Entire.
OCCURRENCE: Common.
RANGE: Maryland to Florida; Texas; West Indies; Brazil.
GEOLOGIC RANGE: Eocene? Miocene to Holocene.
REMARKS: This carnivore does not have a radula but contains its venom in "grooved prickles." The shell can be found under long bulges of sand at low tides.

Flame Auger
Terebra taurina (Lightfoot, 1786), *Cat. Portland Mus.*, pp. 142, 152.
L. *terebra* a boring tool, auger, *taurinus* bull.
SIZE: 100–150 mm.
COLOR: Background cream with axial reddish brown, flame-shaped marks in two spiral rows.
SHAPE: Turriculate, slender.
ORNAMENT OR SCULPTURE: About 14 flattened whorls. Sutures distinct. Two spiral incised lines between sutures. Numerous fine, wavy transverse striations.
APERTURE: Semilunar, oblique, short. Thin outer lip. Columella convexly curved. Anterior or siphonal canal short, recurved.
OPERCULUM: Corneous, brown.
PERIOSTRACUM: Not preserved.
HABITAT: Deeper water offshore. Infaunal.
LOCALITIES: Central, south.
OCCURRENCE: Rare beach shell.
RANGE: Southeastern Florida; Gulf of Mexico; West Indies; Surinam; Brazil.
GEOLOGIC RANGE: ? to Holocene.
REMARKS: Animal is colored yellow. Do not expect to find a perfect specimen of this fine shell. It usually takes a hurricane to bring in the broken shells that are greatly prized. Syn. *T. flammea* Lamarck, 1822. Coll., Texas Memorial Museum, Austin.

Terebra (Strioterebrum) protexta

Hastula maryleeae

Subgenus *Strioterebrum* Sacco, 1891

Fine-Ribbed Auger

Terebra (Strioterebrum) protexta (Conrad, 1846), *Proc. Acad. Natur. Sci. Philadelphia* 3(1):26.
L. *terebra* a boring tool, auger, *pro* before, *textus* texture, fabric.
SIZE: 20–25 mm.
COLOR: Brownish when living.
SHAPE: Turriculate.
ORNAMENT OR SCULPTURE: Thirteen to 15 slightly convex whorls. Suture distinct. Spiral sculpture consists of band below suture similar to but less pronounced than *T. dislocata*. Convex, axial riblets crossed by fine spiral striations.
APERTURE: Small, oblique, oval. Outer lip thin. Parietal area narrow, glossy. Columella short with upturned siphonal notch at base.
OPERCULUM: Corneous, reddish brown.
PERIOSTRACUM: Brownish.
HABITAT: Offshore in 1.8 to 90 meters (1 to 50 fathoms); inlet areas. Infaunal.
LOCALITIES: Entire.
OCCURRENCE: Fairly common.
RANGE: North Carolina to Florida; Texas; Campeche Bank; Yucatán; Caribbean; Brazil.
GEOLOGIC RANGE: Pliocene to Holocene.
REMARKS: Look for this in outer beach drift. Alive at San Luis Pass. Coll., Young.

Genus *Hastula* H. & A. Adams, 1853

Marylee's Terebra

Hastula maryleeae R. D. Burch, 1965, *Veliger* 7(4):242.
L. *hasta* spear; dedicated to Marylee Burch, the collector.
SIZE: 25–51 mm.
COLOR: Variable from ivory white to dark purplish gray. Polished.
SHAPE: Elongate conic.
ORNAMENT OR SCULPTURE: Numerous flat-sided whorls. Sutures distinct; apex very pointed. Numerous small axial riblets near suture. Spiral sculpture consists of microstriations. Rows of punctations typical of *Hastula* are absent.
APERTURE: Small, pear-shaped. Outer lip thin, with deep, recurved siphonal notch at base.
OPERCULUM: Corneous, brown.
PERIOSTRACUM: None visible.
HABITAT: Sandy surf zone. Infaunal.
LOCALITIES: Entire, more to south.
OCCURRENCE: Common.
RANGE: From Galveston, Texas, to Veracruz, Mexico; Yucatán.
GEOLOGIC RANGE: ? to Holocene.
REMARKS: This has only been recognized as a separate species in recent years but was collected in Texas more than a hundred years ago. Holotype collected at Surfside beach, Freeport, Texas, by Marylee Burch on March 16, 1961. *See* Burch 1965, p. 242.

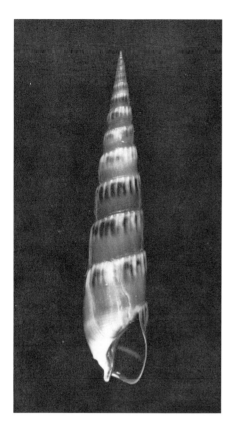

Hastula salleana

Cantharus cancellarius

Sallé's Auger

Hastula salleana Deshayes, 1859, *Proc. Zool. Soc. London* 27:287.
L. *hasta* spear; dedicated to A. Sallé, nineteenth-century collector.
SIZE: 25–51 mm.
COLOR: Dark bluish gray or brownish. Polished.
SHAPE: Elongate conic.
ORNAMENT OR SCULPTURE: Numerous flat-sided whorls. Sutures distinct; apex very pointed. About 30 short, dark ribs below suture of each whorl. Spiral sculpture consists of microscopic rows of punctations; these are more widely spaced than in *H. cinera* Born, 1780.
APERTURE: Small, pear-shaped, dark brown within. Outer lip thin, with deep siphonal notch at base. Sharp ridge runs from notch to mid-columella.
OPERCULUM: Corneous, brown.
PERIOSTRACUM: None visible.
HABITAT: Sandy surf zone. Infaunal.
LOCALITIES: Entire, more to south.
OCCURRENCE: Common.
RANGE: Florida west to Veracruz, Mexico; Colombia; Brazil.
GEOLOGIC RANGE: ? to Holocene.
REMARKS: These quick, burrowing carnivores live in the surf zone in mixed populations of *H. maryleeae* Burch and *Donax* clams. Empty shells have been found inside the starfish, *Luida clathrata*. [*Terebra salleana*]. This shell has been listed as *T. cinerea* Born, 1780. Panamic vicariant is *H. luctosa* (Hinds, 1844). *See* Morrison 1967.

Family BUCCINIDAE Rafinesque, 1815

Genus *Cantharus* Röding, 1798

Cancellate Cantharus

Cantharus cancellarius (Conrad, 1846), *Proc. Acad. Natur. Sci. Philadelphia* 3(1):25.
Gk. *kantharos* drinking cup; L. *cancellare* a lattice.
SIZE: 18–28 mm.
COLOR: Yellowish brown.
SHAPE: Ovate conic.
ORNAMENT OR SCULPTURE: Five to 6 convex, heavy whorls. Spire conical. Spiral sculpture consists of sharp cords that form beads and cross narrow transverse ribs, making a reticulate pattern.
APERTURE: Long oval, glossy white. Outer lip thin, crenulate with fine denticulations on inner edge. Posterior canal weak or absent. Siphonal canal straight, short, slightly upturned. One plica at base of columella.
OPERCULUM: Corneous, brown, concentric with subcentral nucleus.
PERIOSTRACUM: Moderately thin, yellowish brown, arranged in spiral rows.
HABITAT: Shallow water in rocky places, inlet areas. Epifaunal.
LOCALITIES: Entire.
OCCURRENCE: Common seasonally.
RANGE: Western coast of Florida to Texas; Yucatán.
GEOLOGIC RANGE: Pleistocene to Holocene.
REMARKS: Lives on the jetties and has begun to reestablish itself since Hurricane Beulah in 1967. Very active in an aquarium (see fig. 12). Coll., Young.

Pisania tincta

Nassarius (Nassarius) acutus

Genus *Pisania* Bivona, 1832

Tinted Cantharus
Pisania tincta (Conrad, 1846), *Proc. Acad. Natur. Sci. Philadelphia* 3(1):25.
Perhaps from Admiral Pisani or from a native of the coast near Pisa; L. *tinctus* painted.
SIZE: 18–28 mm.
COLOR: Variable: blue gray, yellow, chocolate, milk white; darkest at apex.
SHAPE: Ovate conic.
ORNAMENT OR SCULPTURE: Five to 6 convex, heavy whorls. Spire conical. Spiral sculpture consists of cords with finer threads in between, crossing over weak axial ribs. Weak nodules on whorl shoulder.
APERTURE: Oval. Outer lip thickened, denticulate on inner edge. Parietal lip glazed. Plica on upper part borders small posterior or abaxial canal. Siphonal canal almost straight, slightly upturned.
OPERCULUM: Corneous, pyriform.
PERIOSTRACUM: Thin, brown.
HABITAT: Shallow water, rocks, seaweed close to shore. Epifaunal.
LOCALITIES: Port Aransas, south.
OCCURRENCE: Fairly common.
RANGE: North Carolina to both sides of Florida; Texas; Campeche Bank; West Indies; eastern Brazil.
GEOLOGIC RANGE: Pleistocene to Holocene.
REMARKS: Can be found alive on the jetties, also dead in the rolls of sea whip coral. Less common than *Cantharus cancellaria*. [*C. tinctus*].

Family NASSARIIDAE Iredale, 1916

Genus *Nassarius* Dumeril, 1806
Subgenus *Nassarius* s.s.

Sharp-Knobbed Nassa
Nassarius (Nassarius) acutus (Say, 1822), *J. Acad. Natur. Sci. Philadelphia* 2(1):234.
L. *nassa* a basket for catching fish, *acutus* acute, sharp.
SIZE: 6–12 mm.
COLOR: Cream white to yellowish, occasionally with brown spiral thread.
SHAPE: Ovate conic.
ORNAMENT OR SCULPTURE: Seven convex whorls. Spire pointed and longer than body whorl. Spiral sculpture consists of spiral threads that cross similar transverse ribs, giving beaded, cancellate appearance to shell.
APERTURE: Oval, slightly oblique. Short recurved siphonal canal.
OPERCULUM: Corneous, unguiculate, brown.
PERIOSTRACUM: None visible.
HABITAT: Open lagoon, inlet, along shore. Semi-infaunal.
LOCALITIES: Entire.
OCCURRENCE: Common.
RANGE: Western coast of Florida to Texas.
GEOLOGIC RANGE: Miocene to Holocene.
REMARKS: This scavenger is attracted by the smell of decaying flesh and by light. It feeds on debris, other mollusks, and mollusk egg capsules. The female lays eggs in gelatinous capsules that are attached to the bottom (fig. 24). The young of *Anadara brasiliana* attach themselves with a byssus to the shell of *N. acutus* in a symbiotic relationship (Harper 1970).

Nassarius (Nassarius) vibex

Fasciolaria (Fasciolaria) lilium

Common Eastern Nassa
Nassarius (Nassarius) vibex (Say,
1822), *J. Acad. Natur. Sci. Philadelphia* 2(1):234.
L. *nassa* a basket for catching fish,
vibex the mark of a blow.
SIZE: 12 mm.
COLOR: Gray brown to whitish with
a few splotches of darker brown.
SHAPE: Ovate conic.
ORNAMENT OR SCULPTURE: Seven
convex whorls. Body whorl domi-
nates short, heavy shell. Spiral
sculpture consists of fine threads
that cross about 12 transverse ribs.
Sutures shallow. Apex acute.
APERTURE: Oval, small. Outer lip
with thick varix, denticulate within.
Columella arched, short. Parietal
area well developed, glazed white.
Siphonal canal short, slightly upturned.
OPERCULUM: Corneous, brown, unguiculate.
PERIOSTRACUM: None visible.
HABITAT: In bay and open-sound
margins and inlet areas. Semi-
infaunal.
LOCALITIES: Entire.
OCCURRENCE: Common.
RANGE: Cape Cod to Florida; Gulf
states; Costa Rica; West Indies;
Brazil.
GEOLOGIC RANGE: Pliocene to
Holocene.
REMARKS: These scavengering "mud
snails" are common on the flats but
most move to deeper water in the
winter. Eggs are laid in gelatinous
capsules attached to bottom (fig.
24). *See* Hurst 1963; Gore 1969.

Family FASCIOLARIIDAE Gray,
1853
Subfamily FASCIOLARIINAE
Gray, 1853

Genus *Fasciolaria* Lamarck, 1799
Subgenus *Fasciolaria* s.s.

Banded Tulip Shell
Fasciolaria (Fasciolaria) lilium Fischer
von Waldheim, 1807, *Mus. Demidoff.*
3:205.
L. *fasciola* a band, *lilium* lily.
SIZE: 51–100 mm.
COLOR: Background color cream
with irregular purplish brown and
orange brown mottlings. Widely
spaced, rarely broken, brown spiral
bands.
SHAPE: Elongate fusiform.
ORNAMENT OR SCULPTURE: Seven to
9 rounded whorls. Smooth near
well-defined sutures. Spiral striations on base and fine transverse
growth lines.
APERTURE: Long oval, glazed white
inside. Outer lip thin, brownish
with numerous raised white threads
on inner surface. Parietal area thinly
glazed with white. Moderately long
siphonal canal open. Incurved columella has strong plication toward
end.
OPERCULUM: Corneous, brown, unguiculate.
PERIOSTRACUM: Thin, yellowish
brown.
HABITAT: Inlet areas and offshore.
Epifaunal.
LOCALITIES: Entire, more to south.
OCCURRENCE: Fairly common.
RANGE: North Carolina to western
Gulf of Mexico.
GEOLOGIC RANGE: Pleistocene to
Holocene.
REMARKS: This carnivorous animal is
smaller than *F. tulipa.* It can use its
strong foot to jump out of the unwary collector's pocket. The eggs
are placed in vase-shaped capsules
attached to shell, pilings, and other
structures (fig. 24). The male is

Fasciolaria (Fasciolaria) tulipa

smaller than the female (fig. 49). As observed in an aquarium, he squirts streams of water that set up vibrations which attract the female. This species has been referred to as *F. hunteria* Perry, 1811. *See* Hollister 1957; F. E. Wells 1970; Lyons 1972, p. 99.

True Tulip Shell

Fasciolaria (Fasciolaria) tulipa (Linné, 1758), *Syst. Natur.*, 10th ed., p. 754. L. *fasciola* a band, *tulipa* a flower.

SIZE: 75–125 mm.

COLOR: Cream background with brown blotches and numerous broken spiral bands. Some specimens reddish, orange, or mahogany brown.

SHAPE: Elongate fusiform.

ORNAMENT OR SCULPTURE: About 9 rounded whorls; suture distinct. Smooth appearing but has fine spiral striae just below suture and on base. Transverse sculpture consists of fine, irregular growth lines.

APERTURE: Long oval, flushed with orangish color. Outer lip thin, denticulate on the inner edge. Parietal area thinly glazed. Columella fairly long, curved inward with 2 oblique plicae about midway.

OPERCULUM: Corneous, brown, unguiculate.

PERIOSTRACUM: Thin, yellowish brown.

HABITAT: Grass bottoms from littoral to 9 meters (5 fathoms). Epifaunal.

LOCALITIES: South.

OCCURRENCE: Rare beach shell.

RANGE: North Carolina to southern half of Florida; Texas; Campeche Bank; Yucatán; West Indies; Surinam; Brazil.

GEOLOGIC RANGE: Pliocene to Holocene.

REMARKS: The living animal is a bright flame color. It is only rarely that other than old shells are found on the Texas coast. *See* F. E. Wells 1970.

Pleuroploca gigantea

Busycon spiratum plagosum

Genus *Pleuroploca* P. Fischer, 1884

Florida Horse Conch
Pleuroploca gigantea (Kiener, 1840), *Iconogr. Coq. Viv.*, p. 5.
Gk. *pleura* rib, side, *ploca* wreath, curl; L. *giganteus* gigantic.
SIZE: Up to 150 to 225 mm.
COLOR: Dirty white to chalky salmon. Juveniles bright orange.
SHAPE: Fusiform.
ORNAMENT OR SCULPTURE: About 8 convex whorls. Sutures distinct. Spiral sculpture consists of strong, irregularly spaced cords, with finer threads between. Transverse growth lines.
APERTURE: Oval, polished, orange colored. Outer lip thin, slightly crenulate. Columella has two plicae near base. Siphonal canal long, upturned.
OPERCULUM: Corneous, brown, unguiculate.
PERIOSTRACUM: Heavy, dark brown; flakes when dry.
HABITAT: Offshore and in inlet areas. Epifaunal.
LOCALITIES: Entire.
OCCURRENCE: Uncommon.
RANGE: North Carolina to both sides of Florida; Texas; Campeche Bank.
GEOLOGIC RANGE: Miocene to Holocene.
REMARKS: The largest shell found on the Texas coast. Old specimens are usually covered with calcareous bryozoa and are faded and worn even when living. It has been found living on the jetty at Port Aransas. Panamic vicariant is *P. princeps* Sowerby, 1825. Coll., Young.

Family MELONGENIDAE Gill, 1871 = [GALEODIDAE Thiele, 1925]
Subfamily BUSYCONINAE Finlay & Marwick, 1937

Genus *Busycon* Röding, 1798

Pear Whelk
Busycon spiratum plagosum (Conrad, 1863), *Proc. Acad. Natur. Sci. Philadelphia* 14:583.
Gk. *busycon* a large, coarse fig; L. *spira* coiled, *plagosus* fond of punishing.
SIZE: 75–100 mm.
COLOR: Creamy with irregular brown axial lines.
SHAPE: Pyriform.
ORNAMENT OR SCULPTURE: Spire whorls turreted, producing step at each suture. Suture boxlike. Sharp carina at shoulder finely beaded. Spiral sculpture consists of fine threads.
APERTURE: Pyriform. Outer lip thin. Interior strongly striate, rosy brown except near the lip, where it is white. Siphonal canal long, nearly straight.
OPERCULUM: Corneous, brown, concentric with subcentral nucleus. Arched channel on outer surface running from bottom to top, near outer margin.
PERIOSTRACUM: Thin, brownish.
HABITAT: Offshore and inlet areas in sandy bottoms to 7.2 meters (4 fathoms). Infaunal.
LOCALITIES: Entire.
OCCURRENCE: Fairly common.
RANGE: Mobile Bay to Campeche Bay.
GEOLOGIC RANGE: Miocene to Holocene.
REMARKS: At times these whelks can be found living on sand bars in inlet areas where they will "pop up" after the tide has been out for a while. The female constructs egg capsules in the same manner as *B. perversum*, but they are smaller and have sharply crenulated edges (figs. 23 & 24). Bivalves are the main source of food. *See* Hollister 1958.

Busycon (Sinistrofulgur) perversum pulleyi

Subgenus *Sinistrofulgur* Hollister, 1950

Lightning Whelk
Busycon (Sinistrofulgur) perversum pulleyi Hollister, 1958, *Palaeontograph. Amer.* 4(28):89.
Gk. *busycon* a large, coarse fig; L. *perversus* wrong; dedicated to Dr. Tom Pulley, director of Houston Museum of Natural History.
SIZE: 100–200 mm.
COLOR: Pale fawn to light yellowish gray with long axial, wavy brown streaks. Large adults usually lose color.
SHAPE: Pyriform, sinistral.
ORNAMENT OR SCULPTURE: Body whorl large, spire one-fifth height of shell. Spire turreted, sutures slightly below shoulder. Fine spiral threads. Colored growth lines correspond with spines that circle shoulder.
APERTURE: Pyriform. Outer lip thin, edged in purplish brown. Interior pale yellow to light orange. Siphonal canal long, somewhat twisted and recurved.
OPERCULUM: Corneous, brown, concentric with subcentral nucleus.
PERIOSTRACUM: Thin, brownish.
HABITAT: Intertidal, offshore, in bays. Infaunal.
LOCALITIES: Entire.
OCCURRENCE: Common.
RANGE: Brenton Sound, Louisiana, to Texas and northern Mexican coast.
GEOLOGIC RANGE: Miocene to Holocene.
REMARKS: This carnivorous animal can be caught in the bays with crab lines when it comes to feed on the bait. It buries itself in the sand with the siphonal canal protruding. It feeds on mollusks, opening bivalves by chipping the valve edges with its own shell until it can insert the proboscis (fig. 15). The female constructs long strings of horny, disc-shaped capsules up to the size of a quarter with her black-colored foot, attaching them to the substratum (figs. 23 & 24). There has been much confusion as to the name of the Texas species of *Busycon*. This is probably due to the intergrades which exist at both the northern and southern limits of its range. The typical specimen here does not have the spiral bulge across the body whorl which is typical of *B. perversum* (Linné, 1758) and is more colorful and more strongly spined on the shoulder than *B. contrarium* (Conrad, 1840). The fact that the larvae are not planktonic may account for the development of subspecies where distances are too great for interbreeding. *See* Garriker 1951; Puffer & Emmerson 1954; Hollister 1957; Pulley 1959.

Anachis (Costoanachis) semiplicata

Family COLUMBELLIDAE Swainson, 1840 = [PYRENIDAE Suter, 1913]

Genus *Anachis* H. & A. Adams, 1853
Subgenus *Costoanachis* Sacco, 1890

Semiplicate Dove Shell
Anachis (Costoanachis) semiplicata
Stearns, 1873, *Proc. Acad. Natur. Sci. Philadelphia* 25:344.
L. *anachites* name given by Pliny to the diamond, *semi* half, *plicatus* folded.
SIZE: 8–15 mm.
COLOR: Yellow gray or whitish with reddish brown, irregular markings.
SHAPE: Fusiform.
ORNAMENT OR SCULPTURE: Spire slightly more than one-half of shell length. Whorls almost flat-sided; sutures shallow. Body whorl narrow. Sculpture consists of small number of widely spaced, low axial ribs limited to body whorl. Spire smooth.
APERTURE: Moderately wide. Outer lip barely thickened, distinctly denticulate interiorly. Columella straight with obsolete denticulations.
OPERCULUM: Corneous, oval, brown.
PERIOSTRACUM: Thin, brownish.
HABITAT: On broken shell and rocks in sandy areas. Epifaunal.
LOCALITIES: Entire.
OCCURRENCE: Common.
RANGE: Florida; Texas; Yucatán.
GEOLOGIC RANGE: ? to Holocene.
REMARKS: This carnivore is not timid or nocturnal. On the jetty at Port Mansfield numerous shells were seen hanging by a fine thread of mucus attached to the rock. The animal will also spin this elastic support and hang from seaweed in water. Often found in the bays clustered in algae on dead shell. Lays eggs in single, gelatinous capsule attached to seaweed. The status of the genus *Anachis* in Texas is still dubious. Several species have been reported in the literature as being found here. *A. floridana* Rehder, 1939, is one that is often mentioned. *A. lafresnayi* (Fischer & Bernardi, 1856), formerly *A. translirata* (Ravenel, 1861), is another. With *A. semiplicata* they may be variations of one species. *See* Radwin 1968.

Anachis (Parvanachis) obesa

Mitrella (Astyris) lunata

Subgenus *Parvanachis* Radwin, 1968

Fat Dove Shell
Anachis (Parvanachis) obesa (C. B. Adams, 1845), *Proc. Boston Soc. Natur. Hist.* 2:2.
L. *anachites* name given by Pliny to the diamond, *obesus* fat.
SIZE: 4–8 mm.
COLOR: Variable: some whitish with dark brown bands, others solid reddish brown.
SHAPE: Ovate conic; short fusiform.
ORNAMENT OR SCULPTURE: Five convex whorls, stout, rotund. Spiral sculpture consists of strong spiral cords that do not cross transverse ribs, giving reticulated pattern.
APERTURE: Oval, oblique. Outer lip thickened in adults with denticulations on inner edge. Base of columella denticulate.
OPERCULUM: Corneous, oval.
PERIOSTRACUM: Thin, light brown.
HABITAT: Under shell on sandy bottoms and oyster reefs. Epifaunal.
LOCALITIES: Entire.
OCCURRENCE: Common.
RANGE: Bermuda; Virginia to Florida; Gulf states; Costa Rica; West Indies; Surinam; Brazil.
GEOLOGIC RANGE: Pliocene to Holocene.
REMARKS: *A. ostreicola* may be a subspecies. *See* Radwin 1968.

Genus *Mitrella* Risso, 1826
Subgenus *Astyris* H. & A. Adams, 1853

Lunar Dove Shell
Mitrella (Astyris) lunata (Say, 1826), *J. Acad. Natur. Sci. Philadelphia* 5(1):213.
L. dim. of *mitra*, a miter, *lunatus* crescent-shaped.
SIZE: 5 mm.
COLOR: Glossy white to cream with numerous fine, zigzag brown markings. Occasional specimens have brown markings arranged in definite spiral bands.
SHAPE: Ovate conic.
ORNAMENT OR SCULPTURE: Smooth with about 5 flat-sided, tapering whorls. Spiral striations on base of shell.
APERTURE: Long oval. Outer lip thin on edge, denticulated on interior. Columella short. Edge of siphonal canal dark brown.
OPERCULUM: Corneous, brown.
PERIOSTRACUM: Thin, brownish.
HABITAT: High-salinity shell reef just below low-tide mark, grass flats, inlets. Epifaunal.
LOCALITIES: Entire.
OCCURRENCE: Fairly common.
RANGE: Bermuda; Massachusetts to Florida; Texas; Carmen, Campeche, Mexico; Gulf of Campeche; Yucatán; West Indies; Surinam; northern and northeastern Brazil.
GEOLOGIC RANGE: Pliocene to Holocene.
REMARKS: At times these beautiful little shells are strikingly marked in spiral bands of white below the suture, then brown dots and a row of oblique lines. According to Olsson, Harbison, et al. (1953) *M. lunata* should be placed in the genus *Anachis*, subgenus *Alia*. *See* Leathem & Maurer 1975, p. 74.

Murex (Hexaplex) fulvescens

Family MURICIDAE Rafinesque, 1815
Subfamily MURICINAE da Costa, 1776

Genus *Murex* Linné, 1758
Subgenus *Hexaplex* Perry, 1810

Giant Eastern Murex
Murex (Hexaplex) fulvescens G. B. Sowerby I, 1834, *Conch. Illus.*, p. 7. L. *murex* the purple shellfish, *fulvus* tawny.
SIZE: 125–150 mm.
COLOR: Milky white to dirty gray with reddish brown blotches with spiral threads.
SHAPE: Conic with extended siphonal canal.
ORNAMENT OR SCULPTURE: Six to 7 convex, heavy whorls. Suture distinct, irregular. Spire short. Spiral sculpture consists of strong, brown cords that connect corresponding spines to each varix. Between them are numerous raised threads. Transverse sculpture consists of 6 to 10 highly spinous varices. Largest spines are on shoulder of whorls; all are erect, opened toward outer lip, and irregular in height and size. Numerous fine growth lines.
APERTURE: Oval to subcircular. Outer lip crenulated, thickened into very spinose varix. Parietal lip glazed with low ridge at upper part. Siphonal canal fairly short, broad. Previous canals form series of flutings terminating in false umbilicus. Interior porcelaneous white.
OPERCULUM: Corneous, unguiculate, thick, with numerous concentric growth lines.
PERIOSTRACUM: None visible.
HABITAT: On jetties and just offshore or in inlet areas. Semi-infaunal.
LOCALITIES: Entire.
OCCURRENCE: Fairly common.
RANGE: North Carolina; Florida to Texas; northern Mexico.
GEOLOGIC RANGE: Pleistocene to Holocene.
REMARKS: The female deposits eggs in rubbery capsules attached to some substratum. The larvae have a nonpelagic development. Aquarium observations show that the animal will consume large amounts of food before burying itself for 3 or 4 weeks. When it emerges there will be an addition to the shell with a thin edge. It feeds again, reburies itself, and builds its spiny outer lip. This occurs about 3 times per year. In between additions to the shell it eats little. When feeding it may grasp a clam with its foot and pull the valves open or bore a hole with its radula. *See* Clench & Farfante 1945, p. 42.

Murex (Phyllonotus) pomum

Subgenus *Phyllonotus* Swainson, 1833

Apple Murex
Murex (Phyllonotus) pomum (Gmelin, 1791), *Syst. Natur.*, 13th ed., p. 3527.
L. *murex* the purple shellfish, *pomum* apple.
SIZE: 51–112 mm.
COLOR: Dark brown to yellowish tan with irregular dark brown spiral bands, which are often reduced to spots.
SHAPE: Conic with slightly extended siphonal canal.
ORNAMENT OR SCULPTURE: Seven to 9 solid, convex whorls. Suture not always distinct. Spire extended. Spiral sculpture consists of series of strong cords. Scaly cords form nodules on ridges. Between them are several finer scaly threads. Transverse sculpture consists of 3 prominent, equidistant varices on each whorl. Each varix has row of low, open spines and fluted edge on forward margin. Several ridges between varices.
APERTURE: Oval to subcircular, large. Interior polished, colored pink or ivory, yellow, orange. Outer lip thin, crenulate with varix bordering outer edge. Spotted brown to correspond with spiral bands. Parietal area glazed, adheres to body whorls, except for erect edge. Siphon short, slightly recurved. Dark brown spot on upper end of parietal wall.
OPERCULUM: Corneous, unguiculate, heavy, with strong growth lines.
PERIOSTRACUM: None visible.
HABITAT: Gravelly bottom, 5.4 to 12.6 meters (3 to 7 fathoms). Semi-infaunal.
LOCALITIES: Entire.
OCCURRENCE: Uncommon beach shell.
RANGE: North Carolina to Florida; Texas; Campeche Bank; Yucatán; West Indies; Surinam; Brazil.
GEOLOGIC RANGE: Miocene to Holocene.

REMARKS: This carnivore bores holes in the shells of its prey. The female lays eggs in leathery capsules that are attached to the bottom (fig. 23). Sometimes old shells with hermit crabs inside are found in inlet areas. Panamic vicariant is *Phyllonotus peratus* Keen, 1960. *See* Clench & Farfante 1945, p. 26.

Thais (Stramonita) haemastoma canaliculata

Subfamily THAIDINAE Suter, 1913

Genus *Thais* Röding, 1798
Subgenus *Stramonita* Schumaker, 1817

Hays' Rock Shell
Thais (Stramonita) haemastoma canaliculata (Gray, 1839), *Zool. Blossom*, p. 116.
L. Thais, wife of Ptolemaerus I of Egypt, *haema* blood, *stoma* mouth, *canaliculus* small channel.
SIZE: Up to 112 mm.
COLOR: Grayish with irregular mottling of darker color in either axial or spiral pattern.
SHAPE: Conic.
ORNAMENT OR SCULPTURE: Seven to 8 convex, solid whorls. Sutures usually indented; body whorl has angled shoulder. Spiral sculpture consists of numerous, coarse, incised lines with 2 rows of large nodules on whorl shoulder. Transverse sculpture of fine growth lines.
APERTURE: Subovate. Outer lip thickened with crenulations that run into aperture. Interior light brownish to pinkish orange. Parietal lip glazed, thickened by inductura. At upper edge is ridge that runs into aperture. May be weak plicae on base of straight columella. Siphonal canal short, oblique. Umbilicus closed.
OPERCULUM: Corneous, unguiculate. Underside thickened and shiny along outer edge.
PERIOSTRACUM: Deciduous.
HABITAT: Shallow water on rocks or oyster reefs. Epifaunal.
LOCALITIES: Entire.
OCCURRENCE: Fairly common.
RANGE: Bermuda; Gulf of Mexico from Florida west to Texas.
GEOLOGIC RANGE: Pleistocene to Holocene.
REMARKS: Clench separates this from *T. h. floridana* (Conrad) and names it *T. h. haysae* Clench, 1927, but the characteristics are not always easy to define. Some authors are reluctant to separate the two. *T. h. canaliculata* and *T. h. haysae* may only be variations of *T. h. floridana*. In other areas this mollusk is a serious oyster pest. *See* Clench 1927; Abbott 1975.

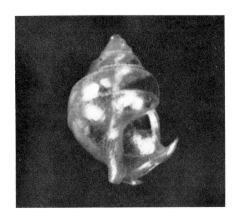

juvenile

Thais (Stramonita) haemastoma floridana

Oliva (Ispidula) sayana

Florida Rock Shell
Thais (Stramonita) haemastoma floridana (Conrad, 1837), *J. Acad. Natur. Sci. Philadelphia* 7:265.
L. Thais, wife of Ptolemaerus I of Egypt, *haema* blood, *stoma* mouth; from Florida.
SIZE: 51–75 mm.
COLOR: Light gray to yellowish, mottled with darker color in axial pattern.
SHAPE: Conic.
ORNAMENT OR SCULPTURE: Six to 7 convex whorls. Sutures in rather heavy shell fine, occasionally indented. Sculpture quite variable. Spiral sculpture may consist of incised lines and 2 rows of small nodules. Transverse sculpture of fine growth lines. Shoulders may be angled or not.
APERTURE: Subovate; interior salmon pink. Outer lip dark brown between denticulations that run into interior of aperture. Parietal lip glazed, smooth, thickened by inductura. Columella straight; may have faint plicae near base. Anal canal short with ridge along parietal wall. Siphonal canal short, oblique. Umbilicus closed.
OPERCULUM: Corneous, unguiculate. Underside thickened and shiny along outer edge.
PERIOSTRACUM: Deciduous.
HABITAT: Intertidal on rocks. Epifaunal.
LOCALITIES: Entire.
OCCURRENCE: Common.
RANGE: North Carolina to Florida; Texas; Yucatán; Central America; West Indies; northern and northeastern Brazil.
GEOLOGIC RANGE: Pleistocene to Holocene.
REMARKS: Carnivorous on bivalves. Sexes separate; lays eggs in purplish capsules clustered together on rocks, cans, bottles, etc. (fig. 23). The first young hatched within the capsule feed on the yolk of the unhatched eggs and emerge as larvae in the veliger stage. Panamic vicariant is *T. biserialis* (Blainville, 1832). *See* Clench 1947, p. 76.

Family OLIVIDAE Latreille, 1825
Subfamily OLIVINAE Swainson, 1840

Genus *Oliva* Bruguière, 1789
Subgenus *Ispidula* Gray, 1847

Lettered Olive
Oliva (Ispidula) sayana Ravenel, 1834, *Cat. Rec. Shells*, p. 19.
L. *oliva* olive; dedicated to Thomas Say (1787–1834), founder of the study of conchology in America.
SIZE: 51–62 mm.
COLOR: Polished cream-colored background with numerous brownish zigzag markings.
SHAPE: Elongate oval.
ORNAMENT OR SCULPTURE: Five to 6 whorls. Body whorl dominates shell. Spire short, acute. Sutures deep.
APERTURE: Long, narrow, purplish within. Outer lip thin. Siphonal canal oblique notch at base. White columella plicated.
OPERCULUM: None.
PERIOSTRACUM: None.
HABITAT: Inlets and offshore. Infaunal.
LOCALITIES: Entire.
OCCURRENCE: Common.
RANGE: North Carolina to Florida; Gulf states; West Indies; Brazil.
GEOLOGIC RANGE: Miocene to Holocene.
REMARKS: Skin divers will find this nocturnal predator plowing along just under the sand. The shell is covered with the propodium and lateral folds of the foot. *See* Pearse et al. 1942, p. 151; Burch & Burch 1967; Olsson & Crovo 1968, p. 31; Zeigler & Porreca 1969.

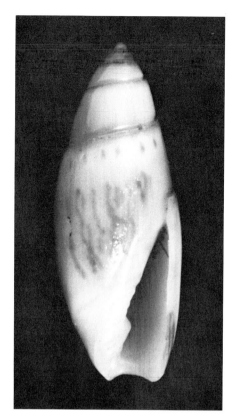

Olivella dealbata

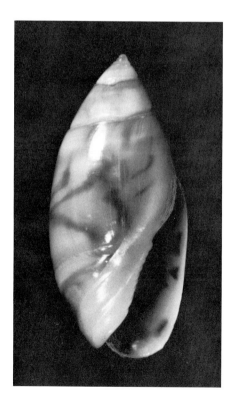

Olivella (Niteoliva) minuta

Genus *Olivella* Swainson, 1831

Whitened Dwarf Olive
Olivella dealbata (Reeve, 1850),
Conch. Icon. 6:25.
L. *oliva* olive, *ella* dim. suffix, *deal-batus* whitened.
SIZE: 6–9 mm.
COLOR: Glossy white or cream. Body whorl faintly marked with brownish zigzag streaks. Color variable.
SHAPE: Elongate oval.
ORNAMENT OR SCULPTURE: Smooth; sutures distinct, slightly canaliculated. Fasciole at base of shell white, bounded with fine raised thread.
APERTURE: Long, narrow, about three-fourths length of body whorl. Outer lip thin. Parietal inductura well developed. Columella slightly concave with 7 to 9 weak oblique plications. Siphonal notch not as pronounced as in *O. minuta*.
OPERCULUM: Corneous, brown, thin.
PERIOSTRACUM: None.
HABITAT: Inlet areas in the sand. Infaunal.
LOCALITIES: Entire, more to east.
OCCURRENCE: Common.
RANGE: North Carolina to both sides of Florida; Texas; Yucatán; West Indies.
GEOLOGIC RANGE: ? to Holocene.
REMARKS: At times in winter months these shells can be found by the thousands in the drift on the outer beaches. They will readily float when you wash and screen the beach drift. This species is closely related to *O. floralia* Duclos, 1835, and may be only a form of it.

Subgenus *Niteoliva* Olsson, 1956

Minute Dwarf Olive
Olivella (Niteoliva) minuta (Link, 1807), *Beschr. Natur.* 4:13.
L. *oliva* olive, *minutus* small.
SIZE: 6–12 mm.
COLOR: Polished grayish white background with purplish brown zigzag line on body whorl and fine brown lines along sutures. Color variable.
SHAPE: Elongate oval.
ORNAMENT OR SCULPTURE: Very smooth. Apex acute. Sutures open and grooved but not as pronounced as in *O. dealbata*. Fine spiral line above base.
APERTURE: Long, narrow, about three-fourths length of body whorl. Outer lip thin. Columella slightly concave with weak oblique plications. Pronounced siphonal notch.
OPERCULUM: Corneous, thin, semiovate.
PERIOSTRACUM: None.
HABITAT: Inlets and surf zone. Infaunal.
LOCALITIES: Entire, more to south.
OCCURRENCE: Common at times.
RANGE: Texas; Costa Rica; Caribbean; West Indies; Brazil.
GEOLOGIC RANGE: Miocene to Holocene.
REMARKS: With a lantern, this nocturnal carnivore can be found plowing along just below the sand of inlet areas at low tides on moonlit nights. This may be *O. mutica* Dall & Simpson, 1901.

Prunum (Leptegouana) apicina

Family MARGINELLIDAE Fleming, 1828

Genus *Prunum* Herrmannsen, 1852
Subgenus *Leptegouana* Woodring, 1928

Common Atlantic Marginella
Prunum (Leptegouana) apicina Menke, 1828, *Syn. Meth. Moll.*, p. 88.
L. *prunum* plum, *apicina* apex.
SIZE: 12 mm.
COLOR: Polished cream, yellowish, or grayish tan with several reddish brown spots on outer lip.
SHAPE: Conic, broad anteriorly.
ORNAMENT OR SCULPTURE: Smooth; spire short; convex body whorl large.
APERTURE: Long, narrow, length of body whorl. Outer lip thickened, notched at base. Columella with 4 strong plicae below.
OPERCULUM: None.
PERIOSTRACUM: None.
HABITAT: Shallow, grassy, inlet-influenced areas. Epifaunal.
LOCALITIES: Port Aransas, south.
OCCURRENCE: Uncommon in beach drift.
RANGE: North Carolina to Florida; Gulf states; Yucatán; West Indies.
GEOLOGIC RANGE: Pliocene to Holocene.
REMARKS: Bleached shells are found in the southern part of the coast. Not recently reported alive, probably fossil. [*Marginella apicina*]. Panamic vicariant is *P. woodbridgei* (Hertlein & Strong, 1951).

Subclass EUTHYNEURA Spengel, 1881 = [OPISTHOBRANCHIA Milne Edwards, 1848, and PULMONATA Cuvier, 1817]
The Euthyneura is the most varied in appearance of any subclass of mollusk. Throughout the geologic history of this group, there has been a tendency toward the loss of shell. The larval stage has both shell and operculum, but either or both may be lacking in the adult. The radula, when present, is of no classificatory value. The Euthyneura are hermaphroditic. Most of them are active carnivores and many are parasitic. Detorsion has taken place in most cases and the shell, if present, is often concealed in the mantle. There is only one gill and often there are respiratory substitutes, such as the outgrowths on many nudibranchs. It is almost impossible to generalize concerning the Euthyneura [opisthobranchs].

As a group, the sluglike nudibranchs have been given little attention along the Texas coast. This is due, in part, to the fact that they have no shell and are not easily recognizable as mollusks. The fleshy body decomposes rapidly, leaving no trace; therefore, unless the collector is on the beach at the time they are washing in and is prepared to transfer them to an aquarium or place them in a preserving solution, their presence may go unrecorded. These remarkably colorful little creatures deserve more attention. Send any specimens found to the University of Texas Marine Science Institute at Port Aransas with the appropriate collection data.

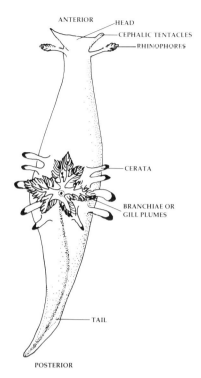

Fig. 35. Dorsal view of a generalized nudibranch

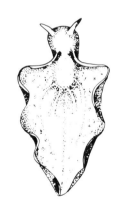

Elysia sp.

Discodoris hedgpethi
(after Marcus & Marcus 1959)

Order SACOGLOSSA Von Ihering, 1876 = [ASCOGLOSSA Bergh, 1877]
Superfamily ELYSIACEA H. & A. Adams, 1854
Family ELYSIIDAE H. & A. Adams, 1854

Genus *Elysia* Risso, 1818

Elysia sp.
L. *elysia* belonging to or like.
SIZE: 12 mm.
COLOR: Green, flecked with white.
SHAPE: Elongate, flattened.
ORNAMENT OR SCULPTURE: Body smooth, with cerata or papillae; foot narrow; tentacles large. Parapodia end at tip of blunt tail.
APERTURE: None.
OPERCULUM: None.
PERIOSTRACUM: None.
HABITAT: Brackish, shallow water on green algae.
LOCALITIES: East.
OCCURRENCE: Uncommon.
RANGE: Not defined.
GEOLOGIC RANGE: ? to Holocene.
REMARKS: First reported by C. Boone (*Texas Conch.* 12[3]:59). A generalized *Elysia* is figured so that the collector will have an idea of what the lettucelike organism might look like. Watch for it on green algae. Its color is due to chlorophyll in the contents of the digestive system.

Order DORIDOIDEA Odhner, 1934 = [HOLOHEPATICA Bergh, 1881]
Suborder CRYPTOBRANCHIA Fischer, 1883 = [EUDORIDOIDEA Odhner, 1934]
Superfamily DORIDACEA Rafinesque, 1815
Family DORIDIDAE Rafinesque, 1815
Subfamily DISCODORIDINAE Bergh, 1891

Genus *Discodoris* Bergh, 1877

Discodoris hedgpethi Marcus & Marcus, 1959, *Pub. Inst. Marine Sci.* 6:254.
L. *discordia* disagreement; dedicated to Dr. Joel W. Hedgpeth, director of Pacific Marine Station, University of the Pacific, Dillon Beach, California.
SIZE: 45–110 mm.
COLOR: Pale olive green with black spots and blotches; sole of foot less spotted.
SHAPE: Oval silhouette.
ORNAMENT OR SCULPTURE: Surface with many stiffened papillae. Foot notched in front.
APERTURE: None.
OPERCULUM: None.
PERIOSTRACUM: None.
HABITAT: Not known.
LOCALITIES: Port Aransas.
OCCURRENCE: Uncommon.
RANGE: Northern Texas.
GEOLOGIC RANGE: ? to Holocene.
REMARKS: Holotype collected by Joel W. Hedgpeth on October 12, 1948, at Port Aransas, Texas. *See* Marcus & Marcus 1959, p. 254.

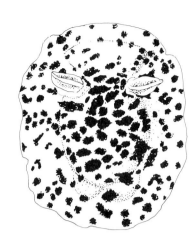

Doridella obscura
(after Marcus 1972a)

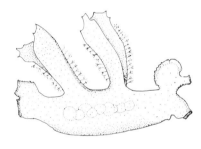

Scyllaea pelagica

Suborder PHANEROBRANCHIA
Von Ihering, 1876
Superfamily ONCHIDORIDACEA
Alder & Hancock, 1845 = [SUC-
TORIA Bergh, 1892]
Family CORAMBIDAE Bergh, 1869

Genus *Doridella* Verrill, 1870

Doridella obscura Verrill, 1870, *U.S.
Fish. Comm. Rep. 1871–72*, p. 307.
Doridella, dim. of Doris; L. *obscura*
darken.
SIZE: 2–4 mm.
COLOR: Reticulated yellow to brown
pattern.
SHAPE: Almost circular.
ORNAMENT OR SCULPTURE: Without
plumes or processes.
APERTURE: None.
OPERCULUM: None.
PERIOSTRACUM: None.
HABITAT: Shallow water on oyster
beds in brackish water.
LOCALITIES: Grand Isle, Louisiana,
and Port Aransas.
OCCURRENCE: Fairly common.
RANGE: Massachusetts to Florida to
Texas.
GEOLOGIC RANGE: ? to Holocene.
REMARKS: First found in Texas by
Harold Harry (1953, pp. 1–9). Syn.
Corambella baratariae Harry, 1953.
Feeds on encrusting bryozoan,
Membranipora. *See* Marcus & Marcus
1959, p. 256; Franz 1967b.

Order DENDRONOTOIDEA Odh-
ner, 1936
Family SCYLLAEIDAE Rafinesque,
1815

Genus *Scyllaea* Linné, 1758

Sargassum Nudibranch
Scyllaea pelagica Linné, 1758, *Syst.
Natur.*, 10th ed., p. 656.
L. Scylla, sea monster on the dan-
gerous rock opposite the whirlpool
Charybdis; Gk. *pelagus* of the sea.
SIZE: 25–51 mm.
COLOR: Yellowish brown to orange
brown, *Sargassum* colored.
SHAPE: Sluglike.
ORNAMENT OR SCULPTURE: No oral
tentacles. Two slender, long
rhinophores. Two series of large
foliaceous gill plumes, or cerata, on
each side of body.
APERTURE: None.
OPERCULUM: None.
PERIOSTRACUM: None.
HABITAT: Pelagic in *Sargassum*. Epi-
faunal.
LOCALITIES: Entire.
OCCURRENCE: Common.
RANGE: Southeastern United States;
other warm seas.
GEOLOGIC RANGE: ? to Holocene.
REMARKS: This creature can be
found by the hundreds clinging to
Sargassum, along with at least 4
other unidentified nudibranchs. It
will live in an aquarium for days
and is a delight to watch. Eggs are
laid in yellow gelatinous strings that
are more zigzag than straight. *See*
photograph in Buchsbaum & Milne
1966, p. 166.

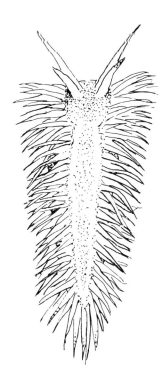

Fiona pinnata

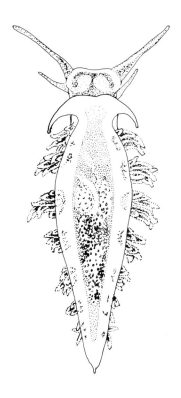

Cratena pilata
(after Franz 1968)

Order EOLIDOIDEA Odhner, 1937
Suborder EOLIDOIDEA Odhner, 1968
Infraorder ACLEIOPROCTA Odhner, 1939
Family FIONIDAE Gray, 1837

Genus *Fiona* Forbes & Hanley, 1851

Atlantic Blue Fiona
Fiona pinnata (Eschscholtz, 1831),
Zool. Atlas 4:4.
L. *fio* to become; *pinnata* feathered.
SIZE: 39 mm.
COLOR: Variable: reddish, bluish, yellowish.
SHAPE: Sluglike.
ORNAMENT OR SCULPTURE: Margins of foot broad, extending beyond body sides; cerata densely situated along margins of notum, leaving large part of back clear. Each of larger cerata has conspicuous longitudinal membrane along posterolateral axis, containing undulating blood vessel.
APERTURE: None.
OPERCULUM: None.
PERIOSTRACUM: None.
HABITAT: Pelagic on floating seaweed.
LOCALITIES: Entire.
OCCURRENCE: Seasonally common.
RANGE: Gulf Stream; Alaska to Peru.
GEOLOGIC RANGE: ? to Holocene.
REMARKS: Brought in by spring winds. Feeds on siphonophores *Velella* and *Lepas*. The generalized *F. pinnata* figured here is based on photographs in Bayer 1963. Syn. *F. nobilis* (Alder & Hancock, 1848). *See* Bayer 1963.

Infraorder CLEIOPROCTA Odhner, 1939
Family FAVORINIDAE Bergh, 1889
Subfamily FAVORININAE Bergh, 1889

Genus *Cratena* Bergh, 1864

Cratena pilata Gould, 1870, *Rep. Invert.*, p. 243.
L. *cratis* basket, box, *pilata* haired.
SIZE: 12–15 mm.
COLOR: Brownish gray on dorsal side with greenish brown gray liver spots in cerata. Underside white.
SHAPE: Elongate, tapered posteriorly; sluglike.
ORNAMENT OR SCULPTURE: Scattered low tubercles on rhinophores. Nine groups of cerata.
APERTURE: None.
OPERCULUM: None.
PERIOSTRACUM: None.
HABITAT: Pelagic in shallow water.
LOCALITIES: Probably entire.
OCCURRENCE: Uncommon.
RANGE: North Carolina to Texas to Brazil.
GEOLOGIC RANGE: ? to Holocene.
REMARKS: This has been found in channels and in a lagoon of variable salinity. *See* Marcus & Marcus 1959, p. 257.

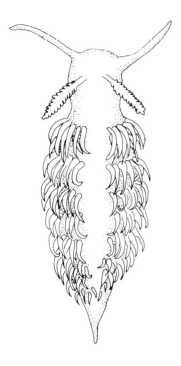

Spurilla neapolitana
(after Marcus & Marcus 1959)

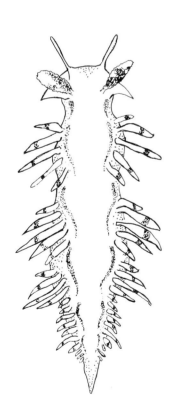

Berghia coerulescens
(after Marcus & Marcus 1959)

Family EOLIDIIDAE Orbigny, 1834

Genus *Spurilla* Bergh, 1864

Spurilla neapolitana (Delle Chiaje, 1823), *Mem. Anim. sans Vert. Napoli* 1(2–4):39.
L. *spurius* false; from Naples.
SIZE: 20–40 mm.
COLOR: Colorful, varying from ivory, yellowish rose, or pinkish with reddish brown to olive green diverticula within cerata which are tipped with white and keeled on side facing midline. Opaque white dots on cerata, head, back.
SHAPE: Elongate, tapered posteriorly; sluglike.
ORNAMENT OR SCULPTURE: Rows of arched cerata on dorsal surface.
APERTURE: None.
OPERCULUM: None.
PERIOSTRACUM: None.
HABITAT: On weeds attached to floating logs. Pelagic.
LOCALITIES: Probably entire.
OCCURRENCE: Occasionally common.
RANGE: Florida to Texas; Caribbean to Brazil; eastern Atlantic; Mediterranean.
GEOLOGIC RANGE: ? to Holocene.
REMARKS: First collected in Texas by Joel W. Hedgpeth at Port Aransas on June 25, 1948. Feeds on sea anemones. *See* Marcus & Marcus 1959, p. 258.

Genus *Berghia* Trinchese, 1877

Berghia coerulescens (Laurillard, 1831), *Guerin Mag. de Zool.*
Dedicated to Ludwig Rudolf Sophus Bergh (1824–1909), German malacologist; L. *coer* sky, becoming blue.
SIZE: 10–40 mm.
COLOR: Yellowish white, bright scarlet and blue "trimmings."
SHAPE: Elongate, tapering posteriorly; sluglike.
ORNAMENT OR SCULPTURE: Rhinophores bear distinct rows of tubercles on posterior surface.
APERTURE: None.
OPERCULUM: None.
PERIOSTRACUM: None.
HABITAT: Pelagic.
LOCALITIES: Probably entire.
OCCURRENCE: Uncommon.
RANGE: North Carolina to Texas; West Indies to Brazil; eastern Atlantic.
GEOLOGIC RANGE: ? to Holocene.
REMARKS: This widely distributed species was first collected in Texas at Port Aransas by Joel W. Hedgpeth in 1948. *See* Marcus & Marcus 1959, p. 258.

Glaucus atlanticus

Genus *Cerberilla* Bergh, 1873

Cerberilla tanna Marcus & Marcus, 1959, *Pub. Inst. Marine Sci.* 6:259.
Gk. *kerberos* doglike; C. *tann* oak, brown.
SIZE: 25 mm.
COLOR: Dirty yellow with orange brown spot on outer surface of many, not all, cerata.
SHAPE: Animal is strongly contracted and curled.
ORNAMENT OR SCULPTURE: Rhinophores minute; tentacles very long, pointed.
APERTURE: None.
OPERCULUM: None.
PERIOSTRACUM: None.
HABITAT: Pelagic.
LOCALITIES: Sabine.
OCCURRENCE: Uncommon.
RANGE: Not defined.
GEOLOGIC RANGE: ? to Holocene.
REMARKS: Holotype collected in Texas by Henry H. Hildebrand off the Sabine Jetties on June 15, 1951. According to E. Marcus (in litt.), there is not, at this time, a total picture of this species because Ceberillae are so like one another that their outer aspect is not needed for classification. It looks somewhat like a shorter version of *Spurilla*. *See* Marcus & Marcus 1959, p. 259.

Family GLAUCIDAE Menke, 1828

Genus *Glaucus* Forster, 1777

Blue Glaucus
Glaucus atlanticus Forster, 1777, *Voy. World* 1:49.
L. *glaucus* bluish gray; of the Atlantic.
SIZE: 51 mm.
COLOR: Shades of blue.
SHAPE: Sluglike body.
ORNAMENT OR SCULPTURE: Tentacles and rhinophores small. Four clumps of bright blue frilled cerata on each side of body.
APERTURE: None.
OPERCULUM: None.
PERIOSTRACUM: None.
HABITAT: Pelagic in warm seas.
LOCALITIES: Entire.
OCCURRENCE: Occasionally common.
RANGE: Worldwide.
GEOLOGIC RANGE: ? to Holocene.
REMARKS: This brightly colored slug is washed ashore by strong southeast winds in the spring when *Janthina* is coming in. Hermaphroditic. Feeds on siphonophores.

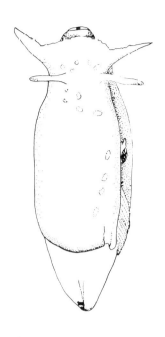

Pleurobranchaea hedgpethi
(after Marcus & Marcus 1959)

Rictaxis ? punctostriatus

Order PLEUROBRANCHIA Von
  Ihering, 1922
Superfamily PLEUROBRAN-
  CHACEA Menke, 1828
Family PLEUROBRANCHIDAE
  Menke, 1828
Subfamily PLEUROBRANCHINAE
  Menke, 1828

Genus *Pleurobranchaea* Leve, 1813

Pleurobranchaea hedgpethi Abbott,
1952, *Florida State Univ. Studies* 7:1.
L. *pleur* side, *branchos* gills or fin;
dedicated to Dr. Joel W. Hedgpeth,
director of Pacific Marine Station,
University of the Pacific.
SIZE: 45 mm.
COLOR: Sepia brown with lighter
mottlings. Light papillae standing
out from dark skin. Dorsal spur
black.
SHAPE: Elongate to elliptical, slightly
flattened.
ORNAMENT OR SCULPTURE: Dorsal
surface covered by semitranslucent
mantle which is shorter and nar-
rower than foot, with very narrow
free edge. Foot has small, gray,
fleshy spur posteriorly on dorsal
surface. No shell.
APERTURE: None.
OPERCULUM: None.
PERIOSTRACUM: None.
HABITAT: Shallow water over mud
bottom. Epifaunal.
LOCALITIES: Port Aransas and Port
Isabel.
OCCURRENCE: Uncommon.
RANGE: South Texas; Bay of Cam-
peche; Surinam.
GEOLOGIC RANGE: ? to Holocene.
REMARKS: Holotype collected at Port
Isabel, Texas by Joel W. Hedgpeth
on March 21, 1947. *See* Abbott 1952;
Marcus & Marcus 1959, p. 253.

Order STEGANOBRANCHIA Von
  Ihering, 1876
Suborder ACTEONOIDEA Or-
  bigny, 1835
Superfamily ACTEONACEA Or-
  bigny, 1835
Family ACTEONIDAE Orbigny,
  1835

Genus *Rictaxis* Dall, 1871

Adams' Baby-Bubble
Rictaxis ? punctostriatus (C. B.
Adams, 1840), *Boston J. Natur. Hist.*
3:323.
Gk. *taxis* classify; L. *punctum* point,
striatus striated.
SIZE: 3–6 mm.
COLOR: White, fragile.
SHAPE: Globose, conic.
ORNAMENT OR SCULPTURE: Four
convex whorls. Sutures deep. Spire
elevated. Body whorl large with fine
spiral striations over basal half.
APERTURE: Elongated pear shape.
Outer lip thin. Little more than
one-half length of body whorl. Col-
umella short with one strong ob-
lique fold.
OPERCULUM: Thin, corneous.
PERIOSTRACUM: Thin.
HABITAT: Inlet areas and outer
beaches. Infaunal.
LOCALITIES: Entire.
OCCURRENCE: Fairly common.
RANGE: Gulf of Mexico; Gulf of
Campeche; Campeche Bank; Brazil.
GEOLOGIC RANGE: Miocene to
Holocene.
REMARKS: According to E. Marcus
(1972), the species that ranges from
Cape Cod to the West Indies is *R.
punctostriatus* (C. B. Adams, 1840).
This Texas species may be the same,
but the animal has not yet been
examined. This little vermivore bur-
rows just below the surface. [*Acteon
punctostriatus*]. *See* Marcus 1972*b*, p.
178.

Bulla striata

Acteocina canaliculata

Suborder BULLOIDEA Lamarck, 1801
Superfamily BULLACEA Lamarck, 1801
Family BULLIDAE Lamarck, 1801

Genus *Bulla* Linné, 1758

Striate Bubble
Bulla striata Bruguière, 1792, *Encycl. Méth.* 1:572.
L. *bulla* bubble, *striatus* striated.
SIZE: 18–25 mm.
COLOR: Whitish with small irregular mottlings of chocolate brown.
SHAPE: Oval with sunken spire.
ORNAMENT OR SCULPTURE: Delicate shell smooth except for microscopic growth lines. Spiral sculpture consists of fine grooves toward base and within sunken apical end.
APERTURE: Longer than body whorl, wider near base. Interior whitish. Outer lip thin. Parietal area covered with glazed white inductura.
OPERCULUM: None.
PERIOSTRACUM: None.
HABITAT: Inlet areas on grass in shallow water. Epifaunal.
LOCALITIES: Entire.
OCCURRENCE: Common.
RANGE: Bermuda; western coast of Florida to Texas; Yucatán; Costa Rica; West Indies to Brazil.
GEOLOGIC RANGE: Miocene to Holocene.
REMARKS: This carnivore completely envelops its shell, looking like a lump of jelly when found alive (fig. 15). Burrows in the bottom near grass roots. Does not like bright sun. Lays eggs in jellylike ribbons.

Family ACTEOCINIDAE Pilsbry, 1921

Genus *Acteocina* Gray, 1847

Channeled Barrel-Bubble
Acteocina canaliculata (Say, 1826), *J. Acad. Natur. Sci. Philadelphia* 5(1):211.
Gk. *actaion* a huntsman; L. *canaliculatus* channeled.
SIZE: 3–5 mm.
COLOR: Glossy white.
SHAPE: Cylindrical with moderately elevated spire.
ORNAMENT OR SCULPTURE: Smooth except for microscopic growth lines. Suture channeled.
APERTURE: Long, narrow, wider at base. Outer lip thin. Columella single, raised fold below parietal inductura.
OPERCULUM: None.
PERIOSTRACUM: None.
HABITAT: Enclosed moderate-salinity bays. Infaunal.
LOCALITIES: Entire.
OCCURRENCE: Common in beach drift.
RANGE: Nova Scotia to Florida; Texas; Campeche Bank; West Indies; Surinam.
GEOLOGIC RANGE: Miocene to Holocene.
REMARKS: Egg masses are gelatinous and attached by a strand to marine grasses. The veligers have a non-pelagic development. Probably on oyster beds. Formerly in the genus *Retusa* (Wells & Wells 1962, p. 87). *See* Franz 1971.

Haminoea antillarum

Haminoea succinea

Family ATYIDAE Thiele, 1926

Genus *Haminoea* Turton & Kingston, 1830

Elegant Paper-Bubble
Haminoea antillarum (Orbigny, 1841), *Hist. d'Ile de Cuba* 1:124.
L. *hamus* hook; from the Antilles.
SIZE: 18 mm.
COLOR: Pale greenish yellow, almost translucent.
SHAPE: Rounded oval; spire insunk.
ORNAMENT OR SCULPTURE: Surface appears smooth but has fine growth striae and microscopic, wavy, spiral lines.
APERTURE: Longer than body whorl, wider at bottom. Outer lip arises to right of apical depression. Columella extremely concave. Parietal area has narrow white inductura.
OPERCULUM: None.
PERIOSTRACUM: None.
HABITAT: Inlet-influenced areas in shallow water. Epifaunal.
LOCALITIES: Entire.
OCCURRENCE: Fairly common.
RANGE: Gulf of Mexico; Yucatán; West Indies; northeastern Brazil.
GEOLOGIC RANGE: ? to Holocene.
REMARKS: This little carnivore cannot withdraw into the shell. Varies its diet with algae.

Conrad's Paper-Bubble
Haminoea succinea (Conrad, 1846), *Proc. Acad. Natur. Sci. Philadelphia* 3(1):26.
L. *hamus* hook, *succinum* amber.
SIZE: 10 mm.
COLOR: White to pale amber.
SHAPE: Cylindrical, thin; spire insunk.
ORNAMENT OR SCULPTURE: Surface covered with minute, wavy, spiral lines.
APERTURE: Longer than body whorl, wider near base. Outer lip thin, sharp. Columella concave with one weak fold above center.
OPERCULUM: None.
PERIOSTRACUM: None.
HABITAT: Inlet influence in shallow water. Epifaunal.
LOCALITIES: Entire.
OCCURRENCE: Uncommon to rare in beach drift.
RANGE: Bermuda; Florida to Texas; Campeche Bank.
GEOLOGIC RANGE: ? to Holocene.
REMARKS: Sift the drift for this little shell. When alive, animal is brown. *See* Marcus 1972a, p. 303.

Volvulella persimilis

Volvulella (Paravolvulella) texasiana

Genus *Volvulella* Newton, 1891

Volvulella persimilis (Mörch, 1875), *Malak. Blätter* 22:179.
L. *volvere* to roll, *persimilis* very like.
SIZE: 3–4 mm.
COLOR: White.
SHAPE: Cylindrical, tapering at each end.
ORNAMENT OR SCULPTURE: Body whorl dominates shell, with sharp, spikelike apex and tapering, rounded anterior end. Rather thin, semitransparent, somewhat lustrous, with 4 or 5 very fine, indistinct, punctate, spiral lines on each end and very indistinct, microscopic striae on intervening surface.
APERTURE: Long, very narrow, expanded anteriorly. Outer lip thin, following curvature of body whorl to just below middle where it continues in straight line and joins inner lip in broad curve. Inner lip very thin, slightly reflected anteriorly over slight umbilical chink.
OPERCULUM: None.
PERIOSTRACUM: Thin, pale yellow.
HABITAT: Seven to 30 meters (17 fathoms), offshore. Infaunal.
LOCALITIES: Entire.
OCCURRENCE: Rare in beach drift.
RANGE: Bermuda; North Carolina to southeastern Florida; Texas; West Indies; Cuba; Surinam; northeastern and eastern Brazil.
GEOLOGIC RANGE: ? to Holocene.
REMARKS: Easily overlooked if drift not screened carefully. Syn. *Volvula oxytata* Bush, 1885. Genus has been called *Rhizorus*. Panamic vicariant is *V. cylindrica* (Carpenter, 1864). *See* Marcus 1960, p. 132; Harry 1967.

Subgenus *Paravolvulella* Harry, 1967

Volvulella (Paravolvulella) texasiana Harry, 1967, *Veliger* 10(2):141.
L. *volvere* to roll; from Texas.
SIZE: 3.94 mm.
COLOR: Gray, translucent, with irregular, opaque white flecks. Ends usually stained with iron, reddish brown.
SHAPE: Cylindrical.
ORNAMENT OR SCULPTURE: Sculpture consists of few narrow spiral bands equally spaced around base and fainter ones on apical end. Microscopic wavy lines cover midsection of shell. Anomphalous. Adult shells not tapering. Small apical spine usually broken but has spiral band about its base.
APERTURE: Narrow, as long as body whorl. Outer lip and side of body whorls flattened. Outer lip quadrate, meeting columella at right angle; basal end strongly arched. No columellar teeth.
OPERCULUM: None.
PERIOSTRACUM: Thin, colorless.
HABITAT: Offshore, 12.6 meters (7 fathoms). Infaunal.
LOCALITIES: Galveston and Port Isabel, probably entire.
OCCURRENCE: Rare in beach drift.
RANGE: Texas.
GEOLOGIC RANGE: ? to Holocene.
REMARKS: A minute shell recently described by Harold Harry of Texas A&M University. Holotype dredged offshore 10 miles south of Galveston, Texas, in 1965 by staff members of the Texas Fish and Game Commission. Panamic vicariant is *V. panamica* Dall, 1919. Coll., Harry. *See* Harry 1967.

Cylichnella bidentata

Aplysia (Varria) brasiliana
(Tryon 1895, 16:pl. 37)

Superfamily CYLICHNACEA A.
Adams, 1850
Family CYLICHNIDAE A. Adams,
1850

Genus *Cylichnella* Gabb, 1873

Orbigny's Baby-Bubble
Cylichnella bidentata (Orbigny, 1841),
Hist. d'Ile de Cuba 1:125.
Gk. *kylix* a drinking cup; L. *bi* twice,
dens tooth (*bidentatus* with two
teeth).
SIZE: 2.5–4 mm.
COLOR: White, fragile.
SHAPE: Cylindrical.
ORNAMENT OR SCULPTURE: Smooth;
spire depressed. Body whorl nar-
rowed above and below.
APERTURE: Long, narrow. Outer lip
thin, slightly flared below. Col-
umella short with 2 plicae at base.
OPERCULUM: None.
PERIOSTRACUM: None.
HABITAT: Inlet areas near low-water
mark. Infaunal.
LOCALITIES: Entire.
OCCURRENCE: Fairly common.
RANGE: North Carolina; Florida;
Gulf states; Yucatán; West Indies;
Brazil.
GEOLOGIC RANGE: Pleistocene to
Holocene.
REMARKS: The maculated mantle of
this minute carnivore completely
envelops the shell. Tiny black eyes
are high on the head. Crawls just
under the sand leaving a raised trail
on the surface. *See* E. Marcus 1958.

Suborder APLYSIOIDEA Lamarck,
1809
Infraorder LONGICOMMIS-
SURATA Pruvot-Fol, 1954
Superfamily APLYSIACEA
Lamarck, 1809
Family APLYSIIDAE Rafinesque,
1815
Subfamily APLYSIINAE Rafinesque, 1815
Color and shape are not reliable for
identification. It "would help in
identification, however, if collectors
would record, in the living animal,
the color and markings, the nature
of the mantle gland exudate (e.g.,
purple, white), the presence or absence of a sucker on the posterior
end of the foot and the length of tail
relative to the body" (Eales 1960, p.
277).

Genus *Aplysia* Linné, 1767
Subgenus *Varria* Eales, 1960

Sooty Sea Hare
Aplysia (Varria) brasiliana Rang, 1828,
Hist. Natur., p. 55.
Gk. *aplysia* that which one cannot
wash, but Linné chose the name
arbitrarily; from Brazil.
SIZE: 100 mm.
EXUDATE: Greenish yellow.
SHELL: Narrow to broad, concave,
dark yellow, with apex hard and
hooked but without spire. Internal.
APERTURE: None.
OPERCULUM: None.
PERIOSTRACUM: None.
HABITAT: Where algae grow abun-
dantly. Epifaunal.
LOCALITIES: Port Isabel.
OCCURRENCE: Uncommon to rare.
RANGE: New Jersey to Brazil; St.
Helena; Ghana.
GEOLOGIC RANGE: ? to Holocene.
REMARKS: Syn. *A. floridensis* (Pilsbry,
1895). A very variable species. Large
bulky body, self-colored or spotted.
Simple cephalic tentacles; slender
rhinophores set close together; long
neck; narrow foot; long tapering
verge; very large parapodia joined
low down posteriorly; mantle aperture tubular; opaline gland compound, uniporous; simple radula
with high narrow rhachidian tooth.
Young specimens may have a hole
in the mantle (Eales 1960).

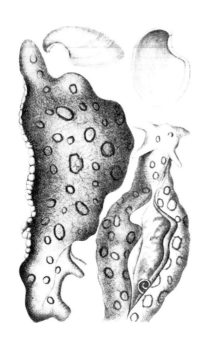

Aplysia (Varria) dactylomela
(Tryon 1895, 16:pl. 32)

Spotted Sea Hare
Aplysia (Varria) dactylomela (Rang, 1828), *Hist. Natur.*, p. 56.
Gk. *aplysia* that which one cannot wash, but Linné chose the name arbitrarily; *dactylos* finger, *mela* black.
SIZE: 100–125 mm.
EXUDATE: Deep purple.
SHELL: Large, broad, rounded, with oblique apex; strongly calcified, with hardly any trace of spire. Internal.
APERTURE: None.
OPERCULUM: None.
PERIOSTRACUM: None.
HABITAT: Where algae grow abundantly. Epifaunal.
LOCALITIES: Port Isabel.
OCCURRENCE: Uncommon.
RANGE: Circumtropical.
GEOLOGIC RANGE: ? to Holocene.
REMARKS: Larger than *A. willcoxi*. Lives only one year. Syn. *A. protea* Rang 1828. Large bulky Aplysias, of basic yellowish green color, with numerous large black rings of irregular sizes on the sides of the body, thick rhinophores with short notched apices, broad foot with blunt tail, frilled swimming lobes joined low down posteriorly, broad spatulate spirally grooved verge, compound uniporous opaline gland, lateral teeth of the radula with long straight smooth cusps (Eales 1960). *See* Buchsbaum & Milne 1966, p. 161; Lederhendler et al. 1974.

Aplysia (Varria) donca Marcus & Marcus, 1959, *Pub. Inst. Marine Sci.* 6:251.
Gk. *aplysia* that which one cannot wash, but Linné chose the name arbitrarily; *don* act.
SIZE: 65 mm.
EXUDATE: Brownish.
SHELL: Thin, flat, with a long sinus. Internal.
ORNAMENT OR SCULPTURE: Smooth mantle and swimming lobes.
APERTURE: None.
OPERCULUM: None.
PERIOSTRACUM: None.
HABITAT: With algae. Epifaunal.
LOCALITIES: Port Aransas.
OCCURRENCE: Rare.
RANGE: Not determined.
GEOLOGIC RANGE: ? to Holocene.
REMARKS: Holotype was collected by Joel W. Hedgpeth on Mustang Island on March 9, 1947. According to E. Marcus (in litt.), a total external illustration of *A. donca* does not exist at this time because the members of the genus *Aplysia* are so alike that their outer aspect is not needed for classification.

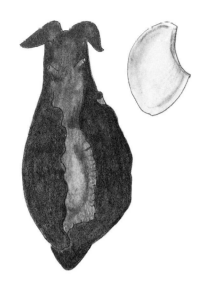

Aplysia (Varria) morio

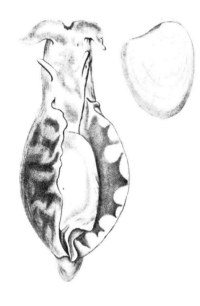

Aplysia (Varria) willcoxi
(Tryon 1895, 16:pl. 35)

Giant Black Sea Hare
Aplysia (Varria) morio Verrill, 1901, *Trans. Connecticut Acad. Arts & Sci.* 11(1):25.
Gk. *aplysia* that which one cannot wash, but Linné chose the name arbitrarily; L. *morio* fool.
SIZE: 212–318 mm.
EXUDATE: Purple.
SHELL: Long and narrow without a spire, strongly ridged, with hardly any anal sinus. Internal.
APERTURE: None.
OPERCULUM: None.
PERIOSTRACUM: None.
HABITAT: Where algae grow abundantly. Epifaunal.
LOCALITIES: Not defined.
OCCURRENCE: Not defined.
RANGE: Bermuda; Rhode Island to Texas; West Indies.
GEOLOGIC RANGE: ? to Holocene.
REMARKS: Large size, deep brown color, soft skin, wide hemispherical tentacles, narrow foot with short tail. Very large, free, thin, swimming parapodia, arising close behind the rhinophores, then becoming wide, rounded and fluted on the edges, to unite low down on the tail. Mantle and visceral regions small. No shell foramen in the adult. Large leaflike siphon, large ctenidium, simple multiporous opaline gland. Shell long and narrow, without spire, strongly ridged, with hardly any anal sinus. Radula with numerous rows and more than 50 teeth on each side in a full row. All teeth, except the few outermost vestigial ones, with elaborate denticulation. Verge sheath anchored by numerous muscle strands, plain internally; verge short, stout, unpigmented (Eales 1960). *See* Marcus & Marcus 1959, p. 253.

Willcox's Sea Hare
Aplysia (Varria) willcoxi (Heilprin, 1886), *Proc. Acad. Natur. Sci. Philadelphia* 38:364.
Gk. *aplysia* that which one cannot wash, but Linné chose the name arbitrarily; dedicated to J. Willcox, nineteenth-century malacologist.
SIZE: 125–225 mm.
EXUDATE: Reddish purple, turns crimson in formalin.
SHELL: Broad, flattened, thin with some calcareous matter. Apex small, curved. Internal.
APERTURE: None.
OPERCULUM: None.
PERIOSTRACUM: None.
HABITAT: Where algae grow abundantly. Epifaunal.
LOCALITIES: Entire.
OCCURRENCE: Common.
RANGE: Bermuda; Cape Cod to both sides of Florida; Texas; West Indies.
GEOLOGIC RANGE: ? to Holocene.
REMARKS: This unusual creature has been seen swimming across the ship channel at Port Aransas with its head breaking the surface of the water. In summer months, a skin diver will be able to observe the animals grazing on algae along the jetties. They are fun to observe in an aquarium, crawling on the bottom or swimming. When disturbed, they expel a purple fluid. Eggs are tangled masses of gelatinous threads laid in grass flats of the bays (fig. 24). Large size, bulky shape, tough skin, dark coloring of all parts with abundance of deep green in the variety *perviridis*. Cephalic tentacles large; rhinophores close together; foot narrow; verge long, filiform; swimming parapodia smooth, joined low down posteriorly; minute mantle foramen; opaline gland compound uniporous; radula large with elaboration of the basal denticles (Eales 1960).

Bursatella leachi pleei
(Tryon 1895, 16:pl. 43, 44)

Infraorder BREVICOMMIS-
SURATA Pruvot-Fol, 1954
Subfamily DOLABRIFERINAE
Pilsbry, 1895

Genus *Bursatella* Blainville, 1817

Ragged Sea Hare
Bursatella leachi pleei Rang, 1828,
Hist. Natur., p. 70.
L. *bursa* pouch, saclike cavity; dedi-
cated to W. C. Leach (1790–1836)
and a Mr. Plee, who found it in the
West Indies.
SIZE: 100 mm.
COLOR: Animal is olive green to
gray, usually with white specks.
SHAPE: Animal is elongate oval.
ORNAMENT OR SCULPTURE: Surface
covered with numerous ragged ap-
pendages. No internal shell in
adult.
APERTURE: None.
OPERCULUM: None.
PERIOSTRACUM: None.
HABITAT: Where algae are abun-
dant. Epifaunal.
LOCALITIES: Port Isabel.
OCCURRENCE: Uncommon.
RANGE: Western and northwestern
Florida; Texas; West Indies to Brazil.
GEOLOGIC RANGE: ? to Holocene.
REMARKS: First reported in Texas by
Breuer (1962). *See* Lowe & Turner
1976.

Order ENTOMOTAENIATA Cossmann, 1896
Superfamily PYRAMIDELLACEA
Gray, 1840
Family PYRAMIDELLIDAE Gray,
1840
This large family of minute gastropods is very confusing to both
novice and expert. A powerful microscope is needed in any attempt
to separate them. They were origi-
nally classified in the Prosobranchia
with the Eulimidae, but recent
study has shown they are more
closely related to the Euthyneura or
Opisthobranchia. They are less removed from the prosobranchs than
other opisthobranch families, with
the exception of the Acteonidae,
and have undergone less evolutionary change. As opposed to other
opisthobranchs, they have opercula, spirally coiled calcareous
shells into which the entire body
can retract, and a large anteriorly
directed mantle cavity. Pyramidellids are ectoparasites. Each species
may feed primarily on a particular
host species, usually a tube-
building polychaete or a bivalve
mollusk to which they attach by
means of an oral sucker. They are
hermaphroditic, laying eggs in
gelatinous masses on their hosts.

The many-whorled shells are distinguished by nuclear whorls that
turn sinistrally and are at right
angles to the later whorls (heterostrophic). The columella has one or
more folds. There is no radula and
the corneous operculum is oval and
few whorled, with an apical nucleus.

The family Pyramidellidae is
represented in Texas by at least 5
genera. Some authors have elevated
many of the subgenera to generic
rank, but this will not be attempted
here. The *Pyramidella* are the largest
and easiest to separate. The elon-
gate-conic shell has regularly increasing, inflated whorls, a columella
with one to three plicae, and an
entire (holostomate) outer lip. The
Odostomia are short and subconic or

Pyramidella (Longchaeus) crenulata

ovate. The complexity of the sculpture and the poor figures available make the *Turbonilla* the most difficult to identify as to species. Until an expert monographs the *Turbonilla*, their correct identity is only a matter of speculation. The shell is cylindro-conic, many whorled, and usually slender with a single columellar fold that varies in strength. The outer lip of this genus is entire and the shell is larger than *Odostomia* but smaller than *Pyramidella*. In *Eulimastoma* Bartsch, 1916, the minute shell is elongate conic with a single columellar fold, a pronounced angulation at the whorl base, no sculpture, and whorls that are slightly convex to flat sided. The heterostropic protoconch is usually immersed in the first postnuclear whorl. Living *Eulimastoma* have been described as *Odostomia*, to which they are closely related. The most strongly sculptured of the family are the *Peristichia*.

In the past, members of this family have often been overlooked because of their size; much of the material is lost in screening. The names assigned to the various members figured here are only "educated guesses" hesitatingly applied.

It is easy to avoid these tiny shells after a few trial identifications and one becomes tempted to agree with Dr. James Lewis, who left an amusing notation on the usually stuffy labels that accompany mollusks in the great study collections when he penciled, "What the hell, who can tell?" (*Nautilus* 55[4]:119).

Genus *Pyramidella* Lamarck, 1799
Subgenus *Longchaeus* Mörch, 1875

Notched Pyram
Pyramidella (Longchaeus) crenulata
(Holmes, 1859), *Post-Plio. Fos. South Carolina*, p. 88.
L. *pyramis* pyramid, *crenulatus* finely notched.
SIZE: 10–12 mm.
COLOR: Pale brown; cream to white when dead. Polished.
SHAPE: Elongate conic.
ORNAMENT OR SCULPTURE: Numerous flat-sided whorls. Sutures distinct, V-shaped channels. Spire acute. Body whorl rounded at base. Posterior margin of each whorl delicately crenulated. Weak basal line meets outer lip at suture. Phaneromphalous.
APERTURE: Small, rather auriform, entire. Outer lip thin. Columella sinuous, 2 oblique folds.
OPERCULUM: Corneous, semicircular, notched to fit plications on columella.
PERIOSTRACUM: None visible.
HABITAT: Ectoparasitic in inlets and hypersaline lagoons. Epifaunal.
LOCALITIES: Entire.
OCCURRENCE: Common.
RANGE: South Carolina to Florida; Texas; West Indies.
GEOLOGIC RANGE: Upper Pliocene to Holocene.
REMARKS: The largest pyram on this coast.

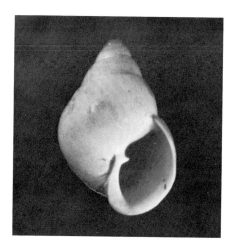

Odostomia (Odostomia) cf. *O. gibbosa*

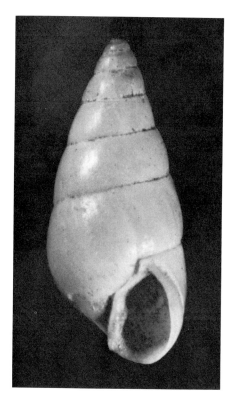

Odostomia (Odostomia) laevigata

Genus *Odostomia* Fleming, 1817
Subgenus *Odostomia* s.s.

Fat Odostome
Odostomia (Odostomia) cf. *O. gibbosa*
Bush, 1909, *Amer. J. Sci.* 27:475.
Gk. *odon, odontis* tooth, *stoma*
mouth; L. *gibbus* a hump.
SIZE: 3 mm.
COLOR: Whitish, polished.
SHAPE: Globose conic.
ORNAMENT OR SCULPTURE: About 5
very convex whorls. Shell rather
fragile. Sutures distinct. Smooth ex-
cept for microscopic growth stria-
tions.
APERTURE: Pear-shaped, fairly large.
Outer lip thin. Columella marked
with single prominent tooth near
insertion.
OPERCULUM: Corneous.
PERIOSTRACUM: None visible.
HABITAT: Ectoparasitic in inlet areas.
Epifaunal.
LOCALITIES: Entire.
OCCURRENCE: Fairly common in
beach drift.
RANGE: Maine to southern Mas-
sachusetts; Texas.
GEOLOGIC RANGE: ? to Holocene.
REMARKS: The rounded shape of this
tiny shell distinguishes it from the
other *Odostomia*.

Smooth Odostome
Odostomia (Odostomia) laevigata (Orbigny, 1842), *Hist. d'Ile de Cuba*
1:227.
Gk. *odon, odontis* tooth, *stoma*
mouth; L. *laevis* smooth.
SIZE: 3–5 mm.
COLOR: Translucent grayish white
alive; opaque white to brownish
dead.
SHAPE: Ovate conic.
ORNAMENT OR SCULPTURE: Four to 6
convex whorls. Suture fairly im-
pressed. Spiral sculpture absent or
microscopic. Nuclear whorls im-
pressed in apex. May have chinklike
umbilicus. Quite variable.
APERTURE: Ovate. Columellar tooth
weak.
OPERCULUM: Corneous.
PERIOSTRACUM: None visible.
HABITAT: Ectoparasitic in inlet-
influenced areas, shallow water.
Epifaunal.
LOCALITIES: Entire.
OCCURRENCE: Fairly common in
beach drift.
RANGE: Southeastern United States
to Lesser Antilles; Texas; Yucatán;
Brazil.
GEOLOGIC RANGE: Pleistocene to
Holocene.
REMARKS: Syn. *O. acutidens* Dall,
1884.

Ex. gr. *Odostomia (Chrysallida) dux*

Odostomia (Chrysallida) seminuda

Subgenus *Chrysallida* Carpenter, 1856

Ex. gr. *Odostomia (Chrysallida) dux* Dall & Bartsch, 1906, *Proc. U.S. Nat. Mus.* 30(1452):350.
Gk. *odon, odontis* tooth, *stoma* mouth; L. *dux* leader, guide.
SIZE: 1.8–3 mm.
COLOR: White.
SHAPE: Elongate conic.
ORNAMENT OR SCULPTURE: Four postnuclear whorls. Each whorl bears 3 rows of tubercles and smooth spiral keel just above suture.
APERTURE: Obliquely oval or pear-shaped. One plica on columella.
OPERCULUM: Corneous.
PERIOSTRACUM: None visible.
HABITAT: Ectoparasitic in bays. Epifaunal.
LOCALITIES: Entire.
OCCURRENCE: Fairly common in beach drift.
RANGE: Massachusetts to North Carolina.
GEOLOGIC RANGE: ? to Holocene.
REMARKS: *O. dux* represents one very large and widely distributed species complex in *Chrysallida*. The specimen figured could be one of several that fall into this subgenus. *See* Dall & Bartsch 1906*b*, p. 350; Wells & Wells 1961.

Half-Smooth Odostome
Odostomia (Chrysallida) seminuda (C. B. Adams, 1839), *Boston J. Natur. Hist.* 2:280.
Gk. *odon, odontis* tooth, *stoma* mouth; L. *semi* half, *nudus* naked.
SIZE: 4 mm.
COLOR: Whitish.
SHAPE: Elongate conic.
ORNAMENT OR SCULPTURE: Six to 7 slightly convex whorls. Whorls shouldered; sutures distinct. Whorls sculptured between sutures by axial ribs cancelled into beads or nodules by 4 low, broad, equidistant ridges. Base of body whorl spirally grooved.
APERTURE: Auriform. Outer lip thick inside but edge thin, entire. Columella strong, twisted, reflexed with oblique plica.
OPERCULUM: Corneous.
PERIOSTRACUM: None visible.
HABITAT: Ectoparasitic in bays and on shallow shelf. Epifaunal.
LOCALITIES: Entire.
OCCURRENCE: Fairly common.
RANGE: Nova Scotia to Gulf of Mexico; Yucatán.
GEOLOGIC RANGE: ? to Holocene.
REMARKS: This nonspecific ectoparasite is known to feed on *Crepidula* and *Pecten*. It can stand less saline waters than some of the other *Odostomia*. Holes in dead specimens indicate that gastropods feed on it in turn. *See* Merrill & Boss 1964.

Odostomia (Menestho) impressa

Odostomia (Evalea) cf. *O. emeryi*

Subgenus *Menestho* Möller, 1842

Impressed Odostome
Odostomia (Menestho) impressa (Say, 1822), *J. Acad. Natur. Sci. Philadelphia* 2(1):244.
Gk. *odon, odontis* tooth, *stoma* mouth; L. *impressus* pressed, imprinted.
SIZE: 4–6 mm.
COLOR: Whitish.
SHAPE: Elongate conic.
ORNAMENT OR SCULPTURE: Eight flattened whorls, shouldered above. Sutures channeled. Nuclear whorls small, partly imbedded in first succeeding turn. Spiral sculpture consists of 3 strong deeply cut grooves; grooves cut by spiral threads. Base rounded, spirally grooved.
APERTURE: Ovate. Outer lip thin, slightly sinuous at edge, showing external sculpture within. Columella stout with strong oblique plica at insertion.
OPERCULUM: Corneous.
PERIOSTRACUM: Thin, yellowish.
HABITAT: Ectoparasitic on oyster reefs. Epifaunal.
LOCALITIES: Entire.
OCCURRENCE: Common.
RANGE: Massachusetts Bay to Gulf of Mexico; Gulf of Campeche.
GEOLOGIC RANGE: Upper Cretaceous to Holocene.
REMARKS: The most common *Odostomia* on this coast. Because of its habit of feeding on *Crassostrea virginica*, this little ectoparasite has been studied considerably. It will also feed on *Diastoma, Crepidula*, polychaete worms, and oyster drills. Probably syn. *O. trifida* Totten, 1834. *See* Allen 1958; H. W. Wells 1959.

Subgenus *Evalea* A. Adams, 1860

Odostomia (Evalea) cf. *O. emeryi* Bartsch, 1955, *Smithsonian Misc. Coll.* 125(2):84.
Gk. *odon, odontis* tooth, *stoma* mouth; dedicated to Daniel L. Emery, Florida malacology student.
SIZE: 2.9 mm.
COLOR: Cream yellow.
SHAPE: Elongate conic.
ORNAMENT OR SCULPTURE: Thin. Nuclear whorls small, obliquely immersed in first postnuclear turn. Postnuclear whorls well rounded and crossed by numerous microscopic spiral lines. Suture deeply impressed. Base inflated, rounded, strongly umbilicated.
APERTURE: Large, oval. Columella slender, curved with internal spiral cord near insertion. Parietal wall covered with thin inductura. Outer lip thin, strongly curved. Rounded body whorl distinctive.
OPERCULUM: Corneous.
PERIOSTRACUM: None visible.
HABITAT: Uncertain.
LOCALITIES: San Luis Pass and south.
OCCURRENCE: Uncommon in beach drift.
RANGE: Known from the Pliocene of North St. Petersburg, Florida.
GEOLOGIC RANGE: ? to Holocene.
REMARKS: Looks like a hydrobiid and may well be because the identification of this specimen has not been verified.

Odostomia (Syrnola) cf. O. livida

Peristichia toreta

Subgenus *Syrnola* A. Adams, 1860

Dark Pyram

Odostomia (Syrnola) cf. O. livida Rehder, 1935, *Nautilus* 48(4):129.
Gk. *odon, odontis* tooth, *stoma* mouth; L. *lividus* black and blue.
SIZE: 3.5–4 mm.
COLOR: Straw yellow with wide subsutural white band.
SHAPE: Elongate ovate.
ORNAMENT OR SCULPTURE: About 6½ moderately convex whorls. Smooth except for microscopic growth lines and spiral sculpture. Whorls closely adpressed at suture. Body whorl half of shell length, with suture considerably below periphery of preceding whorl, which gives shell constricted appearance in middle.
APERTURE: Small, obliquely ovate. Lip thin, thickened anteriorly, proceeding into base of columella, which bears a strong fold. Area surrounding base of columella reddish brown.
OPERCULUM: Not known.
PERIOSTRACUM: None visible.
HABITAT: Ectoparasitic in bays and inlet areas. Epifaunal.
LOCALITIES: Central, probably entire.
OCCURRENCE: Fairly common in beach drift.
RANGE: Florida; Texas.
GEOLOGIC RANGE: ? to Holocene.
REMARKS: The holotype was collected by J. A. Singley in Corpus Christi Bay, Texas, in 1893. [*Sayella livida*]. *See* Rehder 1935, p. 129.

Genus *Peristichia* Dall, 1889

Peristichia toreta Dall, 1889, *Mus. Comp. Zool. Bull.* 18(1):340.
Gk. *peri* around, *stitchos* row, line; L. *toreta* embosser, engraver.
SIZE: 11 mm.
COLOR: White.
SHAPE: Elongate conic.
ORNAMENT OR SCULPTURE: Spiral sculpture of 3 raised, rounded cords on upper whorls, 2 uppermost being nodulated, lower smooth. Only 1 basal cord. Columella without folds.
APERTURE: Rounded.
OPERCULUM: Not known.
PERIOSTRACUM: None visible.
HABITAT: Shallow water.
LOCALITIES: Entire.
OCCURRENCE: Uncommon in beach drift.
RANGE: North Carolina to western Florida; Texas.
GEOLOGIC RANGE: ? to Holocene.
REMARKS: This species has usually been placed with the Turbonillas but is now considered as separate. *See Texas Conch.* 9(1):9.

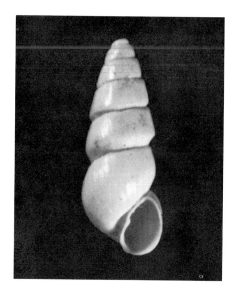

Eulimastoma cf. *E. canaliculata*

Eulimastoma cf. *E. harbisonae*

Genus *Eulimastoma* Bartsch, 1916
Diagnosis: Small to minute, high-spired marine gastropods with a single columellar plication that is generally expressed as a prominent parietal tooth; with a pronounced angulation at the periphery; with or without faint spiral striations; late teleoconch whorls generally attached low on the base of earlier whorls exposing part of the earlier whorl base; protoconch heterostrophic, low spired, generally about two whorls, unornamented, usually deeply and sometimes completely immersed in the first teleoconch whorl; teleoconch whorls slightly convex to flat-sided; aperture generally oval, with or without faint spiral sculpture inside the outer lip; with or without umbilicus; known adult size ranges from about 1.2 to 5.5 mm, average adult size about 2.5 mm (Corgan, 1971, p. 55). The *Eulimastoma* illustrated here are found in Texas; their identification, when attempted, is tentative.

Eulimastoma cf. *E. canaliculata* (C. B. Adams, 1850), *Cont. Conch.* 7:109. Mouth like a *Eulima*; L. *canalis* canal, conduit.
SIZE: 3.2 mm.
COLOR: White, smooth.
SHAPE: Conic, turreted.
ORNAMENT OR SCULPTURE: Apex acute; spire with rectilinear outlines. Six planulate whorls, with suture in small spiral channel; last whorl short, abruptly terminating.
APERTURE: Broadly ovate, columellar plica nearly transverse.
OPERCULUM: Not known.
PERIOSTRACUM: None visible.
HABITAT: Offshore and inlet areas. Epifaunal.
LOCALITIES: Entire.
OCCURRENCE: Uncommon in beach drift.
RANGE: Texas; Jamaica.
GEOLOGIC RANGE: ? to Holocene.
REMARKS: A most variable shell. [*Odostomia canaliculata*]. This has been reported in *Texas Conch.* as being in Texas.

Eulimastoma cf. *E. harbisonae* Bartsch, 1955, *Smithsonian Misc. Coll.* 125(2):82.
Mouth like a *Eulima*; dedicated to Anne Harbison, co-author of *Pliocene Mol. of Florida*.
SIZE: 2.2 mm.
COLOR: Pale brown.
SHAPE: Turreted.
ORNAMENT OR SCULPTURE: Nuclear whorls deeply, obliquely immersed in first postnuclear turn, above which tilted edge of last whorl only projects. Postnuclear whorls moderately rounded and rendered strongly angulated at about one-third of width of turns above suture. Angulation less expressed on last whorl than on preceding turns. Suture strongly constricted. Base rather long, rounded, openly umbilicated. Smooth.
APERTURE: Broadly ovate. Columella oblique, with single plica at insertion. Parietal wall covered by thick callus. Outer lip thin, gently curved.
OPERCULUM: Not known.
PERIOSTRACUM: None visible.
HABITAT: Ectoparasitic in inlet areas. Epifaunal.
LOCALITIES: Entire, more central.
OCCURRENCE: Fairly common in beach drift.
RANGE: Undefined. Holotype is from the Pliocene of North St. Petersburg, Florida.
GEOLOGIC RANGE: Pliocene to Holocene.
REMARKS: Whorls are more convex than in the other *Eulimastoma* found here. *See* Corgan 1971.

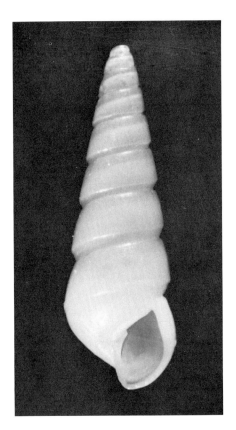

Eulimastoma cf. *E. teres*

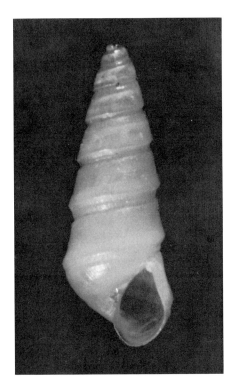

Eulimastoma cf. *E. weberi*

Eulimastoma cf. *E. teres* (Bush, 1885), *Trans. Connecticut Acad. Arts & Sci.* 6(2):465.
Mouth like a *Eulima*; *L. teres* rounded, smooth.
SIZE: 4.5 mm.
COLOR: White, lustrous.
SHAPE: Turreted.
ORNAMENT OR SCULPTURE: About 7½ flattened whorls, sutures canaliculate. Whorls have distinct, impressed, spiral line just below angle. Body whorl distinctly angulated at periphery where there is a prominent, rounded thread, with somewhat elongated, rounded base. Nucleus large, very oblique.
APERTURE: Not so much produced anteriorly. In juveniles plica is very conspicuous. Umbilicus small, deep, nearly concealed by reflected inner lip.
OPERCULUM: Corneous, yellowish.
PERIOSTRACUM: None visible.
HABITAT: Ectoparasitic in low-salinity bays. Epifaunal.
LOCALITIES: Entire.
OCCURRENCE: Fairly common in beach drift.
RANGE: Cape Hatteras; Texas.
GEOLOGIC RANGE: ? to Holocene.
REMARKS: Suture variable. [*Odostomia teres*]. *See* Corgan 1971.

Weber's Eulimastoma
Eulimastoma cf. *E. weberi* (Morrison, 1965), *Proc. Bio. Soc. Washington* 78:221.
Mouth like a *Eulima*; dedicated to Jay A. Weber, Florida collector.
SIZE: 1.4 mm.
COLOR: Vitreous white.
SHAPE: Cylindro-conic.
ORNAMENT OR SCULPTURE: Three postnuclear whorls. Apex and early whorls eroded in adults. Whorls pinched into keel at periphery; peripheral keel, most prominent on early whorls, may be partially obsolete just behind aperture. Second strong keel a little below suture. Flat-sided whorls ornamented only by microspiral striations and microscopic growth lines. Suture like a plowed furrow with narrow but distinct raised ridges bounding open furrow of even width and depth between all remaining whorls.
APERTURE: Ovate, angled posteriorly. Columellar wall thickened internally, but peristome not reflected in any way.
OPERCULUM: Thin, corneous, paucispiral.
PERIOSTRACUM: None visible.
HABITAT: Ectoparasitic in shallow, low-salinity bays. Epifaunal.
LOCALITIES: North, central.
OCCURRENCE: Fairly common.
RANGE: Louisiana to Port Aransas, Texas; Surinam.
GEOLOGIC RANGE: ? to Holocene.
REMARKS: Very variable. [*Odostomia weberi*]. *See* Morrison 1965.

Turbonilla sp. A

Turbonilla sp. D

Turbonilla sp. B

Turbonilla sp. E

Turbonilla sp. C

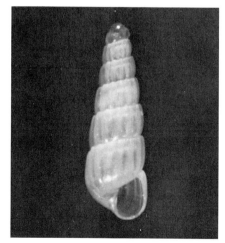

Turbonilla sp. F

Genus *Turbonilla* Risso, 1826, *Hist. Natur. l'Europe Mérid.* 4:224. Shell cylindro-conic, many whorled, generally slender; columellar fold single, varying in strength; outer lip entire; shell usually smaller than in *Pyramidella* and larger than in *Odostomia*. Type, *Turbonilla typica* Dall & Bartsch, 1909. *See* Bush 1899; Bartsch 1909 & 1955.

Key to the subgenera of *Turbonilla*:

A. Spiral sculpture absent or, if present, consisting of exceedingly fine microscopic lines only
  a. Axial ribs obsolete on the later whorls . . . .
           Ptycheulimella
  aa. Axial ribs not obsolete on the later whorls
    b. Axial ribs terminating at the periphery of the last whorl . . . . . .
           Chemnitzia
    bb. Axial ribs continuing over the base of the last whorl . . . .
           Turbonilla

A.A. Spiral sculpture present, always stronger than mere microscopic lines
  c. Spiral sculpture consisting of fine incised lines . .
           Strioturbonilla
  cc. Spiral sculpture consisting of strongly incised grooves . . . . . *Pyrgiscus*

The following *Turbonilla* were found in the drift of Nueces and Aransas bay areas in Texas:

Turbonilla sp. A: 4.25 mm; strong spiral sculpture; strong ribs; no ribs on base; 9 flat-sided whorls; opaque.

Turbonilla sp. B: 4.3 mm; fairly strong, incised spiral sculpture; no sculpture on base; 7 convex whorls; opaque.

Turbonilla sp. C: 4.1 mm; weak spiral sculpture; no ribs on base; 8 flat-sided whorls; ribs extend beyond base of each whorl.

Turbonilla sp. D: 3.7 mm; strong spiral sculpture; faint sculpture on

Turbonilla sp. G

Turbonilla sp. J

Turbonilla sp. H

Turbonilla sp. K

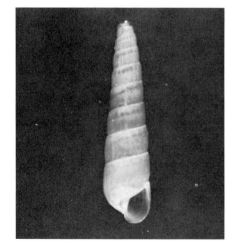

Turbonilla sp. I

base; 6 flat-sided whorls; ribs extend beyond base of each whorl; opaque.

Turbonilla sp. E: 3 mm; no spiral sculpture; weak ribs on base; 5–6 whorls with strong ribs; strong raised spiral cord at whorl shoulder; immersed protoconch; opaque.

Turbonilla sp. F: 3 mm; no spiral sculpture; no ribs over base; 5 slightly convex whorls; ribs project at each whorl shoulder; translucent; protoconch glassy.

Turbonilla sp. G: 5.5 mm; no spiral sculpture; no ribs over base; 11 slightly convex whorls; ribs do not extend beyond shoulder; translucent.

Turbonilla sp. H: 6.3 mm; fine spiral sculpture; no ribs on base; 9 flat-sided whorls; ribs taper into suture; translucent.

Turbonilla sp. I: 4 mm; no spiral sculpture; no ribs on base; 8 flat-sided, closely fitted whorls; ribs weak; translucent.

Turbonilla sp. J: 4 mm; no spiral sculpture; no ribs on base; 7 flat-sided, slightly shouldered whorls; ribs end before reaching abapical suture; translucent.

Turbonilla sp. K: 5.25 mm; microscopic spiral sculpture; no ribs on base; 10 slightly convex whorls; ribs extend full height of whorl; faint appearance of spiral band at adapical side of suture on early whorls; color pale amber.

Turbonilla (Pyrgiscus) cf. T. elegantula

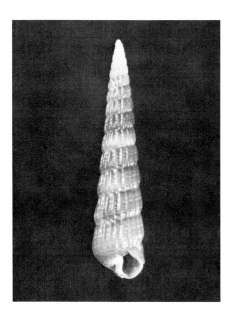

Turbonilla (Pyrgiscus) cf. T. interrupta

Subgenus *Pyrgiscus* Philippi, 1841

Elegant Turbonilla
Turbonilla (Pyrgiscus) cf. *T. elegantula*
Verrill, 1882, *Trans. Conn. Acad. Arts & Sci.* 5:538.
L. dim. of *turbo* a top, *elegans* elegant, fine.
SIZE: 3–5 mm.
COLOR: Amber, semitransparent. Spiral incisions darker.
SHAPE: Elongate conic, slender.
ORNAMENT OR SCULPTURE: Nine rounded whorls. Sutures distinct. Twenty-two nearly perpendicular, rounded transverse ribs, which are separated by about equally wide spaces. Spaces crossed by 5 equal, well-separated, incised spiral lines and 2 very much finer ones. Rounded base incised with 9 unevenly spaced spiral lines.
APERTURE: Elongated oval. Columella nearly straight, slightly reflexed, with slight fold.
OPERCULUM: Corneous.
PERIOSTRACUM: None visible.
HABITAT: Ectoparasitic. Epifaunal.
LOCALITIES: Port Aransas.
OCCURRENCE: Uncommon in beach drift.
RANGE: Texas; West Indies.
GEOLOGIC RANGE: ? to Holocene.
REMARKS: Syn. *T. elegans* Verrill, 1872.

Interrupted Turbonilla
Turbonilla (Pyrgiscus) cf. *T. interrupta*
(Totten, 1835), *Amer. J. Sci.* 1(28):352.
L. dim. of *turbo* a top, *interruptus* interrupted.
SIZE: 6 mm.
COLOR: Brownish.
SHAPE: Elongate conic, slender.
ORNAMENT OR SCULPTURE: About 10 almost flat whorls sculptured with about 22 smooth, axial ribs separated by grooves of a little wider width, and with about 14 subequal, impressed, revolving lines arranged in pairs and entirely interrupted by ribs. Spiral line above periphery heavier than others, forming line of deep pits. Ribs become obsolete below middle of body whorl. Base short, rounded with spiral lines.
APERTURE: Ovate, angular above, regularly rounded below, about one-fifth length of shell. Outer lip sharp, slightly sinuous. Columella slightly curved, weakly reflexed.
OPERCULUM: Corneous.
PERIOSTRACUM: None visible.
HABITAT: Ectoparasitic in inlets and along shore. Epifaunal.
LOCALITIES: Port Aransas, probably entire.
OCCURRENCE: Fairly common.
RANGE: Maine to West Indies; Texas; Carmen, Campeche, Mexico; Gulf of Campeche; Yucatán; Brazil.
GEOLOGIC RANGE: ? to Holocene.
REMARKS: The disappearance of the original shell described by Totten has contributed to the misinterpretation of this species.

Turbonilla (Pyrgiscus) cf. *T. portoricana*

Turbonilla (Strioturbonilla) cf. *T. hemphilli*

Puerto Rican Turbonilla

Turbonilla (Pyrgiscus) cf. *T. portoricana* Dall & Simpson, 1901, *Bull. U.S. Fish. Comm.* 20(1):414.

L. dim. of *turbo* a top; from Puerto Rico.

SIZE: 4.7 mm.

COLOR: Translucent white with narrow yellowish brown spiral band around whorls about one-fourth breadth of whorl above its suture. Pale yellow spiral band on middle of base.

SHAPE: Elongate conic.

ORNAMENT OR SCULPTURE: Ten flattened postnuclear whorls, slightly contracted at sutures. Whorls crossed with almost vertical axial ribs, 16 on fifth and increasing in number toward base. Intercostal spaces broad, wavy, wider than ribs. Base ribbed, crossed with 6 spiral striae.

APERTURE: Subovate. Columella oblique. Outer lip well rounded, meeting columella at right angle. Parietal callus well defined. Strong oblique fold near insertion of columella. Outer sculpture visible through outer lip.

OPERCULUM: Corneous.

PERIOSTRACUM: None visible.

HABITAT: Ectoparasitic in inlet areas. Epifaunal.

LOCALITIES: Port Aransas, south.

OCCURRENCE: Uncommon in beach drift.

RANGE: Texas; West Indies.

GEOLOGIC RANGE: ? to Holocene.

REMARKS: Coll., U.T. Marine Science Institute.

Subgenus *Strioturbonilla* Sacco, 1892

Hemphill's Turbonilla

Turbonilla (Strioturbonilla) cf. *T. hemphilli* Bush, 1899, *Proc. Acad. Natur. Sci. Philadelphia* 51:169.

L. dim. of *turbo* a top; dedicated to H. Hemphill, nineteenth-century California collector.

SIZE: 10–12 mm.

COLOR: White.

SHAPE: Elongate conic, slender.

ORNAMENT OR SCULPTURE: Twelve postnuclear whorls slightly convex, sculptured with about 20 almost perpendicular transverse ribs. Rounded ribs separated by about equally wide, deep, concave spaces ending at periphery of body whorl in clean-cut ends. Base rounded, smooth. Entire surface covered with microscopic striations.

APERTURE: Squarish, somewhat expanded below. Inner lip thickened, reflected.

OPERCULUM: Corneous.

PERIOSTRACUM: None visible.

HABITAT: Ectoparasitic in inlet-influenced areas. Epifaunal.

LOCALITIES: Southern half of range, probably entire.

OCCURRENCE: Fairly common, in beach drift.

RANGE: Western coast of Florida; Texas.

GEOLOGIC RANGE: ? to Holocene.

Cyclostremella humilis

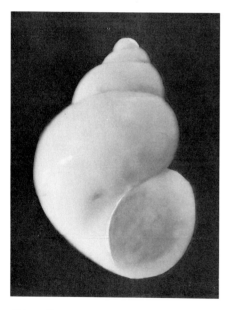

Rissoella sp.

Subfamily CYCLOSTREMELLINAE
D. Moore, 1966

Genus *Cyclostremella* Bush, 1897

Cyclostremella humilis (Bush, 1897), *Trans. Conn. Acad. Arts & Sci.* 10(1):140.
Gk. *kyklos* circle, *trema* aperture; L. *humilis* on the ground.
SIZE: 1.7 mm.
COLOR: White.
SHAPE: Planispiral, slightly depressed.
ORNAMENT OR SCULPTURE: Two postnuclear whorls with several weak spiral cords on periphery and numerous fine, wavy growth lines. Hyperstrophic protoconch. Suture deep, forming channel around spire. Beyond suture, whorl flattened and slopes at 45-degree angle to periphery. Base of shell rounded. Umbilicus widely opened; apex can be seen.
APERTURE: Trigonal. Lip deeply notched at upper inner angle.
OPERCULUM: Paucispiral; nucleus subcentral.
PERIOSTRACUM: Light tan.
HABITAT: Along shore on sandy bottom. Ectoparasitic. Epifaunal.
LOCALITIES: Entire.
OCCURRENCE: Common in beach drift.
RANGE: North Carolina; northwestern Florida; Texas.
GEOLOGIC RANGE: ? to Holocene.
REMARKS: This tiny shell is one of the most abundant on this coast. Robertson transferred D. R. Moore's new subfamily from the Prosobranch family Vitrinellidae to the Euthyneura (opisthobranch) superfamily Pyramidellacea on the basis of the hyperstrophic protoconch and pyramidellid nature of the living *Cyclostremella*. *See* D. R. Moore 1966; Robertson 1973.

Family RISSOELLIDAE Gray, 1847

Genus *Rissoella* Gray, 1847

Rissoella sp.
SIZE: Length 1.4 mm.
COLOR: Translucent.
SHAPE: Conic.
ORNAMENT OR SCULPTURE: Heterostrophic (deviated) nuclear whorl bears sculpture of irregularly arranged elongate vermiform projections. Postnuclear 2½ whorls have irregular fine growth lines, overridden by numerous fine, dense, raised spiral lines that on close inspection are resolved into series of tiny adjoining hemispherical bosses. Narrow open umbilicus bordered by narrow subangulation at base.
APERTURE: Broadly elliptical, slightly narrower above than at base. No fold or plication either externally or internally on columella.
OPERCULUM: Not preserved.
PERIOSTRACUM: Not preserved.
HABITAT: Lower Pecos River valley in late Pleistocene, perhaps in saline water.
LOCALITIES: The same occurrence as 3 species of inland fossil Vitrinellidae.
OCCURRENCE: Not determined.
RANGE: Known from single location in Terrell County, Texas.
GEOLOGIC RANGE: Late Pleistocene only.
REMARKS: Classification and relationships quite uncertain. Found by D. W. Taylor in 1973.

Melampus bidentatus

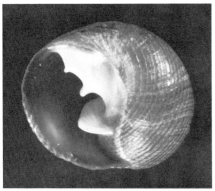

Pedipes mirabilis

Order ACTOPHILA Thiele, 1931
Superfamily ELLOBIACEA Adams, 1855
Family ELLOBIIDAE Adams, 1855
Subfamily MELAMPINAE Stimpson, 1851

Genus *Melampus* Montfort, 1810

Coffee Melampus
Melampus bidentatus Say, 1822, *J. Acad. Natur. Sci. Philadelphia* 2(1):245.
Gk. *melos* black, *pous* foot; L. *bi* two, *dentatis* toothed.
SIZE: 18 mm.
COLOR: Brown with cream-colored bands.
SHAPE: Ovate.
ORNAMENT OR SCULPTURE: Rather thin shell smooth. About 5 whorls; spire low; body whorl predominates. Umbilicate.
APERTURE: Nearly length of body whorl, expanded below. Outer lip thin, curved into columella. Columella short with 2 white plicae. Internal lamellae inside body whorl.
OPERCULUM: None.
PERIOSTRACUM: Thin.
HABITAT: Under vegetation on bay and lagoon shores. Epifaunal.
LOCALITIES: Entire.
OCCURRENCE: Common.
RANGE: Florida to West Indies; Texas.
GEOLOGIC RANGE: Pleistocene? to Holocene.
REMARKS: Examination of stomachs of wild ducks shows this little amphibious snail to be a favorite food. It must go into the water to breed. *See* Hauseman 1932; Holle & Dineen 1959; J. P. E. Morrison 1964; Apley 1970; Russell-Hunter et al. 1970.

Subfamily PEDIPEDINAE Thiele, 1931

Genus *Pedipes* Bruguière, 1792

Stepping Shell
Pedipes mirabilis (Mühlfeld, 1818), *Ges. Natur. Freunde Berlin*, p. 8.
Fr. *pietin* pedestrian, two-stepper; L. *mirabilis* wonderful.
SIZE: 3–5 mm.
COLOR: Light to dark reddish brown.
SHAPE: Globose turbinate.
ORNAMENT OR SCULPTURE: Four to 5 strongly convex whorls. Sculpture consists of numerous incised, spiral lines. Transverse sculpture consists of irregular growth lines. Spire slightly elevated. Anomphalous.
APERTURE: Oval with outer edge thin but thickened on inside. Parietal area has 3 well-developed denticulations, top one being largest. Outer lip has one tooth directly opposite central plica.
OPERCULUM: None.
PERIOSTRACUM: None visible.
HABITAT: Jetties and rocks above tide line. Epifaunal.
LOCALITIES: Entire.
OCCURRENCE: Uncommon.
RANGE: Bermuda; Florida to West Indies; Texas; Costa Rica; northeastern Brazil.
GEOLOGIC RANGE: ? to Holocene.
REMARKS: This little colonial air breather can withstand some environmental changes, but the entire colony will disappear when conditions become extreme. They prefer a hard substratum. *See* Clench 1964, p. 119.

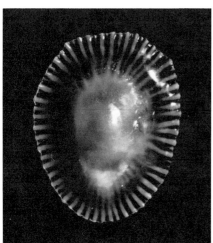

Siphonaria pectinata

Creseis acicula

Order HYGROPHILA Férussac, 1821
Superfamily SIPHONARIACEA Gray, 1840
Family SIPHONARIIDAE Gray, 1840

Genus *Siphonaria* Sowerby, 1824

Striped False Limpet
Siphonaria pectinata (Linné, 1758), *Syst. Natur.*, 10th ed., p. 783.
L. *sipho* siphon, *pecten* comb.
SIZE: 25.6 mm.
COLOR: Whitish with numerous brown bifurcating lines.
SHAPE: Conic, limpet-shaped.
ORNAMENT OR SCULPTURE: Sculpture consists of numerous fine radial threads.
APERTURE: Large, circular. Interior glossy.
OPERCULUM: None.
PERIOSTRACUM: None visible.
HABITAT: Rocks and jetties. Epifaunal.
LOCALITIES: Entire.
OCCURRENCE: Common.
RANGE: Georgia; eastern Florida; Texas; Mexico; West Indies.
GEOLOGIC RANGE: ? to Holocene.
REMARKS: This snail, which is so common on the jetties of the Texas coast (fig. 12), resembles a true limpet, but animal is an air breather. *See* Zischke 1974.

Order THECOSOMATA Blainville, 1824
Suborder EUTHECOSOMATA Meisenheimer, 1905
Superfamily SPIRATELLACEA Thiele, 1926
Family CUVIERIDAE Gray, 1840

Genus *Creseis* Rang, 1828

Straight-Needle Pteropod
Creseis acicula (Rang, 1828), *Annu. Sci. Natur.* 13:318.
Creseis, a mythological name; L. *acicula* small pin, needle.
SIZE: 20–30 mm.
COLOR: White, translucent.
SHAPE: Elongated, straight cone.
ORNAMENT OR SCULPTURE: Smooth, not coiled.
APERTURE: Small, round.
OPERCULUM: None.
PERIOSTRACUM: None.
HABITAT: Pelagic, temperate and tropic seas.
LOCALITIES: Entire.
OCCURRENCE: Common, seasonally, in beach drift.
RANGE: Worldwide.
GEOLOGIC RANGE: Eocene to Holocene.
REMARKS: These shells look like very fine tusk shells and can be easily overlooked if the drift is not carefully screened. At times they may come to shore by the thousands. The animal has a tentacular lobe on anterior fin margin. *See* Tesch 1946; Korniker 1959.

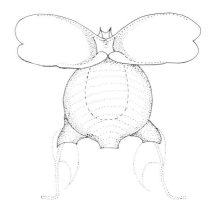

Fig. 36. A living pteropod

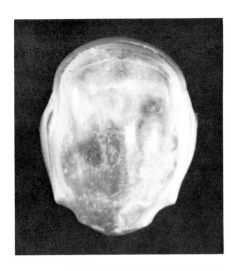

Diacria quadridentata

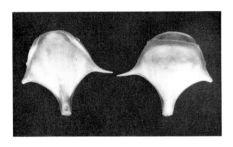

Diacria trispinosa

Subfamily CAVOLINIINAE H. & A. Adams, 1854

Genus *Diacria* Gray, 1850

Four-Toothed Cavoline

Diacria quadridentata (Blainville, 1821), *Dict. Sci. Natur.* 22:81.
Gk. *di* two; L. *akris* hilltop, *quadri* four, *dentata* toothed.
SIZE: 2–4 mm.
COLOR: Transparent with chestnut-colored lip.
SHAPE: Globular.
ORNAMENT OR SCULPTURE: Without prominent lateral spines. Ventral side very globose. Dorsal side sculptured with rounded, radiating ribs. Lateral spines may be straight or fold back obliquely.
APERTURE: Narrow, flattened, ending in slits at lateral spines. Margins of lip thickened.
OPERCULUM: None.
PERIOSTRACUM: None.
HABITAT: Pelagic, temperate and tropical seas.
LOCALITIES: Port Aransas, probably entire.
OCCURRENCE: Uncommon in beach drift.
RANGE: Worldwide.
GEOLOGIC RANGE: Post-Pliocene to Holocene.
REMARKS: This curious-looking little shell is less common than the other species described. There is never an extended hind part and the shape of the shell is much more cavolinalike. *See* Tesch 1964.

Three-Spined Cavoline

Diacria trispinosa Blainville, 1821, *Dict. Sci. Natur.* 22:2.
Gk. *di* two; L. *akris* hilltop, *tri* three, *spinosa* spined.
SIZE: 10 mm.
COLOR: Whitish with chestnut-colored lips.
SHAPE: Lozenge-shaped with extended hind part.
ORNAMENT OR SCULPTURE: Shell somewhat compressed with 3 straight spines, one on either side of aperture and a longer one behind that may or may not be broken off. Longitudinally ribbed on ventral side.
APERTURE: Compressed, thickened. Under lip curved outward.
OPERCULUM: None.
PERIOSTRACUM: None.
HABITAT: Pelagic, temperate and tropical seas.
LOCALITIES: Entire.
OCCURRENCE: Uncommon in beach drift.
RANGE: Atlantic; Gulf of Mexico.
GEOLOGIC RANGE: Post-Pliocene to Holocene.
REMARKS: The animal tends to rid itself of the long hind stalk that would hamper it in swimming. Descends during day, rises at night to feed. Both sides of the Panama land bridge. *See* Tesch 1964.

Cavolina longirostris

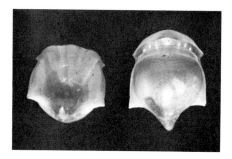

Cavolina uncinata

Genus *Cavolina* Abildgaard, 1791

Long-Snout Cavoline
Cavolina longirostris (Blainville, 1821), *Dict. Sci. Natur.* 22:81.
Dedicated to Cavolini (1756–1810), Italian naturalist; L. *longe* long, far, *rostrum* snout.
SIZE: 4–9 mm.
COLOR: Translucent white.
SHAPE: Triangular when viewed from top.
ORNAMENT OR SCULPTURE: Ventral face of shell nearly round, sculptured with faint concentric ridges; dorsal face longitudinally ribbed, extended in front into long, slightly folded, depressed bead; lateral spines compressed; central spine short, truncated.
APERTURE: Compressed, continued as fissure around side of shell.
OPERCULUM: None.
PERIOSTRACUM: None.
HABITAT: Pelagic, warm and tropical seas.
LOCALITIES: Entire.
OCCURRENCE: Common in beach drift.
RANGE: Worldwide.
GEOLOGIC RANGE: Post-Pliocene to Holocene.
REMARKS: These may be easily overlooked in the beach drift because they do not resemble the usual concept of a sea shell. When living, butterflylike wings extend from either side of long rostrum. *See* Burkenrod 1933; Tesch 1964.

Uncinate Cavoline
Cavolina uncinata (Rang, 1829), *Manu. l'Hist. Natur.*, pl. 93.
Dedicated to Cavolini (1756–1810), Italian naturalist; L. *uncinatus* barbed, bent.
SIZE: 6–11 mm.
COLOR: Pale amber, translucent.
SHAPE: Shield-shaped when viewed from top.
ORNAMENT OR SCULPTURE: Shell very inflated ventrally, surface delicately and regularly reticulated with fine, concentric ridges in front; dorsal face with 3 low, radiating ribs, turned downward and nearly evenly rounded at aperture; lateral spines compressed and curved backward; central spine short, stout, upcurved.
APERTURE: Compressed, continued as fissure around each side of shell.
OPERCULUM: None.
PERIOSTRACUM: None.
HABITAT: Pelagic, warm and tropical seas.
LOCALITIES: Entire.
OCCURRENCE: Fairly common in beach drift.
RANGE: Worldwide.
GEOLOGIC RANGE: Post-Pliocene to Holocene.
REMARKS: *See* Burkenrod 1933; Tesch 1964.

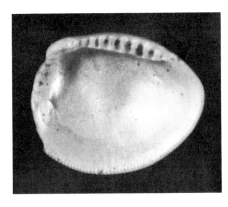

Nucula cf. *N. proxima*

Nuculana acuta

Class BIVALVIA Linné, 1758 = [PELECYPODA Goldfuss, 1820]

Subclass PALAEOTAXODONTA Korobkov, 1954
Order NUCULOIDEA Dall, 1889
Superfamily NUCULACEA Gray, 1824
Family NUCULIDAE Gray, 1824

Genus *Nucula* Lamarck, 1799

Atlantic Nut Clam
Nucula cf. *N. proxima* Say, 1822, *J. Acad. Natur. Sci. Philadelphia*, 2(1):270.
L. *nucula* little nut, *proximus* next of kin, nearest.
SIZE: 6.5 mm.
COLOR: Whitish.
SHAPE: Obliquely trigonal. Equivalve. Inequilateral.
ORNAMENT OR SCULPTURE: Sculpture of faint growth lines and light radiating striae. Margins rounded. Ventral margin crenate.
HINGE AREA: Angular with 12 comb-like teeth anterior to umbones and 18 posterior.
PALLIAL LINE & INTERIOR: Inner surface pearly. Adductor muscle scars but no pallial sinus.
PERIOSTRACUM: Thin, greenish brown.
HABITAT: Sandy mud bottom. Infaunal.
LOCALITIES: East, central.
OCCURRENCE: Fairly common in beach drift.
RANGE: Bermuda; Nova Scotia to Florida; Texas.
GEOLOGIC RANGE: Pliocene to Holocene.
REMARKS: Parker (in litt.) reports this clam common in the Brazos River area.

Superfamily NUCULANACEA H. & A. Adams, 1858
Family NUCULANIDAE H. & A. Adams, 1858

Genus *Nuculana* Link, 1807

Pointed Nut Clam
Nuculana acuta (Conrad, 1831), *Amer. Marine Conch.*, p. 32.
L. *nucula* little nut, *acutus* pointed.
SIZE: 10 mm.
COLOR: White.
SHAPE: Elongate with a pointed posterior rostrum. Equivalve. Inequilateral.
ORNAMENT OR SCULPTURE: Sculpture of well-defined concentric grooves that do not extend over ridge on rostrum.
HINGE AREA: Small triangular chondrophore and numerous chevron-shaped teeth on either side of umbo.
PALLIAL LINE & INTERIOR: Interior polished. Pallial sinus small, rounded.
PERIOSTRACUM: Thin, yellowish brown.
HABITAT: Sandy mud beyond low tide. Infaunal.
LOCALITIES: Entire.
OCCURRENCE: Fairly common in beach drift.
RANGE: Cape Cod to West Indies; Texas; Carmen, Campeche, Mexico; Gulf of Campeche; Campeche Bank.
GEOLOGIC RANGE: Oligocene to Holocene.
REMARKS: This species is more common in the southern part of the state. It is less obese than *N. concentrica*. Very variable; some may lack concentric sculpture. Panamic vicariant is *N. hindsii* (Hanley, 1860). *See* Bird 1965, p. 21.

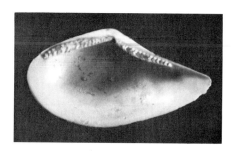

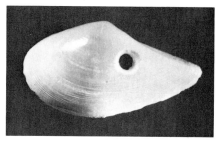

Nuculana concentrica

Concentric Nut Clam

Nuculana concentrica Say, 1824, *J. Acad. Natur. Sci. Philadelphia* 4(1):141.

L. *nucula* little nut, *concentrica* concentric.

SIZE: 12–18 mm.

COLOR: Yellow white, semiglossy.

SHAPE: Rather obese and moderately rostrate. Equivalve. Inequilateral.

ORNAMENT OR SCULPTURE: Adult shells appear smooth; have very fine, concentric growth lines on ventral half of valves. Beaks and area just below smooth. Radial ridge on rostrum smooth, not crossed by strong threads.

HINGE AREA: Numerous chevron-shaped teeth on either side of umbo.

PALLIAL LINE & INTERIOR: Pallial sinus small, rounded. Polished.

PERIOSTRACUM: Thin, yellowish.

HABITAT: Sandy bottoms beyond low tide. Infaunal.

LOCALITIES: Entire.

OCCURRENCE: Fairly common in beach drift.

RANGE: Northwestern Florida to Texas; Surinam.

GEOLOGIC RANGE: Upper Miocene to Holocene.

REMARKS: More common in the eastern part of the state.

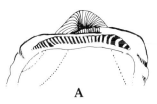

A

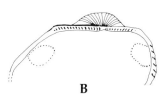

B

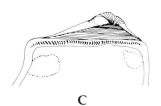

C

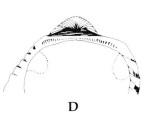

D

Fig. 37. Various types of ark hinges:
A. Noetia ponderosa, beaks point posteriorly, most of ligament area anterior to beaks
B. Barbatia domingensis, ligament long, narrow, and posterior to beaks, fewer than twenty teeth in posterior half of hinge
C. Arca imbricata, ligament area wide, hinge long and narrow with numerous small teeth
D. Anadara brasiliana, beaks face each other, ligament short and transversely striate

Arca (Arca) imbricata

Arca (Arca) zebra

Subclass PTERIOMORPHIA Beurlen, 1944
Order ARCOIDEA Stoliczka, 1871
Superfamily ARCACEA Lamarck, 1809
Family ARCIDAE Lamarck, 1809
Subfamily ARCINAE Lamarck, 1809

Genus *Arca* Linné, 1758
Subgenus *Arca* s.s.

Mossy Ark
Arca (Arca) imbricata Bruguière, 1789, *Encycl. Méth.* 1:98.
L. *arca* box, purse, chest, *imbricare* to cover with overlapping tiles.
SIZE: 25–38 mm.
COLOR: Whitish, concentrically marked with chestnut brown.
SHAPE: Rectangular; hinge long, straight. Equivalve. Inequilateral.
ORNAMENT OR SCULPTURE: Numerous fine, irregular ribs crossed with growth lines giving a beaded appearance. Posteriorly carinate. Large ventral byssal gape.
HINGE AREA: Wide, flat; pearshaped ligamental area between umbones. Umbones more elevated than in *A. zebra*. Hinge margin straight with many small transverse teeth.
PALLIAL LINE & INTERIOR: Interior smooth, dull purplish; muscle scars connected by simple pallial line.
PERIOSTRACUM: Heavy, shaggy, brown.
HABITAT: On rocks or firm substratum. Byssate epifaunal nestler.
LOCALITIES: Entire.
OCCURRENCE: Common.
RANGE: North Carolina; Florida to West Indies; Texas; Campeche Bank; Costa Rica; Surinam; Brazil.
GEOLOGIC RANGE: Oligocene to Holocene.
REMARKS: Attaches with byssal threads; is barely discernable unless the movement of valves closing is seen. Syn. *A. umbonata* Lamarck, 1819.

Turkey Wing
Arca (Arca) zebra (Swainson, 1833), *Zool. Illus.*, 2d ser. 3:118.
L. *arca* box, purse, chest, *zebra* striped.
SIZE: 50.8 mm.
COLOR: Creamy white, streaked, flecked with chestnut brown zebra pattern.
SHAPE: Rectangular; hinge long, straight. Equivalve. Inequilateral.
ORNAMENT OR SCULPTURE: Ventral margin with wide byssal notch opposite umbones; posterior margin sinuate. About 26 narrow, rounded ribs with finely ribbed, flat interspaces. Fine lamellar ridges across both ribs and interspaces.
HINGE AREA: Wide, flat ligamental area between umbones. Numerous small, transverse teeth.
PALLIAL LINE & INTERIOR: Interior smooth, white to purplish. Strong muscle and simple pallial impressions.
PERIOSTRACUM: Heavy, brown, shaggy.
HABITAT: On rocks, shell, roots. Byssate epifaunal nestler.
LOCALITIES: South.
OCCURRENCE: Rare.
RANGE: Bermuda; North Carolina to Lesser Antilles; Texas; Campeche Bank; Yucatán; Surinam; northern Brazil.
GEOLOGIC RANGE: Upper Miocene to Holocene.
REMARKS: Occasionally found washed in on bamboo roots but is more typical of the Mexican coast. Panamic vicariant is *A. pacifica* (Sowerby, 1833).

Barbatia (Barbatia) cancellaria

Barbatia (Barbatia) candida

Genus *Barbatia* Gray, 1847
Subgenus *Barbatia* s.s.

Red Brown Ark
Barbatia (Barbatia) cancellaria (Lamarck, 1819), *Hist. Natur. Anim. sans Vert.* 6:41.
L. *barbatus* bearded, *cancellatus* latticelike.
SIZE: 25.4–38.1 mm.
COLOR: Red brown.
SHAPE: Obliquely rectangular. Equivalve. Inequilateral.
ORNAMENT OR SCULPTURE: Margins irregular; byssal gape on ventral edge. Numerous finely beaded ribs and irregular concentric growth lines.
HINGE AREA: Straight with narrow ligamental area between elevated umbones. Teeth obliquely inclined to center.
PALLIAL LINE & INTERIOR: Interior red brown, smooth. Pallial line simple with muscle scars.
PERIOSTRACUM: Brown, heavy.
HABITAT: Offshore. Byssate epifaunal nestler.
LOCALITIES: Entire.
OCCURRENCE: Rare.
RANGE: Southern Florida; western Gulf of Mexico; Campeche Bank; Yucatán; Quintana Roo; West Indies; Brazilian coast.
GEOLOGIC RANGE: ? to Holocene.
REMARKS: A deep-water species often brought in by shrimpers. Coll., Wilson.

White Bearded Ark
Barbatia (Barbatia) candida (Helbling, 1779), *Abh. Privatgessl. Bohm.* 4:129.
L. *barbatus* bearded, *candidatus* dressed in white.
SIZE: 25.4–50.8 mm.
COLOR: White.
SHAPE: Obliquely rectangular; hinge straight. Equivalve. Inequilateral.
ORNAMENT OR SCULPTURE: Margins irregular; slight byssal gape on ventral edge. Relatively thin for ark. Numerous weak, slightly beaded ribs, those on posterior dorsal area being very strongly beaded. Surface irregular.
HINGE AREA: Straight with narrow, lanceolate ligamental area between umbones, narrower than *Arca*. Teeth not parallel, obliquely inclined to center.
PALLIAL LINE & INTERIOR: Interior white, smooth. Pallial line simple with 2 muscle scars.
PERIOSTRACUM: Brown, heavy, shaggy.
HABITAT: On rocks beyond low tide. Byssate epifaunal nestler.
LOCALITIES: Port Aransas, south.
OCCURRENCE: Rare.
RANGE: North Carolina to West Indies; Texas; Brazil.
GEOLOGIC RANGE: Upper Miocene to Holocene.
REMARKS: Very few hinge teeth for an ark. Coll., Wilson.

Barbatia (Acar) domingensis

Barbatia (Fugleria) tenera

Subgenus *Acar* Gray, 1857

White Miniature Ark
Barbatia (Acar) domingensis
(Lamarck, 1819), *Hist. Natur. Anim. sans Vert.* 6:40.
L. *barbatus* bearded; from Dominican Republic.
SIZE: 12–18 mm.
COLOR: White to cream.
SHAPE: Rectangular; surface irregular. Equivalve. Inequilateral.
ORNAMENT OR SCULPTURE: Very distinctive, coarsely reticulated surface. Shinglelike growth ridges.
HINGE AREA: Ligament long, narrow, posterior to beaks. Chevron-shaped teeth. Umbo curled to edge of hinge.
PALLIAL LINE & INTERIOR: Pallial line simple with 2 muscle scars.
PERIOSTRACUM: Thin, yellowish brown.
HABITAT: On rocks below low tide. Semi-epifaunal.
LOCALITIES: Southern half of coast.
OCCURRENCE: Common.
RANGE: North Carolina to Florida; Texas; Gulf of Mexico to Quintana Roo; Costa Rica; Lesser Antilles; Surinam; Brazil; Brazilian oceanic islands.
GEOLOGIC RANGE: ? to Holocene.
REMARKS: Look for it in holes and crevices of rocks on jetties. *See* Bretsky 1967.

Subgenus *Fugleria* Reinhart, 1937

Doc Bales' Ark
Barbatia (Fugleria) tenera (C. B. Adams, 1845), *Proc. Boston Soc. Natur. Hist.* 2:9.
L. *barbatus* bearded, *tener* thin, tender, delicate, young.
SIZE: 25–38 mm.
COLOR: White.
SHAPE: Trapezoidal, rather fat. Equivalve. Nearly equilateral.
ORNAMENT OR SCULPTURE: Thin shelled. Numerous rather evenly, finely beaded, cordlike ribs, stronger posteriorly. Small byssal gape.
HINGE AREA: Ligamental area fairly wide at umbo, narrowing anteriorly. Typical chevron teeth.
PALLIAL LINE & INTERIOR: Interior polished, white. Pallial line simple with 2 muscle scars.
PERIOSTRACUM: Thin, brown.
HABITAT: Offshore. Byssate epifaunal nestler.
LOCALITIES: Entire.
OCCURRENCE: Uncommon in beach drift.
RANGE: Lake Worth, Florida, to Texas; Caribbean; northern coast of South America.
GEOLOGIC RANGE: ? to Holocene.
REMARKS: Easily confused with *Anadara transversa* but thinner with a more "humped" and beaded surface.

Anadara (Cunearca) brasiliana

Anadara (Cunearca) chemnitzi

Subfamily ANADARINAE
Reinhart, 1935

Genus *Anadara* Gray, 1847
Subgenus *Cunearca* Dall, 1898

Incongruous Ark
Anadara (Cunearca) brasiliana
(Lamarck, 1819), *Hist. Natur. Anim.
sans Vert.* 6:44.
Gk. *ana* without, *dara* gape; from
Brazil.
SIZE: 25–38 mm.
COLOR: White.
SHAPE: Trigonal. Left valve overlaps
right. Inequivalve. Inequilateral.
ORNAMENT OR SCULPTURE: Twenty-
six to 28 radial ribs visible, stronger
at margins.
HINGE AREA: Umbones well sepa-
rated; ligament area wide, exca-
vated. Oblique, comblike teeth be-
come smaller toward center.
PALLIAL LINE & INTERIOR: Interior
white, polished; ribs visible and
stronger at margins. Pallial line
simple with 2 muscle scars.
PERIOSTRACUM: Thin, light brown.
HABITAT: Offshore in shallow water.
Infaunal.
LOCALITIES: Entire.
OCCURRENCE: Common.
RANGE: Southeastern United States;
Texas; West Indies; Surinam; Brazil.
GEOLOGIC RANGE: Miocene to
Holocene.
REMARKS: Most common ark on
Texas coast. Syn. *A. incongrua* Say,
1822. Harper (1970) reports young
A. brasiliana attach by means of a
byssus to *Nassarius acutus* in a sym-
biotic relationship.

Chemnitz's Ark
Anadara (Cunearca) chemnitzi
(Philippi, 1851), *Zeitschr. für
Malakozool.* 8:50.
Gk. *ana* without, *dara* gape; honor-
ing Johann Chemnitz (1730–1800).
SIZE: 25.6 mm.
COLOR: White.
SHAPE: Trigonal. Inequivalve. In-
equilateral.
ORNAMENT OR SCULPTURE: Twenty-
six to 28 broad ribs, strongly re-
curved posteriorly, bearing barlike
beads.
HINGE AREA: Umbones well sepa-
rated, forward of center of ligamen-
tal area. Comblike teeth become
smaller toward center.
PALLIAL LINE & INTERIOR: Interior
white, polished; ribs visible. Pallial
line simple with 2 muscle scars.
PERIOSTRACUM: Thin, light brown,
scaly.
HABITAT: Offshore in shallow water.
Epifaunal.
LOCALITIES: Extreme south.
OCCURRENCE: Uncommon in beach
drift.
RANGE: Texas; Mexico; Greater Antilles to Brazil; Surinam.
GEOLOGIC RANGE: Upper Pleistocene? to Holocene.
REMARKS: Very similar to *A.
brasiliana* but heavier and smaller,
more elevated dorsally. Coll., Wilson.

Anadara (Setiarca) floridana

Anadara (Larkiana) transversa

Subgenus *Setiarca* Olsson, 1961

Cut-Ribbed Ark

Anadara (Setiarca) floridana (Conrad, 1869), *Amer. J. Conch.* 5:108.
Gk. *ana* without, *dara* gape; from Florida.
SIZE: 63.5–127 mm.
COLOR: White.
SHAPE: Obliquely rectangular. Equivalve. Inequilateral.
ORNAMENT OR SCULPTURE: Very heavy shell. Thirty-five square ribs; each rib marked with deep central groove that does not extend over umbones and is not present on more rounded posterior ribs.
HINGE AREA: Umbones incurved, flattened; hinge margin straight. Numerous comblike teeth.
PALLIAL LINE & INTERIOR: Interior marked with delicate lines; margins crenulate. Pallial line simple and 2 muscle scars well defined.
PERIOSTRACUM: Heavy, brown, usually worn off on upper part of shell.
HABITAT: Deeper water offshore. Infaunal.
LOCALITIES: Central, south.
OCCURRENCE: Uncommon to rare beach shell.
RANGE: Southeastern United States; Texas; Greater Antilles.
GEOLOGIC RANGE: Holocene, with forms to Upper Tertiary.
REMARKS: The line down the center of the rib makes this large ark very distinctive and separates it (somewhat doubtfully) from *A. baughmani* Hertlein, 1951, a species from farther offshore. Formerly referred to as *A. secticostata* Reeve, 1844, which has a brown stain. *A. lienosa* Say, 1822, is a similar fossil form. *See* Bird 1965, p. 28.

Subgenus *Larkiania* Reinhart, 1935

Transverse Ark

Anadara (Larkiana) transversa (Say, 1822), *J. Acad. Natur. Sci. Philadelphia* 2(1):269.
Gk. *ana* without, *dara* gape; L. *transversus* crosswise.
SIZE: 12–36 mm.
COLOR: White.
SHAPE: Transversely oblong. Left valve overlaps right. Equivalve. Inequilateral.
ORNAMENT OR SCULPTURE: Thirty to 35 rounded ribs per valve. Ribs on left valve usually beaded, seldom so on right valve.
HINGE AREA: Long, narrow ligamental space separates umbones. Numerous teeth perpendicular to hinge line.
PALLIAL LINE & INTERIOR: Interior polished. Pallial line simple with 2 muscle scars.
PERIOSTRACUM: Brown, thick, usually worn off except at base of valves.
HABITAT: Littoral to 10.8 meters (6 fathoms). Inlet-influenced areas and offshore. Infaunal.
LOCALITIES: Entire.
OCCURRENCE: Common.
RANGE: South of Cape Cod to Florida; Texas to Carmen, Campeche, Mexico; Gulf of Campeche.
GEOLOGIC RANGE: Miocene to Holocene.
REMARKS: Unpaired valve may be hard to identify due to dissimilarity of sculpture on each valve. Coll., Wilson.

Anadara (Lunarca) ovalis

Noetia (Eontia) ponderosa

Subgenus *Lunarca* Reinhart, 1943

Blood Ark

Anadara (Lunarca) ovalis (Bruguière, 1789), *Encycl. Méth.* 1(1):110.
Gk. *ana* without, *dara* gape; L. *ovum* egg.
SIZE: 38–59 mm.
COLOR: White.
SHAPE: Roundish to ovate.
Equivalve. Inequilateral.
ORNAMENT OR SCULPTURE: Ribs have weak groove in center. Strong intercostal ribs. Left valve more heavily sculptured than right. No byssal gape.
HINGE AREA: Ligament very narrow. Umbones close together. Comblike teeth.
PALLIAL LINE & INTERIOR: Pallial line simple with 2 muscle scars. Ribs visible on polished white interior.
PERIOSTRACUM: Heavy, brown, usually worn off at umbones.
HABITAT: Just offshore. Infaunal.
LOCALITIES: Entire.
OCCURRENCE: Common.
RANGE: Cape Cod to West Indies; Gulf states; Costa Rica; Brazilian coast to Rocha, Uruguay.
GEOLOGIC RANGE: Miocene to Holocene.
REMARKS: Animal is bright red. Syn. *A. campechiensis* Gmelin, 1791.

Family NOETIIDAE Stewart, 1930
Subfamily NOETIINAE Stewart, 1930

Genus *Noetia* Gray, 1840
Subgenus *Eontia* MacNeil, 1938

Ponderous Ark

Noetia (Eontia) ponderosa (Say, 1822), *J. Acad. Natur. Sci. Philadelphia* 2(1):267.
From Noe, Noah; L. *ponderosus* heavy.
SIZE: 50.8–63.5 mm.
COLOR: White.
SHAPE: Trigonal. Equivalve. Inequilateral.
ORNAMENT OR SCULPTURE: Heavy, thick shell. Thirty-two flattened square ribs with fine line down center. Posterior margin nearly straight, keeled. Fine concentric intercostal sculpture absent from umbones.
HINGE AREA: Umbones well separated; sides of hinge area slope obliquely downward to straight margin. Teeth comblike.
PALLIAL LINE & INTERIOR: Pallial line simple with 2 strong, raised muscle scars. No byssal threads in adults.
PERIOSTRACUM: Heavy, brown, velvetlike.
HABITAT: Offshore on sandy bottoms. Infaunal.
LOCALITIES: Entire.
OCCURRENCE: Common.
RANGE: Virginia to Key West; Gulf of Mexico.
GEOLOGIC RANGE: Miocene to Holocene.
REMARKS: Often found as paired valves due to strong ligament. I think Gray's name, "Noah's Ark," is much more imaginative than "Ponderous Ark," if not as descriptive.

Brachidontes (Brachidontes) exustus

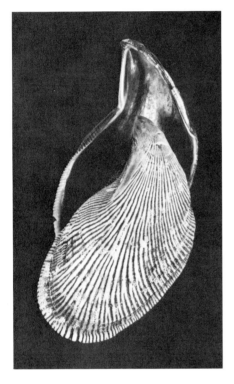

Ischadium recurvum

Order MYTILOIDEA Férussac, 1822
Superfamily MYTILACEA Rafinesque, 1815
Family MYTILIDAE Rafinesque, 1815
Subfamily MYTILINAE Rafinesque, 1815

Genus *Brachidontes* Swainson, 1840
Subgenus *Brachidontes* s.s.

Scorched Mussel

Brachidontes (Brachidontes) exustus (Linné, 1758), *Syst. Natur.*, 10th ed., p. 705.
Gk. *brachys* short, *dontes* teeth; L. *exustium* burn up.
SIZE: 18–38 mm.
COLOR: Yellowish brown to dark brown. Interior metallic purple and white.
SHAPE: Moderately fan-shaped.
ORNAMENT OR SCULPTURE: Numerous rounded, radial ribs that divide as they near ventral margin and are eroded near umbones. Slight byssal gape in ventral margin.
HINGE AREA: Two small teeth at anterior end. At posterior end, beyond ligament, are 5 to 6 tiny teeth on edge of shell.
PALLIAL LINE & INTERIOR: Pallial line weak, simple; posterior muscle scar larger than anterior.
PERIOSTRACUM: Thin, yellowish brown.
HABITAT: On rocks or oyster reefs in bays and inlets. Byssate closely attached epifaunal.
LOCALITIES: Entire.
OCCURRENCE: Common.
RANGE: North Carolina to West Indies; Texas; Yucatán; Quintana Roo; Brazilian coast to Uruguay.
GEOLOGIC RANGE: Pliocene to Holocene.
REMARKS: This small mussel is often confused with *B. citrinus*, Röding, 1798, which is larger and has 4 anterior teeth. It is found attached by its byssus on the jetties and on oyster banks (fig. 17). It does not inhabit brackish water in Texas. *See* Menzel 1955.

Genus *Ischadium* Jukes-Brown, 1905

Hooked Mussel

Ischadium recurvum (Rafinesque, 1820), *An. Gén. Sci. Phys. Bruxelles* 5:320.
Gk. *ischatium* fig-shaped; L. *recurvus* bent, curved.
SIZE: 25.6–63.5 mm.
COLOR: Purplish gray.
SHAPE: Oval with a strong triangular hook on anterior end.
ORNAMENT OR SCULPTURE: Strong radial, rounded ribs that divide as they near ventral margin. Microscopic growth lines cross ribs.
HINGE AREA: Umbones at end of hook. Near umbones are 3 or 4 small teeth. Ligament strong, in large groove extending from umbones to peak of dorsal margin.
PALLIAL LINE & INTERIOR: Interior shiny purple, reddish brown, nacreous. Pallial line simple with 1 large posterior muscle scar.
PERIOSTRACUM: Thin, yellow brown.
HABITAT: Oyster reef in low-salinity bays. Byssate closely attached epifaunal.
LOCALITIES: Entire.
OCCURRENCE: Common.
RANGE: Cape Cod to West Indies; Texas; Carmen, Campeche, Mexico; Gulf of Campeche.
GEOLOGIC RANGE: Pliocene to Holocene.
REMARKS: This species lives on low-salinity reefs of *Crassostrea virginica* (Gmelin, 1792) (fig. 17). During periods of drought *Brachidontes exustus* and *Ostrea equestris* Say, 1834, will completely replace *I. recurvum* and *C. virginica*. *See* Menzel 1955.

Gregariella coralliophaga

Lioberis castaneus

Subfamily CRENELLINAE Adams & Adams, 1857

Genus *Gregariella* Montcrosato, 1884

Common Gregariella
Gregariella coralliophaga (Gmelin, 1791), *Syst. Natur.*, 13th ed., p. 3359.
L. *gregarius* living in flocks, *corallum* coral, *phagen* to eat.
SIZE: 17 mm.
COLOR: Reddish brown. Interior iridescent.
SHAPE: Oval.
ORNAMENT OR SCULPTURE: Smooth except for growth lines. Posterior dorsal area somewhat keeled.
HINGE AREA: Weak, tiny denticulations along hinge.
PALLIAL LINE & INTERIOR: Pallial line simple; inner edges finely serrate.
PERIOSTRACUM: Long, brown, hair-like processes over keeled posterior end.
HABITAT: Bores into rock and coral offshore. Semi-infaunal.
LOCALITIES: Entire.
OCCURRENCE: Fairly common.
RANGE: Cape Hatteras to Brazil; Gulf of Mexico; Yucatán.
GEOLOGIC RANGE: Miocene to Holocene.
REMARKS: Weaves nest of byssal threads. [*Musculus opifex*]. Syn. *G. opifex* (Say, 1815). Coll., Wilson.

Genus *Lioberis* Dall, 1898

Say's Chestnut Mussel
Lioberis castaneus (Say, 1822), *J. Acad. Natur. Sci. Philadelphia* 2(1):226.
Gk. *leios* smooth; L. *berus* water snake, *castanea* chestnut colored.
SIZE: 25 mm.
COLOR: Bluish white.
SHAPE: Elongate oval, inflated.
ORNAMENT OR SCULPTURE: Smooth except for fine, concentric growth lines.
HINGE AREA: Umbones slightly back from anterior end. No teeth.
PALLIAL LINE & INTERIOR: Interior smooth, nacreous. No marginal crenulation. Pallial line simple.
PERIOSTRACUM: Shiny, brown.
HABITAT: Open-bay margins, inlets, along shore. Infaunal.
LOCALITIES: Central, south.
OCCURRENCE: Uncommon in beach drift.
RANGE: South Carolina to Florida Keys and West Indies; Texas; Yucatán; Brazil.
GEOLOGIC RANGE: Holocene.
REMARKS: [*Botula castanea* (Say, 1822)]. Coll., Wilson.

Musculus (Ryenella) lateralis

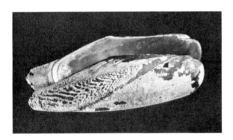

Lithophaga (Diberus) bisulcata

Genus *Musculus* Röding, 1798
Subgenus *Ryenella* Fleming, 1959

Lateral Musculus
Musculus (Ryenella) lateralis (Say, 1822), *J. Acad. Natur. Sci. Philadelphia* 2(1):264.
L. *musculus* muscle, *later* brick, tile.
SIZE: 10 mm.
COLOR: Variable: light brown, pink, or greenish. Interior iridescent.
SHAPE: Oblong.
ORNAMENT OR SCULPTURE: Concentric growth lines over entire surface. Radial ribs on either end leaving disc section with only the finer growth lines.
HINGE AREA: Umbones not terminal. No teeth.
PALLIAL LINE & INTERIOR: Pallial line simple.
PERIOSTRACUM: Thin, yellowish brown to green.
HABITAT: Attached to tunicates. Semi-infaunal.
LOCALITIES: Port Aransas, probably entire.
OCCURRENCE: Uncommon.
RANGE: North Carolina to Florida; Texas; Yucatán; Quintana Roo; West Indies; Brazil.
GEOLOGIC RANGE: Pleistocene to Holocene.
REMARKS: Look in colonies of tunicates (sea pork), where it attaches by its byssal threads. *See* Merrill & Turner 1967; Bertrand 1972.

Subfamily LITHOPHAGINAE
Adams & Adams, 1857

Genus *Lithophaga* Röding, 1798
Subgenus *Diberus* Dall, 1898

Mahogany Date Mussel
Lithophaga (Diberus) bisulcata (Orbigny, 1845), *Hist. d'Ile de Cuba* 2:333.
Gk. *lithos* stone, *phagen* to eat; L. *bisulcus* cloven.
SIZE: 25–38 mm.
COLOR: Mahogany brown.
SHAPE: Elongate cylindrical, coming to a point at one end.
ORNAMENT OR SCULPTURE: Weak concentric growth lines. Two oblique furrows going from dorsal margin to posterior. Covered with gray calcareous deposits.
HINGE AREA: Umbones not terminal. No teeth.
PALLIAL LINE & INTERIOR: Anterior muscle in front of umbo.
PERIOSTRACUM: Smooth, thin, brown, lacquerlike.
HABITAT: In rocks in both shallow and deep water. Infaunal.
LOCALITIES: Entire.
OCCURRENCE: Common.
RANGE: Bermuda; North Carolina to Florida; Texas; West Indies; Surinam; Brazil.
GEOLOGIC RANGE: Oligocene to Holocene.
REMARKS: Bring up rocks from jetties and carefully crush with hammer and chisel to remove these borers. Coll., Young. *See* Turner & Boss 1962, p. 110; Ogle 1976.

Lithophaga (Myoforceps) aristata

Modiolus americanus

Subgenus *Myoforceps* P. Fischer, 1886

Scissor Date Mussel
Lithophaga (Myoforceps) aristata (Dillwyn, 1817), *Cat. Rec. Shells* 1:303.
Gk. *lithos* stone, *phagen* to eat; L. *arista* ear of corn.
SIZE: 25–38 mm.
COLOR: Grayish white.
SHAPE: Cylindrical with one end pointed.
ORNAMENT OR SCULPTURE: Smooth. Points at posterior end that cross each other in scissor-fashion formed by calcareous deposit over periostracum.
HINGE AREA: Umbones not terminal. No teeth.
PALLIAL LINE & INTERIOR: Interior nacreous.
PERIOSTRACUM: Shiny, thin, brown.
HABITAT: In rocks in both shallow and deep water. Infaunal.
LOCALITIES: Central, south.
OCCURRENCE: Fairly common.
RANGE: North Carolina to Florida; Texas; Yucatán; West Indies; La Jolla, California, to Peru.
GEOLOGIC RANGE: Oligocene to Holocene.
REMARKS: Look for this in the same place as *L. bisulcata*. Coll., Young. *See* Turner & Boss 1962, p. 105; Ogle 1976.

Subfamily MODIOLINAE Keen, 1958

Genus *Modiolus* Lamarck, 1799

Tulip Mussel
Modiolus americanus (Leach, 1815), *Zool. Misc.* 2:32.
L. *modiolus* a small measure, or bucket on a water wheel[?]; from America.
SIZE: 25–101 mm.
COLOR: Light brown with blush of rose red and streaks of purple.
SHAPE: Trigonal.
ORNAMENT OR SCULPTURE: Only fine growth lines.
HINGE AREA: Anterior margin without teeth. Umbones away from end of shell. Ligament in groove posterior to umbones.
PALLIAL LINE & INTERIOR: Pallial line weak, simple. Posterior muscle scar larger than anterior.
PERIOSTRACUM: Shiny brown over anterior end, shaggy over posterior end.
HABITAT: Offshore below low-water mark. Byssate closely attached epifaunal.
LOCALITIES: Entire.
OCCURRENCE: Fairly common beach shell.
RANGE: Bermuda; North Carolina to West Indies; Texas; Campeche Bank; Yucatán; Surinam; Brazilian coast to Bahia.
GEOLOGIC RANGE: ? to Holocene.
REMARKS: A strikingly beautiful shell. Color is intense red on Texas coast and purple in Florida. [*Volsella* or *Modiolus tulipa* Lamarck, 1819].

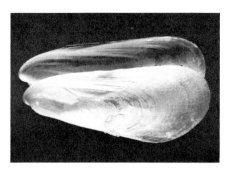

Amygdalum papyria

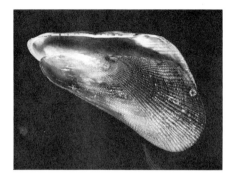

Geukensia demissa granosissima

Genus *Amygdalum* Megerle von Muhlfeld, 1811

Paper Mussel
Amygdalum papyria (Conrad, 1846), *Proc. Acad. Natur. Sci. Philadelphia* 3(1):24.
L. *amygdalum* almond, *papyrus* paper.
SIZE: 25–38 mm.
COLOR: Exterior grayish. Interior iridescent, metallic white.
SHAPE: Elongate fan-shaped.
ORNAMENT OR SCULPTURE: Very delicate and fragile with only fine concentric growth lines.
HINGE AREA: Umbones slightly beyond anterior end. Ligament weak and thin. No teeth.
PALLIAL LINE & INTERIOR: Pallial line simple and muscle scar faint.
PERIOSTRACUM: Thin, deciduous, greenish, lacquerlike.
HABITAT: Open bays and inlet-influenced areas. Semi-infaunal.
LOCALITIES: Entire.
OCCURRENCE: Fairly common.
RANGE: Maryland to Florida; Texas.
GEOLOGIC RANGE: ? to Holocene.
REMARKS: For these nestlers dig carefully in the soft mud around the roots of marine grasses. *See* Allen 1955.

Genus *Geukensia* Poel, 1959

Ribbed Mussel
Geukensia demissa granosissima (G. B. Sowerby III, 1914), *Proc. Malacol. Soc. London* 11:9.
Gk. *geukensia* undetermined derivation; L. *demissus* low lying, humble, *granusus* full of grains.
SIZE: 50.8–101 mm.
COLOR: Brown, shiny.
SHAPE: Elongate trigonal with rounded posterior margin.
ORNAMENT OR SCULPTURE: Numerous strong radial, beaded ribs that divide as they near posterior margin.
HINGE AREA: Long, narrow. No teeth. Ligament in groove posterior to umbones slightly away from end of shell.
PALLIAL LINE & INTERIOR: Interior nacreous. Pallial line rather strong, simple, with small muscle scar at anterior end and larger one at upper part of posterior end.
PERIOSTRACUM: Thin, yellow brown.
HABITAT: Salt marshes. Byssate closely attached epifaunal.
LOCALITIES: East.
OCCURRENCE: Common.
RANGE: Both sides of Florida; Gulf states; Yucatán.
GEOLOGIC RANGE: Pleistocene to Holocene.
REMARKS: Lives in salt marshes imbedded in soil around the roots of grasses. After Hurricane Camille struck the Mississippi area in 1968, uprooting vegetation, the shores of Padre Island were covered with clumps of marsh grass filled with this shell for over 30 miles. They can live up to 3 weeks out of water. Referred to as *Modiola demissus* (Dillwyn, 1817). *See* Lent 1967.

Atrina seminuda

Atrina serrata

Superfamily PINNACEA Leach, 1819
Family PINNIDAE Leach, 1819

Genus *Atrina* Gray, 1840

Half-Naked Pen Shell
Atrina seminuda (Lamarck, 1819), *Hist. Natur. Anim. sans Vert.* 6:131.
L. *atrium* an opening, *semi* half, *nudus* nude.
SIZE: 235–250 mm.
COLOR: Translucent, grayish tan sometimes mottled with purple brown.
SHAPE: Wedge-shaped.
ORNAMENT OR SCULPTURE: Spinose, radiating ribs with ventral slope usually smooth. Ribs often smooth. Growth lines fine.
HINGE AREA: Longest dimension of shell, straight. No teeth.
PALLIAL LINE & INTERIOR: Nacreous area is about one-half to two-thirds length of shell. Small posterior adductor muscle scar lies well within nacreous area, never protruding beyond it. Anterior adductor scar small, nearly as wide as anterior end of shell. Scar separates this shell from *A. rigida*. Pallial line simple.
PERIOSTRACUM: None visible.
HABITAT: Offshore and in inlet-influenced bays. Semi-infaunal.
LOCALITIES: Entire.
OCCURRENCE: Fairly common.
RANGE: Eastern United States; Texas; Yucatán; Surinam; Brazil to Argentina.
GEOLOGIC RANGE: Pliocene to Holocene.
REMARKS: Lives in colonies in the mud attached with byssal threads; only the posterior margin is above substratum. The margin of the mantle is yellow; the foot is a lighter yellow. Sexes separate. Adductor muscle is edible. Less common than *A. serrata*. A small crab is commensal with and lives within the pen shell. Coll., Wilson. *See* Bruce 1972.

Saw-Tooth Pen Shell
Atrina serrata (G. B. Sowerby I, 1825), *Cat. Tank.*, p. 5.
L. *atrium* opening, *serra* a saw.
SIZE: Up to 250 mm.
COLOR: Translucent light tan to medium greenish brown.
SHAPE: Wedge-shaped; thin, fragile, shiny.
ORNAMENT OR SCULPTURE: Uniform sculpture of about 30 low ribs covered with fluted projections. Sculpture much finer on ventral slope.
HINGE AREA: Straight to slightly concave withouth teeth.
PALLIAL LINE & INTERIOR: Interior has nacreous layer usually covering three-fourths length of valve. Posterior adductor muscle scar nearly circular, set well within nacreous layer. Anterior scar small. Pallial line simple.
PERIOSTRACUM: None visible.
HABITAT: Offshore in inner shelf zone. Semi-infaunal.
LOCALITIES: Entire.
OCCURRENCE: Common.
RANGE: North Carolina to West Indies; Texas; Surinam.
GEOLOGIC RANGE: Pliocene to Holocene.
REMARKS: Much thinner and spines more tubular than *A. seminuda*; nacreous area larger. At times this shell is washed up on Gulf beaches by the hundreds (fig. 14). The adductor muscle may be prepared to eat in the same way that scallops are. These mollusks are harvested in Mexico for canning as scallops. A pair of colorless shrimp live commensally with *A. serrata*. *See* Bruce 1972.

Pinctada imbricata

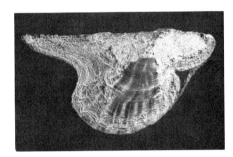

Pteria colymbus

Order PTERIOIDEA Newell, 1965
Suborder PTERIINA Newell, 1965
Superfamily PTERIACEA Gray, 1847
Family PTERIIDAE Gray, 1847

Genus *Pinctada* Röding, 1798

Atlantic Pearl Oyster

Pinctada imbricata Röding, 1798, *Zool. Misc.* 1:98.
Span. *pintado* painted, mottled; L. *imbricare* to cover with lapping tiles.
SIZE: 38–76 mm.
COLOR: Variable: purplish brown or black.
SHAPE: Roundish with 2 short wings. Inequivalve. Inequilateral.
ORNAMENT OR SCULPTURE: Flat with concentrically arranged scaly projections of periostracum. Byssal gape under anterior wing of right valve.
HINGE AREA: Straight with single lateral tooth in left valve, double laterals in right.
PALLIAL LINE & INTERIOR: Interior very nacreous with wide polished border around margins. Pallial line simple.
PERIOSTRACUM: Dark brown, brittle with scalelike projections.
HABITAT: Offshore attached to rock or gorgonia, a soft coral. Byssate free-swinging epifaunal.
LOCALITIES: Southern half of coast.
OCCURRENCE: Uncommon to rare beach shell.
RANGE: Southern half of Florida; Texas; Gulf of Mexico to Quintana Roo; West Indies; Brazil.
GEOLOGIC RANGE: ? to Holocene.
REMARKS: Adults are seldom found. Forms beautiful pearls. Syn. *P. radiata* Leach, 1819. Coll., Young.

Genus *Pteria* Scopoli, 1777

Atlantic Wing Oyster

Pteria colymbus (Röding, 1798), *Mus. Boltenianum*, p. 166.
Gk. *pteron* wing, *kolymbos* a diver.
SIZE: 38–76 mm.
COLOR: Brownish black with broken, radial lines of cream color. Interior highly nacreous.
SHAPE: Oval with a posterior drawn-out wing. Inequivalve. Inequilateral.
ORNAMENT OR SCULPTURE: Smooth surface. Byssal gape near anterior wing.
HINGE AREA: Straight with elongated posterior ear, or wing. Two small cardinal teeth and 1 lateral tooth in each valve.
PALLIAL LINE & INTERIOR: Interior nacreous with single, almost central muscle scar. Pallial line simple.
PERIOSTRACUM: Light brown colored, shaggy with spiny projections extending beyond margin.
HABITAT: Offshore reefs and on "whistling buoy" out of Port Aransas attached to alcyonarians. Byssate free-swinging epifaunal.
LOCALITIES: Southern two-thirds of coast.
OCCURRENCE: Uncommon beach shell.
RANGE: Bermuda; southeastern United States; Texas; Costa Rica; West Indies; Brazil.
GEOLOGIC RANGE: Pliocene to Holocene.
REMARKS: Will wash up on outer beaches attached to gorgonia. Coll., Young.

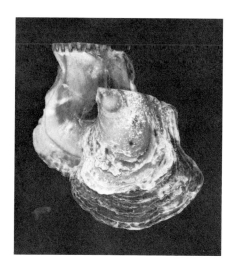

Isognomon alatus

Isognomon bicolor

Family ISOGNOMONIDAE
Woodring, 1925

Genus *Isognomon* Lightfoot, 1786

Flat Tree Oyster
Isognomon alatus (Gmelin, 1791),
Syst. Natur., 13th ed., p. 3339.
Gk. *isos gnomon* equal parallelo-
gram; L. *alatus* winged.
SIZE: 50.8–76 mm.
COLOR: Drab, dirty gray. Interior
nacreous, purplish.
SHAPE: Flat, fan-shaped.
ORNAMENT OR SCULPTURE: Rough
with flaky lamellations.
HINGE AREA: Straight with 8 to 12
oblong grooves into which are set
small, brown resiliums. Byssal gape
on anterior margin near dorsal mar-
gin.
PALLIAL LINE & INTERIOR: Pallial line
simple, discontinuous.
PERIOSTRACUM: None visible.
HABITAT: In crevices on jetties. Bys-
sate free-swinging epifaunal.
LOCALITIES: Port Aransas, south.
OCCURRENCE: Uncommon.
RANGE: Bermuda; southern half of
Florida; Texas; southern Mexico;
Campeche Bank; Central America;
West Indies; Brazilian oceanic is-
lands.
GEOLOGIC RANGE: Pliocene to
Holocene.
REMARKS: Look carefully on jetties;
very undistinguished appearance.

Two-Toned Tree Oyster
Isognomon bicolor (C. B. Adams,
1845), *Proc. Boston Soc. Natur. Hist.*
2:9.
Gk. *isos gnomon* equal parallelogram; L. *bi* two, *color* hue.
SIZE: 12–50 mm.
COLOR: Yellowish with purple
splotches. Variable.
SHAPE: Very irregular, elongated
parallelogram.
ORNAMENT OR SCULPTURE: Rough
with flaky lamellations.
HINGE AREA: Short, straight, with 4
to 8 small, square sockets. Anterior
byssal gape near dorsal margin.
PALLIAL LINE & INTERIOR: Sharply
raised ridge separates central area
from marginal area. Color of interior
frequently different on opposite
sides of ridge. Pallial line simple,
discontinuous.
PERIOSTRACUM: None visible.
HABITAT: In clusters on rocks in
inlet-influenced areas. Byssate
free-swinging epifaunal.
LOCALITIES: Port Aransas, south.
OCCURRENCE: Uncommon.
RANGE: Bermuda; Florida Keys;
Texas; southern Mexico; Campeche
Bank; Yucatán; Costa Rica; Caribbean.
GEOLOGIC RANGE: Pliocene to
Holocene.
REMARKS: More common than *I.
alatus*. Panamic vicariant is *I. recog-
nitus* (Mabille, 1895). Coll., Wilson.

Aequipecten muscosus

Superfamily PECTINACEA
Rafinesque, 1815
Family PECTINIDAE Rafinesque,
1815
Leo G. Hertlein in *Treatise on Invertebrate Paleontology* (ed. Moore, 1969, N348) declines to define the supraspecific units in this family into subfamilies, stating that "to define such groups as subfamilies or to separate them as families would imply relationships and distinctions based chiefly on supposition only." Other authors (Keen 1971 and Abbott 1974) continue with subfamily divisions. According to the *Treatise*, all the pectens found in Texas fall into the chlamys and pecten groups. The subfamily designations will be maintained here. The only justification for this is to maintain consistency of style.

Subfamily CHLAMYDINAE
Korobkov, 1960

Genus *Aequipecten* P. Fischer, 1886

Rough Scallop
Aequipecten muscosus (W. Wood, 1818), *Index Testac.*, p. 47, pl. 2, fig. 2.
L. *aequus*, *aequi* equal, *pecten* a comb, *muscus* moss, covered with sponge.
SIZE: 18–30 mm.
COLOR: Variable from red, orange, yellow, or mottled purple.
SHAPE: Fan-shaped. Inequivalve. Inequilateral.
ORNAMENT OR SCULPTURE: About 20 spinose ribs with spoon-shaped spines arranged in 3 rows. Small spines present in interspaces.
HINGE AREA: Straight. No teeth.
PALLIAL LINE & INTERIOR: One large muscle scar. Pallial line simple.
PERIOSTRACUM: None visible.
HABITAT: Offshore on banks. Free-living epifaunal.
LOCALITIES: South.
OCCURRENCE: Rare.

RANGE: Bermuda; Florida Keys; Texas; Mexico; Campeche Bank; West Indies; Brazil.
GEOLOGIC RANGE: Pleistocene to Holocene.
REMARKS: Only worn and faded valves are found on outer beaches.

Argopecten gibbus

Argopecten irradians amplicostatus

Genus *Argopecten* Monterosato, 1899

Calico Scallop
Argopecten gibbus (Linné, 1758), *Syst. Natur.*, 10th ed., p. 698.
Argo, Jason's ship; L. *pecten* a comb, *gibbus* a hump.
SIZE: 25–50.8 mm.
COLOR: Upper valve mottled with red or purple. Lower valve white with little color.
SHAPE: Almost circular.
ORNAMENT OR SCULPTURE: About 20 squared ribs. Valves inflated.
HINGE AREA: Straight. No teeth. Ears small.
PALLIAL LINE & INTERIOR: Single muscle scar. Pallial line simple.
PERIOSTRACUM: Not preserved.
HABITAT: Offshore on intermediate shelf. Free-living epifaunal.
LOCALITIES: Entire.
OCCURRENCE: Rare beach shell.
RANGE: Bermuda; eastern United States; Gulf of Mexico; Campeche Bank; West Indies.
GEOLOGIC RANGE: Pleistocene to Holocene.
REMARKS: Expect only worn, faded valves. Rarely found alive at Port Isabel. [*Aequipecten gibbus*]. *See* Porter & Wolfe 1971.

Atlantic Bay Scallop
Argopecten irradians amplicostatus (Dall, 1898), *Trans. Wagner Free Inst. Sci.* 3(4):747.
Argo, Jason's ship; L. *pecten* a comb, *irradians* radiating, *amplius* abundant, *costa* a rib.
SIZE: 50.8–76 mm.
COLOR: Upper valve mottled gray and white.
SHAPE: Fan-shaped, almost circular.
ORNAMENT OR SCULPTURE: Twelve to 17 high, squarish ribs. Rather inflated.
HINGE AREA: Straight. No teeth. Ears not as wide as shell.
PALLIAL LINE & INTERIOR: Single muscle scar. Pallial line simple.
PERIOSTRACUM: None visible.
HABITAT: Bays, open lagoons. Free-living epifaunal.
LOCALITIES: Entire.
OCCURRENCE: Common.
RANGE: Central Texas to Tuxpan, Veracruz, Mexico.
GEOLOGIC RANGE: Lower Miocene to Holocene.
REMARKS: This species lives in the bays and is often washed up by the hundreds after a norther. The worn valves found on outer beaches have changed color to orange or black. In the aquarium the "eyes" of this active bivalve are visible around the mantle edge (fig. 15). The tiny juvenile attaches to rock by its byssus; when pulled off it will reattach itself. It will "flap" its valves and skip about the tank. [*Aequipecten irradians amplicostatus*]. *See* Clarke 1965.

Lyropecten (Nodipecten) nodosus

Pecten (Euvola) raveneli

Genus *Lyropecten* Conrad, 1862
Subgenus *Nodipecten* Dall, 1898

Lion's Paw
Lyropecten (Nodipecten) nodosus
(Linné, 1758), *Syst. Natur.*, 10th ed.,
p. 698.
L. *lyro* lyre shaped, *pecten* a comb,
nodus knot.
SIZE: 76–152 mm.
COLOR: Bright red, deep orange, or
maroon red.
SHAPE: Fan-shaped. Nearly
equivalve. Inequilateral.
ORNAMENT OR SCULPTURE: Seven to
9 large, coarse ribs that have large,
hollow nodules. Also numerous
cordlike riblets.
HINGE AREA: Straight. No teeth.
PALLIAL LINE & INTERIOR: Pallial line
simple with single large muscle
scar.
PERIOSTRACUM: Not preserved.
HABITAT: Offshore. Epifaunal
fissure dweller.
LOCALITIES: South.
OCCURRENCE: Rare.
RANGE: Florida Keys; Texas; Mexico;
West Indies; Surinam; Brazil.
GEOLOGIC RANGE: Oligocene to
Holocene.
REMARKS: Halves of this striking
shell are found, rarely, on the
southern part of the coast, but living
specimens have been found by di-
vers on the 7½ Fathom Reef and
other offshore banks. Panamic vi-
cariant is *L. subnodosus* Sowerby,
1835. Coll., Texas Memorial
Museum, Austin.

Subfamily PECTININAE Rafinesque, 1815

Genus *Pecten* Müller, 1776
Subgenus *Euvola* Dall, 1898

Ravenel's Scallop
Pecten (Euvola) raveneli Dall, 1898,
Trans. Wagner Free Inst. Sci. 3(4):721.
L. *pecten* a comb; dedicated to Dr.
Edmund Ravenel, nineteenth-
century collector.
SIZE: 25–51 mm.
COLOR: Variable from pink to purple. Ribs white. Lower valve dark;
upper valve white.
SHAPE: Fan-shaped. Upper valve
very flat; lower valve inflated.
ORNAMENT OR SCULPTURE: About 21
rounded, radiating ribs with wider
interspaces, fine concentric growth
lines. Each rib has groove down
middle.
HINGE AREA: Straight; ears almost
equal. Umbones flat.
PALLIAL LINE & INTERIOR: Interior
smooth with margin beyond pallial
line showing ribs. Pallial line simple
with single muscle scar.
PERIOSTRACUM: Not preserved.
HABITAT: Offshore, 21 to 62 meters
(12 to 35 fathoms). Free-living epi-
faunal.
LOCALITIES: South, mainly Port
Isabel area.
OCCURRENCE: Rare.
RANGE: North Carolina to Gulf of
Mexico; West Indies.
GEOLOGIC RANGE: Pliocene to
Holocene.
REMARKS: Usually washed up only
after storms. Coll., Young. *See*
Verrill 1897.

Plicatula gibbosa

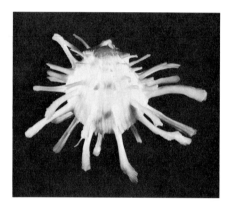

Spondylus americanus

beachworn specimen

Family PLICATULIDAE Watson, 1930

Genus *Plicatula* Lamarck, 1801

Kitten's Paw
Plicatula gibbosa Lamarck, 1801, *Syst. Anim.*, p. 132.
L. *plicatus* folded, *ula* fem. dim., *gibbus* a hump.
SIZE: 25 mm.
COLOR: Whitish with red brown lines on ribs.
SHAPE: Fan-shaped. Inequivalve.
ORNAMENT OR SCULPTURE: Rather heavy with 5 to 7 raised ribs that crenulate margin so that valves interlock. Attached by right valve.
HINGE AREA: Two hinge teeth in each valve lock into corresponding notches in opposite valve, as in *Spondylus*. Ligament internal.
PALLIAL LINE & INTERIOR: Pallial line simple.
PERIOSTRACUM: Not preserved.
HABITAT: Offshore on banks. Cemented epifaunal.
LOCALITIES: Entire.
OCCURRENCE: Uncommon.
RANGE: Bermuda; North Carolina to Florida; Gulf states; Campeche Bank; Yucatán; West Indies; Surinam; Brazil; Uruguay.
GEOLOGIC RANGE: Oligocene? Pleistocene to Holocene.
REMARKS: Dead shells are not uncommon on outer beaches and in spoil banks. Look for it attached to pieces of offshore drilling rigs that are occasionally brought in. Attaches by right valve. Coll., Young.

Family SPONDYLIDAE Gray, 1826

Genus *Spondylus* Linné, 1758

Atlantic Thorny Oyster
Spondylus americanus Hermann, 1781, *Ges. Natur. Freunde Berlin* 16:51.
Gk. *spondylos* vertebra, spines; from America.
SIZE: 76–101 mm.
COLOR: Variable: white with orange or yellow umbones, rose or cream.
SHAPE: Nearly circular to oval. Inequivalve.
ORNAMENT OR SCULPTURE: Adults have spines up to 2 inches in length that are erect, arranged radially. Lower valve larger and deeper than upper.
HINGE AREA: Two large cardinal teeth on either side of ligament in each valve align with sockets in opposite valve.
PALLIAL LINE & INTERIOR: Interior smooth and white with 1 large muscle scar. Pallial line simple.
PERIOSTRACUM: Not preserved.
HABITAT: Offshore attached to reefs. Cemented epifaunal.
LOCALITIES: Southern half of coast.
OCCURRENCE: Uncommon.
RANGE: North Carolina to Florida; Texas; Campeche Bank; Yucatán; Central America; West Indies; Brazil.
GEOLOGIC RANGE: Pleistocene to Holocene.
REMARKS: The worn, faded valves found on Texas beaches bear little resemblance to the spectacular living specimen that is brought up by divers offshore. The ball-and-socket hinge distinguishes these eroded specimens from *Chama*. *See* Logan 1974.

Anomia simplex

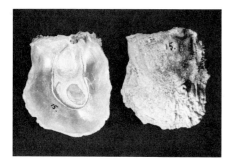

Pododesmus rudis

Superfamily ANOMIACEA
   Rafinesque, 1815
Family ANOMIIDAE Rafinesque,
   1815

Genus *Anomia* Linné, 1758

Common Jingle Shell
Anomia simplex Orbigny, 1845, *Hist. d'Ile de Cuba* 2:367.
Gk. *anomoios* unlike; L. *simplex* simple.
SIZE: 25–51 mm.
COLOR: Variable: translucent yellow or dull orange. Shiny.
SHAPE: Subcircular. Upper valve more convex than flat attached valve.
ORNAMENT OR SCULPTURE: Wavy undulating sculpture. Shape conforms to contours and texture of surface on which attached. Lower valve has hole near umbones from which chitinous byssus projects to anchor shell.
HINGE AREA: Ligament not supported with teeth or ridges.
PALLIAL LINE & INTERIOR: Interior nacreous. Pallial line simple, not distinct. Upper valve has large muscle scar opposite hole and 2 smaller ones below.
PERIOSTRACUM: None visible.
HABITAT: Hypersaline oyster or rock reef. Byssate closely attached epifaunal.
LOCALITIES: Entire.
OCCURRENCE: Common.
RANGE: Bermuda; eastern United States; Gulf of Mexico; Gulf of Campeche; Quintana Roo; West Indies to Brazil; Surinam.
GEOLOGIC RANGE: Miocene to Holocene.
REMARKS: This pretty little shell is often attached to an oyster or old shell. Usually only the top valve is found in the drift. Some old specimens have turned black.

Genus *Pododesmus* Philippi, 1837

Rough Jingle Shell
Pododesmus rudis (Broderip, 1834), *Proc. Zool. Soc. London* 2:2.
Gk. *pous* foot, *desmos* band; L. *rudis* rough.
SIZE: Up to 51 mm.
COLOR: Brownish; lower valve white.
SHAPE: Irregular. Upper valve convex; lower valve flat with a hole near the umbones.
ORNAMENT OR SCULPTURE: Rough, wavy surface arranged somewhat concentrically.
HINGE AREA: Narrow. No teeth.
PALLIAL LINE & INTERIOR: Muscle scar in top valve opposite hole with second large scar diagonally below it. Pallial line simple.
PERIOSTRACUM: None visible.
HABITAT: On rock in inlet-influenced areas. Byssate closely attached epifaunal.
LOCALITIES: South.
OCCURRENCE: Rare.
RANGE: Bermuda; South Carolina to Florida; Texas; Brazilian coast to Argentina.
GEOLOGIC RANGE: Oligocene to Holocene.
REMARKS: Carl Young only recently found this inconspicuous shell while diving off the jetties at Port Isabel. Coll., Young.

Lima (Lima) lima

Lima (Limaria) pellucida

Superfamily LIMACEA Rafinesque, 1815
Family LIMIDAE Rafinesque, 1815

Genus *Lima* Bruguière, 1797
Subgenus *Lima* s.s.

Spiny Lima
Lima (Lima) lima (Linné, 1758), *Syst. Natur.*, 10th ed., p. 699.
L. *lima* file.
SIZE: 25–51 mm.
COLOR: White.
SHAPE: Oblique oval, elongate.
ORNAMENT OR SCULPTURE: Fragile shell. Radial ribs spinose.
HINGE AREA: Oblique. Anterior ear much smaller than posterior ear.
PALLIAL LINE & INTERIOR: Interior polished. Pallial line simple; single muscle scar.
PERIOSTRACUM: Thin, usually lost.
HABITAT: Offshore. Epifaunal byssate fissure dweller.
LOCALITIES: Port Aransas, south.
OCCURRENCE: Rare beach shell.
RANGE: Bermuda; southeastern Florida; southern Texas; Campeche Bank; Yucatán; West Indies; Brazil; Brazilian oceanic islands.
GEOLOGIC RANGE: ? to Holocene.
REMARKS: This is a tropical species that occasionally comes to shore attached to bamboo roots or coconuts. Coll., Wilson. *See* Merrill & Turner 1967.

Subgenus *Limaria* Link, 1807

Antillean Lima
Lima (Limaria) pellucida C. B. Adams, 1846, *Proc. Boston Soc. Natur. Hist.* 2:103.
L. *lima* file, *pelluceo* to be transparent.
SIZE: 18–25 mm.
COLOR: Translucent white.
SHAPE: Oblique oval, elongate.
ORNAMENT OR SCULPTURE: Fragile shell gapes on either side. Radial ribs small, fine, uneven in size and distribution. Margins finely serrate.
HINGE AREA: Oblique, partly external. No teeth. Ears almost equal in length.
PALLIAL LINE & INTERIOR: Interior polished. Pallial line simple; single muscle scar.
PERIOSTRACUM: Thin, light brown, usually lost.
HABITAT: Offshore. Epifaunal byssate fissure dweller.
LOCALITIES: Port Aransas, south.
OCCURRENCE: Rare beach shell.
RANGE: Bermuda; southeastern United States; Texas; Gulf of Mexico to Quintana Roo; West Indies to Brazil.
GEOLOGIC RANGE: ? to Holocene.
REMARKS: The living mollusk has a delicate, "fringed" mantle. It uses these mantle tentacles to move about on the bottom; like the pectens, it flaps its valves to swim about. It has fine byssal threads. Coll., Wilson.

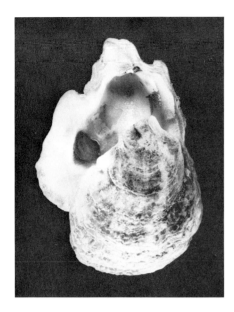

Crassostrea virginica

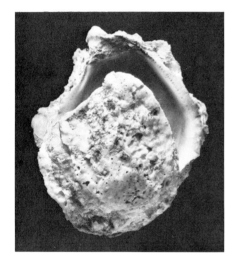

Ostrea equestris

Suborder OSTREINA Férussac, 1822
Superfamily OSTREACEA Rafinesque, 1815
Family OSTREIDAE Rafinesque, 1815

Genus *Crassostrea* Sacco, 1897

Eastern Oyster
Crassostrea virginica (Gmelin, 1791), *Syst. Natur.*, 13th ed., p. 200.
L. *crassus* thick; Gk. *ostrea* oyster; from Virginia.
SIZE: 51–150 mm.
COLOR: Dull gray.
SHAPE: Very irregular and variable from oval to weirdly elongate.
ORNAMENT OR SCULPTURE: Surface rough with leaflike scales. Valve margins slightly undulating or straight. Beaks long, curved. Upper valve smaller, flatter, smoother than lower.
HINGE AREA: Shell attached at umbo of left valve, which is longer than that of right valve. Both umbones have central channel for ligamentary attachment.
PALLIAL LINE & INTERIOR: Muscle scar subcentral, colored deep purple. Interior smooth. Pallial line simple.
PERIOSTRACUM: Eroded.
HABITAT: Brackish bays and estuaries (fig. 17). Cemented epifaunal.
LOCALITIES: Entire.
OCCURRENCE: Common.
RANGE: Gulf of St. Lawrence to Gulf of Mexico; Yucatán; West Indies.
GEOLOGIC RANGE: Miocene to Holocene.
REMARKS: This commercially important bivalve is discussed in Bulletin No. 40 of the Texas Game and Fish Commission. It does not have the interior marginal teeth that *Ostrea equestris* has. *See* Menzel 1955; Galtsoff 1964; Galtsoff 1972; Ogle 1976.

Genus *Ostrea* Linné, 1758

Horse or Crested Oyster
Ostrea equestris Say, 1834, *Amer. Conch.* 6:58.
Gk. *ostrea* oyster; L. *eques* horseman.
SIZE: 25–51 mm.
COLOR: Dull gray to brownish. Interior gray green.
SHAPE: Rather oval, fairly constant shape.
ORNAMENT OR SCULPTURE: Surface rough with raised, crenulated margins. Left valve flatter than right. Six to 12 teeth on larger valve with corresponding cavities on smaller valve.
HINGE AREA: Narrow, curved.
PALLIAL LINE & INTERIOR: Muscle centrally located; scar not pigmented. Pallial line simple.
PERIOSTRACUM: None visible.
HABITAT: High-salinity oyster reef. Cemented epifaunal.
LOCALITIES: Entire.
OCCURRENCE: Common.
RANGE: Southeastern United States; Gulf states; West Indies; Brazilian coast to Argentina.
GEOLOGIC RANGE: Pleistocene to Holocene.
REMARKS: An economically important bivalve. This species requires a more saline environment than *Crassostrea virginica* and will replace the latter during sustained drought. *See* Menzel 1955; Ogle 1976.

Lucina pectinata

Codakia (Codakia) orbicularis

Subclass HETERODONTA
Neumayr, 1884
Order VENEROIDEA H. & A.
Adams, 1858
Suborder LUCININA Dall, 1889
Superfamily LUCINACEA Fleming,
1828
Family LUCINIDAE Fleming, 1828
Subfamily LUCININAE Fleming,
1828

Genus *Lucina* Bruguière, 1797

Thick Lucina

Lucina pectinata (Gmelin, 1791), *Syst.
Natur.*, 13th ed., p. 3236.
Lucina, goddess of childbirth; L.
pecten a comb.
SIZE: 25–63 mm.
COLOR: Pale yellow to orange.
SHAPE: Oval, lenticular.
ORNAMENT OR SCULPTURE: Posterior
dorsal slope rostrate; anterior slope
less rostrate. Sculpture of unequally
spaced lamellate ridges with finer
lines in interspaces.
HINGE AREA: Ligament partially vis-
ible from outside. Lunule small. An-
terior and posterior lateral teeth
strong; cardinals weak.
PALLIAL LINE & INTERIOR: Pallial line
simple with 2 muscle scars; anterior
scar very elongate.
PERIOSTRACUM: Thin, deciduous.
HABITAT: In grass flats in open-bay
margins and hypersaline lagoons.
Infaunal.
LOCALITIES: Entire.
OCCURRENCE: Common.
RANGE: North Carolina to Florida;
Texas; Quintana Roo; West Indies;
Central America to Brazil.
GEOLOGIC RANGE: Pliocene to
Holocene.
REMARKS: This species has a long,
slender foot used for digging.
[*Phacoides pectinatus*]. *See* Dall 1901,
p. 807; Britton 1970.

Genus *Codakia* Scopoli, 1777
Subgenus *Codakia* s.s.

Tiger Lucina

Codakia (Codakia) orbicularis (Linné,
1758), *Syst. Natur.*, 10th ed., p. 688.
After le Codok, a Senegal shell; L.
orbiculatus circular.
SIZE: 63–87 mm.
COLOR: White.
SHAPE: Orbicular, compressed.
Equivalve.
ORNAMENT OR SCULPTURE: Reticulate
sculpture of coarse radial lines
crossed by finer concentric threads.
HINGE AREA: Lunule in front of
beaks is deep, heart-shaped, and
nearly all on the right valve. Right
valve has 2 cardinal teeth and 1 an-
terior lateral close to them. Left
valve has 2 cardinals, a large double
anterior lateral, and small double
posterior lateral.
PALLIAL LINE & INTERIOR: Pallial line
simple with 2 muscle scars.
PERIOSTRACUM: Thin, brownish.
HABITAT: Shallow interreef flats in
sand. Infaunal.
LOCALITIES: Port Aransas, south.
OCCURRENCE: Rare beach shell.
RANGE: Bermuda; Florida; Texas;
Campeche Bank; Yucatán; Costa
Rica; northeastern and eastern
Brazil.
GEOLOGIC RANGE: Pliocene to
Holocene.
REMARKS: This species probably no
longer lives on the Texas coast; the
only specimens found are very
chalky and worn halves, probably
Pleiostocene fossils. Tunnell (1974,
pp. 42–43) tells how the wash of an
outboard motor is used by Mexican
fishermen to dislodge these edible
clams. Panamic vicariant is C. *dis-
tinguenda* (Tryon, 1872). *See* Dall
1901, p. 799; Britton 1970.

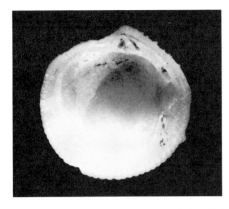

Linga (Bellucina) amiantus

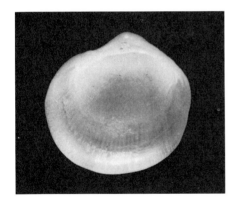

Genus *Linga* De Gregorio, 1884
Subgenus *Bellucina* Dall, 1901

Lovely Miniature Lucina
Linga (Bellucina) amiantus (Dall, 1901), *Proc. U.S. Nat. Mus.* 23(1237):826.
L. *linga* tongue; Gk. *amiantus* unstained.
SIZE: 6–10 mm.
COLOR: White.
SHAPE: Orbicular. Equivalve. Subequilateral.
ORNAMENT OR SCULPTURE: Rather inflated, thickened shell. Sculptured with 8 to 9 wide, rounded ribs, which are crossed by numerous, small concentric threads.
HINGE AREA: Umbones touching; lunule small. Cardinal teeth small, not visible in adults. Laterals well developed in right valve with sockets in left.
PALLIAL LINE & INTERIOR: Pallial line simple with 2 muscle scars. Margin crenulate.
PERIOSTRACUM: Thin, brownish.
HABITAT: Inlet-influenced areas and near shore. Infaunal.
LOCALITIES: Entire.
OCCURRENCE: Common in beach drift.
RANGE: North Carolina to both sides of Florida; Texas; northeastern and eastern Brazil.
GEOLOGIC RANGE: Pleistocene to Holocene.
REMARKS: Sift the drift for this little shell. More abundant in eastern part of coast. [*Lucina amiantus*]. Panamic vicariant is *Lucina cancellaris* Philippi, 1846. *See* Dall 1901, p. 826; Britton 1970.

Genus *Parvilucina* Dall, 1901

Many-Lined Lucina
Parvilucina multilineata (Holmes, 1859), *Post-Plio. Fos. South Carolina*, p. 61.
Lucina, goddess of childbirth; L. *multus* many, *lineas* lines.
SIZE: 6–10 mm.
COLOR: White.
SHAPE: Orbicular. Equivalve.
ORNAMENT OR SCULPTURE: Sculpture of numerous, fine, concentric threads stronger near umbones.
HINGE AREA: Small cardinal and lateral teeth in right and left valves. Umbones small.
PALLIAL LINE & INTERIOR: Pallial line simple with 2 muscle scars. Interior margin finely crenulate.
PERIOSTRACUM: Thin, brownish.
HABITAT: Offshore and inlet-influenced areas. Infaunal.
LOCALITIES: Entire.
OCCURRENCE: Common in beach drift.
RANGE: North Carolina to both sides of Florida; Texas; Yucatán; Quintana Roo; eastern and southern Brazil.
GEOLOGIC RANGE: Pliocene to Holocene.
REMARKS: Sift the drift for this shell. More common to the south. [*Lucina multilineata*]. Syn. *Linga crenella* Dall, 1901. *See* Britton 1970.

Parvilucina multilineata

Anodontia alba

Anodontia philippiana

Subfamily MILTHINAE Chavan, 1969

Genus *Anodontia* Link, 1807

Buttercup Lucina
Anodontia alba Link, 1807, *Beschr. Natur.* 3:156.
Gk. *ano* without, *dontes* teeth; L. *albus* dead white.
SIZE: 38–51 mm.
COLOR: Exterior white. Interior flushed with yellowish orange.
SHAPE: Oval or circular, inflated. Equivalve.
ORNAMENT OR SCULPTURE: Sculpture of weak, irregular concentric growth lines.
HINGE AREA: Hinge with weak teeth. Umbones not prominent. Hinge extended anteriorly to a faint oval lunule.
PALLIAL LINE & INTERIOR: Pallial line simple with 2 muscle scars. Anterior scar elongate, nearly parallel to pallial line. Margins smooth.
PERIOSTRACUM: Thin, brownish.
HABITAT: Inlet-influenced areas, bay margins, hypersaline lagoons. Infaunal.
LOCALITIES: Entire.
OCCURRENCE: Fairly common beach shell.
RANGE: Bermuda; North Carolina to Florida; Gulf states; Campeche Bank; Yucatán; Costa Rica; West Indies.
GEOLOGIC RANGE: Eocene to Holocene.
REMARKS: Unusual on northern half of coast. *See* Britton 1970.

Chalky Buttercup
Anodontia philippiana (Reeve, 1850), *Conch. Icon.* 5(49):pl. 5.
Gk. *ano* without, *dontes* teeth; honoring R. A. Philippi (1808–1904), German malacologist.
SIZE: 51–101 mm.
COLOR: Chalky white.
SHAPE: Orbicular, inflated. Equivalve.
ORNAMENT OR SCULPTURE: Fine concentric growth lines. Interior usually pustulose.
HINGE AREA: Umbones rounded and touching. Hinge with very weak teeth.
PALLIAL LINE & INTERIOR: Pallial line simple with 2 muscle scars. Anterior scar juts away from line at 30° angle instead of being parallel to it as in *A. alba*.
PERIOSTRACUM: Thin, brownish.
HABITAT: Offshore at moderate depths. Infaunal.
LOCALITIES: Port Aransas, south.
OCCURRENCE: Uncommon beach shell.
RANGE: Bermuda; North Carolina to eastern Florida; Texas; Cuba.
GEOLOGIC RANGE: Pleistocene to Holocene.
REMARKS: This species probably no longer lives on the Texas coast; the only specimens found are very chalky and worn valves, possibly Pleistocene fossils. *See* Dall 1901, p. 802; Britton 1970.

Pseudomiltha floridana

Diplodonta (Phlyctiderma) semiaspera

Genus *Pseudomiltha* P. Fischer, 1885

Florida Lucina
Pseudomiltha floridana (Conrad, 1833), *Amer. J. Sci.* 23:344.
Gk. *pseudes* false; *Miltha* (a genus); from Florida.
SIZE: 3.8 mm.
COLOR: White.
SHAPE: Orbicular. Equivalve. Sub-equilateral.
ORNAMENT OR SCULPTURE: Compressed. Rather smooth except for fine, irregular growth lines.
HINGE AREA: Umbones low and pointing forward. Lunule oval. Hinge margin thick but teeth are weakly defined.
PALLIAL LINE & INTERIOR: Pallial line simple with 2 muscle scars; anterior scar elongate.
PERIOSTRACUM: Thin, brownish, deciduous.
HABITAT: Open bays and inlet-influenced areas. Infaunal.
LOCALITIES: Entire, more to south.
OCCURRENCE: Common.
RANGE: Western coast of Florida to Texas.
GEOLOGIC RANGE: Upper Miocene to Holocene.
REMARKS: Pairs are easily found dead in bay drift or by dredging. [*Lucina floridana*]. *See* Dall 1901, p. 809; Britton 1970.

Family UNGULINIDAE H. & A. Adams, 1857

Genus *Diplodonta* Bronn, 1831
Subgenus *Phlyctiderma* Dall, 1899

Pimpled Diplodon
Diplodonta (Phlyctiderma) semiaspera Philippi, 1836, *Arch. für Natur.* 2(1):225.
Gk. *diplos* twofold, *dontes* teeth; L. *semi* half, *asper* rough.
SIZE: Up to 12 mm.
COLOR: Chalky white.
SHAPE: Orbicular, inflated. Equivalve.
ORNAMENT OR SCULPTURE: Thin shell marked with numerous concentric rows of microscopic pimples.
HINGE AREA: Two cardinal teeth in each valve; laterals absent. Left anterior and right posterior ones are split.
PALLIAL LINE & INTERIOR: Pallial line simple with 2 elongate muscle scars.
PERIOSTRACUM: Thin, yellowish brown.
HABITAT: Open-bay centers, jetties, inlet-influenced areas. Infaunal.
LOCALITIES: Entire.
OCCURRENCE: Fairly common.
RANGE: North Carolina to Florida; Texas; Yucatán; West Indies; Brazilian coast to Uruguay.
GEOLOGIC RANGE: Pliocene to Holocene.
REMARKS: These shells may be found by breaking jetty rocks, also in old *Crassostrea* and *Mercenaria* shells. They build nests around themselves of mud and sand held together with mucus. It is not known how the hole has been excavated, because the smooth shells do not appear to be equipped to bore. *See* Dall 1901, p. 794.

Diplodonta (Phlyctiderma) cf. *D. soror*

Chama congregata

Diplodonta (Phlyctiderma) cf. *D. soror*
C. B. Adams, 1852, *Contr. Conch.*
12:247.
Gk. *diplos* twofold, *dontes* teeth; L.
soror sister.
SIZE: 8–18 mm.
COLOR: Translucent white.
SHAPE: Orbicular, inflated.
ORNAMENT OR SCULPTURE: Smooth
with only fine concentric growth
lines. Microscopic roughness on
posterior slope, which is slightly
compressed.
HINGE AREA: Two cardinal teeth in
each valve, no laterals.
PALLIAL LINE & INTERIOR: Pallial line
simple with 2 muscle scars.
PERIOSTRACUM: Thin, yellowish
brown.
HABITAT: Inlet-influenced areas. In-
faunal.
LOCALITIES: Entire, more to south.
OCCURRENCE: Fairly common in
beach drift.
RANGE: Texas to Jamaica; Yucatán.
GEOLOGIC RANGE: Pleistocene to
Holocene.
REMARKS: Possibly the same shell
which has been reported (Parker
1960) as *D. punctata* (Say, 1822). *See*
Clench & Turner 1950*a*, p. 343.

Order HIPPURITOIDEA Newell,
1965 – [PACHYDONTA Stein-
man, 1903]
Superfamily CHAMACEA Blainville, 1825
Family CHAMIDAE Lamarck, 1809

Genus *Chama* Linné, 1758

Little Corrugated Jewel Box
Chama congregata Conrad, 1833,
Amer. J. Sci. 23:341.
Gk. *cheme* to gape; L. *congregatus*
united.
SIZE: Up to 25 mm.
COLOR: Red.
SHAPE: Round. Right, or upper,
valve much smaller than left.
ORNAMENT OR SCULPTURE: Surface
covered with numerous low axial
corrugations. Left valve attached.
Umbones twist to right. Never has
foliaceous appearance of *C.
macerophylla*.
HINGE AREA: Umbones turn from
right to left. Left valve has 2 cardinal
teeth, 1 heavy and rough; in right
are 2 widely separated small teeth.
Both valves have 1 small posterior
lateral tooth.
PALLIAL LINE & INTERIOR: Pallial line
simple, connecting 2 muscle scars.
PERIOSTRACUM: None visible.
HABITAT: Offshore in calcareous
banks. Cemented epifaunal.
LOCALITIES: Entire.
OCCURRENCE: Uncommon beach
shell.
RANGE: North Carolina to Florida;
Texas; West Indies; Central
America.
GEOLOGIC RANGE: Miocene to
Holocene.
REMARKS: Usually only badly
eroded right valves are found in the
drift. The shell is often found at-
tached to the valves of *Atrina serrata*
(Sowerby, 1815). Coll., Young.

Chama macerophylla

Pseudochama radians

Leafy Jewel Box
Chama macerophylla (Gmelin, 1791), *Syst. Natur.*, 13th ed., p. 3304.
Gk. *cheme* to gape; L. *macer* thin; Gk. *phyllon* leaf.
SIZE: 25–76 mm.
COLOR: Variable: white, yellow, purple, or combination of the three.
SHAPE: Roundish. Left, or lower, valve larger and deeper than right.
ORNAMENT OR SCULPTURE: Surface covered with scalelike fronds. Inner margins of valves have tiny crenulations. Attached left valve larger and deeper than right, which serves as a cover.
HINGE AREA: Umbones turn from right to left. Hinge thick with oblique arched cardinal tooth and straight furrow.
PALLIAL LINE & INTERIOR: Pallial line simple, connecting 2 muscle scars.
PERIOSTRACUM: None visible.
HABITAT: Deeper calcareous banks offshore in crevices. Cemented epifaunal.
LOCALITIES: Southern half of coast.
OCCURRENCE: Rare beach shell.
RANGE: Bermuda; southeastern Florida; Texas to southern Mexico; Campeche Bank; Yucatán; Central America; West Indies; northern coast of South America.
GEOLOGIC RANGE: Pleistocene to Holocene.
REMARKS: Only very worn valves of this species are found in outer beach drift.

Genus *Pseudochama* Odhner, 1917

Atlantic Left-Handed Jewel Box
Pseudochama radians (Lamarck, 1819), *Hist. Natur. Anim. sans Vert.* 6:96.
Gk. *pseudes* false, *cheme* to gape; L. *radians* emit rays.
SIZE: 25–76 mm.
COLOR: Cream colored.
SHAPE: Quadrate.
ORNAMENT OR SCULPTURE: Sculpture of 16 to 35 spiny radial ribs. Surface pitted. Attached right valve larger and deeper than left.
HINGE AREA: Umbones turn from left to right. Hinge thick.
PALLIAL LINE & INTERIOR: Pallial line simple, connecting 2 muscle scars.
PERIOSTRACUM: None visible.
HABITAT: Offshore on calcareous banks. Cemented epifaunal.
LOCALITIES: Entire.
OCCURRENCE: Rare.
RANGE: Bermuda; North Carolina to Texas; Yucatán; West Indies; Surinam; Brazil.
GEOLOGIC RANGE: ? to Holocene.
REMARKS: This is a mirror image of *Chama macerophylla* (Gmelin, 1791). Coll., Young.

Arcinella cornuta

Aligena texasiana

Genus *Arcinella* Schumacher, 1817

True Spiny Jewel Box
Arcinella cornuta Conrad, 1866,
Amer. J. Conch. 2(2):105.
L. *arcella* box, *cornus* horn.
SIZE: 25–38 mm.
COLOR: White.
SHAPE: Quadrate, inflated.
ORNAMENT OR SCULPTURE: Seven to
9 radial rows of heavy, short spines.
Shell heavy. Coarse granulations
between ribs.
HINGE AREA: Umbones curved for-
ward over large, wide, heart-
shaped lunule. Large cardinal tooth
in left valve.
PALLIAL LINE & INTERIOR: Pallial line
simple, connecting 2 muscle scars.
PERIOSTRACUM: Not preserved.
HABITAT: Offshore on calcareous
banks. Cemented epifaunal.
LOCALITIES: Entire, more to south.
OCCURRENCE: Fairly common beach
shell.
RANGE: North Carolina; both sides
of Florida; Texas to Carmen, Campeche, Mexico; Yucatán.
GEOLOGIC RANGE: Miocene to
Holocene.
REMARKS: This bivalve starts its life
free swimming, becomes attached
by the right valve for a period, and
ends its life unattached. Near Port
Mansfield jetty it makes up a large
part of the beach shell, probably
Pleistocene fossils. [*Echinochama
cornuta*]. *See* Nicol 1952, 1963.

Superfamily LEPTONACEA Gray,
1847
Family KELLIIDAE Forbes & Hanley, 1848

Genus *Aligena* H. C. Lea, 1843

Texas Aligena
Aligena texasiana Harry, 1969, *Veliger*
11(3):168.
L. *aligenes* epithet of Venus, meaning sea-born; from Texas.
SIZE: 4.8 mm.
COLOR: Chalky white.
SHAPE: Subtrigonal, inflated.
Equivalve. Almost equilateral.
ORNAMENT OR SCULPTURE: Smooth,
except for microscopic, concentric
growth lines. Both posterior and anterior ends rounded. Ventral margin almost straight but shows slight
depression about midway. Valves
very thin.
HINGE AREA: Beaks rounded, touch-
ing. No escutcheon or lunule.
Single tooth in each valve, project-
ing beyond midline and larger in
right valve.
PALLIAL LINE & INTERIOR: Two suboval adductor scars, about equal in
size. Pallial line simple but broken
into series of subtriangular marks.
PERIOSTRACUM: Thin, tan.
HABITAT: Shallow bays. Probably
commensal.
LOCALITIES: Entire.
OCCURRENCE: Fairly common in
beach drift.
RANGE: Louisiana; Texas.
GEOLOGIC RANGE: ? to Holocene.
REMARKS: Holotype collected by
Harold Harry at West Galveston
Bay, Texas, in 1969. Harry (1969)
suggests *A. texasiana* are probably
polychaete worm associates (bur-
rowing invertebrates). Coll., Harry.

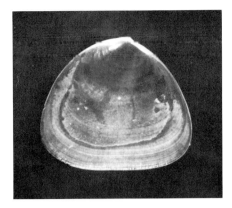

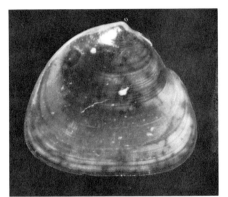

Lepton cf. *L. lepidum*

Mysella planulata

Family LEPTONIDAE Gray, 1847

Genus *Lepton* Turton, 1822

Lepton cf. *L. lepidum* Say, 1826, *J. Acad. Natur. Sci. Philadelphia* 5(1):221.
Gk. *leptos* small, fine; L. *lepidum* graceful, charming.
SIZE: 5 mm.
COLOR: White, translucent.
SHAPE: Trigonal. Equilateral. Equivalve.
ORNAMENT OR SCULPTURE: Smooth and glassy appearing but with numerous microscopic, longitudinal striations that curve toward anterior edge on anterior margin and toward posterior edge on posterior margin.
HINGE AREA: Cardinal teeth obsolete. Lateral teeth prominent.
PALLIAL LINE & INTERIOR: Pallial line simple.
PERIOSTRACUM: None visible.
HABITAT: Along shore. Epifaunal.
LOCALITIES: Entire.
OCCURRENCE: Fairly common in beach drift.
RANGE: Charleston harbor, South Carolina; Texas.
GEOLOGIC RANGE: ? to Holocene.
REMARKS: Commensal with other invertebrates. Attached to the host by means of a byssus.

Family MONTACUTIDAE Clark, 1855

Genus *Mysella* Angas, 1877

Atlantic Flat Lepton
Mysella planulata (Stimpson, 1851), *Shells of New England*, p. 17.
L. dim. of *Mya*, a sea mussel, *planus* level, flat, plain.
SIZE: 3.5 mm.
COLOR: White.
SHAPE: Oblong oval, flattened. Equivalve. Inequilateral.
ORNAMENT OR SCULPTURE: Smooth with only fine concentric growth lines.
HINGE AREA: Small pointed beaks three-fourths of distance back from anterior end. Dorsal margin depressed in front and back of beaks.
PALLIAL LINE & INTERIOR: Pallial line simple with 2 suboval, almost equal muscle scars.
PERIOSTRACUM: Thin, brown.
HABITAT: Attaches to pilings, buoys, grasses in bays and shallow water. Epifaunal.
LOCALITIES: Entire.
OCCURRENCE: Fairly common in beach drift.
RANGE: Greenland to Texas; West Indies.
GEOLOGIC RANGE: Pliocene to Holocene.
REMARKS: Easily overlooked and confused with *Aligena texasiana*. The figure in Parker (1959) is *Aligena* not *Mysella*. Coll., Harry.

215

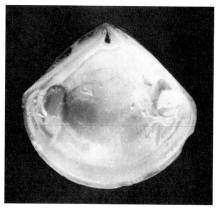

Carditamera floridana

Crassinella lunulata

Superfamily CARDITACEA Fleming, 1820
Family CARDITIDAE Fleming, 1820
Subfamily CARDITAMERINAE Chavan, 1969

Genus *Carditamera* Conrad, 1838

Broad-Ribbed Cardita
Carditamera floridana Conrad, 1838, *Fos. Med. Tert.*, p. 12.
Gk. *kardia* heart; from Florida.
SIZE: 25–63 mm.
COLOR: Whitish, with small bars of chestnut brown arranged concentrically on ribs.
SHAPE: Oval. Equivalve. Inequilateral.
ORNAMENT OR SCULPTURE: Fifteen to 18 strong radiating ribs, beaded by transverse growth lines. Beaks close together.
HINGE AREA: External hinge ligament; hinge oblique; strong cardinal teeth. Right valve has 1 anterior lateral; left valve 1 posterior lateral tooth. Lunule small, deeply indented under beaks.
PALLIAL LINE & INTERIOR: Interior smooth with 2 muscle scars.
PERIOSTRACUM: Grayish, fairly heavy.
HABITAT: Inlet-influenced areas and hypersaline lagoons. Infaunal.
LOCALITIES: Southern half of coast.
OCCURRENCE: Common beach shell.
RANGE: Southern half of Florida; southern Texas to Mexico; Gulf of Campeche; Yucatán; Quintana Roo.
GEOLOGIC RANGE: Pliocene to Holocene.
REMARKS: Attaches by a byssus. On the Texas coast dead shells are common, but to date none have been found alive. Pairs are often found in spoil banks, probably fossil. [*Cardita floridana*].

Superfamily CRASSATELLACEA Férussac, 1821
Family CRASSATELLIDAE Férussac, 1821
Subfamily SCAMBULINAE Chavan, 1852

Genus *Crassinella* Guppy, 1874

Lunate Crasinella
Crassinella lunulata (Conrad, 1834), *J. Acad. Natur. Sci. Philadelphia* 7(1):133.
L. *crassus* thick, *ella* dim. suffix, *luna* moon.
SIZE: 6–8 mm.
COLOR: Whitish or pinkish. Interior brown. Very colorful.
SHAPE: Trigonal. Slightly inequivalve.
ORNAMENT OR SCULPTURE: Beaks at middle. Valves lapped in such a way that posterior dorsal margin of left valve is more visible than that of right. Flattened valves sculptured with well-developed concentric ribs.
HINGE AREA: Ligament internal. Teeth on either side: 2 cardinals in each; 1 anterior lateral in right, 1 posterior lateral in left.
PALLIAL LINE & INTERIOR: Pallial line simple, joining 2 adductor muscle scars.
PERIOSTRACUM: Not reported.
HABITAT: Inlet-influenced areas and channels on shelly bottom. Infaunal.
LOCALITIES: Entire.
OCCURRENCE: Fairly common.
RANGE: Bermuda; Cape Cod south to Florida; northern Gulf of Mexico; Yucatán; Quintana Roo; West Indies; northern and northeastern Brazil.
GEOLOGIC RANGE: Miocene to Holocene.
REMARKS: Panamic vicariant is *C. pacifica* C. B. Adams, 1852. Coll., Young. *See* Harry 1966.

Trachycardium (Trachycardium) isocardia

Trachycardium (Dallocardia) muricatum

Superfamily CARDIACEA
Lamarck, 1809
Family CARDIIDAE Lamarck, 1809
Subfamily TRACHYCARDIINAE
Stewart, 1930

Genus *Trachycardium* Mörch, 1853
Subgenus *Trachycardium* s.s.

Prickly Cockle

Trachycardium (Trachycardium) isocardia (Linné, 1758), *Syst. Natur.*, 10th ed., p. 676.
Gk. *trachys* rough, *kardia* heart, *iso* equal.
SIZE: 76 mm.
COLOR: Exterior light cream with blotches of red brown. Interior has wide band of salmon pink along margins.
SHAPE: Oval, elongated heart-shaped from the side.
ORNAMENT OR SCULPTURE: Thirty-one to 37 strong, radiating ribs that have imbricated scales.
HINGE AREA: Ligament external, posterior. Cardinal teeth arched. Umbones prominent, nearly central.
PALLIAL LINE & INTERIOR: Pallial line simple, connecting 2 muscle scars that are white. Margins crenulate.
PERIOSTRACUM: Thin, brownish.
HABITAT: Offshore. Infaunal.
LOCALITIES: Central, south.
OCCURRENCE: Uncommon beach shell.
RANGE: Bermuda; Texas to Mexico; Campeche Bank; Surinam; West Indies to northern coast of South America.
GEOLOGIC RANGE: Miocene to Holocene.
REMARKS: This species lives offshore and is common along the Mexican Gulf beaches but is only an occasional straggler to the Texas shore. Port Isabel is the most likely spot to find it. Panamic vicariant is *T. consors* (Sowerby, 1833). *See* Clench & Smith 1944, p. 3.

Subgenus *Dallocardia* Stewart, 1930

Yellow Cockle

Trachycardium (Dallocardia) muricatum (Linné, 1758), *Syst. Natur.*, 10th ed., p. 680.
Gk. *trachys* rough, *kardia* heart; L. *muricatus* from *murex* pointed.
SIZE: 51 mm.
COLOR: Light cream with blotches of red brown or shades of yellow. Interior white.
SHAPE: Subcircular, inflated. Equivalve.
ORNAMENT OR SCULPTURE: Thirty to 40 sharply scaled ribs. Scales on anterior slope are on anterior side of ribs, while on central and posterior slopes they are on posterior side of ribs. Separation marked by several ribs with double rows of spines.
HINGE AREA: Umbones prominent, nearly central. Ligament external. Cardinal and lateral teeth present.
PALLIAL LINE & INTERIOR: Interior margin crenate. Pallial line indistinct, simple, connecting 2 equal-sized adductor muscle scars.
PERIOSTRACUM: Thin, brownish, heaviest at margins.
HABITAT: Inlet-influenced areas and bay margins. Infaunal.
LOCALITIES: Entire.
OCCURRENCE: Fairly common.
RANGE: North Carolina to Florida; Texas; Carmen, Campeche, Mexico; Gulf of Campeche; Yucatán; West Indies; Surinam; Brazil to Uruguay.
GEOLOGIC RANGE: Pleistocene to Holocene.
REMARKS: After a sustained freeze these cockles will pop out of the sandy mud along lower bay margins. The double siphons are short and the foot is well developed for digging. Panamic vicariant is *Papyridea aspera* (Sowerby, 1833). *See* Clench & Smith 1944, p. 7.

Laevicardium laevigatum

Laevicardium mortoni

Subfamily LAEVICARDIINAE
Keen, 1936

Genus *Laevicardium* Swainson, 1840

Common Egg Cockle
Laevicardium laevigatum (Linné, 1758), *Syst. Natur.*, 10th ed., p. 680.
L. *laevi* smooth; Gk. *kardia* heart.
SIZE: 25–51 mm.
COLOR: Cream colored or pale yellow variably mottled with brown.
SHAPE: Obliquely egg-shaped.
ORNAMENT OR SCULPTURE: Smooth, polished with obscure radiating ribs.
HINGE AREA: Umbones rounded. Cardinal and lateral teeth present.
PALLIAL LINE & INTERIOR: Interior cream colored with finely serrated margins. Pallial line simple, connecting 2 muscle scars. Ventral margin crenulate.
PERIOSTRACUM: Thin, brownish, usually lost.
HABITAT: Offshore. Infaunal.
LOCALITIES: Central, south.
OCCURRENCE: Uncommon beach shell.
RANGE: Bermuda; North Carolina to both sides of Florida; Texas; Campeche Bank; Yucatán; Central America; West Indies; Surinam; Brazil.
GEOLOGIC RANGE: Oligocene to Holocene.
REMARKS: This shell is another that is common on the upper Mexican coast and is a straggler on the southern part of the Texas coast. *See* Clench & Smith 1944, p. 22.

Morton's Egg Cockle
Laevicardium mortoni (Conrad, 1830), *J. Acad. Natur. Sci. Philadelphia* 6:259.
L. *laevi* smooth; Gk. *kardia* heart; honoring Samuel G. Morton (1799–1851), American malacologist.
SIZE: 16–25 mm.
COLOR: Exterior cream colored, irregularly patterned with brown. Interior yellow with brown mottlings.
SHAPE: Oval, inflated. Equivalve.
ORNAMENT OR SCULPTURE: Smooth, polished with faint concentric lines that are microscopically pimpled. Shell thin.
HINGE AREA: Cardinal and lateral teeth present. Anterior laterals prominent.
PALLIAL LINE & INTERIOR: Pallial line simple, connecting 2 muscle scars. Margins may or may not be crenulated.
PERIOSTRACUM: Thin, brownish, with blisterlike elevations.
HABITAT: Shallow water in inlet-influenced areas and hypersaline lagoons. Infaunal.
LOCALITIES: Entire, more common in south.
OCCURRENCE: Common.
RANGE: Cape Cod to Florida; Texas to Tecolutla, Mexico; Yucatán; Quintana Roo; West Indies.
GEOLOGIC RANGE: Miocene to Holocene.
REMARKS: This little bivalve can swim and hop about in the shallow waters with surprising speed (Baker & Merrill 1965). Ducks love it. *See* Clench & Smith 1944, p. 27.

Laevicardium (Dinocardium) robustum

Mactra fragilis

Subgenus *Dinocardium* Dall, 1900

Giant Atlantic Cockle
Laevicardium (Dinocardium) robustum (Lightfoot, 1786), *Cat. Portland Mus.*, p. 58.
L. *laevis* smooth; Gk. *kardia* heart; L. *robustus* hard and strong.
SIZE: 76–101 mm.
COLOR: Pale tan, mottled with red brown. Posterior slope mahogany brown. Interior salmon pink.
SHAPE: Obliquely ovate, inflated. Equivalve.
ORNAMENT OR SCULPTURE: Thirty-two to 36 rounded, radial smoothish ribs.
HINGE AREA: Umbones rounded. Heavy external ligament. One cardinal tooth in each valve, with 2 anterior lateral and 1 posterior lateral in right valve and complementary arrangement in left valve.
PALLIAL LINE & INTERIOR: Pallial line simple, connecting 2 muscle scars. Margins crenulate.
PERIOSTRACUM: Thin, brownish.
HABITAT: Close to shore and in inlet-influenced areas. Infaunal.
LOCALITIES: Entire.
OCCURRENCE: Common.
RANGE: Virginia to northern Florida; Texas; Carmen, Campeche, Mexico.
GEOLOGIC RANGE: Miocene to Holocene.
REMARKS: This is the largest cockle shell on the Texas coast. Storms will often wash great numbers in alive (fig. 11). Juveniles can be found living in mud flats in the bays around Aransas Pass and adults at San Luis Pass. [*Dinocardium robustum*]. Nomenclature is discussed in *Texas Conch.* 11(4):91. *See* Clench & Smith 1944, p. 9.

Superfamily MACTRACEA Lamarck, 1809
Family MACTRIDAE Lamarck, 1809
Subfamily MACTRINAE Lamarck, 1809

Genus *Mactra* Linné, 1767

Fragile Atlantic Mactra
Mactra fragilis Gmelin, 1791, *Syst. Natur.*, 13th ed., p. 3261.
Gk. *maktra* a kneading trough; L. *fragilis* brittle, fragile.
SIZE: 38–63 mm.
COLOR: White.
SHAPE: Oval. Equivalve. Sub-equilateral.
ORNAMENT OR SCULPTURE: Margins rounded. Sculpture of fine, irregular growth lines. Posterior slope with 2 radial ridges. Fairly large posterior gape.
HINGE AREA: Umbones rounded, almost central. Two ligaments, 1 external, inner cartilaginous ligament housed in spoon-shaped chondrophore posterior to bifid cardinal tooth.
PALLIAL LINE & INTERIOR: Polished white interior with lightly impressed scars of about equal size and shape. Pallial sinus short, broadly rounded.
PERIOSTRACUM: Thin, light brown, heaviest on posterior slope.
HABITAT: Open-bay margins. Infaunal.
LOCALITIES: Entire, more in south.
OCCURRENCE: Fairly common.
RANGE: North Carolina to Florida; Texas; West Indies; Surinam.
GEOLOGIC RANGE: Pliocene to Holocene.
REMARKS: This species has not been as common since the killing freeze in January 1962. Syn. *M. brasiliana* Lamarck, 1818. Odé (1975, 12[1]:12) suggests this species may be a variant of the larger offshore form.

Mulinia lateralis

Rangia (Rangia) cuneata

Genus *Mulinia* Gray, 1837

Dwarf Surf Clam
Mulinia lateralis (Say, 1822), *J. Acad. Natur. Sci. Philadelphia* 2:309.
A meaningless name invented by Gray; L. *lateralis* side.
SIZE: 8–12 mm.
COLOR: Whitish to cream.
SHAPE: Trigonal, inflated. Inequilateral.
ORNAMENT OR SCULPTURE: Smooth except for fine growth lines. Posterior slope marked with distinct radial ridge.
HINGE AREA: Umbones high, almost central. Chondrophore, bifid cardinals, lateral teeth make up hinge complex.
PALLIAL LINE & INTERIOR: Anterior adductor scar more elongate than posterior scar. Pallial sinus short, rounded, oblique.
PERIOSTRACUM: Thin, light brown.
HABITAT: In clayey sediments in every type of assemblage. Infaunal.
LOCALITIES: Entire.
OCCURRENCE: Very common.
RANGE: Maine to northern Florida; Texas; Gulf of Campeche; Yucatán.
GEOLOGIC RANGE: Miocene to Holocene.
REMARKS: This clam is the most abundant and ubiquitous bivalve on the Texas coast due to its ability to withstand a wide range of salinities. The juveniles are thin and opalescent, coming to shore in vast numbers in the winter months. A staple in the diet of the black drum. *See* Castagna & Chanley 1966; Calabrese 1969.

Genus *Rangia* Des Moulins, 1832
Subgenus *Rangia* s.s.

Common Rangia
Rangia (Rangia) cuneata (Gray, 1831), Sowerby, *Gen. Shells* 36:figs. 1–4.
Dedicated to Sander Rang, early-nineteenth-century French malacologist; L. *cuneus* wedge.
SIZE: 25–63 mm.
COLOR: Whitish.
SHAPE: Obliquely ovate. Equivalve. Inequilateral.
ORNAMENT OR SCULPTURE: Heavy, thick shell sculptured with fine concentric growth lines.
HINGE AREA: Deeply excavated chondrophore, cardinals, 2 lateral teeth. Posterior lateral very long, reaching almost to ventral margin, easily separating it from *R. flexuosa*. Umbones prominent, nearer anterior end.
PALLIAL LINE & INTERIOR: Anterior adductor scar smaller than posterior scar. Pallial sinus small but distinct, directed forward and upward.
PERIOSTRACUM: Heavy, smooth, brown.
HABITAT: River-influenced areas. Infaunal.
LOCALITIES: East and central, more prevalent centrally.
OCCURRENCE: Common.
RANGE: Delaware; northwestern Florida to Texas and to Alvarado, Veracruz, Mexico.
GEOLOGIC RANGE: Pliocene to Holocene.
REMARKS: This shell has been found a few miles up the Nueces River, but it is a brackish-water species. Fossils of this shell were found in Pleistocene gravels along the Pecos River at two localities southeast of Malaga, Eddy County, New Mexico (Artie L. Metcalf, Univ. Texas El Paso, report in preparation). Panamic vicariant is the extinct (Pleistocene) *R. lecontei* (Conrad, 1853) of the Colorado Desert, California. *See* Dall 1894; Kane 1961; Fairbanks 1963; Castagna & Chanley 1966; Gallagher & Wells 1969.

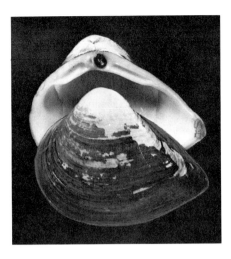

Rangia (Rangianella) flexuosa

Spisula (Hemimactra) solidissima similis

Subgenus *Rangianella* Conrad, 1868

Brown Rangia

Rangia (Rangianella) flexuosa (Conrad, 1839), *Amer. J. Sci.* 38:92.
Dedicated to Sander Rang, early-nineteenth-century French malacologist; L. *flexuosus* bent.
SIZE: 25–38 mm.
COLOR: Whitish.
SHAPE: Obliquely ovate, fairly wedge-shaped. Inequilateral.
ORNAMENT OR SCULPTURE: Thick, heavy shell with sculpture of fine growth lines. Long posterior slope keeled.
HINGE AREA: Umbones prominent. Chondrophore present with cardinal teeth, but laterals much shorter than in *R. cuneata*.
PALLIAL LINE & INTERIOR: Two rounded adductor muscle scars. Pallial sinus almost obsolete.
PERIOSTRACUM: Heavy, smooth, brown.
HABITAT: River-influenced areas. Infaunal.
LOCALITIES: Entire, more to east.
OCCURRENCE: Uncommon.
RANGE: Louisiana to Texas; Veracruz, Mexico.
GEOLOGIC RANGE: Pleistocene to Holocene.
REMARKS: This shell can withstand very low salinity, as does *R. cuneata*, but it is more marine than the latter. Juvenile specimens can easily be confused with *Mulinia lateralis*. The subgenus *Rangianella* is closely related to *Mulinia*. Dall (1894, p. 91) states that it often can be distinguished only by the smaller pallial sinus and the inconspicuous "hook" on the proximal end of the anterior lateral tooth. Some have elevated *Rangianella* to generic rank. Panamic vicariant is *R. mendica* (Gould, 1851). Coll., Young. *See* Dall 1894, pp. 101–103; *Texas Conch.* 7(1):17.

Genus *Spisula* Gray, 1837
Subgenus *Hemimactra* Swainson, 1840

Atlantic Surf Clam

Spisula (Hemimactra) solidissima similis (Say, 1822), *J. Acad. Natur. Sci. Philadelphia* 2:309.
L. *spisus* thick, solid, *solidus* solid, *similis* like.
SIZE: 101–127 mm.
COLOR: Yellowish white.
SHAPE: Oval.
ORNAMENT OR SCULPTURE: Smooth except for fine, concentric growth lines.
HINGE AREA: Large, shallow, triangular umbones acute, more anteriorly located. Chondrophore. Two cardinal teeth, those in left valve fused at upper ends. Lateral teeth have opposite deep socket.
PALLIAL LINE & INTERIOR: Adductor muscle scars rounded, above middle of valve. Pallial sinus short, rounded, almost parallel to pallial line.
PERIOSTRACUM: Thin, yellowish brown, heavier on the slopes.
HABITAT: Near shore, 2 to 12 fathoms. Infaunal.
LOCALITIES: Entire.
OCCURRENCE: Fairly common beach shell.
RANGE: Cape Cod; both sides of Florida; Texas.
GEOLOGIC RANGE: Upper Miocene to Holocene.
REMARKS: An edible bivalve but does not occur in commercial quantities. Syn. *S. s. raveneli* (Conrad, 1831). *See* Castagna & Chanley 1966; Ropes 1967; Jacobson 1972.

Anatina anatina

Raeta plicatella

Subfamily PTEROPSELLINAE
Keen, 1969

Genus *Anatina* Schumacher, 1817

Smooth Duck Clam
Anatina anatina (Spengler, 1802),
Skr. Nat. Selsk. 5(2):92–128.
L. *anatis* a little duck.
SIZE: 50–76 mm.
COLOR: White.
SHAPE: Trigonal. Inequilateral.
ORNAMENT OR SCULPTURE: Thin,
fragile, gaping posteriorly. Fairly
smooth, except for fine growth lines
and concentric ribs near umbones.
Posterior end has distinct radial rib.
HINGE AREA: Prominent chon-
drophore and 3 small cardinal teeth
anterior to chondrophore. Lateral
tooth posterior to chondrophore.
Umbones high, pointed backward.
PALLIAL LINE & INTERIOR: Anterior
adductor scar elongate; posterior
scar rounded. Pallial sinus narrow,
deep.
PERIOSTRACUM: Thin, straw colored,
usually lost.
HABITAT: Two to 12 fathoms
offshore. Infaunal.
LOCALITIES: Entire.
OCCURRENCE: Uncommon beach
shell.
RANGE: North Carolina to northern
two-thirds of Florida; Texas;
Mexico; Puerto Rico; Brazil.
GEOLOGIC RANGE: Miocene to
Holocene.
REMARKS: Seldom found except in
the winter. Less common than *Raeta
plicatella*. Syn. *Labiosa lineata* (Say,
1822). Panamic vicariant is *A. cyp-
rinus* Wood, 1828. *See* Harry 1969*b*.

Genus *Raeta* Gray, 1853

Channeled Duck Clam
Raeta plicatella (Lamarck, 1818), *Hist.
Natur. Anim. sans Vert.* 5:470.
Derivation of *Raeta* not determined;
L. *plicatella* little folds.
SIZE: 50–76 mm.
COLOR: White.
SHAPE: Trigonal. Inequilateral.
ORNAMENT OR SCULPTURE: Thin,
fragile, gaping posteriorly.
Sculpture of evenly spaced,
rounded concentric ribs with fine
striations in intercostal spaces. Fine
radial threads.
HINGE AREA: Prominent chon-
drophore; small, irregular cardinal
teeth. Single lateral tooth posterior
to chondrophore. Umbones high,
pointed backward.
PALLIAL LINE & INTERIOR: Anterior
adductor scar elongate; posterior
scar to about midshell almost paral-
lel to pallial line, somewhat
pointed.
PERIOSTRACUM: Thin, yellowish,
usually wrinkled.
HABITAT: Probably does not burrow
but lives on its side on sandy bottom of outer surf zone. Epifaunal.
LOCALITIES: Entire.
OCCURRENCE: Fairly common.
RANGE: North Carolina to Florida;
Texas; Mexico; West Indies;
Surinam; Brazil to Argentina.
GEOLOGIC RANGE: Miocene to
Holocene.
REMARKS: This species is more
common on the beaches in the
winter. Syn. *Anatina canaliculata*
(Say, 1822). Panamic vicariant is *R.
undulaba* Gould, 1851. *See* Harry
1969*b*.

Ervilia cf. *E. concentrica*

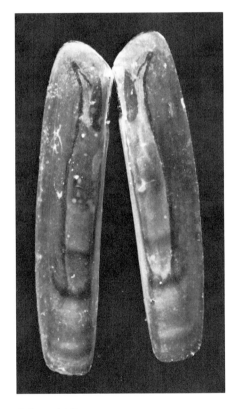

Solen viridis

Family MESODESMATIDAE Gray, 1839
Subfamily ERVILIINAE Dall, 1895

Genus *Ervilia* Turton, 1822

Ervilia cf. *E. concentrica* (Holmes, 1860), *Proc. Boston Soc. Natur. Hist.* 8:281.
L. *ervilia* a small lentil, *concentrica* with concentric lines.
SIZE: 5–6 mm.
COLOR: White.
SHAPE: Elliptical. Equilateral.
ORNAMENT OR SCULPTURE: Sculpture of fine, numerous concentric lines. Quite variable.
HINGE AREA: Umbones central. Resilium small, internal. Cardinal tooth bifid; laterals small.
PALLIAL LINE & INTERIOR: Muscle scars faintly impressed. Pallial sinus rounded, broad, short.
PERIOSTRACUM: Not preserved.
HABITAT: Near shore and open bays. Infaunal.
LOCALITIES: Entire, more to south.
OCCURRENCE: Fairly common in beach drift.
RANGE: Bermuda; North Carolina to both sides of Florida; Texas; Quintana Roo; West Indies to Brazil.
GEOLOGIC RANGE: Pliocene to Holocene.
REMARKS: Due to its similarity to juvenile *Mulinias*, this tiny shell may have been long overlooked on the Texas coast. *See* Davis 1967.

Superfamily SOLENACEA Lamarck, 1809
Family SOLENIDAE Lamarck, 1809

Genus *Solen* Linné, 1758

Green Jackknife Clam
Solen viridis Say, 1822, *J. Acad. Natur. Sci. Philadelphia* 2:316.
Gk. *solen* a channel; L. *viridis* green.
SIZE: Up to 51 mm.
COLOR: White.
SHAPE: Long, narrow, flattened cylindrical. Equivalve.
ORNAMENT OR SCULPTURE: Dorsal edge straight; ventral edge curved. Fragile.
HINGE AREA: Single projecting tooth at very end of valve.
PALLIAL LINE & INTERIOR: Pallial line has 2 muscle scars and pallial sinus.
PERIOSTRACUM: Thin, lacquerlike, greenish brown.
HABITAT: Inlets, near shore. Infaunal.
LOCALITIES: East.
OCCURRENCE: Uncommon.
RANGE: Rhode Island to northern Florida; Gulf states.
GEOLOGIC RANGE: Pleistocene to Holocene.
REMARKS: A western Louisiana species that is easily confused with *Ensis minor* but is much shorter. Figure is that of a juvenile. *See* Dall 1899, p. 107.

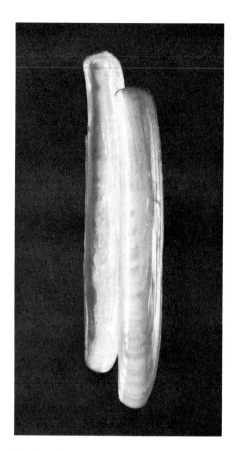

Ensis minor

Tellina (Angulus) tampaensis

Family CULTELLIDAE Davis, 1935

Genus *Ensis* Schumacher, 1817

Jackknife Clam
Ensis minor Dall, 1900, *Trans. Wagner Free Inst. Sci.* 3(5):955.
L. *ensis* sword, *minor* small.
SIZE: Up to 76 mm.
COLOR: Shell white. Interior purplish.
SHAPE: Cylindrical. Equivalve.
ORNAMENT OR SCULPTURE: Long narrow shell smooth, fragile.
HINGE AREA: Left valve has 2 vertical cardinal teeth; each valve has long, low posterior tooth. Teeth in less pointed end.
PALLIAL LINE & INTERIOR: Two adductor muscle scars; pallial sinus shallow.
PERIOSTRACUM: Lacquerlike, brownish green.
HABITAT: Enclosed lagoon and bay margins. Infaunal.
LOCALITIES: Entire.
OCCURRENCE: Common.
RANGE: New Jersey to Florida to Texas.
GEOLOGIC RANGE: Miocene to Holocene.
REMARKS: A favorite food of wading birds. *See* Dall 1899, p. 108.

Superfamily TELLINACEA Blainville, 1824
Family TELLINIDAE Blainville, 1824
Subfamily TELLININAE Blainville, 1824

Genus *Tellina* Linné, 1758
Subgenus *Angulus* Megerle von Mühlfeld, 1811

Tampa Tellin
Tellina (Angulus) tampaensis Conrad, 1866, *Amer. J. Conch.* 2:281.
Gk. *telline* a kind of shellfish; from Tampa, Florida.
SIZE: 13–24 mm.
COLOR: Smooth white, frequently suffused with pale peach coloration. Interior polished.
SHAPE: Ovate subtrigonal. Inequivalve. Inequilateral.
ORNAMENT OR SCULPTURE: Anterior margin broadly rounded; posterior dorsal margin steeply sloping. Sculpture of concentric lines separated by narrow, well-defined sulci.
HINGE AREA: Ligament brown, external. Cardinal teeth present, but no true lateral teeth produced.
PALLIAL LINE & INTERIOR: Adductor muscle scars well impressed. Anterior scar longer, narrower, higher than posterior scar. Pallial sinus descends to pallial line in short, straight drop some distance from anterior scar.
PERIOSTRACUM: None visible.
HABITAT: Hypersaline lagoons from depth of 15.4 centimeters (6 inches) to shore. Infaunal.
LOCALITIES: Entire.
OCCURRENCE: Fairly common.
RANGE: Southern half of Florida to Texas; Bahamas; Cuba.
GEOLOGIC RANGE: Pliocene to Holocene.
REMARKS: Look along Packery Channel. Panamic vicariant is *T. diffusa* Dall, 1900. *See* Boss 1968, p. 302.

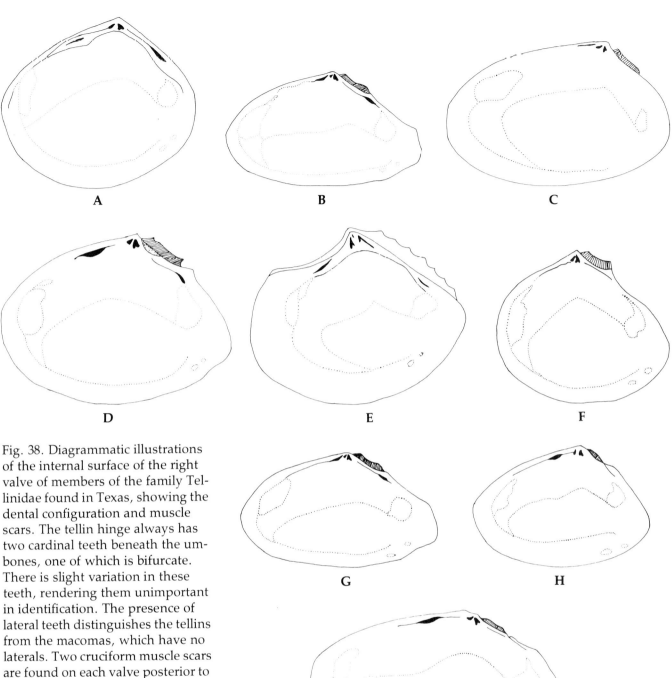

Fig. 38. Diagrammatic illustrations of the internal surface of the right valve of members of the family Tellinidae found in Texas, showing the dental configuration and muscle scars. The tellin hinge always has two cardinal teeth beneath the umbones, one of which is bifurcate. There is slight variation in these teeth, rendering them unimportant in identification. The presence of lateral teeth distinguishes the tellins from the macomas, which have no laterals. Two cruciform muscle scars are found on each valve posterior to and closely aligned with the end of the pallial line; they are found only in the superfamily Tellinacea.

A. *Tellina aequistriata*
B. *T. alternata*
C. *T. iris*
D. *T. lineata*
E. *Tellidora cristata*
F. *T. tampaensis*
G. *T. alternata tayloriana*
H. *T. texana*
I. *T. versicolor* (A, C, & E are original; others after Boss 1968).

225

Tellina (Angulus) texana

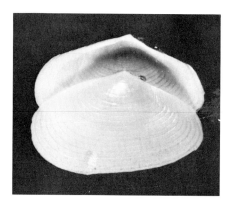

Tellina (Angulus) versicolor

Say's Tellin

Tellina (Angulus) texana Dall, 1900,
Proc. U.S. Nat. Mus. 23(1210):295.
Gk. *telline* a kind of shellfish; from
Texas.
SIZE: 16.5 mm.
COLOR: White with opalescent interior.
SHAPE: Subelliptical to subtrigonal.
Inequivalve. Inequilateral.
ORNAMENT OR SCULPTURE: Anterior
margin rounded; posterior dorsal
margin elongate, steeply inclined.
Sculpture of weak, finely incised,
closely spaced concentric sulci.
HINGE AREA: Ligament yellowish
brown, strong, external. Cardinal
teeth but no true lateral teeth. Umbones posterior to middle, blunt.
PALLIAL LINE & INTERIOR: Adductor
muscle scars fairly well impressed.
Anterior scar elongate, rounded below. Posterior scar rounded. Pallial
sinus convex above, gently inclined
and slightly concave anteriorly, falling in arch to pallial line near but
not touching anterior scar.
PERIOSTRACUM: None visible.
HABITAT: Bay centers. Infaunal.
LOCALITIES: East, central.
OCCURRENCE: Fairly common.
RANGE: North Carolina to southern
half of Florida; Texas; Cuba.
GEOLOGIC RANGE: Lower Pliocene to
Holocene.
REMARKS: Holotype collected by J.
A. Singley at Corpus Christi Bay,
Texas, ca. 1893. Tolerates lower salinity than other Texas tellins. Syn.
T. sayi Dall, 1900. *See* Boss 1968, p.
312.

DeKay's Dwarf Tellin

Tellina (Angulus) versicolor DeKay,
1843, *Zool. New York* 5:209.
Gk. *telline* a kind of shellfish; L.
versicolor changing colors.
SIZE: 14 mm.
COLOR: Translucent with red, white,
or pink rays. Shiny.
SHAPE: Elongate, subelliptical.
ORNAMENT OR SCULPTURE: Anterior
dorsal margin elongate, slightly inclined; posterior dorsal margin
steeply inclined, short, slightly concave. Posterior marked with
rounded keel. Sculpture of widely
spaced, strongly incised concentric
sulci; no radial sculpture.
HINGE AREA: Umbones just posterior
to middle, depressed, pointed. Ligament yellowish brown, external.
Right valve has cardinal teeth and
weak laterals. Left valve has cardinal teeth but no laterals.
PALLIAL LINE & INTERIOR: Anterior
adductor scar elongate, rounded below; posterior scar rounded. Pallial
sinus rises gently posteriorly, convex above, arches down to pallial
line very near anterior scar, at times
touching it.
PERIOSTRACUM: None visible.
HABITAT: Bays and offshore in sandy
mud. Infaunal.
LOCALITIES: Entire.
OCCURRENCE: Common.
RANGE: Rhode Island to southern
half of Florida; Texas; Campeche
Bank; West Indies.
GEOLOGIC RANGE: Pliocene to
Holocene.
REMARKS: Without magnification
this shell can be confused with *T.
iris*, but it lacks the distinctive oblique sculpture of *T. iris*. *See* Boss
1968, p. 313.

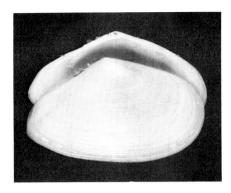

Tellina (Eurytellina) alternata

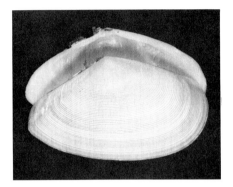

Tellina (Eurytellina) alternata tayloriana

Subgenus *Eurytellina* Fischer, 1887

Alternate Tellin

Tellina (Eurytellina) alternata Say, 1822, *J. Acad. Natur. Sci. Philadelphia* 2:275.
Gk. *telline* a kind of shellfish; L. *alternus* alternating.
SIZE: 70 mm.
COLOR: Glossy white, often with slight blushes of pink or yellow.
SHAPE: Elongate, subtrigonal. Inequivalve. Inequilateral.
ORNAMENT OR SCULPTURE: Outline narrow posteriorly with slight truncation. Sculpture of incised concentric lines separated by broad bands. Left valve has broader bands and fewer lines than right. Posterior ridge occurs in right valve. Every alternate striation disappears at angle of keel.
HINGE AREA: Umbones slightly posterior to center, small, scarcely elevated. Ligament strong, brown, exterior. Three cardinal teeth in right valve. Both valves have internal rib extending from umbo to anterior muscle scar.
PALLIAL LINE & INTERIOR: Adductor muscle scars well impressed. Pallial sinus curves upward toward umbones, extends anteriorly almost to muscle scar.
PERIOSTRACUM: Thin, yellowish brown.
HABITAT: In sand near shore, bay margins, inlets. Infaunal.
LOCALITIES: Entire, more to east.
OCCURRENCE: Fairly common.
RANGE: North Carolina; Florida; Gulf states; Yucatán; Costa Rica; West Indies; southern Brazil.
GEOLOGIC RANGE: Miocene to Holocene.
REMARKS: Until recently this species was considered to be *T. a. tayloriana*, the beautiful pink tellin, and they are closely related. The valves of *T. alternata* are somewhat more inflated than those of *T. a. tayloriana*. The range of this tellin is much wider than that of the pink tellin. Panamic vicariant is *T. laceridens* Hanley, 1844. *See* Boss 1968, p. 283.

Taylor's Tellin

Tellina (Eurytellina) alternata tayloriana Sowerby, 1867, Reeve, *Conch. Icon.* 17:pl. 30, fig. 168.
Gk. *telline* a kind of shellfish; L. *alternatus* alternating; dedicated to Thomas Lambe Taylor (1802–1874), English collector.
SIZE: 63 mm.
COLOR: Glossy pink.
SHAPE: Elongate subtrigonal. Inequivalve. Inequilateral.
ORNAMENT OR SCULPTURE: Outline narrows posteriorly and truncated at end. Sculpture of incised concentric lines, separated by broad bands. Sculpture stronger and closer on right valve.
HINGE AREA: Ligament brown, external. Three cardinal teeth and 2 laterals in right valve. Heavy rib extends from umbones to anterior adductor scar in both valves.
PALLIAL LINE & INTERIOR: Pallial sinus variable but usually about equal in each valve, flattened across top and extending almost to anterior scar, where it drops rather abruptly to pallial line.
PERIOSTRACUM: Thin, blackish.
HABITAT: Near shore, 3.6 to 21.6 meters (2 to 12 fathoms); inlet areas. Infaunal.
LOCALITIES: Entire.
OCCURRENCE: Common.
RANGE: Gulf coast of Texas and Mexico.
GEOLOGIC RANGE: ? to Holocene.
REMARKS: The beautiful pink color is the main distinction between this subspecies and *T. alternata*. The right valve of *T. a. tayloriana* is supposedly much flatter than that of *T. alternata*, but Harold Harry (in litt.) finds no difference in the 2 species. *See* Boss 1968, p. 286.

Tellina (Eurytellina) lineata

Tellina (Merisca) aequistriata

Rose Petal Tellin

Tellina (Eurytellina) lineata Turton, 1819, Conch. Dict., p. 168.

Gk. *telline* a kind of shellfish; L. *linea* line.

SIZE: 25–34 mm.

COLOR: Pink to white.

SHAPE: Elongate subtrigonal. Equivalve. Inequilateral.

ORNAMENT OR SCULPTURE: Anterior margin well rounded. Posterior dorsal margin steeply sloping. Sculpture of close, weak, concentric sulci separated by low, narrow bands. Posterior ridge present but not well developed, stronger on left valve. Twist to right at posterior end.

HINGE AREA: Ligament dark brown, short, wide, sunken. Umbones slightly raised, pointed, inflated, located just posterior to middle. Both cardinal and lateral teeth present, posterior lateral well developed. Variable anterior rib between umbones and anterior scar.

PALLIAL LINE & INTERIOR: Adductor muscle scars well impressed. Pallial sinus convex above, not rising above adductor muscle scars, extending closer to anterior scar than does that of *T. tayloriana*.

PERIOSTRACUM: Thin, brownish.

HABITAT: Offshore or dead in spoil banks. Infaunal.

LOCALITIES: Central.

OCCURRENCE: Uncommon.

RANGE: All of Florida; Texas; Yucatán; Costa Rica; West Indies; Brazil.

GEOLOGIC RANGE: ? to Holocene.

REMARKS: The shape and color of this shell are variable, but the strong twist of the valves to the right posteriorly and the umbones that point to the back are consistent. The specimens found on the Texas coast appear to be very old; it has not been reported living to date. Coll., Wilson. *See* Boss 1968, p. 295.

Subgenus *Merisca* Dall, 1900

Lintea Tellin

Tellina (Merisca) aequistriata (Say, 1824), J. Acad. Natur. Sci. Philadelphia 4(1):145.

Gk. *telline* a kind of shellfish; L. *aequi* equal, *striata* striped.

SIZE: 9–24 mm.

COLOR: White.

SHAPE: Moderately oval. Inequilateral.

ORNAMENT OR SCULPTURE: Sculpture of numerous sharp, concentric ridges. Left valve has 1 posterior radial ridge; right valve has 2. Posterior margin narrow, flexed.

HINGE AREA: Umbones small, sharp. Ligament small. Weak hinge area has 2 long laterals in left valve.

PALLIAL LINE & INTERIOR: Muscle scars small. Dorsal line of pallial sinus meets pallial line near anterior scar.

PERIOSTRACUM: Very thin, yellowish brown.

HABITAT: Offshore in sand, 5 to 15 meters (9 to 28 fathoms). Infaunal.

LOCALITIES: Entire.

OCCURRENCE: Fairly common.

RANGE: North Carolina to both sides of Florida; Texas; Campeche Bank; Yucatán; West Indies; Brazilian coast to Bahia.

GEOLOGIC RANGE: Miocene to Holocene.

REMARKS: Syn. *Quadrans lintea* Conrad, 1837. A very delicate shell distinguished by posterior twist. Panamic vicariant is *T. reclusa* Dall, 1900. *See* Boss 1966, p. 267.

Tellina (Scissula) iris

Tellidora cristata

Subgenus *Scissula* Dall, 1900

Iris Tellin

Tellina (Scissula) iris Say, 1822, *J. Acad. Natur. Sci. Philadelphia* 2:302.
Gk. *telline* a kind of shellfish; L. *iris* the rainbow.
SIZE: 15.3 mm.
COLOR: Transparent to translucent suffused with pink. Two white rays often occur in posterior quarter.
SHAPE: Elongate, elliptical. Equivalve. Inequilateral.
ORNAMENT OR SCULPTURE: Anterior dorsal margin long, gently sloping to rounded anterior margin. Posterior margin obliquely truncated; posterior slope slightly keeled. Sculpture of faint growth lines that are more developed posteriorly. These crossed by well-developed, widely spaced oblique lines.
HINGE AREA: Umbones posterior to middle, small, slightly pointed. Ligament light yellow brown, weak, external. Left valve has cardinal teeth but no true lateral teeth. Right valve has cardinal teeth and anterior lateral tooth but no posterior lateral.
PALLIAL LINE & INTERIOR: Adductor scars weak. Anterior scar irregularly quadrate; posterior scar rounded. Pallial sinus rises abruptly posteriorly, descends gently, arches to pallial line. Well separated from anterior scar.
PERIOSTRACUM: None visible.
HABITAT: Near shore and inlet areas. Infaunal.
LOCALITIES: Entire.
OCCURRENCE: Common.
RANGE: Bermuda; North Carolina to Florida; Gulf of Mexico.
GEOLOGIC RANGE: Pleistocene to Holocene.
REMARKS: This delicate little shell is one of the most common in the winter drift on the Texas beaches. Panamic vicariant is *T. virgo* Hanley, 1844. *See* Boss 1968, p. 333.

Genus *Tellidora* H. & A. Adams, 1856

White Crested Tellin

Tellidora cristata (Récluz, 1842), *Rev. Zool. Soc. Cuvier.* 5:270.
Gk. *telline* a kind of shellfish, *dora* gift or skin; L. *cristatus* crested.
SIZE: Up to 37 mm.
COLOR: White.
SHAPE: Subtrigonal, very compressed. Inequivalve. Inequilateral.
ORNAMENT OR SCULPTURE: Anterior and posterior dorsal margins have triangular spines. Sculpture of strong, narrow, concentric ridges. Spines form deep lunule and escutcheon.
HINGE AREA: Umbones central, acute, elevated. Ligament brown, short, partially internal. Two cardinal teeth in each valve and strong, triangular, anterior lateral tooth in right valve.
PALLIAL LINE & INTERIOR: Adductor scars well impressed. Anterior scar more elongate than posterior. Pallial sinus short, widely separated from anterior scar, arches down to pallial line near posterior end.
PERIOSTRACUM: None visible.
HABITAT: Inlets and channels. Bay margins in sandy bottoms. Infaunal.
LOCALITIES: Entire.
OCCURRENCE: Uncommon.
RANGE: North Carolina to western Florida and Texas; Yucatán.
GEOLOGIC RANGE: Pliocene to Holocene.
REMARKS: The dorsal spines make this little clam unique. Panamic vicariant is *T. burneti* Broderip & Sowerby, 1829. *See* Boss 1968, p. 339.

Strigilla (Pisostrigilla) mirabilis

Macoma tenta

Genus *Strigilla* Turton, 1822
Subgenus *Pisostrigilla* Olsson, 1961

White Strigilla
Strigilla (Pisostrigilla) mirabilis
(Philippi, 1841), *Arch. für Natur.*
7(1):260.
L. *strigil* a scraping tool, *mirabilis*
wonderful.
SIZE: 8 mm.
COLOR: White, translucent, shiny.
SHAPE: Oval, inflated. Inequivalve.
Equilateral.
ORNAMENT OR SCULPTURE: Sculpture
of fine growth lines crossed by oblique lines that meet ventral margin
at about 45 degrees. Posterior slope
patterned with 4 or more zigzag
rows of lines.
HINGE AREA: Umbones rounded,
almost central. Two cardinals and 2
lateral teeth present. Left posterior
cardinal very thin, fragile.
PALLIAL LINE & INTERIOR: Large pal-
lial sinus runs forward but does not
touch anterior muscle scar. Weak
cruciform muscle scars near ventral
margin.
PERIOSTRACUM: None visible.
HABITAT: Offshore. Infaunal.
LOCALITIES: Entire.
OCCURRENCE: Uncommon in beach
drift.
RANGE: Bermuda; southeastern
United States; Texas; Campeche
Bank; West Indies; northeastern
Brazil.
GEOLOGIC RANGE: Miocene to
Holocene.
REMARKS: The typical oblique
sculpture of this tiny clam is distinc-
tive among minute bivalves on the
Texas coast. *See* Boss 1969, p. 362.

Subfamily MACOMINAE Olsson,
1961

Genus *Macoma* Leach, 1819

Tenta Macoma
Macoma tenta (Say, 1834), *Amer.
Conch.*, part 7, pl. 65.
Macoma, a euphonic name in-
vented by Leach; L. *tentus* stretched
out.
SIZE: 12–25 mm.
COLOR: White, slightly iridescent.
SHAPE: Elongate, oblong. Inequilat-
eral.
ORNAMENT OR SCULPTURE: Smooth
except for microscopic growth lines.
Thin. Posterior margin truncated
and flexed to right, marked with
radial ridge.
HINGE AREA: Umbones small, sharp.
Ligament small, brown. Two cardi-
nal teeth in left valve and 1 in right.
One posterior lateral tooth.
PALLIAL LINE & INTERIOR: Anterior
adductor scar elongate; posterior
rounded. Pallial sinus nearly half
confluent, almost reaching anterior
scar.
PERIOSTRACUM: Thin, brownish.
HABITAT: Open-bay margins. Shal-
low hypersaline lagoons. Infaunal.
LOCALITIES: Entire.
OCCURRENCE: Common.
RANGE: Bermuda; Cape Cod to
Florida; Texas; Campeche Bank;
West Indies; Brazil.
GEOLOGIC RANGE: Miocene? Pliocene
to Holocene.
REMARKS: This little clam lives in
mud.

Macoma (Psammacoma) brevifrons

Macoma (Psammacoma) pulleyi

Subgenus *Psammacoma* Dall, 1900

Short Macoma

Macoma (Psammacoma) brevifrons (Say, 1834), *Amer. Conch.*, part 7, pl. 67.
Macoma, a euphonic name invented by Leach; L. *brevifrons* short frond.
SIZE: 25 mm.
COLOR: White to pale peach.
SHAPE: Oval. Inequilateral.
ORNAMENT OR SCULPTURE: Shell smooth except for fine growth lines. Very weak radial ridge posteriorly.
HINGE AREA: Umbones small, pointed, anterior to middle. Ligament brown, small, external. Two cardinal teeth in each valve. Posterior tooth in left much smaller than others. No lateral teeth.
PALLIAL LINE & INTERIOR: Scars and pallial line hardly visible. Elongate anterior scar and small round posterior scar. Pallial sinus large, rounded, almost confluent with pallial line.
PERIOSTRACUM: Thin, yellowish brown, heavier on posterior slope.
HABITAT: Near shore, possibly in bays. Infaunal.
LOCALITIES: Entire.
OCCURRENCE: Fairly common.
RANGE: North Carolina to Texas; Yucatán; Brazil.
GEOLOGIC RANGE: ? to Holocene.
REMARKS: This macoma is much the same color and size as *Tellina tampaensis*, but shape and hinge area differ. Panamic vicariant is *M. aurora* Hanly, 1844. Until a monograph on the macomas is published, *M. brevifrons* and *M. aurora* will be considered synonymous on the basis of published descriptions.

Pulley's Macoma

Macoma (Psammacoma) pulleyi Boyer, 1969, *Veliger* 12(1):40.
Macoma, a euphonic name invented by Leach; dedicated to Dr. Tom Pulley, director Houston Museum of Natural History.
SIZE: 42–55 mm.
COLOR: White.
SHAPE: Elongate, moderately inflated. Equivalve. Inequilateral.
ORNAMENT OR SCULPTURE: Thin. Anterior end longer; anterior dorsal margin almost rectilinear; anterior margin rounded above and more gently and evenly curved below. Ventral margin nearly straight, subparallel to anterior dorsal margin, intersecting posterior margin abruptly. Posterior dorsal margin sloping steeply and meeting posterior margin in curve. Smooth except for very fine growth lines. Rounded ridge running from umbo to posterior ventral angle marks intersection of posterior slope with surface of disc. This ridge stronger in left valve.
HINGE AREA: Hinge plate narrow; left valve with 1 bifid anterior cardinal and 1 lamellar posterior cardinal; right valve with 1 bifid anterior cardinal and 1 smaller, grooved posterior cardinal.
PALLIAL LINE & INTERIOR: Pallial sinus rises obliquely, sinuous above, narrowing and extending forward about three-quarters of distance between adductor muscle scars, about half confluent with pallial line below. Slight posterior gape.
PERIOSTRACUM: Thin, brown.
HABITAT: Offshore, mud substratum in delta-influenced water. Infaunal.
LOCALITIES: East.
OCCURRENCE: Uncommon.
RANGE: Mississippi delta to eastern Texas?
GEOLOGIC RANGE: ? to Holocene.
REMARKS: This species has been confused with *M. tageliformis*, which is

Macoma (Psammacoma) tageliformis

more inequivalve; the ligament area is depressed and does not have the posterior ridge and abrupt ventral angle of *M. pulleyi*. Boyer would be most interested in any Texas findings. Coll., Boyer. *See* Boyer 1969*a*.

Tagelus-Like Macoma

Macoma (Psammacoma) tageliformis Dall, 1900, *Proc. U.S. Nat. Mus.* 23(1210):300.

Macoma, a euphonic name invented by Leach; in the form of the bivalve *Tagelus*.

SIZE: Up to 63 mm.

COLOR: Dull white.

SHAPE: Oblong. Inequilateral.

ORNAMENT OR SCULPTURE: Sculpture of fine, irregular growth lines. Posterior slightly flexed to right. Heavier than other macomas.

HINGE AREA: Umbones toward posterior, pointed. Ligament external, dark brown. Cardinal teeth fairly strong, 2 in each valve. Posterior tooth in left valve thin, often obsolete. No laterals.

PALLIAL LINE & INTERIOR: Anterior adductor scar elongate; posterior scar rounded. Large, convex, rounded pallial sinus one-fourth confluent with pallial line.

PERIOSTRACUM: Thin, brownish, heavier at the margins.

HABITAT: Near shore, 3.6 to 19.8 meters (2 to 11 fathoms) in silty clay. Infaunal.

LOCALITIES: Entire.

OCCURRENCE: Fairly common beach shell.

RANGE: Louisiana; Texas to Tuxpan, Veracruz, Mexico; Yucatán; West Indies; Surinam; Brazilian coast to São Paulo.

GEOLOGIC RANGE: Pleistocene to Holocene.

REMARKS: Longer and larger than most macomas. Holotype collected from Corpus Christi Bay, Texas, by J. A. Singley ca. 1893. Parker's papers identify *M. pulleyi* as this species.

Macoma (Austromacoma) constricta

Macoma (Rexitherus) mitchelli

Subgenus *Austromacoma* Leach, 1961

Constricted Macoma
Macoma (Austromacoma) constricta (Bruguière, 1792), *Encycl. Méth.* 1(3):126.
Macoma, a euphonic name invented by Leach; L. *constrictus* drawn tight.
SIZE: 25–63 mm.
COLOR: White.
SHAPE: Subquadrate. Inequivalve. Inequilateral.
ORNAMENT OR SCULPTURE: Sculptured with irregular, fine, concentric growth lines. Low radial ridge marks posterior slope, which is flexed to right.
HINGE AREA: Umbones rounded. Ligament long, narrow. Cardinal teeth weak. No laterals.
PALLIAL LINE & INTERIOR: Muscle scars and pallial line weak. Two rather high muscle scars. Pallial sinus extended to near anterior scar, convex above and correspondingly curved below.
PERIOSTRACUM: Thin, grayish brown, heavier toward margins.
HABITAT: Open-bay margins and centers. Infaunal.
LOCALITIES: Entire.
OCCURRENCE: Fairly common.
RANGE: Florida to Texas; Yucatán; West Indies; Surinam; Brazil.
GEOLOGIC RANGE: Pleistocene to Holocene.
REMARKS: This species is more tolerant of extremes in salinities and temperatures than the other macomas on the Texas coast.

Subgenus *Rexitherus* Tryon, 1869

Mitchell's Macoma
Macoma (Rexitherus) mitchelli Dall, 1895, *Nautilus* 9(2):33.
Macoma, a euphonic name invented by Leach; dedicated to J. D. Mitchell (1848–1922), early Texas collector.
SIZE: 25 mm.
COLOR: White.
SHAPE: Elongate, subquadrate. Inequilateral.
ORNAMENT OR SCULPTURE: Smooth except for faint concentric growth lines. Weak radial ridge marks posterior slope.
HINGE AREA: Umbones low, pointed, more posterior of center. Cardinal teeth very weak. No laterals.
PALLIAL LINE & INTERIOR: Posterior muscle scar larger and more rounded than anterior. Pallial sinus large, dorsally convex, gently sloping to pallial line before reaching anterior scar.
PERIOSTRACUM: Thin, brownish.
HABITAT: River-influenced areas, estuaries. Infaunal.
LOCALITIES: Central and east.
OCCURRENCE: Common.
RANGE: South Carolina to central Texas.
GEOLOGIC RANGE: Pleistocene to Holocene.
REMARKS: You need to look near rivers in brackish water for this one. Holotype collected from Matagorda Bay, Texas, by J. D. Mitchell ca. 1894. *See* Dall 1895, p. 32.

Donax texasianus

Donax variabilis roemeri

Family DONACIDAE Fleming, 1828

Genus *Donax* Linné, 1758

Fat Little Donax
Donax texasianus Philippi, 1847, *Zeitschr. für Malakozool.* 4:77; Roemer, *Texas*, p. 452.
Gk. *donax* a dart; from Texas.
SIZE: 8–12 mm.
COLOR: Whitish with pale blue, pink, or yellow blushes. Seldom rayed as is *D. variabilis roemeri*.
SHAPE: Unequally trigonal. Inflated.
ORNAMENT OR SCULPTURE: Glossy with fine concentric growth lines. Radial threads on blunt posterior end heavily beaded.
HINGE AREA: Left valve overlaps right on ventral margin. Ligament external. Two cardinal teeth.
PALLIAL LINE & INTERIOR: Interior smooth. Pallial sinus large, rounded.
PERIOSTRACUM: None visible.
HABITAT: Surf-zone sand. Infaunal.
LOCALITIES: Entire sandy portion.
OCCURRENCE: Fairly common.
RANGE: Northern shores of Gulf of Mexico; Mexico.
GEOLOGIC RANGE: Pleistocene to Holocene.
REMARKS: The reduced winter populations of *D. texasianus* and *D. variabilis roemeri* mix, but in the summer they separate and *D. texasianus* stays in deeper water. Holotype collected by F. Roemer at Galveston, Texas, ca. 1846. Syn. *D. tumidus* Philippi, 1848. *See* Loesch 1957; Morrison 1971.

Coquina Shell
Donax variabilis roemeri Philippi, 1847, *Zeitschr. für Malakozool.* 4:77; Roemer, *Texas*, p. 452.
Gk. *donax* a dart; L. *variabilis* variable; dedicated to Ferdinand Roemer (1818–1891).
SIZE: 12–18 mm.
COLOR: Variable: often rayed, pink, purple, yellow, white, bluish, or mauve.
SHAPE: Unequally trigonal or wedge-shaped. Equivalve.
ORNAMENT OR SCULPTURE: Glossy with fine concentric growth lines and radial striae that become stronger on blunt posterior end.
HINGE AREA: Umbones low. External ligament behind umbones. Cardinal and lateral teeth present.
PALLIAL LINE & INTERIOR: Two small muscle scars. Large, rounded pallial sinus adjoining posterior scar, extending to middle of shell. Margins finely crenate.
PERIOSTRACUM: None visible.
HABITAT: Surf-zone sand. Infaunal.
LOCALITIES: Entire sandy portion.
OCCURRENCE: Common.
RANGE: Texas to Alvarado, Veracruz, Mexico.
GEOLOGIC RANGE: Pleistocene? to Holocene.
REMARKS: A delicately flavored chowder is made from this small clam. These mollusks spend the summer at the water's edge and die off in the fall. They feed on minute organisms on the grains of sand. Morrison prefers to call this species *D. romeri romeri* Philippi, 1847. Holotype collected by F. Roemer at Galveston, Texas, ca. 1846. *See* Loesch 1957; Morrison 1971; Tiffany 1972.

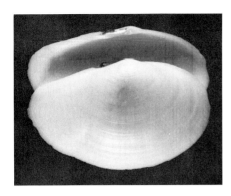

Sanguinolaria sanguinolenta

Semele bellastriata

Family PSAMMOBIIDAE Fleming, 1828

Subfamily SANGUINOLARIINAE Grant & Gale, 1931

Genus *Sanguinolaria* Lamarck, 1799

Atlantic Sanguin
Sanguinolaria sanguinolenta (Gmelin, 1791), Lamarck, *Mém. Soc. Hist. Natur. Paris*, p. 84.
L. *sanguis* blood, *sanguinolenta* filled with blood.
SIZE: 38–50 mm.
COLOR: White. Umbones and area just below bright orangish red fading into white ventrally.
SHAPE: Subovate. Inequivalve. Inequilateral.
ORNAMENT OR SCULPTURE: Thin, gaping shell sculptured with microscopic growth lines. Left valve slightly more compressed than right.
HINGE AREA: Hinge teeth near center of dorsal margin. Two small cardinals in each valve. Ligament external.
PALLIAL LINE & INTERIOR: Large pallial sinus with U-shaped hump at top.
PERIOSTRACUM: Light brown, usually lost.
HABITAT: Offshore. Infaunal.
LOCALITIES: Central, south.
OCCURRENCE: Uncommon.
RANGE: Southern Florida; Gulf states; West Indies; Surinam; almost all of Brazil.
GEOLOGIC RANGE: ? to Holocene.
REMARKS: The color fades rather quickly after this burrowing clam is washed onto shore. Pulley (1952*b*) states that this species is adventitious and does not normally live in Texas. Wrongly referred to as *S. cruenta* (Lightfoot, 1786). Panamic vicariant is *S. bertini* Pilsbry & Lowe, 1932.

Family SEMELIDAE Stoliczka, 1870

Genus *Semele* Schumacher, 1817

Cancellate Semele
Semele bellastriata (Conrad, 1837), *J. Acad. Natur. Sci. Philadelphia* 7:239.
Semele, mother of Bacchus; L. *bellus* pretty, *striata* striped.
SIZE: 12–18 mm.
COLOR: Yellowish white with reddish flecks or all purplish gray. Interior white suffused with mauve or purple.
SHAPE: Oval.
ORNAMENT OR SCULPTURE: Surface sculptured with concentric ridges and radial riblets that are stronger on anterior and posterior slopes, giving cancellate appearance at these extremities.
HINGE AREA: Umbones slightly pointed, just behind center. Horizontal chondrophore and 2 cardinal teeth in each valve. Right valve has 2 lateral teeth.
PALLIAL LINE & INTERIOR: Two rounded muscle scars. Pallial sinus deep, rounded.
PERIOSTRACUM: None visible.
HABITAT: Offshore. Infaunal.
LOCALITIES: Entire.
OCCURRENCE: Uncommon beach shell.
RANGE: Bermuda; North Carolina to southern half of Florida; Texas; Campeche Bank; Yucatán; West Indies; Surinam; northeastern Brazil.
GEOLOGIC RANGE: Pliocene to Holocene.
REMARKS: These have been found after severe northers near the jetties at Port Aransas. Panamic vicariant is *S. pacifica* Dall, 1915. Coll., Young. *See* Boss 1972, p. 20.

Semele proficua

Semele purpurascens

White Atlantic Semele
Semele proficua (Pulteney, 1799),
Hutchins, *Dorsetshire*, p. 29.
Semele, mother of Bacchus; L. *proficuus* useful.
SIZE: 12–35 mm.
COLOR: Whitish to yellowish white.
Interior yellowish, glossy, sometimes flecked with mauve.
SHAPE: Orbicular. Equivalve.
ORNAMENT OR SCULPTURE: Sculpture
of fine, irregular growth lines and
microscopic radial lines.
HINGE AREA: Umbones almost central, pointed. Hinge area has long
chondrophore to house resilium, 2
small, fragile cardinal teeth; right
valve has 2 lateral teeth.
PALLIAL LINE & INTERIOR: Muscle
scars rounded. Pallial sinus deep,
rounded, oblique.
PERIOSTRACUM: None visible.
HABITAT: Open-bay centers, inlet
areas, near shore. Infaunal.
LOCALITIES: Entire.
OCCURRENCE: Fairly common.
RANGE: Bermuda; North Carolina to
southern half of Florida; Texas;
Yucatán; Central America; West Indies; Brazilian coast to Argentina.
GEOLOGIC RANGE: Pliocene to
Holocene.
REMARKS: The most common *Semele*
on the Texas coast. Panamic vicariant is *S. lenticularis* Sowerby,
1833. *See* Boss 1972, p. 8.

Purplish Semele
Semele purpurascens (Gmelin, 1791),
Syst. Natur., 13th ed., p. 3288.
Semele, mother of Bacchus; L. *purpura* purple.
SIZE: 25–38 mm.
COLOR: Variable: cream with
purplish or orange flecks.
SHAPE: Oval. Equivalve.
ORNAMENT OR SCULPTURE: Thin shell
sculptured with concentric striae
that become weaker toward posterior margin. Microscopic lines between striae but no radial ribs. Lines
tend to converge.
HINGE AREA: Umbones posterior of
center, pointed. Hinge with horizontal chondrophore, 2 cardinal
teeth. Right valve has 2 lateral teeth.
PALLIAL LINE & INTERIOR: Muscle
scars irregularly shaped. Pallial
sinus deep, rounded.
PERIOSTRACUM: None visible.
HABITAT: Offshore on sand bottoms
and banks. Infaunal.
LOCALITIES: Entire, more to south.
OCCURRENCE: Uncommon beach
shell.
RANGE: North Carolina to southern
half of Florida; Texas; southern
Mexico; Central America; West Indies; Brazilian coast to Uruguay.
GEOLOGIC RANGE: Pliocene to
Holocene.
REMARKS: Only worn shells found
on beach. Panamic vicariant is *S.
sparsilineata* Dall, 1915. Coll.,
Young. *See* Boss 1972, p. 15.

Abra (Abra) aequalis

Cumingia tellinoides

Genus *Abra* Lamarck, 1818
Subgenus *Abra* s.s.

Common Atlantic Abra

Abra (Abra) aequalis (Say, 1822), *J. Acad. Natur. Sci. Philadelphia* 2:307.
Gk. *habros* graceful, delicate; L. *aequalis* even.
SIZE: 6 mm.
COLOR: White.
SHAPE: Orbicular.
ORNAMENT OR SCULPTURE: Smooth, polished. Anterior margin of right valve grooved.
HINGE AREA: Umbones small, pointed. Two small cardinal teeth in right valve, 1 weak. Lateral teeth absent in left valve, 1 anterior lateral in right valve. Elongate chondrophore extending posteriorly from cardinal teeth.
PALLIAL LINE & INTERIOR: Pallial sinus large, directed forward and upward.
PERIOSTRACUM: Thin, clear, yellowish, usually lost.
HABITAT: Open bays, inlet-influenced areas, along shore. Infaunal.
LOCALITIES: Entire.
OCCURRENCE: Common.
RANGE: Delaware to Florida; Texas; Gulf of Campeche; Yucatán; West Indies; Surinam; northeastern and eastern Brazil.
GEOLOGIC RANGE: Miocene to Holocene.
REMARKS: Next to *Mulinia* this is the most common bivalve on Texas beaches.

Genus *Cumingia* G. B. Sowerby I, 1833

Tellin-Like Cumingia

Cumingia tellinoides (Conrad, 1831), *J. Acad. Natur. Sci. Philadelphia* 6:258.
Dedicated to Hugh Cuming (1791–1865), collector; L. *tellinoides* tellinshaped.
SIZE: 12–18 mm.
COLOR: White.
SHAPE: Trigonal.
ORNAMENT OR SCULPTURE: Thin shell sculptured with fine, slightly raised growth lines. Posterior end slightly pointed, flexed. Radial ridge on posterior slope.
HINGE AREA: Umbones pointed, just posterior to center. Both valves have 1 small, bladelike cardinal tooth, 1 central spoon-shaped chondrophore, elongated anterior and posterior laterals.
PALLIAL LINE & INTERIOR: Anterior adductor scar elongated; posterior scar rounded. Latter largely confluent with pallial line below. Pallial sinus deep, rounded.
PERIOSTRACUM: Thin, yellowish, usually lost.
HABITAT: Bay margins, high-salinity bays, inlet areas. Infaunal.
LOCALITIES: Entire.
OCCURRENCE: Fairly common.
RANGE: Nova Scotia to St. Augustine, Florida; Texas; Cuba.
GEOLOGIC RANGE: Pleistocene to Holocene.
REMARKS: Dead specimens are found in holes in rock and oyster shell but are more apt to be found in mud among roots. Panamic vicariant is *C. mutica* Sowerby, 1833.

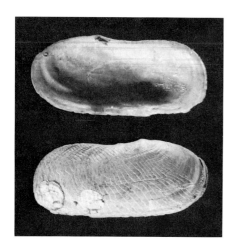

Solecurtus cumingianus

Tagelus (Mesopleura) divisus

Family SOLECURTIDAE Orbigny, 1846

Subfamily SOLECURTINAE Orbigny, 1846

Genus *Solecurtus* Blainville, 1824

Corrugated Razor Clam
Solecurtus cumingianus Dunker, 1861, *Proc. Zool. Soc. London* 29:425. Gk. *solen* a pipe; L. *curtus* short; dedicated to Hugh Cuming (1791–1865), English collector.
SIZE: 25–63 mm.
COLOR: White, dull.
SHAPE: Elongate cylindrical, flattened. Equivalve.
ORNAMENT OR SCULPTURE: Surface of shell sculptured with irregular growth lines crossed by fine, oblique lines. Both rounded ends gape.
HINGE AREA: External ligament posterior to umbones. Right valve has 2 strong cardinal teeth. Left valve with 1 cardinal tooth.
PALLIAL LINE & INTERIOR: Pallial sinus extends forward to point below cardinal teeth.
PERIOSTRACUM: Thin, yellowish gray.
HABITAT: Offshore. Infaunal.
LOCALITIES: Entire.
OCCURRENCE: Uncommon beach shell.
RANGE: Southeastern United States; Texas; Mexico; Campeche Bank; West Indies; Colombia; Brazil.
GEOLOGIC RANGE: Pliocene to Holocene.
REMARKS: Single valves on the beach of mid–Padre Island. Probably fossil.

Genus *Tagelus* Gray, 1847
Subgenus *Mesopleura* Conrad, 1867

Purplish Tagelus
Tagelus (Mesopleura) divisus (Spengler, 1794), *Skr. Nat. Selsk.* 3(2):96. From le Tagal, a name arbitrarily given to a Senegalese shell by Adanson in 1757; L. *dividere* to divide.
SIZE: 25–38 mm.
COLOR: Whitish purple with strong purple radial streak about midshell.
SHAPE: Flattened cylindrical, elongate. Equivalve.
ORNAMENT OR SCULPTURE: Thin, fragile shell unsculptured, gaping at both ends.
HINGE AREA: Umbones posterior of center, suppressed. Cardinal but no lateral teeth in each valve. Purple ray marks position of weak, internal radial rib just anterior to teeth.
PALLIAL LINE & INTERIOR: Two muscle scars. Pallial sinus deep but does not extend to cardinal teeth.
PERIOSTRACUM: Thin, shiny, chestnut brown.
HABITAT: Open sounds, open-lagoon margins. Infaunal.
LOCALITIES: Entire.
OCCURRENCE: Common.
RANGE: Bermuda; Cape Cod to southern Florida; Gulf states; Yucatán; Quintana Roo; Caribbean to Brazil; Surinam.
GEOLOGIC RANGE: Miocene to Holocene.
REMARKS: At low tide one can see herons feeding on this fragile clam in the bays. *See* Dall 1899, p. 112.

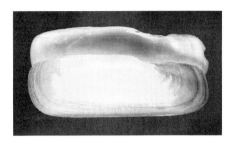

Tagelus (Mesopleura) plebeius

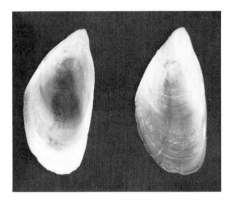

Mytilopsis leucophaeta

Stout Tagelus

Tagelus (Mesopleura) plebeius (Lightfoot, 1786), *Cat. Portland Mus.*, pp. 42, 101, 156.

From le Tagal, a name arbitrarily given to a Senegalese shell by Adanson in 1757; L. *plebeius* common.

SIZE: 50–68 mm.
COLOR: White.
SHAPE: Elongate, rectangular. Equivalve.
ORNAMENT OR SCULPTURE: Strong shell sculptured with faint, irregular growth lines. Gapes at each end. Weak radial ridge on posterior slope.
HINGE AREA: Umbones posterior of center, suppressed. Cardinal but no lateral teeth in each valve. Lacks internal ribs of *T. divisus*.
PALLIAL LINE & INTERIOR: Two muscle scars; pallial sinus deep.
PERIOSTRACUM: Moderately thin, shiny, greenish brown.
HABITAT: Enclosed lagoons, bay margins. Infaunal.
LOCALITIES: Entire.
OCCURRENCE: Common.
RANGE: Cape Cod to southern Florida; Gulf states; West Indies; Surinam; Brazilian coast to Bahia Blanca, Argentina.
GEOLOGIC RANGE: Miocene to Holocene.
REMARKS: Uses its strong foot to bury itself vertically in the mud. Tolerates lower salinities than *T. divisus*. Syn. *T. gibbus* Spengler, 1794. Panamic vicariant is *T. affinis* (C. B. Adams, 1852). *See* Dall 1899, p. 111.

Superfamily DREISSENACEA Gray, 1840
Family DREISSENIDAE Gray, 1840

Genus *Mytilopsis* Conrad, 1858

Conrad's False Mussel

Mytilopsis leucophaeta (Conrad, 1831), *J. Acad. Natur. Sci. Philadelphia* 6:263.

Like the genus *Mytilus*; Gk. *leuco* white, *phaios* brown.

SIZE: 18 mm.
COLOR: Bluish brown to tan.
SHAPE: Mussellike.
ORNAMENT OR SCULPTURE: Exterior very rough. Anterior end much depressed. Byssal opening small. Shelf, or septum, at beak end.
HINGE AREA: Long thin bar under ligament.
PALLIAL LINE & INTERIOR: Pallial line simple with 2 adductor muscle scars.
PERIOSTRACUM: Shiny, light brown.
HABITAT: Brackish water. Epifaunal.
LOCALITIES: Entire.
OCCURRENCE: Fairly common.
RANGE: New York to Florida to Texas and Mexico.
GEOLOGIC RANGE: Pleistocene to Holocene.
REMARKS: The external appearance of this little shell makes it easy to confuse with a mussel, but the internal septum across the end will distinguish it. Attaches in clusters by byssal thread. [*Congeria leucophaeta*]. Breuer's (1962, p. 171) report of *M. sallei* Récluz is probably this species.

Polymesoda caroliniana

Polymesoda (Pseudocyrena) maritima

Superfamily CORBICULACEA Gray, 1847
Family CORBICULIDAE Gray, 1847

Genus *Polymesoda* Rafinesque, 1820

Carolina Marsh Clam
Polymesoda caroliniana (Bosc, 1802), *Hist. Natur. Coq.* 3:37.
Gk. combining form *poly* many, *meso* middle, *odon* tooth; from Carolina.
SIZE: 25–38 mm.
COLOR: White.
SHAPE: Trigonal, inflated. Equivalve. Inequilateral.
ORNAMENT OR SCULPTURE: Rather smooth with weak concentric growth lines.
HINGE AREA: Erosion of umbones typical. Umbones elevated. Each hinge with 3 small, almost vertical, equally sized teeth below umbones and each hinge with 1 anterior and posterior lateral. Dark brown, long, narrow ligament external.
PALLIAL LINE & INTERIOR: Pallial sinus narrow, ascending, fairly deep with 2 equal adductor muscle scars.
PERIOSTRACUM: Heavy, black brown, velvetlike.
HABITAT: Estuaries. Infaunal.
LOCALITIES: All but southern tip of coast, more in Matagorda Bay and east.
OCCURRENCE: Fairly common.
RANGE: Virginia to northern half of Florida and Texas.
GEOLOGIC RANGE: Pleistocene to Holocene.
REMARKS: This clam can stand very brackish to fresh water. It is common in the middle part of the coast, where it can be found alive in Lavaca Bay. It is rare on other parts of coast. Coll., Young.

Subgenus *Pseudocyrena* Bourguignat, 1854

Florida Marsh Clam
Polymesoda (Pseudocyrena) maritima (Orbigny, 1842), *Hist. d'Ile de Cuba* 2:280.
Gk. combining form *poly* many, *meso* middle, *odon* tooth; L. *maritima* of the sea.
SIZE: 25 mm.
COLOR: Whitish flushed with purple pink. Interior white with wide purple margin or all purple.
SHAPE: Trigonal. Equivalve. Inequilateral.
ORNAMENT OR SCULPTURE: Smooth with weak, irregular growth lines. Not heavy. Ventral margin slightly sinuate posteriorly.
HINGE AREA: Each hinge with 3 small almost vertical teeth below umbones and each hinge with 1 anterior and posterior lateral.
PALLIAL LINE & INTERIOR: Pallial sinus narrow, ascending, fairly deep with 2 adductor muscle scars.
PERIOSTRACUM: None visible.
HABITAT: In sand in open hypersaline bays and inlets. Infaunal.
LOCALITIES: Central, south.
OCCURRENCE: Common.
RANGE: Key West to northern Florida; Texas; Yucatán; Quintana Roo.
GEOLOGIC RANGE: Pleistocene to Holocene.
REMARKS: A colorful little clam that is seldom found in the Galveston area. Syn. *Pseudocyrena floridana* (Conrad, 1846). Coll., Young.

Callocardia (Agriopoma) texasiana

Callista (Macrocallista) maculata

Superfamily VENERACEA Rafinesque, 1815
Family VENERIDAE Rafinesque, 1815
Subfamily PITARINAE Stewart, 1930

Genus *Callocardia* A. Adams, 1864
Subgenus *Agriopoma* Dall, 1902

Texas Venus
Callocardia (Agriopoma) texasiana
(Dall, 1892), *Nautilus* 5(12):134.
Gk. *kalos* beautiful, *kardia* heart; from Texas.
SIZE: 38–76 mm.
COLOR: Creamy white to dirty gray. Interior chalky white.
SHAPE: Oval elongate, inflated. Equivalve. Inequilateral.
ORNAMENT OR SCULPTURE: Smooth with only very fine concentric growth lines.
HINGE AREA: Umbones prominent, rolled in under themselves. Weak, tear-shaped lunule. Three cardinal teeth; posterior cardinal S-shaped in right valve. Left anterior lateral small and fitting into socket in right valve.
PALLIAL LINE & INTERIOR: Two small muscle scars; anterior scar very close to margin. Pallial line strong with deep, triangular sinus touching posterior scar. Margin smooth.
PERIOSTRACUM: Weak, inconspicuous.
HABITAT: Clay lagoon centers and along shore in clay. Infaunal.
LOCALITIES: Entire.
OCCURRENCE: Fairly common beach shell.
RANGE: Northwestern Florida to Texas and Mexico.
GEOLOGIC RANGE: Pleistocene to Holocene.
REMARKS: Lives just below the sand. Live specimens are very rare on the Texas shores but worn valves are fairly common in the Galveston area and less so on the rest of the coast. Holotype collected by Wuerdemann ca. 1856 from Galveston, Texas. *See* Boyer 1967.

Genus *Callista* Poli, 1791
Subgenus *Macrocallista* Meek, 1876

Calico Clam
Callista (Macrocallista) maculata
(Linné, 1758), *Syst. Natur.*, 10th ed., p. 686.
Gk. *callista* a nymph; L. *maculatus* spotted.
SIZE: 38–63 mm.
COLOR: Cream with irregular, almost checkered, brown marks. Interior white.
SHAPE: Oval. Equivalve. Inequilateral.
ORNAMENT OR SCULPTURE: Highly polished.
HINGE AREA: Umbones small. Lunule small, impressed. Two unequal cardinals. Short, blunt anterior lateral. Thin posterior lateral.
PALLIAL LINE & INTERIOR: Two muscle scars, posterior larger. Pallial sinus wider at base, angled at end. Margins smooth.
PERIOSTRACUM: Thin, glossy, light brown.
HABITAT: Offshore. Infaunal.
LOCALITIES: South.
OCCURRENCE: Uncommon to rare beach shell.
RANGE: Bermuda; southeastern United States; south Texas; Yucatán; West Indies; Brazil.
GEOLOGIC RANGE: Miocene to Holocene.
REMARKS: A south-of-the-border species, rarely found north of the Port Isabel area. *See* Clench 1942, p. 6.

Callista (Macrocallista) nimbosa

Dosinia discus

Sunray Venus
Callista (Macrocallista) nimbosa
(Lightfoot, 1786), *Cat. Portland Mus.*, p. 175.
Gk. *callista* nymph; L. *nimbus* raincloud.
SIZE: 101–127 mm.
COLOR: Pale salmon with broken, brownish radial lines.
SHAPE: Elongated oval. Equivalve. Inequilateral.
ORNAMENT OR SCULPTURE: Polished. Sculpture of inconspicuous radial and concentric lines.
HINGE AREA: Umbones depressed. Lunule impressed, oval, purplish. Long external ligament. Three cardinal teeth.
PALLIAL LINE & INTERIOR: Two muscle scars. Pallial sinus reflected, wider at base, angled at end. Margins smooth.
PERIOSTRACUM: Thin, lacquerlike, light brown.
HABITAT: Shallow sandy bottoms, inlet-influenced areas. Infaunal.
LOCALITIES: Entire, more to south.
OCCURRENCE: Uncommon beach shell.
RANGE: North Carolina to Florida and Gulf states.
GEOLOGIC RANGE: Pliocene to Holocene.
REMARKS: This beautiful large shell must have been more abundant in the past, because tools and scrapers made from it are found in Indian middens along the bays. It occurs buried in the sand when living, but Texas specimens are probably fossil. *See* Clench 1942, p. 5; Akin & Humm 1960.

Subfamily DOSINIINAE Deshayes, 1853

Genus *Dosinia* Scopoli, 1777

Disk Dosinia
Dosinia discus (Reeve, 1850), *Conch. Icon.* 6:pl. 2.
From Senegalese Dosin, a shell described by Adanson, 1757; L. *discus* quoit, flat round object to be thrown.
SIZE: 50–76 mm.
COLOR: White.
SHAPE: Lenticular, flattened. Equivalve. Inequilateral.
ORNAMENT OR SCULPTURE: Sculpture of numerous fine, concentric ridges.
HINGE AREA: Lunule heart-shaped. Ligament strong, placed in groove. Three cardinal teeth in each valve.
PALLIAL LINE & INTERIOR: Interior smooth, glossy. Two small muscle scars connected by pallial line with large, angular sinus extending to center of shell.
PERIOSTRACUM: Thin, yellowish brown.
HABITAT: Near shore from 3.6 to 21.6 meters (2 to 12 fathoms). Infaunal.
LOCALITIES: Entire.
OCCURRENCE: Common.
RANGE: Virginia to Florida; Gulf states; Mexico; Bahamas.
GEOLOGIC RANGE: Pliocene to Holocene.
REMARKS: The strong ligament is a benefit to beachcombers, as the pairs that are washed ashore in great numbers in the winter are firmly held together. The valves of this shell are often neatly punctured with a hole drilled by a predatory gastropod.

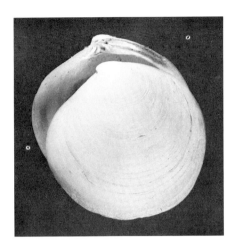

Dosinia elegans

Cyclinella tenuis

Elegant Dosinia

Dosinia elegans Conrad, 1846, *Amer. J. Sci.* 2(2):393.

From Senegalese Dosin, a shell described by Adanson, 1757; L. *elegans* elegant, fine.

SIZE: 50–76 mm.

COLOR: Ivory.

SHAPE: Lenticular, flattened. Equivalve. Inequilateral.

ORNAMENT OR SCULPTURE: Sculpture of regular concentric ribs, which are fewer in number and heavier than in *D. discus*.

HINGE AREA: Umbones prominent. Lunule small, partly submarginal. Three cardinal teeth in each valve with lateral teeth present. Left middle cardinal and right posterior cardinal bifid.

PALLIAL LINE & INTERIOR: Two muscle scars connected by pallial line with long, angular sinus touching posterior scar. Margins smooth.

PERIOSTRACUM: Thin, yellowish brown.

HABITAT: Offshore. Infaunal.

LOCALITIES: Southern half of coast, more near south.

OCCURRENCE: Uncommon beach shell.

RANGE: South Carolina; Florida; south Texas to Isla Mujeres; Yucatán.

GEOLOGIC RANGE: Pliocene to Holocene.

REMARKS: This is an inhabitant of the Texas transitional zone and is seldom found north of Big Shell on Padre Island. May be syn. of *D. concentrica* (Born, 1778). *See* Clench 1942, p. 1.

Subfamily CYCLININAE Frizzell, 1936

Genus *Cyclinella* Dall, 1902

Atlantic Cyclinella

Cyclinella tenuis (Récluz, 1852), *J. Conch.* [Paris] 3:250.

Gk. *kyklos* a circle; L. *ella* dim. suffix, *tenuis* thin.

SIZE: 25–50 mm.

COLOR: Whitish.

SHAPE: Circular, flattened. Equivalve. Inequilateral.

ORNAMENT OR SCULPTURE: Resembles *Dosinia* but smaller and more thin shelled. Surface sculptured with very fine, irregular growth lines.

HINGE AREA: Submarginal hinge ligament. Three cardinal teeth but no laterals as *Dosinia* have. Right posterior tooth bifid.

PALLIAL LINE & INTERIOR: Two muscle scars. Anterior scar much nearer ventral margin than that of *Dosinia*. Pallial sinus ascending, long, narrow. Margins smooth.

PERIOSTRACUM: None visible.

HABITAT: Inlet-influenced areas and bay margins. Infaunal.

LOCALITIES: Entire, more to south.

OCCURRENCE: Fairly common.

RANGE: Eastern United States; Texas; West Indies; Surinam; Brazil.

GEOLOGIC RANGE: Eocene to Holocene.

REMARKS: Easily mistaken for *Dosinia* but much smaller.

Gemma cf. *G. purpurea*

Chione cancellata

Subfamily GEMMINAE Dall, 1902

Genus *Gemma* Deshayes, 1853

Amethyst Gem Clam
Gemma cf. *G. purpurea* Lea, 1842,
Amer. J. Sci. 3:106.
L. *gemma* precious stone, *purpurea*
purplish color.
SIZE: 3 mm.
COLOR: Whitish with purple on um-
bones and posterior areas.
SHAPE: Rounded trigonal.
ORNAMENT OR SCULPTURE: Glossy
with numerous, fine, concentric
ribs.
HINGE AREA: Lunule large. Two
large teeth in left valve with socket
between; 3 teeth in right valve.
PALLIAL LINE & INTERIOR: Small
muscle scars. Pallial sinus points
upward, triangular. Inner margin
faintly crenulate.
PERIOSTRACUM: None visible.
HABITAT: In shallow water, sandy
bottom. Infaunal.
LOCALITIES: Port Aransas area,
probably other locations.
OCCURRENCE: Uncommon in beach
drift.
RANGE: Nova Scotia to Florida;
Texas; Yucatán; Bahamas; introduced to Puget Sound.
GEOLOGIC RANGE: Pleistocene to
Holocene.
REMARKS: One of the smallest
bivalves. Easily overlooked. The
tentative identity of these specimens found in drift along the Aransas Pass ship channel has not been
checked by an expert. *See* Sellmer
1967.

Subfamily CHIONINAE Frizzell,
1936

Genus *Chione* Megerle von
Mühlfeld, 1811

Cross-Barred Venus
Chione cancellata (Linné, 1767), *Syst.
Natur.*, 12th ed., p. 1130.
Chione, mythological personage,
daughter of Boreas; L. *cancellatus* latticed.
SIZE: 25–27 mm.
COLOR: White to gray, often rayed
with brown. Interior glossy white
with blue purple.
SHAPE: Ovate to subtrigonal.
Equivalve. Inequilateral.
ORNAMENT OR SCULPTURE: Surface
sculptured with numerous strong,
bladelike concentric ridges and
many radial ribs. When concentric
ridges become beachworn pattern
appears very cancellate. Heavy,
porcelaneous.
HINGE AREA: Escutcheon long,
smooth, V-shaped. Lunule heart-
shaped. Three cardinal teeth in each
valve; no anterior laterals.
PALLIAL LINE & INTERIOR: Two mus-
cle scars connected by pallial line
with very small, triangular pallial
sinus. Margins crenulate.
PERIOSTRACUM: Weak.
HABITAT: Open bays, bay margins,
inlet-influenced areas. Infaunal.
LOCALITIES: Entire, more to south.
OCCURRENCE: Common.
RANGE: North Carolina to Florida;
Texas; Gulf of Mexico to Quintana
Roo; Costa Rica; West Indies; Brazil;
Brazilian oceanic islands.
GEOLOGIC RANGE: Miocene to
Holocene with related forms in
Jurassic.
REMARKS: The number of dead
shells found in the bay areas indi-
cates that this species was more
abundant in the past than it is to-
day. *See* Moore & Lopez 1969.

Chione intapurpurea

Chione (Lirophora) clenchi

Lady-in-Waiting Venus
Chione intapurpurea (Conrad, 1849),
J. Acad. Natur. Sci. Philadelphia
1:209.
Chione, mythological personage,
daughter of Boreas; L. *inter* within,
purpura a purple dye.
SIZE: 25–38 mm.
COLOR: Glossy white to cream, often
with irregular brown marks. Interior white or with purple splotch in
posterior third.
SHAPE: Ovate to subtrigonal, inflated. Equivalve. Inequilateral.
ORNAMENT OR SCULPTURE: Sculpture
of numerous low, rounded concentric ribs. Ribs marked with tiny serrations at lower edge that give interspaces beaded appearance. Rib
on posterior slope lamellate.
HINGE AREA: Lunule heart-shaped
with raised lamellations. Escutcheon with fine transverse lines.
Ligament exterior. Three cardinal
teeth in each valve, no laterals.
PALLIAL LINE & INTERIOR: Two
shiny muscle scars connected by
pallial line with short, narrow, oblique sinus.
PERIOSTRACUM: None visible.
HABITAT: Near shore, 3.6 to 21.6 meters (2 to 12 fathoms). Infaunal.
LOCALITIES: Entire.
OCCURRENCE: Fairly common beach
shell.
RANGE: Chesapeake Bay to Florida;
Texas; Yucatán; West Indies; Brazil.
GEOLOGIC RANGE: Pleistocene to
Holocene.
REMARKS: More readily found on
Mexican Gulf beaches.

Subgenus *Lirophora* Conrad, 1863

Clench's Chione
Chione (Lirophora) clenchi Pulley,
1952, *Texas J. Sci.* 4(1):61.
Chione, mythological personage,
daughter of Boreas; dedicated to Dr.
William J. Clench, editor of
Johnsonia.
SIZE: 25–63 mm.
COLOR: Cream with irregular brown
splotches. Some rayed with brown.
SHAPE: Subtrigonal. Equivalve. Inequilateral.
ORNAMENT OR SCULPTURE: Sculpture
of 12 to 15 rounded concentric ribs.
Ribs not reflected dorsally or flattened on posterior slope. Ribs
sharply flexed along posterior
slope, producing knobby ridge.
HINGE AREA: Umbones recurved
forward. Ligament sunken. Escutcheon of moderate size, narrow,
with faint growth lines. Three cardinal teeth in each valve.
PALLIAL LINE & INTERIOR: Interior
white, sometimes with purple or
brown blotch under posterior slope.
Pallial line weak with small pallial
sinus and 2 muscle scars. Margin
finely crenulate.
PERIOSTRACUM: None visible.
HABITAT: Offshore. Infaunal.
LOCALITIES: Entire, more to south.
OCCURRENCE: Fairly common.
RANGE: Texas to Campeche, Campeche, Mexico.
GEOLOGIC RANGE: ? to Holocene.
REMARKS: *C. latilirata* Conrad, 1841,
may be the same species. The ribbing is the main difference.
Holotype collected off Port Isabel,
Texas, ca. 1951, by L. A.
Weisenhaus. *See* Clench & Pulley
1952, p. 61.

Chione (Timoclea) grus

Mercenaria campechiensis

Subgenus *Timoclea* Brown, 1827

Gray Pygmy Venus
Chione (Timoclea) grus (Holmes, 1858), *Post-Plio. Fos. South Carolina*, p. 37.
Chione, mythological personage, daughter of Boreas; Gk. *grus* or *griers* gritty, granulose.
SIZE: 6–9 mm.
COLOR: Grayish white, often with pink cast. Interior with broad ray of purple at posterior end.
SHAPE: Oblong. Inequivalve. Inequilateral.
ORNAMENT OR SCULPTURE: Thirty to 40 fine, radial ribs that are crossed by finer, concentric threads. More heavily sculptured on posterior and anterior margins.
HINGE AREA: Lunule narrow, heart-shaped, colored brown. Escutcheon narrow, sunken. Three cardinal teeth in each valve.
PALLIAL LINE & INTERIOR: Two muscle scars connected by weak pallial line with small, oblique sinus. Margins crenulate.
PERIOSTRACUM: Thin, brownish, shaggy at posterior end.
HABITAT: Offshore in intermediate shelf assemblage. Sand and shell bottom. Infaunal.
LOCALITIES: Central, south.
OCCURRENCE: Uncommon in beach drift.
RANGE: North Carolina to Key West to Louisiana; Texas to Cabo Catoche, Mexico; Quintana Roo.
GEOLOGIC RANGE: Miocene to Holocene.
REMARKS: This tiny venus is not easily found. Coll., Wilson.

Genus *Mercenaria* Schumacher, 1817

Southern Quahog
Mercenaria campechiensis (Gmelin, 1791), *Syst. Natur.* 13th ed., p. 3287.
L. *mercenarius* reward, money [Indians made wampum from it]; from Campeche, Mexico.
SIZE: 76–152 mm.
COLOR: Dirty gray to whitish. Interior white, rarely with purple blotches. Porcelaneous.
SHAPE: Ovate trigonal, inflated. Equivalve. Inequilateral.
ORNAMENT OR SCULPTURE: Sculpture of numerous concentric growth lines, farther apart near beaks. Shell very heavy.
HINGE AREA: Lunule as wide as long. Three cardinals in each valve. Left middle cardinal split.
PALLIAL LINE & INTERIOR: Two muscle scars connected by pallial line with small, angular sinus.
PERIOSTRACUM: None visible.
HABITAT: Offshore. Infaunal.
LOCALITIES: Entire.
OCCURRENCE: Common.
RANGE: Chesapeake Bay to Florida; Texas; Yucatán; Cuba.
GEOLOGIC RANGE: Miocene to Holocene.
REMARKS: This clam has not been used commercially as has its northern relative, *M. mercenaria*. Hurricane Carla in 1961 brought thousands of these offshore burrowers up on the beaches. *See* Pratt & Campbell 1956.

Mercenaria campechiensis texana

Anomalocardia auberiana

Texas Quahog

Mercenaria campechiensis texana (Dall, 1902), *Proc. U.S. Nat. Mus.* 26(1312):378.

L. *mercenarius* reward, money; from Campeche, Mexico; from Texas.
SIZE: 76–127 mm.
COLOR: Dirty white, often with brown zigzag marks. Interior white, occasionally marked with purple.
SHAPE: Ovate trigonal.
ORNAMENT OR SCULPTURE: Surface sculptured with irregular, large concentric growth lines. Central area of each valve glossy and smooth in older specimens. Very heavy, porcelaneous.
HINGE AREA: Lunule three-fourths as wide as long. Three cardinal teeth in each valve. Left middle cardinal split.
PALLIAL LINE & INTERIOR: Two muscle scars connected by pallial line with small, angular sinus. Margin faintly crenulate.
PERIOSTRACUM: None visible.
HABITAT: Open bays and inlet-influenced areas. Infaunal.
LOCALITIES: Entire.
OCCURRENCE: Fairly common.
RANGE: Northern Gulf of Mexico to Tampico, Tamaulipas, Mexico.
GEOLOGIC RANGE: Pleistocene to Holocene.
REMARKS: This species lives buried in the bays. The smooth-sided, elongated, pear-shaped siphonal holes were observed while exposed during an extremely low tide. During the day, there was no siphon visible in the opening, but just before sundown, as the light was fading, two slender, white siphons would emerge and lie on the substratum beside the hole. These were quickly withdrawn when approached. It can be used for a chowder if relocated in clear Gulf water so that it can filter enough water to remove the flavor of the muddy bay. The shell of this quahog has a smoother disc than does its relative in the Gulf. Holotype collected by J. A. Singley at Corpus Christi Bay, Texas, in 1893.

Genus *Anomalocardia* Schumacher, 1817

Pointed Venus

Anomalocardia auberiana (Orbigny, 1842), *Hist. d'Ile de Cuba* 2:277.

L. *anomalus* uneven; Gk. *kardia* heart; from the collection of a Mr. Auber.
SIZE: 12–18 mm.
COLOR: Variable: from white to tan with brown rays. Interior white with purplish brown at posterior margin.
SHAPE: Wedge-shaped. Equivalve. Inequilateral.
ORNAMENT OR SCULPTURE: Glossy surface sculptured with rounded concentric ridges and very faint radial lines. Posterior slope slightly rostrate.
HINGE AREA: Umbones small; lunule distinct; escutcheon depressed. Three cardinal teeth in each valve. Right anterior cardinal small and in horizontal position.
PALLIAL LINE & INTERIOR: Two muscle scars connected by pallial line and small, angular sinus. Margins crenulate.
PERIOSTRACUM: Thin, glossy, lacquerlike.
HABITAT: Both enclosed and open hypersaline lagoons. Infaunal.
LOCALITIES: Entire, more to south.
OCCURRENCE: Common.
RANGE: Southern half of Florida; Texas; Yucatán; Quintana Roo; Central America; West Indies; Brazil to Uruguay.
GEOLOGIC RANGE: Pleistocene to Holocene.
REMARKS: This clam can withstand high salinity and is one of the few mollusks that can live in the central Laguna Madre and Baffin Bay. Syn. *A. cuneimeris* Conrad, 1846.

Petricola (Petricolaria) pholadiformis

Petricola (Pseudoirus) typica

Family PETRICOLIDAE Deshayes, 1831

Genus *Petricola* Lamarck, 1801
Subgenus *Petricolaria* Stoliczka, 1870

False Angel Wing
Petricola (Petricolaria) pholadiformis (Lamarck, 1818), *Hist. Natur. Anim. sans Vert.* 5:505.
L. *petra* stone, *colere* to inhabit, *forma* form or shape of a *Pholas*.
SIZE: Up to 50 mm.
COLOR: White.
SHAPE: Elongate, somewhat cylindrical.
ORNAMENT OR SCULPTURE: Sculpture on fragile shell consists of numerous radial ribs and fine growth lines, diminishing posteriorly. Anterior ribs prominently scaled.
HINGE AREA: Umbones low, near anterior end. Small, brown ligament just posterior to umbones. Three cardinal teeth long, pointed in left valve; 2 in right.
PALLIAL LINE & INTERIOR: Both adductor muscle scars somewhat rounded. Pallial sinus fairly narrow and deep with rounded end.
PERIOSTRACUM: None visible.
HABITAT: Open-bay margins, inlet-influenced areas, near shore in clay banks. Infaunal.
LOCALITIES: Entire.
OCCURRENCE: Common.
RANGE: Gulf of St. Lawrence to Gulf of Mexico; Brazil to Uruguay.
GEOLOGIC RANGE: Pleistocene to Holocene.
REMARKS: The external appearance and shape of this shell make it easily confused with a *Pholas*, but a look at the teeth will correct this error.

Subgenus *Pseudoirus* Habe, 1951

Atlantic Rupellaria
Petricola (Pseudoirus) typica (Jonas, 1844), *Zeitschr. für Malakozool.* 1:185.
L. *petra* stone, *colere* to inhabit, *typica* type.
SIZE: 25 mm.
COLOR: White.
SHAPE: Oblong, variable. Inequilateral.
ORNAMENT OR SCULPTURE: Rather heavy shell sculptured with irregularly spaced radial ribs, narrower over anterior area. Valves gape posteriorly.
HINGE AREA: Umbones rounded, not prominent, curved forward. Three cardinal teeth in left valve, 2 in right.
PALLIAL LINE & INTERIOR: Pallial sinus semicircular, somewhat longer than posterior adductor scar.
PERIOSTRACUM: Thin, brownish.
HABITAT: Jetties. Infaunal.
LOCALITIES: Central, south.
OCCURRENCE: Fairly common.
RANGE: North Carolina to southern half of Florida; Texas; Yucatán; West Indies; Brazil.
GEOLOGIC RANGE: Eocene to Holocene.
REMARKS: The shape of this coral- and rock-dwelling bivalve is variable, conforming to its dwelling place. [*Rupellaria typica*]. Coll., Young.

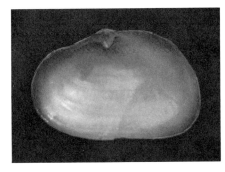

Paramya subovata

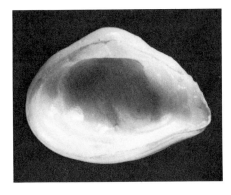

Corbula cf. *C. barrattiana*

Order MYOIDEA Stoliczka, 1870
Suborder MYINA Newell, 1965
Superfamily MYACEA Lamarck, 1809
Family MYIDAE Lamarck, 1809

Genus *Paramya* Conrad, 1861

Paramya subovata (Conrad, 1845), *Foss. Med. Tert. U.S.* 3:65.
L. like a *Mya* shell, or sea mussel; less than oval.
SIZE: 5–10 mm.
COLOR: Grayish white.
SHAPE: Subquadrate.
ORNAMENT OR SCULPTURE: Concentric growth lines and microscopic granules near edge of valves.
HINGE AREA: Chondrophore in either valve.
PALLIAL LINE & INTERIOR: Polished. Pallial line simple, hardly discernable. Large, highly polished, pear-shaped muscle scar located near dorsal area.
PERIOSTRACUM: Not visible.
HABITAT: Offshore; commensal with echiuroid worm, *Thalassema hartmani*.
LOCALITIES: East, central.
OCCURRENCE: Uncommon.
RANGE: Delaware to Florida; Texas.
GEOLOGIC RANGE: Miocene to Holocene.
REMARKS: Collected alive with echiuroid worms at entrance to Bolivar Roads Channel, Galveston, in May 1975 by Clyde A. Henry. *See* Henry 1976, p. 73.

Family CORBULIDAE Lamarck, 1818
Subfamily CORBULINAE Gray, 1823

Genus *Corbula* Bruguière, 1797

Barratt's Corbula
Corbula cf. *C. barrattiana* C. B. Adams, 1852, *Contr. Conch.* 12:237.
L. *corbula* little basket; dedicated to Dr. A. Barratt, friend of Adams.
SIZE: 9 mm.
COLOR: White.
SHAPE: Trigonal. Inequivalve. Inequilateral.
ORNAMENT OR SCULPTURE: Sculptured with small concentric irregular ridges, larger on large valve. Radial ridge on posterior slope.
HINGE AREA: Beaks small, not involute. Umbones with acute angle posteriorly. Teeth moderately developed.
PALLIAL LINE & INTERIOR: Pallial line only slightly sinuate, connecting 2 muscle scars.
PERIOSTRACUM: Deciduous, brownish.
HABITAT: In mud. Infaunal.
LOCALITIES: Entire, more to south.
OCCURRENCE: Uncommon in beach drift.
RANGE: North Carolina to both sides of Florida; Texas; West Indies; northeastern Brazil.
GEOLOGIC RANGE: Pliocene to Holocene.
REMARKS: Adventitious in bamboo roots on the outer beaches. Coll., Johnstone.

Corbula cf. C. contracta

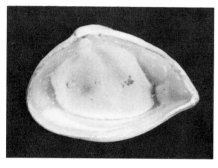

Corbula cf. C. dietziana

Contracted Corbula

Corbula cf. *C. contracta* Say, 1822, *J. Acad. Natur. Sci. Philadelphia* 2:312. L. *corbula* little basket, *contractus* drawn together.

SIZE: 9 mm.

COLOR: Dirty gray.

SHAPE: Trigonal. Very inequivalve.

ORNAMENT OR SCULPTURE: Sculpture of concentric, elevated threads. Posterior slope rostrate. Ventral margin of right valve overlaps that of left.

HINGE AREA: Umbones high, anterior to middle of shell. Right valve has 1 prominent cardinal tooth with corresponding socket in left valve.

PALLIAL LINE & INTERIOR: Two small muscle scars. Pallial sinus only slight depression in pallial line.

PERIOSTRACUM: Thin, yellowish brown.

HABITAT: Open sound on sandy bottom. Infaunal.

LOCALITIES: Entire.

OCCURRENCE: Common in beach drift.

RANGE: Cape Cod to Florida; Texas; Gulf of Campeche; West Indies; Brazil.

GEOLOGIC RANGE: Pliocene to Holocene.

REMARKS: Coll., Johnstone.

Dietz's Corbula

Corbula cf. *C. dietziana* C. B. Adams, 1852, *Contr. Conch.* 12:235. L. *corbula* little basket; dedicated to a Mr. Dietz, identity not determined.

SIZE: 10.5 mm.

COLOR: Pink.

SHAPE: Trigonal. Inequivalve. Inequilateral.

ORNAMENT OR SCULPTURE: Sculpture of fine, irregular concentric lines. Posterior slope has strong radial ridge. Right valve larger than left.

HINGE AREA: Umbones raised, rounded, slightly involute. Strong cardinal tooth in right valve, corresponding socket in left valve. No laterals.

PALLIAL LINE & INTERIOR: Two small muscle scars. Posterior scar thickened, elevated. Pallial line barely indented by pallial sinus.

PERIOSTRACUM: Thin, brownish.

HABITAT: Calcareous banks offshore. Infaunal.

LOCALITIES: Entire.

OCCURRENCE: Uncommon in beach drift.

RANGE: North Carolina to southeastern Florida; Texas; Yucatán; West Indies; Surinam; northeastern and eastern Brazil.

GEOLOGIC RANGE: Pliocene to Holocene.

REMARKS: This species has 2 distinct stages of growth with an abrupt transition from the first to the second. In the first the valves are nearly equal; in the second the right valve grows nearly 3 times as much as the other. Coll., Johnstone.

Corbula cf. *C. krebsiana*

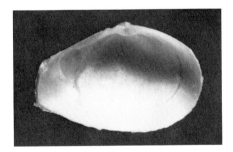

Corbula cf. *C. swiftiana*

Krebs' Corbula

Corbula cf. *C. krebsiana* C. B. Adams, 1852, *Contr. Conch.* 12:234.
L. *corbula* little basket; dedicated to Henry Krebs of Virgin Islands, nineteenth-century collector.
SIZE: 6 mm.
COLOR: Cream. Left valve pinkish, more colored around margins.
SHAPE: Trigonal. Very inequivalve. Inequilateral.
ORNAMENT OR SCULPTURE: Sculpture of strong irregular concentric lines. Right valve more strongly sculptured, much larger, more pointed posteriorly than left valve.
HINGE AREA: Umbones rounded, prominent. One large cardinal tooth in right valve with corresponding socket in left.
PALLIAL LINE & INTERIOR: Two small muscle scars. Pallial line barely indented by pallial sinus.
PERIOSTRACUM: Thin, yellowish brown, heavier on left valve.
HABITAT: On banks offshore. Infaunal.
LOCALITIES: Probably entire.
OCCURRENCE: Uncommon in beach drift.
RANGE: Texas; Jamaica.
GEOLOGIC RANGE: ? to Holocene.
REMARKS: Adventitious in bamboo roots on outer beaches. Coll., Johnstone.

Swift's Corbula

Corbula cf. *C. swiftiana* C. B. Adams, 1852, *Contr. Conch.* 12:236.
L. *corbula* little basket; dedicated to Robert Swift (1796–1872), American.
SIZE: 9 mm.
COLOR: White.
SHAPE: Trigonal. Inequivalve. Almost equilateral.
ORNAMENT OR SCULPTURE: Sculpture of very weak, irregular concentric lines. Posterior slope pointed, marked with sharp radial ridge. Right valve deeper and longer than left.
HINGE AREA: Umbones sharp. Single cardinal tooth in right valve with corresponding socket in left.
PALLIAL LINE & INTERIOR: Two small muscle scars. Pallial line simple.
PERIOSTRACUM: Brownish, deciduous.
HABITAT: Inlet-influenced areas, open-bay margins. Infaunal.
LOCALITIES: Entire.
OCCURRENCE: Fairly common in beach drift.
RANGE: Massachusetts to eastern Florida; Texas; West Indies; Brazil to Argentina.
GEOLOGIC RANGE: Miocene to Holocene.
REMARKS: Probably the most common *Corbula* on this coast. Rios (1970) gives *C. caribaea* Orbigny, 1842, as a syn. Coll., Johnstone.

Corbula (Varicorbula) operculata

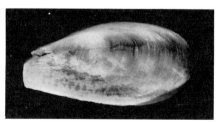

Gastrochaena hians

Subgenus *Varicorbula* Grant & Gale, 1931

Oval Corbula
Corbula (Varicorbula) operculata (Philippi, 1849), *Zeitschr. für Malakozool.* 5:13.
L. *corbula* little basket, *operculata* oval.
SIZE: 9 mm.
COLOR: Whitish.
SHAPE: Subtrigonal, inflated. Inequivalve.
ORNAMENT OR SCULPTURE: Sculpture of strong, concentric ridges. Right valve larger than left, more inflated, stronger sculpture.
HINGE AREA: Umbones high, almost central, curved in. Right valve has single prominent cardinal tooth; left valve has corresponding socket. Ligament internal.
PALLIAL LINE & INTERIOR: Two small roundish muscle scars. Pallial line well impressed; pallial sinus but slight sinuation in pallial line.
PERIOSTRACUM: Not preserved.
HABITAT: Offshore, 36 to 62 meters (20 to 40 fathoms). Infaunal.
LOCALITIES: Central, south.
OCCURRENCE: Fairly common in beach drift.
RANGE: North Carolina to Gulf of Mexico; West Indies; northern and northeastern Brazil.
GEOLOGIC RANGE: Pliocene to Holocene.
REMARKS: A common outer-beach *Corbula*, sometimes found in bamboo-root clumps. Commensal with a Foraminifera. Coll., Young. *See* Bock & Moore 1968.

Superfamily GASTROCHAE-NACEA Gray, 1840
Family GASTROCHAENIDAE Gray, 1840

Genus *Gastrochaena* Spengler, 1783

Atlantic Rocellaria
Gastrochaena hians (Gmelin, 1791), *Syst. Natur.*, 13th ed., p. 3217.
Gk. *gaster* stomach, *chaino* gape; L. *hiatus* opening, to gape.
SIZE: 12–18 mm.
COLOR: White.
SHAPE: Petal-shaped.
ORNAMENT OR SCULPTURE: Sculpture of low, indistinct, fine, concentric lines. Posterior end large, rounded. Entire ventral-anterior end gaping to accommodate foot.
HINGE AREA: Umbones low. Hinge area weak with 1 large toothlike structure in umbonal cavity.
PALLIAL LINE & INTERIOR: Posterior adductor scar large; anterior scar degenerate. Pallial sinus deep, angular.
PERIOSTRACUM: Thin, dark brown.
HABITAT: Offshore. Infaunal.
LOCALITIES: Entire.
OCCURRENCE: Uncommon in beach drift.
RANGE: Bermuda; North Carolina to Florida; Texas; Yucatán; West Indies; Surinam; northeastern and eastern Brazil.
GEOLOGIC RANGE: Pliocene to Holocene.
REMARKS: [*Rocellaria hians*]. This fragile species constructs a hollow "cell" of sand and bits of shell glued together in which it lives. According to Pulley (1953) the mollusk is often found inside empty pecten shells.

Hiatella arctica

Panopea bitruncata

Superfamily HIATELLACEA Gray, 1824
Family HIATELLIDAE Gray, 1824

Genus *Hiatella* Daudin, 1801

Arctic Saxicave
Hiatella arctica (Linné, 1767), *Syst. Natur.*, 12th ed., p. 1113.
L. *hiat* cleft, opening, *ella* dim.; from the Arctic seas.
SIZE: 25 mm.
COLOR: Chalky white.
SHAPE: Irregularly oblong.
ORNAMENT OR SCULPTURE: Sculpture of coarse, irregular growth lines. Weak radial rib on posterior end; may be scaled. Posterior may gape.
HINGE AREA: Umbones close together and about one-third back from anterior end. Teeth indefinite.
PALLIAL LINE & INTERIOR: Pallial line discontinuous; sinus large but irregular.
PERIOSTRACUM: Thin, gray, deciduous.
HABITAT: Inlet areas, hypersaline lagoons, offshore. Boring infaunal.
LOCALITIES: Entire.
OCCURRENCE: Fairly common.
RANGE: Arctic seas to deep waters in West Indies; Yucatán; Brazil; Pacific.
GEOLOGIC RANGE: Miocene to Holocene.
REMARKS: The nestling and boring habits of this bivalve cause its shape and sculpture to vary greatly. Coll., Young.

Genus *Panopea* Menard de la Groye, 1807

Geoduck
Panopea bitruncata (Conrad, 1872), *Proc. Acad. Natur. Sci. Philadelphia* 24:216.
Panope, a sea nymph; L. *bi* two, *truncatus* cut off.
SIZE: 127–228 mm.
COLOR: White.
SHAPE: Quadrate, elongated.
ORNAMENT OR SCULPTURE: Sculpture of concentric, wavy growth lines. Valves gape at both ends.
HINGE AREA: Umbones low, incurved, almost central. One large single, simple "tooth" and broad ledge to which ligament is attached.
PALLIAL LINE & INTERIOR: Anterior adductor muscle scar elongated; posterior rounded, small. Pallial sinus short, rounded.
PERIOSTRACUM: Thin, yellowish.
HABITAT: Offshore and inlet areas. Boring infaunal.
LOCALITIES: Port Aransas, south.
OCCURRENCE: Rare beach shell.
RANGE: North Carolina to Florida and south Texas.
GEOLOGIC RANGE: Miocene to Holocene.
REMARKS: This extremely large bivalve is seldom found alive or dead because it lives so deep in the substratum that the valves rarely wash out of the burrows. Live juvenile specimens have been found in the Aransas Pass channel during a very extreme, extended low tide. The day I found this shell, H. Hildebrand and I were near the Mansfield cut investigating the fish kill resulting from a prolonged freeze in January 1962. *See* Robertson 1957, 1963; Vokes 1969.

Pholas (Thovana) campechiensis

Suborder PHOLADINA Newell, 1965
Superfamily PHOLADACEA Lamarck, 1809
Family PHOLADIDAE Lamarck, 1809
Subfamily PHOLADINAE Lamarck, 1809

Genus *Pholas* Linné, 1758
Subgenus *Thovana* Gray, 1847

Campeche Angel Wing

Pholas (Thovana) campechiensis Gmelin, 1791, *Syst. Natur.*, 13th ed., p. 3216.
Gk. *pholas* a rock-boring mollusk, boring in a hole; from Campeche, Mexico.
SIZE: Up to 128 mm.
COLOR: White.
SHAPE: Subelliptical.
ORNAMENT OR SCULPTURE: This thin, fragile shell sculptured with laminate, concentric ridges and radial ribs. Sculpture becomes weaker posteriorly. Shells gape. Shells rounded at both ends.
HINGE AREA: Umbones prominent, located near anterior fourth of shell, covered by double septate umbonal reflections. Apophyses delicate, short, broad, projecting beneath umbo at sharp posterior angle. Three accessory plates: nearly rectangular protoplax, transverse mesoplax, elongate metaplax.
PALLIAL LINE & INTERIOR: Adductor muscle scars and pallial line well marked. Pallial sinus wide, extending anteriorly almost two-thirds of distance to umbo.
PERIOSTRACUM: Thin.
HABITAT: Offshore in wood and clay. Boring infaunal.
LOCALITIES: Entire.
OCCURRENCE: Fairly common.
RANGE: North Carolina to Gulf states; Mexico; Costa Rica; West Indies; Surinam; Brazil to Uruguay; Senegal to Liberia.
GEOLOGIC RANGE: Pleistocene to Holocene.
REMARKS: This shell is common in beach drift but is seldom found alive. At times it is found in wood on the outer beaches. It is distinguished by the comblike umbonal reflection. The figured specimen is filled with cotton. Panamic vicariant is *P. chiloensis* Molina, 1782. Coll., Wilson. *See* Turner 1954, p. 49.

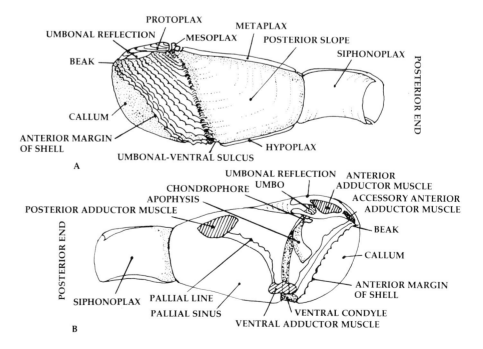

Fig. 39. Diagrammatic pholad shell:
A. external view showing accessory plates
B. internal view showing muscle scars and apophysis (after Turner 1954, p. 11)

Barnea truncata

Cyrtopleura (Scobinopholas) costata

Genus *Barnea* Risso, 1826

Fallen Angel Wing
Barnea truncata (Say, 1822), *J. Acad. Natur. Sci. Philadelphia* 2:321.
Honoring D. H. Barnes, American; L. *truncatus* cut off.
SIZE: 71 mm.
COLOR: White.
SHAPE: Elongate elliptical.
ORNAMENT OR SCULPTURE: Rather thin shell sculptured with radial ribs and concentric ridges. Concentric ridges have lamella anteriorly, becoming weaker toward posterior end. Radial ribs lacking on posterior slope. Imbrications formed where concentric ridges cross radial ribs. Shell beaked anteriorly and truncate posteriorly.
HINGE AREA: Umbones prominent, near anterior third. Apophysis narrow, long, bladelike, curved. Protoplax lanceolate, with posterior nucleus and definite growth lines.
PALLIAL LINE & INTERIOR: Pallial line and muscle scars well marked. Pallial sinus almost as wide as shell is high, extending about halfway to umbones.
PERIOSTRACUM: Thin, yellowish brown.
HABITAT: In clay bottoms of bays. Boring infaunal.
LOCALITIES: Central.
OCCURRENCE: Fairly common.
RANGE: Massachusetts Bay to southern Florida; Texas; Surinam; eastern Brazil; Senegal.
GEOLOGIC RANGE: Pleistocene to Holocene.
REMARKS: Siphons capable of extending 10 to 12 times the length of the shell. Animal cannot withdraw into shell and usually lives in deep burrows in clay but is known to live in wood also. Panamic vicariant is *B. subtruncata* (Sowerby, 1834). Coll., Wilson. *See* Turner 1954, p. 27.

Genus *Cyrtopleura* Tryon, 1862
Subgenus *Scobinopholas* Grant & Gale, 1931

Angel Wing
Cyrtopleura (Scobinopholas) costata (Linné, 1758), *Syst. Natur.*, 10th ed., p. 669.
Gk. *cyrtos* curved, *pleuron* side; L. *costa* rib.
SIZE: 177 mm.
COLOR: White.
SHAPE: Elongate oval.
ORNAMENT OR SCULPTURE: Rather light shell sculptured with concentric ridges and strong radial ribs that extend entire length of shell. Where ribs cross concentric line, imbrications formed, stronger on anterior and posterior slopes.
HINGE AREA: Umbones prominent, located near anterior fourth of shell. Umbones well separated from raised umbonal reflections. Protoplax triangular in outline, mostly chitinous. Mesoplax calcareous. Apophyses large, spoon-shaped, hollow at upper end.
PALLIAL LINE & INTERIOR: Anterior and posterior muscle scars fairly well marked, but pallial sinus not evident.
PERIOSTRACUM: Thin, yellowish, deciduous.
HABITAT: Open-bay margins, inlet-influenced areas. Boring infaunal.
LOCALITIES: Entire.
OCCURRENCE: Common.
RANGE: Massachusetts to Florida; Texas; Mexico; West Indies; Surinam; Brazilian coast to Paraná.
GEOLOGIC RANGE: Pliocene to Holocene.
REMARKS: This beautiful, large bivalve bores into a clay substratum in the bays to a depth of about 46 centimeters (18 inches). Its inability to withdraw into its shell makes it very susceptible to changes of salinity (fig. 14). The fresh-water inundation following Hurricane Beulah in 1967 virtually wiped out the colonies, but they are reestablishing. [*Pholas costata*]. *See* Turner 1954, p. 35.

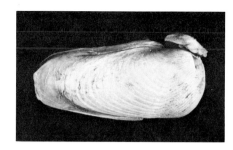

Martesia (Martesia) fragilis

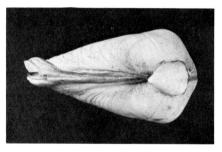

Martesia (Particoma) cuneiformis

Subfamily MARTESIINAE Grant & Gale, 1931

Genus *Martesia* G. B. Sowerby I, 1824
Subgenus *Martesia* s.s.

Fragile Martesia
Martesia (Martesia) fragilis Verrill & Bush, 1890, *Proc. U.S. Nat. Mus.* 20(1139):777.
L. *martes* a marten, a burrowing animal, *fragilis* fragile.
SIZE: 18 mm.
COLOR: White.
SHAPE: Pear-shaped.
ORNAMENT OR SCULPTURE: Valves divided into 2 sections by shallow umbonal-ventral sulcus. Anterior part sculptured with concentric, denticulated ridges and weak radial ribs. Posterior part sculptured with smooth, rounded ridges. Truncated beaks gape. Shell rounded, closed posteriorly.
HINGE AREA: Umbones prominent, located near anterior end of shell in adults. Mesoplax circular to oval, depressed with strong concentric sculpture. Metaplax long, narrow, pointed anteriorly, wider and rounded posteriorly. Apophyses long, thin, extending under umbones anteriorly at angle.
PALLIAL LINE & INTERIOR: Muscle scars strong; pallial sinus wide, deep, extending almost to umbonal-ventral ridge.
PERIOSTRACUM: Thin, yellowish.
HABITAT: Pelagic in floating wood. Boring infaunal.
LOCALITIES: Entire.
OCCURRENCE: Common.
RANGE: Bermuda; Virginia south through Gulf of Mexico; West Indies to Brazil; Surinam; Pacific coast of Mexico; Indo-Pacific.
GEOLOGIC RANGE: Pliocene to Holocene.
REMARKS: This species is easily confused with *M. striata*; however, the mesoplax is depressed, has concentric sculpture, and has sharply keeled edges. *See* Turner 1955, p. 111.

Subgenus *Particoma* Bartsch & Rehder, 1945

Wedge-Shaped Martesia
Martesia (Particoma) cuneiformis (Say, 1822), *J. Acad. Natur. Sci. Philadelphia* 2:322.
L. *martes* marten, a burrowing animal, *cuneus* wedge, *forma* form.
SIZE: 12–21 mm.
COLOR: White.
SHAPE: Pear-shaped.
ORNAMENT OR SCULPTURE: Valves divided into parts by narrow, umbonal-ventral sulcus. Anterior part sculptured with concentric, denticulated ridges. Posterior part sculptured with smooth, rounded, concentric ridges, weak growth lines. Shell gapes anteriorly, rounded, closed posteriorly.
HINGE AREA: Umbones prominent, located near anterior end of shell. Umbonal reflection small, adpressed, not free. Mesoplax cuneiform, or wedge-shaped, with median groove and radiating growth lines. Metaplax long, narrow, divided. Apophyses long, thin, almost parallel with umbonal-ventral ridge.
PALLIAL LINE & INTERIOR: Muscle scars well marked. Posterior adductor scar long, oval; anterior scar kidney-shaped. Pallial sinus broad, extending anteriorly beyond umbonal-ventral ridge.
PERIOSTRACUM: Thin, yellowish.
HABITAT: Pelagic in wood. Boring infaunal.
LOCALITIES: Entire.
OCCURRENCE: Fairly common.
RANGE: Southeastern United States; Texas; West Indies; Brazil; Pacific Panama.
GEOLOGIC RANGE: Miocene to Holocene.
REMARKS: This chubby woodborer is easily confused with *Diplothyra smithii* Tryon, 1862, unless the characteristic wedge-shaped mesoplax is present. The material in which the animal bores readily affects the shape of this genus, causing some problem in identification. *See* Turner 1955, p. 114.

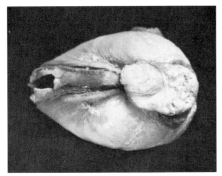

Diplothyra smithii

Jouannetia quillingi

Genus *Diplothyra* Tryon, 1862

Oyster Piddock
Diplothyra smithii Tryon, 1862, *Proc. Acad. Natur. Sci. Philadelphia* 14:450. Gk. *diplos* double, *thyreos* large shield; dedicated to Ed. A. Smith.
SIZE: 15 mm.
COLOR: White.
SHAPE: Pear-shaped.
ORNAMENT OR SCULPTURE: Divided into two parts by umbonal-ventral sulcus. Anterior part triangular in shape, sculptured by fine, close-set, wavy, concentric ridges and numerous weak radial ribs. Posterior part has only growth lines. Widely gaping anteriorly; rounded, closed posteriorly.
HINGE AREA: Umbones prominent, near anterior fourth of shell. Umbones imbedded in callum that extends posteriorly on either side of mesoplax. Apophyses long, thin, fragile. Large chondrophore in left valve. Mesoplax divided into concentrically sculptured posterior section and wrinkled anterior section. Mesoplax and hypoplax forked posteriorly.
PALLIAL LINE & INTERIOR: Adductor scars large. Pallial sinus broad, deep, extending anteriorly past umbonal-ventral ridge.
PERIOSTRACUM: Yellowish, nearly covering pedal gape.
HABITAT: High-salinity oyster reefs. Boring infaunal.
LOCALITIES: Entire.
OCCURRENCE: Common.
RANGE: Massachusetts south to Daytona Beach and Sanibel Island, Florida; west to Texas and Surinam.
GEOLOGIC RANGE: Holocene.
REMARKS: This is similar in appearance to *Martesia cuneiformis* but is not found in wood, preferring shell and coquina rock. It bores into oyster shell but is not commercially damaging. [*Martesia smithii*]. Coll., Wilson. *See* Turner 1955, p. 118; Ogle 1976.

Subfamily JOUANNETIINAE Tryon, 1862

Genus *Jouannetia* Des Moulins, 1818

Quilling's Jouannetia
Jouannetia quillingi R. D. Turner, 1955, *Johnsonia* 3(34):139. Derivation of *Jouannetia* unknown; dedicated to Ben Quilling, original collector of species.
SIZE: 21 mm.
COLOR: White to gray.
SHAPE: Globose, pear-shaped.
ORNAMENT OR SCULPTURE: Valves divided into 2 parts by umbonal-ventral sulcus. Anterior part triangular and sculptured with numerous laminate, imbricate, concentric ridges and weak radial ribs. Shell constricted at sulcus. Posterior part sculptured with thin, concentric ridges and growth lines. Ridges bear long, curved spines.
HINGE AREA: Umbones prominent, near anterior third of shell. Umbonal reflections free, raised. Callum extends dorsally between beaks, on left valve is enlarged to form covering for anterior adductor muscle. Mesoplax small, wedge-shaped. Chondrophore on left valve.
PALLIAL LINE & INTERIOR: Muscle scars barely visible. Pallial sinus extends anteriorly to umbonal-ventral ridge.
PERIOSTRACUM: None visible.
HABITAT: In wood and calcareous rock offshore, pelagic. Boring infaunal.
LOCALITIES: Central.
OCCURRENCE: Rare.
RANGE: North Carolina to Lake Worth, Florida; Texas.
GEOLOGIC RANGE: ? to Holocene.
REMARKS: This unusual species has only recently been found on the Texas coast in floating wood. Coll., Wilson. *See* Turner 1955, p. 139.

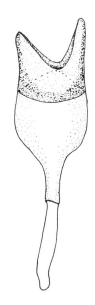

Teredo bartschi
(after Turner 1966, p. 147)

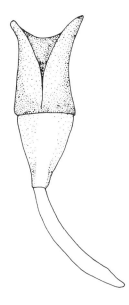

Lyrodus pedicellatus
(after Turner 1966, p. 133)

Fig. 40. Diagram of an entire teredinid indicating relative position of pallets and shell (after Clench & Turner 1946, p. 4)

Family TEREDINIDAE Rafinesque, 1815
Subfamily TEREDININAE Rafinesque, 1815

Genus *Teredo* Linné, 1758

Bartsch's Shipworm
Teredo bartschi Clapp, 1923, *Proc. Boston Soc. Natur. Hist.* 37:33.
L. *teredo* a worm; dedicated to Paul Bartsch, U.S. National Museum.
SIZE: 27 mm.
COLOR: Pallets white.
SHAPE: Stalk long; blade short.
ORNAMENT OR SCULPTURE: Blade deeply excavated at top.
HINGE AREA: None.
PALLIAL LINE & INTERIOR: None.
PERIOSTRACUM: None.
HABITAT: A wood borer. Infaunal.
LOCALITIES: Entire.
OCCURRENCE: Fairly common.
RANGE: Bermuda; South Carolina to northern half of Florida and Texas; introduced to Baja California.
GEOLOGIC RANGE: ? to Holocene.
REMARKS: The shell is not used in identifying this species. *See* Pulley 1953, p. 204; Turner 1966, pl. 8.

Genus *Lyrodus* Binney, 1870

Stalked Shipworm
Lyrodus pedicellatus (Quatrefages, 1849), *Ann. Sci. Natur. (Zool.)* 11:26.
L. *lyricus* lyre, *pediculus* dim. of foot.
SIZE: 6 mm.
COLOR: White.
SHAPE: Stalk long; blade long.
ORNAMENT OR SCULPTURE: Blade very deeply and sharply excavated at top.
HINGE AREA: None.
PALLIAL LINE & INTERIOR: None.
PERIOSTRACUM: None.
HABITAT: In wood. Infaunal.
LOCALITIES: Entire.
OCCURRENCE: Uncertain.
RANGE: New Jersey to West Indies; Gulf of Mexico; Central America to northern coast of South America; San Diego, California.
GEOLOGIC RANGE: ? to Holocene.
REMARKS: Rarely found in the drift because they usually remain in the wood. *See* Pulley 1953, p. 204; Turner 1966, pl. 1.

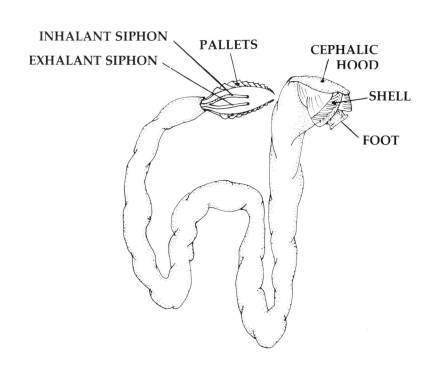

INHALANT SIPHON
EXHALANT SIPHON
PALLETS
CEPHALIC HOOD
SHELL
FOOT

Bankia (Bankiella) gouldi
(after Turner 1966, p. 247)

Pandora (Clidophora) trilineata

Subfamily BANKIINAE Turner, 1966

Genus *Bankia* Gray, 1842
Subgenus *Bankiella* Bartsch, 1921

Gould's Shipworm

Bankia (Bankiella) gouldi (Bartsch, 1908), *Proc. Biol. Soc. Washington* 21:211.
Dedicated to Sir Joseph Banks, British malacologist, and Dr. A. A. Gould (1805–1866), American.
SIZE: 27 mm.
COLOR: White.
SHAPE: Pallet elongate.
ORNAMENT OR SCULPTURE: Blade composed of numerous conelike elements on central stalk.
HINGE AREA: None.
PALLIAL LINE & INTERIOR: None.
PERIOSTRACUM: None.
HABITAT: In wood, mangroves. Boring infaunal.
LOCALITIES: Entire.
OCCURRENCE: Common.
RANGE: New Jersey to Florida; Texas; Central America; West Indies; Brazil; Pacific coast of Mexico.
GEOLOGIC RANGE: ? to Holocene.
REMARKS: Turner (1966, p. 66) states that the shells are helpful in identifying the species only when used in conjunction with the pallets. *See* Clench & Turner 1946; Pulley 1953, p. 204; Turner 1966, pl. 59.

Subclass ANOMALODESMATA Dall, 1889
Order PHOLADOMYOIDEA Newell, 1965
Superfamily PANDORACEA Rafinesque, 1815
Family PANDORIDAE Rafinesque, 1815

Genus *Pandora* Bruguière, 1797
Subgenus *Clidophora* Carpenter, 1864

Say's Pandora

Pandora (Clidophora) trilineata Say, 1822, *J. Acad. Natur. Sci. Philadelphia* 2(1):261.
Gk. Pandora, all-gifted mythological person; L. *trilinea* three-lined.
SIZE: 18–25 mm.
COLOR: White to cream. Interior pearly.
SHAPE: Semilunar, flat. Inequivalve. Inequilateral.
ORNAMENT OR SCULPTURE: Flat, compressed valves sculptured with microscopic, concentric growth lines. Left valve has radial ridge along posterior slope. Strong ridge along hinge margin.
HINGE AREA: Umbones tiny, near rounded anterior end. Hinge internal just below umbones; lamellar plates replace teeth.
PALLIAL LINE & INTERIOR: Two small, round adductor muscles. Pallial line simple, discontinuous.
PERIOSTRACUM: Thin, light colored.
HABITAT: Inlet areas, open-sound and lagoon centers in clayey sediments. Infaunal.
LOCALITIES: Entire.
OCCURRENCE: Common.
RANGE: Cape Hatteras to Florida; Texas.
GEOLOGIC RANGE: Miocene to Holocene.
REMARKS: One wonders how any animal finds space to live between the two flat, half-moon-shaped valves. *See* Boss & Merrill 1965, p. 195.

Lyonsia hyalina floridana

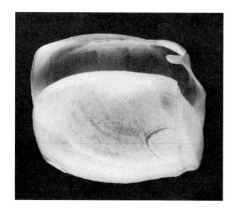

Periploma margaritaceum

Family LYONSIIDAE Fischer, 1887

Genus *Lyonsia* Turton, 1822

Florida Lyonsia
Lyonsia hyalina floridana Conrad, 1848, *Proc. Acad. Natur. Sci. Philadelphia* 4:121.
Dedicated to W. Lyons; L. *hyalus* glass; from Florida.
SIZE: 16 mm.
COLOR: White, translucent.
SHAPE: Elongate, rather tear-shaped. Inequivalve. Inequilateral.
ORNAMENT OR SCULPTURE: Thin shell sculptured with fine growth lines. Valves gape posteriorly.
HINGE AREA: Umbones tiny, pointed. No teeth. Small groove posterior to umbones houses ligament.
PALLIAL LINE & INTERIOR: Two adductor muscle scars. Pallial line indistinct.
PERIOSTRACUM: Thin, with numerous raised radial lines; sand grains usually attached.
HABITAT: Open-bay margins, inlet areas, in grass beds. Infaunal.
LOCALITIES: Central.
OCCURRENCE: Fairly common.
RANGE: West coast of Florida; Texas; Surinam.
GEOLOGIC RANGE: Pleistocene to Holocene.
REMARKS: This fragile bivalve attaches with a delicate byssus.

Family PERIPLOMATIDAE Dall, 1895

Genus *Periploma* Schumacher, 1816

Unequal Spoon Clam
Periploma margaritaceum (Lamarck, 1801), *Syst. Anim.*, p. 137.
Gk. *peri* around, about, *ploimos* fit for sailing; L. *margaritaceum* pearly.
SIZE: 18–25 mm.
COLOR: White, translucent.
SHAPE: Subquadrate. Inequivalve. Inequilateral.
ORNAMENT OR SCULPTURE: Sculpture on rather fragile shell of fine, concentric growth lines. Posterior margin very truncate. Low keel extends from umbones to anterior ventral margin.
HINGE AREA: Umbones small, near posterior end. Ligament internal, located in spoon-shaped "tooth" in each valve.
PALLIAL LINE & INTERIOR: Two small adductor muscle scars. Pallial sinus broad, short, strongly defined.
PERIOSTRACUM: None visible.
HABITAT: Open-sound, open-lagoon centers, inlet areas in sandy bottoms. Infaunal.
LOCALITIES: Entire.
OCCURRENCE: Common.
RANGE: South Carolina to Florida; Texas to Mexico; Costa Rica; West Indies; Brazil.
GEOLOGIC RANGE: ? to Holocene.
REMARKS: Syn. *P. inequale* (C. B. Adams, 1842). At times this fragile little shell is on the outer beaches in large numbers. Most of the valves bear the neat, round hole made by a predatory gastropod.

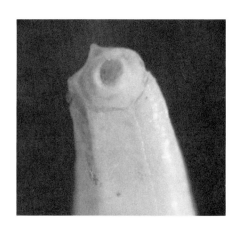

Dentalium (Paradentalium) texasianum

apex

Class SCAPHOPODA Bronn, 1862

Family DENTALIIDAE Gray, 1834

Genus *Dentalium* Linné, 1758
Subgenus *Paradentalium* Cotton &
   Godfrey, 1933

Texas Tusk
Dentalium (Paradentalium) texasianum
Philippi, 1849, *Zeitschr. für
Malakozool.* 5:144.
L. *dens* tooth; from Texas.
SIZE: 18–35 mm.
COLOR: White.
SHAPE: Tapering cylinder. Curved.
ORNAMENT OR SCULPTURE: Hexag-
onal in cross section with 6 main
ribs interspaced with numerous
cordlike riblets on broad in-
terspaces. Apical pipe clearly visible
unless tip broken off.
APERTURE: Hexagonal.
OPERCULUM: None.
PERIOSTRACUM: Not preserved.
HABITAT: Open-bay margins, inlets,
channel in stiff clay sediments.
Semi-infaunal.
LOCALITIES: Entire.
OCCURRENCE: Common.
RANGE: North Carolina to Texas;
Yucatán.
GEOLOGIC RANGE: Pleistocene to
Holocene.
REMARKS: Holotype collected by F.
Roemer near Galveston, Texas, ca.
1846. Petersen (1972) examined live
specimens and noted an enormous
amount of variation in the popula-
tion of West Bay off Galveston Is-
land. *See* R. D. Turner 1961; Gainey
1972; Petersen 1972.

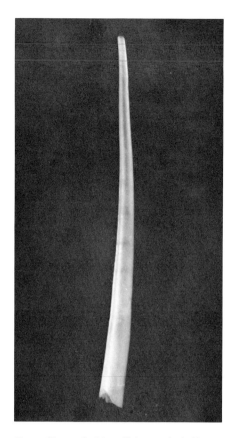

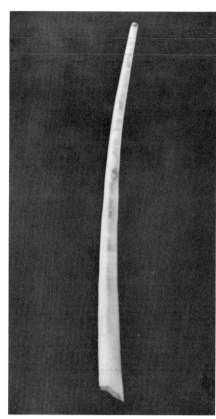

Dentalium cf. *(Antalis)* sp. A & B

apex

apex

Subgenus *Antalis* H. & A. Adams, 1954

Dentalium cf. *(Antalis)* sp. A & B
L. *dens* tooth.
SIZE: Up to 28 mm.
COLOR: Whitish to pale amber.
SHAPE: Very slender, tapered cylinder. Curved.
ORNAMENT OR SCULPTURE: Delicate shell has microscopic longitudinal ribs at apical end; remainder of shell smooth except for growth rings. Growth rings stronger than in *D.* cf. *(Laevidentalium)* sp. C. Apical slit. Some of adult shells do not have microscopic lines.
APERTURE: Round, simple.
OPERCULUM: None.
PERIOSTRACUM: Not preserved.
HABITAT: Inlet areas? Semi-infaunal.
LOCALITIES: Central, south, probably entire.
OCCURRENCE: Fairly common.
RANGE: Not defined.
GEOLOGIC RANGE: ? to Holocene.
REMARKS: Two specimens and details of their apexes are figured. These may or may not be the same species. I have examined some that are the same size, shape, and color which are completely smooth with an apical slit, some with the apical ribs and a slit, and others with apical ribs and no slit. Previously all the *Dentaliums* in Texas without the hexagonal cross section and heavy ribs of *D. texasianum* have been reported as being one species, *D. eboreum* Conrad, 1846. Conrad described *D. eboreum* (*Proc. Acad. Natur. Sci. Philadelphia* 3:27) as having microscopic apical striae but *no* slit. If the absence of the slit in those I have examined is natural and not due to breakage, they could be *eboreum*. However, those with the slit do not fit that description. *See* Pilsbry & Sharp 1897, p. 37; Ludbrook 1960, pp. 37–39; R. D. Turner 1961; Emerson 1962, p. 470; C. P. Palmer 1974.

Dentalium cf. *(Laevidentalium)* sp. C

apex

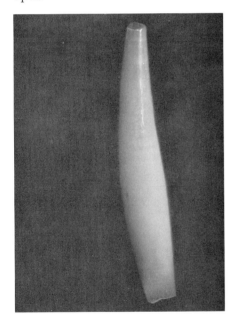

Cadulus cf. *(Gadila)* sp. A

apex

Subgenus *Laevidentalium*
Cossmann, 1888

Dentalium cf. *(Laevidentalium)* sp. C
L. *dens* tooth.
SIZE: Up to 37 mm.
COLOR: White.
SHAPE: Tapered cylinder. Curved.
ORNAMENT OR SCULPTURE: Smooth
except for faint growth rings. No
apical slit. Cross section round.
APERTURE: Round, simple.
OPERCULUM: None.
PERIOSTRACUM: Not preserved.
HABITAT: Inlet areas and near shore.
Semi-infaunal.
LOCALITIES: Central, south.
OCCURRENCE: Fairly common.
RANGE: Not defined.
GEOLOGIC RANGE: ? to Holocene.
REMARKS: This shell was identified
as *D. eboreum* in Andrews 1971 and
has been referred to by other Texas
malacologists as *D. eboreum* Conrad,
1846, but it is larger and has less
definite growth rings. Examination
under a microscope shows an ab-
sence of the longitudinal apical ribs
typical of *eboreum*. *See* Pilsbry &
Sharp 1897, p. 97; Ludbrook 1960,
p. 39; R. D. Turner 1961; Emerson
1962, p. 472; C. B. Palmer 1974.

Family SIPHONODENTALIIDAE
Simroth, 1894

Genus *Cadulus* Philippi, 1844
Subgenus *Gadila* Gray, 1847

Cadulus cf. *(Gadila)* sp. A
L. *cadus* a small pail, jar.
SIZE: Up to 8 mm.
COLOR: White, smooth, glossy.
SHAPE: Cylinder; swollen in middle,
tapering toward each end.
ORNAMENT OR SCULPTURE: Smooth,
polished.
APERTURE: Round, simple.
OPERCULUM: None.
PERIOSTRACUM: Not preserved.
HABITAT: Near shore. Semi-
infaunal.
LOCALITIES: Entire.
OCCURRENCE: Fairly common.
RANGE: Not determined.
GEOLOGIC RANGE: ? to Holocene.
REMARKS: This shell has been mis-
takenly identified as *C. carolinensis*
Bush, 1885, in Andrews 1971 and
other literature on Texas shallow-
water mollusks. The typical "small,
distinct notches, two on each side"
described by Bush (1885, p. 471) are
absent in this small species, which
is often abundant in the beach drift.
However, the typical *C. carolinensis*
is found in deeper offshore waters.
In addition to the notches, it has a
more oblique aperture than do the
specimens which wash up on the
beach. *See* Ludbrook 1960, p. 40; R.
D. Turner 1961; Emerson 1962, p.
478; C. P. Palmer 1974.

Spirula spirula

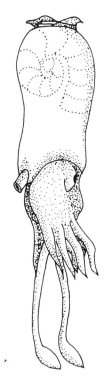

(after Lane 1960, p. 14)

Class CEPHALOPODA Cuvier, 1797

Subclass COLEOIDEA Bather, 1888
Order SEPIOIDEA Naef, 1916
Family SPIRULIDAE Owen, 1836

Genus *Spirula* Lamarck, 1799

Common Spirula
Spirula spirula (Linné, 1758), *Syst. Natur.*, 10th ed., p. 710.
L. *spira* coil.
SIZE: Animal 55 mm, shell 25 mm.
COLOR: Shell porcelaneous white; animal light brown.
DESCRIPTION: Closely coiled and chambered shell enclosed in posterior end of cylindrical body. Two folds cover coiled shell, visible dorsally and ventrally but completely enclosed within mantle. Posterior end of body truncate with two lateral fins. Between fins is circular disc that emits a light. Large head has two eyes that protrude beyond mantle edges. Arms short, stout, pointed, with four rows of suckers. Tentacles short with numerous rows of minute suckers.
HABITAT: Offshore in deep waters.
LOCALITIES: Entire.
OCCURRENCE: Common.
RANGE: Worldwide.
GEOLOGIC RANGE: ? to Holocene.
REMARKS: The coiled shell is often on the outer beaches by the thousands. The normal position for the animal is vertical with the arms hanging down. The living mollusk has seldom been seen. *See* Voss 1956; Haefner 1964; Thomas & Bingham 1972; Ropes & Merrill 1973; Prior 1974.

Order TEUTHOIDEA Naef, 1916
Suborder MYOPSIDA Orbigny, 1840
Family LOLIGINIDAE Orbigny, 1841

Genus *Loliguncula* Steenstrup, 1881

Short Squid
Loliguncula brevis (Blainville, 1823), *J. Phys. Chem. Hist. Natur.* 6:133.
L. *loligo* cuttlefish, *brevis* short.
SIZE: 75 mm.
COLOR: Cream colored with numerous reddish purple spots uniformly distributed over dorsal and ventral surfaces of mantle, head, arms, except for ventral surfaces of fins.
DESCRIPTION: Animal cylindrical, pointed posteriorly; width less than half of length. Anterior mantle edge comes to blunt point at middorsal line. Fins large, about half of mantle length. They form an ellipse and are joined posteriorly by fleshy ridge that encircles posterior end of body. Head small with moderate eyes. Tentacles long, slender, with club-like ends. Arms short, dorsal pair shortest.
HABITAT: Bays and inlets.
LOCALITIES: Port Aransas, south.
OCCURRENCE: Common.
RANGE: Maryland to Florida; Gulf of Mexico; Caribbean; South America to Río de la Plata.
GEOLOGIC RANGE: ? to Holocene.
REMARKS: These soft-bodied animals swim backward by means of jet propulsion. Water is expelled forcibly from a siphon beneath and a little back of the head. A chitinous structure beneath the mantle on the anterior side is called the pen. In the related European cuttlefish this pen is calcareous and is used in bird

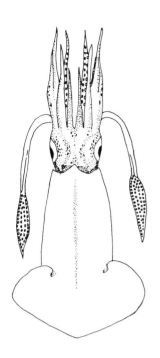

Loliguncula brevis
(after Voss 1956, p. 113)

Octopus vulgaris
(after Lane 1960, p. 6)

cages. As bait this is an economically important mollusk. When you catch it in your seine be careful not to let it nip your fingers with its sharp beak. The tentacles are used to capture food. *See* Voss 1956; Dillon & Dial 1962; Haefner 1964.

Order OCTOPODA Leach, 1817
Suborder INCIRRATA Grimpe, 1916
Family OCTOPODIDAE Orbigny, 1840
Subfamily OCTOPODINAE Grimpe, 1921

Genus *Octopus* Cuvier, 1797

Common Atlantic Octopus
Octopus vulgaris Lamarck, 1798, *Hist. Natur. Anim. sans Vert.* 11:361. Gk. *okto* eight, *pous* a foot; L. *vulgaris* common.
SIZE: 307–900 mm.
COLOR: Reddish brown.
DESCRIPTION: Soft-bodied animal has saclike body with small head and long, tapering arms.
HABITAT: Open-bay centers, inlet areas, the Gulf.
LOCALITIES: Entire.
OCCURRENCE: Fairly common.
RANGE: North and South Atlantic; western Africa; Mediterranean; Atlantic coast of Europe to Great Britain; western Atlantic from New York to Brazil; Gulf of Mexico.
GEOLOGIC RANGE: ? to Holocene.
REMARKS: This small octopus lives among the rocks on the jetties and sea walls. It moves by jet propulsion and exudes a black cloud of ink when frightened. An octopus does not have tentacles as does the squid. It uses its tapering arms to reach into crevices in search of food. The female broods her eggs, which are laid in clusters. Larvae are planktonic. *See* Voss 1956; Lane 1960; Buchsbaum & Milne 1966, p. 170; M. Wells 1969.

4. A Shell Collecting Trip

When planning a shelling trip to the coast of Texas, the first question is—how to get there? Without a boat many of the areas are inaccessible, but the majority can be reached in a passenger car. A map of Texas, then, is the first necessity. The Texas Department of Highways in Austin is only too happy to send its official state highway map. This same agency has also published some delightful maps describing the Texas Trails. The two entitled "Independence Trail" and "Tropical Trail" cover most of the coastal area and are more than worth the trouble it takes to order them. Another map of interest to shellers is Number 1967-306-116/21, published by the United States Department of the Interior, which covers the national seashore on Padre Island. All these maps are free. Other information may be obtained from the Padre Island National Seashore office located at 9405 South Padre Island Drive. (See Appendix C for other map sources.)

Unless one of these maps shows a road to the outer beach there just isn't one. Often maps of the immediate locality are available at motels and eating places along the coast or may be purchased at sporting-goods stores. Simplified maps in this book show the roads to the beaches and back bay areas and can be used to mark the map you keep in your automobile.

Let's begin at Sabine Pass. But, first, check the tide tables. Unless there is a minus tide, the bay areas are not good for collecting, and it will only lead to disappointment if one goes when the tide is high.

State Highway 87 will take you along the beach for about fifty miles from Sabine Pass to Bolivar Peninsula. As you approach Bolivar Pass an old lighthouse built in 1852 will loom up in front of you—turn to the left short of the light toward the north jetty. You may have to ask for directions to the jetty as there are no markings. The area is muddy and marsh grasses grow to the water's edge. When the tide is out a very wide flat is exposed east of the jetty. Another spot exposed by the tides is just to the left of the ferry landing.

The free ferry trip from Port Bolivar to Galveston lasts about fifteen minutes, but during the months of May through September, Friday through Monday, you can expect a wait of up to an hour and a half before boarding; in the Texas heat this delay can be dreadful. Careful planning is recommended. The ferry operates at twenty-minute intervals from 6:00 A.M. to 8:40 P.M. and at forty-minute intervals until midnight. After that it is hourly. Navigators on the ocean-going vessels entering Bolivar Roads and the Houston Ship Channel recognize this passage as one of the most hazardous ship channels in the world and never attempt it during doubtful weather conditions; hence, you often see many large ships anchored nearby waiting to enter the channel.

Galveston is a large city. In 1848, Dr. Ferdinand Roemer, the early German-Texas paleontologist, considered Galveston to be the most important city in Texas. It is still important, but its main attractions are now principally historical and recreational. Texas A&M University's Moody Marine Center and its oceanographic research vessels are located here. A visit to the port on the bay side of the island is an enjoyable experience—mountains of yellow sulphur, bales of cotton, foreign seamen, shrimp boats, and United States Navy ships are but a few of the sights that lend color to the scene.

A wide avenue along the ten-mile-long sea wall is not the least of the attractions to be found in Galveston. Before embarking on this beautiful drive after leaving the ferry, turn left off State Highway 87 onto Seawall Boulevard and drive to the south jetty. Stewart Beach is adjacent to this jetty. The beaches of Galveston are teeming with seashore visitors in the summer, but the winter months find them almost as lonely as the shore of Padre Island. Return to Seawall Boulevard and head west on County Road 3005.

Near the end of this drive is a large, well-stocked marineland. This is a first-class aquarium display that will interest all who love the sea and its creatures. A large fishing pier, the Gulf Coast Pier, is on the Gulf side of the road. The West Beach access road is two miles beyond this point. What was lonely ranch land is being filled with beach cottages and condominiums. A new camping site, the Galveston Island State Park, is located eight miles beyond the big pier. Three miles past the park is a good place to turn on to the beach and drive along the sandy shore for a couple of miles when the tide is low.

You will drive through several growing resort developments on the way to San Luis Pass. The toll bridge spanning San Luis Pass, Vacek Bridge, delivers you to the mainland shore of Brazoria County. The tidal flat at this bridge is the favorite spot for shell collectors in the area, but only at low tide.

The Gulf is never out of sight as you drive to Surfside, and frequent access roads permit driving on the beach. If you would like to sample the beach west of Freeport to the mouth of the Brazos River, turn at Surfside on State Highway 332. At the intersection of 332 and Farm Road 523 turn left on 523 and go to Farm Road 1495. This road will take you over the harbor, past the Freeport Inn, and out to Bryan Beach. There you can drive the beach to the river and return by the same route. The Freeport area has been enclosed with fifty miles of levee to provide hurricane protection to the huge petrochemical industry that dominates the area.

On leaving Freeport follow State Highway 332 to Lake Jackson and spend some time at the Brazosport Museum of Natural Science. This new museum has the most impressive display of shells from the Gulf of Mexico to be found in Texas. You will receive a warm welcome from the volunteers who staff it during the days it is open—Sunday and Wednesday, 2:00 P.M. to 5:00 P.M., and Tuesday, Thursday, Friday, and Saturday, 10:00 A.M. to 5:00 P.M. The museum is at 400 College Drive, off State Highway 288. Look for the Brazosport Center for Arts and Science (P.O. Box 355, Lake Jackson, Tex. 77566).

From Lake Jackson continue on 332 to Brazoria (no motels). Leave Brazoria on the Independence Trail, Farm Road 36, driving past pecan groves and then wide, cultivated fields in an area that was one of the most significant regions of the state during the days when Texas was part of Mexico and then a republic. You will see the huge Clements Unit of the state prison farm, which occupies land in the vicinity of what was the plantation of Stephen F. Austin, the Father of Texas.

At the prison farm turn south on Farm Road 2611, go across Fisherman's High Bridge, and take a left turn onto Farm Road 2918. This road will deliver you to the point where the San Bernard River intersects the Intracoastal Waterway. At present the Gulf may only be reached from this point by a small boat. In the past, before the Intracoastal Waterway separated the mainland from the Gulf beach, there was a settlement at the river's mouth. Today only a few gravestones mark the site. There is a bait stand with cold drinks, but no food or lodging is available. Return to Farm Road 2611 and follow it until it meets Farm Road 457, which will take you to Sargent Beach. Farm roads in Texas are well-maintained, paved roads.

You also could leave Brazoria and go directly to Sargent Beach via Farm Road 521. At Cedar Lane crossroads turn onto Farm Road 457 to reach Sargent Beach, a mainland shore near Caney Creek. Beach erosion has caused a small resort development here to be practically abandoned. There are no tourist facilities; therefore, it is best not to plan to spend the night. Walk the beach. Return by the same road to Cedar Lane and drive back on 521 until you enter Wadsworth. Turn at this village onto State Highway 60 for Matagorda and go beyond the town on Farm Road 2031 to the water.

This beach is at the mouth of the Colorado River and can be a bonanza to the collector at low tides in the winter, but it, too, is crowded on a summer weekend. It is possible to drive a four-wheeled vehicle north on the sand at Matagorda Peninsula for about fifteen miles, but at Brown Cedar Cut you must turn around and come back. Unless you are seeking driftwood, it is a hard drive for the results; pickings are better nearer the Colorado. A one-day trip is all that is recommended for this spot, as there are no overnight facilities. Be sure to pack a lunch!

Back again over State Highway 60 to Farm Road 521 running through fields of rice. At the intersection of 521 and State Highway 35 turn left toward Palacios. The beaches in Palacios may not look very promising to the collector, but a person interested in minute shells will find the stop rewarding. Take First Street to Bay Boulevard, past the old Luther Hotel, built in 1903 and now reopened for guests; beyond a big pier at the corner of Sixth Street and Duson Avenue is a little cove with a beach covered with rock and old oystershell. Stop here. The drift from this spot is worth sifting when you return home and the detour through this little town is an adventure in itself. Return to 35 and travel on to Port Lavaca, over the flat coastal prairie and picturesque bayous.

From Port Lavaca you can make a jaunt to the former site of Indianola by going south on State Highway 35 and turning left on Farm Road 2433, which intersects State Highway 316. Brackish-water species may be collected from the bay shores along this drive, but Indianola itself yields only some old foundations and a few tombstones in the abandoned cemetery. A statue in honor of La Salle stands by the bay that he named La Vaca. After returning to Port Lavaca, continue on 35 to Green Lake, keeping a lookout for the turn onto State Highway 185 to Port O'Connor.

The collector without a boat must content himself with the little jetties along the Intracoastal Waterway, but the flats around them may produce specimens at low tide. It takes a boat and a good knowledge of the waters to reach the Gulf beaches adjoining Pass Cavallo. Shoaling in the pass makes boat passage very tricky for a stranger to the waters, but boats, comfortable lodging, and good food can be had in this fisherman's paradise. Nothing is fancy, but all is new, since Hurricane Carla almost completely destroyed the village in 1961. Waterfowl abound in the extensive marsh areas of this tidal delta. It is not difficult to reach Decros Point on Matagorda Peninsula in your boat, but you are afoot once you are there. A jettied ship channel a few miles north of this point permits exit from the bay into the open Gulf. Not far to the north of this at the site of the ill-starred Matagorda Club, in old World War II air base buildings, is a landing strip and a concrete dock. The flats at Saluria Bayou on the south side of Pass Cavallo are good at low tide for small species. The ruins of a coast guard station called the Cupola and an old lighthouse constructed in 1852 mark this spot. Beyond this point, toward the pass, the going gets rough.

Matagorda Island is not open to the public, for this northernmost island in the chain of barrier islands is privately owned. The state law covering beach usage (Article 5415d—State Beaches) permits the use of all seaward beaches by the people if there is access by public road or ferry. From 1940 until 1975 the United States Air Force maintained a bombing range at the northern end of the island. The discontinuation of this operation has left the future of these 18,999 acres undetermined. The Department of the Interior, General Services Administration, and the state of Texas

are working together to formulate a plan for the future use of this land that will benefit both man and nature. The major part of the remainder of the island is a large ranch owned by Toddie Lee Wynne of Dallas and can be visited only by invitation. Three thousand head of cattle are being raised at the Wynne Star Brand ranch in an operation maintained by air and sea that is a marvel in itself.

The shores of both passes that border either end of the island can be visited by an enterprising collector interested in a lot of boat riding, hard work, and walking. Unless you want to haul a great amount of camping gear overland on your back, these excursions should be planned as long one-day trips. Since so much work and expense is involved to get to these spots, plan your trip carefully to coincide with the lowest tides of the year. Do watch the tide, for shoals can be very hard to see in these murky waters.

On the mainland, just north of the bridge crossing Copano Bay, leave State Highway 35 on Park Road 13 going east to Goose Island State Park. For a small fee you can use very nice picnic and camping facilities, a lighted pier, and a boat ramp. At low tide vast oyster beds are exposed near the pier. Between Park Road 13 and the bridge is a large marina, formerly Mill's Wharf, on the north shore of Copano Bay at the site of the old village of Lamar. A lovely lodge, the Sea Gun (owned by Mr. Wynne), welcomes the traveler just short of the big causeway. Here, you can launch a boat for the voyage to Mesquite Bay. Follow a well-marked channel for four miles to canal marker number 13 in the Intracoastal Canal and then follow the canal north. This part of the canal traverses the Aransas National Wildlife Refuge where whooping cranes feed along the shores, completely unconcerned over the constant flow of tugs and barges. At

a small barrel marker, also number 13, turn right into Mesquite Bay. The channel is not well identified, so hold close to the south shore or you will run aground. Once you are inside, the channel is well marked and maintained all the way to Cedar Bayou because the state Parks and Wildlife Department has established a small experimental station in Cedar Bayou. The Star Brand ranch headquarters are visible to the north at the opening of the pass. A Parks and Wildlife Department sign prohibiting the passage of boats under penalty of $100.00 fine leaves the collector a fairly long, hard walk to the beach—but to trail a low tide behind a norther is worth all the work entailed, including the sore muscles that will follow. The southern shore of Cedar Bayou is San José Island and at times is most rewarding to the shell enthusiast.

San José Island is another privately owned island. The northern end may be explored from Cedar Bayou and the southern end from Port Aransas. We will return to the southern end of the island after we arrive in Port Aransas; in the meantime, back to the Sea Gun and your dependable automobile.

After crossing the causeway on State Highway 35, take the first left turn opposite Farm Road 1781 onto an unmarked, tree-bordered road into the town of Fulton. On one side of the drive is the shallow bay and, on the other, wind-sculptured live oak trees and charming vacation homes. The historic G. W. Fulton mansion, built in 1872, still stands. In 1976 the once grand showplace was rescued from decaying entombment within a surrounding trailer park, and its restoration as a Texas historical site was begun. Fulton and Rockport were once separated by bird-filled marsh flats, but now these havens for birds and marine life have been filled to make room for resort homes with private boat docks.

The state of Texas operates a

THE UNIVERSITY OF TEXAS AT AUSTIN
BUREAU OF ECONOMIC GEOLOGY
W. L. FISHER, DIRECTOR

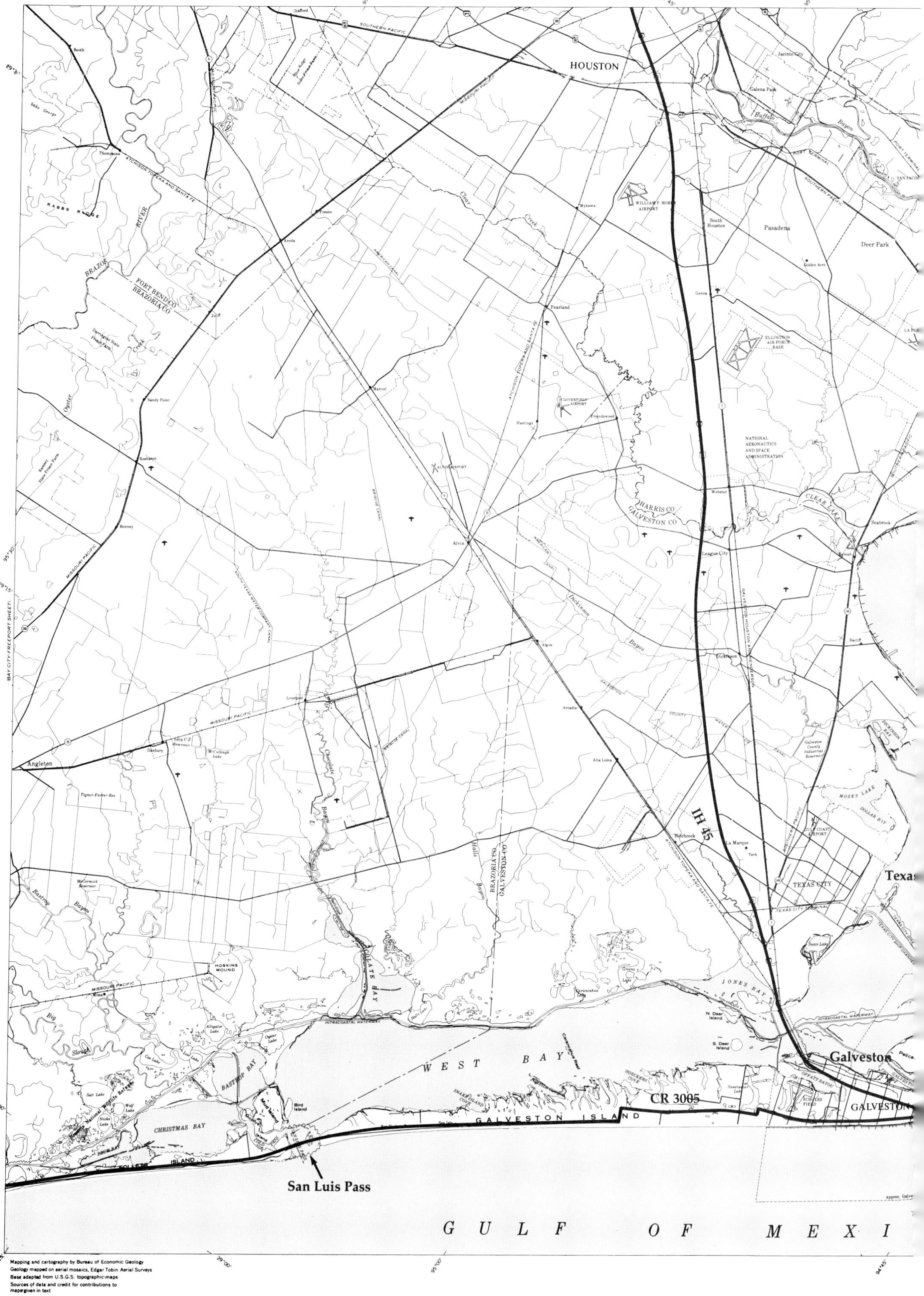

HOUSTON

WILLIAM P. HOBBY
AIRPORT

South
Houston

Pasadena

Deer Park

Galena Park

Pearland

ELLINGTON
AIR FORCE
BASE

NATIONAL
AERONAUTICS
AND SPACE
ADMINISTRATION

HARRIS CO.
GALVESTON CO.

Webster

CLEAR LAKE

Seabrook

Alvin

League City

Dickinson

Alta Loma

Arcadia

IH 45

Hitchcock

La Marque

TEXAS CITY

Texas

Angleton

HOSKINS
MOUND

MOSES LAKE

DOLLAR BAY

JONES BAY

N. Deer
Island

S. Deer
Island

Galveston

GALVESTON

WEST BAY

CR 3005

GALVESTON ISLAND

CHRISTMAS BAY

Bird
Island

San Luis Pass

G U L F   O F   M E X I

Mapping and cartography by Bureau of Economic Geology
Geology mapped on aerial mosaics, Edgar Tobin Aerial Surveys
Base adapted from U.S.G.S. topographic maps
Sources of data and credit for contributions to
maps given in text

north jetty

south jetty

Map 1.   Galveston-Houston Area

Scale 1:250,000

0   1   2   3   4   5   10   15 Miles

BUREAU OF ECONOMIC GEOLOGY-1971

THE UNIVERSITY OF TEXAS AT AUSTIN
BUREAU OF ECONOMIC GEOLOGY
W. L. FISHER, DIRECTOR

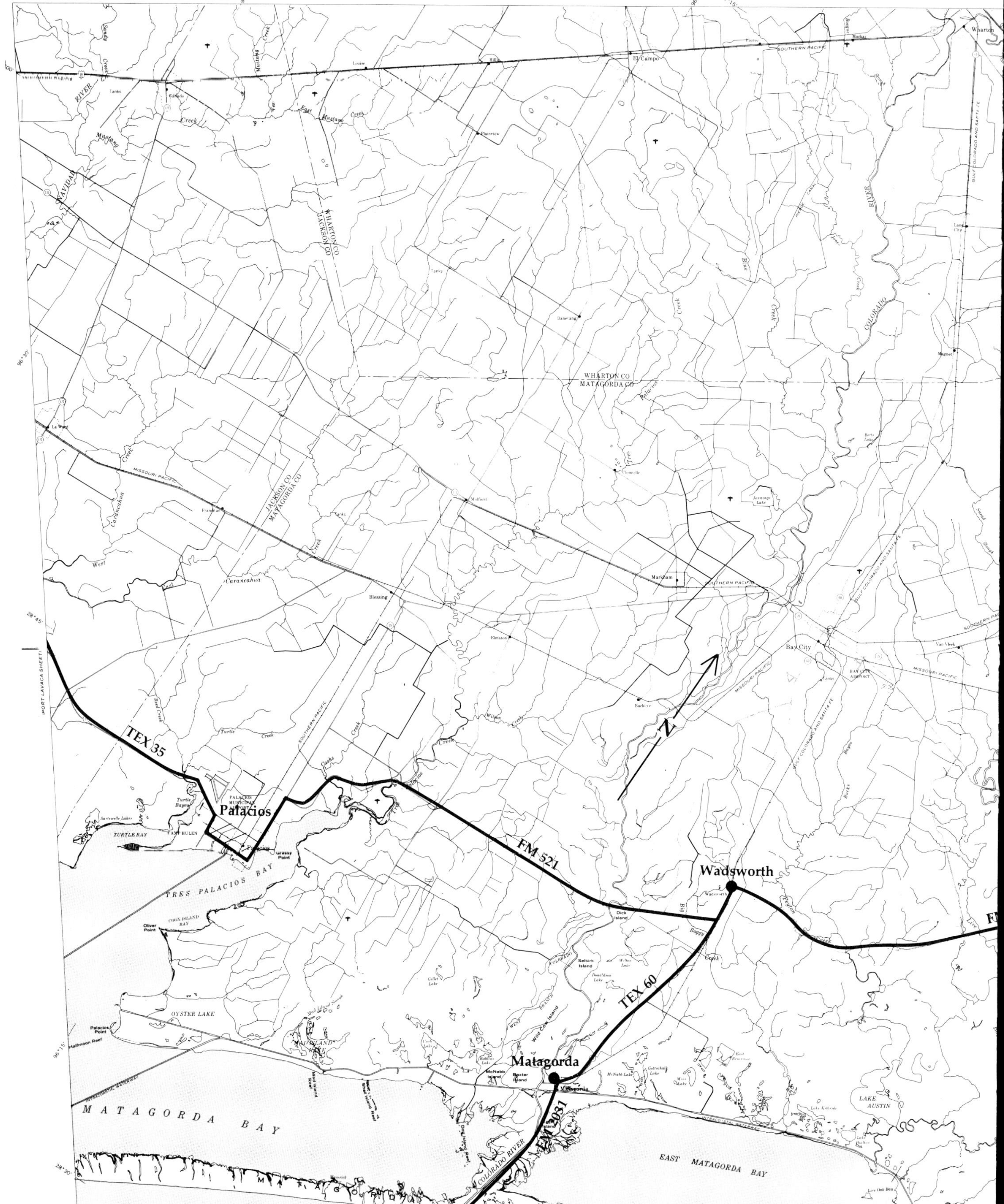

El Campo
Wharton
WHARTON CO
JACKSON CO
WHARTON CO
MATAGORDA CO
JACKSON CO
MATAGORDA CO
SOUTHERN PACIFIC
MISSOURI PACIFIC
GULF COLORADO AND SANTA FE
COLORADO RIVER
NAVIDAD RIVER
Mustang Creek
Carancahua
Danevang
Blessing
Markham
Elmaton
Buckeye
Bay City
Van Vleck
N
TEX 35
Palacios
TURTLE BAY
CAMP HULEN
Grassy Point
TRES PALACIOS BAY
Oliver Point
COON ISLAND BAY
FM 521
Wadsworth
Dick Island
Selkirk Island
TEX 60
OYSTER LAKE
Palacios Point
Halfmoon Reef
Matagorda
McNabb Island
Baxter Island
MATAGORDA BAY
FM 2031
COLORADO RIVER
EAST MATAGORDA BAY
LAKE AUSTIN
MATAGORDA PENINSULA
Matagorda Beach
PORT LAVACA SHEET
Scale 1:250,000
0 1 2 3 4 5 10 15 Miles
GULF OF MEXICO

Mapping and cartography by Bureau of Economic Geology
Geology mapped on aerial mosaics, Edgar Tobin Aerial Surveys
Base adapted from U.S.G.S. topographic maps
Sources of data and credit for contributions to maps given in text

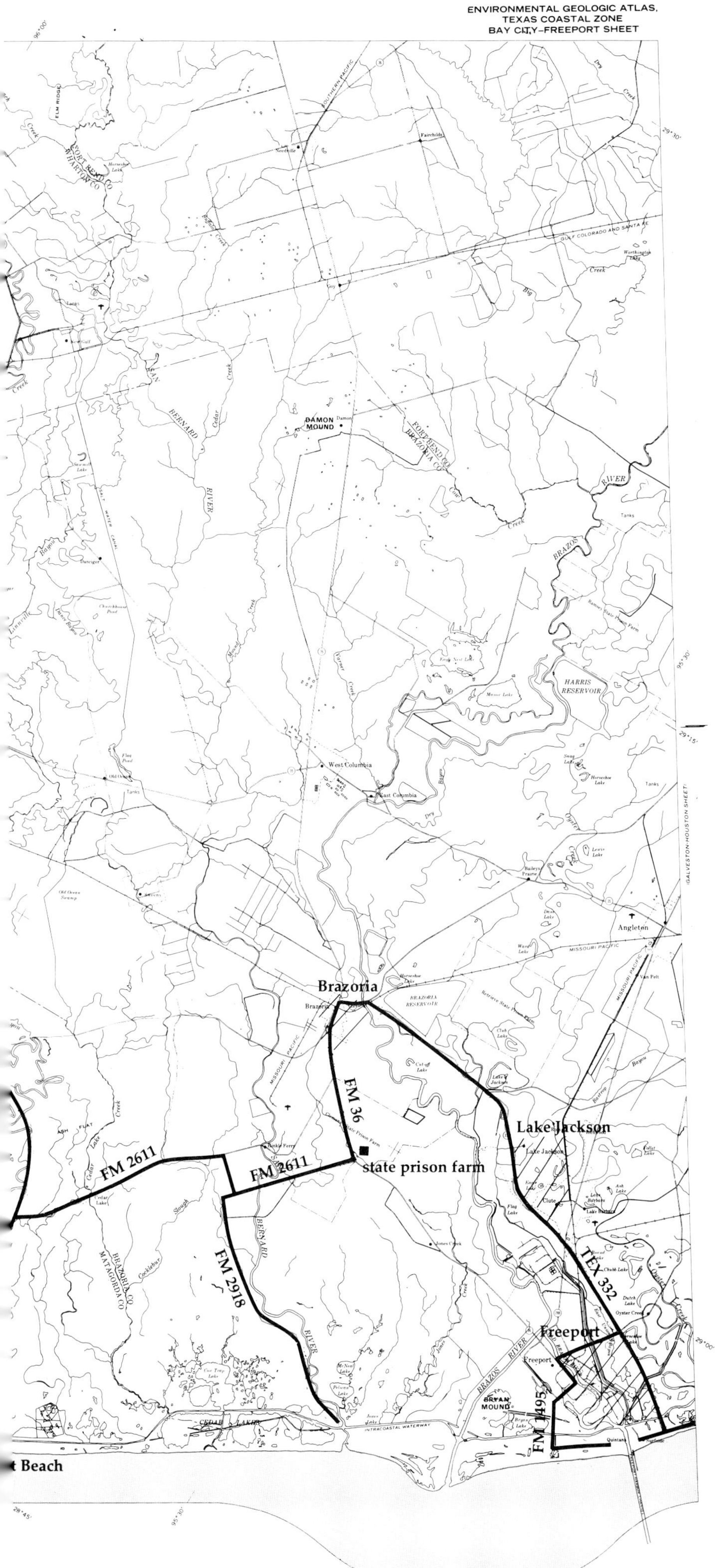

ENVIRONMENTAL GEOLOGIC ATLAS,
TEXAS COASTAL ZONE
BAY CITY–FREEPORT SHEET
Brazoria
FM 36
Lake Jackson
state prison farm
FM 2611
FM 2611
FM 2918
TEX 332
Freeport
FM 1495
BRYAN MOUND
DAMON MOUND
West Columbia
East Columbia
Angleton
HARRIS RESERVOIR
BRAZORIA RESERVOIR
INTRACOASTAL WATERWAY
t Beach

Map 2. Bay City–Freeport Area

GOLIAD CO
BEE CO

GOLIAD CO
REFUGIO CO

Refugio

MISSOURI PACIFIC

VICTORIA CO
REFUGIO CO

GREEN LAKE

MISSION LAKE

GUADALUPE BAY

TEX 113

TEX 185

REFUGIO CO
ARANSAS CO

HYNES BAY

Seadrift

COPANO BAY

TEX 35

Sea Gun

Austwell

LAMAR PENINSULA

BLACKJACK PENINSULA

ARANSAS NATIONAL WILDLIFE REFUGE

Goose Island

SAN ANTONIO BAY

CHARLES BAY

ARANSAS BAY

INTRACOASTAL WATERWAY

Bludworth Island

Sundown Bay

ARANSAS CO
CALHOUN CO

INTRACOASTAL WATERWAY

CARLOS BAY

Ayres Bay

Panther Reef

STEAMBOAT PASS

MESQUITE BAY

SOUTH PASS

ST JOSEPH ISLAND

ranch

MATAGORDA ISLAND

San Jose Island

MATAGORDA ISLAND BOMBING AND GUNN

N

G U L F   O F

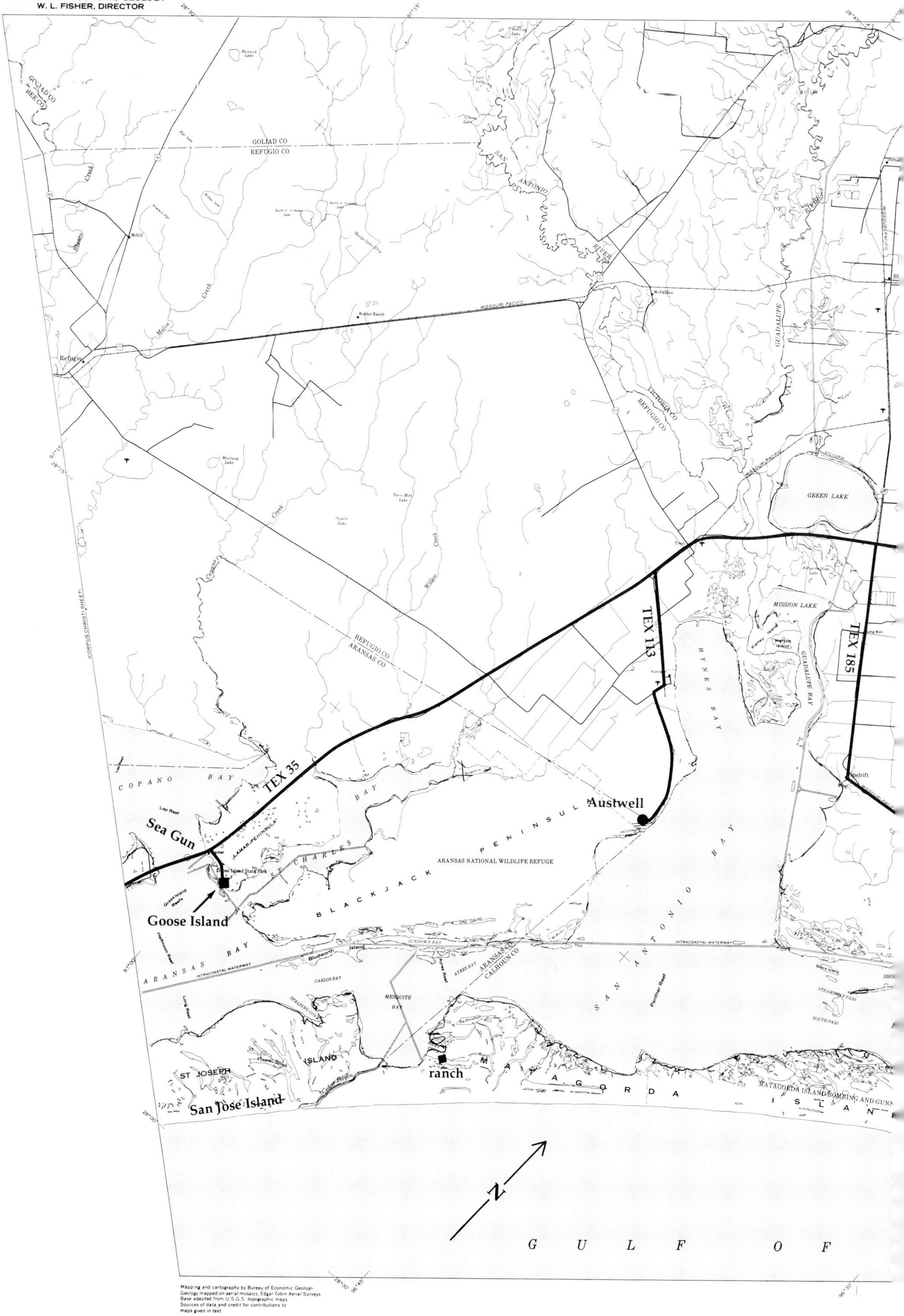

Mapping and cartography by Bureau of Economic Geology
Geology mapped on aerial mosaics, Edgar Tobin Aerial Surveys
Base adapted from U.S.G.S. topographic maps
Sources of data and credit for contributions to
maps given in text

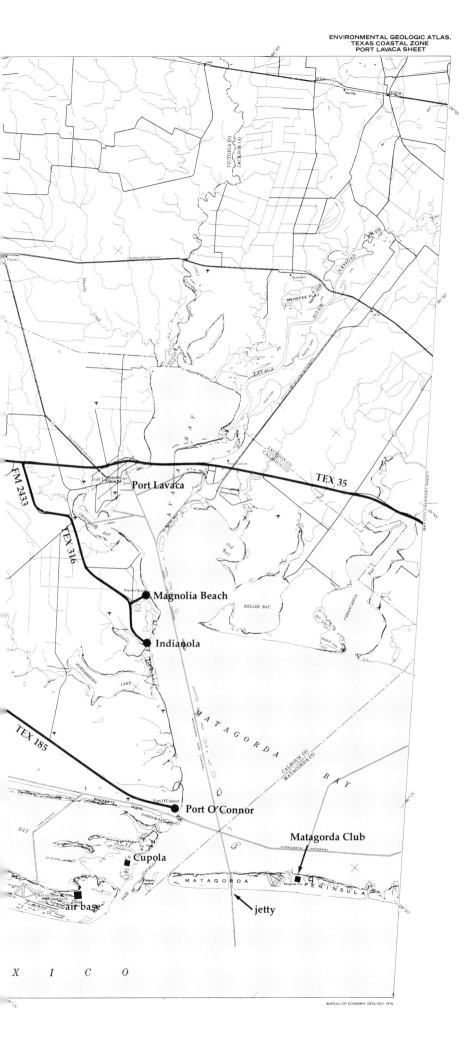

Port Lavaca

Magnolia Beach

Indianola

TEX 35

FM 2433

TEX 316

TEX 185

Port O'Connor

Matagorda Club

Cupola

air base

jetty

Map 3.   Port Lavaca Area

US 77

FM 70

TEX 44

Corpus Christi

TEX 286

CORPUS CHRISTI

Tropical Trail

TEX 358

LAGUNA LARGA

ENCINAL PENINSULA

CORPUS CHRISTI

LAGUNA   MADRE

P 22

P 53

PADRE ISLAND

MUSTANG I

National Seashore

Bob Hall Pier

jetty

GULF   OF   MEX

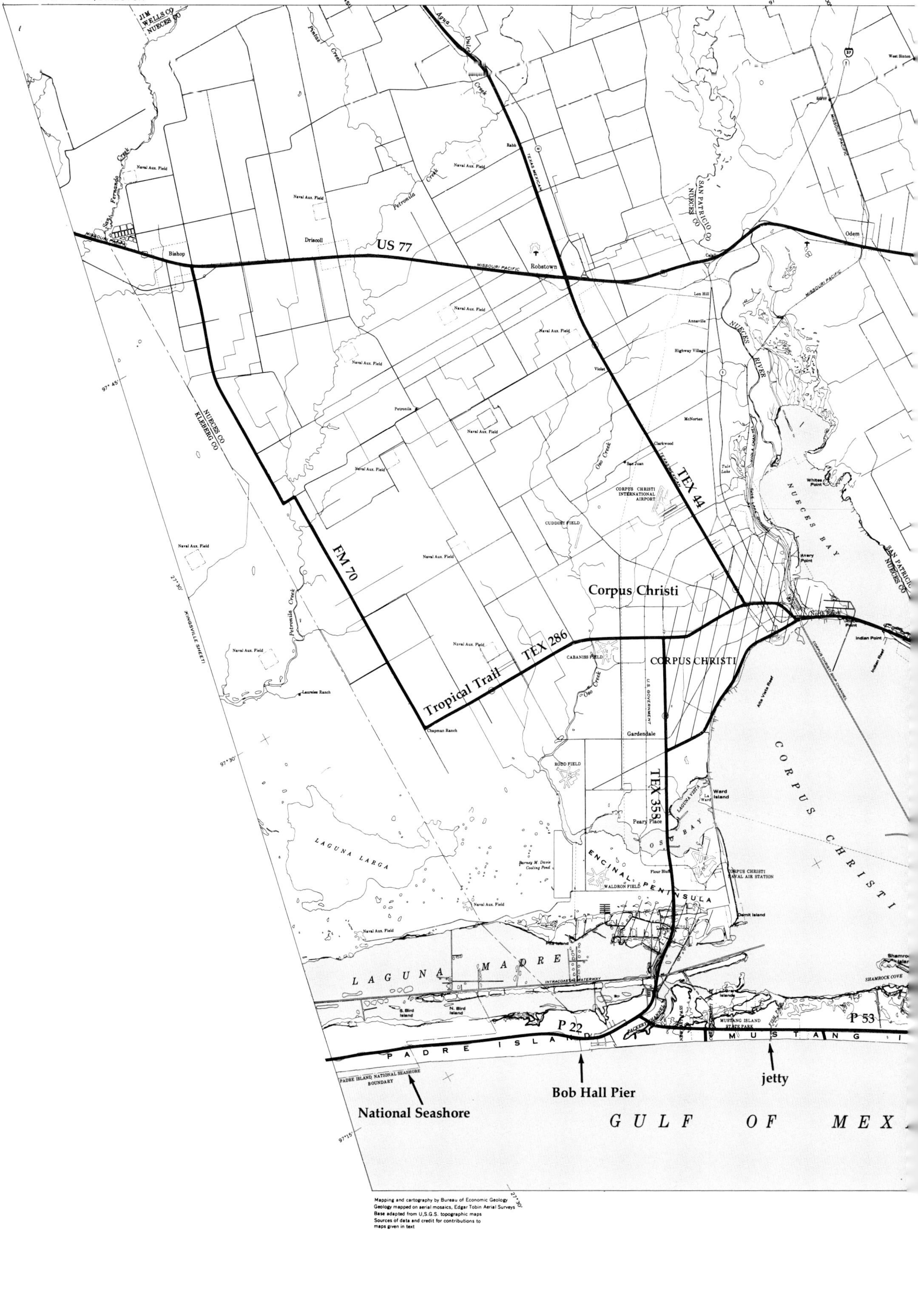

Mapping and cartography by Bureau of Economic Geology
Geology mapped on aerial mosaics, Edgar Tobin Aerial Surveys
Base adapted from U.S.G.S. topographic maps
Sources of data and credit for contributions to
maps given in text

Map 4.   Corpus Christi Area

Scale 1:250,000

2 3 4 5   10   15 Miles

26°45'   27°00'

BROOKS CO
KENEDY CO

Bell Ranch

Candelaria Lake

Cape Lake

U.S. 77

Armstrong   Mifflin

Rudolph   MISSOURI PACIFIC   Norias

97°45'

Armstrong Ranch

El Oso

King Ranch

San Pedro Ranch

Los Indios
Ranch

Marías Islands

97°30'

INTRACOASTAL WATERWAY

LAND-CUT AREA

El Toro
Island

Potrero Lozano

Potrero Farías

Potrero
de los Canales

Camentandes
Ranch

INTRACOASTAL WATERWAY

Potrero Cortado   Potrero Grande

Potrero de los Casos   Boca Nueva

MIDDLE
GROUND

PADRE ISLAND NATIONAL SEASHORE BOUNDARY

L A G U N A   M A D R E

THE HOLE

Cube Island

P A D R E   I S L A N D

BIG SHELL BEACH   BIG SHELL BEACH

PADRE ISLAND NATIONAL SEASHORE BOUNDARY

Big Shell

Yarboroug

← — N — →   G U L F   O F   M E X I

26°45'   27°00'

Mapping and cartography by Bureau of Economic Geology
Geology mapped on aerial mosaics, Edgar Tobin Aerial Surveys
Base adapted from U.S.G.S. topographic maps
Sources of data and credit for contributions to
maps given in text

Kingsville

Loyola Beach

Little Shell

Malaquite Beach

Scale 1:250,000

15 Miles

BUREAU OF ECONOMIC GEOLOGY·1972

Map 5.   Kingsville Area

MEXICO

TEXAS

US 77

Brownsville

TEX 100

port

FM 511

FM 1792

MEXICO

TEXAS

Palmito Hill

TEX 4

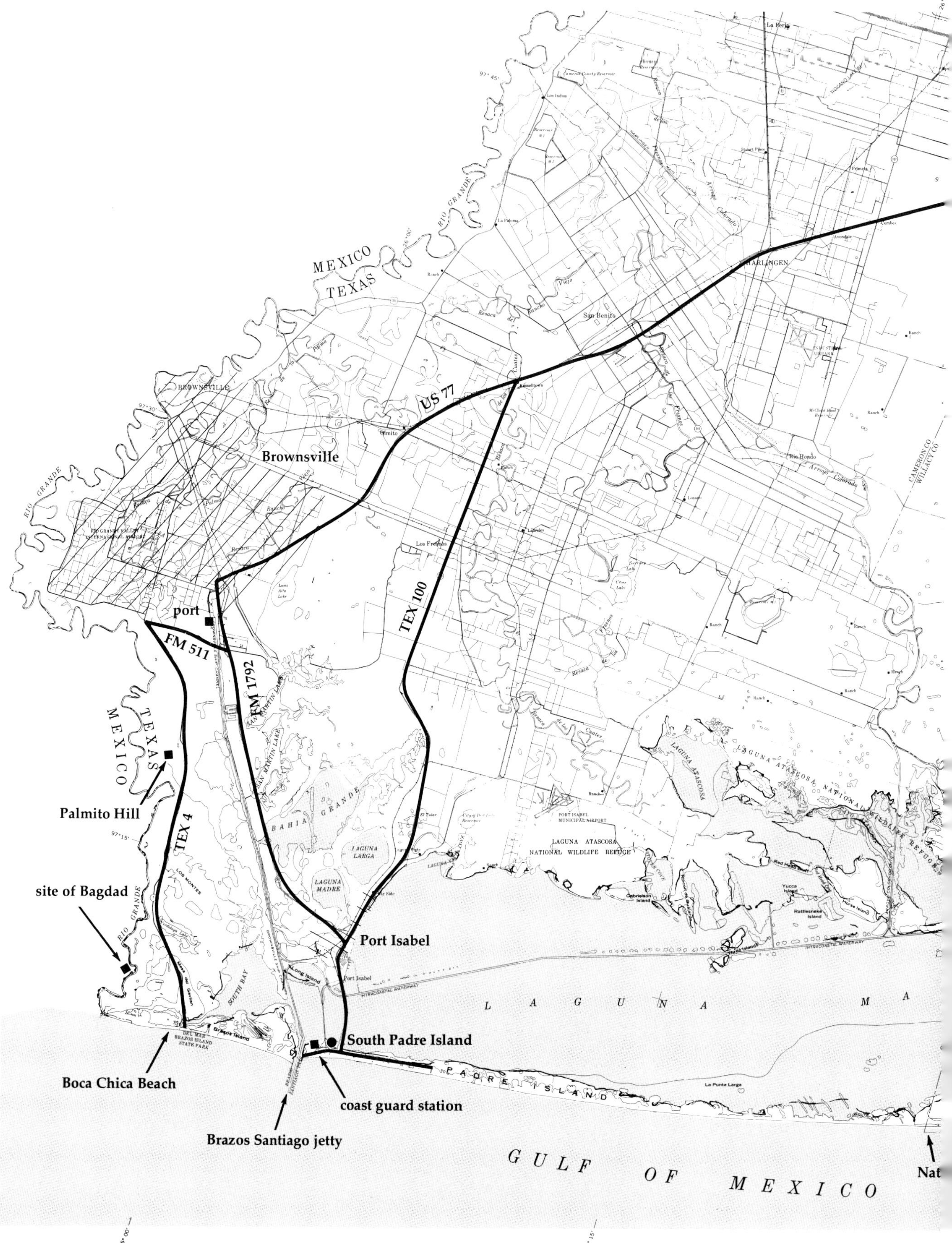

site of Bagdad

BAHIA GRANDE

LAGUNA LARGA

LAGUNA MADRE

Port Isabel

LAGUNA ATASCOSA NATIONAL WILDLIFE REFUGE

LAGUNA MADRE

Boca Chica Beach

South Padre Island

coast guard station

Brazos Santiago jetty

PADRE ISLAND

GULF OF MEXICO

Nat

Port Mansfield

te of Singer ranch

ranger station

Spanish coins

jetty

Nicaragua boiler

TEXAS

Scale 1:250,000

15 Miles

Map 6.　Brownsville-Harlingen
Area

marine biological laboratory in Rockport where welcome visitors will find aquariums filled with local fish and some Texas shells on display. The laboratory owns a notable library on mollusks that is available to the serious collector by prior arrangement. After this stop, return to Business 35 and drive to the post office. Turn south on 35 at the post office, continue for two miles, and turn left onto an unmarked street just after crossing the railroad track. This road winds to the cove, which is a good spot to look for estuarine mollusks at low tide (see Appendix E for habitat). Return to State Highway 35 by the same route and enter the shrimp-fishing port of Aransas Pass. The large shrimp-boat fleet in the harbor is always a picturesque sight. Before taking the causeway to Port Aransas try some bay collecting in the Aransas Pass–Ingleside area.

Aransas Pass has Beasley Avenue as its southern city limit. Winter low tides can make the bay end of this street most profitable for collectors. The flats here are very soft mud, making it easy to bog down to the knees; this can be dangerous to someone wearing waders. The city fathers have recently prohibited the dumping of trash that was despoiling the area, but caution is advised since the area is still used for gun target practice. To be reached by boat (a very short trip from this spot) is Ransom Island, one of the most productive shell sites in Redfish Bay. A hand dredge would be a help here, since the collecting area is the very soft mud along the grassy shores of this little island. A hurricane in the 1930's destroyed the causeway to this former resort site, but the foundations of buildings may still be seen. You will need your own boat to reach many of the other little islands that abound in the area. Pelican and Dagger islands are two of these that are great at low tide, but most of them are bird sanctuaries that cannot be visited

during the nesting season.

Go back to the entrance to Beasley Avenue and turn south on Farm Road 2725. Take samples from the drift at Ingleside Cove (look for oil storage tanks at a turn in the road). On the left is a plant where the massive off-shore drilling platforms and rigs are constructed. Retrace your steps and turn off 2725 on to Farm Road 1069. The grass flats at Bahia Azul Marina, a well-marked spot farther on this road, once the home of the emerald nerite and the spiny pen shell, have been dredged into a channel so that the boats of vacationers living in the adjoining marina may reach the Intracoastal Canal. Recently, both a fertilizer plant and a chemical complex have been built between the Reynolds Plant and Ingleside Cove, and a steel company has plans to follow suit, so it appears that the curtain is rapidly going down on bay collecting here. A turn south, off Farm Road 632 between Ingleside and Gregory, will take you past hideous piles of red sludge from bauxite ore, deposited by the nearby aluminum plant, onto a very bad road to a spot called La Quinta. Many years ago this was the headquarters of the Taft ranch and President William Howard Taft was sometimes a guest at his brother's home there. Now, the mud flats along the shore are the home of the beautiful white angel wing clam. Because of a gate placed across this road in 1968, if you want to reach the angel wing flats you will have to get prior permission from Reynolds Aluminum Company. Better still, go into Portland and find your way down to the bay to an area known as Portland Reef, between La Quinta and Sunset Lake. This is more accessible and equally as good for low-tide collecting as La Quinta. Now, let's return to Aransas Pass.

Along the causeway (State Highway 316) several spots afford good shelling, especially for those interested in the minute mollusks in

the drift. One is opposite a bait stand–restaurant, Fin and Feather, and the other is on the north side of the road at the last bait stand (the name of this one changes frequently).

After crossing on the ferry, we come to the flats on either side of the Port Aransas landing that offer good drift collecting; Cline's Point, north of the coast guard station, was once excellent at low tide but now it has been dredged and a pier has been added, while the rest of it has become inaccessible because of a private road leading to summer homes; however, the jetties are always interesting.

From Port Aransas on the northern tip of Mustang Island it is possible to explore the southern tip of San José Island on foot. In Port Aransas at the water-front bait stand and restaurant one can obtain information about a water-taxi service to the island. This is a new service and may not be regular. Look for signs to the "jetty boat." At one time it was possible to rent one of the old trucks owned by the commercial fishermen who worked on San José. If you were lucky enough to obtain a truck, the entire island could be covered in a day's combing. However, getting a car was something else because these local fishermen have little trust in the strangers who invade their once-sleepy village. At unpredictable intervals the owners of San José have invoked Article 5415d and caused the old cars and fishing huts to be removed from the island. Peace reigned between the two camps for more than ten years, but in late 1968 the owners had the collection of rusting vehicles hauled away and the shacks burned down, which put the seiners out of business for the time being and virtually eliminated the possibility of beach-combing except at either tip of the island.

Mustang Island and the northern twenty miles of Padre Island are

Fig. 41. Four-wheel-drive vehicle in the dunes near the Port Mansfield jetty on Padre Island

completely accessible to the collector in a passenger car. A paved road (Park Road 53) with numbered access roads runs down the center of Mustang Island. The beach is passable at most times, but extremely high tides and water from offshore disturbances occasionally flood the usually firm-packed beach. Natural, wind-formed cusps (ridges of sand perpendicular to the beach road) make excessive speed hazardous. Besides this natural speed hazard an alert police beach patrol also works to this end.

On spring and summer weekends after 3:00 P.M. long lines of automobiles form a creeping procession to the ferry as weary, salty, sand-coated visitors return to the mainland. The trip south down the island and over the causeway with its new high bridge, which replaced the old swing bridge at the Intracoastal Waterway, is easier than formerly but should be made other than at the peak afternoon hours.

The shores of Corpus Christi Bay along Mustang and northern Padre afford the collector opportunities to collect in grass flats that were not there in the years before the flooding of Hurricane Beulah changed the salinity regime of the area. They

are easily reached at the bridges that cross the new Water Exchange Pass, old Corpus Christi Pass, and Packery Channel. Examine the new environmental atlas (see Appendix C) for exact location of grass flats in the area that can be reached by boat.

Eighteen miles south of Port Aransas is fabulous Padre Island. Between Packery Channel and the Nueces County Park on the north end of the island much new development is taking place. Luxury hotels and apartments have been built, a marina is under construction, and residential areas are emerging on this once-barren landscape. A country club is forcing the gulls to vie with whizzing golf balls for air space.

The Bob Hall fishing pier is located in Nueces County Park, as are first aid stations, concession stands, cabanas, and other recreational facilities. Eighteen to twenty miles below the pier the sand becomes so loose that passage is possible only for a four-wheel-drive vehicle (fig. 41). There are times at low tides when the visitor will be tempted to enter this area in his automobile, but it is a foolhardy endeavor that will be rewarded with hours of backbreaking digging under the

sand-stranded car. The public-use buildings of the national seashore located at Malaquite Beach are easily reached by a paved road that terminates there. Below this area you are able to return to the shore and resume the drive over the sandy beach to the Port Mansfield jetties.

The section of Padre Island that makes up the main portion of the national seashore area, Little Shell to Port Mansfield jetty, can be visited only with a four-wheel-drive vehicle. It is seventy-eight miles from Bob Hall Pier to Port Mansfield and seventy-eight miles back over areas of loose shell and deep sand that have been severely gouged by the beach cars of adventurous anglers and other shellers. The vehicle chosen for this jaunt must be in good repair and well equipped with spare parts, gasoline, and water. Current status of conditions in this area may be investigated through the Padre Island National Seashore Area office, Box 8560, Corpus Christi, Texas 78412. Upon arrival stop at the ranger station (map 4) for free maps, safety rules, current tide and weather conditions, and interpretative information. Studies by the Department of the Interior have shown that the Gulf beach itself will tolerate diverse, high-density use. Human footprints and four-wheel-drive vehicle tracks are erased by high tides. Beyond the beach, the resource is fragile and, in several places, is highly vulnerable to even light-to-moderate use. It is imperative that further destruction of the dune vegetation be prevented and that stabilization of damaged areas be initiated. However, natural erosion will be left to heal itself rather than the Park Service undertaking a major stabilization effort. *Four-wheel-drive vehicles and dune buggies must be restricted to the beach zone.* It is important that the visitor understand the island so he will use it properly. The visitor must be kept off the foredunes to prevent erosion.

I have made the trip in as little as two and one-half hours when I was the first to travel it after a hurricane and the beach was firmly packed, but on another occasion, when it had been much in use by the many beach cars in the area during dry weather, my loaded vehicle required thirty-five gallons of gasoline for the round trip (Corpus Christi to the Port Mansfield jetty is about 98 miles) because I had to grind in the deep sand so much of the distance using the "grandma" gear.

A word of caution about travel on these islands—Matagorda, San José, and the middle of Padre are virtually uninhabited. If the beachcomber gets in trouble, he should not panic. Set up some sort of signal—fire, mirror, flag, writing in the sand—and remember that fresh-water wells for cattle run the length of the islands. The park rangers patrol the national seashore between its entrance and Little Shell from 8:00 A.M. until 10:00 P.M. daily with several weekly unscheduled trips to the Mansfield Ship Channel, when weather and Gulf tide conditions permit. After the facilities are in full operation these res-

cue services will be expanded. A paved road down the center of the island to Yarborough Pass is planned, and twelve miles of it have been completed.

Preparations for the trip should include an ample supply of water and enough food for your party, also a jack, shovel, and tow rope. Never visit these islands alone. On one occasion, after being injured when sixty-five miles down the beach, I was fortunate in being able to flag down an airplane, which landed on the beach and flew a message to a rescue party; but you might not be so lucky, especially if the tricky Texas weather finds you stranded there.

A doctor keeps regular hours at Port Aransas and there are twenty-four–hour first aid stations at Port Aransas and the county and national parks on Padre, but travel to them is slow at best. In summer months law officers, with first aid equipment and radio-controlled cars, patrol the area of beach that is passable by automobile. Ambulance service comes from Corpus Christi and Aransas Pass and can take hours. A helicopter evacuation plan is being tried for serious emergencies.

During the winter when there are fewer people on the islands, the coast guard and the park rangers have only praise for the visitor to middle Padre who calls their station before he leaves, to give his destination and an estimated time of return, and then checks in when he returns. Do not forget to call back in, for a search party will be on its way within the hour. This may seem overcautious but history has proved that anything can happen and often does on the barrier islands of Texas.

The Laguna Madre can be traveled by boat down the Intracoastal Canal, but the salinity conditions of these enclosed waters render the search for shells fruitless. The dredging of the Intracoastal Canal caused spoil islands to be built along

the canal from the vast amounts of sediments removed to deepen the waterway. These islands in the Laguna Madre are important wintering and nesting areas for waterfowl. The fishermen's cabins that once squatted on them are being removed to prevent disturbance of these nesting habitats. South Bird Island is particularly important ecologically and no recreational activity is permitted near it. Future plans call for bird observation points.

To reach the southern part of Padre Island you may leave Corpus Christi by several roads that connect with U.S. 77. Try the Tropical Trail. At Raymondville a drive over State Highway 186 and Farm Road 497 will lead you to Port Mansfield where you can go by boat to the Mansfield jetties. There are modest motels and restaurants at Port Mansfield.

Continue on U.S. 77, but turn on State Highway 100 before reaching the border city of Brownsville and take a side trip to Port Isabel. The flat coastal plain leading to the Gulf is dotted with towering yucca and sprawling prickly pear. Across the new four-lane causeway lies the recently incorporated town of South Padre Island, which is beginning to take on the look of a "little Miami Beach" with its tall resort hotels. Collectors in this area find the jetties in Isla Blanca Park, the rocks near the coast guard station, and the grass flats between the two causeways fruitful at low tide. Everything in this well-developed area can be reached by car except the beach drive north to the Mansfield jetties; for this a four-wheel-drive vehicle is necessary. To get to the last of the islands, Brazos, one must leave Port Isabel on Farm Road 1792, which also has markings for State Highway 48. This road follows the Brownsville ship channel with such sights as the colorful shrimping fleet and ocean-going vessels breaking the flatness of the alluvial vista.

Continue to the crossing of Farm Road 511 and turn left to reach Boca Chica Road (on State Highway 4), which returns to the Gulf at Boca Chica Beach.

While you are in the area you may find it worthwhile to cross the border at Brownsville into Matamoros for a trip to the Mexican beach south of the Rio Grande. Before going into the town ask for directions to Playa Lauro Villar (formerly Washington Beach—which was an appropriate name for the beach nearest to the United States). Things change so fast in this border town I do not dare direct you to the beach myself.

Check all this information against the most recent road map. We live in a world of constant change.

Equipment

Special permits and elaborate equipment are not necessary for collecting in Texas. The seasoned collector usually has his favorite essentials, but the beginner will find the following to be handy.

Sun glasses: the glare on the white sand and the water is blinding.
Sun hat: the Texas sun can produce painful burns even on a cloudy day.
Canvas shoes: broken shell, bottles, and cans buried in the sand can be a hazard to bare feet.
Long-sleeved shirt and pants: even if a tan is desired the skin can stand only so much.
Pockets: either built-in or added apron fashion.
Plastic bucket: a light-weight carryall.
Pill bottles, vials, small cotton bags: for small and special specimens.
Plastic bags: for collecting drift or wrapping messy material.
Trowel: for digging in the sand and mud or lifting the layer of drift from the sand.
Small strainer or wire-bottomed boxes: for sifting shells from sand and mud.
Tweezer or toothpicks: to pick up minute shells (wet the end of the toothpick).
Notebook and pencil: to record data.
Thread or string: to tie valves together.
Waders, rubber boots, and thermal underwear: since winter brings the best collecting, these items will make the northers bearable.
Mask, snorkle, and diving gear: to look along the jetties.

Fig. 42. Rigged out for collecting in the bays during a December norther

When and Where to Look

Like fishermen, shell collectors have their favorite haunts and many are reluctant to reveal their trade secrets. However, a few fundamentals can act as a guide to obtaining a representative sample of the shells in Texas waters. Abbott (1958*a*) has said that there are four ingredients to securing good shells:
1. A knowledge of the habits of mollusks
2. A familiarization with the physical conditions of the ocean and seashore
3. A sensible choice of collecting equipment
4. A large proportion of perseverance
A familiarity with the first three of these may be acquired from this book or a similar reference, but the last will come only after hours in the field or at the microscope. The more common forms of shells may be easy to come by for any beachcomber, but the true collector seeks the living shell in its natural habitat (see Appendix E).

If one is fortunate enough to visit the open Gulf beach following a storm or hard freeze, the shore may be strewn with shells that normally live offshore. On an ordinary day, these sparsely inhabited shores may seem unproductive to casual beachcombers. The knowing collector, however, does not pass up a waterlogged piece of wood, for here dwell many boring shells. The tangle of yellow and red sea whip coral will reward the person who stops to shake it (fig. 43)—a tiny yellow *Simnialena* and other such gifts from the sea may drop out. That barnacle-covered coconut or clump of bamboo roots may have a rare tropical species attached. Shore collecting is rewarding in direct proportion to the regularity and persistence of the search. That happy coincidence of time and tide which brings a rare treasure is unpredictable.

The bays and back waters will provide more rewarding collecting any time of the year. On these mud and sand flats the trail of a snail may be followed or the siphon hole of a buried clam investigated. One soon learns to distinguish what animal he is tracking by the type of trail left in the sand (fig. 44). For example, the unbroken line left by the dragging shell of a hermit crab is bordered on either side by rows of dots made by the crab's legs. A snail's track will not have the pattern of dots. Many species are more active on a cloudy day or at night. Many inhabitants of the tidal flats are more in evidence about half an hour after the tide has begun to rise.

Pay attention to the winds, currents, seasons, and tides. Normally, in Texas the winter months are the most productive on the open beaches, but a hurricane during the early fall can bring a windfall of shells. The windy days of March and April drive the pelagic (floating) forms, such as the purple sea snail, to shore. After a quiet tide many small specimens may be encountered in the drift line along the edges of the ship channels and the bays. Wading along the bay edges and raising and examining submerged broken shell, bottles, rocks, and timber often produce fascinating results. Examine any attached algae. Always remember to return the rock or shell to its former position in order not to disturb the ecology of the area.

Another conservation note— don't take more than you need from

Fig. 43. A beached mass of the sea whip coral, *Leptogorgia setacea*, the home of the little yellow or red *Simnialena marferula*

A

B

C

Fig. 44. Trails along a shore:
A. the wide path produced by the plowing motion of *Polinices duplicatus*
B. a raccoon leaves its paw prints after a meal of clams
C. a cerith worms its way across the wet sand
D. a hermit crab in a *Thais* shell traces its punctured trail beside the tracks of a wading bird
E. foot prints of a shore bird beside a row of holes left by its beak as it pursued a mud snail
F. the furrowed path of the mud snail, *Nassarius vibex*
G. live tellins stranded on the beach after a low tide
H. Tellina alternata tayloriana digging in after being stranded
I. trail made by a stranded Taylor's tellin

D

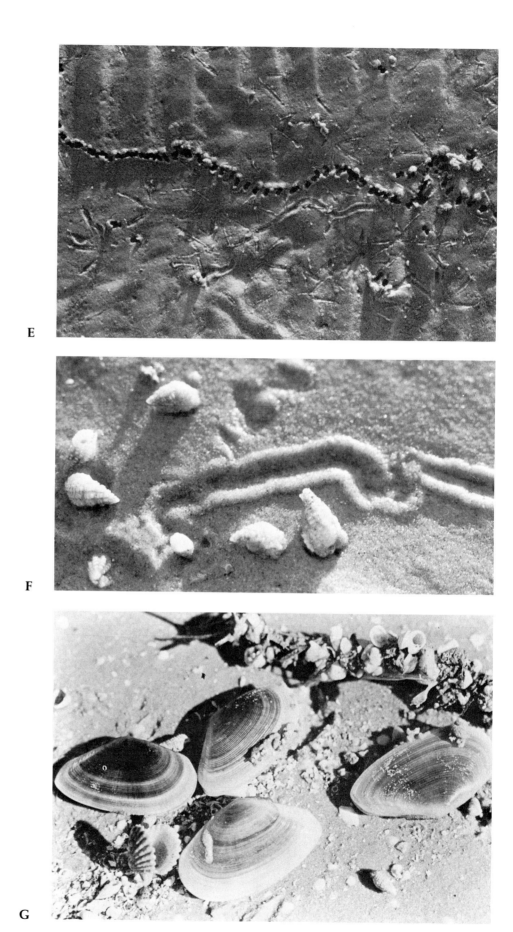

E

F

G

H

I

A

a site where specimens are living. On the open beach where shells have been stranded by the waves, take all you want; these are already doomed and the waves will carry them back to the sea after they are dead. But when you find an exposed flat where *Busycon* and *Mercenaria* are popping up, leave some to repopulate the area. It is hard to understand why some people want a bucket of live whelks. A beautiful specimen or two for your collection should be enough. When you start cleaning all those you lugged home you will probably wish you had left them in the bay or inlet in the first place. It is very sad to watch a shell club on a field trip to a new area practically denude it in one day's hunt. Vast beds of clams like those found in other areas are not the rule in Texas. The collecting of mollusks is not regulated by law in Texas as it is in some other states—do not abuse the privilege. Leave the living in an undisturbed habitat.

Use of the tide tables published annually by the Coast and Geodetic Survey is most beneficial in determining the lowest tides of the year. These tables may be purchased from the United States Department

of Commerce or from a marine supply company. Local newspapers also publish daily tide times and moon phases.

Certain species associate with definite types of environment. For example, the lovely angel wing lives in hard mud flats. The habitat of each species is given with its description in the charts in Appendix E. Work is about to be completed on a set of environmental geologic maps, which are the result of twenty years of research along the Texas coast by the Bureau of Economic Geology of the University of Texas at Austin. The maps will be a most welcome addition to the growing literature on the Texas coast and will facilitate study of the area in the future. In the set the map giving environments and biologic assemblages is of special interest to the shell collector (see Appendix C). To facilitate reference, the six maps of the coast in this chapter are based on these maps.

More than half the shells found in Texas are minute; thus good eyes, a hand lens, or a microscope are needed to identify them. Drift may be taken home to be picked over when you have more time or when

the TV is broken; but be careful, you may become an addict. Trying to identify the tiny shells can be more challenging and frustrating than solving a Russian crossword puzzle or tracing your family tree, and the satisfaction more rewarding when you finally identify a confusing little fellow. First, however, you must gather beach drift.

Beach drift is that unassuming-looking fine rubble or trash deposited by the waves along the high-water line (fig. 45). Usually the last high-water line will hold the richest assortment. Scrape the drift up with your hand or a trowel and put it in plastic bags or a plastic bucket. When you get home wash it with fresh water to remove all traces of salt. Salt left on these tiny shells will eventually cause complete deterioration. Screen the drift through strainers, either homemade or laboratory models. Mine are a nest of simple redwood boxes with rust-resistant wire bottoms in three sizes—hardware cloth, window-screen wire, and marine filter mesh. The washing and screening operations can be done simultaneously.

After your drift is screened and washed, spread it to dry on an old

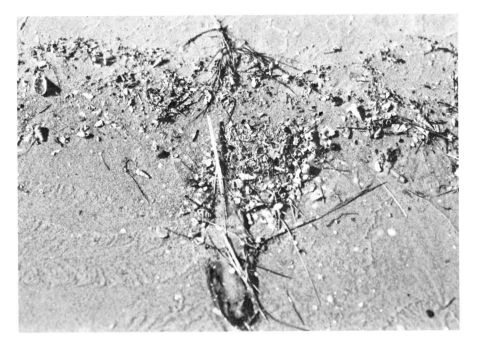

Fig. 45. Beach drift:
A. a collector using a trowel to collect fine drift from the high-tide line along the open Gulf beach to be sorted later under a microscope
B. close-up of beach drift along an inlet area

sheet or other piece of fabric—paper comes apart when wet. The drift must be completely dry before it can be sorted. Do not attempt to dry it in the oven because small particles of asphalt that are present on all Texas beaches will melt and ruin your material. A magnifying glass or microscope (dissecting type) is needed for the sorting. The specimens can be picked up with a wet finger or a damp, fine (no. 000), sable brush. You will soon develop your own method for handling this operation.

In recent years skin diving or scuba diving along the jetties and wharves has become a popular pastime; however, this can be a very dangerous undertaking unless the diver is properly trained, well equipped, and accompanied by another diver. Courses are given at regular intervals at the Corpus

Christi YMCA for those interested in learning this sport. Skin diving has proved very beneficial to science, and marine biology students are using diving as a method of collecting and observing. With the invention of the aqualung much new territory has been opened to the diving scientist. Many species of mollusks once considered to be rare are now more easily obtained by divers.

A mask, fins, and snorkel would be of great help to the collector on a Texas jetty. Choose only simple, rugged, compact equipment that is properly fitted and comfortable. Jetty diving is not a sport for a person alone or the untrained, for the jetties are very treacherous at times as a result of tidal currents sweeping through the passes and currents set up by passing ocean-going vessels. A study of the currents and

tides must be made before a diving trip is planned. It is, however, worth all the trouble to train and equip one's self to see the brightly colored soft corals, the spiny sea urchins, the glowing tunicates, an olive shell plowing under the sand at the base of the jetties, or a shy octopus in a crevice in the rocks.

To me, dredging is unrewarding in proportion to the work and expense involved and it will not be discussed here as a form of collecting. Those interested in attempting dredging can learn from a discussion of the methods and equipment in *American Seashells* by R. Tucker Abbott (1958*a*) or at greater length by reading the benthic sampling methods detailed by Holme (1964). This is a difficult and backbreaking procedure; I leave it to the organized research group.

Cleaning

Cleaning your shell is of great importance, since a beautiful specimen, improperly preserved, can quickly become an unlovely thing. First, consider the mollusk that is taken alive.

Many types of mollusks may be cleaned by simply boiling them and then removing the soft parts. Start them in cold water with a folded piece of cloth on the bottom of the pan to reduce breakage. Boil slowly

until the flesh is firm or the clam has opened. Cool to lukewarm before washing. Boil only a few shells at a time and remove the bodies immediately when cool enough to handle because cooling causes the body to contract and shrink up into the shell. A corkscrew motion will usually get all the soft parts from the winding snail shell. If the visceral portion of the body breaks off, a few drops of 5 percent formalin (formaldehyde gas dissolved in water) placed in the shell will eliminate bad odors. The formalin should then be removed; no shell should be stored in a solution of formaldehyde, because of the destructive action it has on the shell itself. Dental tools, nut picks, and wires are handy for the body-removing operation.

Some highly polished shells like *Strombus*, *Oliva*, or *Cypraea* will craze if boiled. The animals in porcelaneous shells can be killed by placing them in fresh water. Most can then be picked clean, but some are stubborn. These may be dehydrated in the refrigerator. Wrap each shell in a paper towel with extra thickness next to the aperture and place with the aperture down in the refrigerator for a week. At this time the animal should come out easily. If it does not, do not soak it in anything, for this type of shell waterspots easily. Dry it carefully and allow it to sit with the aperture up until the remaining animal has dried up and can be shaken out.

The true collector wants to preserve the operculum or "trap door" of the operculate shell. Not all snails have an operculum, but they are an interesting feature of many. Mark them in some way so that you keep the correct operculum with its own shell. When these have been dried they may be glued in their natural position after the thoroughly clean shell has been stuffed with cotton.

Tiny snails are best preserved by allowing them to remain out of water until they die (fresh water will make them withdraw far into the shell) and then placing them in a solution of 70 percent ethyl, or grain, alcohol or 50 percent methyl or isopropyl alcohol. If they are placed directly in the alcohol the animal will contract and draw the operculum into a position where it will not be visible. After several days in the solution the small snail shells may be drained and spread to dry before storing.

The bivalves or clams are cleaned in the same way, taking care not to break the ligament that holds the two sections together. Many collectors prefer that the shell be dried closed in its natural position. After the soft parts are removed, cotton string is wrapped around the closed valves until the ligament dries. Rubber bands, adhesive tape, and other tapes may prove disastrous. Heat causes the rubber to melt and the adhesive coating on the tape comes off, leaving a hard-to-remove residue on the once-beautiful shell. Other collectors prefer that the bivalve be dried in a butterfly position so that the interior is visible. If one is fortunate enough to have several specimens, it is desirable to dry the clam in both positions. William J. Clench, the editor of *Johnsonia*, recommends preserving bivalves in a solution of four parts alcohol and one part glycerine to keep the periostracum and ligament soft and pliable. An occasional dab of glycerine on the ligament will prevent it from becoming brittle.

The fastidious collector may want to clean off all the foreign matter that is attached to the outside of the shell. This again is a matter of taste, as many desire their shells in the natural state with the exterior uncleaned. It is a good idea to have an example of a cleaned and an uncleaned shell in your collection because cleaning often reveals hidden beauty.

A stiff brush is usually enough to do the job of cleaning. Growth that cannot be removed with the brush can often be removed with a sharp pointed instrument, such as an awl, a knife, or a dental tool. The limey deposits can prove quite stubborn and often one must resort to muriatic acid. Experience has proved that this job must be done with running water at hand. The shell is held with forceps and *quickly* dipped into full-strength acid, then immediately held under running water. Extreme caution must be used with this method. The acid is a poison and can burn your skin. Use it only as a last resort. Apertures and delicate parts of the shell can be coated with melted paraffin to protect them from the acid. Shells overcleaned with acid take on an unnatural sheen and can be spotted a yard away in a shell shop. The composition of shells varies; some will withstand the acid and others, like the lion's paw, will dissolve immediately when put in contact with the powerful caustic. The exterior may also be cleaned with ethyl acetate, a chemical which will not attack the calcium carbonate. It is purchased by the gallon from chemical companies (*Texas Conch.* 8[2]:17).

Often the shell is covered with vegetation and sponge that can be removed by the use of household chlorine compounds. The chlorine will not dissolve the calcium of the shell as do muriatic acid and formalin, but it does have a tendency to bleach the shell if contact is maintained over too long a period. (A note from experience: extended use of chlorine will dissolve your fingernails.)

The following method is not recommended as an enjoyable pastime, but in some cases it may prove necessary. Delicate shells like the purple sea snail may be cleaned by "watering." Place them overnight in fresh water and then rinse away the fleshy parts. This procedure may need to be repeated several times. A word of warning—change the water daily or more often. The decomposition of the animal's body forms corrosives that dull the surface of the shell if it is allowed to remain in the same water for too long a period.

After the shell is cleaned, its natural luster may be restored by rubbing a thin coating of some type of greasy substance on it. Vegetable fats become sticky with age; it is best to use mineral oil, baby oil, or vaseline. Store oiled shells in closed cabinets to avoid the accumulation of dust on the coated surfaces. Most collectors shudder at the thought of a shell that has been coated with varnish or shellac or overcleaned with acids. Don't kill the shell with kindness. A shell carefully cleaned to preserve its natural beauty can be a joy forever.

A word on traveling with a collection of live caught specimens; you may develop your own method but until you do let me recommend a method learned the hard way. Leave the animal in the shell and wrap the individual shell with newspaper, protecting the lip with extra thickness and stuffing the aperture firmly. If paper towels or tissue are available, they work well for the stuffing. Place the wrapped shell in a plastic bag and tie tightly. Plastic garbage-can liners are good for putting several wrapped specimens together and are stronger than smaller bags. Small specimens may be packed in plastic jars in a 30 percent alcohol solution. Carry the whole mess in a garbage can with a tightly fitting lid or cover the top lightly with plastic before putting the lid on. Plan to bring the materials you will use with you from home. Not every place has newspaper. Decomposition of sea life, especially in the Texas climate, is rapid and odorous. In other words, it will stink quickly.

One trip without proper preparation will be enough. A return trip from the west coast of Mexico was ghastly; even the customs agents passed our car without coming near to examine it, waving us on as quickly as possible.

Preserving

In some instances it may be desirable to relax the animal so that its soft parts are preserved in a lifelike manner without excessive contraction or distortion. Magnesium chloride is the anesthetic most highly recommended for marine animals. Try 75 grams of $MgCl_2$ in a liter of fresh water mixed with an equal volume of sea water. If the animal has not been in the solution for more than twelve hours, it may be revived in normal sea water. However, the most readily available material for relaxing is menthol crystals. A few crystals of menthol are added to the water covering the mollusks in a small bottle. Two or three drops of a saturated solution of menthol in 95 percent alcohol may be used. The specimens should be kept cool and undisturbed while being narcotized. After several hours (6 to 48, depending on the number and size of the animals and the volume of water used), to be sure the specimens are insensitive to strong stimuli, such as probing, one or two should be carefully tested in the killing fluid before the entire lot is transferred. It is well to leave them in the menthol for an hour after they become insensitive to the stimuli. If they are left too long, however, the tissue will deteriorate, making the specimens useless for micromorphological studies. When the snails are fully relaxed, the water should be replaced with 5 percent formalin. After a day or so, they can be transferred to 70 percent alcohol. To preserve color in nudibranchs and other opisthobranchs, use an antioxidant (Ionol C.P.-40) 0.3 percent by volume in a solution of 5 percent formalin in sea water (Abbott 1974, p. 349). Each lot of specimens must be accompanied by a data label. Other methods are described by Runham et al. (1956), Emerson and Ross (1965), Rudloe (1971), and Malek and Cheng (1974, p. 366).

Storing

The storing of a sea shell collection presents special problems. Although properly cleaned sea shells do not deteriorate, they do tend to fade in direct sunlight and extreme heat. This feature, combined with their variety of size and shape, makes the shell collection hard to store.

There are several types of collections—the whatnot shelf, the display cabinet, the study collection, the aquarium, and the photograph collection. The first is usually the outcome of a summer's beachcombing by the beginner or it may be an auxiliary to the study collection. The second is generally found in museums, clubs, or libraries and even homes. It is planned for visual appeal, is not overcrowded, is well labeled, has good lighting, and contains choice specimens. The study collection is housed more compactly with the catalog number, scientific name, date found, and location recorded for each specimen.

In a study collection it is essential to record carefully the depth of water, special conditions, occurrence, substratum, and date when the specimen was secured. A shell that cannot be given a definite locality adds no value to a collection. (Not just "Texas" but "beach drift, near jetties, Port Aransas, Nueces Co., Texas.")

The importance of locality data cannot be overemphasized. The potentially valuable material I collected as a novice was unwittingly lost to science because of improper

Fig. 46. Cataloging a shell collection: catalog, vial for small shells with label inside, slide for minute shells, and label to accompany larger specimens.

or careless locality information. Do not trust your memory—jot it down. Distribution maps of the area in which you are collecting can be made by placing dots on standard maps. Without maps, the locality should be accurate to within a quarter of a mile. An example of the importance of this information—in order to avoid frustrating and time-consuming search—is a paper which cited *Busycon perversum* as being from "Obregón, Mexico." The *International Atlas* showed the only two Obregón's to be inland towns. It was not until much valuable time had elapsed that it was determined that the location cited was intended to refer to the fishing port near the Yucatán Peninsula—Puerto Alvaro Obregón, Tabasco, Mexico.

Small plastic pill bottles and gelatin capsules are handy for storing the smaller specimens and may be obtained in a variety of sizes from your pharmacist. Labels made on biological paper withstand time as well as liquid preservatives. Corrugated paper linings in the storage drawers will prevent small bottles and vials from rolling about. Modular plastic boxes with a plastic container to hold a group of them can be ordered from Althor Products, 2301 Benson Avenue, Brooklyn, New York 11214. This company's catalog illustrates a great many types of plastic containers. The tiny shells are best housed in slides. I prefer the micropaleontological slides with glass covers and metal slide holders that can be ordered from W. H. Curtin & Co., P.O. Box 1546, Houston, Texas 77001.

Larger specimens can be stored in drawers with small boxes for dividers. Avoid the use of cotton because it clings to rough surfaces and is difficult to remove. A little more trouble but worthwhile is lining the drawers with a thick (dependent on drawer depth and shell thickness) layer of foam rubber or styrofoam. Using an X-acto knife or razor blade cut a berth to house each individual shell. The drawer is beautiful to look at and chipping is kept to a minimum because the shells never touch each other or jiggle around.

A catalog list in a notebook or a card file is a necessity to prevent the loss of the valuable locality data (fig. 46). You will want to record the precise location, the date, and many other data. The method of collection is important, too. Not all this information can be attached to each shell, hence a numbering system must be used for ease in locating the recorded data. Whatever system is used, you will assign to each shell a specific number. This number can be written in an inconspicuous place on the larger shells with india ink and a fine pen. The Rapidograph pen is excellent for this job and also for recording in your catalog or notebook. Water will not smear dry india ink. Smaller shells can have a number affixed to their containers or written on the slides.

I prefer the double-entry type of catalog, but it is only one of many systems. With it, acquisitions are first entered as received, the number is placed on the shell or its container. Separate localities may be indicated by letters that are added to the numbers. The second entry is in an alphabetical listing of the genera. Care must be taken to allow space between the names for future additions. The numbers are entered opposite the individual species but are not consecutive. Use a loose leaf notebook for this catalog. An excellent paper by Emerson and Ross of the American Museum of Natural History (1965) gives much additional information on the techniques of preparing and cataloging invertebrate specimens.

Aquariums

Salt-water aquarium collectors are a growing breed and are adding much to our knowledge of the habits of marine mollusks by their patient observations. The mollusks' natural resistance to drying will usually permit you to carry them home safely in a small amount of sea water. However, a few added precautions will increase your chances of success. Use only covered containers that have no metal parts, such as styrofoam ice chests. It is important to keep them cool and shaded. An inexpensive, battery-powered aerator with an air stone (from a sporting goods department or an aquarium dealer) will provide needed oxygen. If the trip home is to be long, add fresh salt water occasionally because salt water pollutes rapidly. Handle only with nonmetal equipment.

The basic problems to be solved are pollution, feeding, disease, rust, and corrosion. Of these, corrosion from metal is the most critical. Even condensation on metal aquarium lights dripping into the aquarium can be deadly. The correct selection of a tank will solve some of these problems. An ideal marine aquarium is all glass with a plastic cover to slow evaporation, but those constructed of plywood coated with fiberglass and having a glass front or a plastic or lucite vat are acceptable. All are preferable to the stainless-steel and glass aquarium. The cement on this type of container reacts with the salt water to form a poison, and the salt corrodes the metal creating another toxin to seep into the water. The metal can be coated with an epoxy paint but it will corrode, regardless of the manufacturer's claim.

Once you have the proper tank the next step is a subsand filter, which acts as a false bottom under the sand. It aerates, filters, removes food particles that might decompose, and permits the use of sand without the dangerous formation of toxic gases. Choose a filter with holes small enough to prevent sand from passing through them. It is highly recommended that an outside filter be used in conjunction with the undergravel filter to ensure water quality. If polyester fiber is used with these filters it may not be necessary to rework your tank more than once a year.

Due to the nature of the creatures you will keep in your aquarium, an air pump is necessary to provide oxygen and a moderate current. They will also need some sun or equivalent artificial light, but not too much. Place the tank in a draft-free location that will receive some sun every day but not in strong or direct sunlight, for sunlight encourages the growth of algae. You must also remember that most marine animals live in crevices or reefs or under the sand and are light sensitive.

All equipment used in a marine aquarium must be sterilized. To do this, soak the article (pump, shell, coral, etc.) for several days in fresh water to which three tablespoons of table salt have been added. This removes surface oils. Then rinse thoroughly in fresh water and dry thoroughly in the sun for several weeks before adding them to the aquarium. If your hands must go in the aquarium make certain they are free of soap, hand lotion, oil, rings, and other things that will contaminate the water.

Beach sand is too full of organisms to be used in your aquarium. Choose a builder's sand or some of the nice broken shell from the beach at Big Shell and wash it several times with fresh water in a plastic or enamel bucket. Do not have it over one and one-half inches deep and make certain all air bubbles are removed before adding specimens.

The temperature in the tank should be kept constant between seventy and eighty degrees. If it happens to get over ninety degrees,

Fig. 47. Aquarium observation: This series of the gastropod *Fasciolaria lilium* was raised by Manette Wilson of Corpus Christi in a twenty-gallon salt-water aquarium. The larger female (*next to the rock*) was found stranded on the beach of Mustang Island. Later the smaller male (*next*) was found and added to the aquarium. Following mating, the female constructed vase-shaped egg cases which were attached to a rock over a period of three months. After fifty-eight days the young began to crawl from the gaping egg cases. Within a month 125 snails had been hatched. Those that survived reached a length of 2½ inches the following year.

cool the water with ice, and if it drops under sixty degrees place a heater nearby. Marine animals are able to stand changes in temperature if they are gradual. During warm weather increased aeration is indicated.

A glass cover will prevent your specimens from leaving the tank and will retard evaporation. Extra sea water may be stored for long periods in a glass container in a darkened location. Collect, transport, and store the natural sea water in a nonmetallic container. Filter the water as thoroughly as possible to remove all organic material that might cause the water to foul during storage. Artificial sea water is used with success by many. Also, a fairly constant density (specific gravity) should be maintained. Sea water is heavier than distilled water and evaporation causes the density to increase. The ideal specific gravity is 1.020. Your aquarium dealer will have special hydrometers with which you can measure the density of the water.

When you add a specimen to the

aquarium try not to excite it. Keep it in a small amount of the water in which it was transported and add a cup of water from the tank every fifteen minutes until it is acclimated. Using clean hands or a nonmetallic tool, slowly transfer one specimen at a time to the aquarium. If you have too many specimens you may have to add an air stone. Artificial salt water requires even more care when adding specimens.

Feeding is not the problem it once was; however, overfeeding with failure to remove the excess food particles can present a serious situation. If available, feed the snails a small, live clam every month. You may keep ground clam, oyster, or snail in your freezer to feed to your carnivorous snails. When a supply is abundant, chop it in a blender and place it in an ice cube tray. These frozen cubes are easily added to the tank. A snail does not require frequent feeding, and often after a big meal it will bury itself for days only to emerge with a new growth of shell. Some creatures require algae for food. Small rocks covered with algae or pieces of the seaweed *Ulva* will give herbivorous species something to feed on. Fish eat three to four times a day, but if there are algae in the tank for them to browse on you will only need to feed them in the morning and evening. Do not attempt to grow algae without a subsand filter. Solem (1974, p. 271) gives more extensive information on the care and feeding of mollusks. Also see Appendix E.

A variety of species adds interest to your aquarium, but if you have live clams or scallops in your tank they may become the dinner of a starfish, snail, or crab. Anemones devour any hapless little mollusk, such as a *Cyphoma*, that might come within their reach.

The main causes of aquarium failure are
1. Specimens introduced too quickly
2. Soiled hands in contact with the specimens or water
3. Insufficient aeration
4. Specimens in poor condition when added
5. Painting or spraying in the home
6. Insecticides

However, if you get all this working you can have many pleasurable hours observing the antics of your aquarium's inhabitants. Remember to make notes and sketches of the behavior of these creatures; you may be observing an activity never before recorded. An example of the type of study to be made with an aquarium is illustrated in the growth series shown in figure 47.

Other Collecting Activities

New developments in 35-mm camera lenses make it possible for the camera bug to photograph his collection. This hobby is expensive because the initial equipment is costly; however, collectors so equipped could add greatly to our store of information concerning the various characteristics of the mollusk. These high-quality lenses are often more sensitive than the human eye peering through a microscope and the photograph allows several people to examine the same feature of a specimen under great magnification. The opportunity to photographically record actions of the mollusk living in an aquarium should not be overlooked. Very technical books are written on macro- and microphotography for those interested, but unless you have the patience of a saint do not bother to equip yourself for this type of photography.

The photographs in this book were made by Jean Bowers Gates and me. Mrs. Gates used an Exakta VX II B single-lens reflex camera with an F/2 Zeiss panacolor 50-mm and an F/3.5 Leitz summaron 35-mm lens to produce individual shell shots. Others were made by me using a Nikon F. with Nikon Auto 50-mm F/1.4 lens for the situation shots and the Micro-Nikor for the micromollusks. Both of us added bellows and mounted our cameras on stationary copy stands except in the field. Kodak Panatomic X film developed with Rodinal and printed on Polycontrast paper was found to give the most satisfactory results. The color photographs were made by me with high-speed Ektachrome film.

In taking pictures of extremely high magnification the two main problems encountered are vibration and limited depth of field. The first is more easily overcome than the second. High magnification reduces the depth of field to practically zero and, with a three-dimensional subject like a shell, this can lead to total failure. Lighting can also be difficult and time consuming. For these photographs two side lights were used with reflectors and diffusers when needed; each shell was then individually lighted to bring out its significant characteristics.

Many illustrated references are available for use in identifying your collection (see the Bibliography). The Corpus Christi Museum maintains a labeled display of Texas shells and has a study collection of the smaller species that may be viewed on request. The national seashore office has a display and will have more when the facilities are completed. There is a study collection at the University of Texas Marine Science Institute at Port Aransas and another at the Texas Parks and Wildlife Marine Laboratory in Rockport. Special arrangements must be made in advance to use both these collections. The Brazosport Museum of Natural Science in Lake Jackson also has a beautiful collection. The Houston Museum of Natural History has recently added an excellent library on mollusks. Some museums will identify specimens if you are unable to do so after serious effort. First ask permission of the museum; then send only specimens for which you have exact locality data. If possible, include the animal with the shell to facilitate identification. Wrap the shell in cotton saturated in 30 percent denatured alcohol and place in a vial. Sometimes a living specimen will arrive in good condition if wrapped in damp seaweed and layers of loosely wadded newspaper in a cardboard box.

Members of the various Texas shell clubs are also willing to assist the beginner. Contact any of the following: Coastal Bend Gem and Mineral Society, P.O. Drawer 1232, Bay City, Texas 77414; Coastal Bend Shell Club, Corpus Christi Museum, 1919 North Water Street, Corpus Christi, Texas 78401; Galveston Shell Club, P.O. Box 2072, Galveston, Texas 77550; Houston Conchology Society, Houston

Museum of Natural Science, 5800 Caroline Street, Houston, Texas 77004; San Antonio Shell Club, 9402 Nona Kay Drive, San Antonio, Texas 78217; San Marcos Shell Club, Rt. 1, Box 327C, San Marcos, Texas 78666; South Padre Island Shell Club, P.O. Box 2110, South Padre Island, Texas 78578.

Through the exchange of specimens a collection may be expanded and new friends made. Many people interested in exchanging are listed in *The International Directory of Conchologists* ($3.00 from P.O. Box 29, Falls Church, Virginia 22046). The beginner would do well to "feel out" his prospective exchanger, since many advanced collectors become very choosy. Great care must be given to packaging the material to be shipped. Nothing is more dis-

appointing than to anxiously await an exchange from a distant land only to receive a box full of chipped and broken shells. Wrap the shell in tissues, then in cotton, and pack with loosely wadded newspapers in a stout box.

The earliest recorded shell collection was found in the ruins of Pompeii, which was buried by lava and volcanic ash in A.D. 79. Today the United States National Museum (Smithsonian Institution, Washington, D.C. 20560) contains the largest mollusk collection in the world. Others of note to Gulf collectors are Department of Mollusks, Academy of Natural Sciences of Philadelphia, Nineteenth and the Parkway, Philadelphia, Pennsylvania 19103; Department of Mollusks, Museum of Comparative

Zoology, Harvard University, Cambridge, Massachusetts 02138; Department of Living Invertebrates, American Museum of Natural History, Central Park West at Seventy-ninth Street, New York, New York 10024; Beal-Maltbie Museum, Rollins College, Winter Park, Florida 32789; Division of Mollusks, Museum of Zoology, University of Michigan, Ann Arbor, Michigan 48104; Lowe Invertebrates, Department of Zoology, Field Museum of Natural History, Roosevelt Road and Lake Shore Drive, Chicago, Illinois 60605; and Department of Mollusks, Carnegie Museum, Pittsburgh, Pennsylvania 15213. The splendid collections on the West Coast are of less interest to the collector in this area.

Eating Your Catch

The oyster is the only mollusk regularly found along the Gulf in quantities sufficient to eat but others can sometimes be found, especially after a norther. These mollusks that wash up on the beach in the winter are usually alive and edible. Do not risk cooking those that are dead when found. Check to see that they are living by attempting to pry the valves apart; if the muscles contract, they are alive and therefore safe to eat. In the case of the snails, punch them with your finger; if they draw up into the shell you can eat them.

Oysters may be eaten raw with lemon juice or a cocktail sauce or fried to a golden brown, but have you tried an oyster stew or, better yet, what I call "panned oysters"? Both are simple to prepare.

Oyster Stew

6 oysters per serving, well drained
1 cup half-and-half cream per serving
1 teaspoon butter per serving
Salt and freshly ground pepper to taste

Melt the butter in a heavy stew pan but do not brown. Add a few carefully drained oysters at a time and cook only until the edges curl. Stir in the cream (milk if weight conscious) and simmer until the mixture is thoroughly heated but be careful not to boil. Serve steaming hot with buttered French bread and a tossed green salad.

Panned Oysters

At least 6 oysters per person, but better have more
1 stick butter, not margarine
Freshly ground pepper

In a chafing dish or electric skillet at the table, melt the butter. When ready to eat add about 6 or 8 well drained oysters at a time and sauté until edges curl, turn once. Serve on Ritz-type crackers. Sprinkle with lemon juice if desired. Everyone does his own.

Clam Chowder

Laevicardium, *Tellina*, *Dosinia*, *Mercenaria*, or *Atrina* are sometimes found in enough quantity to make this dish. A mixture of clams may be used. This is my favorite way to prepare coquinas. See coquina recipe for making broth.

1 large onion
4 slices bacon; cut and fry together until onion is golden and translucent. Then add
2 cups diced potatoes with enough water to cover; boil until potatoes are tender. While this is cooking, steam
2 dozen clams; remove from shell, carefully wash out sand, and grind in a food chopper or blender. Strain the broth through a clean cloth and let settle to remove sand. Then combine both mixtures.
1 quart milk; add and heat to a simmer. Never boil. Blend
¼ cup milk and
1 tablespoon flour and stir into chowder to thicken. Salt and pepper to taste. Serve hot with crackers and a green salad. Serves 6.

Stuffed Clams

Any kind of clam or a mixture of clams can be used. Open shells by inserting a thin knife between the valves and severing the adductor muscles. Remove the meat and wash carefully to remove sand. If using *Dinocardium*, cut the foot open and remove visceral material before placing in food chopper.

12 large cockles or a proportionate number of smaller clams, finely chopped. To this add
1 egg, beaten
2 tablespoons tomato catsup
1 tablespoon minced onion
1 tablespoon minced celery
1 cup bread crumbs
Salt and freshly ground pepper to taste

Mix all ingredients together and stuff 4 of the large cockle shells. Cover with half a slice of bacon and bake at 350 degrees until bacon is crisp. Serves 4.

Coquina Chowder

Wash two quarts of *Donax* or coquina clams thoroughly to remove sand. Steam with two cups of water for 20 minutes. Strain the broth through a fine cloth and let settle. Discard the shells. This chowder can be prepared the same way as the clam chowder or as Euell Gibbons, author of *Stalking the Blue-Eyed Scallop*, favored, with wine. Substitute 1 cup of dry white wine for 1 cup of water when steaming the clams.

4 slices bacon, fried crisp and crumbled
1 cup diced boiled potato
½ cup minced white part of green onions

Cook the last two items together in the bacon fat until the potato is a delicate brown and the onion clear and yellow. Drain to remove as much fat as possible.

6 ears of fresh sweet corn; score, scrape on side of mixing bowl to produce corn cream (this can be omitted).

Add the corn cream, bacon, potato, and onion to the broth; reserve ½ cup of broth to mix for thickening. Bring to a boil, reduce heat, and simmer for 20 minutes. Heat 2 cups of half-and-half cream. Make a paste with the reserved broth and 4 tablespoons of flour, stir into chowder until thickened. Add the hot cream, stir again. Season to taste. Serve hot to 4. *Note*: The *Donax* move out to deep water in the cool months but are readily available on the upper shoreface during the summer.

Seviche

I have eaten this in Mexico made of every imaginable combination of seafood. Anything can be substituted for a fish or shellfish mentioned. Great for cocktail snacks on crackers; let your guests dip it from the bowl themselves.

1½ pounds red fish, snapper, trout, or a mixture
2 cups mixed clams, oysters, shrimp, snails, chopped
3 cups lime or lemon juice (Mexican limes preferred)
2 mild, green *jalapeño* peppers, chopped
1 large fresh tomato, chopped
1 large onion, chopped fine
  Fresh cilantro or Chinese parsley if available.

Filet the fish and cut in very narrow thin strips; then chop the shellfish and place both in a large glass or stainless steel bowl. Cover with half the lemon juice and marinate in the refrigerator at least four hours, preferably overnight. Drain and wash in cold water. Drain again. Return to bowl. Pour in remainder of lemon juice and other ingredients. Season to taste. Some like to add sliced stuffed olives and 2 tablespoons of olive oil. Serves 8 to 10.

5. Beachcombing

There are often days when the tides or weather work against the most ardent shell collector. If the collector has not already become a beach-comber as an outgrowth of shelling, he might take it up on such days. It is to the disappointed shell collector that this section is directed. The beachcomber will find every day on a Texas beach rewarding even if the shells are not "coming in" that day. Certain items that might arouse the curiosity of the visitor occur with regularity, even though it often is difficult to ascertain just what the new-found "treasure" is, and the fishermen or baitstand operators whom you might ask for information are not always reliable in their replies. Much of the information received will be "old wives' tales" and "fishermen's stories"—more fiction than fact. To remove some of the mystery surrounding these objects the most common ones will be listed and identified; often, the truth about them is stranger than the fiction.

Treasure hunting is a popular pastime on these isolated beaches.

However, the Antiquities Act of 1906 limits the extent to which treasure hunters can enjoy the fruits of their labors on federally owned property. In other words, the removal of items of historic or prehistoric nature or items of antiquity is not permitted within the Padre Island National Seashore Area, which is federally owned and thus falls under the Antiquities Act. Permission to remove such items as pieces of eight, old ships, Civil War items, or Indian artifacts must come from the Department of the Interior. However, materials not of a scientific or historic nature that are washed in by recurring tides may be taken as beachcomber items. Driftwood, shells, bottles, floats, or other contemporary objects may be lugged home.

For those interested in this romantic pastime, a copy of the Antiquities Act is available at the offices of the Padre Island National Seashore Area, 9405 South Padre Island Drive, Corpus Christi, Texas 78418.

Common law designates all goods lost at sea as *wreck*. *Jetsam* is goods that are cast into the sea and there sink and remain under water; *flotsam* is goods that continue floating on the surface; *lagan* (ligan) is goods that are deliberately sunk at sea but tied to a cork or buoy in order to be found at a later date. In the absence of the true owner flotsam, jetsam, and lagan belong to the sovereign. Wreck (which is stranded on the beach) also belongs to the sovereign because it is said that by loss of the ship the owner loses all right to his property.

The federal government and the state of Texas say you can have all the desirable wreck that does not come under the Antiquities Act. Comb to your heart's content. But if you come across a shrimper or other boat run aground, you should check on who has salvage rights before you start stripping her; that comes under the heading of felony and penalties can be steep. Happy hunting!

From the Animal Kingdom

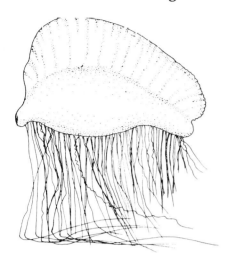

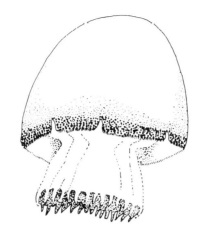

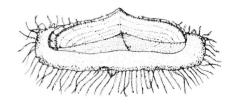

By-the-Wind-Sailor
Velella mutica Bosc is a coelenterate.
When it is alive it is deep blue green
in color but when dead it is transparent and colorless. This colonial
animal is common in the spring
when its chitinous, elongate body,
about 3–4 inches long with keellike
crest, may be encountered in great
numbers on the open beach.

Portuguese Man-of-War
Physalia physalia (Linné), a hydroid
coelenterate, is commonly mistaken
for a true jellyfish (*Scyphozoa*), but it
is really a colony of animals that
sails the sea with its iridescent blue
air bubble (pneumatophore) floating on the waves at the mercy of the
winds. Stretched out, invisible in
the water beneath this colorful
gas-filled float, are stinging tentacles up to twenty feet long. The
man-of-war is an inhabitant of the
Atlantic from the Bay of Fundy to
the Hebrides. Strong offshore
winds drive these creatures up on
the beach in vast numbers from
time to time. It is great sport to pop
the air bladders with the wheels of a
car but the temptation to touch the
balloonlike float should be resisted,
as the result can be a painful sting.

If contact is made with a man-
of-war, wash the affected area with
clean sand and water immediately.
Morphine is effective in relieving
the pain and oral histaminics and
topical cream are useful in treating
the rash. Dilute ammonium hy-
droxide or sodium bicarbonate
might be helpful. Artificial respiration, cardiac and respiratory stimu-
lants, and other forms of supportive
measures may be required if the victim has allergic tendencies. There
are no known specific antidotes.

Jellyfish
Several species of these translucent,
colorless to whitish, jellylike
coelenterates occur in Texas waters.
However, they are *Scyphozoa* and no
relation to fish. They may be seen
by the thousands moving smoothly
in the quiet waters along wharves
and docks or in a melting lump on
the open beach. Give these delicate
organisms wide berth in the water,
for they have stinging tentacles trailing them for several feet. On the
beach, apparently dead, they are
quite capable of inflicting a serious
sting; however, they are not as
painful as the man-of-war, from
which they are easily distinguished
by the absence of blue color.

Three of the most common varieties to be encountered are the cabbagehead, *Stomolophus meleagris*
Agassiz; the moon jelly, *Aurelia au-
rita* Linné, which has a maroon border design; and the beautiful sea
nettle, *Dactylmetra quinquecirrha* De-
sor. After storms remnants of tentacles may be found in the waters,
making swimming very unpleasant.
If stung, wash the affected area with
sand and water first, then apply
ammonia, soda, oil, or alcohol.

Porpita
Porpita linneana Lesson occurs with
the by-the-wind-sailor on the open
beach after high winds in the
spring. When this colonial coelenterate is living the flat disclike body
is a bright blue, shading to green
with a fringe of short tentacles; but
dead, its body becomes a colorless,
transparent piece of chitin about the
size of a quarter. Its sting is not
harmful.

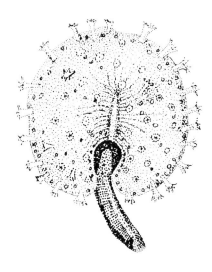

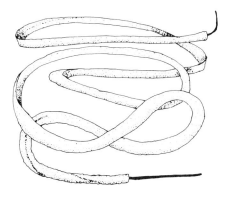

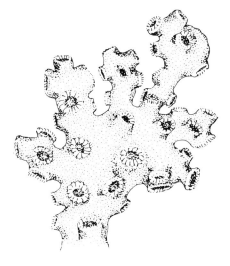

Sea Pansy

Renilla mulleri Gunter is a fleshy, stemmed, rose-colored, pansy-shaped, flat animal about 1.5–2 inches in diameter. The stinging cells of this alcyonarian coelenterate are not powerful enough to affect man. The phosphorescent sea pansy makes its home just offshore on the sandy bottom. Children love to put one in a glass of sea water in a dark room and stir it to produce a glow. The sea pansy will live in a salt-water aquarium or may be preserved by being slowly dried in a warm oven.

Sea Whip Coral

Eugorgia setacea Pallas, a coelenterate, is a soft coral that looks like long yellow or red cords. Large, tangled rolls of this animal are found on the open beach where it lives offshore on the sandy bottom. The dried cores of these colorful strings look like wire. Interesting objects often become entangled in a mass of sea whip, rewarding the person who takes time to stop and shake a pile of it. The sting does not bother man. Some people braid the wiry cores into bracelets or hat-bands.

The shorter, more treelike variety found living on the jetties is *Eugorgia virgulata* Lamarck.

Stony Coral

Astrangia cf. *A. astreiformis* Milne Edwards & Haime is one of the few calcareous corals found along the Texas coast. This solitary coelenterate of the order Madreporaria can be found growing on the jetties. Occasional pieces of this strange animal are found in beach drift.

Starfish

Three relatively small species of starfish occur on the Texas coast. *Luidia clathrata* Say, *Luidia alternata* Say, and *Astropecten duplicatus* Gray are echinoderms. They may be prepared for the collection by slowly drying them on a cookie sheet in a warm oven.

303

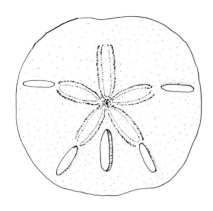

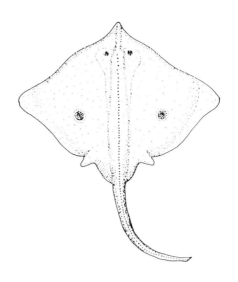

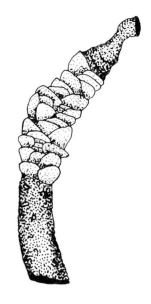

Sand Dollar
Mellita quinquiesperforata Leske (the keyhole urchin), an echinoderm, is a favorite among the beachcombers. The chalky, brittle disc has five perforations in its flat body. When living, the pliable, rose-colored animal may be found in great numbers along the third trough just off the barrier islands. Post cards bearing the legend of the sand dollar are in many shops for those interested in the tale.

Sting Ray and Skate
The skate, *Raja texana*, electric ray, *Narcine brasiliensis*, stingaree, *Dosyatis sabina*, and cownose ray, *Rhinoptera bonasus*, are bat-shaped fish with long barbed tails that hide just under the sand in the bays and open Gulf waters, where they feed on mollusks. These fish may inflict a painful wound in the ankle or foot of the unwary wader. To avoid an injury from stepping on a ray, wade by shuffling your feet along the bottom. The electric ray will shock you if you step on it with bare feet.

Worm Tube
Diopatra cuprea Claparede is a worm that builds a curious tube covered with bits and pieces of small shell. The animal is seldom found, but the odd piece of tube is often found in the drift along bays or open beach. Examine these for living *Epitonium* and *Vitrinella* shells.

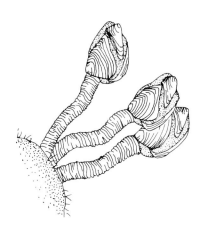

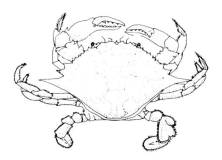

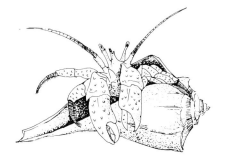

Gooseneck Barnacle
This curious arthropod, *Lepas* several species, has a flattened body, enclosed in a white shell mounted on a more or less slender, fleshy stalk. This animal, with its bright orange and blue colorings, may be found on wood, floats, and ships that have floated onto the beach from tropical waters. The calcareous plates of this animal are found in the drift, often confusing the shell collector.

Crabs
Descriptions of the species common to the Texas coast may be found in a bulletin, *Crabs of Texas*, published by the Texas Parks and Wildlife Service. The species include *Arenaeus cribarius* Lamarck, speckled crab; *Callinectes sapidus* Rathbun, blue crab; *Hepatus epheliticus* Linné, calico crab; *Persephona punctata aquilonaris* Rathbun, purse crab; *Menippe mercenaria* Say, stone crab; and *Libinia emaiginata* Leach, spider crab. Crabs are members of the large invertebrate phylum Arthropoda—animals with jointed legs—and, more specifically, they are the most numerous group of crustaceans representing the order Decapoda, along with the lobster, crayfish, and shrimp. The blue crab is the only one of commercial importance found on the Texas coast.

Hermit Crab
Pagurus floridanus Benedict, in the bays, and *Clibinarius vittatus* Bosc are probably the most common species of the Anomuran family Paguiridae occurring here. These funny little animals live in the cast-off shells of various marine gastropods and are often mistaken for the original inhabitant of the borrowed shell they carry on their backs.

Luminescence of the Waters
The phenomenon of luminescence occurs in salt water but not in fresh water. It is produced by many kinds of sea creatures, such as *Noctiluca*, copepods, bacteria, ctenophores, and other living organisms that make up plankton. On a warm, quiet night this phosphorescence produces a glowing surf that can be an unforgettable sight.

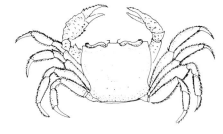

Ghost Crab
Ocypode albicans Bosc is a nocturnal crustacean that feeds on carrion. It can run thirty miles per hour at times. This species is colored like the sand with eyes standing on protruding stalks. When it runs on the beach and suddenly stands still, it seems to disappear; hence, the name "ghost crab." It burrows about two to four feet deep and can live without water for as long as forty-eight hours but must regularly return to the water's edge to moisten its gills.

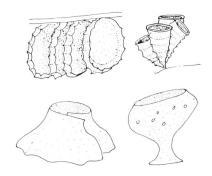

Egg Cases
The egg cases of mollusks take many curious forms to puzzle the finder (figs. 23 & 24). Perhaps the most curious are the long strings of disc-shaped, leathery capsules that are all attached to a cartilaginous band up to three feet in length. Miniature left-handed whelks will be found inside these protective cases formed by the female *Busycon*. The tulip shells will attach their tulip-shaped, bladdery capsules in clusters to old shells or rocks. The *Murex* egg cases look like a wad of dried sponge, but examination shows the individual capsules. Collars of sand are produced by the *Polinices*; groups of purple capsules are formed on old cans or rock by the rock shell; other families lay their eggs in jellylike masses or strings. Another egg case of interest is not that of a mollusk but of the skate. It is a shiny, black rectangular purse with pointed corners.

Land and Fresh-Water Snails
These pulmonates are often the most common shells found in the beach drift, especially with small driftwood. Stream and river drainage is the main source of the thousands of land snails commonly found on Texas beaches. Pilsbry and Hubricht (1956) list the following as occurring on the beach: *Anguispira strongylodes* (Pfeiffer), *Bulimulus alternatus mariae* (Albers), *Cecilioides acicula* (Müll), *Euconulus chersinus trochulus* (Reinh.), *Gastrocopta contracta* (Say), *G. cristata* (Pilsbry & Vanatta), *G. pellucida hordeacella* (Pilsbry), *G. tappaniana* (C. B. Adams), *G. riograndensis* (Pilsbry & Vanatta), *Guppya gundlachi* (Pfeiffer), *Hawaiia minuscula* (Binn.), *Helicina chrysocheila* Binney, *H. fragilis elata* Shuttleworth, *H. orbiculata* (Say), *Helicodiscus eigenmanni* Pilsbry, *H. parellelus* (Say), *H. singleyanus* (Pilsbry), *Holospira montivaga* Pilsbry, *H. roemeri* Pfeiffer, *Lamellaxis mexicanus* (Pfeiffer), *Lucidella lirata* (Pfeiffer), *Polygyra ariadnae* (Pfeiffer), *P. auriformis* (Bland), *P. cereolus* (Mühlfeld), *P. cereolus febigeri* (Bland), *P. dorfeuilliana* Lea, *P. dorfeuilliana sampsoni* Wetherby, *P. implicata* (Martens), *P. leporina* (Gould), *P. mooreana* (W. G. Binney), *P. oppilata* (Morelet), *P. rhoadsi* Pilsbry, *P. scintilla* Pilsbry & Hubricht, *P. texasensis* Pilsbry, *P. texasiana* (Moricand), *P. texasiana tamaulipasensis* Lea, *P. tholus* (W. G. Binney), *Praticolella berlandieriana* (Moricand), *P. griseola* (Pfeiffer), *P. pachyloma* ('Menke' Pfeiffer), *Pupoides albilabris* (C. B. Adams), *Retinella indentata paucilirata* (Morelet), *Stenotrema leai aliciae* (Pilsbry), *Strobilops labyrinthica* (Say), *S. texasiana* (Pilsbry & Ferriss), *Succinea luteola* Gould, *Synopeas beckianum* (Pfeiffer), and *Thysanophora horni* (Gabb).

The most attractive of these snails is the large, globose apple snail, *Pomacea flagellata* (Say), from fresh-water sources in Mexico. It can be up to two inches in diameter, and its grayish white surface is spirally striped with purplish brown lines on the body whorl.

From the Plant World

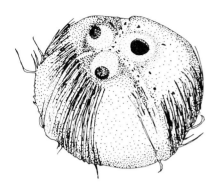

Coconuts

The fruit of the palm tree, coconuts have floated onto the Texas shores from Mexico and the Indies. They are found with and without the thick husk.

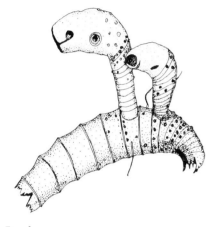

Bamboo

The jointed stems of the bamboo plant that wash ashore from tropical areas are easily recognized and may be utilized in various ways, but the roots are a different matter. The twisted, ribbed roots of the giant bamboo often take the form of weird animals, and the imaginative beachcomber may carry home an entire menagerie to decorate his garden.

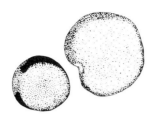

Sea Beans

Entada gigas (syn. *E. scardens*) is the largest and most common of the several types of seeds to be found on Gulf shores. This large, red, kidney-shaped bean that grows on a one-hundred-foot-long woody vine principally in Jamaica is found washed up on the beaches from the West Indies to Norway. The seeds occur in pods five feet long. Medicinal properties are attributed to it and to the several smaller species (*Mucuna sloanei*, brown with dark black band; *Guilandia bonducella*, W. Indies and Cartagena) by primitive peoples. The uncooked kernel is toxic to man.

The journal of the explorer Cabeza de Vaca, who lived among the Karankawas from 1528 to 1536, acting as a trader with tribes in the interior, reports that from the coastal region he took sea shells, "conches used for cutting, and fruit like a bean of the highest value among them, which they use as a medicine and employ in their dances and festivities" (Newcomb 1961, p. 70). In return for this mysterious sea bean, he brought back to the coastal tribes skins, red ocher for painting the face and body, canes for arrows, sinew, flint for weapons and tools, "cement" with which to affix flint tools to handles and shafts, and deer hair, dyed and fixed into tassels. I have seen this distinctive bean in the herb sections of Indian markets throughout Mexico, where its magical powers are still respected. *See* Dennis & Gunn 1972*a*.

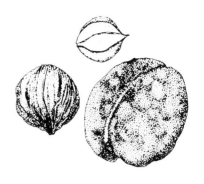

Nuts and Seeds

Lofty pecan, black walnut, and other nut-bearing trees line the shady Texas rivers to have their dropped fruits carried to the barren, sun-soaked beaches. The fastidious coon carries peaches and other fruits to the banks of an inland stream in order to wash them for his dinner. Floods carry these and many other strange seeds to the Texas coast.

Among the most unusual looking is a large, wrinkled, black, hard, oval seed about three and one-half inches in length, which is called cabbage bark. This strange seed is probably *Andira inermis* HBK described in Strandley's book on the flora of British Honduras as from a tree that is widespread in tropical America. *See* Dennis & Gunn 1972*b*; Gunn & Dennis 1973.

Driftwood
Most of the wood found on the beaches north of Big Shell comes from the banks of Texas rivers and may be cottonwood, pecan, cypress, or walnut. The tropical woods, such as bamboo, mahogany, and cedar, are more common south of Big Shell, although both types are mingled in the two areas. Ocean currents bring the tropical woods from southern Mexico and Central America.

Sargassum
Sargassum nutans Meyer is the dominant, large floating seaweed. These floating "weeds" are brown algae that support an entire community of animal life. At times it comes to the shore in enormous quantities, two and three feet deep for miles, obstructing travel along the lower beach.

Miscellaneous Wreck

Pumice
The rounded pieces of this volcanic rock float on the waves to the Texas shores after having been carried to sea by rivers in Africa, Central America, and the region around Tuxla in southern Mexico.

Naval Flares
These flares are often thought to be practice bombs and at times are numerous on the beaches of Padre, Mustang, and San José islands. The eighteen-inch-long aluminum cylinder is a U.S. Navy Marine Location Marker, MK-Mod.3. The navy uses it to simulate the outline of a carrier when landing approaches are practiced in the Gulf. During times of intensive training they are found by the hundreds. It is best to look at them and leave them on the beach; they may be harmless, but that would depend on the use to which they were put when you got them home.

Mud Balls
Strange round balls of hard mud are often found in large numbers along ship channels and near inlets. They are about the size of a baseball and usually covered with broken shell. These balls began as chunks of clay that were eroded by wave action from spoil banks piled up when the channel was dug. Rolling back and forth along the bottom has formed them into neat balls.

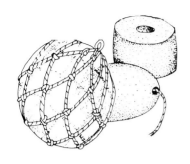

Floats

The highly prized glass floats, along with plastic, cork, metal, styrofoam, and wooden ones, come ashore after breaking away from nets and lines at sea. Contrary to popular opinion the glass floats are not the invention of the Japanese, although most of those in use today are made in Japanese factories. Christopher Faye, a Norwegian, invented them more than 125 years ago to replace the clumsy wooden ones used on cod nets. Today they are used on tuna long lines and for other fishing operations in the Canaries, Puerto Rico, Portugal, North Africa, and North, Central, and South America, being carried to the Texas coast by the North Equatorial Current through the Yucatán Strait to finally become a prized possession of a lucky beachcomber. These hollow, glass balls vary in size depending on the use to which they are put. The more bouyant larger floats are used on tuna long lines that may stretch for as far as fifty miles in the open sea. Medium-sized ones are pressure resistant; hence, they are employed in bottom tangle-net operations. The smaller floats are from gill nets. The colors range from clear, brown, green, and aqua to lavender due to the inexpensive glass used. They are less expensive than the other types of floats, but they are not compatible with the mechanized winch and are consequently being replaced by floats of other materials. Some may be rarities, such as those partially filled with water. There is a high percentage of loss in fishing gear annually

and it is thought that the average glass float picked up on the beach is easily ten or more years old. The spring currents bring in the greatest number. All types of netting from very fine to very makeshift may be used to wrap the float so that it is more easily attached to the net.

The rarest float on the beach is hardly recognizable as such, for it is the crudely hand-carved piece of wood used by the poorer fishermen in the West Indies. They range from one foot to four feet in length, at least those I have seen are this size, and may be riddled with teredo holes. A piece of wood about six inches wide and of various lengths is rounded at one end, while the other is whittled so that it has a narrow neck where the rope attaching it to the net is tied.

Bottles

Since the sixteenth century, when shipping first took place along the Gulf shores, bottles have been collecting in the sands and collectors have been collecting bottles. They were highly prized by the Indians as containers, while the broken pieces were used for arrowheads and scrapers. When early colonists denied the trade of bottles to the Indians, beach bottles became even more highly prized by the natives. Many ancient bottles have been discovered in the dunes of the barrier islands, but it is very difficult to determine the age of a glass bottle from the beach.

This difficulty arises for several reasons, the primary one being that age and deterioration do not change the composition of glass; carbon-14 and other such tests are therefore useless. Beach bottles made in far-away lands and tossed overboard by foreign seamen are difficult to date. Foreign bottles were often made by certain families who passed their secrets of glassmaking from one generation to another so that bottles made hundreds of years ago may have been made by the same formulae and methods as those made yesterday. Molds receive little wear and the same ones may be used for years.

Very primitive methods were used to make bottles until about sixty years ago when great technical strides were made during World War I. Prior to that time all bottles had hand-wrapped necks that were added after the bottle had been formed. The bottlemaking machine formed the neck and lip leaving a mold mark up the sides of the bottle and through the lip. In 1900 the metal bottle cap was invented and the lips were redesigned to accommodate caps instead of corks in certain types of bottles. Prior to the repeal of the prohibition law in 1933, no American bottles bore the mark "Federal law prohibits reuse of this bottle."

To produce a clear glass, bottlemakers would add manganese oxide, which counteracted the natural green color. Glass containing manganese turns a purple color when exposed to the sun, the length of time that it takes to become purple depending on the amount of manganese, the amount of exposure, and the color of the background against which the bottle is placed. When conditions are favorable the change may take place in less than a month. The invention of the bottlemaking machine in the early part of this century made it possible to use materials with fewer impurities, with the result that glass made after this date seldom turns the beautiful purple color. Early wine bottles are green or black because that was the cheapest glass available.

The iridescence of bottles comes from excessive alkalis like sodium in the mix. The rust is an accumulation of iron from the soil as a result of long burial. Hand-blown bottles usually have air bubbles in the glass and some have brown specks caused by iron in the sands used in their manufacture. These bottles will often have a pontil, or punty, mark on the bottom where the glass blower's iron rod was attached.

Asphalt and Petroleum Tars
The beachcomber often finds his feet covered with gooey tar and usually blames ocean-going ships or offshore oil wells for the mess. They are not the only culprits. The Karankawa Indians found this same asphalt and used it to waterproof and decorate pottery. The survivors of De Soto's expedition left us the earliest reference to asphalt on the beaches. Oil slicks in the Gulf of Mexico have been reported long before ships began using oil for fuel. It is said that pieces of tar weighing several hundred pounds have been found and I have seen hunks three feet in diameter, but most pieces are small. (The area of Padre Island near the wreckage of the *Nicaragua* is the site of the greatest stranding of tars on the Texas coast.) Hildebrand and Gunter (1955) suggest

that these deposits float to our coast from natural asphalt seeps from the Tampico-Tuxpan and the Isthmus of Tehuantepec areas of Mexico. Kerosene or any petroleum solvent will remove the accumulation from your feet and your treasures.

Plastic Pellets
The beach drift often yields tiny polyethylene pellets ranging from 3.5 mm to 1 mm in diameter, with colors from dull white to amber. These pellets come from the chemical plants located at Port Arthur, Orange, Houston, Baytown, Texas City, Corpus Christi, Seadrift, and Freeport and are carried by winds and currents along the coast of Texas and into Mexico. Polyethylene, according to the Dow Company, is produced by the polymerization of ethylene, usually at a high temperature and pressure. The hot polyethylene is passed through an extruder where it is cut into pellets and bagged for sale. The purchaser finds it easy to remelt the pellets and mold a finished product. Some of the plants are installing skimming devices to prevent pellets from leaving the plant site; however, they are not known to cause an aquatic loss-of-life problem at this time.

Appendix A

Outline of Classification

Phylum MOLLUSCA Cuvier, 1797
  Subphylum ACULIFERA Hatscheck, 1891 = [AMPHINEURA Von Ihering, 1876, in part]
    Class APLACOPHORA Von Ihering, 1876
        Order CHAETODERMATIDA Simroth, 1893
           Family CHAETODERMATIDAE Von Ihering, 1876
  Subphylum PLACOPHORA Von Ihering, 1876
    Class POLYPLACOPHORA Blainville, 1816 = [AMPHINEURA Von Ihering, 1876, in part]
        Order NEOLORICATA Bergenhayn, 1955
          Suborder ISCHNOCHITONINA Bergenhayn, 1930
            Family ISCHNOCHITONIDAE Dall, 1889
  Subphylum CONCHIFERA Gegenbaur, 1878
    Class MONOPLACOPHORA Wenz, 1940 [none in Texas]
      GASTROPODA Cuvier, 1797
        Subclass PROSOBRANCHIA Milne Edwards, 1848 = [STREPTONEURA Spengel, 1881]
       Infraclass DIOTOCARDIA Mörch, 1865 = [ARCHAEOGASTROPODA Thiele, 1925]
         Order RHIPIDOGLOSSA Mörch, 1865
          Suborder ZEUGOBRANCHIA Von Ihering, 1876
           Superfamily FISSURELLACEA Fleming, 1822
            Family FISSURELLIDAE Fleming, 1822
          Suborder AZYGOBRANCHIA Spengel, 1881
           Superfamily TROCHACEA Rafinesque, 1815
            Family TROCHIDAE Rafinesque, 1815
              PHASIANELLIDAE Swainson, 1840
          Suborder PLANILABIATA Stoliczka, 1868
           Superfamily NERITACEA Rafinesque, 1815
            Family NERITIDAE Rafinesque, 1815
       Infraclass MONOTOCARDIA Mörch, 1865 = [CAENOGASTROPODA Cox, 1959]
        Order CTENOBRANCHIA Schweigger, 1820 = [PECTINIBRANCHIA Blainville, 1814]
         Suborder HOLOSTOMATA Fleming, 1828
           Superfamily VIVIPARACEA Gray, 1847
            Family PILIDAE Conolly, 1927 = [AMPULLARIIDAE Gray, 1824]
           Superfamily LITTORINACEA Gray, 1840
            Family LITTORINIDAE Gray, 1840
           Superfamily RISSOACEA Gray, 1847
            Family RISSOIDAE Gray, 1847
              ASSIMINEIDAE H. & A. Adams, 1856
              LITTORIDINIDAE Thiele, 1929
              STENOTHYRIDAE Fischer, 1885
              TRUNCATELLIDAE Gray, 1840
              VITRINELLIDAE Bush, 1897
              CAECIDAE Gray, 1850
           Superfamily TORNACEA Kuroda, Habe, & Oyama, 1971
            Family TORNIDAE Sacco, 1896
           Superfamily ARCHITECTONICACEA Gray, 1850
            Family ARCHITECTONICIDAE Gray, 1850
           Superfamily TURRITELLACEA Woodward, 1851
            Family VERMETIDAE Rafinesque, 1815
           Superfamily CERITHIACEA Fleming, 1822
            Family MODULIDAE Fischer, 1884
              POTAMIDIDAE H. & A. Adams, 1854
              CERITHIIDAE Fleming, 1822

TRIPHORIDAE Gray, 1847
Superfamily EPITONIACEA S. S. Berry, 1910
Family EPITONIIDAE S. S. Berry, 1910
JANTHINIDAE Leach, 1823
Superfamily EULIMACEA Risso, 1826
Family EULIMIDAE Risso, 1826
ACLIDIDAE G. O. Sars, 1878
Superfamily STROMBACEA Rafinesque, 1815
Family STROMBIDAE Rafinesque, 1815
Superfamily CALYPTRAEACEA Blainville, 1824
Family CALYPTRAEIDAE Blainville, 1824
Superfamily LAMELLARIACEA Orbigny, 1841
Family LAMELLARIIDAE Orbigny, 1841 = [VELUTINIDAE Gray, 1840]
Superfamily TRIVIACEA Gray, 1852
Family TRIVIIDAE Gray, 1852
Superfamily CYPRAEACEA Rafinesque, 1815
Family CYPRAEIDAE Rafinesque, 1815
OVULIDAE Gray, 1853
Superfamily NATICACEA (Swainson), Gray, 1840
Family NATICIDAE (Swainson), Gray, 1840
Superfamily TONNACEA Suter, 1913
Family CASSIDAE Latreille, 1825
TONNIDAE Suter, 1913
Superfamily CYMATIACEA ?Iredale, 1913
Family CYMATIIDAE Iredale, 1913
Suborder SIPHONOSTOMATA Blainville, 1824 = [STENOGLOSSA Troschel, 1848, and NEOGAS-TROPODA Thiele, 1925]
Superfamily CANCELLARIACEA Gray, 1853
Family CANCELLARIIDAE Forbes & Hanley 1853
Superfamily CONACEA Rafinesque, 1815
Family TURRIDAE H. & A. Adams, 1853
TEREBRIDAE Mörch, 1852
BUCCINIDAE Rafinesque, 1815
NASSARIIDAE Iredale, 1916
FASCIOLARIIDAE Gray, 1853
MELONGENIDAE Gill, 1871 = [GALEODIDAE Thiele, 1925]
COLUMBELLIDAE Swainson, 1840 = [PYRENIDAE Suter, 1913]
MURICIDAE Rafinesque, 1815
OLIVIDAE Latreille, 1825
MARGINELLIDAE Fleming, 1828
Subclass EUTHYNEURA Spengel, 1881 = [OPISTHOBRANCHIA Milne Edwards, 1848, and PULMONATA Cuvier, 1817]
Order SACOGLOSSA Von Ihering, 1876 = [ASCOGLOSSA Bergh, 1877]
Superfamily ELYSIACEA H. & A. Adams, 1854
Family ELYSIIDAE H. & A. Adams, 1854
Order DORIDOIDEA Odhner, 1934 = [HOLOHEPATICA Bergh, 1881]
Suborder CRYPTOBRANCHIA Fischer, 1883 = [EUDORIDOIDEA Odhner, 1934]
Superfamily DORIDACEA Rafinesque, 1815
Family DORIDIDAE Rafinesque, 1815
Suborder PHANEROBRANCHIA Von Ihering, 1876
Superfamily ONCHIDORIDACEA Alder & Hancock, 1845 = [SUCTORIA Bergh, 1892]
Family CORAMBIDAE Bergh, 1869
Order DENDRONOTOIDEA Odhner, 1936
Family SCYLLAEIDAE Rafinesque, 1815
Order EOLIDOIDEA Odhner, 1937

Suborder EOLIDOIDEA Odhner, 1968
   Infraorder ACLEIOPROCTA Odhner, 1939
    Family FIONIDAE Gray, 1837
   Infraorder CLEIOPROCTA Odhner, 1939
    Family FAVORINIDAE Bergh, 1889
     EOLIDIIDAE Orbigny, 1834
     GLAUCIDAE Menke, 1828
Order PLEUROBRANCHIA Von Ihering, 1922
   Superfamily PLEUROBRANCHACEA Menke, 1828
    Family PLEUROBRANCHIDAE Menke, 1828
Order STEGANOBRANCHIA Von Ihering, 1876
  Suborder ACTEONOIDEA Orbigny, 1835
   Superfamily ACTEONACEA Orbigny, 1835
    Family ACTEONIDAE Orbigny, 1835
  Suborder BULLOIDEA Lamarck, 1801
   Superfamily BULLACEA Lamarck, 1801
    Family BULLIDAE Lamarck, 1801
     ACTEOCINIDAE Pilsbry, 1921
     ATYIDAE Thiele, 1926
   Superfamily CYLICHNACEA A. Adams, 1850
    Family CYLICHNIDAE A. Adams, 1850
  Suborder APLYSIOIDEA Lamarck, 1809
   Infraorder LONGICOMMISSURATA Pruvot-Fol, 1954
   Superfamily APLYSIACEA Lamarck, 1809
    Family APLYSIIDAE Rafinesque, 1815
   Infraorder BREVICOMMISSURATA Pruvot-Fol, 1954
    Subfamily DOLABRIFERINAE Pilsbry, 1895
Order ENTOMOTAENIATA Cossmann, 1896
   Superfamily PYRAMIDELLACEA Gray, 1840
    Family PYRAMIDELLIDAE Gray, 1840
     RISSOELLIDAE Gray, 1847
Order ACTOPHILA Thiele, 1931
   Superfamily ELLOBIACEA Adams, 1855
    Family ELLOBIIDAE Adams, 1855
Order HYGROPHILA Férussac, 1821
   Superfamily SIPHONARIACEA Gray, 1840
    Family SIPHONARIIDAE Gray, 1840
Order THECOSOMATA Blainville, 1824
  Suborder EUTHECOSOMATA Meisenheimer, 1905
   Superfamily SPIRATELLACEA Thiele, 1926
    Family CUVIERIDAE Gray, 1840
Class BIVALVIA Linné, 1758 = [PELECYPODA Goldfuss, 1820]
  Subclass PALAEOTAXODONTA Korobkov, 1954
   Order NUCULOIDEA Dall, 1889
    Superfamily NUCULACEA Gray, 1824
     Family NUCULIDAE Gray, 1824
    Superfamily NUCULANACEA H. & A. Adams, 1858
     Family NUCULANIDAE H. & A. Adams, 1858
  Subclass PTERIOMORPHIA Beurlen, 1944
   Order ARCOIDEA Stoliczka, 1871
    Superfamily ARCACEA Lamarck, 1809
     Family ARCIDAE Lamarck, 1809
      NOETIIDAE Stewart, 1930
   Order MYTILOIDEA Férussac, 1822
    Superfamily MYTILACEA Rafinesque, 1815

Family MYTILIDAE Rafinesque, 1815
Superfamily PINNACEA Leach, 1819
Family PINNIDAE Leach, 1819
Order PTERIOIDEA Newell, 1965
Suborder PTERIINA Newell, 1965
Superfamily PTERIACEA Gray, 1847
Family PTERIIDAE Gray, 1847
ISOGNOMONIDAE Woodring, 1925
Superfamily PECTINACEA Rafinesque, 1815
Family PECTINIDAE Rafinesque, 1815
PLICATULIDAE Watson, 1930
SPONDYLIDAE Gray, 1826
Superfamily ANOMIACEA Rafinesque, 1815
Family ANOMIIDAE Rafinesque, 1815
Superfamily LIMACEA Rafinesque, 1815
Family LIMIDAE Rafinesque, 1815
Suborder OSTREINA Férussac, 1822
Superfamily OSTREACEA Rafinesque, 1815
Family OSTREIDAE Rafinesque, 1815
Subclass HETERODONTA Neumayr, 1884
Order VENEROIDEA H. & A. Adams, 1858
Suborder LUCININA Dall, 1889
Superfamily LUCINACEA Fleming, 1828
Family LUCINIDAE Fleming, 1828
UNGULINIDAE H. & A. Adams, 1857
Order HIPPURITOIDEA Newell, 1965 = [PACHYDONTA Steinman, 1903]
Superfamily CHAMACEA Blainville, 1825
Family CHAMIDAE Lamarck, 1809
Superfamily LEPTONACEA Gray, 1847
Family KELLIIDAE Forbes & Hanley, 1848
LEPTONIDAE Gray, 1847
MONTACUTIDAE Clark, 1855
Superfamily CARDITACEA Fleming, 1820
Family CARDITIDAE Fleming, 1820
Superfamily CRASSATELLACEA Férussac, 1821
Family CRASSATELLIDAE Férussac, 1821
Superfamily CARDIACEA Lamarck, 1809
Family CARDIIDAE Lamarck, 1809
Superfamily MACTRACEA Lamarck, 1809
Family MACTRIDAE Lamarck, 1809
MESODESMATIDAE Gray, 1839
Superfamily SOLENACEA Lamarck, 1809
Family SOLENIDAE Lamarck, 1809
CULTELLIDAE Davis, 1935
Superfamily TELLINACEA Blainville, 1824
Family TELLINIDAE Blainville, 1824
DONACIDAE Fleming, 1828
PSAMMOBIIDAE Fleming, 1828
SEMELIDAE Stoliczka, 1870
SOLECURTIDAE Orbigny, 1846
Superfamily DREISSENACEA Gray, 1840
Family DREISSENIDAE Gray, 1840
Superfamily CORBICULACEA Gray, 1847
Family CORBICULIDAE Gray, 1847
Superfamily VENERACEA Rafinesque, 1815

Family VENERIDAE Rafinesque, 1815

PETRICOLIDAE Deshayes, 1831

Order MYOIDEA Stoliczka, 1870

Suborder MYINA Newell, 1965

Superfamily MYACEA Lamarck, 1809

Family MYIDAE Lamarck, 1809

CORBULIDAE Lamarck, 1818

Superfamily GASTROCHAENACEA Gray, 1840

Family GASTROCHAENIDAE Gray, 1840

Superfamily HIATELLACEA Gray, 1824

Family HIATELLIDAE Gray, 1824

Suborder PHOLADINA Newell, 1965

Superfamily PHOLADACEA Lamarck, 1809

Family PHOLADIDAE Lamarck, 1809

TEREDINIDAE Rafinesque, 1815

Subclass ANOMALODESMATA Dall, 1889

Order PHOLADOMYOIDEA Newell, 1965

Superfamily PANDORACEA Rafinesque, 1815

Family PANDORIDAE Rafinesque, 1815

LYONSIIDAE Fischer, 1887

PERIPLOMATIDAE Dall, 1895

Class SCAPHOPODA Bronn, 1862

Family DENTALIIDAE Gray, 1834

SPIHONODENTALIIDAE Simroth, 1894

Class CEPHALOPODA Cuvier, 1797

Subclass COLEOIDEA Bather, 1888

Order SEPIOIDEA Naef, 1916

Family SPIRULIDAE Owen, 1836

Order TEUTHOIDEA Naef, 1916

Suborder MYOPSIDA Orbigny, 1840

Family LOLIGINIDAE Orbigny, 1841

Order OCTOPODA Leach, 1817

Suborder INCIRRATA Grimpe, 1916

Family OCTOPODIDAE Orbigny, 1840

Appendix B

Type Terms

Types of families

Type genus: the genus upon which a family is based.

Types of generic categories

Type species: the single species upon which a genus is based.
Genosyntype: one of several species included within a genus at the time of its proposal, if none was designated as type.

Types of specific categories

Holotype: the single specimen taken as "the type" by the original author of a species.
Paratype: a specimen (or specimens), supplementary to the holotype, used by the original author as the basis of a new species.
Syntype: one of several specimens of equal rank upon which a species is based.
Lectotype: a specimen, selected from a syntypic series, subsequent to the original description, to serve as holotype.
Neotype: a specimen selected to re-place the holotype when primary type material of a species is lost or destroyed.
Hypotype: a described, figured, or listed specimen.
Topotype: a specimen from the type locality of a species.
Homeotype: a specimen compared by a competent observer with the holotype, lectotype, or other primary type material of a species and found to be conspecific with it.

Reproductions (for distribution of facsimiles of rare specimens)

Plastotype: a cast of a type.

Appendix C

Map Sources

National topographic maps

1:25,000 scale
U.S. Department of the Interior
 Geological Survey:
Bay City   NH 15-10
Beeville   NY 14-12
Brownsville   NG 14-6
Corpus Christi   NG 14-3
Houston   NH 15-7
Port Arthur   NH 15-8
Free index map and symbols
1:24,000 scale
U.S. Geological Survey
Topographic Division
Map Information Office
Washington, D.C. 20242

Environmental Geologic Atlas of the Texas Coastal Zone

A folio of 63 multicolored geologic and environmental maps accompanied by text explaining use and interpretation. Excellent; not expensive for what they offer.
Bureau of Economic Geology
P.O. Box X
University Station
Austin, Texas 78712

County maps

quarter scale
Department of Highways and Public Transportation
File D-10
Box 5051
West Austin Station
Austin, Texas 78763

American Geographical Society

Map of Hispanic America
107 sheets, vol. 2, no. 5
U.S. Army Map Service Series 1801
Department of the Army
Washington, D.C. 20315

Mexico

1:250,000
1966 northern Mexico for officials of the United States
U.S. Army Map Service Series F501
Department of the Army
Washington, D.C. 20315

U.S. Board on Geographic Names

1956 Gazetteer, no. 15
U.S. Government Printing Office
Washington, D.C. 20401

Appendix D

Publications

Malacological and Marine Science Journals
of Interest to Collectors on the Texas Gulf Coast

Bulletin of Marine Science
Rosenstiel School of Marine and Atmospheric Science
University of Miami, Miami, Florida
P.O. Box 268, Lawrence, Kansas 66044
Printed quarterly

Contributions in Marine Science
University of Texas Marine Science Institute
Port Aransas, Texas 78873
Printed irregularly

Johnsonia
Monographs of the Marine Mollusks of the Western Atlantic
Museum of Comparative Zoology, Harvard University
Cambridge, Massachusetts 02138
Printed irregularly

Nautilus
American Malacological Union
Business and subscriptions: 11 Chelten Road, Havertown, Pennsylvania 19083
Publisher: Delaware Museum of Natural History, Rt. 52, Box 3937, Greenville, Delaware 19807
Quarterly devoted to malacology

Sterkiana
Department of Geology, Ohio State University
155 South Oval Drive, Columbus, Ohio 43210
Quarterly devoted to malacology

Veliger
California Malacozoological Society
Drawer 710, Rancho Santa Fe, California 92067
Quarterly devoted to malacology

Popular Shell Magazines

Of Sea and Shore
P.O. Box 33, Port Gamble, Washington 98364
Quarterly on shells

Sea Frontiers
International Oceanographic Foundation
Rickenbacker Causeway, Virginia Key, Miami, Florida 33149
Printed six times a year

Texas Conchologist
Houston Conchology Society
5238 Sanford Street, Houston, Texas 77035
Printed nine times a year

Appendix E

Molluscan Environments

Legend for the Charts

Habitat/Biotopes

E = Estuarine; 5–30 o/oo

E_u = Upper; 5–18 o/oo, near fresh-water discharge; depth 3–7 ft.

E_t = True; 5–30 o/oo, includes open bay, lower end of bay with tidal influence, bay margin, shoal water bordering bay, grass flats, shallow bay margins with dense grasses, open bay, lower end of bay with tidal influence; depth 3–10 ft.

E_i = Inlet; 25–30 o/oo, includes tidal delta, connects open Gulf and bays; depth <40 ft.

E_o = Oyster reef; 10–30 o/oo, distinct mounds or ridgelike, commonly aligned normal to circulation of bay; depth 8 ft. or less

J = Jetties; 15–35 o/oo, man-made rock structures at the inlets, only rocky habitat on Texas coast; depth to that of channel, 45 ft.

O = Oceanic; 35 o/oo

O_s = Upper shoreface; strong wave action, surf zone, shifting sands; depth low tide to 15 ft.

O_n = Lower shoreface; open marine, moderate wave action; depth 15–30 ft.

O_o = Shelf; offshore, open marine; depth >30 ft.

Salinity

O = Oligohaline; 5/oo–19/oo
E = Euryhaline; 15/oo–40/oo
S = Stenohaline; 25/oo–40/oo
U = Ultrahaline; 40/oo and up

Substratum

A = Algae
A_c = Calcareous algae
C = Clay
D = Under wet debris above water
G = Grass beds
H = Rock or shell
I = Invertebrate
M = Mud; 20% sand
R = Reef
S = Sand
SR = Sand and rubble
W = Wood

Form: Relation to Substratum

E = Epifaunal: exposed above the substratum; may be with or without attachment

S = Semi-infaunal: partially within the substratum and partially without

I = Infaunal: sessile or mobile that spend all or part of their lives buried beneath the sea-floor sediment or in wood, rock, etc.

I_{co} = Commensal
P = Pelagic

Feeding

Feeding methods among the mollusks are many and varied and no attempt to describe them in detail will be made here. They have been organized into a few comprehensive categories. For more specific details, the reader is referred to Fretter & Graham 1962, Wilbur & Younge 1964, Jorgensen 1966, Hyman 1967, Purchon 1968, Cox et al. 1969, and others that are listed in the bibliography. Among the gastropods the range of food eaten and the variety of feeding mechanisms employed are unequaled in any comparable group in the animal kingdom.

C = Carnivore: consumes other animals, such as gastropods, bivalves, barnacles, fish, corals, sponges, echinoderms, etc.; requires living prey but may accept fresh dead corpses. Is either (1) an active predator or (2) scrapes colonial animal growths. Macrophagous.

G = Grazer/scraper: scrapes surface accumulations on rocks and grass; the most primitive method. Microphagous.

H = Herbivore: consumes algae and grass directly by biting off pieces. Macrophagous.

S = Scavenger: consumes dead animal material; usually no living material is consumed. Macrophagous.

EP = Ectoparasite: sucks the juices from its prey; some may be species-specific.

DF = Deposit feeder: feeds on organic debris and small animals and plants within or on the mud or sand of the substratum in or on which they inhabit. Microphagous.

SF = Suspension feeder: filters from the surrounding water the suspended microorganisms and detritus. Most are nonselective and feed continuously when not disturbed. Suspension feeders may be either filtering or mucociliary. Microphagous.
1. Filtering: feeds by passing the surrounding water through structures that retain particles, mainly according to size and shape.
2. Mucociliary: feeds by trapping particles with mucus and transporting them by ciliary action; collectors of plankton.

Gastropod Species	Habitat	Salinity	Substratum	Form	Feeding
Acteocina canaliculata	E_i–O_n	E	S	E	C
Alaba incerta	E_i–O_n	S	SR	E	H
Alabina cerithidioides	E_i–O_n–O_o	S	S	E	H
Amaea mitchelli	O	S	S	E	C
Anachis obesa	E_i–O_n	S	S	E	C
A. semiplicata	E_i–O	E	A, H	E	C
Anticlimax pilsbryi	E_i–O_n	S	SR, G	E	H
Aplysia brasiliana	E_i–O_n	S	M, G	E	H
A. dactylomela	E_i–O	S	M, G	E	H
A. donca	E_i–O_n	S	M, G	E	H
A. morio	?	S	M, G	E	H
A. willcoxi	E_i–O_n	E	M, G	E	H
Architectonica nobilis	O_n–O_o	S	S	E	C_2
Assiminea cf. *A. succinea*	E_u	O	M–S	E	G, DF
Balcis cf. *B. arcuata*	E_i–O_n	S	I	E	EP
B. cf. *B. jamaicensis*	E_i	E	I	E	EP
Berghia coerulescens	O	S	?	E	C
Bulla striata	E_t	E	S–M, G	S	C
Bursatella leachi pleei	E_i–O_n	S	M, G	E	H
Busycon perversum pulleyi	E_i–O_n	S	M–S	S	S
B. spiratum plagosum	E_i–O_o	S	S	S	S
Caecum imbricatum	O	S	SR	E	DF
C. johnsoni	E_o	E	SR	E	DF
C. nitidum	E_i–O_n	S	SR	E	DF
C. pulchellum	E_i–O_o	S	SR	E	DF
Calliostoma euglyptum	O_o	S	H	E	G
Cancellaria reticulata	O_o	S	S	E	C
Cantharus cancellarius	E_i–O_o, J	S	M–S, R	E	C
Cavolina longirostris	O	S	—	E, P	SF
C. uncinata	O	S	—	E, P	SF
Cerberilla tanna	O	S	?	E	C
Cerithidea pliculosa	E_t	E	M	S	DF
Cerithiopsis emersoni	E_t	E	S	E	C_2
C. greeni	E_t	E	M–S, G	E	C_2
*Cerithium atratum**					
C. lutosum	E_t	E	M–S, G, A	S	DF
Cochliolepis parasitica	E_i	E	C	I_{co}	H
C. striata	E_i	E	SR, G	E	H
*Crassispira tampaensis**					
Cratena pilata	E_i	S	?	E	C_2
Crepidula convexa	E, O_n	E	H	E	SF
C. fornicata	E, O_n, O_o	E	H	E	SF
C. plana	E, O_n	E	H	E	SF
Creseis acicula	O	S	—	E, P	SF
Cryoturris cf. *C. cerinella*	E	E?	M–S	E	C
Cyclostremella humilis	O_n	S	S	E	EP
Cyclostremiscus jeaneae	O_o	S	SR	E	H

* Not found alive, probably fossil.

Gastropod Species	Habitat	Salinity	Substratum	Form	Feeding
C. pentagonus	O_n	S	S–M	E	H
C. suppressus	E_i	E	S, G	E	H
Cylichnella bidentata	O_n, O_o	S	M–S	E	C
Cymatium cingulatum	O_o	S	SR	E	C
C. muricinum	O_n	S	R	E	C
C. nicobaricum	O_o	S	SR	E	C
C. parthenopeum	O_o	S	SR	E	C
C. pileare	O_o	S	SR	E	C
Cypraea cervus	O_o	S	R	E	C_2
Cypraecassis testiculus	O_o	S	R	E	C
Depressiscala nautlae	O	S	S?	E	C
Diacria quadridentata	O	S	—	E, P	SF
D. trispinosa	O	S	—	E, P	SF
Diastoma varium	E_i	S	S–M, G	E	H
Diodora cayenensis	E_i–O_n	S	H	E	G
Discodoris hedgpethi	E_i–O_n	S	R	E	C_2
Distorsio clathrata	O	S	SR	E	C
Doridella obscura	O	S	A	E	C_2
Elysia sp.	E_t	E	A	E	H
Episcynia inornata	O_n	S	S	E	H
Epitonium albidum	O	S	S	E	C
E. angulatum	E_i–O	S	S	E	C
E. cf. A. apiculatum	O	S	S	E	C
E. cf. E. humphreysi	E_i–O_n	E	S	E	C
E. multistriatum	E_i–O	S	S	E	C
E. novangliae	O	S	S	E	C
E. rupicola	E_i–O_n	S	S	E	C
E. sericifilum	E_i–O_n	S	S	E	C
E. cf. E. tollini	O	S	S	E	C
Eulima cf. E. bilineatus	O_n	S	I	E	EP
Eulimastoma cf. E. canaliculata	O	S	S, I	E	EP
E. cf. E. harbisonae	E_i–O	S	S	E	EP
E. cf. E. teres	E_t	E	M–S	E	EP
E. cf. E. weberi	E_t	E	M–S	E	EP
Fasciolaria lilium	O	S	S	E	C
F. tulipa	O	S	S, G	E	C
Fiona pinnata	O	S	?	P, E	C
Glaucus atlanticus	O	S	?	E, P	C
Graphis underwoodae	E	E	D	E	?
Haminoea antillarum	E_t	E	A, G	S	C
H. succinea	E_i	E	A, G	S	C
Hastula maryleeae	O_s	S	S	I	C
H. salleana	O_s	S	S	I	C
Heliacus bisulcata	J	S	I	E	C
Henrya goldmani	E	S–U	?	E	?
Janthina globosa	O	S	—	E, P	C
J. janthina	O	S	—	E, P	C

321

Gastropod Species	Habitat	Salinity	Substratum	Form	Feeding
J. pallida	O	S	—	E, P	C
J. prolongata	O	S	—	E, P	C
Kurtziella cf. *K. atrostyla*	O_o	S	?	E	C
K. cf. *K. cerina*	E_i	E?	M–S	E	C
K. cf. *K. limonitella*	E_i–O	E?	M–S	E	C
K. cf. *K. rubella*	O	S	?	E	C
Lamellaria cf. *L. leucosphaera*	J	S	I	E	C
Litiopa melanostoma	O	S	A	E, P	C
Littoridinops sp. A	E_u	O	M–S	E	DF
L. sp. B	E_u	O	M–S	E	DF
Littorina angulifera	E	E	H	E	G
L. irrorata	E_t	E	G	E	G
L. lineolata	J	S	H	E	G
L. meleagris	E_i, J	S	H	E	G
L. nebulosa	E_i, J	S	H	E	G
Lucapinella limatula	E_i–O	E	H	E	G
Macromphalina palmalitoris	O_o	S	A, R	E	DF
Melampus bidentatus	E_t	O	D	S	G
Mitrella lunata	E_t	E	A	E	C?, H
*Modulus modulus**					
Murex fulvescens	O_o	S	R, S	S	C
M. pomum	O_o	S	R, S	S	C
Nannodiella cf. *N. vespuciana*	O	S	?	E	C
Nassarius acutus	O_n–E_i	S	S	S	S
N. vibex	E_t, O_o	E	M–S	S	S, C
Natica canrena	O_o	S	SR	I	C
N. pusilla	O_n–E_i	S	S	I	C
Nerita fulgurans	J	S	H	E	G
Neritina reclivata	E_u	E	G	E	G
N. virginea	E	E	G	E	G
Niso aegless	E_i, O_o	E	I	E	EP
Odostomia dux	E_i	E	I?	E	EP
O. cf. *O. emeryi*	E_i–O	S	I?	E	EP
O. cf. *O. gibbosa*	E_i	S	I?	E	EP
O. impressa	E, O	E	H, I	E	EP
O. laevigata	E_i–O_n	S	I?	E	EP
O. cf. *O. livida*	E_i	E	I?	E	EP
O. seminuda	E_i–O	S	I?	E	EP
Oliva sayana	E_i–O_n	S	S	I	S, C
Olivella dealbata	E_i–O_n	S	S	I	S
O. minuta	O_s–O_n	S	S	I	S
?Parviturboides interruptus	O_n	S	SR	E	H?
Pedipes mirabilis	J	E	H	E	G
Peristichia toreta	O	S	I	E	EP
Phalium granulatum granulatum	O_n	S	S	E	C
Pisania tincta	J	S	H	E	C

* Not found alive, probably fossil.

Gastropod Species	Habitat	Salinity	Substratum	Form	Feeding
Pleurobranchaea hedgpethi	E_i O_o	S	?	E	H
Pleuromalaxis balesi	E_i–O	S	SR	E	H
Pleuroploca gigantea	O–J	S	SR	E	C
Polinices duplicatus	E_i–O	S	S	I	C
P. hepaticus	O	S	S	I	C
*Prunum apicina**					
Pseudocyphoma intermedium	O_n	S	I	E	C_2
Pyramidella crenulata	E_i–O_n	S	S, I	E	EP
Pyrgocythara plicosa	E_o	E	S	E	C
Recluzia rollaniana	O	S	—	E, P	C
Rictaxis ? punctostriatus	E_i–O	S	S?	I	C
Rissoina catesbyana	E_i	E	S, G	E	DF
Scyllaea pelagica	O	S	A	E, P	C
Seila adamsi	E_t	E	M, S	E	H
Simnialena marferula	O	S	I	E	C_2
S. uniplicata	O	S	I	E	C_2
Sinum maculatum	O_o	S	S	I	C
S. perspectivum	E_i–O	S	S	I	C
Siphonaria pectinata	E_i, J	S	H	E	H
Smaragdia viridis viridemaris	E_t	E	S, G	E	G
Solariorbis blakei	E_i–O	S	SR	E	DF
S. infracarinata	E_i	E	SR	E	DF
S. mooreana	O_n	S	SR	E	DF
Spurilla neapolitana	O	S	?	E	C_2
Strombus alatus	O	S	S	E	H
*Tegula fasciata**					
Teinostoma biscaynense	E_i–O	E	SR?	E	DF
T. leremum	E_i	E	SR	E	DF
T. parvicallum	O_n	S	SR	E	DF
Terebra dislocata	O_n	S	S	I	C
T. protexta	O_n–O_o	S	M, S	I	C
T. taurina	O_o	S	S	I	C
Texadina barretti	E_u	O	M	E	DF
T. spinctostoma	E_u	O–E	M	E	DF
Thais haemastoma canaliculata	J	S	H	E	C
T. h. floridana	J–E_i	S	H	E	C
Tonna galea	E_i–O	S	S	E	C
Tricolia affinis cruenta	E_i–O	E	A, H	E	G
Triphora perversa nigrocinta	E_i–E_t	S	M, S	E	C_2
Trivia suffusa	O	S	I, H	E	C_2
Truncatella caribaeensis	E_u	E	D	E	G, DF
Turbonilla cf. *T. elegantula*					EP
T. cf. *T. hemphilli*					EP
T. cf. *T. interrupta*					EP
T. cf. *T. portoricana*					EP

* Not found alive, probably fossil.

Gastropod Species	Habitat	Salinity	Substratum	Form	Feeding
T. sp. A					EP
T. sp. B					EP
T. sp. C					EP
T. sp. D					EP
T. sp. E					EP
T. sp. F } [unidentified but readily found]					EP
T. sp. G					EP
T. sp. H					EP
T. sp. I					EP
T. sp. J					EP
T. sp. K					EP
Vermicularia cf. *V. spirata**					
Vioscalba louisianae	E_u	O	M	E	DF
Vitrinella floridana	E_i–O_o	S	SR	E	DF
V. helicoidea	O_n	S	SR	E	DF
V. texana	O_n	S	SR	I	DF
Volvulella persimilis	O_n–O_o	S	SR	I	C
V. texasiana	O_n–O_o	S	M–C	I	C
Zebina browniana	E_i–O_o?	E	S, G	E	DF

Bivalve Species	Habitat	Salinity	Substratum	Form	Feeding
Abra aequalis	E_i–O_n	S	M, C	I	SF
Aequipecten muscosus	O_n	S	H	E	SF
Aligena texasiana	E_i	E	I	I_{co}	SF
Amygdalum papyria	E_t–O_o	E	G, A, M–C	E	SF
Anadara brasiliana	O_n	S	S	I	SF
A. chemnitzi	O	S	S	E	SF
A. floridana	O	S	A, S	I	SF
A. ovalis	E_i–O	S	M, C	S	SF
A. transversa	E_i–O_n, O_o	S	H, S, SR	I	SF
Anatina anatina	O_n	S	S	I	SF
Anodontia alba	E_u	S	?	I	SF
*A. philippiana**					
Anomalocardia auberiana	E–O	E, S, U	M, S	I	SF
Anomia simplex	E_u, O_o	E	H	E	SF
Arca imbricata	J, O	S	H	E	SF
*A. zebra***	O_o	S	A_c	E	SF
*Arcinella cornuta**					
Argopecten gibbus	E_i–O	S	S	E	SF
A. irradians amolicostatus	E_t	E	G, A	E	SF
Atrina seminuda	E_i	E	S	S	SF
A. serrata	O_n	S	S	S	SF
Bankia gouldi	E–O	E	W	I, P	SF
*Barbatia cancellaria***	O	S	H?	E	SF
B. candida	O	S	H	E	SF
B. domingensis	J, O	S	H	E	SF
B. tenera	O	S	H	E	SF
Barnea truncata	E_t	E	C	I	SF

* Not found alive, probably fossil.
** Adventitious.

Bivalve Species	Habitat	Salinity	Substratum	Form	Feeding
Brachidontes exustus	E_o	E	A	E	SF
Callista maculata	O_o	S	S	I	SF
C. nimbosa*					
Callocardia texasiana	O	S	C, M	I	SF
Carditamera floridana*					
Chama congregata	O_n	S	H	E	SF
C. macerophylla	O	S	H	E	SF
Chione cancellata	E_i–O	E	S	I	SF
C. clenchi	O	S	S	I	SF
C. grus	E_i–O	S	S	I	SF
C. intapupurea	O	S	S	I	SF
Codakia orbicularis	O_o	S	S	I	SF
Corbula cf. *C. barrattiana***	O	S	M, S	I	SF
C. cf. *C. contracta*	E_i, O_o	E	C, S	I	SF
C. cf. *C. dietziana***	O	S	S	I	SF
C. cf. *C. krebsiana***	O	S	S	I	SF
C. operculata	O	S	S	I	SF
C. cf. *C. swiftiana*	E_i	E	S	I	SF
Crassinella lunulata	E_i–O_n	S	S	I	SF
Crassostrea virginica	E_t	E	H	E	SF
Cumingia tellinoides	E_i–O	S	M	I	SF
Cyclinella tenuis	E_i–O_n	S	S?	I	SF
Cyrtopleura costata	E_i–O	E	C, S	I	SF
Diplodonta semiaspera	E_i–J	E	H	I	SF
D. cf. *D. soror*	E_t	E	M	I	SF
Diplothyra smithii	E_t–E_u	E	H	I	SF
Donax texasianus	O_s	S	S	I	SF
D. variabilis roemeri	O_s	S	S	I	SF
Dosinia discus	O_n–E_i	S	S	I	SF
D. elegans	O_o	S	S	I	SF
Ensis minor	E_i–E	E	S	I	SF
Ervilla cf. *E. concentrica*	E_i–O	E	S?	I	SF
Gastrochaena hians	O	S	H	I	SF
Gemma cf. *G. purpurea*	E_t	E	C, S	I	SF
Geukensia demissa granosissima	E_t	E	G	E	SF
Gregariella coralliophaga	O	S	H	S	SF
Hiatella arctica	O	S	W	I	SF
Ischadium recurvum	E_t–E_o	E	H	E	SF
Isognomon alatus	J	S	H	E	SF
I. bicolor	J	S	H	E	SF
Jouannetia quillingi	O	S	W	I, P	SF
Laevicardium laevigatum	O_o	S	S	I	SF
L. mortoni	E_t	E	M, G	I	SF
L. robustum	O_n–E_t	S	S	I	SF
Lepton cf. *L. lepidum*	E_i–O	S	I	I_{co}	SF
Lima lima**	O_n	S	H	E	SF
L. pellucida**	O_o	S	H	E	SF
Linga amiantus	E_i–O_n	S	M, S?	I	SF
Lioberis castaneus	E_i–O	S	H	I	SF

* Not found alive, probably fossil.
** Adventitious.

Bivalve Species	Habitat	Salinity	Substratum	Form	Feeding
Lithophaga aristata	J	S	H	I	SF
L. bisulcata	J	S	H	I	SF
Lucina pectinata	E_t	E	S	I	SF
Lyonsia hyalina floridana	E_i	E	C, S	I	SF
Lyrodus pedicellatus	O	S	W	I, P	SF
Lyropecten nodosus	O_o	S	H	E	SF
Macoma brevifrons	E_i–O	E	S	I	DF
M. constricta	E_i–O	E	M, S	I	DF
M. mitchelli	E_t	E	M	I	DF
M. pulleyi	O	S	M	I	DF
M. tageliformis	E_i–O	S	C, S	I	DF
M. tenta	E_t	E	M, S	I	DF
Mactra fragilis	E_t	E	G, S	I	SF
Martesia cuneiformis	O	S	W	I, P	SF
M. fragilis	E_t	E	G, S	I	SF
Mercenaria campechiensis	O_n	S	S	I	SF
M. campechiensis texana	E_t	E	S, C	I	SF
Modiolus americanus	O	S	H	E	SF
Mulinia lateralis	E–O	E, S, U	C, S	I	SF
Musculus lateralis	E_i–O_n	E	I	I	SF
Mysella planulata	E_t	E	M	E	SF
Mytilopsis leucophaeta	E_u	E	H	E	SF
Noetia ponderosa	E_i–O_n	E	S	I	SF
Nucula cf. N. proxima	E_i	E	C, S	I	DF
Nuculana acuta	E_i–O	S	M, S	I	DF
N. concentrica	E_i–O_n, O_o	S	M	I	DF
Ostrea equestris	E_i	E	H	E	SF
Pandora trilineata	E_i–O_n	S	S	I	SF
Panopea bitruncata	E_i–O	S	C	I	SF
Paramya subovata	O	S	I	I_{co}	SF
Parvilucina multilineata	E_i–O	S	M, S	I	SF
Pecten raveneli	O	S	S	E	SF
Periploma margaritaceum	E_i–O_n	S	S	I	SF
Petricola pholadiformis	E_i	E	C	I	SF
P. typica	O	S	H	E	SF
Pholas campechiensis	O	S	C, W	I	SF
Pinctada imbricata	O	S	I	E	SF
Plicatula gibbosa	O	S	H	E	SF
Pododesmus rudis	J	S	H	E	SF
Polymesoda caroliniana	E_u	O	M	I	SF
P. maritima	E_t	E	M, S	I	SF
Pseudochama radians	J	S	H	E	SF
Pseudomiltha floridana	E_t	E	S	I	SF
Pteria colymbus	O	S	I	E	SF
Raeta plicatella	O_n	S	S	I	SF
Rangia cuneata	E_u	O	C, M	I	SF
R. flexuosa	E_u	O	C, M	I	SF
*Sanguinolaria sanguinolenta***	O_o	S	S	I	SF
Semele bellastriata	O	S	S, A_c	I	DF

** Adventitious.

Bivalve Species	Habitat	Salinity	Substratum	Form	Feeding
S. proficua	E_i	E	S	I	DF
S. purpurascens	O	S	S	I	DF
Solecurtus cumingianus*					
Solen viridis	E_t	E	C, S	I	SF
Spisula solidissima similis	O_n	S	S	I	SF
Spondylus americanus	O_o	S	H	E	SF
Strigilla mirabilis	E_i–O	S	S	I	DF
Tagelus divisus	E_t	E	C, S	I	DF
T. plebeius	E_t	E	C, S	I	DF
Tellidora cristata	E_i	E	S	I	SF
Tellina aequistriata	O_n, O_o	S	S, M	I	SF
T. alternata	O_n	S	S	I	SF
T. a. tayloriana	O_n–E_i	S	S	I	SF
T. iris	O_n–E_i	S	S, SR	I	SF
T. lineata*					
T. tampaensis	E_t	E	S, M	I	SF
T. texana	E_t	E	S, M	I	SF
T. versicolor	E_i–O_n	S	S	I	SF
Teredo bartschi	O	S	W	I, P	SF
Trachycardium isocardia	O_o	S	S	I	SF
T. muricatum	E_i	E	S, M	I	SF

Polyplacophora Species

	Habitat	Salinity	Substratum	Form	Feeding
Chaetopleura apiculata	E_i	E	H	E	G
Ischnochiton papillosus	E_i	E	H	E	G

Scaphopoda Species

	Habitat	Salinity	Substratum	Form	Feeding
Cadulus sp. A	O_n	S	S	S	DF
Dentalium sp. A	E_i–O_n	S	C?	S	DF
D. sp. B	E_i–O_n?	S	C?	S	DF
D. sp. C	E_i–O_n?	S	C?	S	DF
D. texasianum	E_i–O_o	S	C	S	DF

Cephalopoda Species

	Habitat	Salinity	Substratum	Form	Feeding
Lolinguncula brevis	O_n	S	—	E	C
Octopus vulgaris	O_o	S	R	E	C
Spirula spirula	O_o	S	—	E	C

Source: Andrews & Blanton, in press.
Consultant: Granvil D. Treece, University of Texas Marine Science Institute, Port Aransas, Texas.
* Not found alive, probably fossil.

Glossary

ABAPICAL: away from shell apex toward base along axis or slightly oblique to it.

ABERRANT: deviating from the usual type of its group; abnormal, straying, different.

ACCESSORY: aiding the principal design; contributory, supplemental, additional.

ACUMINATE: sharply pointed.

ACUTE: sharp; a spire with an angle of less than ninety degrees.

ADAPICAL: toward shell apex along axis or slightly oblique to it.

ADDUCTOR MUSCLES: muscles that hold the valves of a bivalve together.

ADPRESSED: overlapping whorls with their outer surfaces very gradually converging; preferred to the term *appressed*.

ADVENTITIOUS: Not inherent; accidental, casual.

ANAL: pertaining to or near the anus, or posterior opening of the alimentary canal.

ANALOG: an organism analogous to one in another species group; having a similar function but different in origin and structure.

ANGULATE: having angles, sharp corners, or an edge where two surfaces meet at an angle.

ANNULATED: marked with rings.

ANOMPHALOUS: lacking umbilicus.

ANTERIOR: the forward end of a bivalve shell.

APERTURE: an opening; the cavity of the snail.

APEX (plural APEXES or APICES): the tip of the spire of a snail shell.

APOCRINE: secreting externally; the opposite of endocrine.

APOPHYSIS: a bony protuberance; a fingerlike structure; spoon-shaped, calcareous.

ARCHETYPE: the ancestral type established hypothetically by eliminating specialized characters of known later forms.

ARCUATE: curved, as a bow, or arched, as the ventral edge in some pelecypods.

AURICULATE: having ear-shaped projections.

AURIFORM: shaped like a human ear.

AXIAL: in the same direction as the axis; from apex to the base of a snail shell. Axial ribs are those parallel to the edge of the outer lip. *Transverse* is a preferred term.

BACKSHORE: the part of the shore lying between foreshore and the coastline; covered with water only by exceptional storms or tides.

BASE: in snails, the extremity opposite the apex, the bottom of. In clams, the part of the margin opposite the beaks.

BEAK: the earliest-formed part of a bivalve shell; the tip near the hinge; the umbo.

BENTHOS: the whole assemblage of plants or animals living in or upon the sea bottom.

BICONICAL: similar in form to a double cone; the spire about the same shape and size as the body whorl.

BIFID: divided into two branches, arms, or prongs or into two equal parts by a cleft; separated down the middle by a slit; divided by a groove into two parts.

BIVALVE: a shell with two valves; pelecypod, such as oyster, scallop, or mussel.

BLADE: the broad flat portion of the pallet of all teredinids; the blade and the stalk are the two parts of the pallet.

BODY WHORL: the last and usually the largest turn in a snail's shell.

BUCCAL: pertaining to the mouth or cheek.

BYSSAL GAPE: an opening or a gaping on the ventral margin of bivalves for the passage of the byssus.

BYSSUS: a series or clump of threadlike fibers that serve to anchor the bivalve to some support.

CALCAREOUS: shelly; of hard calcium carbonate.

CALLUM: a sheet of shelly material filling in the anterior gape in adult shells.

CALLUS: a deposit of calcareous, or enamellike, material, mostly around the aperture in snails.

CANAL: a tubular prolongation; e.g., in snails, the siphonal canal is at the base of the shell and contains the siphon.

CANCELLATE: sculpture lines intersecting at right angles.

CARDINAL TEETH: the main, or largest, teeth in a bivalve hinge located just below the beaks or umbones.

CARINATE: with a keellike, elevated ridge, or carina.

CARNIVOROUS: feeding on living animal matter.

CERATA (singular CERAS): external outgrowths, presumably respiratory in nature, along each side of the dorsal surface.

CHITIN: a hard colorless compound that forms the main substance of the hard covering of insects and crustaceans.

CHONDROPHORE: a pit, or spoonlike shelf, in the hinge of a bivalve, such as *Mactra*, into which fits a chitinous cushion, or resilium.

CILIA: hairlike processes on the surface of a cell or organ, shorter and more numerous than flagella.

CIRCUMTROPICAL: throughout the tropics.

COGNATE: allied by deviation from the same source.

COLONIAL: a kind of animal that is organized into associations (colonies) of incompletely separated individuals; e.g., *Physalia*, sponges, and corals.

COLUMELLA: a pillar or column around which the whorls of a snail form their spiral circuit.

COMMENSAL: a symbiotic relationship where only one organism benefits.

COMPRESSED: flattened or "squashed."

CONCAVE: hollow or dished, as opposed to convex.

CONCENTRIC: as in circles or lines of sculpture, one within the other.

CONCHOLOGY: the branch of zoology that embraces the arrangement and description of mollusks based upon a study of the hard parts.

CONFLUENT: flowing together as to form one.

CONIC: cone-shaped, conical, peaked.

CONSPECIFIC: of or pertaining to the same species; members of the same species.

CONSTRICT: draw tight or compress at some point; bind, cramp.

CONVEX: curving outward like a segment of a circle.

COPPICE DUNE: a mound formed by wind in conflict with bunch vegetation.

CORD: coarse, rounded spiral or transverse linear sculpture on the shell surface; smaller than costae.

CORNEOUS: consisting of horn, of a hornlike texture, as the opercula of some mollusks, such as *Busycon*.

CORONATE: encircled by a row of spines or prominent nodes, especially at the shoulder of the last whorl in snails.

COSTAE: ribs.

COSTATE: having ribs.

CRENULATE: notched or scalloped around the margin.

CUSP: a prominence, or point; temporary ridges of sand perpendicular to shoreline.

CUTICLE: an outer layer of cells; the precursor of the calcified shell.

CYLINDRICAL: round, like a cylinder with parallel sides; having the form of a cylinder.

DECIDUOUS: having the tendency to fall off early or before maturity, as the periostracum of most *Cymatium*.

DECK: a septum, or small sheet of shelly substance in the umbonal region connecting the anterior and posterior ends of a valve; also used to describe the diaphragm of *Crepidula*.

DENTICLES: small projections, resembling teeth, around the margin of the gastropod aperture or the pelecypod valve.

DENTICULATED: toothed.

DETRITUS: disintegrated material.

DEXTRAL: turning from left to right; right-handed.

DIAMETER: the greatest width of the shell at right angles to the shell axis.

DIMORPHISM: occurrence of two distinct morphological types in a single population; in sexual dimorphism, male and female forms are different.

DISC: the space between the umbo and the margin of a bivalve shell.

DISCOID: disc-shaped; whorls coiled in one plane.

DORSAL: belonging to the dorsum, or back; the edge of a bivalve in the region of the hinge; the back of a gastropod opposite the aperture.

ECOLOGY: the study of the relationship between organisms and their environment, both animate and inanimate.

ECTOPARASITE: a parasitic animal, such as the snail *Pyramidella*, which infests the outsides of some bivalves, piercing the shell with a buccal stylet and feeding upon the soft parts.

EDENTULOUS: without teeth.

ELONGATE: lengthened; longer than wide.

ENDEMIC: native, not introduced; having the habitat in a certain region or country.

ENTIRE: smoothly arched, without a reentrant curve, sinus, or crenulation.

EPIDERMIS: skin.

EPIFAUNA: animals that normally live exposed, above the substratum surface; may be with or without attachment.

EQUILATERAL: the anterior and posterior ends of each valve being of equal size.

EQUIVALVE: the two valves of a bivalve being of the same shape and size.

ERODED: appearing as if eaten or gnawed away.

ESCUTCHEON: a long, somewhat depressed area of the dorsal area just posterior to the beaks of a bivalve.

EXUDATE: any substance which filters through the walls of living cellular tissue and is available for removal.

FASCIOLE: a small band; a distinct band of color; a spiral band formed in gastropods by the successive growth lines on the edges of a canal.

FATHOM: a nautical unit of measure (six feet), used principally for measuring cables and the depth of the ocean by means of a sounding line.

FLAGELLA: whiplike processes.

FLAMMULATIONS: small flame-shaped spots of color.

FOLIACEOUS: leaflike, flattened, projecting like tiles.

FOOT: muscular extension of body used in locomotion.

FORESHORE: the intertidal zone.

FOSSIL: any hardened remains or traces of plant or animal life of some previous geological period, preserved in rock formations in the earth's crust.

FUSIFORM: spindle-shaped with a long canal and an equally long spire, tapering from the middle toward each end; applied to univalves.

GAMETE: either male or female mature reproductive cells; an ovum or a sperm.

GAPING: having the valves not meet; leaving a space.

GASTROPOD: a univalve; snail, conch, whelk, etc.

GENUS (plural GENERA): a group of species, distinguished from all other groups by certain permanent features called generic characters.

GIBBOSE or GIBBOUS: swollen.

GLABROUS: smooth.

GLAZED: having a shiny surface.

GLOBULAR: globe or sphere-shaped, like a ball.

GRANULATED: having a rough surface of grainlike elevations.

GROWTH LINES: lines on the shell surface indicating rest periods during growth, denoting a former position of the outer lip.

HABITAT: the kind of place where an organism normally lives.

HEIGHT: in gastropods, the greatest length parallel to the shell axis through the columella; in pelecypods, the greatest vertical dimension through the beak at right angles to a line bisecting the adductor scars.

HELICOCONE: distally expanding coiled tube that forms most gastropod shells.

HERBIVOROUS: feeding on vegetable matter.

HERMAPHRODITE: having the sexes united in the same individual.

HETEROSTROPHIC: having the protoconch coiled in a direction that is contrary to the coil of the teleoconch.

HINGE: where the valves of a bivalve are joined.

HOLOSTOMATE: having aperture of the shell rounded or entire, without a canal, notch, or any extension.

HOLOTYPE: the original type; a single specimen upon which a species is based.

HYPOPLAX: an accessory shell piece between the valves ventrally on some burrowing clams.

IMBRICATED: overlapping one another at the margins, shinglelike; to lay or arrange regularly so as to overlap one another.

IMPERFORATE: not perforated or umbilicated; when the spire is quite flat, the umbilicus vanishes entirely; when the whorls are so compactly coiled on an ascending spiral that there is no umbilicus, the shells are termed imperforate. *Anomphalous* is a preferred term.

INCISED: sculptured with one or more sharply cut grooves.

INDIGENOUS: native to the country, originating in a specified place or country.

INDUCTURA: smooth shelly layer secreted by general surface of mantle, commonly extending from inner side of aperture over parietal region, columellar lip, and (in some genera) part or all of shell exterior. Preferred to term often used, *parietal callus*.

INEQUILATERAL: having the anterior and posterior sides of the valves unequal; the umbones nearer one end than the other.

INEQUIVALVE: one valve larger or more convex than the other.

INFAUNA: sessile and mobile animals that spend part or all of their lives buried beneath the substratum.

INFLATED: applied to rotund shells of thin structure; swollen, increased unduly, distended.

INTERCOSTAL: placed or occurring between the ribs.

INTERSPACES: channels between ribs.

INVOLUTE: rolled inward from each side, as in *Cypraea*.

IRIDESCENT: displaying the colors of the rainbow.

KEEL: the longitudinal ridge; a carina, a prominent spiral ridge usually marking a change of slope in the outline of the shell.

LAMELLA: a thin plate or ridge.

LANCEOLATE: long and spearhead-shaped.

LATERAL: to the side of the midline of the body.

LENGTH: in gastropods, the distance from the apex to the anterior end of the shell, same as height; in bivalves, the greatest horizontal dimension at right angles to the height.

LENTICULAR: having the shape of a double convex lens.

LIGAMENT: a cartilage that connects the valves.

LIPS: the margins of the aperture of a snail.

LITTORAL: pertaining to the shore.

LUMEN: the duct or cavity of a tubular organ.

LUNULE: a heart-shaped area, set off by a difference of sculpture, in front of the beaks.

MACROPHAGOUS: consuming large food.

MACULATED: irregularly spotted.

MALACOLOGY: the study of molluscous, or soft, animals; the branch of zoology that deals with the mollusk, the animal within the shell.

MAMMILLIFORM: in the form of a breast.

MANTLES: a fleshy layer or cape that secretes the shell of the mollusk.

MEDIAN: middle.

MESOPLAX: an accessory plate in Pholadacea.

METAPLAX: an accessory plate behind the umbones of some Pholadacea.

MICROPHAGOUS: consuming microscopic food.

MICROSCOPIC: exceedingly minute, visible only under a microscope; opposed to macroscopic.

MILLIMETER (mm): one-thousandth of a meter, 0.03937 of an inch; 25.4 millimeters are equal to one inch.

MORPHOLOGICAL: the structure or form; the morphological features of a spiral shell are the aperture, body whorl, columella, outer lip, and spire.

MUCOCILIARY: a method of feeding associated with sedentary habits. Food particles are entangled with mucus in the gill leaflets and carried in a food groove to the mouth.

MUCUS (adjective MUCOUS): a sticky, slimy, watery secretion.

MULTISPIRAL: consisting of many whorls.

NACRE: an iridescent layer of shell, sometimes called "mother of pearl."

NAUTILOID: resembling the nautilus in shape.

NEOTYPE: a specimen selected to replace the original type if it is lost or destroyed.

NODOSE: having knoblike projections or nodules.

NUCLEAR WHORLS: the first whorls formed in the apex of a snail during the egg or veliger stages.

NUCLEUS: the initial whorl, the protoconch.

OBLIQUE: to deviate from the perpendicular; slanting, as the aperture of some shells.

OMPHALOUS: with umbilicus.

OPERCULUM: a cover or lid; in snails, a shelly or horny plate attached to the foot and used to close the aperture of the shell.

ORBICULAR: round or circular.

ORIFICE: a small opening into a cavity.

OUTER LIP: the apertural margin of the last part of the body whorl of a snail shell.

OVATE: egg-shaped in outline.

PALLET: one of the two lance-shaped plates forming the closing apparatus at the siphonal end of some wood-boring mollusks.

PALLIAL LINE: a groove or channel near the inner margin of a bivalve shell, where the mantle is made fast to the lower part of the shell. When this line is continuous and not marked with a pallial sinus, it is said to be simple.

PALLIAL SINUS: a U-shaped indentation in the pallial line produced by the siphon.

PAPILLA: a small nipplelike projection.

PARAPODIA: lateral expansions of the foot of certain opisthobranchs that can be used for swimming or to envelop the shell.

PARASITISM: *See* SYMBIOSIS.

PARATYPE: a specimen other than the holotype used in the description of a species.

PARIETAL WALL: the area on the whorl of a snail near the columella and opposite the outer lip.

PAUCISPIRAL: with few turns, as some of the opercula.

PELAGIC: pertaining to or inhabiting the open sea far from land; animals living at the surface of the water in mid-ocean.

PELECYPOD: a bivalve; clam, mussel, or scallop.

PENULTIMATE WHORL: the next-to-the-last whorl.

PERIOSTRACUM: the outer layer of a shell, composed of a form of sclerotized protein, or conchiolin.

PERIPHERY: the perimeter of the external surface.

PERISTOME: the margin of the aperture.

PHANEROMPHALOUS: with completely open umbilicus.

PHYLOGENY: the history of the evolution of a species.

PHYLUM: a primary division of the animal or plant kingdom.

PLANKTON: life floating or drifting in the sea.

PLANORBOID: flat; whorls in one plane; discoid. *Planispiral* is not recommended (Cox 1955, p. 200).

PLATH: a chitinous or calcareous accessory of the complicated pholad shell, somewhat flat in shape and held in place by chitinous folds; e.g., protoplax, mesoplax, metaplax, hypoplax.

PLICATE: folded or with plaits, or plicae.

PLICATION: a fold, especially on the columella of a gastropod.

PLUG: the apical closing formed when the Caecidae discard the hindering juvenile portion of the shell.

PORCELANEOUS: having the quality of porcelain; hard and shiny.

POSTERIOR: situated away from the anterior part of the shell.

PROBOSCIS: a long flexible snout.

PROPODIUM: the foremost division of the foot of a gastropod used to push aside sediment as the animal crawls.

PROTANDRIC: reference to a hermaphroditic organism that starts in the male stage.

PROTOCONCH: the larval shell of a univalve, frequently different in design, texture, or color from the adult shell; the rudimentary or embryonic shell of a bivalve mollusk is called a *prodissoconch*.

PROTOPLAX: one of the accessory plates in Pholadacea.

PUSTULOSE: marked with pustules or pimplelike projections.

PYRIFORM: pear-shaped.

QUADRATE: squarish or rectangular in general outline.

RADIAL LINES: lines of color or sculpture fanning out from the beaks to the margins of a valve.

RADULA: a rasplike organ, or lingual ribbon, armed with toothlike processes, found in nearly all mollusks except clams.

RECURVED: bent downward.

REFLECTED: bent backward.

RESILIUM: a triangular ligament structure; a tough chitinous pad, residing in a chondrophore, or pit, along the inner hinge margin of a bivalve which causes the shell to spring open when the muscles relax.

RETICULATE: crossed, like a network.

REVOLVING: turning with the whorls, or spirally.

RHINOPHORES: the posterior pair of tentacles on many opisthobranchs, especially nudibranchs.

RIB: a long and narrow ridge, strip; a firm riblike elevation.

ROSTRATE: drawn out, like a bird's beak.

ROSTRUM: a beaklike process or part; usually used describing the anterior end of bivalves.

RUFOUS: reddish.

RUGOSE: rough or wrinkled.

SCULPTURE: a pattern of raised or depressed markings on the shell's surface.

SEPTUM: a calcareous plate or partition; one of the transverse partitions of a chambered shell; a dividing wall.

SHOULDER: the top, or largest part, of the outline of a whorl.

SINISTRAL: turning counterclockwise; left-handed.

SINUOUS: undulating, winding and turning in an irregular course.

SINUS: a bend, or embayment, either in growth lines or in the attachment scar of the mantle.

SIPHON: a tubular structure through which water enters or leaves the mantle cavity.

SIPHONOSTOMATOUS: with apertural margin interrupted by canal, spout, or notch for protrusion of siphon.

SLOPE: refers to the face of a bivalve shell; e.g., central, anterior, or posterior slope.

SOCKET: a cavity in the hinge of a bivalve to receive the tooth of the opposite valve.

SPECIES: the subdivision of a genus, distinguished from all others of the genus by certain permanent features called specific characters.

SPINE: a pointed process or outgrowth; stiff, sharp.

SPINOSE: with spines.

SPIRAL: revolving, as lines going in the direction of the turning of the whorls.

SPIRE: the upper whorls, from the apex to the body whorl, but not including the body whorl.

SPOIL BANKS: banks and islands formed as a result of dredging operations.

STRIATED: marked with rows of fine grooves, often microscopic in size.

SUB-: a prefix indicating "somewhat" or "almost"; as subglobular—almost round.

SUBSTRATUM: an underlying layer; the sea floor; preferred to *substrate*.

SUFFUSED: overspreading; to overspread as with color; to cover the surface.

SULCUS: a slit or fissure.

SUTURE: a spiral line, or groove, where one whorl touches another.

SYMBIOSIS: to live together; a condition in which two animals, two plants, or a plant and an animal live in partnership. At one time, and occasionally today, the term was restricted to an association supposed to be to the mutual advantage of both organisms. The relationship can be that of *commensalism*, where one organism benefits from the activities of the other; *parasitism*, where one organism lives on another to the detriment of its host; or *mutualism*, where both organisms benefit from the association.

SYNONYM: having the same meaning; or being a different name for the same species.

SYNTYPE: one of several specimens of equal rank upon which a species is based.

TAXONOMY: the systematic classification of organisms.

TEETH: in a bivalve, the shelly protuberances on the dorsal margin of a valve that fit into corresponding sockets of the opposite valve.

TELEOCONCH: the entire gastropod shell except the protoconch.

THREAD: a slender linear surface elevation; the silky fibers of the byssus.

TOPOTYPE: a specimen collected at the same locality where the original type was obtained.

TORSION: a 180° counterclockwise rotation of the gastropod visceral hump and mantle cavity occurring in early larval stage.

TRANSLUCENT: allowing light to pass through, but not transparent.

TRIGONAL: somewhat triangular in shape.

TRUNCATE: having the end cut off squarely.

TUBERCULES: small, raised projections.

TUMID: swollen, enlarged.

TURBINATE: conical with a round base.

TURRICULATE: having the form of a turret; tower-shaped; spire whorls regularly stepped in outline forming a long spire with somewhat shouldered whorls.

TYPE: a fundamental structure common to a number of individuals, having the essential characteristics of its group; a specimen or specimens upon which a description of a species is based (see Appendix B).

UMBILICUS: a small hole, or depression, in the base of the body whorl of a snail shell.

UMBO (plural UMBONES): the upper, or early, part of the bivalve shell as seen from the outside, at the hinge.

UNDULATE: having a wavy surface.

UNGUICULATE: resembling a claw, or talon.

UNIVALVE: a snail shell; gastropod.

VALVE: one of the shelly halves of a clam shell or one of the eight plates of a chiton.

VARIX (plural VARICES): a prominent raised rib on the surface of a snail shell, caused by a periodic thickening of the lip during rest periods in the shell's growth.

VELIGER: a mollusk in the larval stage, in which it has a ciliated swimming membrane or membranes; free-swimming young.

VENTER: the abdomen, or belly; hence, the ventral surface.

VENTRAL: the lower side, opposite the dorsal area.

VENTRICOSE: swollen.

VERGE: penis, male copulatory organ.

VERMICULATION: surface sculpture of irregular wavy lines.

VERMIFORM: like a worm in shape.

VICARIANT: species with common ancestry for the closely related pair, usually very similar, that occupy adjacent areas separated by a barrier (Croizat et al. 1974).

VITREOUS: glassy.

VIVIPAROUS: producing live young.

WHORL: a complete turn, or volution, of a snail shell.

WIDTH: the maximum dimension measured at right angles to the length or height of the shell.

WING: a more-or-less triangular projection or expansion of the shell of a bivalve, either in the plane of the hinge line or extending above it.

Bibliography

Abbott, R. T.
1944.   The genus *Modulus* in the western Atlantic. *Johnsonia* 1(14):1–6.
1952.   Two new Opisthobranch mollusks from the Gulf of Mexico belonging to the genera *Pleurobranchaea* and *Polycera*. *Florida State Univ. Stud.*, no. 7.
1954.   *American seashells*. Princeton: Van Nostrand.
1958.   *The marine mollusks of Grand Cayman Island, B.W.I.* Acad. Natur. Sci. Philadelphia Monogr., no. 11. Philadelphia.
1963.   The janthinid genus *Recluzia* in the western Atlantic. *Nautilus* 76(4):51.
1964.   *Littorina ziczac* (Gmelin) and *L. lineolata* (Orbigny). *Nautilus* 78(2):65–66.
1968a.   The helmet shells of the world (Cassidae): I, *Indo-Pacific Mollusca* 2(9):7–202.
1968b.   *Seashells of North America: A guide to field identification of the seashells of North America*. New York: Golden Press.
1972.   *Kingdom of the seashell*. New York: Crown Publ.
1974.   *American seashells*. 2d ed. New York: Van Nostrand–Reinhold.
1975.   Notes on *Thais haemastoma*. *Texas Conch.* 12(2):31.
Abbott, R. T., and H. S. Ladd
1951.   A new brackish-water gastropod from Texas (Amnicolidae: *Littoridina*). *J. Washington Acad. Sci.* 41(10):335–338.
Abbott, R. T., and M. E. Young, eds.

1973–74.   *American malacologists*. Greenville, Md.: Amer. Malacol.
Adams, A.
1855.   Further contributions toward the natural history of the Trochidae. *Proc. Zool. Soc. London* 22[for 1854]:37–44.
Adams, C. B.
1849–52.   *Contributions to conchology*. 12 vols. Privately printed. [See Clench and Turner 1950a for Adams's descriptions and complete bibliography.]
Aguayo, C. G.
1949.   Malacology and the official list of generic names. *Nautilus* 63(1):17.
Akin, R. M., and H. J. Humm
1960.   *Macrocallista nimbosa* at Alligator Harbor. *J. Florida Acad. Sci.* 22(4):226–228.
Alder, ——
1848.   *Moll. Northumberland and Durham. See* Forbes and Hanley 1849–53, 3:237.
Allee, W. C.
1923.   Studies in marine ecology: III, Some physical factors related to the distribution of littoral invertebrates. *Biol. Bull. Marine Biol. Lab., Woods Hole* 44:205–253.
Allen, J. F.
1955.   A note on *Amygdalum papyria* Conrad in Maryland waters of Chesapeake Bay. *Nautilus* 68(3):83–87.
1958.   Feeding habits of two species of *Odostomia*. *Nautilus* 72(1):11–15.
Altena, C. O. van R.
1969.   The marine Mollusca of Suriname (Dutch Guiana)

Holocene and Recent: I, General introduction. *Zoologische Verhandelingen* (Leiden) 1(101):1–49.
1971.   The marine Mollusca of Suriname (Dutch Guiana) Holocene and Recent: II, Bivalvia and Scaphopoda. *Zoologische Verhandelingen* (Leiden) 2(119):1–99.
1975.   The marine Mollusca of Suriname (Dutch Guiana) Holocene and Recent: III, Gastropoda and Cephalopoda. *Zoologische Verhandelingen* (Leiden) 3(139):1–104.
Amos, W. H.
1966.   *The life of the seashore*. New York: McGraw-Hill.
Anderson, A. A.
1960.   *Marine resources of the Corpus Christi area*. Bur. Bus. Res., Univ. Texas Monogr., no. 21. Austin.
Andrews, E. W.
1969.   *The archeological use and distribution of Mollusca in the Maya lowlands*. Middle American Res. Inst. Pub., no. 34. New Orleans: Tulane Univ.
Andrews, J.
1963.   *See* Wasson, J. A.
1971.   *Sea shells of the Texas coast*. Austin: Univ. Texas Press.
Andrews, J., and W. G. Blanton
In press.   Marine molluscs from shallow-water environments off the southern Texas coast, including the Padre Island National Seashore. In *A biological survey of the Padre Island National Seashore*. Nat. Park Serv. Sci. Monogr., no. 3. Washington, D.C.: U.S. Dept. Int.

Ansell, A. D.
1969   Leaping movements in the Bivalvia. *Proc. Malacol. Soc. London* 38:387–399.

Apley, M. L.
1970.   Field studies on life history, gonadal cycle, and reproductive periodicity in *Melampus bidentatus* (Pulmonata: Ellobiidae). *Malacologia* 10(2):381–397.

Armstrong, L. R.
1965.   Burrowing limitations in Pelecypoda. *Veliger* 7(3):195–200.

Arnold, A. F.
1901.   *The sea beach at ebbtide*. Reprint, New York: Dover Pub., 1968.

Arnold, W. H.
1965.   A glossary of a thousand and one terms used in conchology. *Veliger* 7:suppl.

Baker, E. B., and A. S. Merrill
1965.   An observation of *Laevicardium mortoni* actually swimming. *Nautilus* 78(3):104.

Bandel, K.
1974.   Studies on Littorinidae from the Atlantic. *Veliger* 17(2):92–114.
1976.   Observations on spawn, embryonic development, and ecology of some Caribbean lower Mesogastropoda (Mollusca). *Veliger* 18(3):249–271.

Bartsch, P.
1909*a*.   More notes on the family Pyramidellidae. *Nautilus* 23:54–59.
1909*b*.   Pyramidellidae of New England and the adjacent region. *Proc. Boston Soc. Natur. Sci.* 34(4):67–113.
1912.   A zoogeographic study based on the pyramidellid mollusks of the west coast of America. *Proc. U.S. Nat. Mus.* 42(1909):297–349.
1916.   *Eulimastoma*: a new subgenus of pyramidellids and remarks on the genus *Scalenostoma*. *Nautilus* 30(7):73–74.
1920.   The west American mollusks of the families Rissoellidae and Synceratidae and the rissoid genus *Barleeia*. *Proc. U.S. Nat. Mus.* 58(2331):159–176.

1934.   Mollusks: Shelled invertebrates of the past and present. *Smithsonian Inst. Ser.* 10(3).
1947.   A monograph of west Atlantic mollusks of the family Aclididae. *Smithsonian Misc. Coll.* 106(20).
1955.   The pyramidellid mollusks of the Pliocene deposits of north St. Petersburg, Florida. *Smithsonian Misc. Coll.* 125(2).

Bartsch, P., and H. A. Rehder
1939*a*.   Mollusks collected on the presidential cruise of 1938. *Smithsonian Misc. Coll.* 98(10):1–18.
1939*b*.   New turritid mollusks from Florida. *Proc. U.S. Nat. Mus.* 87(3070):127–138.

Baughman, J. L.
N.d.   Taps for Texas lighthouses. *Houston Chronicle Magazine*.

Baughman, J. L., and B. B. Baker
1951.   Oysters in Texas. *Bull. Texas Game Fish & Oyster Comm.* 29:1–37.

Bayer, F. M.
1943.   The Florida species of the family Chamidae. *Nautilus* 56(4):116–124.
1963.   Observations on pelagic mollusks associated with the siphonophores *Velella* and *Physalia*. *Bull. Marine Sci. Gulf & Caribbean* 13(3):454–466.

Bayer, F. M., and G. L. Voss
1971.   *Studies in tropical American mollusks*. Coral Gables: Univ. Miami Press.

Bedichek, R.
1950.   *Karánkaway country*. Reprint, Austin: Univ. Texas Press, 1975.

Behrens, E. W., and R. L. Watson
1969.   Differential sorting of pelecypod valves in the swash zone. *J. Sedim. Petrol.* 39(1):159–165.

Bequaert, J. C.
1942.   *Cerithidea* and *Batillaria* in the western Atlantic. *Johnsonia* 1(5):5–11.
1943.   The genus *Littorina* in the western Atlantic. *Johnsonia* 1(7):1–27.

Bernard, H. A., and R. J. LeBlanc, Sr.
1970.   *Recent sediments of southeast Texas: A field guide to the Brazos alluvial and deltaic plains and the Galveston barrier complex*. Bur. Econ. Geol., Univ. Texas Guidebook, no. 11. Austin.

Berrill, N. J.
1964.   *The living tide*. Greenwich, Conn.: Fawcett Pub.

Bertrand, G. A.
1972.   The ecology of the nest-building bivalve *Musculus lateralis* commensal with the ascidian *Molgula occidentalis*. *Veliger* 14(1):23–29.

Bingham, F. O.
1972.   Several aspects of the reproductive biology of *Littorina irrorata* (Gastropoda). *Nautilus* 86(1):8–10.

Bingham, F. O., and H. D. Albertson
1974.   Observations on the beach strandings of *Physalia* (Portuguese-man-of-war) community. *Veliger* 17(2):220–224.

Bird, S. O.
1965.   Upper Tertiary Arcacea of the mid-Atlantic coastal plain. *Palaeontograph. Amer.* 5(34):1–62.
1970.   Shallow-marine and estuarine benthic molluscan communities from area of Beaufort, North Carolina. *Amer. Assoc. Pet. Geol. Bull.* 54(9):1651–1676.

Blainville, H. M.
1816–30.   Vers et zoophytes. In *Dictionnaire des sciences naturelles*. Part 2, *Règne organisé*. 60 vols. Paris.

Blanton, G. W.; T. J. Culpepper; H. W. Bischoff; A. L. Smith; and C. J. Blanton
1971.   *A study of the total ecology of a secondary bay, Lavaca Bay*. Final Rep., Aluminum Co. of America. Fort Worth: Texas Wesleyan Coll.

Bock, W. D., and D. R. Moore
1968.   A commensal relationship between a foraminifer and a bivalve mollusk. *Gulf Res. Rep.* 2(3):273–279.

Borkowski, T. V., and M. R. Borkowski
1969. The *Littorina ziczac* species complex. *Veliger* 11(4):408–414.

Born, Ignatius
1778. *Index rerum naturalium musei caesarei vindobonensis*. Part 1, *Testacea*. Vienna. [For notes on date of publication, see R. Rutsch, *Nautilus* 69(3):78–79.]
1780. *Testacea musei caesarei vindobonensis*. Vienna.

Borradaile, L. A.; F. A. Potts; et al.
1961. *The Invertebrata: A manual for the use of students*. 4th ed. Cambridge: Univ. Press.

Bosc, A. G.
1802. *Histoire naturelle des coquilles,* . . . 5 vols. Paris.

Boss, K. J.
1966. The subfamily Tellininae in the western Atlantic: The genus *Tellina* (part I). *Johnsonia* 4(45):217–272.
1968. The subfamily Tellininae in the western Atlantic: The genera *Tellina* (part II) and *Tellidora*. *Johnsonia* 4(46):273–344.
1969. The subfamily Tellininae in the western Atlantic: The genus *Strigilla*. *Johnsonia* 4(47):345–366.
1971. Critical estimate of the number of recent Mollusca. *Occ. Pap. Moll., Mus. Comp. Zool.* 3(40):81–135.
1972. The genus *Semele* in the western Atlantic. *Johnsonia* 5(49):1–32.

Boss, K. J., and A. S. Merrill
1965. The family Pandoridae in the western Atlantic. *Johnsonia* 4(44):181–216.

Boss, K. J.; J. Rosewater; and F. S. Ruhoff
1968. *The zoological taxa of Wm. Healey Dall*. U.S. Nat. Mus. Bull., no. 287. Washington, D.C.

Bowditch, N.
1958. *American practical navigator*. U.S. Navy Oceanogr. Off. Washington, D.C.: G.P.O.

Boyer, P. S.
1967. Some observations on the ecology of *Callocardia texasiana*. *Nautilus* 80(3):79–81.

1969a. *Macoma (Psammacoma) pulleyi*: A new clam from Louisiana. *Veliger* 12(1):40.
1969b. Pelecypod beak wear: An indication of post mortem transportation. *Texas J. Sci.* 20(4):385–388.

Branson, B. A.
1967. Notes on and measurements of river drift snails from Texas. *Texas J. Sci.* 19(3):292–300.

Bretsky, S. S.
1967. Environmental factors influencing the distribution of *Barbatia domingensis* (Mollusca: Bivalvia) on the Bermuda Platform. *Postilla*, no. 108.

Breuer, J. P.
1957a. An ecological survey of the Baffin and Alazan bays, Texas. *Pub. Inst. Marine Sci.* 4(1):134–155.
1957b. An ecological survey of the upper Laguna Madre of Texas. *Pub. Inst. Marine Sci.* 4(2):156–200.
1962. An ecological survey of the lower Laguna Madre of Texas. *Pub. Inst. Marine Sci.* 8:153–183.

Briggs, J. C.
1974. *Marine zoogeography*. New York: McGraw-Hill.

Bright, T. J., and L. H. Peguegnat, eds.
1974. *Biota of the west Flower Garden Bank*. Univ. Texas Marine Biomed. Inst., Galveston. Houston: Gulf Publ.

Britton, J. C., Jr.
1970. The Lucinidae (Mollusca: Bivalvia) of the western Atlantic Ocean. Ph.D. dissertation, George Washington Univ.

Brown, L. F., Jr., coord.
1973–. *Environmental geologic atlas of the Texas coastal zone*. Austin: Bur. Econ. Geol., Univ. Texas.

Brown, R. W.
1954. *Composition of scientific words*. Privately printed.

Bruce, J. J.
1972. Shrimp that live with mollusks. *Sea Frontiers* 18(4):218–227.

Bruguière, J. G.
1782–1832. *Encyclopédie méthodique*, by J. G. Bruguière, J. B. P. A. de M. de Lamarck, et al.

196 vols. in 186. Paris. [For collation and dates, see E. V. Coan 1966, *Veliger* 9(2):132–133.]

Buchsbaum, R.
1967. *Animals without backbones: An introduction to the invertebrates*. Chicago: Univ. Chicago Press.

Buchsbaum, R., and L. J. Milne
1966. *The lower animals: Living invertebrates of the world*. Garden City, N.Y.: Doubleday & Co.

Burch, J. Q., and R. D. Burch
1967. The family Olividae. *Pacific Sci.* 21(4):503–522.

Burch, R. D.
1965. New terebrid species from the Indo-Pacific Ocean and from the Gulf of Mexico. *Veliger* 7(4):241–253.

Burkenroad, M. D.
1931. Notes on the Louisiana conch *Thais haemostoma* in its relation to the oyster *Ostrea virginiea*. *Ecology* 12(4):656–664.
1933. Pteropoda from Louisiana. *Nautilus* 47(2):54–57.

Bush, K. J.
1885a. Additions to the shallow-water Mollusca of Cape Hatteras, N.C., dredged by the U.S. Fish Commission steamer *Albatross* in 1883 and 1884. *Trans. Connecticut Acad. Arts & Sci.* 6(2):453–481.
1885b. List of deep-water Mollusca dredged by U.S. Fish Commission steamer *Fish Hawk* in 1880, 1881, 1882 with their range in depth. *Annu. Rep. U.S. Comm. Fish.* [for 1883]. Washington, D.C.
1897. Revision of the marine gastropods referred to [the vitrinellids] . . . *Trans. Connecticut Acad. Arts & Sci.* 10(1):97–144.
1899. Descriptions of new species of *Turbonilla* of the western Atlantic fauna, with notes on those previously known. *Proc. Acad. Natur. Sci. Philadelphia* 51:145–177.

Butler, P. A.
1954. A summary of our knowledge of the oyster in the Gulf of Mexico. In *The Gulf of Mexico: Its origin, waters, and marine life*, ed.

P. S. Galtsoff, pp. 479–489. Fishery Bull., no. 89. U.S. Fish & Wildlife Serv. Washington, D.C.: G.P.O.

Calabrese, A.
1969.   Reproductive cycle of the coot clam *Mulinia lateralis* (Say) in Long Island Sound. *Veliger* 12(3):265–269.

Cameron, R. W.
1961.   *Shells*. New York: G. P. Putnam's Sons.

Carnes, S. F.
1975.   Mollusks from southern Nichupté Lagoon, Quintana Roo, Mexico. *Sterkiana* 59:21–50; 60:1–40.

Carr, J. T., Jr.
1967.   *Hurricanes affecting the Texas Gulf coast*. Texas Water Devel. Board Rep., no. 49. Austin.

Carriker, M. R.
1951.   Observations on the penetration of tightly closing bivalves by *Busycon* and other predators. *Ecology* 32(1):73–83.
1967.   Ecology of estuarine benthic invertebrates: A perspective. In *Estuaries*, ed. G. H. Lauff, pp. 442–489. Amer. Assoc. Adv. Sci. Pub., no. 83. Washington, D.C.

Carson, R. L.
1950.   *The sea around us*. New York: Oxford Univ. Press.
1955.   *The edge of the sea*. Boston: Houghton Mifflin.

Caspers, H.
1967.   Estuaries: Analysis of definitions and biological considerations. In *Estuaries*, ed. G. H. Lauff. Amer. Assoc. Adv. Sci. Pub., no. 83. Washington, D.C.

Castagna, M., and P. Chanley
1966.   Salinity tolerance and distribution of *Spisula solidissima*, *Mulinia lateralis*, and *Rangia cuneata*, family Mactridae. In *Annu. Rep. Amer. Malacol. Union*, p. 35. N.p.

Castañeda, C. E.
1936.   *Our Catholic heritage in Texas*. Austin: Von Boeckmann–Jones.

Cate, C. N.
1973.   A systematic revision of the recent cypraeid family Ovulidae (Mollusca: Gastropoda). *Veliger* 15:suppl.

Catlow, A.
1845.   *The conchologist's nomenclator*. London: Reeve Bros.

Cernohorsky, W. O.
1972.   Comments on the authorship of some subfamilial names in the Turridae. *Veliger* 15(2):127–128.

Chambers, G. N., and A. K. Sparks
1960.   An ecological survey of the Houston Ship Channel and adjacent bays. *Pub. Inst. Marine Sci.* 6:1–22.

Chanley, P. E., and J. D. Andrews
1971.   Aids for identification of bivalve larvae of Virginia. *Malacologia* 11(1):119.

Ciampi, E.
1960.   *The skin diver: A complete guide to the underwater world*. New York: Ronald Press.

Clark, J.
1974.   *Coastal ecosystems: Ecological considerations for management of the coastal zone*. Washington, D.C.: Conservation Found.

Clarke, A. H., Jr.
1965.   The scallop superspecies *Aequipecten irradians* (Lamarck). *Malacologia* 2(2):161–188.

Clench, W. J.
1927.   A new subspecies of *Thais* from Louisiana. *Nautilus* 41(1):6–8, pl. 2, figs. 10–11.
1931.   Cephalopods. *Bull. Boston Soc. Natur. Hist.* 60:10.
1942.   The genera *Dosinia*, *Macrocallista*, and *Amiantis* in the western Atlantic. *Johnsonia* 1(3):1–8.
1944.   The genera *Casmaria*, *Galeodea*, *Phalium*, and *Cassis* in the western Atlantic. *Johnsonia* 1(16):1–16.
1947.   The genera *Purpura* and *Thais* in the western Atlantic. *Johnsonia* 2(23):61–92.
1964.   The genera *Pedipes* and *Laemodonta* in the western Atlantic. *Johnsonia* 4(42):117–128.

Clench, W. J., and R. T. Abbott
1941.   The genus *Strombus* in the western Atlantic. *Johnsonia* 1(1):1–15.
1943.   The genera *Cypraecassis*, *Morum*, *Sconsia*, and *Dolium* in the western Atlantic. *Johnsonia* 9(3):1–8.

Clench, W. J., and I. P. Farfante
1945.   The genus *Murex* in the western Atlantic. *Johnsonia* 1(17):1–58.

Clench, W. J., and T. E. Pulley
1952.   Notes on some marine shells from the Gulf of Mexico with a description of a new species of *Conus*. *Texas J. Sci.* 1:59–62.

Clench, W. J., and L. C. Smith
1944.   The family Cardiidae in the western Atlantic. *Johnsonia* 1(13):1–32.

Clench, W. J., and R. D. Turner
1946.   The genus *Bankia* in the western Atlantic. *Johnsonia* 2(19):1–28.
1948.   The genus *Truncatella* in the western Atlantic. *Johnsonia* 2(25):149–164.
1950a.   The western Atlantic marine mollusks described by C. B. Adams. *Occ. Pap. Moll., Mus. Comp. Zool.* 1(15):233–403.
1950b.   The genera *Sthenorytis*, *Cirsotrema*, *Acirsa*, *Opalia*, and *Amaea* in the western Atlantic. *Johnsonia* 2(29):221–248.
1951.   The genus *Epitonium* in the western Atlantic, part I. *Johnsonia* 2(30):249–288.
1952.   The genus *Epitonium* in the western Atlantic, part II. *Johnsonia* 2(30–31):221–356.
1957.   The family Cymatiidae in the western Atlantic. *Johnsonia* 3(36):189–244.
1960.   The genus *Calliostoma* in the western Atlantic. *Johnsonia* 4(40):1–80.
1962.   *Names introduced by H. A. Pilsbry in the Mollusca and Crustacea*. Acad. Natur. Sci. Philadelphia Spec. Pub., no. 4. Philadelphia.

Coker, R. E.
1954.   *This great and wide sea*.

Chapel Hill: Univ. North Carolina Press.

Collier, A.
1959. Some observations on the respiration of the American oyster *Crassostrea virginica* (Gmelin). *Pub. Inst. Marine Sci.* 6:92–108.

Collier, A., and J. W. Hedgpeth
1950. An introduction to the hydrography of tidal waters of Texas. *Pub. Inst. Marine Sci.* 1(2):121–194.

Compton, J.
1966. Bottle collectors check county find. *Corpus Christi Caller Times*, July 14, sect. B.

Conrad, T. A.
1831–32. *American Marine Conchology*. Philadelphia.
1838. *Fossils of the Medial Tertiary of the United States*, nos. 1–4. Philadelphia: J. Dobson. Reprint, Philadelphia: Wagner Free Inst. Sci., 1893.

Cooke, A. H.; A. E. Shipley; and F. R. C. Reed
1895. *Molluscs and brachiopods*. Cambridge Natur. Hist. Ser., ed. S. F. Harmer and A. E. Shipley. London: Macmillan & Co. Reprint, Codicote, Eng.: Wheldon & Wesley, 1959.

Coomans, H. E.
1963. The marine Mollusca of St. Martin, Lesser Antilles, collected by H. J. Krebs. *Stud. Fauna Curaçao & Other Caribbean Islands* 16(72):59–87.

Copeland, B. J.
1965. Fauna of the Aransas Pass inlet, Texas: I, Emigration as shown by tide trap collections. *Pub. Inst. Marine Sci.* 10:9–21.

Corgan, J. X.
1967. Quaternary micromolluscan fauna of the Mudlumps Province, Mississippi River delta. Ph.D. thesis, Louisiana State Univ.
1971. Review of *Paradostomia, Telloda, Goniodostomia*, and *Eulimastoma* (Gastropoda: Pyramidellacea). *Nautilus* 85(2):51–59.

Corpus Christi Caller Times
1959. Seventy-fifth anniversary edition, January 18.

Cox, L. R.
1955. Observations on gastropod descriptive terminology. *Proc. Malacol. Soc. London* 31:190–202.
1960. Gastropoda: General characteristics of Gastropoda. In *Treatise on invertebrate paleontology*, Part I, *Mollusca 1*, ed. R. C. Moore, pp. 184–269. Boulder, Col.: Geol. Soc. Amer.

Cox, L. R.; C. P. Nuttall; and E. R. Trueman
1969. General features of Bivalvia. In *Treatise on invertebrate paleontology*, Part N, *Mollusca 6*, ed. R. C. Moore, pp. 2–128. Boulder, Col.: Geol. Soc. Amer.

Croizat, L.; G. Nelson; and D. E. Rosen
1974. Centers of origin and related concepts. *Syst. Zool.* 4:265–287.

Cross, E. R.
1956. Underwater safety. *Healthways* (Los Angeles).

Crovo, M. E.
1971. *Cypraea cervus* and *C. zebra* in Florida: One species or two? *Veliger* 13(3):292–295.

Dall, W. H.
1886–89. Report on the results of dredging under the supervision of A. Agassiz . . . by the . . . *Blake* . . . Report on the Mollusca. *Mus. Comp. Zool. Bull.* 12(6):11–318; 18(1):1–492.
1889. *A preliminary catalog of the shell-bearing marine mollusks and brachiopods of the southwestern coast of the United States*. U.S. Nat. Mus. Bull., no. 37. Washington, D.C.
1890–1903. *Tertiary fauna of Florida. Trans. Wagner Free Inst. Sci. Philadelphia* 3(1–6).
1894. Monograph of the genus *Gnathodon* Gray (Rangia). *Proc. U.S. Nat. Mus.* 17(988):89–106.
1895. Three new species of *Macoma* from the Gulf of Mexico. *Nautilus* 9(2):32–34.
1896. On some new species of *Scala. Nautilus* 9(10):110–112.
1898. A new species of *Terebra* from Texas. *Nautilus* 12(4):44–45.

1899. Synopsis of the Solenidae of North America and the Antilles. *Proc. U.S. Nat. Mus.* 22(1185): 107–112.
1901a. Synopsis of the family Cardiidae and of the North American species. *Proc. U.S. Nat. Mus.* 23(1214):381–392.
1901b. Synopsis of the Lucinacea and of the American species. *Proc. U.S. Nat. Mus.* 23(1237): 779–833.
1902a. Illustrations and descriptions of new, unfigured, or imperfectly known shells, chiefly American in the U.S. National Museum. *Proc. U.S. Nat. Mus.* 24(1264):199–566.
1902b. Synopsis of the family Veneridae and of the North American recent species. *Proc. U.S. Nat. Mus.* 26(1312):335–412.

Dall, W. H., and P. Bartsch
1906a. Notes on Japanese, Indopacific, and American Pyramidellidae. *Proc. U.S. Nat. Mus.* 30(1452):321–328.
1906b. *Odostomia (Chrysallida) dux*, new species. *Proc. U.S. Nat. Mus.* 30(1452):350.
1909. *A monograph of west American pyramidellid mollusks*. U.S. Nat. Mus. Bull., no. 68. Washington, D.C.

Dall, W. H., and C. T. Simpson
1901. The Mollusca of Porto Rico. *Bull. U.S. Fish. Comm.* 20(1):351–524.

Dance, S. P.
1966. *Shell collecting: An illustrated history*. Berkeley: Univ. California Press.

Davis, J. D.
1967. *Ervilia concentrica* and *Mesodesma concentrica*: Clarification of synonymy. *Malacologia* 6(1–2):231–241.
1973. Systematics and distribution of western Atlantic *Ervilia* with notes on living *E. subcancellata. Veliger* 15(4):307–313.

Day, J. H.
1951. The ecology of South African estuaries, Part I. *Trans. Royal Soc. South Africa* 33:53–91.

DeKay, J. E.
1843. *Zoology of New York*. Part V, *Mollusca*. Albany: Carroll & Cook.

Delle Chiaje, S.
1823. In *Memorie animales sans vertèbre Napoli* 1(2–4):39.

Dennis, J. V., and C. R. Gunn
1972. New interest in Florida's stranded seeds and fruits. *Florida Natur.* 45(1):11–14, 45.

Dillon, J. S., and R. O. Dial
1962. Notes on the morphology of the common Gulf squid *Lolliguncula brevis* (Blainville). *Texas J. Sci.* 14:156–166.

Dillwyn, L. W.
1817. *A descriptive catalogue of recent shells arranged according to the Linnean method; with particular attention to the synonymy*. London.

Eales, N. B.
1960. Revision of the world species of *Aplysia* (Gastropoda: Opisthobranchia). *Bull. Brit. Mus. (Natur. Hist.) Zool.* 5(10):267–404.

Edwards, D. C.
1974. Preferred prey of *Polinices duplicatus* in Cape Cod inlets. In *Bull. Amer. Malacol. Union*, pp. 17–20. N.p.

Edwards, P.
1970. *Illustrated guide to the seaweeds and sea grasses in the vicinity of Port Aransas, Texas*. Contr. *Marine Sci.* 15:suppl. Reprint, Austin: Univ. Texas Press, 1976.

Ekdale, A. A.
1974. Marine mollusks from the shallow-water environments (0–6 m.) off the northeast Yucatan coast, Mexico. *Bull. Marine Sci.* 24(3):638–668.

Emerson, W. K.
1952. Generic and subgeneric names in the molluscan class Scaphopoda. *J. Washington Acad. Sci.* 42(9):296–303.
1962. A classification of the scaphopod mollusks. *J. Paleontol.* 36(3):461–482.

Emerson, W. K., and A. Ross
1965. Invertebrate collection: Treasure or trash. *Curator* 8(4):333–346.

Eschscholtz, J. F. von
1831. *Zoologischer Atlas . . . Beschreibungen neuer Thierarten Zweiter Reise um die Welt.* N.p.

Fairbanks, L. D.
1963. Biodemographic studies of the clam *Rangia cuneata* (Gray). *Tulane Stud. Zool.* 10(1):3–47.

Farfante, I. P.
1943a. The genera *Fissurella*, *Lucapina*, and *Lucapinella* in the western Atlantic. *Johnsonia* 1(10):1–20.
1943b. The genus *Diodora* in the western Atlantic. *Johnsonia* 1(11):1–20.

Fischer von Waldheim, G.
1807. *Museum Demidoff. Mis en ordre systématique et décrit par G. Fischer.* Vol. 3, *Végétaux et animaux*. Moscow: Impr. l'Univ. Impériale.

Florkin, M., and B. T. Scheer, eds.
1964. *Chemical zoology*. Vol. 7, *Mollusca*. New York: Academic Press.

Forbes, E., and S. Hanley
1849–53. *A history of British Mollusca and their shells*. 4 vols. London: Van Voorst.

Forster, J. G. A.
1777. *A voyage round the world in H.M.S. "Resolution," commanded by Capt. J. Cook, during . . . 1772–75*. 2 vols. London.

Fotherington, N., and S. Brunenmeister
1975. *Common marine invertebrates of the northwestern Gulf coast*. Houston: Gulf Publ.

Fox, L. E.
1944. "Sea beans" collected at Cameron, Louisiana. *Proc. Louisiana Acad. Sci.* 8:76–77.

Franz, D. R.
1967a. Substrate diversity and the taxonomy of *Crepidula convexa* (Say) (Gastropoda: Prosobranchia). *Univ. Connecticut Occ. Pap.* 1(4):281–289.
1967b. On the taxonomy and biology of the dorid nudibranch *Doridella obscura. Nautilus* 80(3):73–79.

1968. Taxonomy of the dorid nudibranch *Cratena pilata* (Gould). *Chesapeake Sci.* 9:264–266.
1971. Development and metamorphosis of the gastropod *Acteocina canaliculata. Trans. Amer. Micros. Soc.* 90(2):174.

Fretter, V., ed.
1972. *Studies in the structure, physiology, and ecology of molluscs.* New York: Academic Press.

Fretter, V., and A. Graham
1949. The structure and mode of life of the Pyramidellidae parasitic opisthobranchs. *J. Marine Biol. Assoc. U.K.* 28:493–532.
1962. *British prosobranch molluscs.* London: Ray Soc.

Gainey, F. L., Jr.
1972. The rise of the foot and the captucala in the feeding of *Dentalium* (Mollusca: Scaphopoda). *Veliger* 15(1):29–34.

Gallagher, J. S., and H. W. Wells
1969. Northern range extension and winter mortality of *Rangia cuneata. Nautilus* 84(1):22–25.

Galtsoff, P. S.
1954. Historical sketch of the explorations in the Gulf of Mexico. In *The Gulf of Mexico: Its origin, waters, and marine life*, ed. P. S. Galtsoff, pp. 1–36. Fishery Bull., no. 89. U.S. Fish & Wildlife Serv. Washington, D.C.: G.P.O.
1964. The American oyster *Crassostrea virginica* (Gmelin). *U.S. Fish Bull.* 64:1–480.
1972. *Bibliography of oysters and other marine organisms associated with oyster bottoms and estuarine ecology.* Boston: G. K. Hall & Co.

García-Cubas, A., Jr.
1963. Sistemática y distribución de los micromoluscos recientes de la Laguna de Términos, Campeche, México. *Bol. Inst. Geol., Mex.* 67(4).

Garriker, M. R.
1951. Observations on the penetration of tightly closed bivalves by *Busycon* and other predators. *Ecology* 32(1):73–83.

Gatschitt, A. A.
1891.   The Karankawa Indians: The lost people from Texas. *Peabody Mus. Arch. Ethnol. Pap.* 1(2):21–103.

Geiser, S. W.
1937.   *Naturalists of the frontier.* Dallas: Southern Methodist Univ. Press.
1939.   A century of scientific exploration in Texas: Part Ib, *1820–1880. Field & Lab.* 7:29–52.

Gibbons, E.
1964.   *Stalking the blue-eyed scallop.* New York: David McKay.
1967.   *Beachcomber's handbook.* New York: David McKay.

Gilbert, S. A.
1861.   *Report of the superintendent of the coast survey showing the progress of the survey during the year 1860,* append. 33–34. Washington, D.C.: G.P.O.

Gmelin, J. F.
1791.   *Caroli a Linné systema naturae per regna tria naturae.* 13th ed. Leipzig.

Godfrey, G. H.
1966.   Sea heart. *Sea Frontiers* 12(1):55–57.

Goode, B.
1876.   *Animal resources of the United States.* U.S. Nat. Mus. Bull., no. 6. Washington, D.C.

Gore, R. H.
1969.   Scavengers of the mud flats. *Sea Frontiers* 15(4):242–248.

Gould, ———
1870.   *Report on the invert. of Massachusetts.* 2d ed. Boston.

Gould, S. J.
1968.   Phenotypic reversion to ancestral form and habit in a marine snail. *Nature* 5(220):804.
1969.   Ecology and functional significance of uncoiling in *Vermicularia spirata. Bull. Marine Sci.* 19(2):432–445.

Graham, A.
1955.   Molluscan diets. *Proc. Malacol. Soc. London* 31:144–159.

Grassé, P. P., ed.
1968.   *Traité de zoologie.* Vol. 5, fasc. 3, *Mollusques gastéropodes et scaphopodes.* Paris: Masson & Cie.

Gray, J. E.
1832.   In *The conchological illustrations,* ed. G. B. Sowerby. London, 1832–41.
1839.   *Zoology of Captain Beechey's voyage: Molluscous animals and their shells* [*Zoology of the Blossom*]. N.p.

Green, J.
1968.   *The biology of estuarine animals.* London: Sidgwick & Jackson.

Guest, W. C.
1958.   *The Texas shrimp fishery.* Texas Game & Fish Comm. Bull., no. 36, ser. no. 5, Marine Lab. Austin.

Gunn, C. R.
1968.   Stranded seeds and fruits from the southeastern shore of Florida. *Garden J.* 18(1):43–54.

Gunn, C. R., and J. V. Dennis
1973.   Tropical and temperate stranded seeds and fruits from the Gulf of Mexico. *Contr. Marine Sci.* 17:111–121.

Gunter, G.
1942.   Seasonal condition in Texas oysters. *Proc. Trans. Texas Acad. Sci.* 25:89–93.
1950.   Seasonal population changes of certain invertebrates of the Texas coast, including the commercial shrimp. *Pub. Inst. Marine Sci.* 1(2):7–51.
1951*a*.   The species of oyster in the Gulf, Caribbean, and West Indian region. *Bull. Marine Sci. Gulf & Caribbean* 1:40–45.
1951*b*.   Historical changes in the Mississippi River and adjacent marine environment. *Pub. Inst. Marine Sci.* 2(2):119–139.

Gunter, G., and R. A. Geyer
1955.   Studies on fouling organisms of the northwest Gulf of Mexico. *Pub. Inst. Marine Sci.* 4(1):37–67.

Gunter, G., and H. H. Hildebrand
1951.   Destruction of fishes and other organisms on the south Texas coast by the cold wave of January 28–February 3, 1951. *Ecology* 32(4):731–736.
1954.   The relation of total rainfall to the state and catch of the marine shrimp (*Penaeus setiferus*) in Texas waters. *Bull. Marine Sci. Gulf & Caribbean* 4(2):95–103.

Haefner, P. A.
1964.   Morphometry of the common Atlantic squid, *Loligo pealei,* and the brief squid, *Lolliguncula brevis,* in Delaware Bay. *Chesapeake Sci.* 5(3):138–144.

Hall, C. A., Jr.
1964.   Shallow-water marine climates and molluscan provinces. *Ecology* 45(2):226–234.

Hall, J. R.
1974.   Intraspecific trail following in the marsh periwinkle *Littorina irrorata* Say. *Veliger* 16(4):72–75.

Halstead, B. W.
1959.   *Dangerous marine animals that sting, bite, are non-edible.* Cambridge, Md.: Cornell Maritime Press.

Halter, R. E.
1873.   Records of the Office of Civil Assistants and of Superintendents relating to R. E. Halter and his activities in and near Corpus Christi and Padre Island, 1873–1881. Microfilm, G.S.A., Nat. Arch. & Rec. Serv., R.G. 23, 1958.

Hanks, J. E.
1953.   Comparative studies on the feeding habits of *Polinices heros* and *Polinices duplicatus* relative to temperature and salinity. In *Fourth Annu. Conf. Clam Res.,* pp. 88–95. Boothbay Harbor, Maine: U.S. Fish & Wildlife Serv.

Harger, J. R. E.
1972.   Competitive coexistence among intertidal invertebrates. *Amer. Sci.* 60:600–697.

Harper, D. E., Jr.
1970.   Ecological studies of selected level-bottom macroinvertebrates off Galveston, Texas. Ph.D. dissertation, Texas A&M Univ.

Harry, H. W.
1942.   List of Mollusca of Grand Isle, La., recorded from the Louisiana State University Marine Laboratory, 1929–1941.

Occ. Pap. Marine Lab. Louisiana State Univ. 1:1–13.

1953.   Corambella baratariae, a new species of nudibranch from the coast of Louisiana. Occ. Pap. Marine Lab. Louisiana State Univ. 8:1–9.

1966.   Studies on bivalve molluscs of the genus Crassinella in the northwestern Gulf of Mexico: Anatomy, ecology, and systematics. Pub. Inst. Marine Sci. 11:65–69.

1967.   A review of the living tectibranch snails of the genus Volvulella, with descriptions of a new subgenus and species from Texas. Veliger 10(2):133–147.

1968a.   An alternate view of the phylogeny of the Mollusca. In Proceedings of the symposium on Mollusca, part I, pp. 170–187. N.p.

1968b.   Reconciling biological nomenclature and the phylogeny of organisms. In The echo: Abstracts and proceedings of the third annual meeting of the Western Society of Malacologists, pp. 41–53. N.p.

1968c.   Marine Mollusca of Galveston: Tentative and preliminary list. 2d ed. Galveston: Marine Lab., Texas A&M Univ.

1969a.   A review of the living leptonacean bivalves of the genus Aligena. Veliger 11(3):164–181.

1969b.   Anatomical notes on the mactrid bivalve Raeta plicatella Lamarck, 1818, with a review of the genus Raeta and related genera. Veliger 12(1):1–23.

1976.   Correlation of benthic Mollusca and substrate composition in lower Galveston Bay, Texas. Veliger 19(2):135–152.

Harry, H. W., and S. F. Snider
1969.   Cuttlebones on the beach at Galveston. Veliger 12(1):89–94.

Hauseman, S. A.
1932.   A contribution to the ecology of the salt-marsh snail Melampus bidentatus Say. Amer. Natur. 99:541–545.

Hayes, M. O.
1967.   Hurricanes as geologic agents:

Case studies of hurricanes Carla, 1961, and Cindy, 1963. Univ. Texas Bur. Econ. Geol. Rept. Inv. 61. Austin.

Hedgpeth, J. W.
1947.   The Laguna Madre of Texas. In Transactions of the 12th North American Wildlife Conference, pp. 364–380. N.p. [See also Pub. Inst. Marine Sci. 3(1):107–224.]

1950.   Notes on the marine invertebrate fauna of salt flat areas in Aransas National Wildlife Refuge, Texas. Pub. Inst. Marine Sci. 1(2):103–109.

1953.   An introduction to the zoogeography of the northwestern Gulf of Mexico with reference to the invertebrate fauna. Pub. Inst. Marine Sci. 3(1):107–224.

1954.   Bottom communities of the Gulf of Mexico. In Gulf of Mexico: Its origin, waters, and marine life, ed. P. S. Galtsoff, pp. 203–214. Fishery Bull., no. 89. U.S. Fish & Wildlife Serv. Washington, D.C.: G.P.O.

1957a.   Estuaries and lagoons: II, Biological aspects. In Treatise on marine ecology and paleoecology, ed. K. O. Emery et al., 1:693–749. Geol. Soc. Amer. Mem. 67. Boulder.

1957b.   Classification of marine environments. In Treatise on marine ecology and paleoecology, ed. K. O. Emery et al., 6:17–27. Geol. Soc. Amer. Mem. 67. Boulder.

1967.   Ecological aspects of the Laguna Madre, a hypersaline estuary. In Estuaries, ed. G. H. Lauff, pp. 408–419. Amer. Assoc. Adv. Sci. Pub., no. 83. Washington, D.C.

Hedley, C.
1899.   The Mollusca of Funafuti: Part 1, Gastropoda. Mem. Austral. Mus. 3(7):398–488.

Helbling, ——
1779.   Abh. privatgessl. Bohm. N.p.

Hendricks, A.; W. M. Parsons; et al.
1969.   Bottom fauna studies in the lower Sabine River. Texas J. Sci. 21(2):175–187.

Henry, C. A.
1976.   The commensal clam, Paramya subovata (Bivalvia: Myidae) and Thalassema hartmani (Echuroidea) off Galveston, Texas. Nautilus 90(2):73–74.

Henry, W. S.
1847.   The campaign sketches of the war with Mexico. New York: Harper & Bros.

Hermann, ——
1781.   In Gesellschaft Naturforschender Freunde zu Berlin, vol. 16.

Hildebrand, H. H.
1954.   A study of the fauna of the brown shrimp (Penaeus aztecus Ives) grounds in the western Gulf of Mexico. Pub. Inst. Marine Sci. 3(3):231–366.

1955.   A study of the fauna of the pink shrimp (Penaeus duorarum Burkenroad) grounds in the Gulf of Campeche. Pub. Inst. Marine Sci. 4(1):171–231.

1958.   Estudios biologios preliminares sobre la Laguna Madre de Tamaulipas. Ciencia (Mex.) 17(7–9):151–173.

Hildebrand, H. H., and G. Gunter
1952.   Correlation of rainfall with the Texas catch of white shrimp Penaeus setiferus. Trans. Amer. Fish. Soc. 82:151–203.

1955.   A report on the deposition of petroleum tars and asphalts on the beaches of the northern Gulf of Mexico, with notes on the beach conditions and the associated biota. Report at Univ. Texas Marine Sci. Inst., Port Aransas.

Hodge, F. W.
1907.   Narrative of Alvar Núñez Cabeza de Vaca. In Original narratives of early American history: Spanish explorers in southern United States, 1528–1542, ed. J. F. Jameson. New York: Scribner's Sons.

Hoese, A. D.; B. S. Copeland; F. N. Moseley; and E. D. Lance
1968.   Fauna of Aransas Pass inlet: Part 3, Diel. and seasonal variation in trawlable organisms in the adjacent area. Texas J. Sci. 20(1):33–60.

Hoese, A. D., and R. S. Jones
1963.   Seasonality of larger animals in a Texas turtle grass community. *Pub. Inst. Marine Sci.* 9:37–47.

Hofstetter, R. P.
1959.   *The Texas oyster fishery.* Texas Game & Fish Comm. Bull. no. 40, ser. no. 6. Reprint, Texas Parks & Wildlife Dept. Bull., no. 40, 1965. Austin.

Holland, J. S.; N. J. Maciolek; R. Kalke; and C. H. Oppenheimer
1974.   A benthos and plankton study of the Corpus Christi, Copano, and Aransas Bay systems: Report on data collected during the period of July 1973 to April 1974. In *Second Annual Report to the Texas Water Development Board from the University of Texas Marine Science Institute at Port Aransas.* N.p.

Holland, J. S.; N. J. Maciolek; and C. H. Oppenheimer
1973.   Galveston Bay benthic community structure as an indicator of water quality. *Contr. Marine Sci.* 17:169–188.

Holle, P. A.
1957.   Life history of the salt-marsh snail *Melampus bidentatus* Say. *Nautilus* 70(3):90–95.

Holle, P. A., and C. F. Dineen
1959.   Studies on the genus *Melampus* (Pulmonata). *Nautilus* 73(1):28–35; 73(2):46–51.

Hollister, S. C.
1957.   On the status of *Fasciolaria distans* Lamarck. *Nautilus* 70(3):73–84.
1958.   Illustrated contributions to the paleontology of America: A review of the genus *Busycon* and its allies. *Palaeontograph. Amer.* 4(28):59–126.

Holme, N. A.
1964.   Methods of sampling the benthos. In *Advances in marine biology,* 2:171–260. London: Academic Press.

Holmes, F. S.
1858–60.   *Post-pleiocene fossils of South Carolina.* Charleston: Russell & Jones.

Houbrick, J. R.
1968.   A survey of the littoral marine mollusks of the Caribbean coast of Costa Rica. *Veliger* 11(1):4–23.
1970.   Reproduction and development in Florida *Cerithium.* In *Amer. Malacol. Union Annu. Rep.,* p. 74. N.p.
1974a.   Growth studies on the genus *Cerithium* (Gastropoda: Prosobranchia) with notes on ecology and microhabitats. *Nautilus* 88(1):14–27.
1974b.   The genus *Cerithium* in the western Atlantic. *Johnsonia* 5(50):33–84.

How to Collect Shells
1975.   Pub. Amer. Malacol. Union. Buffalo: Buffalo Mus. Sci. [P.O. Box 394, Wrightsville Beach, N.C. 28480.]

Hubricht, L.
1960.   Beach drift land snails from southern Texas. *Nautilus* 74(2):82–83.

Huebner, J. D.
1972.   Physiological ecology and bioenergetics of *Polinices duplicatus.* Ph.D. dissertation, Univ. Massachusetts.

Hulings, N. C.
1955.   An investigation of the benthic invertebrate fauna from the shallow waters of the Texas coast. M.S. thesis, Texas Christian Univ.

Hunt, C. B.
1959.   Dating of mining camps with tin cans and bottles. *Geotimes* 3(8):8–9.

Hurst, A.
1963.   The feeding habits of *Nassarius vibex* (Say). *Proc. Malacol. Soc. London* 36:313–317.

Hutchens, ———
1799.   *Dorsetshire.* N.p.

Hyman, L. H.
1967.   *The invertebrates.* Vol. 6, *Mollusca* 1. New York: McGraw-Hill.

Jackson, J. B. C.
1972.   The ecology of the molluscs of *Thalassia* communities, Jamaica, West Indies: I, Molluscan population variability along

an environmental stress gradient. *Marine Biol.* 14(4):302–337.
1973.   The ecology of molluscs of *Thalassia* communities, Jamaica, West Indies: II, Distribution, environmental physiology, and ecology of common shallow-water species. *Bull. Marine Sci.* 23(2):313–350.

Jacobson, M. K.
1972.   Observations on the siphonal behavior of young surf clams *Spisula solidissima. Nautilus* 86(1):25–26.

Jaeger, E. C.
1960.   *The biologist's handbook of pronunciations.* Springfield, Ill.: Charles C. Thomas.

James, B. M.
1972.   Systematics and biology of the deep-water Paleotoxodonta (Mollusca: Bivalvia) from the Gulf of Mexico. Ph.D. dissertation, Texas A&M Univ.

Johnson, C. W.
1934.   List of marine Mollusca of the Atlantic coast from Labrador to Texas. *Proc. Boston Soc. Natur. Hist.* 40(1):1–203.

Johnson, J. K.
1972.   Effect of turbidity on the rate of filtration and growth of the slipper limpet *Crepidula fornicata* Lamarck. *Veliger* 14(3):315–320.

Johnson, R. I.
1961.   *The recent Mollusca of Augustus Addison Gould.* U.S. Nat. Mus. Bull., no. 239. Washington, D.C.

Jonas, ———
1844.   In *Zeitschrift für Malakozoologie,* vol. 1.

Jones, F. B.
1975.   *Flora of the Texas coastal bend.* Corpus Christi: Mission Press.

Jones, F. B.; C. M. Rowell, Jr.; and M. C. Johnston
1961.   *Flowering plants and ferns of the Texas coastal bend counties.* Sinton, Tex.: Rob & Bessie Welder Wildlife Found.

Jordan, D. S.
1905.   *Guide to the study of fishes.* New York: Columbia Univ. Press

Jordan, T. G.
1972.   The origin of "motte" and

"island" in Texas vegetational terminology. *South. Folklore Quart.* 3:121–135.

Jorgensen, C. B.
1966.   *Biology of suspension feeding.* Oxford: Pergamon Press.

Kane, H. E.
1961.   Occurrence of *Rangia cuneata* and *Crassostrea virginica* (Gmelin) in Sabine Lake, Texas, Louisiana. *J. Sedim. Petrol.* 31(4):627.

Kauffman, E. G.
1969.   Form, function, and evolution. In *Treatise on invertebrate paleontology*, Part N, *Mollusca 6*, ed. R. C. Moore, pp. 129–203. Boulder, Col.: Geol. Soc. Amer.

Keen, A. M.
1961.   What is *Anatina anatina*? *Veliger* 4(1):9–12.
1966.   What's the difference? *Veliger* 9(4):444.
1971.   *Sea shells of tropical west America*. 2d ed. Stanford: Stanford Univ. Press.

Keen, A. M., and E. Coan
1974.   *Marine molluscan genera of western North America*. Stanford: Stanford Univ. Press.
1975.   *Additions and corrections to 1975 to sea shells of tropical west America*. Occ. Pap. West. Soc. Malacol., no. 1. N.p.

Keith, D. E., and N. C. Hulings
1965.   A quantitative study of selected nearshore infauna between Sabine Pass and Bolivar Point, Texas. *Pub. Inst. Marine Sci.* 10:33–40.

Kennedy, E. A.
1959.   A comparison of the molluscan fauna along a transect extending from the shoreline to a point near the edge of the continental shelf of the Texas coast. Masters thesis, Texas Christian Univ.

Kiener, L. C.
1834–70.   *Spécies général et iconographie des coquilles vivantes . . . (continué par . . . P. Fischer)*. 11 vols. Paris.

Kimsey, J. B., and R. F. Temple
1963.   Currents on the continental shelf of the northwestern Gulf of Mexico. In *Annu. Lab. Rep.*, pp. 25–27. U.S. Fish & Wildlife Serv. Biol. Lab., Galveston, Tex.

Korniker, L. S.
1959.   Observations on the behavior of the pteropod *Creseis acicula* (Rang). *Bull. Marine Sci. Gulf & Caribbean* 9(3):331–336.

Korniker, L. S., and N. Armstrong
1959.   Mobility of partially submerged shells. *Pub. Inst. Marine Sci.* 6:171–185.

Korniker, L. S.; F. Bonet; R. Cann; and C. M. Hoskin
1959.   Alacran reef, Campeche Bank, Mexico. *Pub. Inst. Marine Sci.* 6:1–22.

Korniker, L. S.; C. Oppenheimer; and J. T. Conover
1958.   Artificially formed mud balls. *Pub. Inst. Marine Sci.* 5:148–150.

Kraeuter, J. N.
1973.   Notes on mollusks *Ostrea* and *Siphonaria* from Georgia. *Nautilus* 87(3):75–77.

Kurtz, J. D.
1860.   *Catalogue of recent marine shells found on the coasts of North and South Carolina*. Portland, Maine: David Tucker.

Kuykendall, J. H.
1903.   Reminiscences of early Texans. *Quart. Texas Hist. Assoc.* 6:236–253.

Ladd, H. S.
1951.   Brackish water and marine assemblages of the Texas coast with special reference to mollusks. *Pub. Inst. Marine Sci.* 2(2):125–163.

Lamarck, J. B. P. A. de M. de
1799.   Prodrome d'une novelle classification des coquilles. *Mém. Soc. Hist. Natur. Paris*, an. VII.
1801.   *Système des animaux sans vertèbres*. Paris.
1815–22.   *Histoire naturelle des animaux sans vertèbres*. 7 vols. Paris.

Lane, F. W.
1960.   *Kingdom of the octopus*. New York: Sheridan House.

Laursen, D.
1953.   *The genus "Janthina": A monograph*. Carlsberg Found. Dana Rep., no. 38. Copenhagen.

Leach, W. E.
1814–17.   *The zoological miscellany; being descriptions of new, or interesting animals*. 3 vols. London.

Leathem, W., and D. Maurer
1975.   The distribution and ecology of common marine and estuarine gastropods in the Delaware Bay area. *Nautilus* 89(3):73–79.

Lederhendler, I., et al.
1974.   Behavior of *Aplysia dactylomela* in Bimini waters. *Veliger* 17(4):347–373.

Leipper, D. F.
1954.   Physical oceanography of the Gulf of Mexico. In *The Gulf of Mexico: Its origin, waters, and marine life*, ed. P. S. Galtsoff, pp. 119–137. Fishery Bull., no. 89. U.S. Fish & Wildlife Serv. Washington, D.C.: G.P.O.

Lemche, H., and K. G. Wingstrand
1959.   The anatomy of *Neopilina galatheae* Lemche, 1937. *Galathea Rep.* 3:9–17.

Lent, C.
1967.   Effect of habitat on growth indices in the ribbed mussel *Modiolus (Arcuatula) demissus*. *Chesapeake Sci.* 8(4):221–227.

Lewis, H.
1972.   Notes on genus *Distorsio* (Cymatiidae) with descriptions of new species. *Nautilus* 86(2–4):27–50.

Lightfoot, J.
1786.   In *A catalogue of the Portland Museum, lately the property of the Dowager Duchess of Portland deceased; which will be sold by auction, etc.* London. [Usually attributed to D. Solander. See Keen 1971, p. 1001.]

Link, H. F.
1806–08.   *Beschreibung de naturalien: Sammlung der Universität zu Rostock*. Rostock. [See Tomlin & Winckworth 1936, *Proc. Malacol. Soc. London* 22:27–48.]

Linnaeus, C. [Linné]

1758.   *Systema naturae per regna tria naturae*. Vol. 1, *Regnum animale*. 10th ed. Stockholm. [12th ed., 1767.]

1771.   *Mant. Plant.* 2:548. N.p.

Lipka, D. A.

1974.   Mollusca. In *Biota of the west Flower Garden Bank*, ed. T. J. Bright and L. H. Peguegnat. Univ. Texas Marine Biomed. Inst., Galveston. Houston: Gulf Publ.

Loesch, H. G.

1957.   Studies on the ecology of two species of *Donax* on Mustang Island, Texas. *Pub. Inst. Marine Sci.* 4(2):201–227.

Logan, A.

1974.   Morphology and life habits of the recent cementing bivalve *Spondylus americanus* Hermann from the Bermuda Platform. *Bull. Marine Sci.* 24(3):568–605.

Lowe, F. E., and R. L. Turner

1976.   Aggregation and trail-following in juvenile *Bursatella leachii pleii* (Gastropoda: Opisthobranchia). *Veliger* 19(2):153–155.

Ludbrook, N. H.

1960.   Scaphopoda. In *Treatise on invertebrate paleontology*, Part I, *Mollusca 1*, ed. R. C. Moore, pp. 37–41. Boulder, Col.: Geol. Soc. Amer.

Lynch, S. A.

1954.   Geology of the Gulf of Mexico. In *The Gulf of Mexico: Its origin, waters, and marine life*, ed. P. S. Galtsoff, pp. 67–83. Fishery Bull., no. 89. U.S. Fish & Wildlife Serv. Washington, D.C.: G.P.O.

Lyon, W. G., et al.

1971.   *Preliminary inventory of marine invertebrates collected near the electric generating plant, Crystal River, Florida, in 1969.* Prof. Pap. Ser., no. 14. Florida Dept. Natur. Res., Marine Res. Lab. St. Petersburg.

1972.   A new *Fasciolaria* from the northeastern Gulf of Mexico. *Nautilus* 85(3):96–100.

MacGinitie, G. E., and N. Mac-Ginitie

1949.   *Natural history of marine animals*. New York: McGraw-Hill.

McKenna, V. J.

1956.   *Old Point Isabel lighthouse: Beacon of Brazos Santiago*. Harlingen, Tex.: Privately printed.

McLean, J. H.

1972.   A revised classification of the family Turridae with the proposal of new subfamilies, genera, and subgenera from the eastern Pacific. *Veliger* 14(1):114–130.

McLean, R. A.

1951.   The Pelecypoda or bivalve mollusks of Puerto Rico and the Virgin Islands. In *Scientific survey of Puerto Rico and the Virgin Islands* 17:1–183. New York: N.Y. Acad. Sci.

Malek, E. A., and T. C. Cheng

1974.   *Medical and economic malacology*. New York: Academic Press.

Marcus, E.

1958.   On western Atlantic opisthobranchiate gastropods. *Amer. Mus. Novitates* 1906:1–82.

Marcus, E. du B.-R.

1960.   Opisthobranchs from American Atlantic warm waters. *Bull. Marine Sci. Gulf & Caribbean* 10(2):129–203.

1972a.   Notes on some opisthobranch gastropods from the Chesapeake Bay. *Chesapeake Sci.* 13(4):300–317.

1972b.   On some Acteonidae (Gastropoda: Opisthobranchia). *Pepeis Avulsos Zool.* (São Paulo) 25(19):167–188.

1972c.   On some opisthobranchs from Florida. *Bull. Marine Sci.* 22(2):84–308.

1972d.   On the Anaspidea (Gastropoda: Opisthobranchia) of the warm waters of the western Atlantic. *Bull. Marine Sci.* 22(4):841–874.

1974.   On some Cephalaspidea (Gastropoda: Opisthobranchia) from the western and middle Atlantic warm waters. *Bull. Marine Sci.* 24(2):300–371.

Marcus, E. du B.-R., and E. Marcus

1959.   Some opisthobranchs from the northwestern Gulf of Mexico.

Pub. Inst. Marine Sci. 6:251–264.

1960.   On *Tricolia affinis cruenta*. *Bol. Fac. Fil. Cien. Letr. S. Paulo* 23:171–198.

1967a.   Some opisthobranchs from Sapelo Island, Georgia, U.S.A. *Malacologia* 6(1–2):199–222.

1967b.   Opisthobranchs from the southwestern Caribbean Sea. *Bull. Marine Sci.* 17(3):597–628.

Marland, F. C.

1958.   An ecological study of the benthic macrofauna of Matagorda Bay, Texas. Masters thesis, Texas A&M Univ.

Marmer, H. A.

1954.   The tides and sea level in the Gulf of Mexico. In *The Gulf of Mexico: Its origin, waters, and marine life*, ed. P. S. Galtsoff, pp. 101–114. Fishery Bull., no. 89. Fish & Wildlife Serv. Washington, D.C.: G.P.O.

Maurer, D.; L. Walling; and G. Aprill

1974.   The distribution and ecology of common marine and estuarine pelecypods in the Delaware Bay area. *Nautilus* 88(2):38–45.

Maury, C. J.

1920.   Recent mollusks of the Gulf of Mexico and Pleistocene and Pliocene species from the Gulf states: Part I, Pelecypoda. *Bull. Amer. Paleontol.* 8(34):3–115.

1922.   Recent mollusks of the Gulf of Mexico and Pleistocene and Pliocene species from the Gulf states: Part II, Scaphopoda, Gastropoda, Amphineura, Cephalopoda. *Bull. Amer. Paleontol.* 9(38):1–140.

Mayr, E.

1942.   *Systematics and the origin of species*. New York: Columbia Univ. Press.

1969.   *Principles of systematic zoology*. New York: McGraw-Hill.

Menke, K. T.

1828.   *Synopsis methodica molluscorum generum omnium et specierum earum quae in Museo Menkeana adservabitur . . .* Pyrmont.

1829.   *Verzeichniss der ansehnlichen*

Conchylien-Sammlung des Freiherrn von der Malsburg. Pyrmont: Heinrich Gelpke.

Menzel, R. W.

1955.   Some phases of the biology of *Ostrea equestris* Say and a comparison with *Crassostrea virginica*. *Pub. Inst. Marine Sci.* 4(1):68–153.

Merrill, A. S., and K. J. Boss

1964.   Reactions of hosts to proboscis penetration by *Odostomia seminuda* (Pyramidellidae). *Nautilus* 78(2):42–45.

Merrill, A. S., and R. D. Turner

1967.   Nest building in the bivalve genera *Musculus* and *Lima*. *Veliger* 6:55–59.

Miner, R. W.

1950.   *Field book of seashore life*. New York: G. P. Putnam's Sons.

Mitchell, J. D.

1894.   *List of Texas Mollusca collected by J. D. Mitchell, Victoria, Texas*. Privately printed.

1895.   List of Texas Mollusca, marine. *Natur. Sci. News* 1(8):31–36.

Mobius, K.

1874.   *Zoologische ergebnisse*. Vol. 5, *Vermes*. Jahresbricht Comm. Wissensch. Untersuchungen Dtsch. Meere, Kiel, Jahrgang II.

Moore, D. R.

1955.   Observations of predation on echinoderms by three species of Cassididae. *Nautilus* 69(3):73–76.

1958.   Additions to Texas marine Mollusca. *Nautilus* 71(4):124–128.

1961.   The marine and brackish water Mollusca of the state of Mississippi. *Gulf Coast Res. Rep.* 1(1):1–58.

1962.   The systematic position of the family Caecidae. *Bull. Marine Sci. Gulf & Caribbean* 12:695–701.

1964.   The family Vitrinellidae in south Florida and the Gulf of Mexico. Ph.D. dissertation, Univ. Miami.

1965.   New species of Vitrinellidae from the Gulf of Mexico and adjacent waters. *Nautilus* 78(3):73–79.

1966.   The Cyclostremellidae, a new family of prosobranch mollusks. *Bull. Marine Sci. Gulf & Caribbean* 16(3):480–484.

1969.   Systematics, distribution, and abundance of the West Indian micromollusk *Rissoina catesbyana* d'Orbigny. *Trans. Gulf Coast Assoc. Geol. Soc.* 19:425–426.

1972a.   *Cochliolepis parasitica*, a nonparasitic marine gastropod, and its place in the Vitrinellidae. *Bull. Marine Sci.* 22(1):100–112.

1972b.   Ecological and systematic notes on Caecidae from St. Croix, U.S. Virgin Islands. *Bull. Marine Sci.* 22(4):881–899.

Moore, H. B., and N. N. Lopez

1969.   The ecology of *Chione cancellata*. *Bull. Marine Sci.* 19(1–4): 131–148.

Moore, R. C., ed.

1960.   *Treatise on invertebrate paleontology*. Part I, *Mollusca 1 (Mollusca: General features)*. Boulder, Col.: Geol. Soc. Amer.

1964.   *Treatise on invertebrate paleontology*. Part K, *Mollusca 3 (Cephalopoda: General features)*. Boulder, Col.: Geol. Soc. Amer.

1969a.   *Treatise on invertebrate paleontology*. Part N, *Mollusca 6 (vol. 1 [of 3], Bivalvia)*. Boulder, Col.: Geol. Soc. Amer.

1969b.   *Treatise on invertebrate paleontology*. Part N, *Mollusca 6 (vol. 2 [of 3], Bivalvia)*. Boulder, Col.: Geol. Soc. Amer.

1971.   *Treatise on invertebrate paleontology*. Part N, *Mollusca 6 (vol. 3 [of 3], Bivalvia)*. Boulder, Col.: Geol. Soc. Amer.

Mörch, O. A. L.

1874.   *Vidensk. medd. naturhist. Forening i Kjöbenhavn*, no. 17.

1875.   Synopsis molluscorum marinorum occidentalium. *Malakozoologische blätter*, vol. 22.

Morris, P. A.

1973.   *A field guide to the shells of our Atlantic and Gulf coasts*. Ed. W. J. Clench. Peterson Field Guide Series. 3d ed. Boston: Houghton Mifflin.

Morrison, J. P. E.

1939.   Two new species of *Sayella* with notes on the genus. *Nautilus* 53:127–130.

1964.   Notes on American Melampidae. *Nautilus* 77(4):119–121.

1965.   New brackish water mollusks from Louisiana. *Proc. Biol. Soc. Washington* 78:217–224.

1967.   Notes on American *Hastula*. In *Annu. Rep. Amer. Malacol. Union*, pp. 49–50. N.p.

1968.   Four American *Hastula* species. *Texas Conchol.* 4(9):67–70.

1971.   Western Atlantic *Donax*. *Proc. Biol. Soc. Washington* 83(48): 545–586.

1973.   New name for a Texas *Hydrobia*. *Nautilus* 87(1):28.

Morton, J. E.

1960.   *Molluscs: An introduction to their form and function*. Harper Torchbooks, Science Library. New York: Harper & Bros.

Morton, J. E., and C. M. Yonge, eds.

1964.   *Physiology of Mollusca*, vol. 1. New York: Academic Press.

Mühlfeld, J. C. M. von

1818.   Beschreibung einiger neuen Conchylien. *Gesellschaft Naturforschender Freunde zu Berlin*.

Naef, A.

1926.   Studien zur generellen: Part 3, Die typischen Beziehtung der Weichtierklassen untereinander und das Verhaltnis ihrer Urformen zu anderen Coelomaten. *Ergeb. u. Fortschr. d. Zool.* 6:17–124.

National Science Foundation

1973.   Managing coastal lands. *Mosaic* 4(3):26–32.

Neave, S. A.

1939.   *Nomenclator zoologicus: A list of the names of genera and subgenera in zoology from the tenth edition of Linnaeus 1758 to the end of 1935*. 4 vols. London: Zool. Soc. London.

Newcomb, W. W., Jr.

1961.   *The Indians of Texas: From prehistoric to modern times*. Austin: Univ. Texas Press.

Nicol, D.

1952.   Revision of the pelecypod genus *Echinochama*. *J. Paleontol.* 26(5):803–817.

1953. The scientific role of the amateur malacologist. *Nautilus* 67(2):41–44.

1965*a*. Nomenclature note on *Arcinella* versus *Echinochama*. *Nautilus* 78(4):15–16.

1965*b*. Ecologic implications of living pelecypods with calcareous spines. *Nautilus* 78(4):109–115.

1968. Are pelecypods primarily infaunal animals? *Nautilus* 82(2):37–43.

1972. Geologic history of deposit-feeding pelecypods. *Nautilus* 86(1):11–15.

Nowell-Usticke, G. W.

1959. *A check list of the marine shells of St. Croix, U.S. Virgin Islands with random annotations.* Burlington, Vt.: Lane Press.

1969. *A supplementary listing of new shells.* Wynnewood, Pa.: Livingston Publ.

Nowlin, W. D., Jr.

1971. Water masses and general circulation of the Gulf of Mexico. *Oceanology Inter.* (Feb.):28–33.

Oberholser, H. C.

1974. *The bird life of Texas.* Ed. E. B. Kincaid, Jr., et al. Austin: Univ. Texas Press.

Odé, H.

1974–. Distribution and records of the marine Mollusca in the northwest Gulf of Mexico. *Texas Conch.* 11(2,3,4,–). [A continuing monograph.]

Odé, H., and A. B. Speers

1964–74. Notes concerning Texas beach shells. *Texas Conch.* 1–10.

Odum, E. P.

1971. *Fundamentals of ecology.* 3d ed. Philadelphia: W. B. Saunders.

Ogle, J.

1976. The occurrence of the date mussel, *Lithophaga bisulcata* (Mytilidae), in living oysters off Galveston, Texas. *Nautilus* 90(2):74–76.

Olsson, A. A.

1961. *Mollusks of the tropical eastern Pacific: Panamic-Pacific Pelecypoda.* Ithaca, N.Y.: Paleo-Research Inst.

Olsson, A. A., and L. E. Crovo

1968. Observations on aquarium specimens of *Oliva sayana* Ravenel. *Veliger* 11(1):31–33.

Olsson, A. A.; A. Harbison; W. G. Fargo; and H. A. Pilsbry

1953. *Pliocene Mollusca of southern Florida, with special reference to those from north St. Petersburg.* Acad. Natur. Sci. Philadelphia Monogr., no. 8. Philadelphia.

Oppenheimer, C. H.

1963. Effects of hurricane Carla on the ecology of Red Fish Bay, Texas. *Bull. Marine Sci. Gulf & Caribbean* 13:59–72.

Orbigny, A. d'

1834–47. *Voyage dans l'Amérique méridionale.* Vol. 5, pt. 3: *Mollusques.* Paris: P. Bertrand.

1841–46. Mollusques. In *Histoire physique, politique, et naturelle de l'Ile de Cuba,* by R. de la Sagra. 2 vols. N.p.

Palmer, C. P.

1974. A supraspecific classification of the scaphopod Mollusca. *Veliger* 17(2):115–123.

Palmer, K. V. W.

1966. Who were the Sowerbys? *Sterkiana* 23:1–6.

Pan American Health Organization, W.H.O.

1968. *A guide for the identification of the snail intermediate hosts of Schistosomiasis in the Americas.* Sci. Pub., no. 168. N.p.

Papp, C. S.

1968. *Scientific illustration: Theory and practice.* Dubuque: Wm. C. Brown.

Parker, L. P., ed.

1976. Environmental assessment of South Texas outer continental shelf: Chemical and biological survey component. Rep. to Bur. Land Manage., state of Texas. Univ. Texas, Texas A&M Univ., and Rice Univ. N.p.

Parker, R. L.

1955. Changes in invertebrate fauna, apparently attributable to salinity changes in the bays of central Texas. *J. Paleontol.* 29:193–211.

1956. Macro-invertebrate assemblages as indicators of sedimentary environments in east Mississippi delta region. *Bull. Amer. Assoc. Petrol. Geol.* 40(2):295–376.

1959. Macro-invertebrate assemblages of central Texas coastal bays and Laguna Madre. *Bull. Amer. Assoc. Petrol. Geol.* 43(9):2100–2166.

1960. Ecology and distributional patterns of marine macro-invertebrates, northern Gulf of Mexico. In *Recent sediments, northwest Gulf of Mexico,* ed. F. P. Shepard, F. B. Phleger, and T. H. van Andel, pp. 302–337. Tulsa: Amer. Assoc. Petrol. Geol.

1967. Benthic invertebrates in tidal estuaries and coastal lagoons. In *Lagunas costeras: Un simposio,* pp. 563–590. Mexico City: UNAM-UNESCO.

Parker, R. L., and J. R. Curray

1956. Fauna and bathymetry of banks of continental shelf, northwest Gulf of Mexico. *Bull. Amer. Assoc. Petrol. Geol.* 40(10):2428–2439.

Patch, J. D.

1962. *The concentration of General Zachary Taylor's army at Corpus Christi, Texas.* Corpus Christi: Mission Print.

Patton, W. K.

1972. Studies on the animal symbionts of the Gorgonian coral *Leptogorgia virgulata* (Lamarck). *Bull. Marine Sci.* 22(2):419–432.

Pearse, A. S.; H. Humm; and G. W. Wharton

1942. Ecology of sand beaches at Beaufort, N.C. *Ecol. Monogr.* 12:136–190.

Pelseneer, P.

1906. Mollusca. In *A treatise on zoology,* ed. E. R. Lankester. London: Adams & Black.

Perry, L. M., and J. S. Schwengel

1955. *Marine shells of the western coast of Florida.* Ithaca: Paleontol. Res. Inst.

Petersen, R. L.

1972. Anatomical studies on the scaphopod *Dentalium texasianum.* M.S. thesis, Texas A&M Univ.

Peterson, R. T.
1960.   *The birds of Texas*. Boston: Houghton Mifflin.

Petuch, E. J.
1976.   An unusual molluscan assemblage from Venezuela. *Veliger* 18:322–325.

Pew, P., and Staff of Marine Laboratory
1954.   *Food and game fishes of the Texas coast*. Texas Game & Fish Comm. Bull., no. 33, series no. IV, Marine Lab. Austin.

Pfeiffer, K. G. L.
1839–40.   In *Archiv. für Naturgeschichte*, vols. 5 & 6. N.p.
1840.   In *Zeitschrift für Malakozoologie*. N.p.

Philippi, R. A.
1836–41.   In *Archiv. für Naturgeschichte*, vols. 2 & 7. N.p.
1847–51.   In *Zeitschrift für Malakozoologie*, vols. 4–8. N.p.

Pickford, G. E.
1946.   *Vampyroteuthis infernalis* Chun, an archaic dibranchiate cephalopod. I, Natural history and distribution. Carlsberg Found. *Dana Rep.*, no. 29:1–40. Copenhagen.
1949.   *Vampyroteuthis infernalis* Chun, an archaic dibranchiate cephalopod. II, External anatomy. Carlsberg Found. *Dana Rep.*, no. 32:1–132. Copenhagen.

Pierce, W. E.
1967.   Flower Garden Reef. *Texas Parks & Wildlife* 25(12):6–9.

Pilsbry, H. A., and L. Hubricht
1956.   Beach drift Polygyridae from southern Texas. *Nautilus* 69(3):93–97.

Pilsbry, H. A., and T. L. McGinty
1945–50.   Cyclostrematidae and Vitrinellidae of Florida, parts I–V. *Nautilus* 59(1):1–13; 59(2):52–59; 59(3):77–83; 60(1):12–18; 63(3):77–86.

Pilsbry, H. A., and B. Sharp
1897–98.   Scaphopoda. In *Manual of conchology*, ed. G. W. Tryon, Jr., pp. i–xxxii, 1–280. Philadelphia: Acad. Natur. Sci.

Poirier, H. P.
1954.   *An up-to-date systematic list of 3200 sea shells from Greenland to Texas*. Hudson View Gardens, N.Y.: Villedieu.

Ponder, W. F.
1973.   The origin and evolution of the Neogastropoda. *Malacologia* 12(2):295–338.

Porter, H. J., and D. A. Wolfe
1971.   Mollusca from the North Carolina commercial fishing grounds for the calico scallop *Argopecten gibbus* Linné. *J. Conchyl.* 109(3):91–109.

Potiez, V. L. V., and A. L. G. Michaud
1838–41.   *Galerie des mollusques, ou catalogue . . . Muséum de Dovai.* 2 vols. Paris.

Pounds, S. G.
1961.   *The crabs of Texas*. Texas Fish & Game Comm. Bull., no. 33, ser. no. VII, Marine Lab. Austin.

Pratt, D. M., and D. A. Campbell
1956.   Environmental factors affecting growth in *Venus mercenaria*. *Limnol. Oceanogr.* 1:2–17.

Price, W. A.
1933.   Role of diastrophism in topography of Corpus Christi area, south Texas. *Bull. Amer. Assoc. Petrol. Geol.* 17(8):907–962.
1954.   Shorelines and coasts of the Gulf of Mexico. In *The Gulf of Mexico: Its origin, waters, and marine life*, ed. P. S. Galtsoff, pp. 39–98. Fishery Bull., no. 89. U.S. Fish & Wildlife Serv. Washington, D.C.: G.P.O.

Prior, D. J.
1974.   Role of the incurrent siphonal valve in the surf clam, *Spissula solidissima* (Mactridae). *Nautilus* 88(4):115–117.

Pritchard, D. W.
1967.   What is an estuary: Physical viewpoint. In *Estuaries*, ed. G. H. Lauff, pp. 3–5. Amer. Assoc. Adv. Sci. Pub., no. 83. Washington, D.C.

Puffer, E. L., and W. K. Emerson
1953.   The molluscan community of the oyster-reef biotope on the central Texas coast. *J. Paleontol.* 27(4):737–544.
1954.   Catalogue and notes on the gastropod genus *Busycon*. *Proc. Biol. Soc. Washington* 67:115–150.

Pulley, T. E.
1952a.   A new species of *Chione* from the western Gulf of Mexico. *Texas J. Sci.* 4(1):61–62.
1952b.   An illustrated check list of the marine mollusks of Texas. *Texas J. Sci.* 4(2):167–199.
1953.   A zoogeographic study based on the bivalves of the Gulf of Mexico. Ph.D. dissertation, Harvard Univ.
1959.   A review of *Busycon perversum* (Linné, 1758). *Texas Conch.* 9(2):34.

Purchon, R. D.
1968.   *The biology of the Mollusca*. Oxford: Pergamon Press.

Quatrefages, A. de
1849.   Mémoire sur le genre Taret (*Teredo*). *Ann. Sci. Natur. (Zool.)* 11:26.

Radwin, G. E.
1968.   A taxonomic revision of the family Columbellidae (Mollusca: Gastropoda) in the western Atlantic exclusive of the genus *Astyris*. Ph.D. dissertation, George Washington Univ.

Rang, P. C. S. A. L.
1828.   Histoire naturelle des Aplysiens, première famille de l'ordre de Tectibranches. In *Histoire naturelle gen. et partic. des mollusques-pteropodes*, ed. Férussac, pp. 1–84. Paris.
1829.   *Manuel de l'histoire naturelle des mollusques et de leurs coquilles, ayant pour base de classification celle de M. le baron Cuvier*. Paris.

Raven, C. P.
1958.   *Morphogenesis*. London: Pergamon Press.

Raven, P. H.; B. Berlin; and D. E. Breedlove
1971.   The origins of taxonomy. *Science* 174(3013):1210–1213.

Ravenel, E.
1875.   *Catalogue of the recent and fossil shells in the cabinet of the late Edmund Ravenel*. Ed. L. R. Gibbes. Charleston, S.C.: Walker Evans & Cogswell.

Rayburn, J. C., and V. K. Rayburn, eds.
1966.   *Century of conflict, 1821–1913*. Waco: Texian Press.

Récluz, C. A.
1842.   Description de quelques nouvelles espèces de Nérites vivantes. *Rev. Zool. Soc. Cuvierienne*, no. 5.

Reed, C. T.
1941.   *Marine life in Texas waters*. Texas Acad. Pub. Natur. Hist. Houston: Anson Jones Press.

Reese, P.
1938.   The history of Padre Island. Masters thesis, Texas Col. Arts & Industries.

Reeve, L. A.
1841–42.   *Conchologia systematica; or, complete system of conchology*. 2 vols. London: Longmans, Brown, Green, & Longmans.
1843–78.   *Conchologia iconica; or, illustrations of the shells of molluscous animals*. London: Lovell Reeve.

Rehder, H. A.
1935.   New Caribbean marine shells. *Nautilus* 48(4):127–130.
1939.   New marine mollusks from the west Atlantic. *Nautilus* 53(1):16–21.
1943.   New marine mollusks from the Antillean region. *Proc. U.S. Nat. Mus.* 93(3161):187–203.
1954.   Mollusks. In *The Gulf of Mexico: Its origin, waters, and marine life*, ed. P. S. Galtsoff, pp. 469–478. Fishery Bull., no. 89. U.S. Fish & Wildlife Serv. Washington, D.C.: G.P.O.

Rehder, H. A., and R. T. Abbott
1951.   Some new and interesting mollusks from the deeper waters of the Gulf of Mexico. *Rev. Soc. Malacol. "C. de la Torre"* 8(2):53–66.

Reid, G. K.
1955.   A summer study of the biology and ecology of East Bay, Texas. *Texas J. Sci.* 7:316–343.

Reinhart, P. W.
1943.   *Mesozoic and Cenozoic Arcidae from the Pacific slope of North America*. Geol. Soc. Amer. Spec. Pap., no. 47. N.p.

Rice, W. H.
1960.   A preliminary checklist of the mollusks of Texas. Report at Univ. Texas Marine Sci. Inst., Port Aransas.

Rice, W. H., and L. S. Kornicker
1962.   Mollusks of Alacran Reef, Campeche Bank, Mexico. *Pub. Inst. Marine Sci.* 8:366–393.
1965.   Mollusks from the deeper waters of the northwestern Campeche Bank, Mexico. *Pub. Inst. Marine Sci.* 10:108–172.

Richards, H. G.
1939.   Marine Pleistocene of Texas. *Bull. Geol. Soc. Amer.* 50:1885–1898.
1962.   Studies on the marine Pleistocene: Part II, The marine Pleistocene mollusks of eastern North America. *Trans. Amer. Philos. Soc.* 32(3).

Ricketts, E. F., and J. Calvin
1968.   *Between Pacific tides*. Rev. J. W. Hedgpeth. 4th ed. Stanford: Stanford Univ. Press.

Rios, E. C.
1970.   *Coastal Brazilian sea shells*. Rio Grande, R.S.

Risso, A.
1826.   *Histoire naturelle des principales productions de l'Europe méridionale et particulièrement de celles des environs de Nice et des alpes maritimes*. N.p.

Robertson, R.
1957.   Gastropod host of an *Odostomia*. *Nautilus* 70(3):96–97.
1958.   The family Phasianellidae in the western Atlantic. *Johnsonia* 3(37):245–283.
1963.   Bathymetric and geographic distribution of *Panopea bitruncata*. *Nautilus* 76(3):75–82.
1973.   *Cyclostremella*: A planispiral pyramidellid. *Nautilus* 87(3):88.

Robson, G. C.
1929.   *A monograph of the recent cephalopods*. British Mus. Natur. Hist. Oxford: Oxford Univ. Press.

Röding, P. F.
1798.   *Museum boltenianum . . . ; pars secunda continens conchylia . . .* Hamburg. [See also H. A. Rehder 1945, *Nautilus* 59(2):50–52.]

Roemer, F.
1849.   *Texas; mit besonderer Rücksicht auf deutsche Auswanderung und der physische Verhältnisse des Landes nach eigener Beobachtung geschildert*. Bonn: Adolph Marcus. [Trans. Oswald Mueller as *Roemer's Texas*. San Antonio: Standard Print., 1935.]

Ropes, J. W.
1967.   The locomotion and behavior of surf clams *Spisula solidissima*. *Proc. Nat. Shellfish Assoc.* 57:4. [Abstract.]

Ropes, J. W., and A. S. Merrill
1973.   To what extent do surf clams move? *Nautilus* 87(1):19–21.

Rosewater, J., and B. J. Vermeij
1972.   The Amphi-Atlantic distribution of *Littorina meleagris*. *Nautilus* 86(2–4):67–69.

Rothschild, N. M.
1961.   *A classification of living animals*. New York: John Wiley & Sons.

Rudloe, J.
1968.   *The sea brings forth*. New York: Alfred A. Knopf.
1971.   *The erotic ocean*. New York: World Publ.

Runham, N. W.; K. Isarankura; and B. J. Smith
1956.   Methods for narcotizing and anaesthetizing Gastropoda. *Malacologia* 2(2):231–238.

Russell, H. D.
1937.   Living rainbows of the sea. *Bull. New England Mus. Natur. Hist.* 82:3.
1966.   *Index Nudibranchia: A catalog of the literature, 1554–1965*. Greenville, Del.: Delaware Mus. Natur. Hist.

Russell-Hunter, W. D.; M. L. Apley; and R. D. Hunter
1970.   Semilunar and other factors influencing hatching from egg masses of *Melampus bidentatus* in the field and laboratory. *Biol. Bull. Marine Biol. Lab., Woods Hole* 138:434.

Salis Marschlins, C. V. von
1793.   *Reisen in versch. prov. Königreich Neapel 1*. Trans. Anthony Autrere as *Travels through various*

provinces of the Kingdom of Naples in 1789. London.

Say, T.

1822.   An account of some of the marine shells of the United States. *J. Acad. Natur. Sci. Philadelphia*, vol. 2.

1830–34.   *American conchology, or descriptions of the shells of North America.* New Harmony, Ind.: School Press.

1858.   *The complete writings of Thomas Say on conchology of the United States.* Ed. W. G. Binney. New York: H. Baillière. [A reprint of Say's scattered papers and descriptions.]

Scheltema, A. H.

1968.   Redescriptions of *Anachis avara* (Say) and *Anachis translirata* (Ravenel) with notes on some related species. *Breviora* 304:1–19.

Schenk, E. T., and J. H. McMasters

1958.   *Procedure in taxonomy.* Stanford: Stanford Univ. Press.

Schilder, F. A.

1966.   Personal views on taxonomy. *Veliger* 8(3):181–188.

Schwengel, J.

1942.   New Floridian marine mollusks. *Nautilus* 56(1):62–66.

Sellmer, G. P.

1967.   Functional morphology and ecological life history of the gem clam *Gemma gemma* (Eulamellibranchia: Veneridae). *Malacologia* 5(2):137–223.

Sheldon, P. G.

1916.   Atlantic slope arcas. In *Palaeontographica Americana*, vol. 1. Ithaca: Harris.

Shepard, F., and G. A. Rusnak

1957.   Texas bay sediments. *Pub. Inst. Marine Sci.* 4(2):5–13.

Sherborn, C. D.

1902–33.   *Index animalium*, Part I (1758–1800) and Part II (1800–1850). London: British Mus.

Shoemaker, A. H.

1972.   Reef mollusks of South Carolina. *Nautilus* 85(4):114–119.

Simmons, E. G.

1957.   An ecological survey of the upper Laguna Madre of Texas. *Pub. Inst. Marine Sci.* 4(2):156–200.

Simmons, E. G., and J. P. Breuer

1962.   A study of red fish (*Scaniops ocellata* [Linnaeus]) and black drum (*Pogonias cromis* [Linnaeus]). *Pub. Inst. Marine Sci.* 8:184–211.

Simmons, E. G., and H. D. Hoese

1959.   Studies on the hydrography and fish migrations of Cedar Bayou. *Pub. Inst. Marine Sci.* 6:56–80.

Singley, J. A.

1893.   Contributions to the natural history of Texas: Part 1, Texas Mollusca. In *Fourth Annu. Rep. Geol. Surv. Texas, 1892.* Austin: Ben Jones & Co.

1894.   List of Mollusca collected in Texas in 1891. In *Fishes of Texas and Rio Grande Basin*, ed. B. W. Evermann and W. C. Kendall, pp. 123–125. Bull. U.S. Fish Comm., vol. 12 for 1892. Washington, D.C.

Smith, L. A.

1958.   Ecological catalogue and bibliography of the invertebrate fauna and environments of the Gulf of Mexico with special reference to the Mollusca. In *Paleoecological significance of tertiary molluscan fauna*, vol. 1, part 2. Sun Oil Co. prelim. rep. Dallas.

Smith, M.

1937.   *East coast marine shells.* Rev. ed., Ann Arbor: Edwards Bros., 1951.

Smylie, V.

1964.   *The secrets of Padre Island.* Corpus Christi: Texas News Syndicate Press.

Solander, D. *See* Lightfoot, J.

Solem, A.

1961.   Hydrobiid snails from Lake Pontchartrain, Louisiana. *Nautilus* 74(4):157–160.

1974.   *The shell makers: Introducing mollusks.* New York: John Wiley & Sons.

Sowerby, G. B. [I]

1825.   *A catalogue of the shells contained in the collection of the late Earl of Tankerville.* London.

1828.   On recent species of the genus *Ovulum. Zool. J. London* 4:145–162.

1830.   In *Species conchyliorum; or, concise original descriptions and observations . . . on all of the species of recent shells . . . ,* ed. Broderip, vol. 1. London.

1832–41.   *The conchological illustrations.* London.

Sowerby, G. B., Jr. [II]

1842.   *A conchological manual.* London: Henry G. Bohn.

1847–87.   *Thesaurus conchyliorum; or, monographs of genera of shells,* ed. G. B. Sowerby, Jr., completed by G. B. Sowerby III, London.

Sowerby, J. de C., and G. B. Sowerby

1825–34.   *The genera of recent and fossil shells.* London: Bernard Quaritch.

Spengler, L.

1794–1802.   *Skr. Nat. Selsk.* (Copenhagen), vols. 3–5.

Stanley, S. M.

1970.   *Relation of shell form to life habits in the Bivalvia (Mollusca).* Geol. Soc. Amer. Mem. 125. N.p.

Stanton, R. J., and I. Evans

1971.   Environmental controls of benthic macrofaunal patterns in the Gulf of Mexico adjacent to the Mississippi delta. *Trans. Gulf Coast Assoc. Geol. Soc.* 21:371–378.

1972.   Recognition and interpretations of modern molluscan biofacies. In *Contributions on the geophysical oceanography of the Gulf of Mexico*, ed. R. Rezak and V. J. Heary, pp. 203–222. Texas A&M Univ. Oceanogr. Stud., no. 3. College Station.

Stasek, C. R.

1961.   Studies on feeding and form in the bivalved Mollusca. Ph.D. dissertation, Univ. Calif., Berkeley.

1972.   The molluscan framework. In *Chemical zoology*, ed. M. Florkin and B. T. Scheer, pp. 1–41. New York: Academic Press.

Stasek, C. R., and W. R. McWilliams

1973.   The comparative morphology and evolution of the molluscan mantle edge. *Veliger* 61(1):1–19.

Stenzel, H. B.

1940. Mollusks from Point Isabel in Texas. *Nautilus* 54(1):20–21.

1971. Oysters. In *Treatise on invertebrate paleontology*, Part N, *Mollusca 6 (Bivalvia, vol. 3)*, ed. R. C. Moore, pp. 953–1224. Boulder, Col.: Geol. Soc. Amer.

Stimpson, W.

1851. *Shells of New England*. Boston.

Stohler, R.

1966. Ethics for the collector. *Veliger* 8(3):203.

Story, D. A.

1968. *Archeological investigations at two central Texas Gulf coast sites*. State Bldg. Comm. Archeol. Prog. Rep. 13. Austin.

Straughn, R. P. L.

1964. *The salt-water aquarium in the home*. New York: A. S. Barnes & Co.

Strecker, J. K.

1935. Notes on marine shells of Texas (misc. papers by Strecker, posthumous). *Baylor Bull.* 38(3):vii–79.

Sverdrup, H. V.; M. W. Johnson; and R. H. Pheming

1942. *The oceans*. New York: Prentice-Hall.

Swainson, W.

1820–33. *Zoological illustrations; or, original figures and descriptions of new, rare, or interesting animals, selected chiefly from the classes of ornithology, entomology, and conchology*. Ser. 1, vols. 1–3, 1820–23; ser. 2, vols. 1–3, 1829–33. London.

Sweet, W. E., Jr.

1971. Water circulation study in the Gulf of Mexico. In *Texas A&M Univ. study of naturally occurring hydrocarbons in the Gulf of Mexico*. College Station.

Taki, I.

1950. Morphological observation on the gastropod operculum. *Jap. J. Malacol.* 16(1–4):32–48.

Taylor, D. W.

1966. A remarkable snail fauna from Coahuila, Mexico. *Veliger* 9(2):152–228.

1975. *Index and bibliography of late Cenozoic freshwater Mollusca of western North America*. Contrib. no. 43, Pacific Marine Sta., Univ. Pacific. Dillon Beach, Calif.

Taylor, D. W., and N. F. Sohl

1962–64. An outline of gastropod classification. *Malacologia* 1(1):7–32.

Taylor, W. R.

1954. Sketch of the marine algal vegetation of the shores of the Gulf of Mexico. In *The Gulf of Mexico: Its origin, waters, and marine life*, ed. P. S. Galtsoff, pp. 177–192. Fishery Bull., no. 89. U.S. Fish & Wildlife Serv. Washington, D.C.: G.P.O.

Tesch, J. J.

1946. *Thecosomatous pteropods*. Carlsberg Found. *Dana Rep.*, no. 28. Copenhagen.

Texas, General Land Office

1974. *An annotated bibliography of research activities in the coastal zone*. Austin: Off. Coastal Zone Manage.

Texas, Governor's Office

1972–73. *The management of bay and estuarine systems*. 2 parts. Austin: Coastal Res. Manage. Prog., Div. Plan. Coord.

1973. Bay and estuarine system management in the Texas coastal zone. In *Project report summaries, Texas coast*. Austin: Coastal Res. Manage. Prog., Div. Plan. Coord.

Texas Almanac

1965. Dallas: A. H. Belo Corp.

Texas Conchologist

1964–76. Vols. 1–12. Houston: Houston Conchology Society.

Thiele, J.

1929–35. *Handbuch der systematischen Weichtierkunde*, vols. 1–2. Jena: Gustav Fischer.

Thomas, R. F., and F. O. Bingham

1972. Shell structure in *Spirula spirula* (Cephalopoda). *Nautilus* 86(2–4):63–66.

Thompson, F. G.

1968. *The aquatic shells of the family Hydrobiidae of peninsular Florida*. Gainesville: Univ. Florida Press.

Thorne, R. F.

1954. Flowering plants of the waters and shores of the Gulf of Mexico. In *The Gulf of Mexico: Its origin, waters, and marine life*, ed. P. S. Galtsoff, pp. 193–202. Fishery Bull., no. 89. U.S. Fish & Wildlife Serv. Washington, D.C.: G.P.O.

Thorson, G.

1955. Modern aspects of marine level-bottom animal communities. *J. Marine Res.* 14:387–397.

1956. Marine level-bottom communities of recent seas: Their temperature adaptation and their "balance" between predators and food animals. *N.Y. Acad. Sci. Trans.* ser. 2, 18:693–700.

1957. Bottom communities (sublittoral or shallow shelf). In *Treatise on marine ecology and paleoecology*, ed. K. O. Emery et al., 1:461–534. Geol. Soc. Amer. Mem. 67. N.p.

Tiffany, W. J.

1972. The tidal migration of *Donax variabilis* Say (Mollusca: Bivalvia). *Veliger* 14(1):82–85.

Tolbert, F. X.

1961. *An informal history of Texas*. New York: Harper & Bros.

Torre, A. de la

1960. Caribbean species of *Truncatella*. *Nautilus* 73(3):79–88.

Treece, G. D.

1976. Bathymetric records of marine shelled Mollusca from the outer northeastern shelf and upper slope of Yucatan. Masters thesis, Texas A&M Univ.

Tryon, G. W., Jr.

1862. A sketch of the history of conchology in the United States. *Amer. J. Sci.* 2(33):161–180.

1878–98. *Manual of conchology: Structural and systematic*. 17 vols. Philadelphia: Acad. Natur. Sci.

Tunnell, J. W., Jr.

1969a. Vertebrate Pleistocene fossils from the continental shelf, northwestern Gulf of Mexico. *Taius* 2(1).

1969b. The mollusks of Seven and

One-Half Fathom Reef. M.S. thesis, Texas A&I Univ.

1972.   Molluscan populations of a submerged reef off Padre Island, Texas. In *Bull. Amer. Malacol. Union*, p. 25. N.p.

1974.   Ecological and geographical distribution of Mollusca of Lobos and Enmedio coral reefs, southwestern Gulf of Mexico. Ph.D. dissertation, Texas A&M Univ.

Tunnell, J. W., Jr., and A. H. Chaney

1970.   Checklist of the mollusks of Seven and One-Half Fathom Reef, northwestern Gulf of Mexico. *Contr. Marine Sci.* 15:193–203.

Turner, H. J., Jr.

1958.   The effect of nutrition on the color of the callus of *Polinices duplicatus*. *Nautilus* 72(1):1–3.

Turner, R. D.

1948.   The family Tonnidae in the western Atlantic. *Johnsonia* 2(26):165–192.

1954–55.   The family Pholadidae in the western Atlantic. *Johnsonia* 3(33):1–64; 3(34):65–160.

1956.   *Melongena corona* Gmelin: An excellent marine laboratory mollusk. *Turtox News* 34(6):106–108.

1959a.   Notes on the feeding of *Melongena corona*. *Nautilus* 73(1):11.

1959b.   The genera *Hemitoma* and *Diodora* in the western Atlantic. *Johnsonia* 3(39):334–343.

1961.   Scaphopods of the *Atlantis* dredgings in the western Atlantic. In *Papers in marine biology and oceanography*, pp. 309–320. London: Pergamon.

1965.   Mussel. In *Encyclopaedia Britannica*. Chicago: Encyclopaedia Britannica.

1966.   *A survey and illustrated catalogue of the Teredinidae*. Cambridge, Mass.: Harvard Univ. Mus. Comp. Zool.

1967.   The Xylophagainae and Teredinidae: A study in contrasts. In *Annu. Rep. Amer. Malacol. Union*, pp. 46–48. N.p.

1973.   Wood-boring bivalves: Opportunistic species in the deep sea. *Science* 180:1377–1379.

Turner, R. D., and K. Boss

1962.   The genus *Lithophaga* in the western Atlantic. *Johnsonia* 4(41):81–116.

Turner, R. D., and J. Rosewater

1958.   The family Pinnidae in the western Atlantic. *Johnsonia* 3(38):285–324.

Turney, W. I., and B. F. Perkins

1972.   *Comparison of molluscan distribution in Florida Bay*. Univ. Miami Comp. Sedimentol. Lab, Sediments II. Coral Gables.

Turton, W.

1819.   *A conchological dictionary of the British Islands*. N.p.

Usticke, F. N. *See* Nowell-Usticke, G. W.

Vanatta, E. G.

1903.   A list of shells collected in western Florida and Horn Island, Mississippi. *Proc. Acad. Natur. Sci. Philadelphia* 55:756–759.

Verrill, A. E.

1897.   A study of the family Pectinidae, with a revision of the genera and subgenera. *Trans. Connecticut Acad. Arts & Sci.* 10:41–95.

1901.   Additions to the fauna of the Bermudas, from the Yale expedition of 1901. *Trans. Connecticut Acad. Arts & Sci.* 11(1):15–62.

Vokes, H. E.

1967.   Genera of the Bivalvia: A systematic and bibliographic catalogue. *Bull. Amer. Paleontol.* 51(232):111–394.

1969.   Notes on the occurrence of *Panopea bitruncata* (Conrad). *Tulane Stud. Geol. Paleontol.* 7(1):41–42.

Voss, G. L.

1954.   Cephalopoda. In *The Gulf of Mexico: Its origin, waters, and marine life*, ed. P. S. Galtsoff, pp. 475–478. Fishery Bull., no. 89. U.S. Fish & Wildlife Serv. Washington, D.C.: G.P.O.

1955.   The cephalopods obtained by the Harvard-Havana expedition off the coast of Cuba in 1938–39. *Bull. Marine Sci. Gulf & Caribbean* 5(2):81–115.

1956.   Gulf of Mexico cephalopods. *Bull. Marine Sci. Gulf & Caribbean* 6(2):359–363.

1960.   Biologist collects shells. *Sea Frontiers* 6(2):66–77.

1971.   Shy monster, the octopus. *National Geographic* 140(6):776–800.

1974.   On the absence of cuttlefish in the western Atlantic. *Veliger* 16(4):367–369.

1976.   In [cephalopod symposium volume of the Zoological Society of London]. In press.

Wagner, R. J. L., and R. T. Abbott

1965.   *Van Nostrand's standard catalog of shells*. Princeton: D. Van Nostrand.

Waller, T. R.

1973.   The habits and habitats of some Bermudian marine mollusks. *Nautilus* 87(2):31–52.

Warmke, G. L., and R. T. Abbott

1962.   *Caribbean seashells: A guide to the marine mollusks of Puerto Rico and other West Indian islands, Bermuda, and the lower Florida keys*. Narberth, Pa.: Livingston Publ.

Wasson, J. A. [J. Andrews]

1963.   Notes on the finding of an addition to the marine mollusks of Texas. *Texas J. Sci.* 15(1):119–120.

Watling, L., and D. Maurer

1973.   *Guide to the macroscopic estuarine and marine invertebrates of the Delaware Bay region*. Ed. F. Polis. Delaware Bay Rep. Ser., vol. 5. Newark: Col. Marine Stud., Univ. Delaware.

Watson, R. L., and E. W. Behrens

1970.   Nearshore surface currents southeastern Texas Gulf coast. *Contr. Marine Sci.* 15:133–144.

Watson, R. S.

1971.   Origin of shell beaches, Padre Island, Texas. *J. Sedim. Petrol.* 41(4):1105–1111.

Weisbord, N. E.

1962.   Late Cenozoic gastropods from northern Venezuela. *Bull. Amer. Paleontol.*, vol. 42.

1965.   Late Cenozoic pelecypods

from northern Venezuela. *Bull. Amer. Paleontol.*, vol. 45.

Wells, F. E.
1970.   An ecological study of two sympatric species of *Fasciolaria*. *Veliger* 13(1):95–107.

Wells, H. W.
1959.   Notes on *Odostomia impressa* (Say). *Nautilus* 72(4):140–144.

Wells, H. W., and M. J. Wells
1961.   Three species of *Odostomia* from North Carolina, with descriptions of new species. *Nautilus* 74(4):149–157.
1962.   The distinction between *Acteocina candei* and *Retusa canaliculata*. *Nautilus* 75(3):87–93.

Wells, H. W.; M. J. Wells; and I. E. Gray
1964.   The calico scallop community in North Carolina. *Bull. Marine Sci. Gulf & Caribbean* 14:561–593.

Wells, M.
1969.   Memory traces in the octopus. *Sea Frontiers* 15(5):295–307.

Wenz, W.
1938–44.   Gastropoda. *Handbuch Paläozool*. 6(1–2). Berlin: Borntraeger.

Wheeler, H. E.
1949.   Ferdinand Röemer. *Nautilus* 63(2):54–56.

Whitehouse, E.
1962.   *Common fall flowers of the coastal bend of Texas*. Dallas: Privately printed.

Whitten, H. L.; H. F. Rosene; and J. W. Hedgpeth
1950.   The invertebrate fauna of the Texas coast jetties: A preliminary survey. *Pub. Inst. Marine Sci.* 1(2):53–99.

Wilbur, K. M., and C. M. Yonge, eds.
1964.   *Physiology of Mollusca*. 2 vols. New York: Academic Press.

Wolfe, D., and N. Wolfe
1970.   *Molluscs of North Carolina: A checklist of marine and brackish species with notes on geographic and ecological distribution*. Publ. with Regional Marine Sci. Proj., Carteret County Public Schools. N.p.

Wood, A. L.
1967.   *Beachcombing for Japanese glass floats*. Portland, Ore.: Binfords & Mort.

Wood, W.
1818.   *Index testaceologicus; or, a catalogue of shells, British and foreign, arranged according to the Linnean system*. London.

Woodring, W. P.
1965.   Endemism in middle Miocene Caribbean molluscan faunas. *Science* 148:961–963.
1966.   The Panama land bridge as a sea barrier. *Proc. Amer. Phil. Soc.* 110(6):425–433.

Work, R. C.
1969.   Systematics, ecology, and distribution of the mollusks of Los Roques, Venezuela. *Bull. Marine Sci.* 19(3):614–711.

Writer's Round Table
1950.   *Padre Island*. San Antonio: Naylor.

Yonge, C. M.
1960.   General characters of Mollusca. In *Treatise on invertebrate paleontology*, Part I, *Mollusca 1*, ed. R. C. Moore, pp. 13–136. Boulder, Col.: Geol. Soc. Amer.
1963.   *The sea shore*. New York: Atheneum.

Yount, J. T.
1967.   *Bottle collector's handbook and pricing guide*. San Angelo, Tex.: Action Print.

Zeigler, R. F., and H. C. Porreca
1969.   *Olive shells of the world*. North Myrtle Beach, S.C.: Privately printed.

Zim, H. S., and L. Ingle
1955.   *Seashores: A guide to shells, sea plants, shore-birds, and other natural features of American coasts*. Golden Nature Guide, sponsored by the Wildlife Manage. Inst. New York: Simon & Schuster.

Zischke, J. A.
1974.   Spawning, development, and growth in the pulmonate limpets *Siphonaria pectinata* Linné 1758 and *S. alternata* Say 1822. *Veliger* 16(4):399–404.

Index

357